WHAT REVIEWERS SAID ABOUT

THE FIRST EDITION ...

"Jam-packed with facts and figures, larded with maps and direct quotations from diaries and official dispatches, illustrated with photographic reproductions of the portraits of the outstanding figures of this war as well as of the famous battle scenes, this book must rank among the better historical works produced in this country."

Montreal *Gazette*

"... a good book, lavishly illustrated, and its author is pleasantly unimpressed by conventional wisdom."

The Times Literary Supplement

"[This book] has given us what is, to date, the most satisfactory Canadian account of the War of 1812 ... [Hitsman] has the knack of keeping his main theme clearly in sight while clothing his narrative in fascinating detail. He has made profuse use of primary sources with a liberal insertion of quotations, and he offers many excellent analyses and judgements. He sees the defence of Canada as soldiers of that day saw it; and he conveys to the reader a considerable image of military life in the nineteenth century."

University of Toronto Quarterly

Front cover

The painting by Peter Rindlisbacher portrays a crucial moment during the naval battle on Lake Ontario on September 28, 1813. Commodore Isaac Chauncey's flagship, the U.S.S. *Pike*, had crippled British commodore Sir James Yeo's flagship, H.M.S. *Wolfe*. He was prevented from finishing the job by the quick thinking of Captain William Mulcaster, who interposed his vessel, H.M.S. *Royal George*, between the two flagships and held Chauncey off long enough for Yeo to make crucial repairs that allowed him to get under way.

Books by J. Mackay Hitsman

The Incredible War of 1812: A Military History
(University of Toronto Press, 1965)

Safeguarding Canada, 1763-1871
(University of Toronto Press, 1968)

Broken Promises: A History of Conscription in Canada
(with J.L. Granatstein, Copp Clark Pitman, 1985)

Other Books by Donald E. Graves

ORIGINAL WORKS

Century of Service: The History of the South Alberta Light Horse
(South Alberta Light Horse Foundation / Robin Brass Studio, 2005)

(with Werner Hirschmann) *Another Place, Another Time: A U-boat Officer's Wartime Album*
(Robin Brass Studio, 2004)

In Peril on the Sea: The Royal Canadian Navy and the Battle of the Atlantic
(Canadian Naval Memorial Trust / Robin Brass Studio, 2003)

Guns Across the River: The Battle of the Windmill, 1838
(Friends of Windmill Point / Robin Brass Studio, 2001)

Field of Glory: The Battle of Crysler's Farm, 1813
(Robin Brass Studio, 1999)

South Albertas: A Canadian Regiment at War
(Robin Brass Studio, 1998)

Where Right and Glory Lead! The Battle of Lundy's Lane, 1814
(Robin Brass Studio, 1997)

Redcoats and Grey Jackets: The Battle of Chippawa, 1814
(Dundurn Press, 1994)

(with Michael Whitby) *Normandy 1944: The Canadian Summer*
(Art Global, 1994)

EDITED WORKS

More Fighting for Canada: Five Battles, 1760-1944
(Robin Brass Studio, 2004)

Quebec, 1759: The Siege and the Battle by C.P. Stacey
(Updated by Donald E. Graves; Robin Brass Studio, 2002)

Fighting for Canada: Seven Battles, 1758-1945
(Robin Brass Studio, 2000)

Soldiers of 1814: American Enlisted Men's Memoirs of the Niagara Campaign
(Old Fort Niagara Press, 1996)

*Merry Hearts Make Light Days: The War of 1812 Journal
of Lieutenant John Le Couteur, 104th Foot*
(Carleton University Press, 1993)

1885. Experiences of the Halifax Battalion in the North-West
(Museum Restoration Service, 1985)

J. MACKAY HITSMAN

The

INCREDIBLE
WAR OF 1812

A MILITARY HISTORY

Updated by

DONALD E. GRAVES

Foreword by

SIR CHRISTOPHER PREVOST

ROBIN BRASS STUDIO
Toronto

First published 1965 by University of Toronto Press.

This revised edition published 1999
by Robin Brass Studio Inc.
www.rbstudiobooks.com

ISBN-10 1-896941-13-3
ISBN-13 978-1-896941-13-4

Reprinted in 2000 (twice), 2002 (with minor corrections), 2003, 2005

Printed and bound in Canada by Marquis Imprimeur,
Cap-Saint-Ignace, Quebec

Canadian Cataloguing in Publication Data

Hitsman, J. Mackay, 1917–1970
    The incredible War of 1812 : a military history

Rev. ed.
Includes bibliographical references and index.
ISBN 1-896941-13-3

1. Canada – History – War of 1812.* 2. United States –
History – War of 1812. 3. Canada – History, Military.
I. Graves, Donald E. (Donald Edward). II. Title.

FC442.H57 1999   971.03'4   C99-932424-1
E354.H57 1999

This edition of *The Incredible War of 1812*

is dedicated to the memory of

John Mackay Hitsman (1917–1970):

soldier, historian, father, friend

Contents

PART IV – 1814: ON THE OFFENSIVE

APPENDICES

MAPS

Foreword

I was very honoured to be asked by Donald E. Graves to write a foreword to this new edition of John Mackay Hitsman's book *The Incredible War of 1812*. I have always considered Hitsman's work to be fairly balanced in its treatment of the military leadership of my ancestor, Sir George Prevost. After his successful campaigns in the West Indies, particularly his notable defence of Dominica in 1805, the government considered that Sir George was the ideal man to succeed Sir James Craig as the governor-general and commander-in-chief of British North America. He spoke fluent French, having passed through the French military academy at Colmar, and was considered ideally suited to govern French-speaking Canadians. This he achieved in his civil administration with considerable success, but at the expense of losing support from certain sectors of the English-speaking population.

During the early part of the War of 1812, Sir George Prevost necessarily fought on the defensive but when troops were released to him from the greater conflict in Europe, he was able to plan offensive operations to secure the frontier.

At the same time he was instructed by "Secret Orders" from Earl Bathurst, the colonial secretary, on behalf of the British government, "not to prejudice his lines of communication by too extended a line of advance." These orders, dated 3 June 1814, appear to have been missing from the official records in 1905 when Rear-Admiral Alfred T. Mahan was writing his book *Seapower in its Relations to the War of 1812*. Mahan subsequently obtained a copy from my grandfather, but received it too late to include it in his book. It is also possible that other previous historians of the war did not have access to these "Secret Orders" which Hitsman reproduces in full in *The Incredible War*.

As a final comment on Sir George's role in the war, I would like to emphasize the comments by the Duke of Wellington which are quoted by Hitsman and which approve the conduct of military operations in North America in 1812-1814.

*   *   *

On a personal note, as a young boy, brought up in the countryside of England, one of the first books given to me by my grandmother to read was *Rolf in the Woods* by Ernest Thompson Seton. Along with James Fenimore Cooper's *Last of the Mohicans*, it is still jealously preserved on my bookshelves. Both these books gave me an insight into the way the early settlers lived in North America and the hardships they endured. In later years, in school, by coincidence, one of my subjects was "American History and the War of Independence."

It was a subject of interest to me as my ancestor, Major-General Augustin Prevost, successfully defended Savannah, Georgia, against a French and American siege in 1779. It was his son, Sir George Prevost, who became commander-in-chief and governor-general of British North America. Another son, also called Augustin, was his father's adjutant in the 60th Royal American Regiment during the Revolutionary War and settled with his family at Greenville, New York, after the termination of hostilities. He had friends in high places in America!

As more information about my family's history became known to me, the more questions I asked. My aunt was the family historian and she told me that when my grandfather died in 1939, the family papers marked "Secrets" were burnt! I have often wondered if these referred to Sir George's recall in 1815 to answer charges after his withdrawal from Plattsburgh. We will never know, unfortunately, but it is odd that no personal papers of Sir George appear to have survived relating to his defence against the charges levelled at him after the naval court martial concerned with the defeat on Lake Champlain. Unfortunately, he died a day before his own hearing, at which he confidently expected to be completely exonerated. After his death, his widow entered into a spirited defence of his character and reputation and insisted that this hearing should proceed. This was not allowed but the Prince Regent bestowed a rare honour of "Supporters" to the family armorials as a mark of his respect and esteem.

In September 1998 my wife and I were invited by the Mayor of Plattsburgh to attend the anniversary celebrations of the battle. These included raising the anchor of the main British warship, H.M.S. *Confiance*, from the waters off Cumberland Head and a service in the graveyard where Captain Robert Downie, RN, and Major James Wellington, both killed in action during the engagement, are buried.

It gave me great pleasure to place a commemorative stone in the River-walk Gardens at Plattsburgh in memory of Sir George Prevost after 184 years! He was born in Paramus, New Jersey, and I feel it is ironic that, as far as I am aware, Plattsburgh is the only place on North American soil where there is now an exhibit to his memory!

Sir Christopher Prevost, Bart.
London, August 1999

"Mac" Hitsman, Sir George Prevost and the Incredible War of 1812

John Mackay Hitsman, the author of *The Incredible War of 1812*, was born in Kingston, Canada, in April 1917. He was the son of Samuel Hitsman, a teacher at Kingston Collegiate Institute and the descendant of an old Loyalist family that had settled along the St. Lawrence in the 1780s, and Minnie Hitsman (née Mackay) from Smiths Falls, Ontario. "Mac," as he was always known to friends and family, grew up in this picturesque little city at the eastern end of Lake Ontario. He was an active boy who liked canoeing and camping, and playing baseball and football, and in these pursuits he was evincing a determination to overcome the physical infirmity that would plague him throughout his life, for he had been born with a neurological disability that affected his spinal column and to a certain extent his lower limbs. As befitted the son of a teacher and parents who were both university graduates, Mac Hitsman's other boyhood interests were more intellectual – he enjoyed reading, writing short stories and drama, and he also became very interested in history, particularly military and naval history. This predilection may have been inspired by his home town, as Kingston, site of the Royal Military College of Canada and dominated by the grey stone mass of Fort Henry that overlooks its harbour, provided a constant reminder of the past.[1]

Following graduation from Kingston Collegiate Institute in 1935, Mac Hitsman entered Queen's University in that city to study history. His interest in athletics did not wane and, although his state of health did not permit him to actively compete, he served as the sports editor for the *Queen's Journal*. He received his honours degree in 1939 and immediately commenced graduate studies – his chosen field being Canadian naval policy – which culminated in a master's degree in 1940.

Like many university students in those fateful years, Mac Hitsman joined the Canadian Officers' Training Corps in preparation for military service. For him, it was not long in coming: he was appointed a probationary lieutenant in the Canadian Active Service Force in the spring of 1941 and after graduation from an Officer Candidate Training Unit he was commissioned a lieutenant in the Royal Canadian Artillery. Hitsman's infirmity precluded his being sent to a combat unit, and in the spring of 1942 he was transferred to the Royal Canadian Ordnance Corps and posted to National Defence Headquarters in Ottawa. Here he laboured as a junior staff officer for a year before being sent to Britain to take up an appointment at the Army Historical Section.

Created in 1940 by Charles P. Stacey, a young Canadian academic and militia officer, the Historical Section was part of Canadian Military Headquarters in London. Stacey was determined that, in terms of its history, the army of the Second World War would not suffer the same fate as its First World War predecessor – because of government indifference and a lack of funding only three of a planned eight-volume history of the Canadian Army in that conflict had appeared in print by 1939.[2] To avoid a repetition of that fiasco, Stacey resolved that the official record of the army's activities in this new war would see publication, and to do so he assembled a collection of historians-turned-soldiers who would not only bring the project to a successful conclusion but would dominate the writing of military history in Canada for nearly four decades.[3] Hitsman therefore joined the ideal organization for someone of his personal interests and academic background, and he functioned as the section's chief archivist and records manager.

By the end of the war, Mac Hitsman was a captain and, wishing to remain in the Historical Section, he transferred to the peacetime army in 1946. Unfortunately, his physical state had been harmed by an accident suffered in training and from this time on he exhibited signs of a slow but progressive deterioration. He was unable to drive and his left side became very weak, which required him to make use of a cane to walk. He was therefore released on medical grounds from the army in 1947 but Stacey wanted to retain his services and the following year Hitsman was reappointed to the Historical Section as a civilian archivist, a position he would hold for twenty-two years. He was liked and respected by his colleagues, who invariably use the word "gentle" when describing him.[4]

The immediate postwar period was a lively time for the writing of military history in Canada. The Army Historical Section in Ottawa provided a focus for its study and the results were disseminated in the Section's periodical, *The Canadian Army Journal*. It was inevitable that the historians in the Section would begin to examine earlier conflicts, including the War of 1812. In doing so, they encountered one of the great national historical beliefs – the so-called "militia myth," which held that the successful defence of the Canadas (particularly Ontario) in 1812-1814 was the result of the heroic efforts of the brave Canadian militia (Loyalists to the man) who repelled the American invaders with just a little help from the regular British army. The origins of this myth have been traced back to a sermon attributed to the Reverend John Strachan and delivered at York (present-day Toronto) in 1812. Not six months after the war had commenced, Strachan was confident that:

> It will be told by the future Historian, that the Province of Upper Canada, without the assistance of men or arms, except a handful of regular troops, repelled its invaders, slew or took them all prisoners, and captured from its enemies the greater part of the arms by which it was defended. ... And never, surely, was greater activity shewn in any country, than our militia have exhibited, never greater valour, cooler resolution, and more approved conduct; they have emulated the choicest veterans, and they have twice saved the country.[5]

Strachan's prediction came true. With the exception of William James, who wrote vitriolic histories of both the naval and land wars that were shamelessly chauvinistic, most British and Canadians (particularly Canadians) who published on the conflict in the years that followed it, embellished the myth Strachan had started in 1812.[6] In their eyes, the war assumed the trappings of the classical age, and these authors waxed eloquent about "Spartan bands of Canadian Loyalist volunteers" who, "aided by a few hundred English soldiers," repulsed "the Persian thousands of democratic American invaders" and preserved "the virgin soil of Canada unpolluted by the boot of the plundering invader."[7] By the turn of the century, when American historians of the calibre of Henry Adams and Alfred T. Mahan were writing substantial studies of the war that discussed not only its military and naval operations but also its political, diplomatic and economic elements, Canadian authors were still wrapping themselves in the Union Jack and defending the pass at Thermopylae.[8] It is almost embarrassing to compare Adams's delineation of the interplay between diplomatic and political developments or Mahan's magisterial analysis of naval operations and their economic consequences, with that of their Canadian contemporary, James Hannay, who wrote a blatantly biased history of the war in 1905 but was unflinching about possible complaints about his partiality. "No doubt," he commented, some critics might say that "I have been too severe on the Americans, who invaded our country, burnt our towns, ravaged our fields, slaughtered our people and tried to place us under a foreign flag," but he could see no reason why any American would be offended by his "absolutely truthful" book.[9]

Canada's answer to such historians of the first rank as Adams and Mahan was a narrow specialist, Ernest Albert Cruikshank. A well-educated militia officer from the Niagara area, Cruikshank began to actively publish on the war in the 1880s and continued without pause until his death in 1939 at the age of eighty-six. During this sixty-year span he produced dozens of books, monographs and pamphlets and hundreds of articles on War of 1812 topics.[10] He was able to do this because his methodology was of the "scissors and paste" variety – with the exception of his document collections, almost all his writing consists of strung-together quotations or paraphrases of quotations, and in the rare instances where he provides source references, they are maddeningly obscure. Cruikshank's three published document collections remain useful, although care must be taken as Cruikshank was not above altering the record if it contained matters that displeased him.[11] Cruikshank's impressive but mindless industry was given further impetus in 1908 when he was appointed keeper of military records at the Public Archives of Canada (as it was then known). Here he organized, classified and indexed that institution's extensive holdings of British records of the war, and this labour was put to good use by William Wood, who published a three-volume documentary history of the war in the 1920s that contained much material not in Cruikshank's earlier efforts.[12] Although even the most cursory perusal of the works of these two men (who were basically compilers, not historians) reveals that the greater part of the fighting (and the dying) in 1812-1814 was done by the regulars, not the militia, neither drew any substantial conclusions from this evidence.[13]

It was Charles Stacey who began the needed task of demolishing the militia myth and its verdant covering of heroic ivy. In an article published in 1958 Stacey admitted the essential part played by the militia in the defence of Canada but emphasized that the successful preservation of British North America was not due to "youngsters fresh from the tail of the plough" but trained soldiers. To Stacey the war was "essentially a contest between ill-organized numbers on the American side and professional skill on ours." Canada remained British because it was better prepared for war than the United States since Britain had provided "essentials for successful defence" – a naval force on the Great Lakes and "an efficient body of regular troops" commanded by officers who provided "skilful and energetic professional leadership."[14]

Stacey's re-evaluation of the conflict was paralleled by his colleagues or former colleagues of the Army Historical Section who published on various aspects of the War of 1812 in the immediate postwar years – not least among them being Hitsman, who contributed eight articles on the aspects of the conflict between 1959 and 1962.[15] This was a remarkable output for one historian, particularly so because Mac Hitsman was then not only completing his first book, *Military Inspection Services in Canada, 1855-1950*, which appeared in 1962, but had also commenced a part-time doctoral program in history. As if this was not enough, Hitsman had also married and now had three sons to raise.

It was one of these articles, "Sir George Prevost's Conduct of the Canadian War of 1812," that led directly to the writing of the book that follows. This article was an outgrowth of Hitsman's research for the doctoral dissertation he completed under the direction of Dr. Arthur Vanasse at the University of Ottawa between 1960 and 1964. Later published as *Safeguarding Canada*, it was a survey of British defence strategy in North America from the end of the Seven Years' War in 1763 to the Treaty of Washington in 1871.[16] In the course of his research, which was based extensively on primary sources, Hitsman became suspicious that Sir George Prevost, the British commander-in-chief in North America from 1811 to 1815, "had been greatly maligned by Canadian historians and that his conduct of the War of 1812 and events in it had been in many respects different from what they had been in many places declared to be."[17] Hitsman was the first historian to go carefully through the official correspondence between Prevost and his superiors and subordinates and stressed that this officer, often derided for his timidity by earlier British and Canadian authors, was under orders from London to remain on the defensive throughout most of the war. Only in the late spring of 1814, when the end of the great conflict in Europe permitted Britain to send sizeable reinforcements to North America, was Prevost instructed to act on the offensive, and even then, such operations were to be restricted. Hitsman also noted that the Duke of Wellington, the greatest British soldier of his time, entirely approved Prevost's direction of the defence of Canada. It was Hitsman's opinion that Prevost had been unfairly condemned by historians obsessed with his "ineptness as a field commander before Plattsburgh, and his curbing of rash or incompetent subordinates," and they therefore "failed to recognize or appreciate the extremely competent defensive strategy displayed in his overall direction of the war."[18]

He presented his findings in a paper delivered at the 1962 conference of the Canadian Historical Association, and it attracted the notice of Francess G. Halpenny, an editor with the University of Toronto Press. Francess Halpenny was very much aware of the militia myth and its pernicious influence on Canadian historiography and wanted to "clarify" this legend. She was intrigued by Mac Hitsman's views on Prevost, which "seemed to have a strong, persuasive story," and asked him if he would be interested in writing a history of the war. The response was positive, and in the summer of 1962 Mac Hitsman began work on the manuscript that would eventually become *The Incredible War of 1812.*

It took him about two years to complete, which is actually a fairly short gestation period for a project of this scope, but Mac Hitsman had the advantage of having done much preliminary work, particularly concerning the higher direction of the war, while completing his doctoral dissertation, which he wrote concurrently. Most of the research was done at the Public Archives of Canada, the single largest repository for British records of the War of 1812, which in Mac Hitsman's time was open to researchers twenty-four hours a day, 365 days a year.[19] He relied heavily on the records of the Colonial Office for evidence concerning British strategical decisions, and Record Group 8, I, *the source* for operational and tactical matters. He was also fortunate enough to be able to consult the original documents – modern historians must make do with microform copies. As, by this time, he was unable to type with his left hand, Mac wrote his drafts in pencil on legal pads which were later typed up by his wife, Kaye. His favourite working place was a table covered with books and papers in the glassed-in back porch of the Hitsman family home in Ottawa, and his middle son, Ted, remembers that he would head straight there every day when he returned from his office at the Historical Section.[20]

What Mac Hitsman produced in that porch was a compact (the main text is just over 100,000 words) but thorough history of the War of 1812. The book is written primarily from the British and Canadian point of view but Hitsman's treatment of the American aspirations, politicians and generals is very even-handed. In a preliminary section of three chapters he traces the settlement and development of British North America, discusses its connection with the origins of the conflict, outlines the preparations for its defence and provides a concise but thorough analysis of its defenders. The remaining twelve chapters are devoted to an examination of wartime operations from the highest political and strategical level down to the tactical aspects of individual battles. Hitsman concentrated on operations along the Canadian border, which is not surprising as for the contenders this was the main theatre of war – two-thirds of the regular troops of *both* Britain and the United States were deployed in this area in 1812-1814. He did not entirely neglect other theatres, however, nor did he overlook the maritime aspects of the conflict, but surveyed naval operations on the high seas and inland waters and their relationship with land operations. Mac Hitsman's history of the war was not only sound, it was also detailed, for as a colleague later remarked, Hitsman possessed a "remarkable capacity for boiling a great mass of miscellaneous and complicated official records down into a lucid and readable narrative."[21] He was also gifted with a refined but clear style that is still a delight to read, and when dealing with difficult personalities, Hitsman revealed a wicked but restrained sense of cynical irony (read very carefully what he says about Sir James Lucas Yeo).

One of the major strengths of Hitsman's manuscript was that, unlike many previous studies of the War of 1812, it contained a thorough examination of the higher direction of the British war effort. Hitsman discussed and quoted the documents (and reproduced the two most important in an appendix) that formed the guidelines for the unfairly vilified Sir George Prevost, British commander-in-chief in North America. He expanded the thesis begun in his earlier article and emphasized that Prevost's options were limited by specific instructions from his superiors not to undertake offensive operations except "for the purpose of preventing or repelling Hostilities" (what modern soldiers call "pre-emptive strikes").[22] He was also careful to emphasize that, throughout the war, Prevost was aware that the British government was confident it could resolve its differences with the United States by diplomatic, not military means, and aggressive actions might endanger the positive outcome of possible negotiations.[23] Hitsman discussed the British commander's relations with his senior subordinates – Brock, Sheaffe, De Rottenburg, Drummond, Yeo and the uninspiring Procter – and went a long way to redress errors made by previous historians who, without consulting the full historical record, had castigated

Prevost for restraining or not supporting them. By providing the wider historical context for Prevost's record in command, Hitsman for the first time produced an objective view of that officer, an "amiable, well-intentioned and honest" administrator who had done his best in very difficult circumstances.[24]

Although Hitsman was more favourable to the British commander than almost every historian who had preceded him (with the possible and interesting exception of Alfred Thayer Mahan), he was aware of Prevost's weaknesses and did not ignore his mistakes.[25] Prevost's rather mediocre performance at Ogdensburg in February 1813, at Sackets Harbor in May 1813 and, above all, at Plattsburgh in September 1814, are discussed at length, as is his penchant for adjusting in his own favour the administrative record of any problem he experienced with a subordinate. Mac Hitsman was too professional to become adulatory – his is always the reasoned and balanced view – and this quality is best seen in his treatment of Prevost during the Plattsburgh campaign, to which he devoted almost an entire chapter. It is an honest appraisal of the man's inability to command the best army Britain ever sent to North America in the major British offensive of the war. But it is also empathetic to an officer not up to the task he had been given, and Hitsman's overall conclusion, which appeared in another book, that if the army was "now strong enough in Canada to take the offensive, the defensively minded Prevost should have been provided with an aggressive senior officer to command his field army" is entirely pertinent.[26]

Two aspects of the war that Mac Hitsman did not cover in detail were the role of the native peoples, and the war and civilian society. Concerning his treatment of the First Nations, he was reflecting his time as, in the 1960s, there was only limited knowledge of the participation of the aboriginal peoples and much ethnocentric bias, but within these restrictions Hitsman's discussion of the native peoples is basically sound. Nor did he spend much time on the civilian side of the war although he touched on the main points in both Upper and Lower Canada. It must be remembered that Hitsman was tasked with preparing a comparatively short history that required concision and it has to be accepted that his limited coverage of some topics resulted from his need to produce a fairly tight narrative addressing his central thesis.[27]

After much labour, which was not made easier by the fact that Mac Hitsman's physical condition was getting progressively worse, the manuscript was finished and submitted to the University of Toronto Press for publication. Mac had, of course, prepared proper and detailed references for his text but they were not to appear in the printed version. As Francess Halpenny comments, the book was planned for the press's general list and intended for a wide audience. This being the case, length and cost were major considerations and the decision was made to publish *The Incredible War of 1812: A Military History* without any sources but with a bibliographical note.[28] This decision apparently annoyed Mac Hitsman because it meant that his book would not have its proper scholarly underpinnings in place, and friends still remember his bitter invective about the matter.

When it was released in hard and softcover form in 1965, *The Incredible War* was well received. One scholarly reviewer thought Mac Hitsman had "given us, what is to date, the most satisfactory Canadian account of the War of 1812" and praised the author's "knack of keeping his main theme clearly in sight while clothing his narrative in fascinating detail."[29] The *Montreal Gazette*, with typical journalistic licence, enthused about a book "Jam-packed with facts and figures, larded with maps and direct quotations from diaries and official dispatches" which "must rank among the better historical works produced in this country." The reviewer for *The Times Literary Supplement* was more restrained, as befits the august stature of that periodical, but still aware the work contained much new material: "it is a good book, lavishly illustrated, and its author is pleasantly unimpressed by conventional wisdom." The first printing of *The Incredible War* quickly sold out, and it was reprinted in 1968 and 1972.[30]

Sadly, Mac Hitsman did not long enjoy his book's success. By the time it appeared, his physical movement was becoming very restricted and he had difficulty holding a pen. Worse was to follow. Shortly after publication of *The Incredible War*, he was diagnosed with cancer and began a long struggle against that terrible enemy which ended with his death in February 1970 at the untimely age of fifty-three. Mac Hitsman kept working as long as he could and his fourth book, *Broken Promises: A History of Conscription in Canada*, co-authored with J.L. Granatstein, appeared posthumously. The task of summing up this gentle man, who had faced daunting problems throughout his life but had carried on, fell to his longtime associate Charles Stacey:

Mac Hitsman's friends will remember him best, not for his contributions to military scholarship, important as those were, but for the extraordinary courage and resolution with which over a long period of years he confronted and overcame physical miseries that would have reduced most men to utter inaction. Almost to the end, he went on producing – and producing first-class work – in spite of these handicaps. In this case the well-worn phrase rings true: he was an example to us all.[31]

John Mackay Hitsman's *Incredible War of 1812* remains possibly the best single-volume account of that strange and far-off conflict. It is certainly the best overall study of the war from the British point of view and, since its appearance in 1965, only one other major history of the war has been published by a British or Canadian historian: George Stanley's *War of 1812: Land Operations*. Brought out by the Canadian War Museum in 1983, this handsome publication written by one of Hitsman's former colleagues was notable because it provided coverage of neglected aspects of the war: logistics and distant operations along the New Brunswick border and the Pacific coast. As its author admits, however, he ignored operations that did not take place along the international boundary, nor did he touch on naval operations in any detail, because these were to be covered in a companion volume by another historian.[32] At least four popular histories of the war by Britons or Canadians have seen print since 1965, and they make for entertaining reading, but none is of the quality of *The Incredible War*.[33]

Most recent British and Canadian scholarship on the conflict is more specialized in its subject matter, and to date no historian has equalled Hitsman's achievement. For those who wish to understand the British and Canadian experience of the War of 1812, particularly the command decisions, *The Incredible War of 1812* remains the standard against which all other works must be judged.[34] Thirty years after its first publication, one Canadian historian felt it had "yet to be surpassed" as it offered an "incisive and balanced view of the war and of wartime occurrences."[35] In the time since its last printing, the book has become increasingly rare, and with this in view, the decision by Robin Brass Studio of Toronto to revise and again make available this established classic is a matter of considerable celebration.[36] It is also a fitting memorial to a brave man and a fine historian.

Donald E. Graves
Thanksgiving Day,
Almonte, Canada

EDITORIAL NOTE AND ACKNOWLEDGEMENTS

In preparing this new edition of *The Incredible War of 1812*, I resolved at the outset that Mac Hitsman's book would be preserved as intact as possible and any changes to it would be only cosmetic. This new edition contains the author's original preface, main text and appendix complete. The major change I have made to the text is to divide it into four parts instead of the original two. I have also offset the many lengthy quotations to render them more readily apparent. This required slight changes to the punctuation of the lead-in sentences to these quotes but corrected an aspect of the original edition in which they were printed in a smaller typeface that resulted in a format that could be confusing to the reader. Other changes were limited to silent correction of the remarkably few inaccuracies in dates and spelling.

I then turned to the problem of the missing sources. As Mac Hitsman was a conscientious and careful scholar (and also an archivist of much experience) I thought it entirely possible that at some point he would have left a copy of his original draft with sources intact for the benefit of future researchers. I therefore searched among his surviving papers and the collections of the Department of National Defence in Ottawa. Nothing was found in Hitsman's personal papers, but a tantalizing reference to a document on the War of 1812, authored by him and some 478 typescript pages in length, turned up in the records of the main DND reference library. Unfortunately, this interesting trail led nowhere as this document (if it existed as more than a note on a catalogue card) seems to have disappeared during a recent large transfer of material from that library to the collections of the Museum of Civilization.

This being the sad case, I decided that if I could not provide the original references for the text, I would at least make an effort to identify the sources for the many quotes. Fortunately for me, four fellow historians, each a specialist in an aspect of the War of 1812, assisted in this laborious undertaking. Carl Benn, author of *The Iroquois in the War of 1812*, dealt with the role of the native peoples during the war – a subject that did not receive prominent enough mention in the original edition – and compiled Appendix 5. René Chartrand, author of *Canadian Military Heritage*, made contributions on topics concerning military organization, weapons, uniforms and illustrations. Robert Malcomson, author of *Lords of the Lake:*

The Naval War on Lake Ontario, 1812-1814, covered naval and maritime topics and compiled Appendix 7. And last but certainly not least, Stuart Sutherland, author of the forthcoming *His Majesty's Gentlemen: A Directory of Regular British Army Officers of the War of 1812*, solved some of the most difficult identification problems and bestowed his extensive knowledge of the military machinery of Britain during the Napoleonic era. This team effort has allowed me to identify sources for all but about a half dozen of the hundreds of quotations in Hitsman's text.

In the last three decades, our knowledge of the War of 1812 has increased at an exponential rate. Much new and exciting scholarship has appeared, not only concerning military, naval and diplomatic matters, but also on such topics as the war and civilian society, the internal political and economic aspects of British North America at war and, above all, the role of the native peoples of North America. Mac Hitsman's work remains sound (which is comment sufficient on its quality), but I have included in the notes to this new edition additional information and commentary that elaborates on aspects of the war he did not cover in depth and which draws attention to new material published since 1965. Again, I was assisted in this labour by the historians noted above, and where they have offered comment at length, I have identified their contribution by placing their initials at the end of the note in which it appears.

For similar reasons, to bring this new edition in accord with recent scholarship and enhance its utility, the maps, illustrations and bibliography have been upgraded and new appendices provided. Many of the 1965 maps, particularly the tactical maps of military actions, had become outdated and have been replaced by revised versions. There are twenty maps as compared to ten in the first edition. The 1965 book had only eleven illustrations; the 1999 version has more than fifty and they not only cover a wider range of subjects but have been placed near the text that applies to them. A more extensive bibliography of unpublished and published sources, which includes titles dealing with British, Canadian and native participation in the war that have appeared since 1965, has been substituted for the brief bibliographical note of the original. Finally, seven new appendices have been added which are concerned with the military and naval forces of the Crown in 1812-1815, and their native allies. Here the interested reader can find information on the organization, strength and service of units that fought in the war, their modern successors and the awards, medals and honours that were granted.

It is my hope that my labours have not injured *The Incredible War of 1812* but, instead, given it a new lease on life.

In closing, I wish to acknowledge those who assisted in these tasks. I have noted above the contributions of four fellow scholars, but I also have others to thank. Sir Christopher Prevost of London, the descendant of the British commander-in-chief during the War of 1812, wrote the foreword that graces this new edition and provided much information on the history of his family. The author's sons, Ted Hitsman of Merrickville, Ontario, and Canon Tony Hitsman of Harrington Harbour, Quebec, searched their father's papers and answered many questions about his life. Lieutenant Colonel Charles Nutting of The King's Royal Hussars and Major Andrew Hart of The Royal Irish Regiment, both officers of the British army currently serving in Canada, helped unravel the complexities of the modern British order of battle. Syd Wise of Ottawa and Francess G. Halpenny of Toronto shared with me their memories of Mac Hitsman as a scholar and friend, while Michael Whitby of the Directorate of History in Ottawa helped track down source material. John Grodzinski of Kingston risked lending a mint copy of the hardcover first edition for editorial purposes, and George Henderson of the Queen's University Archives in that city was instrumental in providing details of Mac Hitsman's family. Stephen Pallas of Ottawa proved a fount of information on anything to do with medals and awards and Robert Henderson loaned documents from his personal files. Finally, I must yet again pay tribute to my long-suffering wife, Dianne, who accepted with the best of grace my breaking a solemn promise that I would not tackle another major book project so soon after completing the previous one.

D.E.G.

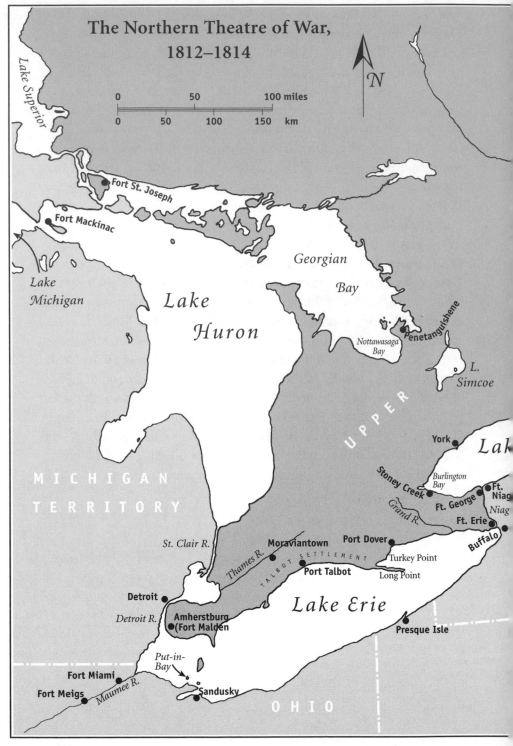

The Northern Theatre of War, 1812–1814

Lake Superior

Fort St. Joseph

Fort Mackinac

Lake Michigan

Lake Huron

Georgian Bay

Nottawasaga Bay

Penetanguishene

L. Simcoe

UPPER

York

Lak

Burlington Bay

Stoney Creek

Ft. George

Ft. Niag

Grand R.

Niag

Ft. Erie

Buffalo

MICHIGAN TERRITORY

St. Clair R.

Thames R.

Moraviantown

TALBOT SETTLEMENT

Port Dover

Turkey Point

Port Talbot

Long Point

Detroit

Detroit R.

Amherstburg (Fort Malden)

Lake Erie

Presque Isle

Put-in-Bay

Fort Miami

Fort Meigs

Maumee R.

Sandusky

OHIO

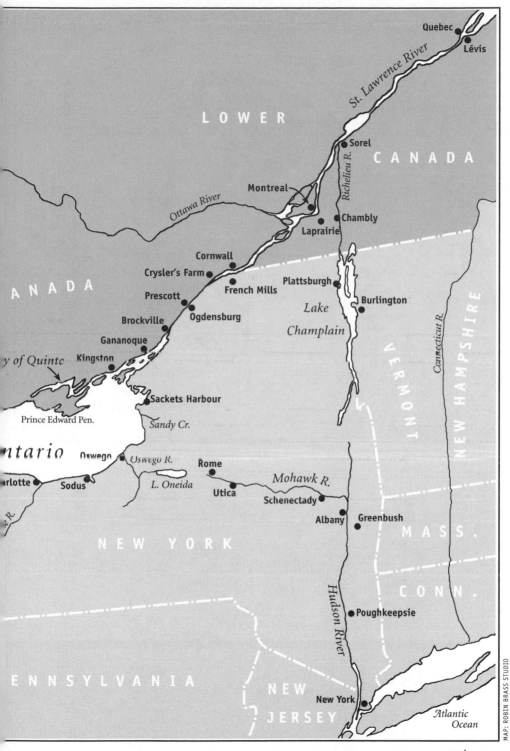

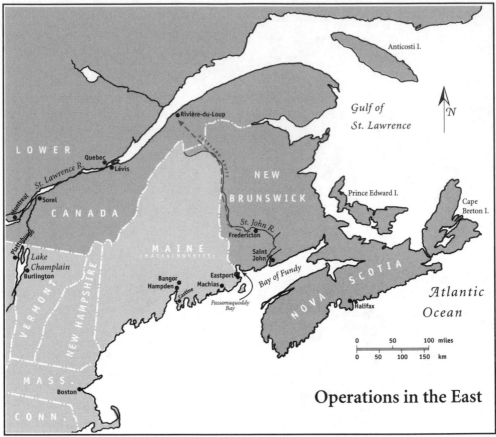

Operations in the East

Author's Preface

I began writing this book in July 1962, after receiving a long distance telephone call from the Editor of the University of Toronto Press, Miss Francess G. Halpenny, who had heard me deliver a paper before the annual meeting of the Canadian Historical Association on "Sir George Prevost's Conduct of the War of 1812." Delivery of this paper had been prompted by a growing conviction, based on material available in the Public Archives of Canada at Ottawa, that Sir George Prevost had been greatly maligned by Canadian historians and that the conduct of the War of 1812 and events in it had been in many respects different from what they had been in many places declared to be. I found several statements by the Duke of Wellington, Britain's greatest soldier, to support my thesis and my overall findings seemed to be confirmed by the two-volume account of the war written by the great American naval historian, Rear-Admiral A.T. Mahan.

Residence in the greater Ottawa area made it possible for me to carry on further spare-time research on manuscript sources, since the Public Archives is open to students seven days and nights every week. Members of its staff went out of their way to give me a helping hand with my varied problems. Additional material was obtained on microfilm from the Public Record Office in London and the National Archives in Washington. Other material was made available by the Librarians of the Department of National Defence in Ottawa, the Royal Military College of Canada in Kingston, the New York Historical Society in New York City, and the St. Lawrence University in Canton, New York. The first two of these librarians, Mr. Charles H. Stewart and Mr. John W. Spurr, were particularly helpful. Professor A.M.J. Hyatt and Mr. I. Maxwell Sutherland allowed me to read their unpublished theses. All this material is detailed in my bibliography.

Quotations from unpublished Crown-copyright material in the Public Record Office have been made by permission of the Controller of H.M. Stationery Office.

Illustrations were obtained from the Library of the Department of

National Defence, the Public Archives of Canada, the McCord Museum in Montreal, and the Company of Military Historians in the United States. The artists of the last named, Messrs. Ted Chapman and Hugh McBarron, agreed that their work might be reproduced freely in a Canadian book. The maps are the work of Major C.C.J. Bond, a longtime friend in whose company I had wandered over several of the battlefields. His map of the Battle of Châteauguay is based on one now hanging in the Archives of the Province of Quebec.[1]

Lieutenant-Colonel H.F. Wood and Mrs. W.O. Sorby were kind enough to read and comment on each chapter as the work progressed. Mr. T. Thorgrimsson answered endless telephone queries about naval matters and then provided detailed comments on the whole manuscript. Miss Halpenny's editorial advice and her criticism of the manuscript have been a stimulating guide throughout the writing of the text. Colonel C. P. Stacey provided helpful suggestions on the completed text. Responsibility for what now appears in print is mine, and mine alone.

J.M.H.

PART I

The Origins of a Conflict

NOTICE.

Wanted for His Majesty's CANADIAN FENCIBLE REGIMENT, *commanded by* BRIGADIER GENERAL THOMAS PETER, *now raising in Canada, to serve in America and not elsewhere.*

A FEW young men willing to engage for seven years, in terms of a late Act of Parliament. If under the age of Eighteen years, the difference between that, and the Actual Age of the recruit to be added to the above Period of service.

Now is your time loyal Canadians to shew yourselves worthy of the glorious constitution under which you enjoy so much happiness. The Lieutenant Colonel requests that none will offer themselves but Canadians ; the sons and relations of actual settlers in the Canadas, or other British American Colonies, and natural born subjects, as none of a different discription will be acceptable or sought after. Every man who inlists will receive a bounty of FIVE POUNDS, and six pence sterling appropriated according to the Recruiting Instructions. No man will be taken who is above thirty years of age, or under five feet three inches high. Such as are qualified to act as non-commissioned Officers, and who prove themselves intelligent and active may expect speedy promotion, and all may rest assured of the best usage, and will receive every advantage granted to His Majesty's Forces in this Country.—Application to be made to LIEUT. COLONEL SHANK at Three Rivers, or to the different Recruiting Parties in the Country.

GOD SAVE THE KING.

Quebec, 9th April, 1807

Recruiting advertisement, Canadian Fencibles, 1807

1

Quebec during the War of 1812
The capital of British North America, its preservation was regarded by British commanders as being paramount. (National Archives of Canada, C-138099)

CHAPTER ONE

Years of Tension:
The Road to War, 1783-1811

The War of 1812 was a result of long-standing disputes and, like many wars before and since, failed to resolve them. The oldest of these disputes dated back to the American Revolution. Less than thirty years had elapsed since the conclusion of that conflict, not long enough to soften bitter memories in the continuing colonies of British North America and the new United States of America. Great Britain had, it is true, agreed to very favourable Articles of Peace late in 1782, in an effort to weaken the rebellious colonists' wartime alliance with France and Spain and to regain American goodwill and trade, but there remained potentially troublesome points of argument. Both the United States and Great Britain were to violate from the outset the terms of the final Treaty of Paris signed on September 3, 1783.

According to this Treaty, those colonists who had fought for Britain and been dispossessed of their property and civil rights were to have had these restored to them, but the weak central government established by the Americans in their Articles of Confederation could not coerce individual states who refused to honour this promise. The plight of the British loyalists was a convenient excuse for Britain to refuse to evacuate most of the inland forts built in territory which the Treaty recognized as part of the United States. The new international boundary now followed the ill-defined St. Croix River to its height of land, and continued westward along it and the 45th parallel of latitude to the St. Lawrence River, whose crooked route it then followed through the Great Lakes region to the northwest corner of the Lake of the Woods. The most important of the so-called "western posts" now on the American side of this boundary were Oswegatchie [Ogdensburg], Oswego, Niagara, Presque Isle [Erie], Sandusky, Detroit and Mackinac. They had been rendezvous for Britain's Indian Allies, who travelled to these forts each spring to receive presents from officers of the Indian Department and to barter their furs with the Montreal traders,

3

now loosely organized as the North West Company so that they might better control the economy of what was known as the Old Northwest.

The British Government soon realized that the Mother Country herself would have to compensate the dispossessed loyalists, many of whom had now decided on a new life in what remained of British North America; but what she should do about her Indian Allies, whose hunting grounds were located in what was now American territory, was a much more difficult matter to decide. The Indians had not been consulted about the peace negotiations and indeed, through an oversight on the part of the British negotiators, had not even been mentioned anywhere in the Treaty of Paris. It was useless to expect that the United States would assist in placating tribes of what most Americans considered to be bloodthirsty savages, particularly when land-hungry citizens were streaming westward. Ultimately Britain might have to provide new homes for these Indians, as had been done for the Mohawks led to Canada by Joseph Brant during the Revolution. But Governor Frederick Haldimand, surveying his uneasy province from Quebec, had felt that the situation could not wait for such a solution. Disgruntled Indians had once turned on the British, in the [1763] rising led by Pontiac, and the havoc wrought then might be repeated. Haldimand was convinced he must lull the chiefs into believing that their "white father" had not forsaken them by holding on to the western posts indefinitely and by continuing a liberal distribution of presents. This view he managed to persuade the British Government in far off London to accept.[1]

Inevitably the Americans protested, but to no avail. Most Englishmen tended to regard the new United States as an immature and inconsequential nation which need not be taken seriously. And certainly it did not have the military strength to lend weight to its protests. "Standing armies in time of peace," Congress had decided, "are inconsistent with the principles of republican government"; so only a battery of artillery from Washington's army was retained to guard the stores at Fort Pitt and West Point, and a weak regiment of infantry recruited to garrison frontier forts.[2] Responsibility for defence was left to the militias of the individual states. There was no navy whatsoever.

Thus the British Government did nothing about the concern evinced periodically by Haldimand's successor, Lord Dorchester, for the continued safety of the western posts, even though these wooden forts were falling into ruin and he had only 2,000 British regular troops extended along 1,100 miles of frontier where communication was impossible in wintertime.[3]

A much more serious problem was government of the greatly increased population of the inland province. By 1784 the 65,000 French-speaking Canadians of 1760 had increased to 113,000; their numbers had thus almost doubled since the Conquest but, except for a few settled along the Detroit River, they were restricted to the same seigniories and these were still far from being completely under cultivation. By now the majority was resigned to British rule, if hardly happy about it. The English-speaking inhabitants numbered 20,000, about two-thirds of whom were in the more westerly settlements along the north shore of the upper St. Lawrence River and the Bay of Quinte, in the Niagara Peninsula, and around Detroit; here the original loyalists were still being joined by families from the United States. These English-speaking inhabitants were united in a desire to live under English civil law and customs, and enjoy freehold tenure of land. Some division between predominantly French-speaking and English-speaking areas was obviously indicated, but just where this should occur was disputed. The influential Montreal merchants, for example, were opposed to any division that would disrupt their trade with the interior.

Lord Dorchester was not able to produce any practical solution and eventually the British Government decided to divide the Province of Quebec along the line of the Ottawa River and the Seigniory of Longueuil. Its so-called Constitutional Act of 1791 made it possible to create separate provinces of Upper and Lower Canada, each of which was to have the form of representative government already enjoyed by Nova Scotia, New Brunswick and St. John's Island (Prince Edward Island). Lower Canada continued the existing laws and methods of holding land, but Upper Canada promptly adopted English laws and freehold tenure. Indeed the latter's first Lieutenant-Governor, John Graves Simcoe, misguidedly strove to turn the backwoods into a replica of the contemporary English scene.[4]

The people who were to develop Upper Canada were a mixed lot. The overwhelming majority of loyalist settlers were of humble origin, just as the French-speaking *habitants* had been.[5] They were not unfamiliar with hard work, or with want and privation, and were mostly able to make an eventual success of life in their new homes. Many ex-officers of the loyalist corps had been merchants or tradesmen before taking up arms in the American Revolutionary War, and with the half-pay they now received to keep them on the army's reserve they were able to become relatively affluent. Many British half-pay officers, however, had dreamed of living in the backwoods like English country gentlemen. They soon discovered their error. Fortunately there were a number of official appointments for which such inept gentlemen could qualify.[6]

More settlers were needed to develop the large empty spaces and in both provinces almost identical proclamations were issued by the Lieutenant-Governors of Upper and Lower Canada on February 7, 1792. These offered 200-acre farms to individuals who would take up residence within six months and large tracts of land to enterprising speculators who would act as developers. Large-scale emigration from the British Isles was not yet being encouraged by the Government; these were years before the Industrial Revolution had progressed sufficiently to cause mass unemployment among home weavers and other skilled artisans.

Thus the only promising source of English-speaking settlers was the United States, where both Lieutenant-Governors believed there were thousands of people disillusioned with a republican form of government and still retaining fond memories of life under British rule. They were sanguine about motives (more sanguine than later leaders were to be) and those desiring free land found it easy to satisfy the light demands of loyalty made upon them. The new arrivals had all sorts of excuses for not having fought during the American Revolution, even for having fought on the wrong side. There was land for all, and most of the earlier loyalists welcomed the newcomers into the great unoccupied spaces of Upper Canada, which attracted the majority of these new immigrants. All of them were interested primarily in good farms. Caring little what flag waved overhead, each immigrant was only too willing to "promise and declare that I will maintain and defend to the utmost of my power the authority of the King in His Parliament as the supreme Legislature of this Province."[7] Lieutenant-Governor Simcoe particularly encouraged the immigration into Upper Canada of Quakers, Mennonites and Dunkers as being good farmers and sober citizens; they, of course, had conscientious objections against military service and were to be excepted by successive Militia Acts.

Everyone who had lived in North America since the first settlements of the early 17th century was accustomed to the idea of serving in a local militia, and in the new province of Upper Canada a similar defence organization was set up. All physically fit males aged 16 to 60 belonged to a local militia company, unless they were clergymen, crown officials or such essential workers as millers and ferrymen. Except in a time of dire emergency, local militia companies were expected mainly to provide designated quotas of men whenever a particular service was required. There were annual training days, but these were little more than musters of the local inhabitants. Quotas for service were filled by ballot (or lot) whenever there were insufficient volunteers. Those doing duty were then normally excused further service until the balance of their company had been balloted. The provision that each man must provide his own musket and ammunition was widely honoured in the breach. The Lieutenant-Governor of New Brunswick soon found that most of the loyalist veterans had to sell their army muskets in order to buy necessities following their arrival at Saint John. This, however, was less a cause for concern because, although the marksmanship of militiamen could be an important factor on the field of battle, in time of conflict the militia's principal role was expected to be the transportation of supplies by bateau, cart or sleigh and the building of roads or fortifications.[8]

These duties involved arduous physical labour for the pittance paid British soldiers, hence the provision that prospering members of the community could hire substitutes to perform their militia service. Militia officers, of course, received pay of rank merely for performing simple administrative tasks. Older officers would have served in regular or loyalist regiments and their experience was essential for any military role they might possibly have to play, but newly commissioned officers were youngsters recommended to the attention of the lieutenant-governor by the officer commanding the local militia battalion. Everywhere, acquisition of a militia commission was the first step towards a career in politics or a profitable position under the Crown.

The real defence of British North America would be conducted by men serving in Britain's regular forces. The first shield was the Royal Navy, with a considerable strength based on the West Indies, Halifax, and Newfoundland. The Navy always had to be ready to meet changing needs in particular areas, but its position in the New World in wartime would depend on its ability to control and command the narrow seas of western Europe against the navies of France and Spain. Thus all the first-rate ships of the line, mounting 90 guns or more, were required close to home. A proportion of the much more numerous third-rate and fourth-rate ships, the last mounting only 50 guns, was positioned in the West Indies and at Halifax. Newfoundland generally had to be content with one or two of the single-decked ships, known as frigates and mounting from 24 to 38 guns. Also serving everywhere were variously rigged sloops and brigs, otherwise miniature frigates mounting 10 to 20 guns. These smaller vessels were commanded by officers having the rank of commander or only lieutenant, but commonly called "captain." Ships of the line and larger frigates were commanded by proper captains, who were known as post captains because of the superior status of their posts.[9] Commanders-in-Chief of naval stations and even lesser commodores holding small independent commands of a temporary nature, might appoint an officer to fill a captain's vacancy and receive pay and allowances of that rank, but he would not become a post captain until his rank was confirmed by the Admiralty in London.

The importance of the large inland waterways in North America necessitated fresh water navies. Yet the nondescript British collection of small armed vessels which had existed on the Great Lakes and Lake Champlain since the conclusion of the Seven Years' War was hardly a navy. This self-styled Provincial Marine was really maintained by the Quartermaster-General's Department of the British Army to transport personnel and supplies for its several inland forts. The Provincial Marine's schooners also freighted goods for the fur traders based on these posts because there was still a shortage of privately owned vessels and it was desirable to provide maximum employment for the crews.

Ten years after the American Revolution the British Army had four companies of artillery and six regiments of foot in Upper and Lower Canada, although the reduced peace-time strengths totalled only 2,500 officers and other ranks. Upper Canada also had a revived corps of Queen's Rangers, consisting of 350 officers and other ranks specially engaged for service there as military pioneers.[10] There were a further four regiments of foot and three companies of artillery in "Nova Scotia and Its Dependencies." Because of the wooded terrain of British North America and the few roads there were no cavalry regiments.

The enemy against which this thinly stretched force might have to act was not much in doubt and seldom out of the mind of governors who were usually military men: it was the young and expanding republic to the south. Plans for the defence of British North America were based on a simple premise: so long as the Royal Navy was supreme in the North Atlantic and Quebec was properly garrisoned, "any American attempts to conquer the colonies must be impotent and abortive."[11] General George Washington himself had pointed out to the Continental Congress, as early as January 30, 1776, that any force invading Nova Scotia was likely to be cut off from its base by the Royal Navy. A great expanse of forest and wilderness separated the settlements now in the interior of New Brunswick from those of Maine. An American army advancing down the Lake Champlain route could hardly reduce both Montreal and Quebec before the coming of winter put an end to campaigning. Spring would bring up the St. Lawrence River a British fleet and an army capable of regaining whatever had been lost, as it had in May 1776.[12]

This scheme, according to a letter of Lord Dorchester's of October 7, 1793, to Lieutenant-Governor Simcoe, would involve the withdrawal of all regular troops from Upper Canada as soon as a crisis arose, to avoid their being cut off by an American army advancing against Montreal and having to surrender. Simcoe, however, argued in a despatch of December 2 to the British Government that, rather than deceive his militia into taking part in a hopeless conflict, the two Canadas should be defended. A well constructed and garrisoned fort at the rapids on the Richelieu River would delay any American force moving against Montreal. British ships navigating the St. Lawrence River as far as Montreal could bring supplies and reinforcements from Quebec and harass an approaching enemy force. From Montreal to Oswegatchie [Ogdensburg], the St. Lawrence was interrupted by formidable rapids, but there were no Americans settled along its south shore. Absence of American armed vessels ensured the Provincial Marine's superiority on Lake Ontario and control of the St. Lawrence River above Oswegatchie. The only weak spot was Kingston, whose harbour could not be defended with the forces and fortifications likely to be available, particularly during winter when the lake was frozen from shore to shore and an enemy could cross on the ice. Simcoe had already concentrated his military pioneer corps of Queen's Rangers as a mobile reserve at York; the defence of advanced posts was being left to the more elderly among the regulars and the veterans settled in the province.

Despatches from London soon assured Simcoe that there would be no need to abandon Upper Canada in an emergency. The Secretary of State for War and the Colonies was impressed by Simcoe's argument for a naval force on the Great Lakes, as being the "cheapest mode of defence" for Upper Canada.[13] In consequence, Simcoe's supplementary Militia Act of 1794 provided that Upper Canadian militia detachments might be employed in time of war upon the inland waterways, to reinforce the Provincial Marine. The Governor-in-Chief and Commander of the Forces in British North America, Lord Dorchester, was authorized to recruit two provincial battalions of Royal Canadian Volunteers for service in either of the Canadas. These were similar to the Royal Nova Scotia Regiment and the King's New

Brunswick Regiment which had been raised for purely local service in 1793, when the outbreak of war between Britain and Revolutionary France had necessitated withdrawal of three of the four regiments of foot from the Nova Scotia district for service in the West Indies.

These years of tension and conflict in Europe had made colonial governors nervous. Would a French fleet ever attack Halifax or other Nova Scotian ports? Would it try to transport an army up the St. Lawrence to attempt a re-conquest of Quebec? Would American forces co-operate with an overland invasion of Canada? Anglo-American friction had mounted as a result of the Royal Navy's enforcement of Orders in Council intended to stop the Americans' provision trade with France and their assumption of the carrying trade with the French West Indies. International law had been evolving since the early years of the 17th century, but there was still no agreement among nations of the western world as to whether a warring party had any right to interfere with the trading activities of citizens of a neutral country with its enemy, and, if it had, whether items other than munitions should be classed as contraband. The American contention of "free ships, free goods" was effectively denied by the Royal Navy, whose captains took merchantmen into the nearest British port so that a Vice-Admiralty Court might rule whether or not they should be confiscated as prizes.

There was, at the same time, a vigorous trade between the United States and the British North American colonies. The busy channels of trade brought American timber, pot and pearl ash, grain and provisions to Montreal. They also brought propaganda, circulated for a time by agents of Citizen Genêt who was the representative of Revolutionary France in the United States. By the spring of 1794 rumour was widespread that an invasion from Vermont was to coincide with the arrival of a French fleet in the Gulf of St. Lawrence. Lord Dorchester alerted the militia of Lower Canada. The English-speaking citizens of Montreal and Quebec came forward with great alacrity; but there were alarming disturbances among the *habitants* who were primarily interested in remaining neutral, as they had done during the American Revolution, despite the efforts of their leaders. The clergy in Lower Canada, shocked by the attacks made upon the Roman Catholic Church in France by the revolutionary régime and fearful of the growing influence exerted by American Protestants among the *habitants*, was more than ever determined on loyalty to Great Britain. The French-speaking lay leaders were similarly disposed. The rumoured invasion was a false alarm, however, and Dorchester soon reverted to a favourite theme by crediting the disorders "to a long disusc of Military Services, rather than to a spirit of discontent or disloyalty."[14]

Meanwhile the situation in the interior had become very threatening. At the instigation of Joseph Brant the Indians of the Old Northwest had joined in a confederacy to resist the advance of American settlement.[15] In each of 1790 and 1791 they had inflicted shattering defeats on American military forces sent against them.[16] Yet their confederacy dissolved two years later because Brant had become convinced that it would be in their own best interests to make peace with the United States while they could still bargain. Discussions had been opened but the western tribes refused the American proposals for boundaries offered during the summer of 1793, and Major-General "Mad Anthony" Wayne now prepared a punitive expedition, built around a mixed regular force of cavalry, artillery and infantry known as the Legion of the United States. Lord Dorchester delivered a bellicose address to an Indian gathering at Quebec on February 10, 1794, with the deliberate intention of making them believe that war between Great Britain and the United States was imminent and that they must revive their confederacy to resist American aggression. A week later Dorchester wrote Simcoe to guard Detroit and its communication with Lake Erie by establishing a regular garrison at the rapids on the Maumee (or Miami) River.

As soon as Simcoe learned of Wayne's actual advance into Indian country he called out the militia in the Western District of Upper Canada and ordered militia from Detroit to reinforce the new and still incomplete Fort Miami. On the morning of August 20, "Mad Anthony" Wayne's advancing column vanquished the western Indians at Fallen Timbers, on the opposite side of the Maumee rapids from Fort Miami and near the site of the present city of Toledo, Ohio. The British commander of the fort had kept his troops aloof and even closed the gates against Indian fugitives, leaving the Indians to draw obvious conclusions about the practical help they might expect in their campaigns. Even though the Canadian militiamen from Detroit had joined in the battle, in defiance of orders, Wayne in turn refrained from attacking the few British regulars in Fort Miami. He knew that President Washington did not want war and that Chief Justice John Jay was even then in London to negotiate a general settlement of Anglo-American differences.

Disheartened by their defeat at Fallen Timbers and by British failure to succour them, the Indians of the Old Northwest accepted the Peace of

Greenville offered them by the United States on August 3, 1795. This pushed the boundary of the Indian country northward from the Ohio River to the watershed separating its tributaries from the streams flowing into Lake Erie, and thus opened a large area for American settlement. These Indians, whose hunting grounds were now confined to what was left of the Old Northwest, also recognized the exclusive protection of the United States. This, however, did not end border intrigues: agents of the Indian Department in Upper Canada encouraged them to look still to the British for assistance and advice, since allies would be vital for the sustenance of Canada in any future Anglo-American conflict.

Jay's Treaty, signed in London on November 19, 1794, provided for British surrender of the disputed western posts by June 1, 1796. Britain's navigation laws were relaxed sufficiently to permit American vessels to engage in limited trade with the West and East Indies. The question of the Royal Navy's interference with American merchant ships on the high seas was shelved until two years after Britain's war with France should be concluded.

In the more confident period after Jay's Treaty the two regiments of foot which had been in Upper Canada were withdrawn, leaving less than 500 rank and file of the Queen's Rangers and the Royal Canadian Volunteers. These were few enough for continuing garrison duty at Kingston, York, and Fort Erie, and for manning the new forts required to replace certain of the western posts being relinquished: Fort George in the Niagara Peninsula, Fort Malden at Amherstburg on the Canadian shore of the Detroit River, and Fort St. Joseph on that island in the mouth of the St. Mary's River.

New causes of anxiety were soon to appear. The Anglo-American reconciliation achieved by Jay's Treaty had angered the French because they could no longer play off one against the other. They renewed and intensified the decrees authorizing their warships and privateers to prey on American merchantmen, and finally severed diplomatic relations. The United States struck back. A Navy Department was created on April 30, 1798. During the undeclared naval war which lasted until 1801, a small American navy was outfitted and several single ship actions were fought. This navy then took on the Barbary Pirates, while a general European peace was being concluded at Amiens in early 1802.

Again the respite was short. Barely had the several under-strength provincial corps and the Queen's Rangers been disbanded in British North America, and the regular regiments of foot placed on a reduced establishment, when a new and what was to be a greater threat to peace appeared. Napoleon's open contempt for British diplomacy and obvious intention of annexing more of Europe forced Great Britain to declare war on May 16, 1803. There was alarm for the safety of British North America, because British regiments would be heavily committed in Europe. Early in August authority was given to raise regiments of fencible infantry in each of New-foundland, Nova Scotia, New Brunswick and Canada. During earlier wars the British Army had raised so-called "fencible" regiments of cavalry and infantry for local defence only, chiefly in Scotland which had no militia prior to 1797; but the fact that certain of these Scottish units volunteered to replace overseas units of regulars during the war with Revolutionary France established a precedent: recruits now volunteered to serve "in North America but not elsewhere."[17] Recruiting parties for these regi-ments, whose officers were obtained in stipulated proportions from the regular army, half-pay list and local gentry, wandered anywhere for men and paid little attention to provincial boundaries. Brigadier-General Mar-tin Hunter soon realized that there was little hope of recruiting more than 200 men locally of the 1,100 other ranks authorized for his New Brunswick Fencibles, so he directed Lieutenant-Colonel George Johnstone, who had been a major in the 29th Foot, and other regular officers acquired in Great Britain to seek recruits in the Scottish Highlands. Other recruiting parties later obtained about 400 men in Upper and Lower Canada. Recruiting was slower for the Nova Scotia Fencibles, which numbered only 312 rank and file (corporals and privates) on January 1, 1805. That summer the Nova Scotia Fencibles exchanged stations with the Royal Newfoundland Fenci-ble Infantry and recruiting was continued among the fishermen and squatters in Newfoundland. As late as the end of 1806, however, the Cana-dian Fencibles had recruited only 124 men – too few for the unit to be placed upon the Army's establishment of employable regiments.

The problems of recruitment for service were only part of the difficul-ties facing those charged with making the best use of the British Army in Canada during these years. Their problems of discipline and morale were set forth in a submission made by Colonel Isaac Brock of the 49th Regi-ment of Foot to Field-Marshal H.R.H. Frederick, Duke of York, Com-mander-in-Chief of All His Majesty's Forces early in 1806:

A regiment quartered in Upper Canada is generally divided into eight different parts, several hundred miles asunder, and in this situation it remains at least three years. Great as is the evil incidental to a state of separation, even where the mind is in no danger of being debauched, what may not be apprehended in a country where both the divided state of the regiment, and the artifices employed to wean the soldier from his duty, conspire to render almost ineffectual every effort of the officer to maintain the usual degree of order and discipline? The lures to desertion continually thrown out by the Americans, and the facility with which it can be accomplished, exacting a more than ordinary precaution on the part of the officers, insensibly produce mistrust between them and the men, highly prejudicial to the service.

The soldier, in his intercourse with the inhabitants, soon learns that many of them, who a few years before possessed no kind of property, are become opulent, by having obtained extensive grants of land. He will also find that these men generally speaking, had no claim to favor, being either utter strangers, or known only as our enemies in the war of the rebellion. ...

The young and thoughtless give too much credit to what the designing are continually repeating to them – that they need only desert to secure an independence. ...

Experience has taught me that no regular regiment, however high its claims to discipline, can occupy the frontier posts of Lower and Upper Canada without suffering materially in its numbers. It might have been otherwise some years ago; but now that the country, particularly the opposite shore, is chiefly inhabited by the vilest characters, who have an interest in debauching the soldier from his duty, since roads are opened into the interior of the States which facilitate desertion, it is impossible to avoid the contagion. A total change must be effected in the minds and views of those who may be hereafter sent on this duty, before the evil can be surmounted.[18]

Brock's suggestion was that the vital centre of the defence of Canada – Quebec – should have the main concentration of regular troops and that a veteran battalion of older soldiers could assume garrison duty at frontier posts. Such old soldiers of good character and long service towards a pension would be unlikely to desert their posts. Nine such battalions were already in use by the British Army. On December 25, 1806, a 10th Royal Veteran Battalion was formed for service in North America. Volunteers of existing veteran battalions, men discharged from other regiments but fit for garrison duty, or men whose time had expired but wished to re-enlist made up its 10 companies totalling 650 rank and file.

The great conflict in Europe and elsewhere continued to overshadow events in North America. Napoleon's armies seemed capable of over-running continental Europe at will, but they could not cross the few miles of English Channel, guarded by a Royal Navy strong enough to keep bottled up in port the enemy ships of the line that had survived Nelson's great victory at Trafalgar in 1805. The Royal Navy could make the blockade of continental Europe effective simply by apprehending enemy or neutral ships attempting to enter or leave port: there was no necessity for warships patrolling outside enemy ports in all sorts of weather.

This blockade, however, merely intensified grievances that had been grating on far too many Americans since Britain had resumed war in 1803, and here again world events were to have an effect on the concerns of British North America. The major points at issue between Britain and the United States were the Royal Navy's refusal to permit neutral ships to enter ports of French-dominated Europe, its insistence on searching them on the high seas for contraband and deserters, and its impressment of American seamen. The British Government insisted that the Royal Navy was interested in removing from American ships only British fugitives – deserters from what was often a life of floating hell in its ships, or merchant seamen who had escaped impressment by signing on American ships where wages were higher. The Government of the United States had made an attempt to provide bona fide American sailors with certificates of citizenship, but these were easy for anyone to obtain and were often lost or sold. British naval officers used their own judgment, particularly if they were short-handed, and undoubtedly several thousand Americans were kidnapped over the years. These naval officers also decided whether neutral ships and cargoes consigned to a French destination might also be taken into the nearest British port for probable confiscation.

The position of neutral traders became impossible after Napoleon issued his Berlin Decree of November 21, 1806. By confiscating all British goods entering the ports of French-dominated Europe whether carried in British or in neutral ships, he hoped to cripple the economy of the world's greatest trading nation. The British Government retaliated with a new series of Orders in Council which extended its naval blockade to every port from which British ships were excluded: any ship which tried to enter any continental port without going first to the British Isles would be regarded as an enemy. Napoleon countered with his Milan Decree, which declared that all vessels searched by British warships or obeying the Orders in Council would lose their neutral character and be subject to seizure. Both belligerents were coercing neutrals from necessity, and with equal severity, but the Americans suffered in practice far more from British restrictions because the only French ships at sea were a few commerce-raiding privateers. Many Americans were also impressed by Napoleon's propaganda that British enforcement of the Orders in Council was really more than an act of war and was intended to establish the economic supremacy of Britain in the world.

During the early spring of 1807 this explosive situation threatened darkly. A British naval squadron was waiting in Chesapeake Bay, watching for French ships which would sooner or later have to leave American territorial waters. Several sailors managed to escape ashore from the British warships; they promptly enlisted in the United States Navy and were soon strutting about the streets of Norfolk, Virginia. Official representations for American assistance in apprehending these deserters met with flat refusals. The captain of the 38-gun American frigate *Chesapeake* knew that he had deserters among his crew, but believed them to be American citizens who had been pressed into the Royal Navy. The refusal incensed Vice-Admiral the Hon. George Cranfield Berkeley who, from Halifax, exercised command of "His Majesty's Ships and Vessels employed & to be employed in the River St. Lawrence, along the coast of Nova-Scotia, the Islands of Prince Edward and Cape Breton, in the bay of Fundy & the Islands of Bermuda."

In pursuance of the order he issued, H.M.S. *Leopard* tried to search U.S.S. *Chesapeake* when she cruised beyond the three-mile limit on June 22. When *Chesapeake* refused to heave to, the British 50-gun ship opened fire, killing three and wounding eighteen crew members before the American captain struck his colours. A British party then went aboard and carried off four men. This flagrant violation of American sovereignty caused a national uproar and a heated demand for war. Even the "most temperate people and those most attached to England," reported the English Minister to the United States, "say that they are bound as a nation and that they must assert their honor on the first attack upon it, or subject themselves to an imputation which it may be difficult ever to remove."[19] Fortunately Congress was not in session and President Jefferson refused to summon it. The British Government promptly disavowed the action and recalled Vice-Admiral Berkeley. It had never claimed the right to search ships of war; it

War scare, 1807
When H.M.S. *Leopard* made an unprovoked attack on U.S.S. *Chesapeake* in June 1807, it brought Britain and the United States to the brink of war. (Sketch by F.S. Cozzens, courtesy of the U.S. Naval Historical Center, NH-74526)

was willing to indemnify the wounded and next of kin of those killed; it was prepared to restore the abducted seamen.

News of this stormy incident reached Canada in July, embellished with all sorts of wild rumours. The acting Commander of the Forces was Colonel Isaac Brock.[20] Brock was then in his thirty-eighth year (he was born in Guernsey, one of the Channel Islands, on October 6, 1769) and a soldier of long standing, for he had been commissioned in the 8th (or King's) Regiment of Foot at 15 years of age. At 28 he was lieutenant-colonel of the 49th Regiment and commanded it in the Low Countries where he had a distinguished part in the Battle of Egmont-op-Zee in 1799. Two years later he was at the naval attack on Copenhagen. Brock brought the 49th Foot to Canada in 1802 and spent the next three years in garrison at Montreal, York, Fort George, and Quebec, thus acquiring considerable experience of the frontier he might now have to defend. A keen soldier, he was also a humane and considerate commanding officer. Late in 1805 he had been promoted to be a colonel in the Army. Now, as acting Commander of the Forces, he requested Mr. Thomas Dunn, the elderly Administrator of Lower Canada in the absence of a Governor, to call out sufficient militia to repair the crumbling defences of Quebec and to train for any emergency.

Only on August 20 [1808] did Dunn finally order that one-fifth of the militia, or about 10,000 men, should be drafted by ballot and hold themselves in readiness to march whenever required. Bishop Plessis of Quebec followed this with a *mandement*,[21] which was read in all the churches of his diocese. The *Quebec Mercury* of August 31 described the draft in exalted and rousing tones:

> The first draught was, in consequence, made, on the Esplanade, from the first battalion, of the Canadian militia, on Tuesday [25th August], from the second battalion on Friday, and from the British battalion, by ballot, yesterday. We should be wanting in justice to our compatriots did we say less than that, never, on a similar occasion, could there be manifested more cheerful alacrity and zeal, than were shewn on these occasions, as well by the Canadians as by the British. Numbers volunteered their services. The Artillery company, the two flank companies, and Captain Burn's battalion company, who are the strongest and best disciplined of the British have, to a man, formally tendered their services. Sums of money were offered by individuals for prize-tickets, for such the tickets were called which, in balloting, were for service. Some young batchelors procured prize-tickets from the married men, who had drawn for service; but the greater part of the latter insisted on keeping their tickets, notwithstanding that offers of exchange were made to them by other batchelors.
>
> Too much praise cannot be given to the animating language of the field officers and others, in their speeches, addressed to the different battalions and companies, on the occasion. The whole has been attended with much festivity and hilarity.
>
> We hear that equal cheerfulness and ardour have manifested themselves in the different country parishes.[22]

A disgusted Brock pointed out, however, that nothing actually was done. "The men thus selected for service being scattered along an extensive line of four or five hundred miles, unarmed and totally un-acquainted with anything military, without officers capable of giving them instruction, considerable time would naturally be required before the necessary degree of order and discipline could be introduced among them."[23] Obviously little more could be expected from the small companies of English-speaking and French-speaking volunteers who had been drilling at Quebec, Trois-Rivières, and Montreal since the summer of 1803 with muskets loaned by the Board of Ordnance.[24]

Lieutenant-Governor Francis Gore[25] of the more exposed Upper Canada hastened down to Montreal to consult Brock, but all this one-time cavalry major could get was a promise that 4,000 stands of arms would be sent forthwith from Quebec.[26] In the meantime there were practically no weapons in Upper Canada to issue to his untrained militia. Gore wrote the Secretary of State for War and the Colonies that he was refraining from calling out any part of the militia, "that the Americans may not be made acquainted with our weakness."[27]

On October 18 Lieutenant-General Sir James Craig arrived at Quebec to assume the long vacant appointments of Captain-General and Governor-in-Chief of British North America.[28] The career of this 59-year-old soldier had followed the general pattern of those serving Britain's far-flung interests in these years. Service in the American Revolution, including the Burgoyne expedition, had been followed by fighting at the Cape of Good Hope, in India and the Mediterranean. At the same time as his arrival in Canada further troops became available. The 10th Royal Veteran Battalion had arrived at Quebec a few weeks earlier than previously scheduled. No further reinforcement could be expected from Britain that season, but the position of the Canadas was strengthened when the 98th Foot and the Royal Newfoundland Fencibles shortly arrived from Halifax and joined the Quebec garrison. The over-all plan was that, should the under-strength New Brunswick Fencibles and the untrained militia be unable to halt possible American invasion from Maine, they were to retreat on Halifax, where there were still 600 regulars and the Royal Navy. About 2,000 militia were embodied in Nova Scotia, including 500 to work on the fortifications of Halifax. The approach of winter, however, made an invasion unlikely, so Craig merely warned the inhabitants of Lower Canada, in a Militia General Order of November 24, to be on their guard against strangers and the "portion of the Militia, amounting to one-fifth, directed to be balloted for … to continue to hold itself in readiness to assemble, on the shortest notice."[29]

With the arrival of the promised arms in Upper Canada, Gore took more forthright action early in December. "Our militia has been mustered, and arms issued out to them," wrote an inhabitant of Kingston on January 3, 1808, "also every fourth man draughted, which draughts are to keep themselves in Constant readiness, in case Jonathan should attempt an invasion. We are now learning the Exercises and are drilled twice a Week by a Sergeant from the Garrison – and are already much improved Considering our Awkwardness."[30]

Craig had arrived in October but it was not until January 3 that Gore finally received a letter from him, explaining his secret instructions from the Secretary of State for War and the Colonies. These laid the familiar stress on the pivot of Quebec. Craig wrote that they pointed out

> the preservation of Quebec as the object of my first and principal con-
> sideration, and that to which all others must be subordinate. It is the
> only Post, defective as it is in many respects, that can be considered ten-
> able for a moment, nor is the preservation of it of less consequence to
> the Province under your immediate direction, than it is to this, as af-
> fording the only door for the future entry of that force which it might
> be found expedient, and which the King's Government might be then
> able to send for the recovery of both or either … for if the Americans
> are really determined to attack these Provinces, and employ those
> means which they may so easily command, I fear it would be vain for us
> to flatter ourselves with the hopes of making any effectual defence of the
> open country, unless powerfully assisted from home.[31]

Craig suggested sending into Upper Canada the loyal militia of Lower Canada and any regulars not involved directly in the defence of Quebec. These, and Gore's present troops and militia, might then harry the rear of the American invaders who, after having occupied Montreal, would be moving down river against Quebec.

In his reply dated January 5, Gore agreed that the whole disposable force in Upper Canada might be so employed. Since the Americans had no naval vessels on the Great Lakes, he could retain supremacy there for some time. To give effect to such a policy, the consolidated Militia Act approved by the Legislature of Upper Canada on March 16 provided that

> It shall not be lawful to order the militia or any part thereof, to march out
> of this Province, except for the assistance of the Province of Lower
> Canada, (when the same shall actually be invaded or in a state of insur-
> rection) or except in pursuit of an enemy who may have invaded this
> Province, and except also for the destruction of any vessel or vessels built
> or building, or any depot or magazine, formed or forming, or for the at-
> tack of any enemy who may be embodying or marching for the purpose
> of invading this Province, or for the attack of any fortification now
> erected, or which may be hereafter erected, to cover the invasion thereof.[32]

Gore's letter of January 5 had also conceded the obvious: it would be impracticable to defend Upper Canada against anything except a "partial or sudden incursion." This truth, however, "must be carefully concealed from Persons of almost every description in this colony, for there are few People here that would act with Energy were it not for the purpose of defending the lands which they actually possess."[33]

Craig and Gore also revived the almost dormant policy of conciliating the western Indians. Napoleon had sold Louisiana to the United States in 1803 and had thus seemed to withdraw French interest from North America, but he was believed to be now considering intervention in the New World; this might lead to French agents reviving old alliances and unloosing the Indians upon the "defenceless frontier of Upper Canada." Therefore, as Craig wrote to Gore, it was more imperative than ever to win over the Indians; but as usual the commitment would be partial: "the means that are pursued should be such as are of general conciliation and attachment without any particular allusion for the present to any possible state of hostilities with Americans."[34]

Craig also re-submitted a proposal rejected a year earlier by the Secretary of State for War and the Colonies that a corps be raised from among the Scots settled in Glengarry county of Upper Canada, some of whom had been members of the Glengarry Fencibles disbanded in Scotland following the [1802] Treaty of Amiens. A month after issuing a letter of service on his own authority, however, Craig had to withdraw it because he realized that the unit's officers were unable to raise the required number of men as quickly as they had claimed possible. He also tried to improve his position by getting the Canadian Fencibles to a usable strength, and to this end ordered from the province the more zealous recruiting parties of the New Brunswick Fencibles. On June 14 approval was given at the Horse Guards in London for the Canadian Fencibles to be placed upon the establishment of the Army whenever there should be 400 rank and file, with the usual proportion of officers and non-commissioned officers.[35] A strength return of November 11, 1808, showed 24 sergeants, 22 drummers and 411 rank and file.

Similar concern for troops was evident below the border. During the years 1802-1807 the Congress of the United States had enacted several measures envisaging the employment of militia and volunteers in case of national emergency, but had ignored the regular army which had been allowed to decline to only 175 officers and 2,389 enlisted men. Congress now authorized an increase of five regiments of infantry, one regiment of rifle-men, one regiment of light artillery and one regiment of dragoons – the men to serve five-year engagements unless discharged sooner. Recruiting proved difficult, however, and these units long continued under-strength. Nor did the fledgling navy increase its power greatly. Congress remained convinced that gunboats could provide a more satisfactory and cheaper defence of the American coast than a proper ocean-going navy of ships of the line.

Neither President Jefferson nor his Republican party's majority in Congress really believed in taking adequate defensive measures because of firm conviction about the efficacy of economic pressure to ensure American rights in the world. Their answer to the Orders in Council of Britain and the Decrees of Napoleon was an Embargo Act hurriedly enacted by Congress and proclaimed on December 22, 1807. This put a legal end to virtually all land and seaborne commerce with foreign nations. American ships were forbidden to leave for foreign ports. Importation in foreign ships was not prohibited, but it was almost outlawed by the provision that foreign vessels could not carry goods out of an American port.

This retaliation was most unpopular among local traders. Serious internal disturbances resulted from the attempts by federal officials to prevent smuggling. Enraged citizens at Sackets Harbor forcibly prevented customs officers and troops from interfering with the trade across Lake Ontario and the St. Lawrence River. Armed guards ensured the safe delivery of lumber rafts and produce floated down Lake Champlain into Lower Canada. Unprecedented storms forced New England coastal vessels to seek shelter in Nova Scotian ports, while Passamaquoddy Bay became an even better place for smuggling. The election of 1808 provided a means whereby the mercantile interests in New England, New York, New Jersey and Delaware could express their preoccupation with trade; they supported the Federalist party. It again failed to secure a majority of the seats in Congress, but there was now sufficient opposition to the Republican party to cause repeal of the Embargo Act. Jefferson's successor, James Madison, persuaded the new Congress to pass a lesser Non-Intercourse Act. This Act of March 1, 1809, re-opened trade with all nations except Great Britain and France, but authorized the President to proclaim resumption of trade with either or both these belligerents, whenever they should cease to violate neutral rights. Napoleon refused to revoke his Berlin and Milan Decrees, however, and the British Government stood by its Orders in Council.

Attempts continued to be made to improve Anglo-American relations, but they foundered because neither government would yield or compromise sufficiently on fundamental issues. Impressment of an American sailor from a coastal vessel by H.M.S. *Guerrière* on May 1, 1811, raised another outcry in the United States. This act was avenged on May 16 when U.S.S. *President* mistook the much smaller H.M.S. *Little Belt* for the frigate *Guerrière* and battered her into submission, killing nine and wounding twenty-three. The new British Minister *en route* to Washington was able to effect a settlement of the long-drawn-out *Chesapeake* Affair, but otherwise deadlock continued. British impressment of sailors from American ships was the root of the trouble.

There did, however, seem to some Americans to be a more promising way of getting back at Britain. Although totally unprepared to go to war, the United States might well effect an easy conquest of Canada. The militia of the neighbouring states could quickly take possession of Upper Canada, leaving a regular force free to reduce Quebec. Even should the worst come to the worst and the all-powerful Royal Navy make possible British capture of New York and New Orleans, these could be recovered at the inevitable peace conference in exchange for returning the Canadas

These alarums and excursions had convinced Sir James Craig that war was inevitable. He himself felt too old and unhealthy to direct the defence of British North America and he had already requested permission to resign. He was pessimistic about the outcome, having unhappy memories of the *habitants* as militiamen during the American Revolution and because his experiences later in governing the Canadas had given him a low

President James Madison (1751-1836)
A decent and humane man, Madison came to the conclusion that war was the only way to resolve America's problems with Britain.
(Portrait by Gilbert Stuart, U.S. Naval Historical Center, NH-48047)

opinion of the French-speaking population, which now numbered almost 275,000 men, women, and children.

Gore was almost as pessimistic about the loyalty of the population in Upper Canada, for a different reason of course. He put his fears of the effect of American influences in his letter to Craig of January 5, 1808:

> I think I may venture to state that the generality of the Inhabitants from Kingston to the Borders of the lower province may be depended upon, but I cannot venture, from the industry that has been used by certain characters now and lately in this Province, to assert that the Inhabitants about the Seat of this Government [York], Niagara and Long Point [on Lake Erie] are equally to be relied on. I have also to observe that excepting the Inhabitants of Glengarry and those Persons who have served in the American War and their Descendents, which form a considerable body of men, the residue of the Inhabitants of this colony consist chiefly of Persons who have emigrated from the States of America and of consequence, retain those ideas of equality and insubordination much to the prejudice of this government, so prevalent in that country.[36]

Although population figures can only be estimated, there would seem to have been nearly 77,000 men, women and children in Upper Canada by 1811. An American itinerant Baptist minister, who shortly thereafter compiled a *Geographical View of the Province*, estimated that loyalist stock accounted for only one-sixth of the population and emigrants from the British Isles and their children for another one-fifth.[37]

Increasing ill health caused Craig to sail for England on June 19, 1811, on the ship which had delivered a letter from the Secretary of State for War and the Colonies finally acquiescing in his request to resign. Until his designated successor, Lieutenant-General Sir George Prevost, should arrive from Nova Scotia where he was serving as Lieutenant-Governor, the elderly Mr. Thomas Dunn who had vacillated during the *Chesapeake* incident would again administer the government of Lower Canada. The situation was tense and uneasy, but the British Government was confident that the Minister *en route* to Washington would be able to restore amicable Anglo-American relations without a repeal of the Orders in Council. British North America could only wait, its peace and security absolutely dependent on the moves of greater powers.

CHAPTER TWO

"A General Outline for Defence": Preparations for War, 1811-1812

Lieutenant-General Sir George Prevost, one of the leading actors in the drama soon to unfold, reached Quebec to take up his new duties on September 13, 1811.[1] The extent of the responsibilities he was about to assume may be inferred from what were soon to be his official titles: "Captain-General and Governor in Chief in and over the Provinces of Upper & Lower Canada, New-Brunswick, Nova-Scotia, and the Islands of Prince Edward and Cape Breton, and their several Dependencies, Vice-Admiral of the same, Lieutenant-General and Commander of all his Majesty's Forces in the Provinces of Lower and Upper Canada, Nova-Scotia & New-Brunswick, and in the Islands of Prince Edward, Cape Breton, Newfoundland and the Bermudas."

Prevost was the eldest son of French-speaking Swiss Protestant parents; his father had served in the British Army, was wounded during the siege of Quebec in 1759, and had climaxed his long career by a successful defence of Savannah, Georgia, against the Americans and French in 1778. He himself had been born in New Jersey on May 19, 1767, when his father was a lieutenant-colonel in the predominantly Swiss-officered 60th (or Royal American) Regiment of Foot. After being educated in England and on the Continent, George was commissioned in June 1783. When war with France broke out ten years later he was commanding the 3rd Battalion of the 60th Regiment on the island of Antigua. During the fighting in the West Indies, Lieutenant-Colonel Prevost distinguished himself. He was wounded twice in January 1796, while his regiment was fighting the French who had landed on St. Vincent. Two years later he obtained his colonelcy and an appointment as brigadier-general. He was subsequently as popular a governor of St. Lucia, until its return to France by the Treaty of Amiens in 1802, as any conqueror could be. Successful defence of Dominica against a determined French assault during the winter of 1805

25

**Lieutenant-General Sir George Prevost
(1767-1816)**
As governor-general of the Canadas, he
had the difficult task of reconciling the
French- and English-speaking segments
of the population; as commander-in-
chief of British North America, he bore
the responsibility for its defence during
the War of 1812. (National Archives of
Canada, C-6152)

brought his promotion to the rank of major-general and a baronetcy, and
a short tour of duty in England. He changed the scene of his operations
when the *Chesapeake* Affair led to his being ordered to Nova Scotia with
reinforcements in the spring of 1808; he was to command the troops there
with the rank of lieutenant-general and to succeed the elderly Sir John
Wentworth as Lieutenant-Governor. However, he returned to the West
Indies late in 1808, when he temporarily left Halifax with part of its garrison and served as second-in-command of the successful expedition
against Martinique.[2] Sir George Prevost and his English wife were popular
throughout their sojourn in Nova Scotia. Suave and diplomatic by nature,
Prevost was next expected to undo the harm done in Lower Canada by
Craig's brushes with the Legislative Assembly and the Roman Catholic
clergy. Back of Craig's suppression of the radical newspaper *Le Canadien*,
the arrest and confinement of its editors without trial, and the dissolution
of the Assembly when its French-speaking majority persisted in obstruc-
tive tactics, had been Craig's firm conviction that the province was a conquered territory which should be governed in accordance with the best interests of the English-speaking commercial oligarchy or *Château Clique.*

The men holding senior appointments under Prevost had also pursued
careers in many parts of the world. His successor in Nova Scotia, Lieutenant-General Sir John Coape Sherbrooke, three years older, had served in
the Netherlands, in India, in Sicily, and in the Peninsular War under Sir
Arthur Wellesley until ill health had forced his return to England.[3] The

military commanders in New Brunswick, Cape Breton, Newfoundland, and Bermuda were immediately responsible to Sherbrooke; as civil administrators as well, however, the first two officers were directly responsible to Prevost, as was the elderly Lieutenant-Governor of Prince Edward Island.

Since the summer of 1810 a still older and more experienced soldier-of-fortune, Major-General Francis, Baron de Rottenburg, had been in Lower Canada.[4] Born in Danzig on November 4, 1757, he had served in the French Army of Louis XVI and in Kosciuszko's unsuccessful fight against the Russians. In 1795 he had been commissioned into one of the foreign corps being added to the British Army to make up for its deficiency of light infantry. Three years later he raised a 5th Battalion for the 60th Royal Americans. He had written, in German, a book of *Regulations for the Exercise of Riflemen and Light Infantry* which was really an unofficial drill manual until the Duke of York ordered that it be translated into English and brought to the attention of all British officers.[5] Just before coming to Lower Canada, De Rottenburg had commanded a brigade of light infantry during the Walcheren Campaign of 1809.

Major-General Sir John Coape Sherbrooke (1764-1830)
The commander in the Atlantic provinces, the veteran Sherbrooke was one of Prevost's most reliable subordinates. (Benson Lossing, *Pictorial Field-Book of the War of 1812*, 1869)

Major-General Francis de Rottenburg (1757-1832)
A German veteran serving in the British army, he was Prevost's senior subordinate and would command in Upper Canada in 1813. (*Journal of the Society for Army Historical Research*, 1931)

Major-General Isaac Brock (1769-1812)
As the commander in Upper Canada at the outbreak of war, Brock had the task of defending a province nearly surrounded by American territory. (National Archives of Canada, C-36181)

In Upper Canada the recently promoted Major-General Isaac Brock became Administrator as well as commander of its forces on October 9, 1811, so that Lieutenant-Governor Francis Gore could attend to private business in England (where he was to remain until the summer of 1815). Off and on since the summer of 1808, Brock had been requesting employment in an active theatre of war. "I must see service," he wrote in one letter to his brothers, "or I may as well, and indeed much better, quit the army at once, for no one advantage can I reasonably look to hereafter if I remain buried in this inactive, remote corner, without the slightest mention being made of me."[6] By the time word was received that the Duke of York had approved of his return to Europe, however, Brock agreed with Prevost's suggestion that he decline: "Being now placed in a high ostensible situation, and the state of public affairs with the American government indicating a strong presumption of an approaching rupture between the two countries, I beg leave to be allowed to remain in my present command."[7]

Viewed from Canada, the situation developing in Washington did appear ominous. Congress had assembled earlier than usual, on November 4, 1811, and the younger Republican element had immediately gained control of the House of Representatives. Representing agrarian interests in the south and west for the most part, and clamouring for war with Great Britain, its members were quickly dubbed "War Hawks." Even the staunchest Federalists, however, were now less pro-British: France had claimed to have revoked the offending Berlin and Milan Decrees, and they felt that Britain should cancel its Orders in Council aimed at neutral traders. The message which President Madison sent to Congress stressed the seriousness of the situation and his conviction of the rectitude of the American cause:

> ... the period is arrived, which claims from the legislative guardians of the national rights a system of more ample provisions for maintaining them. Notwithstanding the scrupulous justice, the protracted modera-tion, and the multiplied efforts on the part of the United States to sub-stitute for the accumulating dangers to the peace of the two countries, all the mutual advantages of re-established friendship and confidence; we have seen that the British cabinet perseveres, not only in withhold-ing a remedy for other wrongs so long and so loudly calling for it; but in the execution, brought home to the threshold of our territory, of meas-ures which, under circumstances, have the character, as well as the effect, of war on our lawful commerce.
>
> With this evidence of hostile inflexibility, in trampling on rights which no independent nation can relinquish – congress will feel the duty of putting the United States into an armour, and an attitude de-manded by the crisis, and corresponding with the national spirit and expectations.[8]

President Madison asked for increases to the regular army, the acceptance of volunteer corps, an improvement in the navy, and an augmentation of the already satisfactory supply of cannon, muskets and ammunition.

Although news of it was to travel slowly from the Old Northwest, a de-cisive action was fought between land-hungry Americans and Indians of a new confederacy on November 8. The Indians had been preparing a final stand for their rights under the leadership of the Shawnee warrior known as Tecumseh.[9] This remarkable Indian, now forty-three years of age, had fought in many border skirmishes and at Fallen Timbers. He had even fa-vourably impressed many Americans, one of whom would later write:

> His carriage was erect and lofty – his motions quick – his eyes penetrat-ing, his vision stern, with an air of hauteur in countenance, which arose from an elevated pride of soul. His eloquence was nervous, concise,

impressive, figurative and sarcastic; being of a taciturn habit of speech, his words were few but always to the purpose.

Unfortunately Tecumseh was busy elsewhere organizing his confederacy when William Henry Harrison, Governor of the Indiana Territory, led a mixed force of regulars and militia against his headquarters at the village of Tippecanoe, about 80 miles due south of Lake Michigan. The 38-year-old Harrison had been a promising young regular army lieutenant until he switched his career to politics.[10] A continuing student of military history and a firm believer in unorthodox tactics, he managed to beat off a dawn attack inspired by Tecumseh's younger brother, a visionary known as the Prophet. Harrison's force then advanced on and burned the defenceless village of Tippecanoe. Tecumseh and the remains of his abortive confederacy sought help from British officers of the Indian Department at Amherstburg and soon came to constitute a part of the defence of Upper Canada.

Obviously one of Sir George Prevost's most pressing tasks in these days of threatened invasion was to conciliate the French-speaking Canadians who had now become a solidly knit opposition to the English-speaking oligarchy in Lower Canada. Three of his new appointees to the Legislative Council were French-speaking Canadians. Only two were included among the seven new members appointed to the Executive Council, but this body was designed to reflect the wealthier class who were now mostly English-speaking merchants. Prevost had no illusions that his French-speaking appointees were disinterested *patriotes*; he regarded them, and those later selected for positions of trust, as politicians who were only too anxious to earn both official and popular favour. By managing some improvement in the official status of Bishop Plessis as head of the Roman Catholic clergy in the province, Prevost further ensured its support. Bishop Mountain of the Church of England, however, was enraged by such friendliness to the Roman Catholic clergy and soon became Prevost's bitter enemy. Although the Prevosts liberally entertained the leading English-speaking residents of Quebec City at the Château St. Louis, and Sir George paid particular attention to the leading merchants and fur traders in Montreal, most of these preferred to remember happier days when they had been the confidants of Sir James Craig.

Military preparedness also claimed Prevost's attention very soon after his arrival. During a visit to the Montreal District in October, he inspected the forts at Chambly, St. Johns, and Sorel (or William Henry). As a precaution against the future possibility of having to transfer troops from Halifax to Quebec, Prevost ordered two officers to test the canoe and portage route across New Brunswick to Rivière-du-Loup on the lower St. Lawrence. He sought and obtained authority from London to continue with the works of fortification commenced by Craig. Prevost requested a further 10,000 muskets and accoutrements for possible issue to the militia, as well as 200 sabres, saddles and bridles to equip inhabitants who had volunteered to serve as cavalry. He had, however, been disconcerted to learn one of the characteristic oddities of these years of conflict: a great part of the provisions required for the Canadian garrisons were normally purchased from the United States.

Fortunately the Provincial Marine enjoyed naval preponderance on the Great Lakes. The Americans had nothing on the upper lakes to oppose the 16-gun brig *Queen Charlotte* and the schooner *General Hunter* of six guns. The United States Navy had a 16-gun brig *Oneida* at Sackets Harbor on Lake Ontario, but obviously this was no match for the Provincial Marine's 22-gun corvette *Royal George* which was really a miniature ship-rigged frigate.[11] The Provincial Marine's additional three armed schooners on Lake Ontario, and the single one on Lake Champlain, however, were neither manned nor maintained properly and were no longer able to compete for commercial cargoes with privately owned shipping. Seamen were lured away from the Provincial Marine by merchants who offered higher wages. There were no opportunities for promotion. One captain was actually 87 years of age; other elderly masters were equally disinterested in retirement. Prevost finally retired the commodore and the two captains in charge of operations, on full pay pending referral to London, but much more was needed before the Provincial Marine could become a truly combatant organization.

Considering that Britain was engaged in a life-and-death struggle with France and that there was always the possibility of trouble erupting elsewhere in the British Empire, the military manpower already available in North America was the most that Sir George Prevost had any right to expect. The British regulars, including fencibles, in the Canadas totalled roughly 5,600 effectives: four companies of Royal Artillery numbering less than 450 gunners, the 1st Battalion of the 8th (or King's) Regiment, the 41st, 49th and 100th Regiments of Foot, the 10th Royal Veteran Battalion,[12] the Royal Newfoundland Regiment of Fencible Infantry and the Canadian

Fencibles.[13] Only about 1,200 all ranks, however, were in Upper Canada, which was most exposed to attack; and these were scattered widely in small garrisons. The Royal Artillery did not come completely under Sir George Prevost's command. Its commander, Major-General George Glasgow, recently promoted, was directly responsible to the Board of Ordnance in London, as well as to Sir George Prevost. So was the Commanding Royal Engineer, Lieutenant-Colonel R. H. Bruyeres. His Engineer Department actually comprised only four captains: unless and until Prevost's request for a company of Royal Military Artificers should be granted, it would have to depend upon civilian or militia labour.[14] The Commissariat, Barrackmaster and Paymaster staffs were correspondingly small and responsible to Treasury officials in London for their expenditures. Medical and hospital arrangements were rudimentary by modern standards.

Since correspondence had to be written in long hand, staff officers kept it to a minimum and were not yet swamped by paper work; they could be given field commands of a temporary nature. The Adjutant General, Colonel Edward Baynes, was often to perform other than administrative duties when required by Prevost and he more closely resembled a modern Chief of Staff.[15] The then parallel appointment of Quartermaster General, however, was held by a recently appointed nonentity who had previously been Deputy Barrackmaster General and would not long continue in his new duties.[16]

Sir John Sherbrooke's subordinate command in "Nova Scotia and Its Dependencies" had 161 officers and 4,220 other ranks, including 560 Royal Artillerymen and 119 Royal Military Artificers. The 104th Regiment of Foot[17] was in New Brunswick (less companies on each of Cape Breton and Prince Edward Island); the 2nd Battalion of the 8th Regiment, the 98th Regiment (less about 300 all ranks in Bermuda) and the 99th Regiment were in Nova Scotia; the Nova Scotia Fencibles were still in Newfoundland.

What were the qualities of these regulars on whom so much reliance had to be placed? Something of the background of their service might help in realizing these. In peacetime most infantry regiments of the line had possessed only one battalion, commanded by a lieutenant-colonel, who had a major as second in command. A battalion would have eight companies, each of which was limited to a captain, lieutenant, ensign (who originally had carried the company's own flag), two sergeants, a drummer and 42 rank and file. To this total of 384, would be added a regimental staff of

Colonel Edward Baynes (1768-1829)
Long associated with Prevost, Colonel
Edward Baynes was one of the British
commander's closest associates but not a
popular officer. (Richardson's *War of
1812*, 1902)

adjutant, quartermaster, surgeon, paymaster and a few orderlies. Following
the outbreak of war with France, battalions were increased to 10 larger
companies with an optimum strength of better than 1,100 all ranks. Extra
battalions were added to most regiments and additional regiments were
authorized. As we have seen, however, the regiments in North America
were seldom up to strength.

The private soldiers traditionally were recruited from the labouring
classes in the British Isles. Many were Irish peasants. Knowing only drudg-
ery and want, they were often attracted to soldiering by the tall tales of recruiting sergeants, the free drinks prior to attestation, or the enlistment
bounty. This bounty money was, however, soon expended treating the
temporarily solicitous old soldiers and the company sergeants. Thence-
forth soldiering was almost as poor a means of subsistence as civilian life,
since the meagre pay was subject to all manner of deductions, including
amounts for food and clothing: in 1797 the daily pay of a private soldier
had been increased to the trifling sum of one shilling and he was guaranteed four shillings per week for himself. Although normal enlistment ages
were between 18 and 30, boys could be enlisted as young as 14 years of age.
Enlistment had been for an indeterminate period during peacetime; it was
actually a life-time engagement unless the Crown should be pleased to discharge a soldier from service sooner, or he should become a deserter and
manage to make a success of civilian life elsewhere. Long years of war had
depleted this reservoir of men, but fortunately the British Army was then

able to enlist large numbers of home craftsmen and artisans thrown out of work by the spreading Industrial Revolution. Parliament's abhorrence of standing armies and preference for shorter service enlistments resulted in a number of special Recruiting Acts designed to augment the military establishment for a limited period only. That of 1806 authorized enlistments of seven years for infantry, ten years for cavalry and twelve years for artillery. Discipline in the army was strict, and might be brutal if a commanding officer believed that flogging was the only answer to both laxity and legitimate complaints. Barracks were crowded and there was little or no privacy in them even when men had their wives with them. Wives were permitted to accompany a regiment abroad in peacetime, or might be found from the local population. They nursed the sick and eked out their husbands' pay by serving as laundresses for the rest of the men. Even in wartime, six wives per company were generally allowed to accompany a regiment and lots were drawn for the privilege of enduring the rigours of active service. Those unlucky enough to be left behind, with or without children, often acquired new husbands to avoid becoming destitute.[18]

Under these circumstances the British soldier's superiority as a fighting man is best attributed to his being better disciplined and trained than his opponents. The elaborate drill movements, learned to perfection, were designed to enable an advancing column to form line immediately an enemy was discovered, to the front or either of the flanks. Experiments in North America and India had demonstrated that infantrymen formed in two ranks possessed firepower equal to that of the three ranks used by European armies. In 1809 official approval was belatedly given to the two-rank line in the British army although its use had been *common* practice among commanding officers anxious to form a longer line of battle with the limited manpower available. The "Brown Bess" musket was superior to the muzzle-loaders used by every other army.[19] The maximum effective range of these smooth-bored weapons, which a soldier merely pointed at a target because there were no sights, was only 100 yards. Yet three volleys a minute fired by soldiers standing shoulder to shoulder could almost be guaranteed to halt an enemy advancing in similar close order.[20]

This improvement in firepower had made it possible to discard the clumsy hand grenade as an infantryman's weapon; the name grenadier, however, continued to be used to designate the right flank company containing the tallest and physically best developed soldiers. In North America during the Seven Years' War the best shots had been grouped into special companies of lightly armed and equipped troops and these companies had also proved their worth during the American Revolution: henceforth a light infantry company formed the left flank of every battalion of infantry. These flank companies gave a necessary flexibility to any field force; tasks demanding initiative were often assigned to distinct flank battalions especially formed from the regiments available, while the mass of battalion companies merely fired volleys straight ahead at a visible enemy who was within 100 yards range.

The officers who exercised command were mostly drawn from the privileged classes of society. When a young man of family wished to join a cavalry or infantry regiment he purchased his commission and subsequently his promotion up to the rank of lieutenant-colonel; thus an officer's rise normally depended upon his having the purchase price available whenever a vacancy occurred in his own regiment, or in any one whose colonel would accept him. This meant having private means at his disposal, for his pay would be too low for him to save anything as a junior officer or even really "enjoy life" in the officers' mess. A profitable marriage could, of course, help him to improve his circumstances greatly. Since regimental promotion depended primarily on possession of adequate financial means rather than on military considerations, gradations of rank could almost disappear off duty and mess life resembled that of any gentlemen's club. Eventually, sale of a commission brought what was virtually a small retirement annuity. Colonial service, which fell to the lot of most units at some time, was not attractive to many of these "clubmen": the more wealthy and socially conscious managed to arrange transfers to other regiments, for a financial inducement, whenever a unit was ordered on colonial service in peacetime. Those who actually served on such stations therefore were either run of-the-mill officers who could not afford to avoid it, or keen officers to whom soldiering was a way of life and upon whom fortune might yet shine. Military success had come both to Haldimand and to Prevost's own father while serving in North America.[21]

A colonel, though he usually did not in practice command his regiment, virtually owned it and expected to profit from the allowances given for its clothing and other maintenance. Frequently he was actually a general officer who might be serving on a different continent. He might even be unemployed. A lieutenant-colonel, major and senior captains might be given a higher rank because of distinguished service or in order to fill a particular staff appointment away from regimental duty. This was known as army or brevet rank. For example, Lieutenant-General Josiah Champagne was colonel of the 41st Regiment of Foot, whose 1st Battalion was serving in Upper Canada; Lieutenant-Colonel Henry Procter of the same battalion was employed there as a colonel on staff; the senior major was commanding the battalion as a brevet lieutenant-colonel; four of the regiment's senior captains were elsewhere as brevet majors.[22]

This closed system did occasionally have openings. Vacancies created by death could be filled without purchase. Battlefield commissions could be given to deserving and intelligent sergeants, although such instances were comparatively rare. Appointments as adjutants, quartermasters, and paymasters, however, normally went to men who had risen from the ranks.[23]

The Royal Artillery and Royal Engineers were also exceptions, for their officers did not have to purchase commissions or promotion. For the most part they were more intelligent sons of middle-class families and had received mathematical and scientific training at the Royal Military Academy, Woolwich. These R.A. and R.E. officers, responsible to the Board of Ordnance rather than the Commander-in-Chief, were promoted on seniority and merit, both in their own corps and in the army. The senior colonels-commandant in each corps had army rank and lieutenant-generals and most colonels were major-generals in the army.[24]

The local levies provided a sharp contrast to the regular army. According to Sir George Prevost's information, the militia of Lower Canada numbered upwards of 60,000 on paper, "ill armed and without discipline." That of Upper Canada was calculated at 11,000 men, "of which it might not be prudent to arm more than 4000," since large numbers were recent immigrants from the United States.[25] The British Army provided Inspecting Field Officers for the militia, but up to now these appointments in the Canadas had been treated as sinecures by the fortunate incumbents, and they had not made it their business to supervise militia training with any great care.[26] About 6,000 of the 11,000 militia in Nova Scotia had been provided with arms and accoutrements since the *Chesapeake* Affair and given rudimentary training. Few of the 4,000 widely scattered militia in New Brunswick had received any training. The militia of Cape Breton and Prince Edward Island did not "amount to any considerable number deserving to be noticed."[27]

When he viewed the manpower available to him, Prevost decided he should revive the proposal to raise a fencible corps in Glengarry county of

Upper Canada. Without waiting for a "yes" or "no" from London, he directed Captain "Red George" Macdonell of the 8th (or King's) Regiment of Foot to attempt the formation of a small battalion of 376 rank and file, which he might command in the rank of major.[28] The corps was to be organized and uniformed (in green) like the 95th Rifles, which had been added to the British Army as an experimental corps in 1800.

Recruiting for the Glengarry Light Infantry Fencibles officially began in February 1812. Captain Macdonell naturally sought assistance from his kinsman, Father Alexander Macdonell, who had been chaplain of the earlier Glengarry Fencibles in Scotland and instrumental in bringing many of its discharged men to Upper Canada. The captains and all but two of the lieutenants were selected from officers of regular or fencible regiments serving in North America: the former had to enlist 30 and the latter 15 men each for their rank. Officers were forbidden to enlist French-speaking Canadians or recent arrivals from the United States; these were to be referred to the Canadian Fencibles. Prevost shortly accepted Brock's suggestion of authorizing two further company parties for the new Glengarry Fencibles in Upper Canada. One of these was given to Mr. Alexander Roxburgh, a resident of Kingston and the only non-serving officer to get a captaincy. These additional companies increased the establishment to 600 men, which made a colonelcy necessary and this Prevost gave to his Adjutant-General, Colonel Baynes. The lieutenant-colonelcy and actual command went to Major Francis Battersby of the 8th Regiment; the more junior and disgruntled Macdonell had to be content with a majority.

Recruiting parties did not confine their efforts to the Canadas; they also visited the Scottish and Acadian settlements in Nova Scotia, New Brunswick, and Prince Edward Island. Prevost subsequently admitted that, although most of the men were of Scottish extraction, "not a sufficient portion has been raised in Glengarry to give the Corps claim to bear that Name"; but obviously he had more important things to do than worry about a more appropriate name.[29] By May the companies were being concentrated for training at Trois-Rivières. Prevost's action in promising recruits a grant of 100 acres of land after the war, in addition to the four pounds bounty money, drew a congratulatory comment from the *Quebec Gazette* on May 28:

> The terms of this Levy exact a service, but little more than what every man may be called on in time of war to perform, as a militia man, while it holds out the substantial recompense at its completion, of a valuable

grant of Crown Lands, making every soldier in this favoured corps an Independent Freeholder.[30]

Meanwhile Prevost had been busy humouring and conciliating the members of Lower Canada's Legislative Assembly. Fearing possible internal disturbances if an emergency arose, Prevost had asked the Assembly to renew Craig's act permitting a temporary suspension of *habeas corpus* at the Governor's discretion. It refused. Eventually, as Prevost had requested, the Legislature did agree to a new Militia Act. This authorized him to have 2,000 bachelors aged 18 to 25 selected by lot and embodied for 90 days training during each of two successive summers. In the event of war or its imminence, this Select Embodied Militia could be retained on service for a maximum of two years, although half should be replaced annually. Men would receive the same rates of pay as British regulars and would not again be liable for service until all members of that age group had served. One of the strongest objections to this new act voiced in the Assembly had been that Canadians might contract military habits, and the Militia Act as passed specified that such militiamen were not to be enlisted into regular or fencible regiments. The Assembly voted £12,000 for other measures needed to secure the safety of Lower Canada; should war actually erupt, a further £30,000 would be made available to Prevost.

Once the Militia Act was passed by the Legislature on April 4, Prevost, still seeking ways of increasing his troops, decided to raise a Provincial Corps of Light Infantry or Voltigeurs. This was to serve during the war, or apprehension of war, with the United States, under the rules and articles for the better government of the militia of Lower Canada. A member of a well-known French-speaking family, Captain (Brevet Major) Charles Michel de Salaberry of the 60th Royal Americans, then serving as *aide-de-camp* to Major-General de Rottenburg, was appointed major-commandant.[31] Major de Salaberry's immediate family had an impressive record with the British Army. One of his brothers was killed while serving in Spain and two brothers died in India. He himself had served against the French in the West Indies and in the Walcheren expedition. Except for the adjutant and quartermaster, who were to be obtained from regular or fencible regiments, De Salaberry selected his officers from among the leading families of Lower Canada.[32] They were to be junior to all regular and fencible officers of the same rank, and were to have no subsequent claim to half-pay. The six captains and eighteen lieutenants would receive their commissions as soon as they had recruited their quotas (36 men for captains and 16 for lieutenants). Recruits were to be between the ages of 17 and 36, and not shorter than five feet three inches in height. Besides a bounty of £4, men were promised 50 acres of land on discharge. There were to be a ser-geant-major, sergeant armourer, bugle major, 25 sergeants, 25 corporals, 10 buglers, 475 privates or more if they could be obtained. If one were to believe the report in the *Quebec Gazette* of April 23, 1812, the call to serv-ice had only needed to be given to receive immediate response:

> This Corps now forming under Major De Salaberry, is completing with a dispatch worthy of the ancient warlike spirit of the Country. Capt. Perrault's company was filled up in 48 hours, and was yesterday passed by His Excellency the Governor; and the companies of Capts. Duchesnay, Panet, and L'Ecuyer, have very nearly their complement. The young men move in solid columns towards the enlisting officers, with an expression of countenance not to be mistaken. The Canadians are awakening from the repose of an age, secured to them by good gov-ernment and virtuous habits. Their anger is fresh; the object of their preparation simple and distinct. They are to defend their King, known to them, only by acts of Kindness, and a native country long since made sacred by the exploits of their forefathers.[33]

Journalistic exaggeration, which has been repeated by later accounts, had been used to add enthusiasm to a news report. By June 9 only 309 of the 538 authorized other ranks had been enlisted. Prevost then ordered that recruiting be suspended, Until war should actually come, what funds could be spared from the military chest were to be used for the Glengarry Light Infantry Fencibles.

Prevost had had some success as a result of his dealings with the Assem-bly in Lower Canada, Brock had had less success with the Legislature of Upper Canada, because of the "great influence which the numerous settlers from the United States" possessed over the decisions of the Assembly and the prevalent belief that war was unlikely.[34] It was, indeed, his fears about the possible actions of former Americans which were behind some of his requests. His bill for a temporary suspension of *habeas corpus* was lost, as was a restrictive measure aimed at aliens. Supplementary clauses to the Militia Act, which was renewed, did authorize the formation of flank com-panies of volunteers for each militia battalion. They were to train six days per month until proficient. There was no provision for payment, but there were certain compensations: a volunteer should "not be liable to any personal Arrest on any Civil Process, or to serve as Juror, or to perform duty as a Town or Parish Officer, or Statute labour on the Highways, during the time he shall continue in such flank Companies, any law to the contrary in no wise notwithstanding."[35] Flank companies initially consisted of one captain, two subalterns, two sergeants, one drummer, and 35 rank and file. In a circular letter which Brock sent to all commanding officers, he told them that he did not expect full military competence from these companies, but merely partially trained and disciplined cadres around which the rest of the militia might be embodied in an emergency:

> It is my earnest wish that the little the men have to learn may be acquired by way of a pastime, and not looked upon in the light of an irksome restraint. The generality of the Inhabitants being already acquainted with the use of the Musket, have the less to learn, You may therefore under existing circumstances, limit the Parade of the Companies to three in each Month.
>
> A little attention on the part of the men will very soon enable you to reduce even that short term of attendance.
>
> The chief object of the Flank Companies, is to have constantly in readiness, a force composed of Loyal, Brave, and Respectable Young Men, so far instructed as to enable the Government, on any emergency, to engraft such portions of the Militia as may be necessary, on a stock capable of giving aid in forming them for Military service.[36]

A uniform would assist in the creation of the necessary esprit de corps and since clothing for these militiamen would be some time coming from England, Brock's Adjutant General of Militia sent out another circular suggesting that each man provide himself with a "Short Coat of some dark colored Cloth made to button well round the body, and Pantaloons suited to the Season, with the addition of a Round Hat." Such clothing was eminently practical: it would be equally suitable for civilian use. Officers were further advised, when in the field, to dress in conformity to the men In order to avoid the bad consequences of a conspicuous dress."[37] Brock planned to form a troop of cavalry from the "many respectable young men" who had offered their services and their own horses.[38] He counted on getting the necessary pistols and swords from Quebec, where the Ordnance establishment was busy converting its surplus holding of highland broadswords into cavalry sabres.

Since taking over the Administration of Upper Canada, Brock had become convinced that the existing concept of the defence of the Canadas should be modified. He disliked the thought of having to abandon his province and as early as December 2, 1811, less than two months after his appointment, argued in a long letter to Prevost that a strong stand should be made in Upper Canada. "The military force which heretofore occupied the frontier posts being so inadequate to their defence," he wrote, "a general opinion prevailed that, in the event of hostilities, no opposition was intended. The late increase of ammunition and every species of stores, the substitution of a strong regiment [41st Foot], and the appointment of a military person to administer the government, have tended to infuse other sentiments among the most reflecting part of the community."[39] If the western Indians were supplied by the British and encouraged to make war, the strong force which the Americans were about to assemble for the defence of the frontier could not be later employed against Upper Canada. "But before we can expect an active co-operation on the part of the Indians," his letter continued, "the reduction of Detroit and Michilimackinac must convince that people, who conceive themselves to have been sacrificed, in 1794, to our policy, that we are earnestly engaged in the war." Naval superiority on the Great Lakes was also essential for a successful defence. If the continuance of this could be assured by augmenting the Provincial Marine on both Lake Ontario and Lake Erie, the only likely place for an attack on Upper Canada would be along the Niagara River, which American troops could cross in small boats.

The instructions Prevost had recently received from the Prince Regent, however, had been very specific on an opposite line: he was not to commence offensive operations – "except it be for the purpose of preventing or repelling Hostilities or unavoidable Emergencies."[40] On purely military grounds, Prevost agreed in his reply to Brock, there would be advantages in attacking Detroit and Mackinac while they were only weakly held, "rather than receiving the first blow."[41] At the moment, however, there seemed to be a distinct divergence of opinion among Americans about the question of war or peace, so particular care must be taken to avoid giving offence. Unlike his more venturesome and carefree subordinate, Prevost faced a dilemma which had been common to colonial governors since the beginning of recorded history: heavy casualties to inadequate defensive forces during the opening campaign might make it impossible for war to be continued until reinforcements could arrive, and in his case those reinforcements would have to travel hundreds of miles, and only during the months when the St. Lawrence River was free of ice.

Before Prevost had time to visit Upper Canada to see for himself, a letter arrived from the Secretary of State for War and the Colonies requesting a detailed appreciation of the military situation in North America and Prevost's intentions. Prevost's lengthy reply was dated May 18, 1812, the day before he prorogued the Legislature of Lower Canada, but did not find its way on a ship bound for England for another two weeks. This lengthy and important document is printed in full in the Appendix but the salient points are detailed here.[42]

Prevost commenced with Upper Canada, which was "more liable to immediate attack in the event of war," and he described the various places at which strength had been concentrated. The palisaded house on the Island of St. Joseph, garrisoned by a few artillerymen and one company of the 10th Royal Veterans, served as a protected depot for the North West Company fur traders and friendly Indians. Amherstburg, on the Detroit River, was the Provincial Marine's dockyard for the Upper Lakes. Its dilapidated Fort Malden, in the process of being renovated, was manned by a subaltern's detachment of artillery and about 120 all ranks of the 41st Regiment of Foot. There were about 400 men of the 41st Foot and a captain's command of artillery at Fort George at the head of Lake Ontario. Smaller detachments of the same manned the inadequate field works of Chippawa and Fort Erie. In order to secure the navigation of the Niagara River, it would be necessary to capture the same Fort Niagara which had been relinquished to the Americans by Jay's Treaty. The provincial capital, York, was without fortifications, but was too removed from the frontier for its garrison of three companies of the 41st Foot to be easily attacked. Kingston's four companies of the 10th Royal Veteran Battalion numbered about 200 all ranks. They were, however, exposed to sudden attack from the American settlements on the eastern end of Lake Ontario; if this were successful, there could be no further communication between Upper and Lower Canada. A fortified post would have to be established above the rapids on the St. Lawrence River to ensure continued use of this vital water route. As for the Provincial Marine, five companies of the Royal Newfoundland Fencibles were *en route* from Quebec to Upper Canada to help man its vessels at Kingston and Amherstburg.

Prevost considered that Montreal would be the "first object of attack" in the event of war. Its garrison consisted of the 49th Regiment of Foot and a brigade of light artillery. This last, which was the only field battery in the Canadas, had five 6-pr. guns and one 5.5-in. howitzer, with 6 officers, 17 N.C.O.s, and 123 gunners, but only 30 drivers.[43] Nevertheless Montreal did not possess "any means of defence" and its security depended upon "our being able to maintain an impenetrable line on the South Shore, extending from La Prairie to Chambly, with a sufficient Flotilla to command the Rivers St. Lawrence and the Richelieu." The field works at St. Johns, occupied by a company of the 49th Foot and one of the 10th Royal Veterans, were not worth repairing because the position was tactically indefensible. Chambly was important only as a supporting depot and assembly point for the militia; it was occupied by the recently organized Canadian Voltigeurs. Of far more importance was Sorel. It was garrisoned by four companies of the 100th Regiment, but would have to be strengthened.

At Trois-Rivières, on the north bank of the St. Lawrence River, the Glengarry Light Infantry Fencibles was being organized, but only 400 of its recruits were yet in camp and the unit would not be ready for service until it had been properly trained.

The only permanent fortress in the Canadas was at Quebec, where there were 2,300 regulars. Its existing fortifications were not suited to withstand a "vigorous and well conducted" siege, however, and bombproof casemates were needed for the troops, since the town was completely commanded from the south shore at Levis (where Wolfe had erected batteries in 1759). Yet Prevost's despatch emphasized that the security of Quebec was the key to his whole plan:

To the final defence of this position, every other Military operation ought to become subservient, and the retreat of the Troops upon Quebec must be the primary consideration. ...

In framing a general outline of Co-operation for defence with the forces in Upper Canada, commensurate with our deficiency in Strength, I have considered the preservation of Quebec as the first object, and to which all others must be subordinate: Defective as Quebec is, it is the only post that can be considered as tenable for a moment, the preservation of it being of the utmost consequences to the Canadas, as the door of Entry for that Force the King's Government might find it expedient to send for the recovery of both, or either of these Provinces, altho' the pressure of the moment in the present Extended range of Warfare, might not allow the sending of that force which would defend both, therefore considering Quebec in this view, its importance can at once be appreciated.

If the Americans are determined to attack Canada, it would be in vain the General should flatter himself with the hopes of making an effectual defence of the open Country, unless powerfully assisted from Home:– All predatory or ill concerted attacks undertaken presumptuously without sufficient means can be resisted and repulsed:– Still this must be done with caution, that the resources, for a future exertion, the defence of Quebec, may be unexhausted.

As will be seen, Prevost's defence was dependent on the 41st and 49th Regiments, which were due to return to England shortly after having had a lengthy tour of duty in Canada. In the event that war should erupt, however, Prevost had been authorized to retain these regiments and treat the two replacement regiments as an augmentation of strength.

"The province of New Brunswick and the peninsula of Nova Scotia present so many vulnerable points to an invading army," Prevost's letter continued, "that it is difficult to establish any precise Plan for the defence of either, and consequently much must depend upon Contingencies in the event of Invasion: – Their security very materially depends upon the Navy, and the vigilance of our Cruizers in the Bay of Fundy." The towns of Fredericton and Saint John were indefensible and the 104th Regiment might have to vacate New Brunswick if American invaders were sufficiently numerous. In view of the strength the Royal Navy could assemble at Halifax, its imperfect land defences could be safely left to its garrison of 1,500 regulars, which included three companies of artillery. The safety of Newfoundland, too, although it was garrisoned by the Nova Scotia Fencibles and a company of Royal Artillery, depended on continued British naval superiority, as did that of Cape Breton and Prince Edward Island. There were 3 ships of the line, 23 frigates, and 53 sloops, brigs and schooners of the Royal Navy in North American waters, even though they were spread between the West Indies, Halifax and Newfoundland.

Prevost would have been surprised, and also reassured, had he known how little was being done in Washington to prepare the United States for the conflict being demanded by the War Hawks. Congress had agreed early in January 1812, after much debate, to increase the establishment of the regular army to 35,603 officers and enlisted men, but practically everyone doubted whether the necessary numbers of Americans would enlist for a five-year period while the nation was still at peace. Actual strength was then only about 4,000 officers and enlisted men. Therefore on February 6, Congress empowered the President to accept 30,000 volunteers for one year's service and to organize them into battalions, regiments and brigades. The question of whether these volunteers, like the several state militias from which they would be drawn, could be compelled to serve beyond the boundaries of the United States was, however, left unsettled. On April 8 President Madison was authorized further to accept 15,000 short enlistments of only 18 months for the regular army. Two days later he was empowered to require the governors of states to hold in readiness to march at a moment's notice as many as 80,000 militia. New York had already been asked to furnish volunteers or militia for service along the Niagara frontier, at Oswego and Ogdensburg, and for the harbour defences of New York City; Ohio had been asked to reinforce the regular garrison of Detroit with volunteers or militia. Yet as late as June 6 most of this strength was in paper men: there were only 6,744 officers and men serving on regular establishments and about 5,000 on the newly authorized establishments. These included a large number of newly commissioned officers who were as inexperienced in military matters as the enlisted recruits. Counting a few companies of rangers in the west, the total strength was roughly the same as that of the trained British regulars, including fencibles, in a much smaller area of North America.

The U.S. Navy had only 5 frigates in commission and 5 laid up in need of repair; there were also 3 sloops, 7 brigs and 62 of the ineffectual coastal gunboats in commission. There were 4,000 seamen and boys in the Navy and about 1,800 enlisted men in the Marine Corps. A request by Secretary of the Navy Paul Hamilton for 12 74-gun ships of the line and 20 frigates had been rejected. Congress merely authorized the repair of the laid-up frigates and the purchase of timber for new vessels of undetermined specifications to be built at some indefinite time in the future. Strangely enough, it was the War Hawks who opposed creation of an ocean-going navy which alone could counter the Royal Navy's strength in the North Atlantic.

Then, as now, the President of the United States was titular Commander-in-Chief of the Armed Forces. Both the War and Navy Departments were administered by civilian members of his Cabinet, but there was then no uniformed head of each service, corresponding to the modern Chief of Staff, U.S. Army, and Chief of Naval Operations, to tender professional advice.

The absence of detailed plans for war may be attributed to the paucity of proper staff officers in Washington. Until now the Secretary of War, William Eustis, had also been discharging the duties of Quartermaster General, Commissary General, Indian Commissioner, Commissioner of Pensions and Commissioner of Public Lands – all with a staff of about a dozen subordinates. Changes were now initiated, but newly appointed officers could become proficient only with time. The senior combatant officer was 61-year-old Henry Dearborn, a distinguished veteran of the American Revolution and long-time politician. After eight years in President Jefferson's cabinet and three years as the Collector of Taxes for the Port of Boston, he had been appointed major-general in the regular army on January 27, 1812, to command the Northern Department.[44] The other major-general, Thomas Pinckney, was two years older; another veteran of the American Revolution, he had shown to better advantage as a politician and diplomat than he was destined to do as a soldier in the Southern Department. The 60-year-old Governor of the Michigan Territory, William Hull, now acceded very reluctantly to President Madison's request that he accept appointment to the regular army as a brigadier-general and a North Western Army command separate from that of General Dearborn. Hull's military service was also limited to the American Revolution, when he had performed creditably but in junior capacities. There were only 29 field officers in the regular army: many of these were too old for active service or too benumbed by the humdrum life in small frontier garrisons to be competent to command even regiments. The highest naval rank was captain, although an appointment as commodore could be given temporarily to a captain who was commanding the largest ship in a small squadron or who was engaged in other independent operations. The handful of captains corresponded directly with the Secretary of the Navy, Paul Hamilton.

Both President Madison and his Secretary of War seemed satisfied with Major-General Dearborn's suggestion that operations could be launched simultaneously by troops of the Northern Department against Montreal, Kingston and Niagara. Brigadier-General Hull was confident that an advance by his North Western Army from Detroit into the Western District of Upper Canada would be welcomed by the inhabitants who were mostly

recent arrivals from the United States. Easy conquest of Canada would offset any gains accruing from British supremacy at sea.

Interest in these schemes was kept very much alive by the continuing
international tensions. Britain had refused to repeal her controversial Orders in Council, because of evidence that the Napoleonic Decrees actually
were still in force, and her continued impressment of American sailors
angered even those Americans who did not want war. Southern Congressmen had the further grievance that their essential exports of cotton and
tobacco were being kept out of European markets by the Royal Navy. Except for northern New York and Vermont, where local views were coloured
by the profitable commercial intercourse with Canada, the Congressmen
representing the frontier constituencies could afford to be bellicose: they
had no interest in the seaborne trade which influenced thinking in maritime New England, New York, New Jersey and Delaware, and nothing to
fear from the guns of the Royal Navy; moreover, very few voters lived in the
remote areas actually menaced by the Indians who were supposedly being
egged on by British agents.

Fruitless interviews with the British Minister at Washington in late May,
1812, convinced President Madison that further discussion was pointless.
On June 1, therefore, he sent Congress a message requesting an immediate
declaration of war. The four major charges against Great Britain were impressment of American seamen; violation of American neutral rights and
territorial waters in order to harass commerce; employment of "pretended
blockades" whose real aim was to plunder American commerce; refusal to
revoke the "sweeping system" of Orders in Council.[45] On June 4 the House
of Representatives voted 79 to 49 for war. Action in the Senate was delayed
by an unsuccessful attempt of the Federalists and older Republicans to approve only a limited war at sea by privateers; the waverers then made up
their minds and on June 17 the Senate, after making some amendments to
the bid, voted 19 to 13 for war. The next day the House of Representatives
approved the Senate's amendments and the President signed the bill. President Madison's formal proclamation of war was dated June 19, and issued
on behalf of the 7,500,000 white men, women and children inhabiting the
seventeen states and six frontier territories which then comprised the
United States of America. The British Minister sought a suspension of hostilities until word could get to England by fast sailing ship, but he was unsuccessful. "This extraordinary measure," he then wrote the Foreign Secretary, "seems to have been unexpected by nearly the whole Nation; & to

have been carried in opposition to the declared sentiments of many of those who voted for it, in the House of Representatives, as well as in the Senate, in which latter body there was known to have been at one time, a decided Majority against it."[46]

On the very day that the Minister took his formal leave of the United States, June 23, a new British Government headed by Lord Liverpool provisionally repealed the Orders in Council.

Private soldier, 4th U.S. Infantry, 1812
The only regular American regiment in the field on the northern frontier at the outbreak of war, the 4th Infantry went into captivity when Detroit surrendered. (Painting by Don Troiani, courtesy of the Department of National Defence)

PART II

1812: The Canadas at Bay

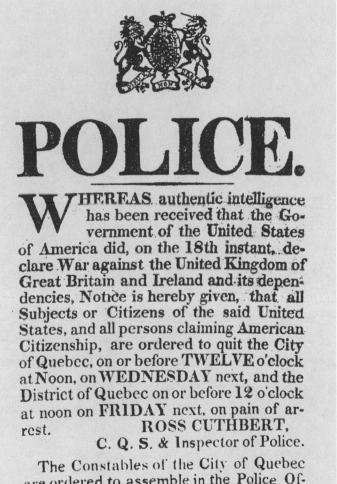

Police notice, Montreal, June 1812

Private soldier, 1st Regiment of Foot, The Royal Scots
The British regular bore the brunt of the fighting and suffered the heaviest casualties throughout the war. Well trained and well led, he was more than a match for the American opponent for the first two years of the war. (Painting by G.A. Embleton, courtesy Parks Canada)

CHAPTER THREE

Opening Moves:
June and July 1812

The first intimation in British North America that the United States had declared war on Great Britain was received on June 24 by two Montreal merchants from fur trade associates in New York City. Word was at once relayed to Quebec City, where Sir George Prevost immediately began to implement his existing plans for a defensive campaign. No one was under any illusions as to where the United States would choose to carry on the fighting against Britain.

Scheduled withdrawal of the 41st and 49th Regiments for despatch to Europe and transfer of the 100th Regiment to Halifax were cancelled. The flank companies of the regular and fencible regiments in Lower Canada were formed into a flank battalion to man an advanced line of posts stretching from St. Johns to Laprairie. Most of the battalion companies of these regiments were shortly concentrated forward of Montreal. Half a brigade of artillery (two 6-pounder guns and one 5.5-inch howitzer) was made available as a supporting force. Command of the whole was given to Major-General de Rottenburg.[1] Garrison duty at Quebec and Montreal was temporarily left to volunteers from the local sedentary militia units, serving in weekly rotation.

Command at Quebec itself devolved on Major-General George Glasgow, R.A.[2] Sir George Prevost had agreed that he might remain in Canada, where he had served nearly twenty-three years without an opportunity for active service, rather than now return to Britain and a mundane Board of Ordnance appointment. Prevost was very short of experienced and capable officers for command and staff appointments, and even mediocre regulars familiar with the proper procedures were likely to be more useful than enthusiastic but untrained militia officers. Rank for rank, regulars and fencibles were senior to militia officers.

Thus lieutenant-colonels in the British Army took precedence over the commanders of all but a few militia regiments in Upper Canada; where the latter had been mistakenly granted the rank of colonel, this could be circumvented by giving the British officers a higher local rank. Even British majors commanding the smaller forts were later to be advanced to the local rank of lieutenant-colonel so that they would experience less difficulty with nearby militia.

Unfortunately the 41st and 49th Regiments of Foot, which had been in Canada since 1799 and 1802 respectively, were short of experienced officers. The only regimental field officer of the 41st Foot in Upper Canada was employed on the staff as a brevet colonel, while two captains were elsewhere as brevet lieutenant-colonels and two as brevet majors. Two captains of the 49th were employed on staff in Canada and five more were on leave in Great Britain, expecting to rejoin the regiment when it returned there. In consequence, most of the companies of both regiments were actually being commanded by lieutenants.

Except for disturbances in a few parishes near Montreal, there was no difficulty finding the quotas required for the four battalions of Select Embodied Militia earlier ordered to mobilize. Presumably in the parishes where there was trouble, the balloting was badly handled and some young men felt they were being victimized as their forbears had been by the hated *corvée*.[3] Thus a company of the 49th Foot had to open fire on an angry crowd intent upon rescuing those who refused to be embodied at Lachine. This display of force, backed by the arrival of 450 sedentary militia from Montreal, quickly restored peace and quiet. The greater number of those who had absented themselves at Pointe-aux-Trembles returned voluntarily on learning that the United States had declared war. Elsewhere, according to the *Quebec Gazette*, conscientious parents insisted that would-be recalcitrants do their duty. After some rudimentary training, these four battalions joined the troops in front of Montreal.

Another immediate problem was currency. In paying for the prosecution of the war, the public coffers would soon be drained of specie and none could be expected from England. The Legislature of Lower Canada, which was called into special session on July 16, was asked to approve Prevost's suggestion for the issuance of Army Bills.[4] The Assembly generously voted £15,000 to pay interest as it became due on the £250,000 worth of Army Bills authorized for circulation. Another £25,000 was voted to defray the expense of handling these bills. Large numbers of the French-speaking inhabitants proved mistrustful of this new tender but when

**Major-General Henry Dearborn
(1751-1829)**
The senior American general in 1812, he
was a veteran of the Revolutionary War
who was well past his prime. (Lossing,
Field-Book, 1869)

Prevost appealed to Bishop Plessis he was able to convince them that Army
Bills should be accepted as legal.

Tension eased when no invaders appeared on the borders of Lower
Canada. Major-General Dearborn, commanding the Northern Department, had returned home to Boston after establishing a headquarters at
Albany, the capital of New York State, in early May. The instructions sent
him by the Secretary of War on June 26 had not suggested any need for
haste:

> Having made the necessary arrangements for the defence of the sea-
> coast, it is the wish of the President that you should repair to Albany and
> prepare the force to be collected at that place for actual service. It is un-
> derstood that being possessed of a full view of the intentions of Govern-
> ment, and being also fully acquainted with the disposition of the force
> under your command, you will take your own time and give the neces-
> sary orders to the officers on the sea-coast. It is altogether uncertain at
> what time General Hull may deem it expedient to commence offensive
> operations. The preparations it is presumed will be made to move in a
> direction for Niagara, Kingston, and Montreal. On your arrival at
> Albany you will be able to form an opinion of the time required to pre-
> pare the troops for action.[5]

Slowness of recruiting and the refusal of the Governors of Massachusetts
and Connecticut to furnish the militia quotas sought by President Madison do not seem to have worried Dearborn unduly, although he was to

express concern over the defenceless state of the eastern seaports. Not until July 26 did Dearborn return to Albany, where there were still only 1,200 men, without organization, training or equipment. Meantime the people of northern Vermont had let it be known in Lower Canada that they wished to continue with normal trade, obtaining British manufactured goods in exchange for the agricultural products so necessary to feed the British Army.

Prevost was further encouraged in his proposed course of defence by intelligence from Nova Scotia and New Brunswick. News of President Madison's declaration of war had reached Halifax on June 29, along with the heartening information that the nearby inhabitants of New England were generally opposed to it and desired to continue normal trading relations. Word received at Saint John indicated that the inhabitants of Eastport, Maine, had met and unanimously agreed "to preserve a good understanding with the Inhabitants of New Brunswick, and to discountenance all depredations upon the Property of each other."[6] Since New Brunswick depended on trade with New England for its very sustenance, its Executive Council requested the newly appointed Administrator, Major-General George S. Smyth, to permit the import of provisions in unarmed American ships.[7] After consulting his own Executive Council of Nova Scotia, Sir John Sherbrooke issued a proclamation on July 3, giving official sanction to this lack of hostilities and continuing friendship:

Whereas every species of predatory warfare carried on against Defenceless Inhabitants, living on the shores of the United States contiguous to this Province and New Brunswick, can answer no good purpose, and will greatly distress Individuals: I have therefore thought proper by and with the advice of His Majesty's Subjects under my Government, to abstain from molesting the Inhabitants living on the shores of the United States contiguous to this Province and New Brunswick: and on no account to molest the Goods, or unarmed Coasting Vessels, belonging to the Defenceless Inhabitants on the Frontiers, so long as they shall abstain on their parts, from any acts of Hostility and Molestation towards the Inhabitants of this Province and New Brunswick, who are in a similar situation. It is therefore my wish and desire, that the Subjects of the United States, living on the frontiers, may pursue in peace their usual and accustomed Trade and occupations, without Molestation, so long as they shall act in a similar way towards the frontier Inhabitants of this Province and New Brunswick.

And I do hereby order and command all His Majesty's Subjects, within my jurisdiction, to govern themselves accordingly, until further orders.[8]

A week later Smyth issued an almost identical proclamation. "I have not yet actually enroled any part of the Militia," he reported to London, "as depriving the Country of its labour at this Season would occasion the most alarming scarcity, if not the total want of food, during the remainder of this year."[9] Sherbrooke had embodied about 180 militiamen and had ordered guns mounted at the entrance of each principal harbour in Nova Scotia, but he also recognized the importance of harvesting the local crops. The American need for manufactured goods would, he felt, result in both provisions and much needed specie coming into Nova Scotia from New England: that is, should the Royal Navy be ordered not to interfere with coastal trade.

Actually the Royal Navy was momentarily too busy with defensive measures in the North Atlantic to take offensive action against American ports and the coastal trade. Only one ship of the line, 6 frigates and 16 smaller vessels were immediately available between Halifax and Bermuda. Moreover the situation was complicated by another of the anomalous policies about wartime trade which were pragmatic answers in these years to real needs for food and supplies. Thus Vice-Admiral Herbert Sawyer issued such licences as the following:

Whereas, Mr. Andrew Allen, his Majesty's consul at Boston, has recommended to me Mr. Robert Elwell, a merchant of that place AND WELL INCLINED TOWARDS THE BRITISH INTEREST, who is desirous of sending provisions to Spain and Portugal, for the use of the allied armies in the Peninsula; and whereas I think it fit and necessary that encouragement and protection should be afforded him in so doing.

These are, therefore, to require and direct all captains and commanders of his Majesty's ships and vessels of war, which may fall in with any American, or other vessel bearing a neutral flag, laden with flour, bread, corn and pease, or any other species of dried provisions, bound from America to Spain and Portugal, and having this protection on board, to suffer her to proceed without unnecessary obstruction or detention in her voyage: *Provided*, she shall appear to be steering a due course for those countries, and it being understood this is only to be in force for one voyage, and within six months from the date thereof. Given under my hand and seal, on board his Majesty's ship *Centurion*, at Halifax, this fourth day of August, 1812.[10]

Herbert Sawyer

Vice-Admiral

On June 22 the United States Navy's three frigates, sloop and brig in New York harbour put to sea as two separate squadrons under Commodores John Rodgers and Stephen Decatur. They hoped to protect the return of American merchantmen from abroad and to attack British convoys then sailing between England and North America or the West Indies under inadequate escort against anything except French privateers. "We have been so completely occupied in looking for Commodore Rodgers' squadron," wrote an officer in H.M.S. *Guerrière*, "that we have taken very few prizes."[11] Rodgers admitted to capturing "only seven merchant vessels, and those not valuable," but the super-frigate U.S.S. *Constitution* was later, on August 20 and near Bermuda, to smash H.M.S. *Guerrière* into a helpless hulk to achieve the first single-ship victory of the war.[12] The "44-gun" *Constitution* actually mounted 55 guns and had a 30 per cent heavier broadside than the 38-gun *Guerrière*, which also carried extra but smaller guns and whose crew had been badly depleted by the need to put prize crews on earlier captured merchantmen.

Control of British naval operations was now facilitated by the appointment of Admiral Sir John Borlase Warren as Commander-in-Chief of the

Medal awarded to Captain Isaac Hull by Congress
Hull's victory in the *Constitution* against the British frigate *Guerrière* was acclaimed throughout the United States. (Lossing, *Field-Book*, 1869)

combined North America and West Indies Stations.[13] The 59-year-old Warren had a long and good fighting record, even if he was considered to be an indifferent seaman. He had studied at Cambridge and received his M.A. before becoming a naval officer during the American Revolutionary War, and had acquired some diplomatic experience as an ambassador extraordinary to Russia in 1802. He now authorized the granting of licences to New England vessels trading with Nova Scotia, but did not yet have sufficient ships to interfere seriously with American coastal trade emanating from more southerly ports such as New York city.

The people of New York State were sharply divided in their initial reaction to "Mr. Madison's War." Congressmen representing the settlements fronting on the St. Lawrence River and the eastern end of Lake Ontario had voted against war, as had those representing the maritime constituencies at the opposite end of the state. Yet the 13,500 militia requested by the President had appeared on the summons of Governor Daniel D. Tompkins. This energetic and enterprising Republican politician even managed to manoeuvre a leading Federalist opponent into accepting command of the northern frontier from the Indian Reserve at St. Regis on the St. Lawrence River to the western border with Pennsylvania.[14] Major-General Stephen Van Rensselaer of Albany was well aware that his only qualification for promotion to that rank in the militia had been his status as a successful politician.[15] Therefore he insisted that his kinsman, Colonel Solomon Van Rensselaer, who had observed some military operations in Europe, should be his Chief of Staff.[16] All state governors considered themselves equally responsible with the President of the United States for local defence, which was the only obligation many citizens believed the militia to have. In consequence command arrangements were completely different from those in Canada, where considerable pains had been taken to prevent the possibility of British troops in a mixed force having to serve under ill-trained militia colonels. New York's energetic Governor Tompkins expressed their arrangements succinctly in a letter to Major-General Dearborn:

> When the Militia and Regular troops come together in the service of the United States, each organized Corps of Militia is to be commanded by officers of the Militia exclusively, but the officer of superior rank whether of the Militia or Regulars will command the whole. The Regular officers of the same grade taking rank, though holding Junior commissions of that grade.

Major-General Jacob Brown (1775-1828)
A pre-war militia officer, Brown won more pitched battles against British regulars than any other American general of the war. (National Archives of Canada, C-100390)

Actually time was to make such amateurs as Brigadier-General Jacob Brown of the New York militia much better fighting soldiers than company grade officers who had continued in the regular army while energetic civilians were pushing back the frontier. Born of Quaker parents in 1775, Brown had been successively a school teacher and land speculator before becoming the founder and leading citizen of Brownville near Sackets Harbor. During the period of the Embargo and Non-Intercourse Acts, he had given his name to "Brown's Smugglers Road," and had acquired the nickname "Potash Brown." Now he was to put the same energy into learning to soldier.[17] Instinctively he realized that his militia brigade should not be widely scattered along the frontier from St. Regis to Sackets Harbor. Therefore he concentrated on creating a semblance of order at the incipient naval base of Sackets Harbor, while Colonel Thomas Benedict of Ogdensburg had rude gun emplacements of cordwood built around the two 6-pr. guns there.

The inhabitants of the little border communities on the river had been terrified at first by the prospect of what the British garrison at Kingston might attempt and many had fled inland. Brown was personally just as worried, but he had successfully persuaded them to return to their homes. He positioned a large standing patrol at Cape Vincent, almost opposite on the American shore of the St. Lawrence River but hidden by the considerable Wolfe Island. Acting without orders, three local farmers had already surprised the four soldier caretakers of the former British naval base on nearby Carleton Island, to achieve the first American success of the war. In consequence of these moves, news of war did not reach Kingston from American sources.

As soon as the news from Montreal finally did circulate at Kingston on July 3, the 1st Regiment of Frontenac Militia mustered to reinforce Major Donald Macpherson's garrison of less than 200 effectives of the 10th Royal Veterans.[18] Major Macpherson had only 34 pistols and 1,130 muskets for issue to the sedentary militia that quickly turned out almost to a man in the predominantly loyalist settlements stretching along the upper St. Lawrence River and as far west as the Bay of Quinte. Yet parties of these, manning bateaux among the Thousand Islands, managed to capture two of thirteen American sailing vessels trying to make a dash up river to the safety of Sackets Harbor; this loss persuaded the remainder to turn back and shelter at Ogdensburg. There were also seven troops of militia cavalry scattered along the Canadian shore, but since they had received no training as such, Major Macpherson wisely ordered them to provide a courier service. Men were posted in pairs at convenient intervals, westward as far as there was settlement and eastward to the boundary of Lower Canada.

The true pioneer era was coming to an end in these districts and substantial houses were replacing the original log cabins. One military traveller from Montreal to Kingston by the road, which mostly kept within sight of the St. Lawrence River, recorded that the "streets of Cornwall were wide and straight. It has a church, a court house, a jail and neat houses, all built of wood. ... The roads are good enough, particularly so from Cornwall westward."[19] Six miles above the present city of Brockville, however, the woods began. Here, he wrote, the roads were "unpleasant; long stretches of corduroy bridge the swamps and low grounds, bridges remarkably solid, some long and lofty, span creeks and fairly wide rivers." The wet weather of spring and autumn could render such roads impassable, but even at other times it was easier to transport supplies by boat or by horse and sleigh over the snow-covered ice.

Major Macpherson's request of July 5 for further stocks of arms and ammunition was reinforced by a personal letter addressed to Sir George Prevost by [the] Hon. Richard Cartwright. As well as being colonel of the Frontenac militia, the elderly Cartwright was Kingston's leading merchant and a member of the Executive Council of Upper Canada. His letter emphasized the defenceless state of Kingston and the necessity of retaining command of the river communications to Montreal; the desirability of having a regular officer of some seniority and ability to exercise command; and the inability of the militia to do more than escort boatloads of stores sent up river, construct strong points at convenient overnight stopping places and work on what roads there were. Cartwright's letter then got to a central problem of those organizing the defence of the Canadas, the concern of the militia for their farms and the best way of taking advantage of their limited usefulness:

> In the first fervor of their zeal it has not perhaps occurred that it is not possible to keep on military service for a considerable length of time the whole male population of a country and arms put into the hands of people not actually arrayed for service are soon allowed to become unserviceable. Yet it might be expedient to have depots in the different counties to be resorted to in the case of emergency. Every man along the frontier supposes that his property will be the object of immediate attack but it is to be presumed that mere predatory warfare will be wholly discountenanced on both sides.[20]

These letters had the desired effect at Montreal, and small quantities of arms and ammunitions were sent up river for distribution to the militia battalions of the counties of Cornwall, Stormont, Dundas, Glengarry, and Prescott. On July 10 Colonel Robert Lethbridge, an elderly half-pay officer serving as an Inspecting Field Officer of Militia for Lower Canada, was ordered to take command at Kingston and to exercise a "vigilant general superintendence of the whole district."[21] *En route* he was to ascertain the efficiency of the several militia units and make such arrangements as should be necessary to ensure the general defence and security of the line of communication with Lower Canada. A convoy system would be instituted to ensure the safe transit of bateaux and other supply boats.[22] Colonel Lethbridge was to be responsible directly to Major-General Isaac Brock. It might, of course, be difficult for anyone in a position such as Kingston to keep in touch with so energetic a superior officer and Lethbridge's instructions specifically gave him some liberty of judgment:

> From the extent of the several posts placed under your command, the difficulty of communicating promptly either with the headquarters of the Upper Province or with the Commander of the Forces, you must under all circumstances not expressly provided for, guide yourself to the

best of your judgment, observing as a general line of conduct that the post of Kingston is the object of primary importance committed to your charge. The general defence and security of the line of frontier should form the next object of your attention.[23]

Above all, he was not to provoke hostilities: "Under the existing state of affairs it is not desirable that you should engage the enemy, on the contrary use every precaution to preserve the tranquility of that part of the Province which does not in itself afford an eligible position for offensive operations." In the unlikely event that Kingston should become untenable, Lethbridge was to retreat either west or east after destroying his stores.

Colonel Lethbridge subsequently reported on the uniform zeal of the militia of the counties of Grenville, Stormont, Dundas and Glengarry "to exert their best endeavours for the defence of their country, tho' as yet almost in the infancy of discipline with the exception of the manual & platoon exercise owing to the general want of instructors."[24] Bare amenities as well as munitions were lacking: at Prescott, where a stockade and battery were being erected to control river navigation, and to offset any American enterprise attempted from nearby Ogdensburg, the men were without blankets. Colonel Lethbridge decided to retain only the volunteer flank companies for continuous service, and allow the rest of the militia to return home for the harvest. The flank companies guarded all points where the river channel was narrow, or where there were rapids, and provided relay escorts for the convoys of bateaux which were to bring up supplies for the balance of the war, except during the winter months when sleighs took over.

Brock's first reaction upon receipt of the news of war, which reached him at Fort George from an unofficial American source on June 25, had been to undertake offensive operations. Then he remembered Prevost's strict injunction and wrote his superior officer on July 3 that upon

the reflection that at Detroit and St. Josephs the weak state of the garrisons would prevent the Commanders from accomplishing any essential service connected in any degree with their future security, and that my only means of annoyance on this communication, was limited to the reduction of Fort Niagara, which could easily be battered at any future period, I relinquished my original intention, and attended only to defensive measures.[25]

The militia in the Niagara Peninsula turned out cheerfully to the number of 800 men to supplement the 500 regulars of the 41st Foot garrisoning Fort George, Chippawa and Fort Erie. There were no tents for the militia guarding the river bank, however, and blankets, hammocks and kettles had to be purchased from local merchants. Brock believed that there were at least 1,200 American regulars and militia mobilized along the opposite shore; in reality the equally confused commander of the small American garrison at Fort Niagara expected to be attacked hourly and was frantically pleading for reinforcements.

On July 12 Brock wrote Prevost that his militiamen were becoming impatient with inactivity. In response to a widespread clamour to return to their farms, he had released many; but he was afraid the remainder would leave as soon as the harvest was ready, without permission and in defiance of the Militia Act. Unfortunately that Act authorized only fines to be levied against delinquents. Yet, his letter continued, the "alacrity and good temper with which the militia, in the first instance, marched to the frontier have tended to infuse in the mind of the enemy a very different sentiment of the disposition of the inhabitants."[26] He was led to believe that "on the first summons, they would declare themselves an American State."

Thanks to the warning letter sent him by Brock on June 25, the British commander at Amherstburg learned of the declaration of war on June 28, well ahead of Brigadier-General William Hull who was plodding overland towards Detroit with three regiments of Ohio volunteers and one regiment of regulars. Hull's advance was plagued by almost continuous rain, by the near mutiny of Ohio volunteers who had not been paid and by friction resulting from the fact that their colonels outranked the lieutenant-colonel commanding the regulars. On July 1 Hull finally decided to increase the speed of his march by loading his heavy baggage, official papers and sick men on a schooner which he chartered on impulse. It was intercepted opposite Fort Malden on the following morning, however, and forced to surrender to the Provincial Marine's brig *General Hunter*. This news was relayed by Brock to Prevost at Montreal.

So far as Prevost could judge from a distance, this unwanted war was not going badly. Yet his answer of July 10 to Brock's first despatch emphasized caution. The numbers of troops available did not allow for offensive campaigns and it was in their best interest to let the Americans attempt the initiative:

Our numbers would not justify offensive operations being undertaken, unless they were solely calculated to strengthen a defensive attitude. I consider it prudent and politic to avoid any measure which can in its effect have a tendency to unite the people in the American States. Whilst disunion prevails among them, their attempts on these Provinces will be feeble:– it is therefore, our duty carefully to avoid committing any act, which may, even by construction, tend to unite the Eastern and Southern States, unless by its perpetration, we are to derive a considerable and important advantage. But the government of the United States, resting on public opinion for all its measures, is liable to sudden and violent changes; it becomes an essential part of our duty to watch the effect of parties on its measures, and to adapt ours to the impulse given by those possessed of influence over the public mind in America.

Notwithstanding these observations, I have to assure you of my perfect confidence in your measures for the preservation of Upper Canada. All your wants shall be supplied as fast as possible, except money, of which I have so little, as to be obliged to have recourse to a paper currency.[27]

Nevertheless, Prevost's letter continued, the "mode of conducting the war" was suited only to the "existing circumstances"; "as they change, so must we vary our line of conduct, adapting it to our means of preserving entire the King's Provinces."

Lord Bathurst's directives of August 10 approved what he had read in the first wartime despatches from North America. Although the Secretary of State for War and the Colonies hoped that war with the United States would be brought to a speedy end, once news of the conditional repeal of the Orders in Council reached Washington, Prevost was to do the best he could with what men and munitions could be spared him. Because of the worldwide danger facing the British Empire, there was no possibility of despatching either specie or reinforcements from Great Britain; but two battalions of infantry were already *en route* from elsewhere, one to Quebec and one to Halifax, and 10,000 stands of arms were being diverted to the former and 5,000 to the latter. "Your own Military Experience and local information will make you the best judge of the mode in which those means can be supplied with the greatest Prospect of ultimate success," Bathurst wrote to Prevost. "It is sufficient for me to express my concurrence in the general Principles upon which you intend to conduct operations, by making the Defence of Quebec paramount to every other consideration, should the Threat of Invasion be put into Execution."[28] Prevost was, however, to pay the "strictest and most unremitting attention to Economy" and to wait until he received authority from London for incurring new expenditures. Sherbrooke in Nova Scotia and Smyth in New Brunswick were directed to continue a policy of "cultivating an amicable and liberal Communication with the neighbouring States, and of promoting any friendly disposition which may appear to you best calculated to rensure its Continuence."[29]

The only question mark in what otherwise seemed a reassuring situation was the western extremity of the province of Upper Canada. Communication from the west to Prevost at Montreal could be almost as slow as it was between Quebec and London, and no one could be sure what might be happening there or what success, if any, the Americans might achieve.

Gunner, United States Artillery, 1812
The four regular artillery regiments were the best units in the American army and often functioned as infantry during the war. (Painting by H.C. McBarron, courtesy Parks Canada)

CHAPTER FOUR

Victories in the Old Northwest: August 1812

SANDWICH / MACKINAC / MAGUAGA / DETROIT

On July 12 Brigadier-General William Hull crossed the Detroit River to the Canadian shore with the bulk of his command and took peaceful possession of the village of Sandwich. At once he issued a flamboyant proclamation which described his arrival as that of a liberator ready and able to give the benefits of independence to those who welcomed them, or the perils of war to those who opposed:

> In the name of my Country and by the authority of my Government I promise you protection for your *persons, property* and *rights.* Remain at your homes. Pursue your peaceful and customary avocations. Raise not your hands against your brethren, many of your fathers fought for the freedom & *Independence* we now enjoy. Being children therefore of the same family with us, and heirs to the same Heritage, the arrival of an army of Friends must be hailed by you with a cordial welcome. You will be emancipated from Tyranny and oppression and restored to the dignified station of freemen. Had I any doubt of eventual success I might ask your assistance, but I do not. I come prepared for every contingency. I have a force which will look down all opposition and that force is but the vanguard of a much greater. If, contrary to your own interest & the just expectation of my country, you should take part in the approaching contest, you will be considered and treated as enemies, and the horrors and calamities of war will stalk before you.[1]

Hull had reason to believe that many of the settlers would, as American-born recent arrivals to the Western District of Upper Canada, not oppose but rather welcome his advance. The few Canadian militia on duty at

Sandwich had scurried away as the first American boats approached. Foraging parties, sent out to seize supplies in nearby government warehouses and the storehouses of the North West Company, were accompanied back to Sandwich by settlers willing to organize a cavalry troop. About 50 mounted men were recruited and these led other foraging parties against their erstwhile neighbours. "The Canadian militia are deserting in large parties," Hull reported to Washington on July 21, "about sixty came in yesterday. I send them to their homes and give them protection."[2] The correspondence of the British commander at Amherstburg verifies this transfer of loyalties. Lieutenant-Colonel Thomas Bligh St. George was writing on the same day to Major-General Brock at Fort George and admitted that "the Militia have been going off in such numbers, that I have not more than 471 in all this morning – and in such a state as to be totally inefficient in the field."[3] He could depend only on his own 300 officers and men of the Royal Artillery, 41st Regiment of Foot and Royal Newfoundland Fencibles. There were, of course, about 400 Indian survivors of Tecumseh's confederacy with a deadly hatred for the Americans who had driven them from their hunting grounds. Indians, however, had never demonstrated either willingness or ability to submerge themselves in a proper military organization under a single commander, thus Tecumseh was merely the most forceful of several tribal chiefs, all of whom continually had to be persuaded to co-operate with his own band of Shawnee braves and with British officers of the Indian Department.[4]

Brock wrote Prevost on July 20 that he had never been "very sanguine" in his hopes of assistance from the militia: "a general sentiment prevails

Brigadier-General William Hull, U.S. Army
Unaggressive, uninformed by his superiors and plain unlucky, Hull's invasion of Upper Canada came to an abrupt end in August 1812. (Lossing, *Field-Book*, 1869)

Tecumseh (c. 1768-1813)
The great Shawnee chief whose vision of
a pan-native confederacy stretching from
Canada to the Gulf of Mexico inspired his
followers. (Lossing, *Field-Book*, 1869)

that with the present force resistance is unavailing."[5] And in another letter the same month he also referred to the "critical situation" created by the "prepossession" of the public: "Most of the people have lost all confidence – I however speak loud and look big."[6]

Yet, though a few settlers actually joined the invading forces, and others played safe by expressing support while they stayed on their farms, only a few hundred of the American-born settlers in the whole of Upper Canada took the decisive step of returning to American territory. American newspaper despatches, such as one which appeared later in the *New York Statesman*, made much of those who did:

> Canadians arrive daily. The Niagara river which in peaceable times can only be crossed in safety in boats, flats, &c., can now be passed in apparent safety on logs, rails, slabs and even by many without any buoy whatever. Lakes Ontario and Erie, formerly considered extremely dangerous to cross with open boats, no longer present any obstacle to those who are so fortunate as to get possession of a boat – the perils of the sea are absorbed by the fear of being taken by their friends.[7]

The feeling of defeatism in the Western District was a serious problem for those entrusted with its defence. It increased when the flank companies of the Norfolk militia refused to move to Amherstburg at the behest of Colonel Thomas Talbot, although part of this reaction may have been to the autocratic colonel himself, who had tried to act like a feudal baron in his settlement. Even the Indians of the Six Nations, considerably disillusioned by British policy during the years since the American Revolution, decided to remain on their Grand River Reserve.[8] The possibility that these Indians might actually espouse the enemy cause was a further deterrent to the rallying of the militia, who were afraid to leave their homes and families unprotected. The proclamation issued by Brock on July 22, as a rebuttal to that of Hull, was a poor effort. A demoralized people was hardly likely to be influenced by either the logical suggestion that prosperity depended on continuance of the British connection, or the illogical suggestion that victorious Americans would return Canada to France. The following paragraph was probably ignored as being merely Brock's effort to "speak loud and look big":

> The same spirit of Justice, which will make every reasonable allowance for the unsuccessful efforts of Zeal and Loyalty, will not fail to punish the defalcation of principle: every Canadian Freeholder is by deliberate choice, bound by the most solemn Oaths to defend the Monarchy as well as his own property; to shrink from that engagement is a Treason not to be forgiven; let no Man suppose that if in this unexpected struggle his Majesties Arms should be compelled to yield to an overwhelming force, that the Province will be eventually abandoned; the endeared relation of its first settlers, the intrinsic value of its Commerce and the pretensions of its powerful rival to repossess the Canadas are pledges that no peace will be established between the United States and Great Britain and Ireland, of which the restoration of these Provinces does not make the most prominent condition.[9]

Brock expected Amherstburg to be an early loss: "Your Excellency will readily perceive the critical situation in which the reduction of Amherstburg is sure to place me," his letter to Prevost of July 20 had continued,

> I do not imagine General Hull will be able to detach more than one thousand Men, but even with that trifling force I much fear he will succeed in getting to my rear. The Militia will not act without a strong Regular force to set them the example, and as I must now expect to be seriously threatened from the opposite shore [i.e. Niagara], I cannot, in prudence, make strong detachments; which would not only weaken my line of defence, but in the event of a retreat endanger their safety.[10]

The Detroit Frontier

MICHIGAN TERRITORY

UPPER CANADA

Lake St. Clair

Detroit
Sandwich
Detroit R.

Maguaga
Fort Malden
Amherstburg

Raisin R.

Frenchtown

Lake Erie

Pelee Island

Maumee R.

Put-in-Bay

Fort Miami
▲ Ft. Meigs 6 mi.

OHIO

Fort Stephenson
Sandusky R.

Sandusky

TERRITORY

0 5 10 15 miles
0 10 20 km

MAP: ROBIN BRASS STUDIO

Recalling to duty at Niagara the portion of the militia which he had earlier released for the harvest would, however, be unpopular. "I am prepared to hear of much discontent in consequence," he wrote Prevost on July 26; "the disaffected will take advantage of it and add fuel to the flame but it may not be without reason that I may be accused of having already studied to the injury of the Service, their convenience and humour."[11]

Brock had done what he thought was practicable. He had sent his most capable subordinate, Colonel Henry Procter of the 41st Foot, to supersede Lieutenant-Colonel St. George as commander at Amherstburg.[12] About 50 men of the same regiment were sent to the Moravian Town on the bank of the Thames River, under Captain Peter Chambers, to rally the militia against further American raiding parties. Yet Brock, according to his letter of July 26, was now a victim of the general gloom: "unless the enemy be driven from Sandwich it will be impossible to avert much longer the impending ruin of the Country."[13]

Meanwhile Brigadier-General Hull was sitting in Sandwich trying to make up his mind what to do next – or if he should do anything. Admiral Mahan was later to write charitably that "though a soldier on occasion, he [Hull] probably never had the opportunity to form correct soldierly standards."[14] Hull had hoped that occupation of Sandwich would have important results: it would permit him to control river traffic with guns mounted on both banks; provide him with much needed stores and provisions; ensure him support from American-born settlers of the Western District; and give him time to train his raw volunteers and militia for a subsequent attack on Fort Malden. The Secretary of War believed that naval command of the upper lakes could be secured by capturing the Provincial Marine's dockyard at Amherstburg, and this had prompted from him a letter of June 24 which had sent Hull across the river: should the "force under your Command be equal to the Enterprize, consistent with the Safety of your own post you will take possession of Malden and extend your conquests as circumstances may justify."[15] Yet, as this letter had at the same time warned, there was no large American force available at Niagara to create a diversion and thus prevent British reinforcements being rushed westward. Moreover, as Hull knew, the armed vessels of the Provincial Marine still commanded Lake Erie and could disrupt pack trains from Ohio moving along the road which ran beside the water for many miles. This knowledge had prompted Hull to reply, immediately after receipt of the Secretary of War's letter on July 9, and three days before his army had crossed the Detroit River: "The British command the water and the savages. I do not think the force here equal to the reduction of Amherstburg. You therefore must not be too sanguine."[16]

Fort Malden had recently been strengthened under the supervision of Captain M. C. Dixon, R.E., and its garrison was capable of beating off anything except a storming attack by good troops. Apart from the 400 regulars of the 4th U.S. Infantry, Hull's army was anything but that. Most of the Michigan militia had been left at Detroit. More than 100 of the Ohio men had refused to cross into Canada: as militiamen compulsorily embodied to complete quotas for the volunteer regiments, they were legally liable for duty only within the United States; a few who had earlier deserted from British Army posts in order to make their fortunes in the United States knew what would be their fate if captured. The bulk of the Ohio Volunteers

Amherstburg, 1813
The British naval base on Lake Erie, it formed one of Hull's primary objectives in the summer of 1812. (Watercolour by Margaret Reynolds, 1813, courtesy, Parks Canada)

were still enthusiastic for action, but little interested in undergoing the rigorous training necessary to make them the equivalent of regulars. The expeditionary force was thus a very mixed and dwindling bag of 1,200. On the evening of July 14, two days after the landing a Council of War summoned by Hull had voted to delay an assault on Fort Malden until heavy guns could be sent over from Detroit and put into position. Such procrastination was typical of councils of war and the reason that the practice of summoning senior subordinates for an exchange of opinions, desirable originally because commanders lacked trained staff officers, was now in disrepute among European armies. Only the vacillating Hull, and equally inexperienced American senior officers who would later fight along the Canadian border during this war, would make use of councils of war to cloak personal indecision.

The Ohio colonels became involved in a few skirmishes with patrols from Fort Malden, but Hull himself did nothing beyond send fatuous messages to Washington. One, that of July 22, suggested he was hurrying preparations for a siege, then continued with a typical excuse for delay:

> I find that entirely new carriages must be built for the 24-pounders and mortars. It will require at least two weeks to make the necessary prepa-

rations. It is in the power of this army to take Malden by storm, but it would be attended in my opinion with too great a sacrifice under the present circumstances. … if Malden was in our possession, I could march this army to Niagara or York in a very short time.[17]

The situation was, however, to be drastically altered by the news shortly received from Fort Mackinac. Here Lieutenant Porter Hanks and his 61 U.S. regulars, who had not heard that war had been declared, had been merely "showing the flag" as usual. The log fort, situated on a high limestone bluff overlooking the harbour on the southeastern end of Mackinac Island, was only capable of beating off Indian attacks. Its 9-pr. guns could not command the water passage from Lake Huron to Lake Michigan, or even the local spring visited by the garrison for water. A higher hill less than a mile distant was undefended.

On July 8 news of war had reached the British commander at Fort St. Joseph, on the island in the St. Mary's River where the most westerly British garrison had moved in 1796. Brock's letter, dated June 26, had ordered Captain Charles Roberts to make an immediate attack upon Mackinac, if practicable; or, in the event of an attack by the Americans upon St. Joseph, to defend it to the utmost. On June 28 Brock wrote countermanding these instructions, but changed his mind again on June 28 and instructed Roberts to adopt the "most prompt and effectual measures to possess himself of Michilimackinac" and to make full use of friendly Indians and fur traders in doing so.[18] To add to the instructions being directed at Roberts, and arriving by successive couriers, was a letter from Quebec, written on June 25 by the Adjutant General on behalf of Prevost. It instructed Roberts to observe "the greatest vigilance and Caution" in the protection of his fort.[19] The North West Company had promised its active co-operation in the war, and Roberts was, in turn, to "afford every assistance and Protection Possible to Promote the Interest and Security of the North West Company, Consistent with a due regard to the Security of the Post and in Case of Necessity the ultimate retreat of your Party."[20]

The local Nor' Westers had already mustered their resources at Roberts' bidding. These included 180 Canadian and *métis* employees and nearly 300 Ojibway and Ottawa Indians who were in the process of bartering their furs for trade goods. Mr. Robert Dickson had arrived from the area bordering Lake Michigan which is now Wisconsin with upwards of 110 Sioux, Menominee and Winnebago Indians.[21] Fortunately for the commander's peace of mind, on July 15 a further letter arrived from Brock authorizing Captain Roberts to use his own discretion. Roberts realized that the stockaded blockhouse of Fort St. Joseph was even less defensible than Fort Mackinac; the American garrison might receive reinforcements and then attack him; the Indians, "whose minds had been prepared for hostilities," would not remain unless he acted.[22] He therefore did use his own discretion and on the morning of July 16 he embarked every man he could muster in the North West Company's schooner *Caledonia* and in sundry canoes for the 50-mile journey. These numbered 45 of his 10th Royal Veterans, the 180 fur traders and some 400 Indians.

By this time rumours of an Indian concentration at St. Joseph's Island and possible attack had reached Lieutenant Hanks, who was sufficiently impressed to send a local resident to investigate. However, this man was captured by the advancing flotilla. It landed its nondescript force on Mackinac Island shortly after three o'clock on the morning of July 17. The prisoner was released so that he might warn the villagers that their only hope of securing British protection from the Indians was to congregate at the far end of the island. Instead the local doctor took it upon himself to alert Fort Mackinac; but it was now too late to do any good. The Canadians had managed to manhandle a 6-pr. gun to the top of the hill overlooking the fort and at ten o'clock Captain Roberts summoned Lieutenant Hanks to surrender. Hanks knew that he was not prepared to withstand a lengthy siege, and that his small garrison might not even be able to beat off an initial assault. He also fully realized that aroused Indians might take matters into their own hands and massacre all those who eventually surrendered, a practice which had become something of a tradition in the annals of North American warfare. He therefore agreed to a capitulation which granted the honours of war to his men and provided for their parole, on the understanding that they would not serve again until regularly exchanged for troops the Americans might capture elsewhere. Three known deserters from the British Army were, however, taken into custody. Private property and two merchant vessels in harbour were left unmolested, but a considerable quantity of ammunition, supplies and provisions was taken from the U.S. Government storehouse. "It is a circumstance without precedent," Roberts wrote Brock, "and demands the greatest praise for all those who conducted the Indians, that although these people's minds were much heated, Yet as soon as they heard the Capitulation was signed they all returned to their Canoes, and not one drop either of Man's or Animal's Blood was Spilt, till I gave an Order for a certain number of Bullocks to be purchased for them."[23]

Captain Roberts quickly decided that Fort Mackinac was a better base from which to fight the war, and only one officer and six men were relegated to Fort St. Joseph to look after its buildings. He was soon to become worried about the behaviour of the Indians: many of those who had come with him were anxious to get back to hunting and trading, while the band of Ottawas had gone so far as to remain completely aloof from the rest of the expedition until a winner was declared. Roberts hoped to win active support from enough Chippewas to make him independent of an alliance with the unreliable Ottawas, but reported that even so he was desperately in need of "active troops" to reinforce his position. "The men I have here," he wrote of his own Royal Veterans, "tho' always ready to obey my orders are so debilitated and worn down by unconquerable drunkenness that neither the fear of punishment, the love of fame or the honor of their Country can animate them to extraordinary exertions."[24]

News of the capture of Mackinac reached Brock on July 29. Two days earlier he had convened a special session of the Legislature of Upper Canada at York, to obtain assistance for a successful prosecution of the war. "A more decent House had not been elected since the formation of the province," he wrote Prevost on July 28, "but I perceive at once that I shall get no good out of them. They evidently intend to remain passive."[25] The measures Brock considered necessary, justifiably or not, to further the war effort, he felt he had little hope of obtaining. "The repeal of the Habeas Corpus will not pass — And if I have recourse to the Martial Law I am told the whole armed force will disperse." The rest of this letter was just as despondent about the attitude of the scattered communities to the west of Kingston:

> The population, though I had no great confidence in the Majority, is worse than I expected to find it — And all Magistrates &c &c appear quite confounded and decline acting — the consequence is the most improper conduct is tolerated — The officers of Militia exert no authority, everything shews as if a certainty existed of a change taking place soon. But I still hope the arrival of reinforcements may yet avert such a dire calamity — Many in that case would become active in our cause who are now dormant.[26]

Even the welcome news from Mackinac failed to alter the attitude displayed by the Assembly. Members persisted in continuing their debate on a school bill, instead of discussing the war measures requested by Brock and bringing them to a vote, so he finally gave up in disgust and prorogued the Legislature on August 5. Late that night he prepared to leave for Long Point on Lake Erie, where he had ordered a force to assemble for the relief of Amherstburg. He had been encouraged to do so by the enthusiasm which Captain Roberts' bloodless victory had engendered among the flank companies of militia on duty at York. All had volunteered for active service, but he had selected only 100 men because York could not be left without defenders. Fortunately two experienced officers despatched by Prevost to assist him had arrived: Lieutenant-Colonel Christopher Myers, who had been transferred from Jamaica to assume the appointment of Quartermaster General, and Major-General Roger Hale Sheaffe who had returned from leave in Britain.[27] Sheaffe, who had been born in Boston in 1763, had already seen service in Canada; from 1787 to 1797 he was with the 8th Regiment, and he had returned in 1803 as Brock's immediate subordinate in the 49th Foot; he was now placed in charge of the vulnerable Niagara frontier, where Lieutenant-Colonel Myers had already been posted.

News of the loss of Mackinac had first come to Brigadier General Hull by way of friendly Indians; it was confirmed on August 2 when the paroled garrison reached Detroit by schooner. On the same day the hitherto trusted Wyandot Indians living close to Detroit went over to the British and were escorted by a detachment of the 41st Foot to Amherstburg. Hull at once realized that the Indians of the whole Northwest would join the British unless he could restore American prestige by a speedy capture of Fort Malden. To facilitate this, he wrote imploring the Governors of Ohio and Kentucky to send him militia reinforcements. At the same time, however, Hull sent orders for the abandonment of the isolated and indefensible Fort Dearborn, on the site of the present city of Chicago.

On August 5 Colonel Procter, who had now reached and assumed command at Amherstburg, sent Tecumseh across the Detroit River with two dozen braves to intercept a supply train known to be proceeding slowly under a small escort from Ohio. The Indians also successfully ambushed and scattered the troops Hull had sent out to meet it. As an added gain, Procter got possession of official despatches going to and from Hull.

Brigadier-General Hull assembled another Council of War on August 6.

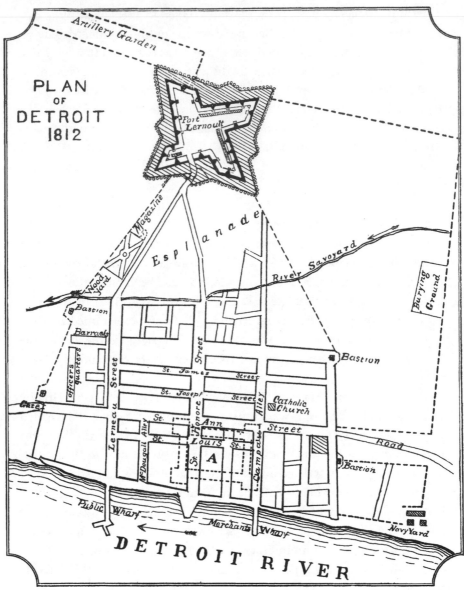

PLAN
OF
DETROIT
1812

RICHARDSON'S WAR OF 1812, 1902

This time the majority voted for an immediate assault on Fort Malden, supported by the heavy guns now mounted on rafts and ready to be floated into firing position. Hull agreed to implement this verdict. Intelligence that Brock was on the way with help for Amherstburg, however, caused Hull once again to change his mind. On August 8 he re-crossed the Detroit River with most of his force.

The town of Detroit was the centre for about half the 4,800 inhabitants of the Michigan Territory, living along the river from five miles above to ten miles below the town. Its collection of about 150 houses was surrounded by a palisade of pickets. Unfortunately the town lay between the river and the fort, whose guns had to fire overhead at long range against river traffic. This location also lessened the defensive possibilities of the fort, which was otherwise sturdy enough to withstand any likely attacker.

Hull was anxious to withdraw further from Detroit, to the line of the Raisin or Maumee rivers, there re-form the severed supply route with Ohio, and await the requested reinforcements. The colonels of the Ohio regiments were vehemently opposed to any retreat, however, as were their men. Instead a picked force of 600 – about half of Hull's effectives – was sent to protect another supply train moving forward from the Raisin River.

During the early afternoon of August 9, near the Indian village of Maguaga, this force blundered into an ambush set by Captain Adam Muir's detachment of 150 British regulars and Canadian militia which, with an indeterminate number of Indians led by Tecumseh, had been ordered to prey upon the American line of communications. The Americans managed to drive off Muir's men; the regulars and militia retreated to their boats and returned to the Canadian shore, while the Indians disappeared into the forest. American losses were 18 killed and 64 wounded; Muir, himself wounded, reported 6 killed, 21 wounded and 2 taken prisoner. Thirty years later, Major John Richardson, then a "gentleman volunteer"[28] attached to the 41st Foot, was to describe this encounter and to emphasize the disadvantages of employing British regulars in forest fighting:

Here it was that we had first an opportunity of perceiving the extreme disadvantage of opposing regular troops to the enemy in the woods. Accustomed to the use of the rifle from his infancy – dwelling in a measure amid forests with the intricacies of which he is wholly acquainted, and possessing the advantage of a dress which renders him almost undistinguishable to the eye of a European, the American marksman enters with comparative security into a contest with the English soldier whose glaring habiliment and accoutrements are objects too conspicuous to be missed, while his utter ignorance of a mode of warfare, in which courage and discipline are of no avail, renders the struggle for mastery even more unequal. The ... levies of men taken from the forests of Ohio [are] scarcely inferior as riflemen to the Indians. Dressed in woollen frocks of a gray color, and trained to cover their bodies behind the trees from which they fired, without exposing more of their persons than was absolutely necessary for their aim, they afforded us, on more than one occasion, the most convincing proofs that without the assistance of the Indian Warriors, the defence of so great a portion of Western Canada ... would have proved a duty of great difficulty and doubt.[29]

Having beaten off the ambush, the Americans might well have continued on to meet their much-needed supplies. Instead they made camp where they were, and then, after passing a tentless and foodless night in pouring rain, they headed back towards Detroit. Along the river road they were harassed by gunfire from the brig *Queen Charlotte* and schooner *General Hunter*. On the following day, August 11, Hull ordered the last of his command to vacate Sandwich and return to Detroit. Shortly thereafter, "round robin" petitions circulated among the Ohio officers requesting the arrest or displacement of General Hull.

Meanwhile Brock was hurrying to Amherstburg with the 50 regulars, 250 militia and one 6-pr. gun that had awaited him at Long Point on August 8. The trip along the shore of Lake Erie in small boats took five days, hampered by heavy rain and adverse winds. Shortly before midnight on August 13 Brock arrived at Amherstburg, and the delight of the Indians was such that they fired off their muskets in a straggling *feu de joie*. Brock must have been relieved himself after this unpleasant trip, but he quickly explained to Tecumseh, whom he now met for the first time, that this was really an unnecessary waste of ammunition when Detroit had to be captured. Legend has made much of this meeting of two undeniably imposing figures. Tecumseh may have turned to his braves and said "This is a man" – whether he did or did not is immaterial.[30] Brock and Tecumseh developed a respect for each other and Brock was to write subsequently that "a more sagacious or a more gallant Warrior does not I believe exist."[31]

Undoubtedly Colonel Procter had been acting in too cautious a fashion to suit the Indians. He was, however, only a subordinate entrusted with his first independent command and should not be censured for refusing to endanger unduly his too few redcoats. Major-General Brock, however, was the British military commander for the whole of Upper Canada. Moreover Brock was bold by nature, and the contents of the captured American despatches indicated that Hull's position at Detroit would remain precarious until such time as large reinforcements should arrive from Kentucky and

Ohio. Therefore Brock quickly devised a plan of attack, which he subsequently explained to the several Indian chiefs and Lieutenant-Colonel Matthew Elliott of the Indian Department. When he had finished, Tecumseh took it upon himself to agree on behalf of the other chiefs of the small bands of Shawnees, Miamis, Delawares, Potawatomis, and Wyandots. Except for the leaders of the Wyandots, who had crossed over from American territory only a few days earlier, these chiefs had accompanied Tecumseh to Amherstburg after the defeat at Tippecanoe.[32]

Brock also struck the right note to improve morale in the order issued to the troops, and did not fail to point out to the militiamen the duties and rewards of loyal service:

> The Major General congratulates the troops on the evacuation of the country by the enemy. He is persuaded that nothing but the spirit manifested by those who have remained doing duty, and the judicious measures adopted by Colonel Procter have compelled him to do so disgraceful a retreat.
>
> Colonel Elliott and Major McKee and the officers of the Indian Department are entitled to his best thanks for their judicious management of the Indians, and for the example of galantry [sic] which they have uniformly shown before the enemy.
>
> The Major General cannot avoid expressing his surprise at the numerous desertions which have occurred from the ranks of the militia, to which circumstance the long stay of the enemy on this side of the river must in a great measure be ascribed. He is willing to believe that their conduct proceeded from an anxiety to get in their harvests and not from any predilection for the principles or Government of the United States. He requests officers commanding corps to submit to him the names of such militiamen as have remained faithful to their oath and duty, that immediate measures may be taken to discharge their arrears of pay.
>
> The enemy still being in the neighborhood, the whole physical force of the country will be employed to drive him to such a distance as will ensure its tranquility.[33]

Brock now organized his disposable field force of 300 regulars and 400 militia into three tiny brigades. These bore no resemblance to modern formations of that name. The first consisted of the 50 officers and men of the Royal Newfoundland Fencibles and members of the Oxford and Kent militia regiments; the second included 50 all ranks of the 41st Foot and militia detachments from the counties of York, Lincoln, Oxford and Norfolk; the third comprised the remaining 200 of the 41st Foot. Command of each of these "battle groups" was entrusted to a regular officer: Lieutenant-Colonel St. George and two captains of the 41st Foot who were given the local rank of major. The subaltern's detachment of 30 artillerymen had three 6-prs. and two 3-prs. for employment in a mobile role. Command of the whole was given to Colonel Procter, although he would function directly under Brock's watchful eye.

On the following day, August 15, Brock despatched his *aide-de-camp* under a flag of truce to Detroit, with a demand that Hull surrender immediately. "It is far from my intention to join in a war of extermination," Brock had written deliberately, "but you must be aware, that the numerous body of Indians who have attached themselves to my troops will be beyond control the moment the contest commences."[34] Naturally Hull refused, but he was worried by what Brock's Indian allies might do and thus delayed his answer. As soon as the flag of truce did return, a battery of three guns and two mortars, erected at Sandwich under the direction of Captain Dixon, R.E., opened fire on Detroit. This was returned from the American shore. Such was the range, however, that no damage was done on either side.

Hull was made more uneasy by the protracted absence from Detroit of Colonels Lewis Cass and Duncan McArthur with 400 of the best Ohio men. Both colonels were involved in the plot to depose Hull and only very reluctantly had agreed to lead a picked force to meet a supply column *en route* from the Raisin River staging point. Finding no one at the designated rendezvous, Cass and McArthur decided to return. However, they neither sent word of this to Hull nor made any haste to get back to Detroit.

Obsessed by the notion that the Indians would attack his weakened garrison during the hours of darkness, Hull disposed his remaining Ohio volunteers and Michigan militia about the town and fort on the landward side; the regulars were congregated within the fort or the shore batteries. Most of the women and children were moved to a root cellar in a nearby orchard. In consequence, he had no men left to guard the logical spot for Brock to attempt a crossing with his regulars and militia – where the river was narrowest. This was at Spring Wells, about three miles below Detroit.

During the night of August 15/16 about 600 Indians did cross the Detroit River. These were acting under the direction, rather than the orders, of Lieutenant-Colonel Elliott of the Indian Department: even tribal chiefs could exercise little enough control over undisciplined braves on the war-path. Shortly after daybreak on August 16, a Sunday morning, Brock's 700 regulars and militia crossed in boats, under the cover of fire from the shore battery at Sandwich and from the guns of *Queen Charlotte* and *General Hunter*. An unopposed landing was made at Spring Wells. As soon as Brock learned from local residents that Colonels Cass and McArthur were still absent with 400 of their Ohio men, he ordered an immediate advance against Detroit. Led by Colonel Procter, the three brigades advanced to within less than a mile of the town and then halted so that the troops could eat the cold breakfasts carried with them. Many of the militiamen were decked out in part-worn red tunics, obtained in one way or another from the regulars at Fort Malden, and the sections moved with double the usual distance between them, so that the appearance of the little force was for-midable.

Hull certainly thought it so when news of the landing came to him. He decided that he did not have enough men immediately available to risk a battle in the open. Desertion of the Michigan militia from their posts and the appearance of Indians in the outskirts of the town soon suggested that even a successful defence would be impossible. Hull was a Brigadier-General in the United States Army, but he was also Governor of the Michigan Ter-ritory and responsible for the welfare of its inhabitants. The menace posed by the Indians of the Northwest had undoubtedly become an obsession with him and he feared for the safety of the women and children with him. His apprehension was heightened when an 18-pound shell landed in the officers' mess and killed four: the shore battery at Sandwich had finally found the correct range.[35] Hull had a flag of truce hoisted at once and pro-posed one hour's cessation of hostilities.

Terms were quickly arranged with Brock. Hull agreed to surrender his whole command, including the detachment commanded by Colonels Cass and McArthur. These officers had not hurried back to help Hull, even when they heard the early morning cannonade, but they subsequently complained bitterly that they would have insisted on fighting. About 1,600 Ohio volunteers were paroled to their homes and escorted beyond possi-ble danger from the Indians, who had again behaved quietly. Brigadier-General Hull and 582 regulars, however, shortly began the long trip as pris-oners of war to Quebec City where alone there were facilities to accommo-date them. The 33 artillery pieces, 2,500 muskets and considerable military stores surrendered to Brock were vital to his continued defence of Upper

Canada and most of the capture was soon transferred to Fort Erie by ship. The American brig *Adams* was taken over by the Provincial Marine and renamed *Detroit*. Needless to say, the attacking force had suffered no battle casualties.

Brock now issued the inevitable proclamation advising the inhabitants of the Michigan Territory that the "Laws heretofore in existence shall continue in force until His Majesty's pleasure be known, or so long as the peace and security of the said territory will admit thereof."[36] Colonel Procter was delegated to govern Michigan, in addition to continuing in command at Amherstburg, since Fort Malden was a far better defensive position than Detroit. Brock himself, fearing that trouble might erupt any time at Niagara, hurried back, taking with him as many regulars as the changed situation on the Detroit frontier seemed to make feasible.

Acting on the orders earlier sent by Brigadier-General Hull, the American commander at distant Fort Dearborn had commenced the withdrawal of his 54 regulars, 12 militia, 9 women and 18 children on the morning of August 15. The local Potawatomi Indians had received word of the British victory at Mackinac, however, and excited by the news 400 braves attacked the retreating column. In what was virtually a massacre, 26 regulars, all the militia, 2 women and 12 children were killed; those taken prisoner either later escaped or were ransomed by the British.

Fort Wayne was now the only American post in the Old Northwest. Even this small post on the Maumee River, commanded by an alcoholic captain with a mere 70 regulars, was soon invested by hostile Indians. The military situation had been quickly and decisively reversed, and for this credit must be given to the initiative of British officers in command of makeshift forces built around an essential core of regular troops.

CHAPTER FIVE

Brock and the Niagara: September and October 1812

QUEENSTON HEIGHTS

On the evening of August 1, a ship reached Quebec from Halifax with the first news that the British Government had conditionally repealed its controversial Orders in Council. A letter from the erstwhile British Minister to the United States informed Sir George Prevost that he was trying, from Halifax, to open negotiations with the American Government for peace. The letter suggested that Prevost take similar action, which he did by sending his Adjutant General under a flag of truce to Major-General Henry Dearborn's headquarters to arrange an armistice.

Colonel Edward Baynes reached Dearborn's headquarters at Greenbush, across the Hudson River from Albany, on August 8 and delivered Prevost's proposal. The politically astute Dearborn agreed with the suggestion that the United States was hardly likely to want to continue a needless war, although his agreement was undoubtedly influenced by the fact that his own preparations had not advanced sufficiently to make offensive operations feasible. Yet, as he told Baynes on the following day, he did not possess the authority to conclude a proper armistice. Dearborn offered, however, to give positive orders to the officers commanding frontier forts to confine themselves to defensive measures until further orders were received. Should this arrangement not prove acceptable to the President of the United States, hostilities would be resumed after four days' notice had been given. Dearborn explained further that he possessed no authority over Brigadier-General Hull, but would write and suggest that he take similar action. The latest developments on the frontier, of course, were unknown to the negotiators. "I consider the agreement as favorable at this period," Dearborn reported to the Secretary of War in Washington on August 9, "for we could not act offensively except at Detroit for some time, and there it will not probably have any effect on General Hull or his movements."[1]

Similarly, as Prevost was to explain in a despatch of August 17 to the Secretary of State for War and the Colonies, "I have not thought it necessary to restrain Major-General Brock from adopting any measures he might judge fit for repelling the Invasion of the Upper Province & for compelling General Hull to retire from it."[2]

Whether or not President Madison would approve Dearborn's action, important advantages accrued to Prevost, as he carefully explained in his letter of August 24 to Lord Bathurst. His military situation had already improved and could continue to improve; encouraged by this the mood of the civilians had become more cheerful:

> In the absence of Instructions from His Majesty's Government founded on their knowledge of an actual state of hostility with America, Your Lordship must be aware that I am necessarily obliged to confine myself to measures of defence, & to combine every movement with that object.
>
> A suspension of hostilities therefore on a considerable portion of the extremely extensive line of Frontier which I have to defend has enabled me rapidly to strengthen the Flank attacked. The decided superiority I have obtained on the Lakes in consequence of the precautionary measures adopted during the last winter has permitted me to move without interruption, independently of the arrangement, both Troops & supplies of every description towards Amherstburg, while those for Genl. Hull having several hundred miles of wilderness to pass before they can reach Detroit, are exposed, to be harassed and destroyed by the Indians. Another consequence of the Mission of Col. Baynes and of the arrangement resulting from it, has been a Discovery of the inability of the Government of the United States to overrun the Canadas & of their unprepared state for carrying on the war with vigour; this has become so manifest that His Majesty's Subjects in both Provinces are beginning to feel an increased confidence in the Government protecting them, and as the means & resources which have been displayed appear to have far exceeded their expectations, so has it effectually secured their best exertions for the defence of their Country against any tumultuary force – In the mean time from a partial suspension of hostilities I am enabled to improve & augment my resources against an Invasion, whilst the Enemy distracted by Party broils & intrigues are obliged to remain supine & to witness daily the diminution of the Force they had so much difficulty in collecting.[3]

Major-General Brock received the news of the cessation of hostilities during his return to the Niagara frontier from Amherstburg. Naturally an impulsive man, and now flushed with triumph, he was disconcerted at this turn of events. Yet his correspondence was discreet. "However wise and politic the measure must be admitted to be," he wrote to the Secretary of State for War and the Colonies on August 29, "the Indians, who cannot enter into our views, will naturally feel disheartened and suspicious of our intentions. Should hostilities recommence I much fear the influence the British possess over them will be found diminished."[4] To his brothers, Brock was only slightly more explicit: "Should peace follow, the measure will be well; if hostilities recommence, nothing could be more unfortunate than this pause."[5]

The cease-fire arrangements concluded between Dearborn and Prevost were that no offensive measures were to be undertaken, but that otherwise the opposing forces would carry on as before. When Brock reached Niagara, however, he found that Major-General Sheaffe had failed to observe "religiously" the instructions issued on Prevost's orders and had made his own supplementary agreement with Major-General Stephen Van Rensselaer. On August 20 Sheaffe had accepted Van Rensselaer's suggestion that "no reinforcements of men or supplies of ammunition" be sent by either party higher than Fort Erie, and that no troops should be moved from any station to the westward, without four days' previous notice being given to the other party.[6] Sheaffe considered himself smart to have made this bargain, since he knew that Brock had captured Detroit – information which had not yet reached Van Rensselaer. But Prevost was incensed when he heard

Major-General Sir Roger Hale Sheaffe (1763-1851)
He performed well at Queenston Heights but not so well when he replaced Brock as the commander in Upper Canada.
(National Archives of Canada, C-111307)

of the bargain, since, he wrote to Brock on August 30, "it had been expressly stated to General Dearborn and clearly understood by him, that our mutual supplies and reinforcements should move unmolested, with the contemplation of succouring Amherstburg."[7] Yet Prevost's letter to Brock admitted also that considerable embarrassment would result from disavowal of Sheaffe's action. So nothing was done about it.

At this stage Brock was convinced that he could sweep away the small enemy forces scattered along the line of the Niagara River any time he pleased. The Canadian inhabitants of the Niagara Peninsula felt the same way, after they had talked to the victorious regulars and militia returned from Detroit and seen the long lines of American prisoners. According to Reverend Michael Smith, an itinerant Baptist minister who had left the United States to labour in Upper Canada in 1808, the service of King George III now assumed a new respect and doubts about allegiance were no longer noised about:

> The surrender of the fort at Detroit and all the Michigan Territory, were events which the people of Canada could scarcely believe, even after they were known to be true. Indeed, when I saw the officers and soldiers returning to Fort George, with the spoils of my countrymen, I could scarcely believe my own eyes. ...
>
> After this event, the people of Canada became fearful of disobeying the government – some that had fled to the wilderness returned home – and the friends of the United States were discouraged, and those of the King encouraged. ...
>
> The army now became respectable, and a dread fell on those who had opposed the government. The people now saw that it was as much as their property and lives were worth to disobey orders, and now what they had been compelled to do, after a while they did from choice.[8]

It might indeed have seemed to a quick observer that Brock should have been given an opportunity to follow up his success at once rather than remain idle. But Prevost's understanding with Dearborn was based firmly on his appreciation that for him the war had essentially to be a defensive struggle. His conduct was to be defended by a distinguished veteran of the Peninsular and Waterloo campaigns, Major-General Sir James Carmichael-Smyth, R.E., who spent several months of 1825 reporting on the defence of British North America. According to the confidential study he prepared for the Duke of Wellington, any operations by Brock at this time could have had little effect on the war as a whole and might even have been an embarrassment:

It has been said that General Brock, after his return to the Niagara frontier, on the 24th August, might have immediately taken Fort Niagara, which would have had the happiest effects upon the campaign, if not upon the war. General Brock's force was not more than 1200 men upon the Niagara River, one-half of whom were militia. The Americans had 6,300. Offensive operations were, therefore, not likely to have been undertaken by the British. The capture of the fort at Niagara could not, moreover, at any rate, even if it had taken place, have prevented the Americans from passing the Niagara, above the Falls, between the Chippeway and Fort Erie, or below the Falls, from Lewis Town to Queen's Town. In fact, it would, in General Brock's possession, have been rather an inconvenience, compelling him to deprive himself of 300 or 400 men from his already too small disposable force for its garrison. In defensive warfare, delay is everything. The war was essentially defensive on the part of the British.[9]

President Madison had, however, unhesitatingly condemned Major-General Dearborn's action. The British Government's conditional repeal of the controversial Orders in Council had eliminated only one of the major American grievances and there was no guarantee that similar Orders in Council might not be imposed at a later date. There had been no suggestion that impressment of American sailors would cease forthwith, nor had any sop been given to injured national pride. Above all, Madison and his supporters in Congress would lose face if he called off the war. Therefore on August 13 the Secretary of War replied to Dearborn's despatch that "after the receipt of this letter and allowing a reasonable time in which you will inform Sir George Prevost thereof, you will proceed with the utmost vigor in your operations."[10] Both the President and his Secretary of War doubted whether Dearborn possessed sufficient resources to implement the existing scheme of attacking Montreal, Kingston and the Niagara Peninsula simultaneously. Dearborn should, however, seize Kingston and the Niagara Peninsula, and make at least a feint against Montreal to keep Prevost's attention concentrated there.

Dearborn duly notified Prevost as directed and hostilities were resumed on September 4, but he made no forward move. Prevost had been right to assume that Dearborn did not possess the necessary manpower. In what is still the best American account of the War of 1812, Henry Adams was much later to describe how the lack of interest of the country at large and the meagre pay for service made it difficult to draw men into the ranks of worthwhile military forces:

> The country refused to take the war seriously. A rich nation with seven million inhabitants should have easily put one hundred thousand men into the field, and should have found no difficulty in supporting them; but no inducement that the Government dared offer prevailed upon the people to risk life and property on a sufficient scale in 1812. The ranks of the army were to be filled in one of two ways, either by enlistment in the regular service for five years, with pay at five dollars a month, sixteen dollars bounty, and on discharge three months pay and one hundred and sixty acres of land; or by volunteer organizations to the limit of fifty thousand men in all, officered under State laws, to serve for one year, with the pay of regular troops but without bounty, clothes, and in the case of cavalry corps mounted, at their own expense. In a society where the day-laborers' wages were nowhere less than nine dollars a month, these inducements were not enough to supply the place of enthusiasm. The patriotic citizen who wished to serve his country without too much sacrifice, chose a third course, – he volunteered under the Act of Congress which authorized the President to call one hundred thousand State militia into service for six months.[11]

Even prominent War Hawks in Congress, such as the young Henry Clay from Kentucky, knew also that farmers had to be home to plant and harvest their crops. This line of reasoning had prompted the Secretary of War's letter of August 22 authorizing Major-General Pinckney, at Charleston in South Carolina, to reduce the number of militia on duty in his Southern Department: his remaining regulars could do most of the necessary garrison duty, instead of being sent north as originally contemplated, since there now seemed little likelihood of a British-Canadian force taking the offensive.

Brock had been paying a whirlwind visit to Kingston on September 4 when he received Prevost's letter announcing that hostilities would resume that day. In consequence he sailed that night for Fort George to take over personal command of the Niagara frontier from Major-General Sheaffe who, however, continued to serve there as a major-general on staff. Accepting at face value Sheaffe's dismal reports, which greeted his arrival on September 6, of growing enemy strength along the American shore, Brock immediately sent word to both Amherstburg and Kingston for whatever troops could be spared. "I expect an attack almost immediately," he wrote Prevost on the following day.[12] "I stand in want of more artillery men and a thousand regulars." This letter took four days to reach Sir George Prevost at Montreal, where he had again moved his headquarters.

Brock's next letter, written on September 13, was in a far different vein. It advised Prevost that the enemy, though greatly reinforced, now seemed determined on "defensive measures." Brock's best intelligence corroborated the stories of deserters that sickness was rampant and that discipline was bad. The New York militia were complaining of "bad usage, bad and scanty food, and a total want of pay."[13] Unknown to Brock, of course, an inspecting officer's report on the newly mobilized 14th Regiment of U.S. Infantry was soon to complain that it "is composed entirely of recruits; they appear to be almost as ignorant of their duty as if they had never seen a camp, and scarcely know on which shoulder to carry the musket. They are mere militia, and, if possible, even worse; and if taken into action in their present state, will prove more dangerous to themselves than to their enemy."[14]

Neither was the American build-up in Ohio and Kentucky yet as serious a threat to Colonel Procter as was being suggested in his letters, which Brock was forwarding to Prevost. Yet there could be no thought of further reducing Procter's command to assist Brock, even though the commander of the new American North Western Army was another incompetent veteran of the Revolutionary War, James Winchester, who had also been appointed to the regular army as a brigadier-general only a few months previously.[15] The sole American in whom westerners possessed confidence, Governor William Harrison of the Indiana Territory, had been appointed a major-general in the Kentucky state militia in a deliberate attempt to outrank Winchester. Harrison had little difficulty talking Brigadier-General Winchester into devoting his time to recruiting and letting him relieve Fort Wayne. The Indian besiegers evaporated in the face of Harrison's advance and he reached the fort without a fight on September 12, while the force belatedly sent by Procter to assist them was still some miles distant.

Meanwhile Sir George Prevost had been extremely annoyed by the receipt of Brock's first and pessimistic letter from Fort George. Since the commencement of hostilities, Prevost had been doing his best to augment Brock's military resources. Clothing for 2,000 militia and a few guns had been forwarded from Montreal late in June. The subsequent arrival of the 103rd Regiment at Quebec had not added appreciably to Prevost's strength in Lower Canada since, as he explained in a letter of July 27 to Brock, it was composed of "about 750 very young Soldiers and Boys."[16] Yet "for the preservation of the communication between Upper and Lower Canada, thereby securing, in an extreme case of being attacked by an overwhelming force, a retreat for the Regulars, & Loyalists embodied" towards Quebec, Prevost had sent a considerable reinforcement to Kingston. This movement was staged over several weeks and also served as armed escorts for supply convoys of bateaux. One company of the 49th Foot had left Lachine late in July; three further companies had set out on August 6; a fifth company had travelled with the flank companies of the Royal Newfoundland Regiment and 50 of the 10th Royal Veterans on August 13. Colonel John Vincent had moved to Kingston with the remaining five companies of his 49th Regiment before the end of the month, and there assumed command. Colonel Vincent had 31 years of commissioned service behind him and was considered a competent officer, but like Brock he had only very limited experience of war.[17] As soon as Vincent had assumed the command at Kingston, Colonel Lethbridge moved to Prescott, whence he would superintend the flank companies of militia stationed at the several convoy staging points for boats along the upper St. Lawrence River.

Prevost had been able to send these detachments to Upper Canada only because he had received some reinforcements at Quebec and thus was able to forward other troops to the Montreal area. He had explained these movements in a letter despatched to Lord Bathurst from Montreal on August 17:

The arrival of the First Battalion of the Royals from the West Indies with the exception of one Transport captured by the United States Frigate Essex but afterwards ransomed & sent to Halifax has principally afforded me the means of furnishing Genl. Brock with the reinforcements I have sent to him. The 8th or King's Regiment has arrived this morning from Quebec to relieve the 49th Regt. – This fine & effective Regt. of the 8th together with a chain of Troops established in the vicinity of this place consisting of regular & Militia Forces, the whole amounting to near Four thousand five hundred men, effectually serve to keep in check the Enemy in this Quarter where alone they are in any strength, & to prevent any Attempt to carry on a predatory Warfare against this flourishing portion of Lower Canada.[18]

After their lengthy service in the fever-ridden West Indies, the upwards of 1,100 all ranks of what were popularly known as the 1st Royal Scots were in poor health, but Prevost hoped that a spell of garrison duty at Quebec would remedy this.

Prevost's reply to Brock's letter of September 7 was not despatched until September 14. "I have already afforded reinforcements to the full extent of my ability," Prevost wrote; "you must not, therefore, expect a further supply of men from hence until I shall receive from England a considerable increase to the present regular force in this province [i.e. Lower Canada]; the posture of affairs, particularly on this frontier, requires every soldier who is in the country."[19] Should the situation still appear serious at Niagara, Prevost suggested that Brock abandon Detroit and the Territory of Michigan: "by this measure you will be enabled to withdraw a greater number of the troops from Amherstburg, instead of taking them from Colonel Vincent, whose regular force [at Kingston] ought not, on any account, to be diminished." Brock was free to make up his own mind about reinforcing Fort Mackinac.

Brock decided to send on to Mackinac, by schooner from Fort Erie, the sergeant and 25 rank and file of the 10th Royal Veterans forwarded from Kingston by Colonel Vincent in response to his appeal. The flank companies of the Royal Newfoundland Regiment, which had joined him from there at the same time, were sent to Colonel Procter at Amherstburg, since he had decided not to abandon Detroit. He kept at Niagara, however, the six companies of the 49th Foot which Vincent had also sent to him.

Prevost was disturbed when he learned of Vincent's action in reducing the Kingston garrison to four companies of the 49th Regiment and Major Macpherson's original four companies of Royal Veterans. He had intended that only one company of the 49th, from the reinforcements ordered to Kingston, should continue to the Niagara frontier. Prevost now decided to strengthen the line of communication between Cornwall and Kingston by sending a company of the Glengarry Light Infantry Fencibles to Prescott.

"Under present circumstances," he wrote Brock on September 25, "you are not to expect further aid."[20] Nor did Prevost feel that Brock needed any, after receiving the optimistic letter of September 13, which even hinted that this was the time to launch an offensive across the Niagara River. "I agree in opinion with you," Prevost now continued,

> so wretched is the organization and discipline of the American army, that at this moment much might be effected against them; but as the government at home could derive no substantial advantage from any disgrace we might inflict on them, whilst the more important concerns of the country are committed in Europe, I again request you will steadily pursue that policy which shall appear to you best calculated to promote the dwindling away of such a force by its own inefficient means.

By the time this letter reached Fort George, the growing numbers of American troops, whatever their quality, had made the situation critical and Brock was glad to have better than half his own old 49th Foot with him. "Although the regiment has been ten years in this country, drinking rum without bounds," he wrote to one of his brothers, "it is still respectable, and apparently ardent for an opportunity to acquire distinction."[21]

With the arrival of Brigadier-General Alexander Smyth's 1,650 regulars at Buffalo on September 29, the American forces along the Niagara frontier had reached the strength of 6,000 which Major-Generals Dearborn and Van Rensselaer deemed necessary for an advance into Upper Canada. Van Rensselaer had 900 regulars and 2,650 militia concentrated in and around the village of Lewiston, below Niagara Falls and opposite to the Canadian village of Queenston. Here the Niagara River ran swiftly between high banks, but it was only 250 yards wide and could be crossed in a few minutes. Seizure of the commanding Queenston Heights, a great natural feature running at right angles to the river and across it, would, Van Rensselaer expected, give him command of the immediate area and a firm base from which to mop up the whole Niagara Peninsula.

The newly arrived Smyth more correctly appreciated that the Niagara River should be crossed above the Falls, where its banks are low and the current less swift. A regular soldier, he had no intention of taking orders from a major-general in the New York militia; he even refused to meet Van Rensselaer and discuss plans for an invasion. Yet the 47-year-old Smyth had forsaken politics and the legal profession only in 1808 to become colonel of

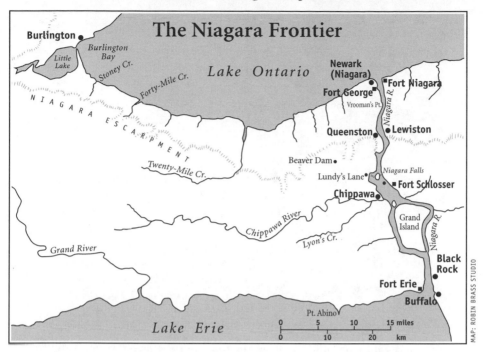

The Niagara Frontier

the rifle regiment then added to the United States Army, and he had never seen a day's serious fighting.[22] This snub only persuaded Van Rensselaer to go ahead on his own, since the resources immediately available to him at Lewiston were greater than those with which Brock was guarding the whole line of the Niagara River.

Brock's major concentrations were at Fort Erie and Chippawa, above the Falls where a crossing would be most easy, and at Fort George near the mouth of the Niagara River. Only the two flank companies of the 49th Foot and an approximately equal number of Lincoln militia, with a tiny 3-pr. gun, were disposed in and around Queenston, a village of nearly 100 houses below the towering Heights; an 18-pr. gun was in a tiny earthwork or redan on the long, north slope leading up from the village, far enough below the crest to prevent it having a silhouette at which the enemy guns at Lewiston might aim; a 24-pr. gun was located about a mile down river on Vrooman's Point.

Brock had become convinced that a major attack was pending, but where? On the night of October 9 a party of American sailors and soldiers headed by Lieutenant Jesse D. Elliott, U.S.N., managed to cut out two armed vessels of the Provincial Marine from under the guns of Fort Erie. The smaller *Caledonia*, which had taken part in the capture of Mackinac,

Infantryman, United States Army, 1812
In two years of campaigning on the northern frontier, the American regular infantry evolved from a collection of raw amateurs into a well trained force capable of tackling their British opponents on equal terms. (Painting by C.H. McBarron, courtesy Parks Canada)

was successfully towed away into captivity, but the larger *Detroit*, the brig surrendered by Hull to Brock, ran aground and had to be burned. This reduction in the Provincial Marine's strength meant that Lieutenant Elliott might soon be able to contest its hitherto undisputed naval command of Lake Erie with the makeshift vessels he was converting to war purposes at Buffalo.

During the night of October 10/11, the garrison at Queenston were eager listeners to the confusion attending an abortive assault crossing from Lewiston. Van Rensselaer's planning for the operation he was mounting had been poor and his men had not had any boat drill. Confusion increased when several of the boats were found to be without oars. A heavy rainstorm then drenched everyone, and made both officers and men impatient to get back to camp. The boats continued in position along the shore, for all to see, but common sense suggested to Brock that this attempt should be taken as merely a feint. He expected that the real attack would be launched closer to Fort George, about seven miles down river, where the Americans could be supported by the guns of the opposing Fort Niagara. Therefore Brock remained at Fort George with his small staff. Major-General Sheaffe also was here.

On October 12, however, Brock did have cause to worry about Queenston. He had sent a staff officer to investigate the mutinous state of the detachment there of the 49th Foot, whose men had threatened to shoot their officers because they were fed up with isolated duty. He was to bring back half a dozen of the "most culpable" so that Brock could make an example of them.[23] This staff officer was also instructed to visit Van Rensselaer's headquarters and arrange for the exchange of the prisoners captured during the recent attack on *Caledonia* and *Detroit*. His brief and unsuccessful visit to the American encampment convinced him that the enemy would try again to cross the river at Queenston. Therefore he returned to Fort George and reported to Brock that he had taken it upon himself to release the imprisoned soldiers of the 49th's grenadier company, "on the specious plea of their offence proceeding from a too free indulgence in drink" and after "appealing to them for proof of their loyalty and courage, which they were assured would be severely tested ere another day dawned."[24]

Van Rensselaer may have been sufficiently discouraged to call it quits, but circumstances would not let him. His men were bordering on mutiny and demanding action. His political opponent, Governor Tompkins of New York, was hounding him and Brigadier-General Smyth of the regular army was ignoring him. He gave the order for a new attack.

At three o'clock on the morning of Tuesday, October 13, and under the cover of an intense artillery bombardment from the American shore, the first of an assault wave of 300 volunteers and 300 regulars embarked at Lewiston in the 13 boats available. Three of these were carried too far downstream, but the others landed a short distance above Queenston as planned. Colonel Solomon Van Rensselaer was soon badly wounded and his volunteers driven to ground by the fire of the 49th Regiment's grenadier company; but Captain John E. Wool managed to find and lead his company of the 13th U.S. Infantry Regiment up a winding footpath that led to the top of the Heights, some 350 feet above the river.

Awakened at Fort George by the sound of the American guns supporting the crossing from Lewiston, Brock waited until he felt sure the real attack was not aimed at Fort George, then mounted his horse and galloped into the dawn. He paused *en route* only long enough to order forward the flank companies of York militia and to send back word for Sheaffe to bring up most of the garrison of Fort George.

Brock's first act at Queenston was to order down the light company of the 49th Foot from the Heights into the village to support its hard-pressed grenadier company. There was little reason for Brock to imagine that, in the half-light, an enemy party would be able to find the steep path and make its way to the top. He himself rode up the slope to the one-gun redan and dismounted in order to get a better look at the situation. Across the river at Lewiston he could now see large masses of the enemy waiting their turn to cross in the boats, which were plying back and forth while round shot from the redan's gun and the larger gun at Vrooman's Point landed in the water around them. Suddenly, Captain Wool and his leading American regulars came over the crest of the Heights; there was a loud yell and they charged down on the redan. There was time only for the gunners to drive a spike into the touch hole of the gun, rendering it unserviceable, before they fled down the hill. Brock ran along beside them, leading his horse into the village.

There was no time to waste, as Brock knew only too well. Unless the redan could be recaptured before the enemy had a chance to consolidate this commanding position, all would be lost. Brock had only about 100 men of the 49th Regiment and an equal number of tired and dazed Lincoln militia, but these would have to suffice. He formed his little command into line and gave the order to advance.

There was no hesitation about following this commanding figure. Yet the cocked hat, red coat, gold epaulettes, and the decorative scarf given him by Tecumseh after the capture of Detroit, made him the obvious target for enemy marksmen as the little group moved up the hillside. A bullet in the wrist made him pause only momentarily. He pressed on, waving his sword, until a sharpshooter's bullet pierced his left breast. He died almost instantly. The nearest men clustered around for a moment and then everyone started back down the hill.

His *aide-de-camp*, Lieutenant-Colonel John Macdonell, who had just arrived on the scene with the two flank companies of York militia, quickly launched a second attack. It managed to recapture the redan and drive the enemy up the hillside. At the crucial moment, however, the Americans received reinforcements from below and Macdonell was fatally wounded. Once again the redcoats and militia retreated down the hill, and then towards Vrooman's Point to await reinforcements. The newly arrived York men have since become one of the legends of the war. The dying Brock is supposed to have urged those near him to "Push on the York Volunteers" who were, he knew, coming towards Queenston, and folklore has turned a simple command into the ringing exhortation, "Push on, brave York Volunteers."[25]

The American commander, Captain Wool, also was now badly wounded but another young regular officer, Lieutenant-Colonel Winfield

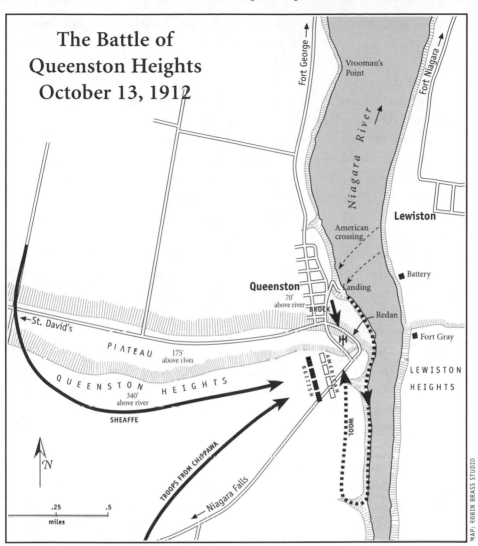

The Battle of
Queenston Heights
October 13, 1912

Fort George →

Vrooman's
Point

Fort Niagara →

Niagara River

Lewiston

American
crossing

■ Battery

Queenston
70'
above river

Landing

BROCK

Redan

■ Fort Gray

←St. David's

PLATEAU   175'
above river

LEWISTON
HEIGHTS

QUEENSTON   HEIGHTS
340'
above river

AMERICAN

BRITISH

SHEAFFE

WOOL

N

TROOPS FROM CHIPPAWA

← Niagara Falls

.25   .5

miles

MAP: ROBIN BRASS STUDIO

In the early hours of October 13, 1812, American troops crossed the Niagara and
landed at the small village of Queenston. An initial attempt to take the commanding
heights above the village was rebuffed but Captain John Wool of the 13th Infantry
found an alternate route and captured the high ground. A counter-attack led in
person by Isaac Brock failed, but later in the day General Roger Sheaffe assembled
troops from the surrounding area and gradually compressed the American position
until the invaders surrendered.

Scott, arrived to take command. Scott was a 26-year-old Virginian, who was to distinguish himself in the later campaigns of this war, capture Mexico City in 1847, and be still serving as Chief of Staff in Washington when the Civil War erupted in 1861.[26] Van Rensselaer visited the position briefly and then returned to Lewiston, leaving Brigadier-General William Wadsworth of the New York militia in charge.

By mid-morning the American militiamen still waiting their turn to cross in the boats, which continued under fire from the single 24-pr. gun at Vrooman's Point, were refusing to embark. They had also heard the noise of battle and wanted no part of it. Despite harangues and appeals, they insisted on their legal right to serve only on American soil for its defence. Even a few of the 1,300 Americans who had crossed earlier now managed to return to Lewiston; others insisted on remaining in the village of Queenston. Only about 350 regulars and 250 militia were in position on the Heights and they were running short of ammunition.

The guns of Fort George had been duelling all morning with those of the opposing Fort Niagara. Several houses in Newark village were set on fire by red-hot shot from the American guns only 900 yards away. The garrison of Fort Erie continued alert for signs of an invasion attempt from Black Rock but obviously could spare no one for the battle down river.

Major-General Roger Sheaffe reached Vrooman's Point around noon. He had brought from Fort George about 300 officers and men of the 41st Foot, a so-called Car Brigade of artillery which was a battery of field guns drawn by draught horses belonging to local farmers, and 250 militia. These last included the Niagara Light Dragoons, Captain Robert Runchey's Company of Coloured Men[27] and further flank companies of Lincoln and York militia. Instead of risking another frontal attack Sheaffe decided to follow a circuitous path recommended by the Indians and thus gain the Heights well to the west of the American position. *En route* he met the grenadier company of the 41st Foot from the Chippawa garrison and a band of Indians. Altogether Sheaffe now had better than 400 regulars, about the same number of militia, and nearly 300 Indians of the Six Nations. Joseph Brant's son John was one of the Mohawk leaders. Sending the Indians ahead as skirmishers, Sheaffe followed with his regulars and militia in an extended line of advance. It was now about three o'clock in the afternoon.

This time it was the Americans who were taken completely by surprise. A new front was formed, after a fashion, on their left flank and with their backs to the river, but there was no time to start rearranging their breast-

The Battle of Queenston Heights, October 13, 1812
British victory in this engagement, which cost Brock his life, ended the second
American invasion of Upper Canada. (Courtesy of the Weir Foundation, Queenston)

works before Sheaffe's troops fired a volley and came on with the bayonet.
Some of the Americans broke and ran after firing their muskets only once,
in the hope of reaching the shore and getting across somehow. The majority was equally afraid of what the Indians might do, but stayed huddled in
a mass at the edge of the precipice until Winfield Scott's waving white
handkerchief of surrender was recognized.[28]

American losses for the whole day were 958 prisoners and more than
300 killed and wounded. British and Canadian losses were 14 killed, 77
wounded and 21 missing. Sheaffe agreed with Van Rensselaer's request for
a three-day armistice, because he was hampered by having more prisoners
than troops. The practical solution again adopted was to release the
American militia to their homes on parole and send only the captured
regulars to Quebec and captivity.

Canadian history has emphasized the death of Brock while leading an
unsuccessful and hurried counter-attack, but the British Government rewarded Sheaffe with a baronetcy for the skilful manner in which he mar-
shalled and manoeuvred his little army to victory. Brock had actually been

made a Knight of the Bath for his capture of Detroit, but the news did not reach Upper Canada in time for him to know it.

Van Rensselaer quickly decided that he had enough and sent an offer of resignation to Major-General Dearborn. This was accepted and command at Niagara was given to Brigadier-General Smyth, who secured a further armistice which either side could terminate on 24 hours notice.

American command had also changed in the distant Northwest. It was put into the more capable hands of Brigadier-General William Harrison, now holding a regular commission in that rank by virtue of presidential action. Brigadier-General Winchester was relegated by President Madison to command merely the left wing of the new North Western Army. Harrison had grandiose ideas about recapturing Detroit and moving into Upper Canada, but there could be no advance until adequate stores were received and a proper forward base was established. His choice for this last was the rapids on the Maumee River, where he hoped to concentrate a million rations, as well as adequate reserves of ammunition and winter clothing.

In Upper Canada there was an end to defeatist talk after the events at Queenston. On November 23 Sheaffe wrote Prevost that the number of militiamen remaining in the field had considerably increased: "they are very alert at their several posts, and continue generally to evince the best disposition. Some old Loyalists who bore arms in the American War, have come in tho' exempt from service in the Militia. I retain them for the present, as they are still capable of stationary Service, and their lessons and example will have a happy influence on the youth of the Militia Ranks."[29]

Contrast this with the situation on the opposite shore of the Niagara River, where Brigadier-General Smyth had cancelled the armistice with effect from November 20, and was making widely publicized preparations for another invasion attempt. According to an inspecting officer's report, the state of one militia brigade was

such as to be little better than an undisciplined rabble, and it may be a question whether they are not of more disservice than of use; the total want of order no doubt proceeds from the ignorance of the officers, and the great familiarity that exists between them and their men; that this can be remedied, perhaps is impossible, while such materials are employed for officers. I have endeavoured to select and retain in service the best, and such as I am told will not shrink from duty.[30]

Consequently Smyth considered it wise to follow Major-General Dearborn's suggestion and ask whether any companies would refuse "to serve the United States in Canada."[31] After consulting the field officers of his Pennsylvania Volunteers, Brigadier-General George A. Tannehill replied on November 22 that the "prevailing opinion appears to be that, if an efficient force can be had to cross into Canada, a very general embarkation may be expected; if on the contrary, it is difficult for me to say what number may be calculated on."[32] Yet Smyth continued to issue bombastic public statements, suggesting that his men were "accustomed to obedience, silence, and steadiness" and that they will "conquer or will die."[33]

Smyth made his attempt before dawn on November 28, a Saturday. The crossing was made this time above the Falls and initial success was obtained by the American assault party landing two and a half miles below Fort Erie, where there were only 50 British regulars with two light guns. A second party, however, failed to destroy the bridge over Frenchman's Creek, nearer to Chippawa. Then, while Smyth was trying to embark his main force after sunrise, both advanced parties were driven back across the river by counter-attacking British regulars and Canadian militia from the Fort Erie garrison under the command of Lieutenant-Colonel Cecil Bisshopp. Formerly a major in the 1st Regiment of Foot Guards, he was one of the Inspecting Field Officers of Militia given a higher local rank to prevent command of mixed forces being assumed by a militia officer.[34] The casualties to Bisshopp's force were considerable, however: 17 other ranks killed, 4 officers and 43 other ranks wounded, and 35 other ranks reported

Major-General William Henry Harrison (1773-1841)
Harrison understood the importance of logistics in campaigning on the frontier and solved supply problems before all else. Like Jackson and Brown, he was a prewar militia officer. (Lossing, *Field-Book*, 1869)

as missing. By lunch time only about 1,200 of Smyth's main force were actually embarked and a council of war voted against an assault on Fort Erie with this small number. Smyth called off the operation.

About 1,500 Americans embarked when Smyth scheduled another assault crossing on November 30, but once again the operation was abandoned following a council of war. It is difficult not to find these attempts ludicrous. Half a century later, Winfield Scott wrote in his *Memoirs* that "though well read, brave and honorable he [Smyth] showed no talent for command, and made himself ridiculous on the Niagara frontier."[35] Yet there was a great deal of truth in the lengthy statement Smyth issued on December 3 in reply to local critics. In it he placed the blame on the state of his troops, many of them exhausted, others ill, others again interested only in the excitement and far from ready for the reality of war:

My orders were to pass into Canada with 3000 men *at once*. On the first day of embarkation not more than 1100 men were embarked, of whom 400, that is, half the regular infantry, were exhausted with fatigue, and want of rest. On the second embarkation, only 1500 men were embarked, and these were to have put off immediately, and to have descended the river to a point where reinforcements were not to be expected. On both days, many of the regular troops were men in bad health, who could not have stood one days march; who, although they were on the sick report, were turned out by their ardent officers. The affair at Queenston is a caution against relying on crowds who go to the bank of Niagara to look on a battle as on a theatrical exhibition; who if they are disappointed of the sights, break their muskets: or if they are without rations for a day desert [as had 600 of Brigadier-General Tannehill's brigade].[36]

Dearborn readily granted Smyth leave to visit his family and he never returned to duty.

In Upper Canada it was now possible for Sheaffe to deal with American-born residents who had refused to take the oath of allegiance and claimed exemption from service in the sedentary militia. A proclamation of November 9 had already specified that "every citizen of the United States" who did not report himself to one or other of the examination boards being convened at Niagara, York and Kingston before January 1, 1813 "should be considered as an alien enemy and become liable to be treated as a prisoner of war or a spy as circumstances might dictate."[37] Those reporting were required to make statements, and when satisfied that the statements made were true, boards could issue passports for them to cross into the United States.

Several American-born officers in the militia of Upper Canada lost their commissions for having failed to do their duty during the period of Hull's invasion. Henceforth they would be liable for the more menial duty of privates in the sedentary militia.

Thus far, compulsory militia service had involved only the guarding of American prisoners and the forwarding of supplies whenever called upon. Even the flank companies had mostly performed such mundane duties. The exploits of the militia flank companies which accompanied Brock to Detroit and those which fought as auxiliaries at Queenston Heights, stalwart as they were, were soon exaggerated by local patriotism and seem to be the basis for the hardy myth that Canada in this war was successfully defended by the militia, with only small help from the British Army. We can see the myth taking shape even before the assault across the river was abandoned, in the remarks credited to Reverend John Strachan, Rector of York, following his sermon of November 22, 1812:

> the Province of Upper Canada, without the assistance of men or arms, except a handful of regular troops, repelled its invaders, slew or took them all prisoners, and captured from its enemies the greater part of the arms by which it was defended. ... And never, surely, was greater activity shewn in any country than our militia has exhibited, never greater valour, cooler resolution, and more approved conduct; they have emulated the choicest veterans, and they have twice saved the country.[38]

CHAPTER SIX

Supply Routes:
August to December 1812

GANANOQUE / ST. REGIS / KINGSTON

The surrender of Brigadier-General Hull's North Western Army at Detroit and the listless behaviour within Major-General Dearborn's Northern Department strongly suggested to those in charge of the American war effort that it was time for the United States Navy to take a hand with inland operations. Captain Isaac Chauncey, U.S.N., received orders on September 3, 1812, "to assume command of the naval forces on lakes Erie and Ontario, and to use every exertion to obtain control of them this fall."[1] He was also given the courtesy title of commodore.

Chauncey, who had just passed his fortieth birthday, was considered to be one of the most efficient and versatile officers in the United States Navy. His service at sea had included the closing stages of the undeclared naval war with France and the conflict with the pirates of Tripoli.[2] The four years previous to this new appointment he had spent in command of the New York navy yard. He at once prepared to go to Sackets Harbor, which he reached on October 6, although about 170 sailors and marines, 140 ship carpenters, more than 100 cannon and other stores had gone forward much earlier. The absence of decent roads across country made it necessary for this train of men and supplies to travel by a roundabout water route up the Hudson River to the Mohawk, thence to Wood Creek, down the Oswego River to Lake Ontario, and along its eastern shore to Sackets Harbor.

British commanders in Upper Canada had long appreciated the advantages possessed by Sackets Harbor as a naval base. On July 19, the Provincial Marine's makeshift squadron from Kingston had tried to shoot up the naturally well protected harbour, but had been driven off. A few days later Brigadier-General Jacob Brown's militia brigade at Sackets Harbor was reinforced by a company of grey-clad riflemen, the first regular troops to

**Commodore Isaac Chauncey
(1772-1840)**
Chauncey was primarily responsible for
the establishment of American naval
power on the Great Lakes, but having
constructed a fleet, he proved reluctant
to risk it in action. (Courtesy, Toronto
Reference Library, T-15206)

reach northern New York State. It was led by Captain Benjamin Forsyth, a big, dashing daredevil from North Carolina, who had got his captaincy in the Regiment of Riflemen which had been added to the United States Army in 1808.[3]

The only other early exchange across the water had been a skirmish which, according to the *Kingston Gazette* of August 11, "took place not long since in the river opposite Elizabethtown [soon to be renamed Brockville], between a small American schooner and a party of Government Boats, with ammunition, on their way to this place. Several shots were exchanged, but we cannot ascertain that any material damage was done on either side."[4] Otherwise tranquillity reigned along the upper St. Lawrence during the weeks of 1812 that Colonel Robert Lethbridge commanded at Kingston, before his relegation to a lesser militia command at Prescott and replacement at Kingston by Colonel John Vincent. During the period of so-called armistice arranged between the troops of Dearborn and Prevost on August 9, the American schooners which had earlier been chased back to Ogdensburg had been able to make their way to Sackets Harbor. The largest and best were purchased by Lieutenant Melancthon Woolsey, U.S.N., for conversion into war vessels or for use as transports. Woolsey was then in charge of the small navy yard, where the brig U.S.S. *Oneida*[5] had been built during the Embargo troubles of 1809.

Those in charge of the defence of the Canadas were bound to feel uneasy at all times about the exposed state of the St. Lawrence water route, by which alone supplies could be moved with any degree of ease or speed to Upper Canada. Boats had been restricted to travelling in convoy under arrangements made by the Corps of Voyageurs, which had been formed from employees of the North West Company. The boats were held at Lachine, immediately above the rapids, until a sufficient escort of militia should be available for the trip to Kingston. Fortunate were the convoys whose escort included a detachment of regular troops destined for service in Upper Canada. Overnight stops were arranged to rest the tired boatmen at staging points guarded by flank companies of the local militia. Several of these stops also coincided with the beginning or end of each of the succession of rapids, which extended almost as far as the village of Prescott and made it necessary for men to go ashore and drag the boats with long ropes through the rough water. At such times a convoy was particularly vulnerable to attack.

On September 16, 1812, a party of American militia in boats managed to surprise a convoy of bateaux as it was passing Toussaint Island, a few miles below Prescott. Its escort reacted quickly and drove off the attackers as was only to be expected since it comprised regular soldiers, even if odds and ends, of the 49th Foot, Royal Newfoundland Fencibles and 10th Royal Veterans.

The next week, on Monday, September 21, the last convoy staging point, at Gananoque in the heart of the Thousand Islands and only 17 miles below Kingston, was attacked just after dawn. Captain Benjamin Forsyth's company of regular riflemen and about 30 militia from Sackets Harbor had easily crossed the St. Lawrence in small boats from Cape Vincent and landed west of the tiny village. The flank companies of Leeds militia turned out as soon as the alarm was given, but as no entrenchments or other form of fortification had been erected to protect the makeshift harbour they fled after firing their muskets at the charging American regulars. Forsyth had one man killed and one wounded. Four of the Leeds men were wounded and eight taken prisoner. Some of these militiamen had been wearing red coats discarded by the Kingston garrison, and Forsyth naturally reported that his adversaries had included British regulars. The Americans seized the small quantity of arms and ammunitions left behind, and then burned a small store in which were a few barrels of flour and a small quantity of beef. According to the next issue of the *Kingston Gazette*, their depredations did not stop at this:

Their conduct at Col. Stone's house was truly disgraceful. They fired into his house and wounded Mrs. Stone, who was the only person in it. They broke open and ransacked his Trunks, and had his Bedding and other articles carried down to the shore with an intention of carrying them off with them; but this was prevented by their officers. ....[6]

The *Gazette* went on to criticize the unprotected state of Gananoque:

It unfortunately happened that Capt. Scholfield and Lieut. Braddish with 12 men of the detachment at Gananoque were here [Kingston] at the time, by which means that station was deprived of the assistance of these two excellent officers. But it is a matter of astonishment that these two officers should have quitted their post to take the direction of so very small a party [on escort duty].

Forsyth's men were rewarded from state funds by Brigadier-General Jacob Brown, who was in command at Sackets Harbor. Governor Tompkins himself sent his approval. The Governor had already decided to accept Brown's advice to strengthen the garrison at Ogdensburg in order that convoys from Montreal could be attacked more easily. So later that week Brown was transferred there, with some of his militia and Forsyth's riflemen, while Brigadier-General Richard Dodge and another militia brigade took over the defence of Sackets Harbor.

The military advantages to be gained by harassment across the narrow waters of the river were not appreciated by the people of Ogdensburg, whose Federalist representative to Congress had voted against war. Thus Brown found on his arrival that the more prosperous inhabitants were trying their best to ignore the fact that a war was going on, and particularly the existence of the small garrison of ragged militiamen. Canadians from Prescott were still crossing the 1,800 yards of the St. Lawrence River, to shop at Parish's store and take tea or dinner at his mansion – under the protection of a white flag of truce. David Parish was another of the colourful figures who gravitated towards a new frontier: a German-born financial adventurer, he had invested a first American fortune made by smuggling gold from Mexico to Paris into a scheme to develop 200,000 acres of northern New York State.[7]

Brown soon put an end to this state of undeclared peace. He ordered the shore batteries to fire at all convoys of bateaux moving up along the Canadian shore, and Forsyth's riflemen ventured onto the river in small boats to exchange shots with the escorts of British troops and Canadian militia.

Sir George Prevost blamed this outbreak of predatory warfare on Colonel Vincent's unauthorized despatch of most of the regular troops from Kingston to Niagara. He now sent two companies of the Glengarry Light Infantry Fencibles and two light gunboats to strengthen Colonel Lethbridge's militia garrison at Prescott. Unfortunately, as events turned out, he did not consider it necessary to repeat the earlier injunction to Lethbridge that any unnecessary offensive operations might drive the peace-loving Federalist voters of the area into the ranks of the War Hawks. Lethbridge seems to have been too incensed over the local situation to think clearly about what action, if any, he should take and the arrival of the reinforcements determined him to retaliate against Ogdensburg.

The preparations being made at Prescott on Saturday, October 3, could be watched by Brigadier-General Brown from an upper window of Parish's store on the Ogdensburg waterfront, with the "aid of an excellent glass of Mr. Parish."[8] So far as Brown could judge, all the Canadian militia for miles around were moving into Prescott. Yet the attack launched on Sunday morning was a complete fiasco. Lethbridge's two companies of fencibles and 600 militia set off well enough but hesitated when their boats were in mid-stream and finally turned back from the hail of grape shot from the American shore batteries. Correspondents to the *Montreal Herald* charitably called this unlucky affair "a rash undertaking ... as the force was not adequate to the attainment of the object."[9] Colonel Lethbridge was quickly recalled to Montreal and succeeded by a younger man, Lieutenant-Colonel Thomas Pearson, who was also an Inspecting Field Officer of Militia.[10]

Later in October a detachment of Canadian Voyageurs established an outpost at St. Regis, almost across the river from Cornwall, where the 45th parallel met the St. Lawrence to form the international boundary. Here, there was an Iroquois reservation, but these Indians had received little consideration in the past from either belligerent and were undecided as to their course of action. Sides were soon drawn, however, following a surprise attack launched by American militia from nearby French Mills during the early hours of October 23. Ensign Pierre Rototte and seven voyageurs were left dead and the other 23 Canadians made captive. A considerable quantity of blankets, muskets and other items intended as presents for the Indians was taken away by the departing Americans. Most of these Iroquois subsequently favoured the British cause.[11]

**Admiral Sir John Borlase Warren
(1753-1822)**
The flag officer or commander of the
Royal Navy's North American and West
Indies station from the outbreak of war
to 1814. (*Naval Chronicle,* 1800)

Meanwhile, the war at sea had not taken on much significance. It was
still limited to the occasional single ship action: seldom did British warships make contact with American privateers preying on merchant shipping and the U.S. Navy's frigates managed to elude British ships of the line.
The Royal Navy's new combined North America and West Indies Command now had 11 ships of the line, 34 frigates, 38 sloops, and 14 smaller
vessels.

Following his arrival at Halifax on September 26, Admiral Sir John Warren had followed his instructions to the letter and made overtures for
peace to the American Government. These were rejected, however, and
even Warren knew only too well that British public opinion would never
agree to the acceptance of President Madison's own prerequisites for peace.
Madison's conditions were the stoppage of impressments, the release of
impressed seamen, indemnity for war damage to date and abandonment
of the policy of blockading enemy ports to neutral shipping. In consequence the British Government authorized Lieutenant-General Sir John
Sherbrooke and Major-General George S. Smyth to issue letters of marque
to Nova Scotia and New Brunswick shipowners interested in fitting out
privateers. Yet Sherbrooke and Smyth could still continue the pragmatic
policy of issuing licences to merchants wishing to exchange British goods
imported into Halifax for provisions from New England. The British
Government's circular of November 9 authorizing its governors in the
West Indies to issue licences for the importation of essential commodities
was also slanted in favour of New England: "Whatever importations are

proposed to be made, under the order, from the United States of America, should be by your licenses confined to the ports in the Eastern States exclusively, unless you have reason to suppose that the object of the order would not be fulfilled if licenses are not also granted for the importations from the other ports in the United States."[12]

The naval situation on Lake Ontario was to change decidedly and naval command was soon to change hands as a result of the exertions made by Commodore Chauncey at Sackets Harbor. There he had found only U.S.S. *Oneida* and the several lake schooners now undergoing conversion. He shortly visited Oswego and purchased four more schooners. Their hulls and decks were also strengthened and one or two 32-pr. long guns were mounted on each. These had an effective range of 3,000 yards with an elevation of less than 15 degrees.

Chauncey's tactics would, nevertheless, have to be governed by the fact that his brig *Oneida's* 18 32-pr. carronades could be employed only in a close action, since carronades had an accurate range of only 400 to 600 yards.[13] Otherwise they possessed great advantages over long guns. There was a useful saving of metal, a 32-pr. carronade being shorter and lighter than the ordinary long 12-pr. gun. Its carriage took up less deck space. Unlike the long gun too, the carronade was never known to burst in action, even when double-shotted. Carronades of all natures required a gun crew of four, whereas anywhere from six to 14 men were needed to man the various calibres of long guns. Thus carronades presented less of a transportation problem from the New York navy yard to Sackets Harbor and more could be crowded onto the small warships designed for service on the Great Lakes. Those in charge of the Provincial Marine felt the same way: the corvette *Royal George* at Kingston was then armed with 20 carronades and two 9-pr. long guns, and the smaller *Earl of Moira* had 10 smaller 18-pr. carronades and four 9-pr. guns.

A month after his arrival at Sackets Harbor, Chauncey began his campaign. On November 8 he sailed from Sackets Harbor with *Oneida* and six armed schooners, hoping to intercept the Provincial Marine's *Royal George* and schooners *Prince Regent* and *Duke of Gloucester* which were out on the water returning to Kingston from the head of Lake Ontario. Two days later he did catch up with *Royal George* and chased her right into Kingston harbour, where his little squadron came under fire from the handful of 6-pr. and 9-pr. guns mounted in two shore batteries and a blockhouse under construction on Point Henry. Colonel Vincent had ample warning of

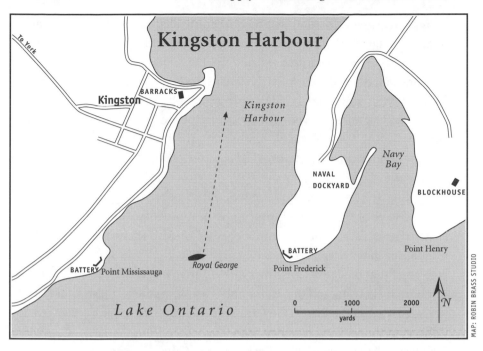

Kingston Harbour

To York

Kingston

BARRACKS

Kingston Harbour

Navy Bay

NAVAL DOCKYARD

BLOCKHOUSE

Royal George

BATTERY

Point Henry

BATTERY Point Mississauga

Point Frederick

Lake Ontario

0   1000   2000
yards

N

MAP: ROBIN BRASS STUDIO

Chauncey's approach and the town was swarming with militia, who had flocked in from the surrounding countryside to reinforce his 459 regulars. After two hours of exchanging fire, at too great a range for appreciable damage to be done on either side, Chauncey broke off the engagement. According to his hastily written report to the Secretary of the Navy, the casualties were light:

> We lost in this affair [in *Oneida*] 1 man killed and 3 slightly wounded, with a few shot through our sails. The other vessels lost no men and received but little injury in their Hull and sails with the exception of the *Pert*, whose gun bursted in the early part of the action and wounded her Commander (sailing master Arundel) badly, and a midshipman and 3 men slightly. Mr. Arundel who refused to quit the Deck although wounded, was knocked overboard in beating up to our anchorage and I am sorry to say was drowned.[14]

The defenders also had only one man killed and a few wounded. Indeed the action was very inconclusive. *Royal George* certainly did not suffer the "very considerable damage" claimed by Chauncey elsewhere in his report in an obvious effort to gloss over his failure to capture her.

111

Yet Chauncey's assertion that he now controlled Lake Ontario was correct. Although *Earl of Moira* did manage to get into Kingston a few days later, no vessel then ventured outside the harbour, the entrance of which was blockaded by the enemy for the balance of the navigation season. Both *Prince Regent* and *Duke of Gloucester* remained at York for the winter. Moreover, Chauncey was potentially strengthened by the launching of the corvette U.S.S. *Madison* on November 26. She had been built at Sackets Harbor in the short space of 45 days and was armed with 24 32-pr. carronades.

At Kingston the naval situation was felt to be anything but promising. "The officers of the Marine appear to be destitute of all energy and spirit, and are sunk into contempt in the eyes of all who know them," was the evaluation shortly reported to Sir George Prevost.[15] "The want of seamen is so great that the *Royal George* has only 17 men on board who are capable of doing their Duty, and the *Moira* only 10 able seamen." Prevost had earlier suggested to the British Government the importance of having "tried Officers of the rank of Lieutenant and trusty men from the Navy" available for service on the Great Lakes during 1813: he had also proposed that his own brother, a post captain in the Royal Navy "at present unemployed," be made superintendent of the establishment.[16] He now urged that the Royal Navy should take over the Provincial Marine completely.

As this letter was being written on November 21, Major-General Dearborn's long-heralded invasion of Lower Canada was petering out. Undoubtedly Dearborn felt that he had to justify his many protestations to the Secretary of War in Washington. Whether he had intended a serious attempt to coincide with Brigadier-General Smyth's attempt at Niagara, or whether he moved his 3,000 regulars and 3,000 militia forward from Plattsburgh merely for appearance's sake is a moot point.

Word of the advance reached Major de Salaberry, commanding the forward defences of the Eastern Townships, on November 17. He hastened with his own Canadian Voltigeurs and 300 Caughnawaga Indians to Lacolle, where a clash might be expected.[17] Not until the early hours of November 20, however, did Dearborn's advanced guard cross the border from the nearby village of Champlain and attack the Canadian outposts. The Canadian militia and Indians reacted promptly, helped by the fact that one party of American regulars persisted in firing on the other in the darkness; the whole of the enemy advanced guard soon retreated back to Champlain. As a further discouragement the Vermont and New York militia flatly refused to cross into Canada. Dearborn waited three days, and then tamely withdrew to Plattsburgh and ordered his troops into winter quarters.

As support for the field force in front of Montreal, Lieutenant-Colonel Patrick Murray's 5th Battalion of Select Embodied Militia, only recently organized in the Montreal area from 560 drafted militiamen, had been ordered forward, along with companies of the several sedentary militia battalions. David Thompson, the North West Company's recently retired explorer who was now adjutant of the 2nd Terrebonne Battalion of sedentary militia, recorded in his Journal on November 21 that a few of the men drafted for the two companies he had despatched had mutinied and returned home. A troop of militia cavalry and four volunteer companies, formed earlier by merchants and tradesmen of the 1st Montreal Battalion of Sedentary Militia to avoid more rigorous and lasting service in the Select Embodied Militia, naturally gave no trouble. Indeed, when they returned home on November 28, after the emergency was officially deemed to be at an end and the sedentary militia of the whole province was dismissed, these emergency soldiers jokingly referred to their week of service at Laprairie as a "party of pleasure." On the same day Prevost wrote Lord Bathurst that this American threat had a value: "use had been made of and confidence placed in" the French-speaking Canadians by calling them out for service and giving them weapons to defend their homes.[18]

This letter also mentioned a successful attack on the American militia post on the Salmon River, near French Mills on the St. Lawrence, on November 23. The flank companies of Cornwall and Glengarry militia had prevailed upon Captain Andrew Gray and a party of 70 regulars escorting a convoy of bateaux up river to help them avenge the affair at St. Regis a month earlier. Captain Gray, who was proceeding to Upper Canada in his capacity as acting Deputy Quartermaster General to investigate the state of the Provincial Marine, reported that the militiamen had performed creditably after he had "got them in motion, and all properly arranged." Initially suffering from too much zeal and not enough discipline, the officers and men had been insistent that the attack should be made from the river side. "I saw what would happen by following their advice," Gray's report continued. "The only difference between us was, that I saw it before, and they after the capture of the place. They were all fully convinced of their error – had we gone by the River, we would have been shamefully beaten, as they expected us in that direction, and had a Picquet of 20 men on the River banks, that might have killed the whole Party."[19]

Certainly, with the possible exception of the blockade of Kingston, the Americans had not distinguished themselves. Governor Tompkins of New York had earlier written David Parish that "the command by the enemy of the water communication and the almost impassable state of the roads between the Black River and the St. Lawrence, will retard the occupation of Ogdensburg, with a force proportioned to its importance, until spring."[20] Brigadier-General Brown and his militia brigade returned home in time for Christmas, having fulfilled their six months' service. This left Captain Forsyth with only his own regular company of riflemen, and a few volunteer gunners and some local militia.

The need for experienced officers and at least a nucleus of trained regulars to stiffen local militia might not yet be fully appreciated in Washington, but the British Government in far-off London was well aware of their importance to Sir George Prevost's successful conduct of defensive operations. "In estimating, however, the force under your Command as compared with that of the Enemy," Lord Bathurst had written him on November 16, "I cannot so entirely confine myself to numerical Calculation, as to put out of the Question the vast superiority which the general composition & discipline of the British Army supported as it is by the good disposition of all classes of the inhabitants must give to any Military operation against an American Force acting beyond their frontiers."[21]

Yet Lord Bathurst had no thought of detracting from Prevost's achievement. When the year 1812 came to an end, the only American servicemen still on Canadian soil were a few hundred prisoners of war being held in captivity at Quebec. The Union Jack waved over Detroit and Fort Mackinac and most of the Indian tribes had decided to support this flag. Events of the autumn had convinced the majority of both English-speaking and French-speaking Canadians that a continued defence was possible against their much bigger neighbour to the south; provided, of course, that further British help should arrive with the re-opening of the St. Lawrence River to navigation in the spring and that naval supremacy should be regained on Lake Ontario.

PART III

1813: Holding the Line

GREAT ADVANTAGES,
to those who enlift for
Capt. LIDDELL's Company of the
GLENGARY
LIGHT INFANTRY FENCIBLES.

EVERY Young Man who afpires to ferve His Majefty in this fine Regiment now raifing, will do well to confider without delay, the very advantageous terms on which he enlifts. He is to receive FIVE GUINEAS BOUNTY, and is only required to ferve in the *Canadas* for *Three Years*, or *during the War*, which probably may not laft fo long, when he will, beyond a doubt, receive the Reward of his Services, by obtaining an allotment of the rich and fertile Lands of Upper Canada, or Lower Canada, if more convenient. This important Grant will make every Soldier of the Corps an Independant Man, at the expiration of his Service; enabled thereby to settle comfortably on his own Farm, in a fhort time he will have every Luxury of Life about him : he will be able to take his Wife and Family to Church or Market in his own Cariole, and if he has not a Wife, it will be the fure means of getting him a good one, for Fortune always favors the Brave, and flinty muft be the heart of that Damfel, and vain her pretenfions to tafte, who could refift a *Light Boh of the Glengary's* when equipped in his new *Green Uniform,* which will unqueftionably be the *neateft in the Service.*

Look around you! See how many rich and refpectable Inhabitants of Canada, who were formerly Soldiers, that are now enjoying the reward of their Services, and who date their Profperity from the time when they received their Grants of Land on being difcharged. The fame advantages will be yours. Such of you, on the reduction of the Corps, as are not then Officers, and who prefer the tranquil Pleafures of a Rural Life, may, by induftry and good management, hope to reach the higheft honours which the Province can beftow. In this happy Country, Merit and Ability muft ever lead to Preferment, and the Man poffeffed of thefe qualities, may have it in his power to chufe whether he will be a Colonel of Militia, a Juftice of the Peace, or a Member of the Houfe of Affembly. Brave Countrymen! you muft be quick in your acceptance of fuch Offers as thefe, or you will certainly miss the Golden Opportunity; terms fo evidently advantageous muft foon complete the Regiment, and thofe who are too late, will have caufe all their lives to reproach themfelves for being fo blind to their own intereft. No deception is intended; for the affurance of General SIR GEORGE PREVOST, as certified by *Colonel Baynes*, Adjutant General, muft convince the moft incredulous, that His Royal Highnefs the PRINCE REGENT will gracioufly attend to His Excellency's Recommendation, by beftowing a Grant of Lands upon every Soldier who has faithfully ferved for the ftipulated period.

N. B. A few Taylors, Shoemakers, Carpenters and Black Smiths, will meet with great encouragement in the Corps; a Serjeant Armourer. Quarter Mafter Serjeant, Serjeant Major, Bugle Major, Paymafter's Clerk and Ten Pay Serjeants will be wanted, and fuch men as are qualified for thefe Offices, will see the neceffity of an early application.

Recruiting poster, Glengarry Light Infantry, 1813

Soldier, Glengarry Light Infantry Fencibles
A regular unit raised in Upper Canada, the green-uniformed Glengarries saw continous action during the war. (Painting by G.A. Embleton, courtesy Parks Canada)

CHAPTER SEVEN

Across the Ice: January and February 1813

THE MARCH OF THE 104TH / FRENCHTOWN / OGDENSBURG

On January 9, 1813, the Prince Regent finally issued a Declaration decrying the war started by the United States of America, and now officially recognized as likely to continue for some time. The bulk of the British people were convinced, as were many Federalists in the United States, that President Madison had been acting as a tool of Napoleon. That discomfited Emperor was now known to be trying to replace the *Grande Armée* lost in the Russian snows, but there was a growing hope that Europe might soon be freed from his domination.[1]

Thus Lord Bathurst was able to advise Sir George Prevost in successive letters that more and more help would be sent to Canada following the reopening of the St. Lawrence River for navigation in early May. Militarily this added up to the 19th Light Dragoons, a company of Royal Artillery, detachments of the Corps of Royal Artillery Drivers and of the Corps of Royal Sappers and Miners (formerly the Royal Military Artificers), battalions of the 13th, 41st, 70th, 89th, 98th, 101st and 103rd Regiments of Foot, the overstrength foreign regiments of De Watteville and De Meuron, and reinforcement drafts for the existing four companies of Royal Artillery and regiments of regular infantry.[2] The extent to which any or all of these might be able to participate in the season's campaigning would, however, be another matter: distances to be travelled varied all the way from the relatively close islands of Bermuda, through the ports of Ireland and Great Britain, to those of Spain and Italy, and meant that troop transports would likely be entering the St. Lawrence until late in the summer. Actual strengths would vary from the 445 rank and file of the 2nd Battalion of the 41st Regiment at Bermuda to nearly 1,300 for De Watteville's Regiment in Spain.

The British Government had accepted Prevost's recommendation that the Admiralty should take over the conduct of naval operations on the inland waters of North America and 200 officers and seamen were now under orders to sail from England. Most of them had been employed previously with a flotilla of gunboats for the defence of Riga on the Baltic Sea, under conditions not unlike those they would meet in a Canadian winter. Early in March the size of the Royal Navy's contingent was more than doubled. On March 19 the appointments of commodore and commander-in-chief were given to Captain Sir James Lucas Yeo, R.N. This 30-year-old veteran of many small ship actions had gone to sea at the age of 10 and had been promoted post captain shortly after his 25th birthday. The most successful of his exploits, the siege and capture of Cayenne in French Guiana in 1809 with an Anglo-Portuguese force, had brought him a knighthood.[3] Yeo's last command had been H.M.S. *Southampton,* a frigate which hit a reef in the West Indies and sank on November 27, 1812, shortly after having captured the American brig *Vixen.* Yeo's contingent, sailing for Quebec in late March, 1813, comprised three commanders, eight lieutenants, two masters, two pursers, two surgeons, four assistant surgeons, two boatswains, two gunners, two carpenters, two master mates, 18 midshipmen, and 400 seamen.[4] Obviously, however, these could furnish only nucleus crews for the existing vessels and those that would have to be constructed by civilian shipwrights and carpenters.

Yeo's instructions from the Admiralty specified that the "first and paramount object" was defence of the North American provinces:

> We do hereby require and direct you in the Employment thereof to cooperate most cordially with His Excellency, the Captain General and Governor in Chief of the said Provinces, not undertaking any operations without the full concurrence and approbation of him or of the Commanders of the Forces employed under him; and on all occasions conforming yourself and employing the Force under your command according to the Requisitions which you may from time to time receive to this Effect, from the said Governor or Commander of the Forces.[5]

Although Yeo was responsible directly to the Admiralty in London, he could request assistance from Admiral Sir John Warren. The latter had already agreed to supply Sir George Prevost with nine lieutenants and a few gunners from ships on his own North America and West Indies Stations for service with the Provincial Marine. "They are all active, zealous young officers," Warren had written on March 5, "and I doubt not, will cheerfully promote the service they are appointed to, with all the exertion of their power."[6] Warren appointed the three senior lieutenants – Robert H. Barclay, Daniel Pring and Robert Finnis – to be "captains of Corvettes" on Lake Ontario. These experienced but still young lieutenants had been waiting to obtain regular promotion to the next rank of commander because they had not had such sensational careers as that of Sir James Yeo. Barclay, who was in charge of the party, had merely lost an arm at Trafalgar.[7]

The British Government had sent Warren orders early in January to attempt a diversion in Prevost's favour, by harrying the American coast with a landing force of soldiers and marines from his fleet. This force was to be commanded by Colonel Sir Sidney Beckwith, a Peninsular veteran who was slated to assume the vacant appointment of Quartermaster General in North America. The likely scene of operations would be Chesapeake Bay and the Delaware River, the ports and harbours of which were placed under blockade "in the most strict and rigorous manner" by Admiral Warren on February 6, 1813.[8] It was Congressmen from these areas who had clamoured for war, and President Madison's own state of Virginia and the city of Washington adjoined Chesapeake Bay.

On February 10, 1813, the Marquess of Wellington wrote from Portugal to Lord Bathurst that, although he hated to lose De Watteville's Regiment, he was "very glad to find" that Sir George Prevost was going to be reinforced. Britain's foremost soldier approved of what he had learned about Prevost's conduct of the war in Canada and stressed the need for continued caution and defensive strategy:

> I only hope that the troops will go in time; and that Sir George will not be induced by any hopes of trifling advantages to depart from a strong defensive system. He may depend upon it that he will not be strong enough either in men or means, to establish himself in any conquest he might make. The attempt would only weaken him, and his losses augment the spirits and hopes of the enemy, even if not attended by worse consequences; whereas by the other system, he will throw the difficulties and risk upon them, and they will most probably be foiled. If they should be so, and they should receive a check at sea, their arrogance will be lowered a little, which will give me more satisfaction than any thing that has occurred for a length of time, and they will be obliged to ask for peace.[9]

Considerable time would elapse, however, before any or all of this information about reinforcements could actually get to Sir George Prevost at Quebec. The letters would have to travel across the Atlantic by ship to Halifax, across Nova Scotia and up the St. John Valley by sleigh, and finally by a courier wearing snowshoes along the Madawaska-Temiscouata portage route to the settlement at Rivière-du-Loup on the lower St. Lawrence River.

Lieutenant-Colonel John Harvey had arrived at Quebec via this route during the first week of January, so that he could assume his new appointment as Deputy Adjutant General without delay. He confirmed the advice tendered Prevost a year earlier that troops could negotiate it on snowshoes. Major-General Dearborn was rumoured to be contemplating a winter campaign and, in consequence, Sir John Sherbrooke was directed to send forward the Royal Artillery detachment and companies of the 104th Regiment then in New Brunswick, as the only possible reinforcement for Lower Canada. Sherbrooke was to replace them by troops from Halifax. Only six companies of the 104th Foot actually made this winter trip, on snowshoes, with a strength of 550 rank and file. The remainder of the regiment, together with the wives and children, later travelled by ship to Quebec.

On February 16 the regimental headquarters and grenadier company left Fredericton. Another company started on each of the next five days. It was an unusually cold winter and enough snow kept falling to make it necessary for each company to break trail afresh. Even the officers carried their personal kit in knapsacks. Provisions and other common stores were hauled on toboggans. The march generally began at daybreak and continued only until mid-afternoon so that camp could be made before dark. For the first week the troops were able to sleep in houses or barns, but as they left settlement behind they had to erect shelters in the woods and sleep closely packed about their fires for warmth. Many were frostbitten and food ran short as they neared the boundary with Lower Canada. One subaltern, recalling the hardships of the march, tells of the relief towards the end of the worst of it:

No dinner that day, no supper that night, no breakfast the next morning; but in the afternoon, we were agreeably surprised, when crossing the River de Loup, to find two men, with bags of biscuits and two tubs of spirits and water, handing out a biscuit and about a half pint of grog. I found it very acceptable after a march of two days and a fast of upwards of thirty hours.[10]

From Rivière-du-Loup to Quebec the troops travelled on well-packed roads and were well provided with food. Each company completed the march of more than 350 miles in 24 days, with the first reaching Quebec on March 15. One man had died *en route*, actually from causes other than the cold weather. Private Rogers was left at Lake Temiscouata, so badly frozen that "he was quite a hideous spectacle, altogether one ulcerated mass, as if scalded all over from boiling water."[11] By the time he rejoined the regiment six weeks later, it should be noted, a corporal and 19 men had died from conditions probably aggravated by the journey. The regiment was then at Kingston, having marched a further 360 miles from Quebec over snow-covered roads during the last days of March and first two weeks of April.

That this whole journey had been a great feat physically there can be no doubt, and it indicated that winter warfare was not out of the question for regular troops who were properly acclimatized. On the other hand, it must be remembered that this unit had served in New Brunswick for eight years and that most of the men had been recruited in North America. Furthermore, it had been able to make the march on its own terms: there had been no fleeting enemy to plague the marchers, in striking contrast to the trials of Napoleon's veterans retreating through the Russian snows from Moscow.

Meanwhile Lieutenant-Colonel Bruyeres, R.E., had conferred with David Thompson at Montreal and persuaded this experienced winter traveller to help the military by devising models of a sled for conveying artillery pieces by manpower where horse were not available. Thompson demonstrated a model for a 9-pr. gun at Montreal in early January, but the Commanding Royal Engineer was then ordered to inspect the defences of Upper Canada and there is no record of actual trials ever having been conducted by troops on snowshoes.

Fortunately the intelligence that the sleighs being collected by Major-General Dearborn at Plattsburgh were for a winter campaign proved to be wrong. This news had come from those engaged in the substantial smuggling operations along the border of Lower Canada. As soon as the snow fell and the St. Lawrence River was frozen over for the winter, more and more American farmers were encouraged to cross into Canada by the higher prices paid by the British Army's Commissariat Department for food. Sir George Prevost would much later admit in a despatch that "two thirds of the Army in Canada are, at this moment [August 27, 1814], eating Beef provided by American Contractors, drawn principally from the

States of Vermont and New York."[12] Sometimes American farmers had their sleighs commandeered at Montreal to transport supplies and troops as far as Kingston. Naturally enough, on their return home they reported what they had seen. Whether or not their intelligence was accurate was something American commanders would have to judge for themselves.

Merchants and enterprising farmers in both the Canadas at the same time made large profits from legitimate contracts for supplying clothing, fuel, food and forage to the Army. Even those men who did the actual physical labour were benefiting from the new prosperity, while tavern keepers in garrison towns were doing a flowing business.

The French-speaking *habitants* were glad to transport stores on *corvée* for militia pay during the winter months when they normally had little to do. Prevost might have described this necessary and utilitarian work by the sedentary militia of Lower Canada in his letter of February 8 to Lord Bathurst, instead of merely referring to "the zeal and alacrity with which the Militia both embodied and sedentary continue to discharge their several duties; The Sedentary Militia who have been called out to do duty for a short period in this Garrison [Quebec] as well with a view to relieve the King's Troops as to obtain the instruction so necessary for them have obeyed the call with the greatest cheerfulness."[13] A subsequent letter to Lord Bathurst, this time about Upper Canada, seems more realistic. "In Upper Canada," Prevost wrote on April 21,

the difficulties in forming an efficient Militia, inseparable from a scanty population spread over an extensive surface, and from the emigration to the United States of many who were discontented with, or disaffected to the Government, have rendered it expedient to organize more regular corps to serve during the war with America, and subject to such regulations, as should ensure the establishment of good order and discipline in them.[14]

In Lower Canada the five battalions of Select Embodied Militia were placed on a more regular basis. Prevost had promised to release 900 of the conscripts in June 1813, when their year of service was complete, but everyone would have to draw lots on parade all over again and those drawing the wrong ballot would have to complete a second year in uniform. They would be joined by 2,200 newcomers from the sedentary militia. A 6th Battalion of Quebec Embodied Militia was similarly raised for garrison duty there. Three troops of Canadian Light Dragoons and a tiny Corps of Provincial Royal Artillery Drivers recruited volunteers in the Montreal district for 18 months service or the duration of the war.[15] The Corps of Commissariat Voyageurs, which replaced the Corps of Canadian Voyageurs on April 8, had an establishment of 14 officers and 410 men. Two volunteer companies of Frontier Light Infantry, recruited on similar terms from the six sedentary militia battalions of the Eastern Townships, and an Independent Company of Militia Volunteers were subsequently attached to the Canadian Voltigeurs. Lieutenant-Colonel de Salaberry reported the Voltigeurs as being 438 strong, "independent of many recruits not yet formed."[16]

Major-General Sir Roger Sheaffe had shared Prevost's hope that three similar Volunteer Incorporated Militia battalions might be raised in Upper Canada. The Legislature could only spare $8.00 bounty money, but Sheaffe added an additional $10.00 bounty money from his military chest and promised a land grant to all ranks following disbandment. Yet only enough men materialized for one battalion. Command and the rank of lieutenant-colonel went to Captain William Robinson of the 8th (or King's) Regiment of Foot. The adjutant and quartermaster were found from the 41st Foot, and a paymaster was acquired from the Glengarry Light Infantry Fencibles. Most of the officers and men for the battalion's 10 companies had previous service in the militia flank companies formed a year earlier. Captain Merritt's volunteer troop of Dragoons had difficulty "getting young men to enlist as private soldiers who were able to keep a horse," but he did finally obtain two subalterns, one sergeant-major, three sergeants, two corporals, one trumpeter and forty troopers.[17] Captain Alexander Cameron's Incorporated Militia Artillery Company acquired four officers and 31 gunners; a troop of Provincial Royal Artillery Drivers managed five officers and 48 men. These all engaged to serve for 18 months or the duration of the war.

The Provincial Marine continued in both the Canadas to offer a bounty of $20.00 for able-bodied seamen and $12.00 for ordinary seamen. Part of its duty was now to man gunboats for the convoy service on the upper St. Lawrence and on the Richelieu Rivers. Armed with a 24-pr. carronade and equipped with oars, they were really small galleys.

Captain Alexander Roxburgh advertised in the weekly *Kingston Gazette* that the Glengarry Light Infantry Fencibles would give seven guineas bounty and 100 acres of crown land on discharge to "young men of good character" who would enlist for three years or until there was a general peace. "As every man is liable to be called upon to carry arms during this *unjust* and *unprovoked* war," his advertisement continued, "the advantages held out by this liberal offer, are too evident to require any comment."[18] A total of 730 men had been recruited for this corps during the year 1812, but there already was considerable wastage: 31 deaths, 66 deserters, 5 claimed by other corps, 7 sentenced to general service elsewhere as punishment, and 22 discharged as unacceptable when the unit had been placed on the army establishment in October. Thus, on February 6, 1813, Colonel Baynes informed Sir George Prevost that his Fencibles had an effective strength of only 36 sergeants, 19 buglers and 550 rank and file. As a result of Baynes's representations, the bounty money was increased to eight guineas, to place his regiment on an equal footing with the other fencible regiments seeking reinforcements. Recruiting parties again visited Prince Edward Island, where the Lieutenant-Governor had vainly suggested the creation of a new corps.

A new fencible corps was authorized in New Brunswick and Sir George Prevost agreed that it also might recruit anywhere, because he was very pessimistic about the chances of it obtaining 600 rank and file. Farming, fishing and lumbering were essential services, which could not safely be interfered with, and militiamen in both New Brunswick and Nova Scotia were embodied only for the time needed to escort to Halifax the prisoners of war landed from ships at various ports. British war expenditure at Halifax had forced civilian wages upwards, until masons demanded 10 shillings a day and even ordinary labourers could get seven shillings and sixpence. Small wonder then that the New Brunswick Fencibles was able to interest fewer than 200 men in soldiering for a shilling a day. Many of these were "old crocks" unfit for any strenuous activity; the youngest of the boys recruited was only 11 years old.

Adventurous youth and seafarers generally could do much better by privateering. Even service in a warship of the Royal Navy was made to sound attractive by the following notice in the *Acadian Recorder*:

NOW OR NEVER

All able bodied SEAMEN and sturdy LANDSMEN, willing to serve His Majesty, and enrich themselves; are invited forthwith to enter for His Majesty's ship *Tartarus*,[19] Captain John Pascoe, fitting with all expedition to take more American Indianmen; she will be ready for sea in a few days. Those fond of pumping and hard work had better not apply – the *Tartarus* is as tight as a bottle, sails like a witch, scuds like a Mudian, and lays like a Gannet[20] – has one deck to sleep under and another to dine on – Dry Hammocks, regular meals, and plenty of Grog – the main brace always spliced when it rains or blows hard – A few months more cruising just enough to enable her brave crew to get Yankee Dollars enough to make them marry their sweethearts, buy farms and live snug during the Peace that is now close aboard of us.

HIS MAJESTY'S AND PROVINCIAL BOUNTIES

Able Seamen.... £10. 5. 0

Ordinary 2. 10. 0

Landsmen 1. 16. 0

Halifax, Feb. 16th, 1813

GOD SAVE THE KING[21]

The legislatures of all provinces, called into session during the coldest weeks of winter when most civilian pursuits were at a standstill, had proved quite willing to vote money for the militia. The Assembly of the populous Lower Canada voted £15,000 to equip its Select Embodied Militia, £1,000 to provide hospitals for the militia, and £25,000 for the support of the war. The Army Bill Act was renewed and extended, with £500,000 worth authorized for circulation. Yet the French-speaking majority in the Assembly persisted in continuing its wrangle with the Legislative Council, over grievances stemming from Sir James Craig's day. Thus nothing was done about revising the Militia Act and providing against a possible need for martial law, as Prevost had requested in his opening speech to the Legislature on December 29, 1812. On behalf of the Prince Regent he had then expressed "confidence in the courage and loyalty of His Majesty's Canadian subjects which made him equally fearless of the result of any direct attack upon them, and of any insidious attempts to alienate their affection from his government," but wished to be prepared for any emergency.[22] Prevost tried not to show his annoyance with the Assembly, but he was anxious to put an end to useless talk and finally pay a visit to Upper Canada, which he had not yet managed to see. Captain Gray had brought back further unfavourable reports on the Provincial Marine, and Lieutenant-Colonel Bruyeres, R.E., was then making a survey of the defences of Kingston, York and the Niagara frontier. Construction of a 20-gun corvette was well under way at Kingston, but progress on a similar ship at York was far from satisfactory.

Good news, however, had arrived from the Detroit frontier, against which Brigadier-General Harrison had been making a winter advance with 6,300 infantry of his new North Western Army. With the Detroit River frozen and thus easily crossed, and the Provincial Marine's vessels immobilized, Harrison had promised in letters to the Secretary of War to capture both Detroit and Fort Malden from Colonel Procter's greatly inferior garrisons. Unfortunately for Harrison's hopes, however, the elderly Brigadier-General Winchester blundered badly. On January 18 he had led his advanced guard of some 900 American regulars and militia to the attack of a Canadian outpost at Frenchtown and with no difficulty had driven off the few Canadian militia and Indians. Detroit was only 26 miles away and he should have considered the possibility of Procter launching a counter-attack, but no precautions were taken to guard against surprise.

The attack came before dawn on the Friday morning of January 22, Procter having managed to cross the ice from Fort Malden with a make-shift force of 273 regulars, 61 fencibles, 212 militia, 28 sailors of the Provincial Marine and possibly 600 of the Indians now permanently encamped with him. Procter, however, did not make the most of his opportunity for surprise: he ordered his 3-pr. sleigh-drawn guns to open fire instead of having his troops rush upon the unsuspecting and sleeping enemy with the bayonet. In consequence Winchester's regulars managed to form behind a picket fence and kill or wound 185 of the attackers with their Kentucky rifles. The American militia, however, was quickly overcome and only 30 or 40 managed to escape through the deep snow from pursuing Indians. Brigadier-General Winchester was among those captured. Colonel Procter suggested that his Indians might get out of hand if the battle was continued, so Winchester sent word to the American regulars to surrender. Owing to Procter's nonchalance or negligence, however, drunken Indians did subsequently murder about 30 prisoners too badly wounded to walk, something which would not have happened had the humane Tecumseh been a member of the expedition. This raised the American death toll to almost 400. About 500 remained as prisoners. The Kentucky militiamen were soon paroled to their homes, on the understanding that they would not serve again until regularly exchanged.[23]

Brigadier-General Harrison hurriedly retreated, after burning his stores at the Maumee rapids; but the withdrawal of Procter's badly mauled little

**Secretary of War John Armstrong
(1758-1843)**
A frustrated general with presidential
ambitions, Armstrong brought order to the War
Department but, although he could pick the
correct objectives, he proved incapable of
maintaining American strategical aims.
(Portrait by J.W. Jarvis, National Portrait
Gallery, NPG 72.12)

force to Fort Malden, to resume its defensive role, soon encouraged him to return and construct a proper fortification. This he named Fort Meigs. Harrison would not admit his inability to recapture Detroit and announced that there would be another attempt. Meantime he would raid Fort Malden across the ice and destroy the Provincial Marine's vessels there. When the scheduled day arrived, however, the ice was no longer safe. In Washington no one seemed eager to push him into activity. President Madison had reorganized his Cabinet in early January in response to widespread clamour about winning the war but, as the new Secretary of War, John Armstrong, subsequently explained: "The Cabinet, not inexpert at deciphering military diplomacy, and particularly shy of incurring any responsibility it could avoid, determined, with perhaps less of patriotism than of prudence, to leave the question of continuing the winter campaign exclusively with the General."[24]

Sir George Prevost was so relieved to learn that all threat of immediate danger had been removed from the Detroit area that he took the first opportunity to grant Colonel Procter the local rank of brigadier-general. He seems to have accepted Procter's version of the battle of Frenchtown without question and to have made no comment as to why casualties had been so heavy when the enemy had been taken by surprise. Allowance could, it is true, be made for the fact that this had been Procter's first opportunity to command in battle. Prevost, of course, had never had an opportunity to meet the man and size him up as a soldier.

Prevost was soon able to learn a good deal from American newspapers. On January 26 Congress had authorized a first War Loan of $16,000,000 and this was successfully floated with considerable assistance from that international financier and land promoter, David Parish. Congress had subsequently appointed six additional major-generals to the regular army (including Harrison) and an equal number of brigadier-generals; it had authorized the President to raise 20 new regiments for one year's service; and it had substituted nine military districts for the Northern and Southern Departments into which the United States had hitherto been divided. Military District No. 9, the most important, embraced "Pennsylvania, from the Alleghany mountains to its western limit, New-York, north of the highlands, and Vermont."[25] In practice it included the principal operational portion of the previous Northern Department, and therefore it was the responsibility of Major-General Dearborn. Military District No. 1 was obviously one of the least important, since it embraced New Hampshire, Massachusetts and Maine, where the war was being virtually disregarded. Major-General Harrison's Military District No. 8 included Kentucky, Ohio, Indiana, Michigan, Illinois and Missouri. This all sounded impressive; but Prevost could not have suspected that the new Secretary of War was endeavouring to keep the control of field operations in his own hands. The 54-year-old Armstrong had already displayed considerable ability as a diplomat in Paris and as a brigadier-general in command of the harbour defences of New York, and there was, of course, no single military head of the United States Army to give overall supervision; but something in his character always created distrust in those associated with him.[26]

Congress had also approved the construction of four ships of the line, six super-frigates and six sloops for the war at sea, and an unlimited number of vessels for service on the inland lakes. Since most of the U.S. Navy's ocean-going frigates were then confined to port because of the Royal Navy's overwhelming supremacy at sea, considerable drafts of experienced officers and seamen could be and were despatched to Commodore Chauncey's inland command. One of the first letters sent to Chauncey by the new Secretary of the Navy, William Jones, an experienced ship-owner from Philadelphia, emphasized that "the success of the ensuing campaign will depend absolutely upon our superiority on all the lakes & every effort & resource must be directed to that object."[27] A subordinate, Oliver Hazard Perry, was now preparing a squadron for service on Lake Erie and this, Secretary Jones's letter of January 27 continued, would be important for the success of Major-General Harrison's summer campaign. Perry, then possessing only the naval rank of master-commandant, which was equivalent to a commander in the Royal Navy, had served in the naval wars against France and the Barbary pirates, like Chauncey, but afterwards had been mostly with gunboats.[28]

Chauncey had visited Black Rock during December, 1812, and during January, 1813, had transferred the naval base thence to Presque Isle, which was across a tiny bay from the town of Erie, Pennsylvania. The guns and stores for the two 20-gun brigs under construction and the three converted schooners could be transported more easily by road and water from Philadelphia and Pittsburgh to Presque Isle, than from the New York navy yard to either Sackets Harbor or Black Rock.[29]

Following his return to Sackets Harbor on January 19, Chauncey complained to the Secretary of the Navy in Washington that little had been done in his absence to alleviate the "exposed position" of his own squadron during the winter.[30] "Altho' I think the Vessels with their crews are fully competent to protect themselves against any attacks of musketry," he had written as early as December 1. 1812, "yet if the Enemy by any desperate effort should succeed in obtaining possession of the Forts in this Town, the vessels must fall of course, as they could not be moved for the ice."[31] Furthermore, this letter of December 1 had explained, the importance of Lake Ontario would encourage such an attempt, which the winter would make all the easier:

> Viewing the immense importance of the command of this Lake to the Enemy, no one can doubt but that he will make a desperate effort to regain the ascendancy that he has lost, and really the accomplishment of the object is not a difficult Task to an Enterprising officer. Closed up as we shall be within about 30 miles of Kingston where the enemy can, (and most likely will) collect a force of from 3 to 4000 men for the express purpose of destroying our naval ascendancy on this Lake, he can with great ease ... cross from Kingston to Long or Grand Island [now Wolfe Island] on the Ice, from thence to Gravelly Point [or Cape Vincent], so along the shore to Chaumont Bay, across that Bay to this Harbor in about 12 hours as all their Troops are exercised to walk with Snow Shoes. Now, Sir, suppose 2 or 3000 men cross in the way pointed out, what can save us here? Nothing but a re-enforcement of Regular Troops sufficient to repel any attack that may be made upon us, and so preserve our little Fleet from otherwise certain destruction.[32]

Actually consideration had been given by Colonel Vincent at Kingston to attacking Sackets Harbor in much the manner envisaged by Chauncey. There were, however, no snowshoes available for the Kingston garrison and at least one battalion trained in their use would have to be sent forward from Montreal, with three or four guns mounted on sleighs, to spearhead such an operation. Moreover, when the proposal was sent to him, the naturally cautious Prevost was dubious about the wisdom of any unnecessary offensive move, which might cause heavy casualties to his already inadequate forces. Lieutenant-Colonel Bruyeres was, however, directed to look into the matter during his trip west.

Yet there was now a fairly widespread American belief that trouble was being brewed at Kingston. On January 22 the *New York Evening Post* carried the following item, purporting to give signs of preparation on the Canadian side:

Look out: From information we have received, we think it highly probable, that the British are preparing to make a descent on Sacket's Harbor with a view of destroying the American vessels which are hauled up there for the winter – Their destruction, would be important to the British, as thereby they may retain the command of Lake Ontario, which they cannot do, if our little fleet is well found in the spring. A great number of sleighs, loaded with British troops, have been seen to pass up on the other side of the St. Lawrence, and as soon as the river is frozen over, it is apprehended they will cross.[33]

A company of the Glengarry Light Infantry Fencibles and a few artillerymen had travelled from Montreal to Kingston in early January, in order that a company of the 49th Foot with "a proportion of Artillery" could be sent ahead to reinforce the militia flank companies at York. Four companies of the 8th Regiment joined the Kingston garrison at the end of the month. Two more companies of the 8th Foot reached Prescott on Sunday, February 21, a few hours before Sir George Prevost's own arrival. He had left Quebec four days earlier, having finally managed to prorogue the Legislature, and his sleigh party had made excellent time by spending long hours on the road. Sheaffe's illness had prevented him from conducting any military or civil business in Upper Canada for several weeks and therefore Prevost had decided to transfer Colonel John Vincent to the Niagara frontier, replace him at Kingston by Lieutenant-Colonel Thomas Pearson from Prescott, and give Major "Red George" Macdonell this last command. Each of these three officers was granted a higher local rank. Pearson was ordered to accompany Prevost to Kingston.

Both Pearson and Macdonell urged the desirability of putting an end to the American menace from across the St. Lawrence at Ogdensburg. Captain Forsyth's riflemen and militia had surprised the Canadian militia post at Brockville during the early hours of February 7 and returned across the ice with 52 prisoners, most of whom were, however, shortly released to their homes. Forsyth had been promoted a major for this exploit. A smaller American night patrol had snatched three farmers and a team of horses from the Canadian side of the river and Major Macdonell had been insulted when sent with a flag of truce to remonstrate. There were known to be many desertions from the New York militia regiment recently called out to augment the garrison at Ogdensburg, and this would, it was felt, assist a surprise attack, which thus appeared to be a practical operation of war.

News of Prevost's journey was hardly likely to remain a secret. Indeed it was expected that Ogdensburg would have heard of his arrival in Prescott from two soldiers who had deserted from the Prescott garrison only that evening. Prevost agreed early next morning that Macdonell might make a demonstration on the ice to attract attention away from his own small party travelling towards Brockville. Only if the situation at Ogdensburg

Lieutenant-Colonel "Red George" Macdonell (1780-1870)
A veteran light infantry officer, he mounted a successful raid across the frozen St. Lawrence against Ogdensburg in February 1813. (National Archives of Canada, C-19719)

changed should an actual attack be made, since the Commander of the Forces was loath to see the revival of predatory warfare.

As soon as Prevost departed, before daylight, Lieutenant-Colonel Macdonell decided instead to implement an existing plan of attack. Captain John Jenkins was to lead his own company of Glengarry Light Infantry Fencibles and about 70 militiamen against the fort and barracks alongside the Oswegatchie River at the western edge of Ogdensburg. This was known to house Forsyth's riflemen. Macdonell's main column, consisting of about 120 officers and men of the 8th Foot, 30 of the Royal Newfoundland Fencibles and 230 of the local militia flank companies, would cross the river farther down and attack the enemy from the flank. Both columns were to be supported by small field guns mounted on sleighs and drawn by horses.

Since the Prescott garrison often drilled on the ice, which made an ideal parade ground, the American sentries paid little attention to the force when it appeared. The St. Lawrence is here more than a mile wide and the two columns were more than halfway across before the Americans opened fire. "Their firing had not much effect as their gunners were undisciplined, most of their shots going over our heads," later wrote Sergeant James Comins of the 8th Foot, which was with Macdonell's main column.[34] "On our nearer approach their soldiers abandoned their posts, leaving the Inhabitants to Protect their own Property; some of them fired upon our men from their windows, but they suffered for their Temerity, every one was bayoneted; all this time the soldiers were retreating and some of ours was ordered to pursue them while others took possession of the town."[35]

However, Captain Jenkins's column had meanwhile run into difficulties and he himself had an arm torn off by a cannon ball. Forsyth's riflemen were able to hold their own in the fort, which could not be assaulted because all but one of the British sleigh-mounted guns had got stuck in the deep snow and could not be brought into action. Forsyth realized, however, that Macdonell's men would soon cut off all possible means of retreat, so he abandoned the fort and retired southwest into the woods towards Black Lake. American losses were 20 killed and 70 captured, with most of the latter being wounded. The attackers had 7 officers wounded, including Lieutenant-Colonel Macdonell as well as Captain Jenkins; 3 sergeants and 38 rank and file also were wounded; 7 other ranks were killed.

A message was now delivered to Macdonell in Ogdensburg from the naturally cautious Prevost, who had stopped to write it before reaching Brockville. It specifically ordered Macdonell not to undertake "any offensive operations against Ogdensburg without previous communication with Major-General de Rottenburg [at Montreal], unless the imbecile conduct of your enemy should offer you an opportunity for his destruction and that of his shipping, batteries, and public stores, which does not admit of any delay in availing yourself of it."[36]

The American schooners and gunboats frozen into the ice were soon set on fire; the military stores were loaded onto sleighs and removed to Prescott. Human nature being what it is, in such a situation there was some plundering. "At one time," reported David Parish's local agent, a Belgian named Joseph Rosseel, "they were carrying off some of my property and hurrying my person off to Canada when a British officer who knew me, happening to pass by my house, perceiving my embarrassment, rushed in, bid the ruffians desist and dispersed them."[37] There is also little doubt that some of the poorer citizens of Ogdensburg helped themselves to the contents of Parish's store before Macdonell led his troops back to Prescott.

Major Forsyth's riflemen were too few in number to attempt re-occupation of Ogdensburg, so he led them on to Sackets Harbor. For the balance of the war Ogdensburg was without an American garrison, and soon the more prosperous citizens of Prescott were back shopping at Parish's store. Joseph Rosseel and other neutral-minded inhabitants of Ogdensburg frequently crossed the river to dine with Lieutenant-Colonel Macdonell.[38]

Sir George Prevost was having a late dinner at Kingston when a courier arrived from Prescott with news of Macdonell's victory that morning. The news being good, Prevost overlooked Macdonell's disobedience and sent him a personal note of congratulation. Prevost also considered it advisable to attach a doctored version of Macdonell's first report to his next despatch to Lord Bathurst, lest anyone should suspect that he was too defensive-minded to take advantage of any ready-made opportunity for an easy victory. Macdonell had written the Deputy Adjutant General "for the information of His Excellency the Commander of the Forces, that immediately after his departure from this post I made a demonstration of crossing to Ogdensburg by advancing on the right of the Enemys line with my principal Column. ... Finding that the Enemy's means ensured success to the respectable force I had with me, I availed myself of the conditional permission I had received this morning from His Excellency to undertake the measure & accordingly moved on to the attack."[39] The revised version stated, "that in consequence of the Commands of his Excellency to retaliate, under favourable Circumstances, upon the Enemy for his late wanton aggressions on this Frontier, I this morng about 7 o'clock cross'd the River St. Lawrence on the Ice & attacked & carried, after little more than an hour's action, his position in & near the opposite Town of Ogdensburg."[40]

As soon as the news from Ogdensburg reached Albany on February 25, Major-General Dearborn began drawing the wrong conclusions. Brigadier-General Jacob Brown was ordered to call out 300-400 of his militia brigade to act as a screening force. Colonel Zebulon Pike was ordered to reinforce Sackets Harbor with 800 of his regulars, travelling across country by sleigh from Plattsburgh. Troops at Greenbush also were put in motion for Sackets Harbor. Dearborn hurried there himself, hourly becoming more convinced that Prevost now had 6,000 to 8,000 men, including 3,000 regulars, at Kingston and would cross Lake Ontario on the ice.

Commodore Chauncey's initial reaction was that Prevost was in Kingston "more for the purpose of superintending the defense of that post than for any attack upon us."[41] Dearborn's gloom seems to have been contagious, however, for Chauncey wrote the Secretary of the Navy on March 12 from Sackets Harbor that we "hourly expect a visit from the other side. The enemy is obviously collecting a large Force at Kingston and by every account that we can collect from deserters and others a visit is contemplated. Sir George Prevost is to command in person and has assured his friends that he will destroy our little Fleet here or perish in the attempt. The latter I have no objection to, but the former I shall endeavour to prevent."[42]

Actually on this very day Sir George Prevost returned to Kingston, his visit to York and inspection of the Niagara frontier completed. Two days later he departed for Montreal, a fact that did not become known to those at Sackets Harbor for another week.

Dearborn never renounced his belief that the danger of attack had been real, even though he was finally satisfied that no attempt would be made. His letter of March 14 to the Secretary of War in Washington merely suggested that it was now too late in the season for the British to risk launching an attack across the ice. Sackets Harbor had been reinforced by nearly 1,200 American regulars. Chauncey was convinced, as he had written to the Secretary of the Navy on March 12, that "the Enemy does not intend an attack upon this place but keeps up the appearance of it" to mask an early offensive against Major General Harrison.[43] This last was equally faulty reasoning, but the balance of Chauncey's letter had been sound enough: "We have accounts that 6,000 men passed up on Sunday last. This cannot be true, for taking all the accounts together they would make out more than 20,000 men at Kingston. This force we know that they cannot raise in so short a time. I presume that the truth is that the people on the other side are as credulous as our own countrymen, and that they magnify a few Sleighs loaded with stores and accompanied by guards into a Brigade of Regular Troops."

Prevost now did order a considerable troop movement to Upper Canada, since he had finally received Lord Bathurst's despatches detailing the considerable military and naval efforts to be made on his behalf. The six companies of the 104th Regiment recently arrived at Quebec and the remaining companies of the 8th Regiment still at Montreal were ordered to proceed westward. The lst (or Royal Scots) moved from Quebec to Montreal and one of its flank companies continued to Prescott. The two companies of the 8th (or King's) Regiment already there then continued to Kingston. Four companies of the Canadian Voltigeurs were also alerted, Prevost wrote Bathurst, in order to "afford an early proof of the disposition of the Canadians of the Lower Province, to contribute to the defence of Upper Canada."[44] Sheaffe was advised by Prevost that these various re-inforcements would help him to repel enemy raids. He was not, however, to dissipate his forces and thus run the risk of the separate components being beaten successively should there be a major invasion attempt. In other words, caution was still to be the watchword. The risks could be left to the enemy, who would have to accept them if he was to get anywhere at all.

CHAPTER EIGHT

See-Saw in the Canadas:
April to June 1813

YORK / FORT MEIGS / FORT GEORGE /
SACKETS HARBOR / STONEY CREEK /
LAKE CHAMPLAIN / BEAVER DAM

The plan approved in Washington for operations against Upper Canada during 1813 called for the capture of Kingston as the first objective, the seizure of York and destruction of the ships there as the second, and the reduction of Fort George and Fort Erie on the Niagara River as the third. About 7,000 of the 18,945 officers and men actually serving in the United States Army were to be concentrated at Sackets Harbor and Buffalo by April 1, to carry out these successive operations in conjunction with Commodore Chauncey's naval squadron.

This sound plan was the work of the Secretary of War, John Armstrong. As Rear-Admiral Mahan was later to agree in his two-volume study of *Sea Power in Its Relations to the War of 1812*, the capture of Kingston would solve "at a single stroke every difficulty" in the inland theatre of operations. "No other harbor was tenable as a naval station; with its fall and the destruction of shipping and forts, would go the control of the lake, even if the place itself were not permanently held. Deprived thus of the water communications, the enemy could retain no position to the westward, because neither reinforcements nor supplies could reach them."[1] The subsequent attacks on York and the Niagara Peninsula would then be little more than mopping up operations.

Commodore Chauncey and Major-General Dearborn had accepted Armstrong's plan while the former was visiting the latter at Albany early in February, but the winter alarum at Sackets Harbor had caused both to doubt their ability to capture a strongly reinforced Kingston. They suggested a rearrangement of the objectives. Dearborn in a letter to Armstrong explained why he now thought York should be the first objective, to be followed by Niagara and finally Kingston:

> To take or destroy the armed vessels at York will give us the complete command of the Lake. Commodore Chauncey can take with him ten or twelve hundred troops to be commanded by Pike; take York; from thence proceed to Niagara and attack Fort George by land and water, while the troops at Buffalo cross over and carry Forts Erie and Chippewa, and join those at Fort George; and then collect our whole force for an attack on Kingston.[2]

The Secretary of War replied on March 29 that the "alteration in the plan of campaign so as to make Kingston the last object instead of making it the first, would appear to be necessary or at least proper."[3]

As early as January 19, Lieutenant-Colonel Bruyeres, R.E., had reported from Kingston to Sir George Prevost the expectation that "the first effort of Commodore Chauncey will be to endeavour to destroy York previous to the Ice being dispersed in the narrow part of the Lake towards this place, and then to proceed here; but I hope we shall be well prepared to resist him."[4] Another letter from Bruyeres of February 13, written at York, had little to say in its favour as a naval base, "as it is too remote and distant a Port to obtain the necessary resources to carry on any great undertaking. … Nature has done very little to the position as a Military Post, or to the Harbor for the purposes of a Dock yard; everything must be created which will require considerable time, and Expense."[5] Its defences were equally unsatisfactory. As late as April 5, Major-General Sir Roger Sheaffe wrote to Lord Bathurst from York that he wished "particularly to see this place put into a more respectable state of defence before my departure [for Fort George], as I think it probable that the Enemy will make some attempt on it in the Spring."[6]

There was indeed little respectable about York's defences. The outline of a fort had been dug on the triangular point where Garrison Creek emptied into Lake Ontario. It was intended to enclose the Government House but only the magazine had been completed. On the lakeside, however, a semi-circular earthwork battery had been erected and two 12-pr. guns mounted. This was known as the "Government House" Battery. The "old garrison" of barrack huts and blockhouse east of the creek had never been defensible except against Indians, but the authorities assumed that any attacker would land west of the town where there was a good beach. A Western Battery was therefore being constructed 600 or 700 yards west of the unfinished fort and two 18-pr. guns were in position. These guns had long ago been condemned and lacked trunnions; clamped to a log base, however, they could be fired at a fixed range. Only two 6-pr. field guns were available to support the mixed garrison of about 700 all ranks. This comprised two companies of the 8th (or King's) Regiment, a company-sized detachment of the Royal Newfoundland Regiment, a company of Glengarry Light Infantry Fencibles and about 300 dockyard workers and militiamen. The last of these were the companies of the 3rd York Militia Regiment. There also seem to have been anywhere from 40 to 50 Mississauga and Chippawa Indians.

Unfortunately for Sir Roger Sheaffe's reputation and subsequent career, he was still at York when Commodore Chauncey's 15 vessels carrying 1,700 American regular troops appeared on the afternoon of Monday, April 26, and the alarm was sounded. Sheaffe's only hope for a successful defence was to keep his small force concentrated behind his unfinished fort until the Americans began landing and then to launch a counter-attack before they had time to consolidate their bridgehead. Therefore only the Indians and a company of Glengarry Light Infantry were ordered westward initially to a clearing about the ruins of the old French fort (Rouille or Toronto), in what is now the grounds of the Canadian National Exhibition. Here, Sheaffe thought from the movement of Chauncey's vessels during the early hours of daylight on April 27, the enemy might attempt to land.

The small boats carrying the American assault landing force were carried too far west by the wind and missed the clearing. The Glengarry Light Infantry had in any case followed the wrong route and got lost in the woods, and only the Indians were able to engage Major Forsyth's grey-clad riflemen coming ashore near the modern Sunnyside at about 8 A.M. They were followed ashore by Brigadier-General Zebulon Pike at the head of three companies of blue-coated infantrymen. The whole pushed up the steep bank to secure the high ground. The grenadier company of the 8th Regiment now appeared, having been ordered to the scene by Sheaffe, and immediately charged with the bayonet to force the foremost Americans to retire. Numbers quickly told against them, however, and the surviving grenadiers had to retreat towards the town. Sheaffe failed to keep his force under proper control and companies kept arriving piecemeal to join the fighting, only to be repulsed in detail as they attacked in succession. Sheaffe

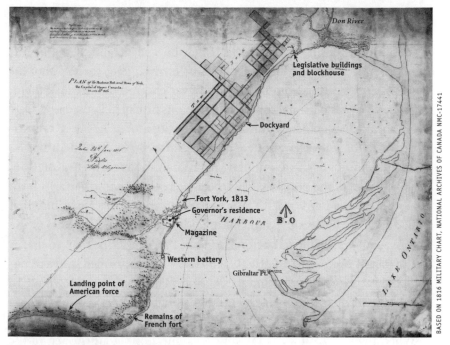

The attack on York, April 27, 1813

later wrote that he "succeeded in rallying them several times, and a detachment of the King's with some Militia, whom I had placed near the edge of the wood to protect our left flank repulsed a column of the Enemy which was advancing along the bank at the Lake side: but our troops could not maintain the contest against the greatly superior and increasing numbers of the Enemy."[7] An American officer wrote that Chauncey's 12 armed schooners "kept up so well directed and incessant a fire of grape on the woods, as to effectually cover our right flank, and afforded us great facility in forming our platoons: besides producing the greatest consternation among the Indians … owing to shallowness of the water, neither the ship nor brig could be brought to participate in the action; but the commodore himself was through the whole of the action, in his boat, encouraging and giving orders to the different schooners."[8]

Retreating British troops had crowded the Western Battery and further disaster now struck there. While its makeshift 18-prs. were doing their best to reply to Chauncey's schooners, the open magazine was accidentally detonated. About 20 men were killed instantly, others were badly mangled, and one of the guns was put out of action.[9] Three hours had elapsed since the first landing and Pike was now able to bring forward his own field guns

139

to fire on the Western Battery. It soon fell and the victorious Americans pushed forward to engage the 12-pr. battery at the unfinished fort.

All this time Sheaffe continued to display his usual coolness, but he was later to be accused by civilian onlookers of having "kept too far from his troops after retreating from the woods, never cheered or animated them, nor showed by his personal conduct that he was hearty in the cause."[10] Certainly Sheaffe was no Brock. Casualties to his little force, however, now totalled 62 killed and 94 wounded, and common sense indicated that he should abandon York and withdraw his remaining regulars to Kingston, while retreat was still possible. The troops were therefore withdrawn from the fort area. The flag was left flying to mislead the Americans, a ruse that would turn out to be successful. Sheaffe advised the senior officers of the militia, who were being left behind, to seek the best terms they could for the town and people of York. He then ordered the unfinished ship and naval storehouse to be burned and the "Grand Magazine" to be blown up, to prevent them falling into enemy hands. Time might well have seemed to pass quickly since the American landing, but it was still only early afternoon.

When the magazine went up, Pike was questioning a prisoner, in the hope of finding out how many redcoats remained in the fort area where the flag was still flying. Huge stones thrown skyward by the detonation crashed into the ranks of the Americans.[11] Pike had his own back and ribs crushed by falling debris; 38 members of his brigade were killed outright and 222 were wounded. Pike was quickly evacuated, to die in U.S.S. *Madison*. Major-General Dearborn, who then came ashore to assume personal command, was appalled by this unexpected loss, which increased American casualties to 320 killed and wounded. He was in no mood to discuss surrender terms with anyone.[12]

The Canadian militia officers were paroled to their homes for the night, but the men were cooped up and the wounded got no attention. By the next afternoon Dearborn had cooled down sufficiently to sign a capitulation guaranteeing private property. Henceforth Dearborn did his best to prevent looting and supported the civil authorities who tried their best to carry on as usual during the remaining days of American occupation. The American soldiers and sailors behaved much better than expected: not a single case of murder or rape was reported and most of the robberies were of empty houses whose residents had fled. "I kept my Castle, when all the rest fled,"' wrote Penelope Beikie, "and it was well for us I did so, – our little property was saved by that means. Every house they found deserted was completely sacked."[13] The burning of the Parliament Buildings on the evening of April 30 was probably the unauthorized work of American sailors, but the military buildings and Government House were deliberately burned by the departing Americans on May 1.

The Americans were longer at York than they planned for a gale blew up and prevented the departure of Chauncey's vessels. So crowded were the schooners with troops that only half could go below at a time to escape the rain and waves which continued to wash over the decks. The crossing to Fort Niagara was finally made on May 8, but the troops were now in too "sickly and depressed" a state to make an attempt against Fort George.[14] The element of surprise had been lost anyway, so Chauncey took his squadron back to Sackets Harbor.

More by good luck than good management, Brigadier-General Procter now secured a minor success over Major-General Harrison's North Western Army. Harrison had been ordered to continue in his winter quarters until May, when the naval squadron being prepared on Lake Erie should be ready to help him redeem American fortunes in the west. Had Procter moved during the winter, after the Kentucky militia had returned home, the unfinished Fort Meigs could have been captured from its continuing small garrison of sickly men. Procter's own force had suffered severely at Frenchtown, however, and he was content to remain on the defensive until the two flank companies of the 41st Foot joined him from Niagara. Only then did he decide to nip Harrison's coming offensive in the bud, and it was April 28 before the six vessels, two gunboats and flotilla of bateaux carrying his force of 550 regulars, 63 fencibles and 464 militia, reached the mouth of the Maumee River. Batteries were quickly erected on both banks. They opened fire on Fort Meigs on May 1, while 1,200 Indians led by Tecumseh and other chiefs surrounded it.

The besiegers failed to invest Fort Meigs completely, however, and Harrison was able to communicate with a Kentucky brigade of 1,200 men moving down the Maumee River to his support. About nine o'clock on the morning of May 5 some 900 of these Kentuckians quickly overran the besieging batteries on the north bank, while the defenders sallied forth and captured a British battery on the south bank. On the north bank, however, three companies of the 41st Foot and some Canadian militia did stand firm, and the Indians closed in on the Kentuckians who were nearly all killed or captured. On the south bank the American sortie party was finally driven back into the fort. Over 600 Americans were taken prisoner and another 400 were either killed in battle or subsequently massacred by the Indians.[15] Procter's losses were insignificant: his 15 killed and 46 wounded included five militiamen.

Yet Procter's siege had to be broken off on May 9. About half his militia had already deserted to their homes and the remainder had declared their intention of doing likewise. The need to plant their crops was a convenient excuse to avoid unpopular, and possibly dangerous, militia service. Only Tecumseh and a score of Indians remained. Procter reported that "under present circumstances at least, our Indian Force is not a disposable one, or permanent, tho' occasionally a most powerful Aid. ... Daily experience more strongly proves that a regular force is absolutely requisite to ensure the Safety of this District."[16]

That same May 5, Sir James Yeo had landed at Quebec and been greeted with the news that York had been captured and part of the Provincial Marine destroyed. The next day he set out for Kingston with 150 of his officers and seamen. He soon caught up with Sir George Prevost who had left Quebec only the day before. They reached Kingston together on May 15 and found that Captain Robert H. Barclay had accomplished wonders in the two weeks since his own arrival from Halifax. During the intervening fortnight, the other two captains appointed by Admiral Warren to command corvettes on Lake Ontario, Daniel Pring and Robert A. Finnis, had reached Kingston, together with four of the six lieutenants sent from Halifax. These officers, incidentally, had followed the same overland route across New Brunswick as the 104th Regiment of Foot. At Kingston the youthful Midshipman David Wingfield of Commodore Yeo's first contingent had "expected to find nothing but large gunboats; but to our surprise,

Commodore Sir James Lucas Yeo (1782-1818)
Like his counterpart, Chauncey, Yeo had the energy to construct a fleet on the lakes but was hesitant about risking it in action. (Engraving after painting by A. Buck, courtesy, Toronto Reference Library, T-15241)

on opening Navy Bay, we saw two Ships of 23 and 21 guns, a Brig of 14 and two Schooners of 14 and 12 guns, comprising every sort of calibre, from a 68, to a 4 pounder."[17] These were *Wolfe* launched on April 20 and waiting for her guns, the existing *Royal George, Earl of Moira* (lately re-rigged), *Prince Regent* (soon to be re-named *General Beresford*) and *Sir Sidney Smith*. Plans had been made to lay down a ship to replace that destroyed at York, and six gunboats were on order.[18] Since Commodore Yeo wished to promote his own three commanders to be captains on Lake Ontario, the more junior Barclay was sent to command on Lake Erie, shortly to be followed by Finnis, and Pring was ordered to Lake Champlain. The remainder of Yeo's officers and men arrived in successive detachments within a week. The guns and naval stores which would be required for the war vessels still under construction could not, however, be moved up river quickly from Quebec.

From the outset Sir James Yeo was aware that Chauncey's war vessels mounted more 32-pr. and 18-pr. long guns than those of the Provincial Marine. Once Chauncey's new corvette was completed and armed with 26 24-pr. long guns "for the purpose of battering the forts at Kingston," Yeo knew that the American squadron would be too strong for him to attack.[19] Yeo wrote to the Admiralty on May 26 that he would "put to sea" while the opposing navies were still roughly even, "as the possession of Upper Canada must depend on whoever can maintain the Naval Superiority on Lake Ontario."[20]

Sir George Prevost's letter of May 27 to Lord Bathurst was equally frank about his constant problem of providing a dependable defence, with too few regulars and a militia whose service was uncertain:

The growing discontent & undissembled dissatisfaction of the Mass of the People of Upper Canada, in consequence of the effects of the Militia Laws upon a population thinly scattered over an extensive range of Country, whose zeal was exhausted & whose exertions had brought want and ruin to the doors of many, & had in various instances produced a considerable Emigration of Settlers to the United States from whence most of them originally came, have compelled me for the Preservation of that Province to bring forward my best and reserved Soldiers to enable me to support the positions we hold on the Niagara and Detroit Frontier. I have also been induced to adopt this measure from the further consideration that the Militia has been considerably weakened by the frequent desertion of even the well disposed part of them to their farms, for the purpose of getting seed into the ground before the short summer of this country had too far advanced.[21]

This movement into Upper Canada was now possible because the promised reinforcements had already begun to arrive at Quebec by ship; indeed the 2/41st and 98th Regiments had arrived from the West Indies only a few days before they were placed under orders for Upper Canada. Also ordered to proceed to Kingston were a car brigade of light artillery, Captain Coleman's Troop of Volunteer Light Dragoons, the balance of the 1st Royal Scots, four grenadier companies of other regiments and the 1st Light Battalion of Infantry.

This last unit, and a 2nd Battalion, had been organized six weeks earlier from the flank companies of the five battalions of Select Embodied Militia and the light infantry companies of the regular regiments then in Lower Canada. Both battalions were intended for employment in lesser mixed detachments of regulars and militia, with the same companies always kept together "to create more intimately that Esprit de Corps and mutual confidence so essentially necessary to insure success in the Field."[22] Another car brigade of light artillery[23] was to be formed at Quebec and sent forward to Montreal, along with six companies of the 103rd Regiment, the Canadian Fencibles, the 19th Light Dragoons which had recently arrived with only a few horses, and De Meuron's Regiment.

Shortly after these despatches had left Kingston for Montreal, word reached the town that Commodore Chauncey's tiny fleet was off the mouth of the Niagara River. It began cannonading Fort George on the morning of May 25 and soon managed to set fire to all the log buildings within. The American assault landing finally was made on the early morning of May 27. It was led by Colonel Winfield Scott, who had been appointed Adjutant General to Major-General Dearborn following his exchange as a prisoner of war, and included Major Forsyth's riflemen. Dearborn being ill and none of Brigadier-Generals John P. Boyd, John Chandler or William A. Winder being competent to command even a brigade, Scott was really in charge of the whole operation.

The defenders were a polyglot force: about 1,000 all ranks of the 8th and 49th Regiments of Foot, Royal Newfoundland Fencibles and Glengarry Light Infantry Fencibles, and 300 continuing members of militia flank companies. Brigadier-General John Vincent had earlier divided his garrison into three groups and decided to launch counter-attacks wherever the

Canadian Light Dragoon, 1813
Raised in Lower Canada, this
provincial unit saw considerable
action in the Niagara and along the
Detroit River in 1813. (Painting by
G.A. Embleton, DND, Canada)

enemy should effect a landing, rather than allow himself to be bottled up in an inadequate fortress which could be demolished by the guns of Chauncey's naval squadron.[24]

This plan, however, was not given a chance of execution. When the assault came, the detachment of British troops and Indians stationed nearest the American landing place "were obliged to fall back, and the fire from the Shipping so completely enfiladed and scoured the plains that it became impossible to approach the beach."[25] Scott's assault force was followed ashore by the brigades of Boyd, Winder, and Chandler. After suffering considerable casualties, 52 killed and 306 wounded or missing, Vincent withdrew his troops from the fort to a concentration area out of range of Chauncey's naval guns. "There after waiting the approach of the Enemy for about half an hour," Vincent subsequently reported to Prevost,

> I received authentic information, that his force consisting of four to five thousand men had reformed his columns and was making an effort to turn my right flank – At this critical juncture not a moment was to be lost, and sensible that every effort had been made by the officers and Men under my command to maintain the Post of Fort George, I could not consider myself justified in continuing so unequal a contest, the issue of which promised no advantage to the interests of His Majesty's Service. Having given orders for the Fort to be evacuated, the Guns to

be spiked, and the Ammunition destroyed, the Troops under my Command were put in motion and marched across the Country in line parallel to the Niagara River, towards the position near the Beaver Dam beyond Queenston Mountain.[26]

Here he had earlier established a supply depot in a large stone house. And here he was joined by Lieutenant-Colonel Bisshopp with all the detachments from Chippawa to Fort Erie, two more companies of the 8th Regiment and Captain Barclay's naval party headed for Amherstburg. This last comprised three lieutenants, one surgeon, one purser, one master's mate, seven British seamen and twelve from the Provincial Marine's establishment at Kingston. The next morning Vincent changed the direction of his movement and retreated overland towards Burlington at the head of Lake Ontario, with what now totalled 1,600 regulars and fencibles. The continuing militia had been dismissed to their homes, to be recalled when needed.

The American army had only 40 killed and 120 wounded, but otherwise had little to show for its assault on Fort George. Vincent's force was far from being destroyed and was encamped at Burlington by the time Brigadier-General Winder was finally ordered in pursuit on June 1. Major-General Dearborn had gained only one immediate advantage by occupying the Niagara frontier: the naval vessels at Black Rock, hitherto unable to get past the guns of Fort Erie, now joined Captain Perry's squadron at Presque Isle.

Commodore Chauncey had hurried back to Sackets Harbor on May 31, following receipt of word that Sir George Prevost and Sir James Yeo had been there with an expedition from Kingston. As soon as they had verified Chauncey's absence, Prevost decided to create a diversion in Vincent's favour by attacking Sackets Harbor. With luck he could destroy its dockyard and the corvette under construction. There was not time to wait for the reinforcements *en route* from Montreal so the greater part of the existing garrison of Kingston was embarked in *Wolfe, Royal George, Earl of Moira*, two armed schooners, two gunboats and 30 bateaux on May 27. They crossed the eastern end of Lake Ontario during the night. Colonel Baynes was to command the assault force of about 750 all ranks. This consisted of the grenadier company of the 100th Foot with a section from the 1st Royal Scots, two companies of the 8th, four companies of the 104th, one company of the Glengarry Light Infantry Fencibles, two companies of the Canadian Voltigeurs and an artillery detachment with two 6-pr. guns.

The expedition was in position off Sackets Harbor before daylight on

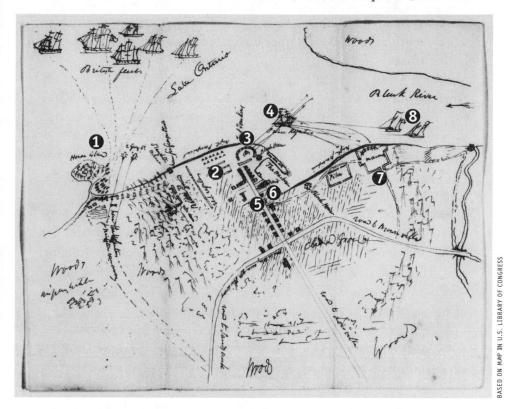

The attack on Sackets Harbor, May 29, 1813
1. British landing point. 2. Blockhouses. 3. Fort Tompkins. 4. H.M.S. *Beresford*.
5. Village. 6. New ship. 7. Fort Volunteer. 8. U.S. schooners.

Friday, May 28. Prevost's subsequent despatches state that "light and adverse winds preventing their nearing the Fort until the evening, arrangements were made for the attack at the dawn of the following morning."[27] Commodore Yeo disagreed: having participated in combined operations elsewhere, he knew that conditions were never likely to be perfect and that it would be bad for morale to keep the troops cooped up for at least another 12 hours. But he was only the naval commander.

The only gain during the day of waiting was the capture of 12 American barges with supplies bound for Sackets Harbor from Oswego. Another seven barges gained Sackets Harbor which was now thoroughly alerted. Militia were thronging in from the countryside to reinforce the 400 regulars in garrison. Major-General Jacob Brown had come from his nearby home to assume command, in accordance with an arrangement made earlier by Major-General Dearborn. The senior American regular officer left by Dearborn at Sackets Harbor was only too glad to see this doughty militia officer.[28]

Brown guessed correctly that the British would attempt to land on Horse Island, a wooded 24 acres joined by a fordable neck of sand and gravel to the mainland about a mile southwest of the tiny harbour and dockyard. These were ringed by batteries and blockhouses. Therefore Brown lined his 500 militia along the water's edge by the ford. The few regulars spared from the fixed defences were posted along the edge of the woods to the rear of the small clearing beside the shore.

Shortly after daylight on May 29, Baynes's force was able to get ashore on Horse Island, despite the complete absence of surprise and with the troops in poor spirits after being exposed most of the night to drizzling rain. They quickly formed up and charged across the ford. Most of the American militia fired too soon and then fled, as Brown had expected; but he managed to withdraw about 100 in a formed body.

With these he tried to work around the flank of the invaders who were now closely engaged with the American regulars under the trees. The British intention was to swing left and force the line of the nearest blockhouses from the landward side, and then destroy the dockyard installations. The action became confused but the Americans slowly but surely were pushed back on the line of blockhouses. Captain Andrew Gray was killed leading an assault on one of these, which proved impervious to attack by men in the open. A continuing off-shore breeze prevented Yeo's squadron from getting close enough for its guns to batter these defensive works, and the carronades of the smaller gunboats, never intended for firing at other than level targets, were completely ineffective. Brown's handful of militia began pressing from behind Baynes's right flank, and Prevost apparently became convinced in his own mind that there was no chance of success. According to his report, he "reluctantly ordered the Troops to leave a Beaten Enemy, whom they had driven before them, for upwards of three hours, and who did not venture to offer the slightest opposition to the re-embarkation, and in perfect order."[29] Three captured 6-pr. field guns and 154 prisoners were also brought away. Casualties had, however, been considerable: 47 killed, 154 wounded and 16 missing.

Not all the attacking force shared Prevost's conviction that abandonment of the attack was well judged. "We brought all our wounded away it was possible to remove," Sergeant Comins of the 8th Regiment wrote, and embarked on board ship tired, hungry, wet and thirsty, highly mystified and looking very sheepish at one another; you would hardly have heard a whisper until that powerful stimulant grog was served out when the Tower of Babel was nothing like it, everyone blaming another, nay some of them were rash and imprudent to lay the blame on anyone but themselves. As for my part, I thought much but said little, having got a wound in my thigh which began to pain me as soon as I got cold.[30]

Mystification indeed continued long after the event and the timing of the attack on Sackets Harbor has been one of the more confused moments in a war not noted for clarity.

The American version, of course, was greatly different. "Had not General Prevost retreated most rapidly under the guns of his vessels," Jacob Brown wrote in his report, "he would never have returned to Kingston."[31] Brown's own conduct led to his being appointed a brigadier-general in the regular army. American losses had been 21 killed and 85 wounded. At the height of the action, when the attackers appeared likely to win, the naval officer in charge of the dockyard had set fire to the new ship under construction, a captured schooner, and a large quantity of naval stores. Fortunately for Commodore Chauncey, the fires were extinguished before too much damage was done.[32]

On June 4 Chauncey, now back at Sackets Harbor from Niagara, wrote the Secretary of the Navy that his 14 vessels mounted 62 guns; but Yeo had seven, which with six gunboats, carried 106 guns. "If he leaves Kingston, I shall meet him. The result may be doubtful but worth the risk."[33] Actually Sir James Yeo had sailed for the head of Lake Ontario on the previous day to harass Major-General Dearborn's army on behalf of Brigadier-General Vincent. On board his vessels were nearly 220 regulars of the 8th Regiment and a quantity of stores and ammunition for Vincent's division of the army in Upper Canada.

"The Enemy having dared to pursue this Division by moving a Corps of 3500 Men with 4 Field Guns and 150 Cavalry to Stoney Creek," Lieutenant-Colonel John Harvey strongly urged Vincent at Burlington to "make a forward movement for the purpose of beating up this encampment."[34] Harvey's reconnaissance of June 5 had revealed that the Americans had encamped at Stoney Creek for the night in a field beside the road: their sentries were few and badly placed, and it would be easy to mount a night attack from the surrounding forest. Vincent agreed and gave Harvey 700

**Lieutenant-Colonel John Harvey
(1778-1852)**
Shown here in a postwar illustration, Harvey
was a highly competent soldier who planned
the British attack on the American camp at
Stoney Creek in June 1813. (National
Archives of Canada, C-2733)

regulars of the 8th and 49th Regiments, or nearly half his force, for the enterprise. Harvey's men moved silently into position before two o'clock on the morning of June 6. The American password had been learned from a paroled prisoner, and the leading files were thus able to approach the unsuspecting sentries. These were quickly bayoneted, and then the redcoats burst into the centre of the encampment. In their excitement, forgetting the strict orders to keep quiet, a few of the men let out shouts of victory and fired their muskets. This roused the Americans who were astonished to see masses of redcoats illuminated by the flames of the blazing camp fires while they tried to load their muskets. The Americans reacted quickly, and the targets were too good to miss. Major Charles Plenderleath of the 49th Regiment stormed and captured the enemy's field guns with 40 of his own men, but elsewhere the British officers began to lose control over their men and the fighting became very confused. Friend fought friend rather than foe. The two American brigadier-generals, Winder and Chandler, were, however, taken prisoner. Only as dawn broke was Lieutenant-Colonel Harvey able to concentrate his scattered troops and retire into the woods. His losses had been considerable – 23 killed, 134 wounded and 5 missing; only 55 Americans were killed or wounded and another 100 reported as missing.

Subsequent American action was explained by Colonel James Burn of the 2nd Light Dragoons in a letter to Major-General Dearborn. "On the return of day-light," he reported,

> I found the command of the army had devolved on me, and, being at a
> loss what steps to pursue in the unpleasant dilemma, occasioned by the

capture of our Generals, finding the ammunition of many of the troops nearly expended, I had recourse to a council of the field officers present, of whom a majority coincided in opinion with me, we ought to retire to our former position at the Forty Mile Creek, where we could be supplied with ammunition and provisions, and either advance or remain, until further orders.[35]

On the afternoon of June 7, however, Sir James Yeo's squadron shelled the American camp established at Forty Mile Creek and destroyed or captured 16 boatloads of supplies *en route* from Niagara. This threat to their line of communications caused the Americans to retreat to Fort George on the following day. The next night the enemy set fire to and abandoned Fort Erie; he also withdrew from Chippawa and began preparing Fort George for a siege. Brigadier-General Vincent now moved forward his whole force to Forty Mile Creek "to give encouragement to the Militia and Yeomanry of the Country who are everywhere rising upon the fugitive Americans, making them Prisoners & *withholding* all Supplies from them and lastly (and perhaps *chiefly*) for the purpose of sparing the resources of the Coun try in our rear and drawing the Supplies of the Army as long as possible from the Country immediately in the Enemy's possession."[36] This was in marked contrast to the report Dearborn had made to the Secretary of War immediately following his capture of Fort George. He had then written that "the inhabitants came in numbers, and gave their paroles. I have promised them protection. A large number are friendly to the United States, and fixed in their hatred against the Government of Great Britain."[37]

The British now re-occupied the depot at Beaver Dam. Meanwhile, another small reinforcement was proceeding up Lake Ontario from Kingston: commanded by Major Peter W. De Haren of the Canadian Fencibles, it consisted of the flank companies of the 104th Regiment, a company of the Glengarry Light Infantry Fencibles, and drafts of recruits for the 8th and 49th Regiments. This made it possible for Vincent to send the balance of the 41st Foot – its headquarters and 100 rank and file – to join Procter at Amherstburg.

The provision of timely assistance and close support for Vincent's military efforts was not Commodore Yeo's only contribution during the month of June. Cruising along the American shore of Lake Ontario, his naval squadron captured two schooners and several bateaux loaded with supplies off Fort Niagara, seized a depot of provisions and a trading vessel at the mouth of the Genesee River, burned a further store house to the westward after carrying off 600 barrels of provisions, and managed to secure two more small lake schooners before heading back to Kingston late in June.

Chauncey's earlier resolution to follow Yeo and provoke battle had quickly evaporated and he remained safely in Sackets Harbor during the whole of June. The explanation sent to the Secretary of the Navy on June 11 sounded reasonable enough, if rather too carefully developed:

> on the one hand I had the prospect, (if I succeeded against the enemy) of immortalizing myself; on the other hand if I was beaten, the loss and disappointment to my country would be irreparable. The only question was whether I was to fight for my own aggrandizement or that of my country? If the latter there could be no question as to the course that I ought to pursue, which was to put nothing to hazard; for by remaining here four weeks I could prepare the new ship for service, and with her I should consider myself as having the complete and uncontrolled command of the lake; without her the enemy has near a fourth more guns than I have, as many men and as good, and his officers are experienced and brave. With such a disparity of force I trust you will approve of my determination of putting nothing at hazard until the new ship is fitted.[38]

Caution had been thrown to the winds on Lake Champlain, however, by over-zealous subordinates of Lieutenant Thomas Macdonough, U.S.N. In an effort to put a stop to the smuggling of cattle and provisions into Lower Canada, the American armed schooners *Growler* and *Eagle* entered the wide mouth of the Richelieu River on the morning of June 3. Foolishly they continued downstream until the river narrowed within sight of Isle aux Noix. This was garrisoned by a small detachment of Royal Artillery and six companies of the 100th Regiment of Foot; the Provincial Marine's establishment consisted of an armed schooner and three gunboats, but very few seamen. (Captain Pring, R.N., had not yet arrived to take naval command on Lake Champlain.) Personnel of the 100th Foot now rowed out in the gunboats, with Royal Artillerymen manning the 6-pr. gun in each, and engaged the enemy. *Growler* and *Eagle* soon decided to withdraw, but the navigable channel was narrow, and their efforts to tack against the breeze took them close to the high ground on each bank, where parties of infantrymen and militia fired their muskets into them each time they came within range. The pursuing gunboats were too low in the water to make good targets for the American gunners. On the other hand, the gunboats managed to secure enough hits to render both *Growler* and *Eagle* unmanageable and cause them to surrender. According to the *Quebec Gazette*, men due to be discharged that day from service in the 1st Battalion of Select Embodied Militia "volunteered their services and marched in a style honorable to themselves and to the Canadian Character."[39] American casualties were one killed and 19 wounded; only three of the attackers were wounded. Renamed *Shannon* and *Broke*, the captured vessels were soon able to range Lake Champlain at will, since Macdonough was left with only one armed sloop and two gunboats.

Sir George Prevost took advantage of the lull which followed the American withdrawal in the Niagara peninsula and Yeo's successes to switch his senior subordinates in the Canadas. "The support I have received from the General Officers in command since the Death of Major-General Sir Isaac Brock, I am sorry to say has not always corresponded with my expectations," Prevost complained to the Duke of York in a letter of June 23,

Circumstances indicating an insufficiency on the part of Major General Sir R. H. Sheaffe to the arduous task of defending Upper Canada, have induced me to place Major-General de Rottenburg in the Military Cmd and civil administration of that province ... except Sir John Sherbrooke [in Nova Scotia] the Major General is the only General Officer of high character and established reputation serving in the Army in the North American Provinces, to whom I could entrust this important duty, without embarrassing myself with it to the prejudice of the other possessions of His Majesty committed to my care.[40]

Prevost neglected to add that his difficulties were not lessened by the fact that Sherbrooke, De Rottenburg and Sheaffe were older than himself, and that the first two had seen much more active service. His letter of the following day to the Secretary of State for War and the Colonies merely stated that having found on arrival at Kingston that Sheaffe had "lost the confidence of the Province by the measures he had prescribed for its defence, I deemed it most conducive to the good of the public service to remove that Officer to Montreal & to substitute Major General De Rottenburg in his place."[41]

Undoubtedly, however, this action was influenced by the long and indignant account of the battle and occupation of York written with characteristic force by the Reverend John Strachan and also signed by six other prominent citizens. "A new commander and more troops" was its prescription for saving Upper Canada, since Sheaffe "has lost entirely the confidence of the regulars and militia and his very name is odious to all ranks of people."[42]

Major-General de Rottenburg had assumed his new responsibilities with effect from June 19. Henceforth the force serving under Brigadier-General Procter at Amherstburg was to be styled the Right Division of the Army of Upper Canada; the troops at Niagara and York were to be known as the Centre Division; the garrisons at Kingston and below that post were to form the Left Division of the Army of Upper Canada. For the time being, Sir George Prevost continued with his headquarters at Kingston and left Major-General Glasgow to administer the government of Lower Canada.

Major-General Dearborn continued to report disasters to Washington. The next unfortunate event for his army was the surrender on Thursday, June 24, of Lieutenant-Colonel C. G. Boerstler's punitive force sent from Fort George to attack Brigadier-General Vincent's advanced post near the Beaver Dam. Here there was one company of the 49th Foot commanded by Lieutenant James Fitzgibbon, who had been commissioned from the ranks while Brock was still its commanding officer. Boerstler's force of 575 cavalry and infantry, with two field guns, did not set out before midday on Wednesday, but secrecy had been sacrificed by loose talk earlier. At daybreak on Tuesday, June 22, a Queenston housewife named Laura Secord started across country on foot to warn Lieutenant Fitzgibbon. Neither the exact route followed by this determined little woman nor her exact time of arrival at the Beaver Dam can be verified, but she did reach Fitzgibbon some time that evening.[43]

Mrs. Secord was naturally unable to provide details of the American plans so there was nothing Fitzgibbon could do but await developments. Not until early on the morning of June 24 were the advancing Americans discovered by Indian scouts and their whereabouts reported to Captain Dominique Ducharme of the Indian Department. He sent a messenger to alert Fitzgibbon, and about nine o'clock his 300 Caughnawaga Indians attacked the enemy rear. They were soon joined by 100 Mohawks led by Captain William Kerr. After three hours of firing at shadows in the surrounding woods and listening to war whoops, the Americans were ready to surrender, but afraid to trust themselves to the mercy of the warriors.[44]

Fortunately for them Lieutenant Fitzgibbon then appeared with about 50 of his own 49th Regiment. "Not a shot was fired on our side by any but

Laura Secord, c. 1860
Her famous walk to warn Lieutenant
James Fitzgibbon of the American
advance on the Beaver Dam has become
one of the enduring Canadian epics of
the war. (Lossing, *Field-Book*, 1869)

the Indians," he later wrote. "They beat the American detachment into a
state of terror, and the only share I claim is taking advantage of a favourable moment to offer them protection from the tomahawk and the scalping knife."[45] Apparently the only reason why Captain Ducharme had not
demanded the American surrender earlier was his inability to speak English fluently. Major P. W. De Haren arrived with a larger force of regulars in
time to accept the actual surrender.

An officer of the Indian Department later suggested that the "*Cognawaga
Indians* fought the *battle*, the *Mohawks* or Six Nations got the *plunder* and
Fitzgibbon got the credit."[46] Legend, however, has placed the credit elsewhere. Stories told many years later were elaborated in successive versions
by Mrs. Secord and members of her family and came to include many in-
triguing details such as her driving a milk cow part of the way as a means
of concealing her errand.

Major-General Dearborn had now worn out his welcome, as well as his
health. Everyone in Washington agreed that this sick and elderly veteran
must be removed from so important a command. On July 6 the Secretary
of War wrote: "I have the President's orders to express to you the decision
that you retire from the command of District No. 9, and of the troops
within the same, until your health be re-established and until further orders."[47] Dearborn's successes at York and Fort George, with the help of
Commodore Chauncey, had been good for morale; but on both occasions
he had failed to capture or destroy his redcoated enemy and thus had not
improved the American strategical position in Upper Canada. The same
thin red line was still there to plague whomever the Secretary of War
should pick as his successor.

CHAPTER NINE

Defeats in the West:
June to October 1813

CHESAPEAKE vs. SHANNON /
LAKES CHAMPLAIN, ONTARIO AND ERIE /
FORT MEIGS /MORAVIAN TOWN

The importance of sea power for the several theatres of this war was amply demonstrated during the summer weeks of 1813. Along the Atlantic seaboard the British Government had promised a diversion to relieve the American military pressure upon Sir George Prevost. On Lakes Ontario and Erie opposing naval squadrons were to jockey for control of the vital freshwater communications by which the rival armies were supplied.

The British Government and people had been exasperated by the loss of the frigates *Guerrière*, *Macedonian* and *Java*, in single ship engagements, to American super-frigates. "It is of the highest importance to the *character* and interests of the country that the naval force of the enemy should be quickly and completely disposed of," read an Admiralty communication of January 9, 1813, to Admiral Sir John Warren, Commander-in-Chief of the North America and West Indies Stations.[1] "Their Lordships have therefore thought themselves justified at this moment in withdrawing ships from other important services, for the purpose of placing under your command a force with which you cannot fail to bring the naval war to a termination, either by the capture of the American national vessels, or by strictly blockading them in their own waters."

Early in April an advanced squadron under Rear-Admiral George Cockburn began moving up Chesapeake Bay to effect a close blockade of its ports as intended by Admiral Warren's previously mentioned proclamation of February 6.[2] By another proclamation of May 26, the Admiral extended his "strict and rigorous blockade" to the "ports and harbours of New York, Charleston, Port Royal, Savannah, and the River Mississippi."[3]

This still left free for commerce the more northerly American ports, from which ships were carrying supplies vital to the British war effort. Rear-Admiral Mahan was to describe the expedient later:

> The needs of the British armies in the Spanish Peninsula and in Canada, and the exigencies of the West India colonies, induced the enemy [the British] to wink at, and even to uphold, a considerable clandestine export trade from the United States. Combined with this was the hope of embarrassing the general government by the disaffection of New England, and of possibly detaching that section of the Country from the Union. For these reasons, the eastern coast was not included in the commercial blockade of 1813.[4]

The trade between various American ports, carried on by coastal vessels, was another matter. Admiral Mahan continues, in his description of the British naval strategy:

> But no motive existed for permitting the egress of armed vessels, or the continuance of the coasting trade, by which always, now as then, much of the intercourse between different parts of the country must be maintained, and upon which in 1812 it depended almost altogether. With the approach of spring in 1813, therefore, not only was the commercial blockade extended to embrace New York and all south of it, together with the Mississippi River, but the naval constriction upon the shore line became so severe as practically to annihilate the coasting trade, considered as a means of commercial exchange. It is not possible for deep-sea cruisers wholly to suppress the movement of small vessels, skirting the beaches from headland to headland; but their operations can be so much embarrassed as to reduce their usefulness to a bare alleviation of social necessities, inadequate to any scale of interchange deserving the name of commerce.[5]

Thus there were no buyers for the cotton and rice piling up in southern warehouses; the price of imported tea more than doubled during the year; by December 1813 the sugar quoted at $9.00 a hundredweight in New Orleans came to fetch $40.00 in New York. American Government revenue was proportionately affected by the decreased volume of trade.

Two American frigates did manage to escape from Boston into the

North Atlantic on April 30, but their raids on commerce proved highly unprofitable that summer because most British merchantmen were travelling through the dangerous shipping areas in heavily guarded convoys. Smaller privateers were ultimately to be relatively more successful, once American captains realized that the Royal Navy tended to relax precautions as soon as the merchantmen they had escorted were close to port.

The recognition that such a laxity existed in the Gulf of St. Lawrence caused the Secretary of the Navy in Washington to order the U.S.S. *Chesapeake* to go and intercept ships headed for Quebec. When this order reached Boston in early May, this large frigate had just come under command of Captain James Lawrence, U.S.N.; the first, third, and fourth lieutenants and many of the seamen were also newcomers. Very different was the situation of Captain Philip Vere Broke, R.N., then commanding H.M.S. *Shannon*, blockading Boston against American warships. He had had his frigate for seven years and his was a well-trained crew.

On the afternoon of June 1, *Chesapeake* set out on her mission. Her captain had not received the challenge sent into Boston that day by Captain Broke for a single-ship duel. Yet Captain Lawrence made no effort to avoid the waiting *Shannon* and, although *Chesapeake* carried more guns and men than the 38-gun *Shannon*, superior seamanship and gunnery told. The contest lasted only 15 minutes. *Chesapeake* was given a bad battering, and Captain Lawrence and his senior subordinate were mortally wounded. *Shannon* then ran alongside. Her boarders quickly put an end to further resistance in *Chesapeake*, despite the dying American captain's plea "Don't give up the ship!" American casualties were 48 killed and 96 wounded. British losses were fewer: 23 killed and 60 wounded.[6]

Captain Broke's success at once improved morale in the Royal Navy. It was to receive more lasting fame as the inspiration for a patriotic song which English schoolboys were to sing with gusto for many a year. According to the author of *Tom Brown's Schooldays*, the boys at Rugby got really noisy when they reached the words:

Brave Broke he waved his sword, crying, now my lads aboard,
And we'll stop their playing Yankee-doodle-dandy oh!

Great was the excitement at Halifax when H.M.S. *Shannon* brought *Chesapeake* into port. Historians of Halifax of a later day have seemed to imply that the citizens were somehow contributing to the war effort by their wild cheering. Rather the war effort was contributing to their own cheer for Haligonians were busily taking advantage of the unprecedented prosperity, occasioned both by government spending and by the presence of eight or ten thousand sailors, soldiers and paroled prisoners of war who were eager to spend their money in taverns, dance halls and brothels. Recalling these days when he was a boy, Thomas Akins would write nearly half a century later:

> A portion of Grafton Street was known under the appellation of Hogg Street, from a house of ill-fame kept by a person of that name. The upper street along the base of Citadel Hill between the north and south barracks was known as "Knock him Down" Street in consequence of the number of affrays and even murders committed there. No person of any character ventured to reside there, nearly all the buildings being occupied as brothels for the soldiers and sailors. The streets of this part of the town presented continually the disgusting sight of abandoned females of the lowest class in a state of drunkenness, bare headed, without shoes and in the most filthy and abominable condition.[7]

But if most Haligonians preferred not to see such sights, they were filled with the "greatest alarm" on one single July night that summer when two Independent Companies of Foreigners created a wild disturbance in the part of the city known as "Dutch Town."

These Independent Companies had been formed in England from captured French prisoners for garrison duty in the fever-ridden West Indies, but had been added to the expedition with which Admiral Warren was to create a diversion in Chesapeake Bay in favour of Sir George Prevost. The foreigners had been trouble-makers from the outset. The military commander of the force to be landed from the fleet, Colonel Sir Sidney Beckwith, had suggested that they be named Canadian Chasseurs, in the hope that an expectation of being sent later to soldier in the temperate Canadian climate, instead of being returned to the West Indies, would persuade them to moderation. The device, however, had not had the desired result. A number had deserted to the Americans on June 22 during an unsuccessful assault landing against Craney Island, which guarded the entrance to Hampton Roads. Three days later Colonel Beckwith had led a successful attack against the village of Hampton, which was then systematically looted. The so-called Canadian Chasseurs were responsible for most of the atrocities against the men, women, and children of defenceless Hampton. Lieutenant-Colonel Charles Napier, commanding one of the brigades, recorded in his Journal that the 102nd Regiment of Foot, his own men, almost mutinied against his refusal to permit them to join in the pillage, but they and the Royal Marines "behaved like soldiers." Sir Sidney Beckwith "ought to have hanged several villains," he also wrote; "had he so done, the Americans would not have complained: but every horror was committed with impunity, rape, murder, pillage: and not a man was punished!"[8]

American protests, however, did result in an investigation. "The murder of the old *bedridden* Man, and his Aged Wife were but too true," Beckwith had to admit to Admiral Warren, "and repeated Circumstances have transpired since ... to prove it was their [the Chasseurs] Intention to desert in a Body to the Enemy, most probably at the same time murdering Capt. Smith and such of his Officers as had interfer'd, or endeavoured to check their horrid proceedings."[9] The misnamed Canadian Chasseurs were now divorced from the expedition and shipped to Halifax, where they continued troublesome until their return to England was finally authorized. Admiral Warren advised Brigadier-General Robert B. Taylor of the Virginia militia that future "military operations should be carried on with all the liberality and humanity which becomes the respective nations. Any infringement of the established usage of war will instantly be noticed and punished."[10]

In the early weeks of its summer activities the British fleet had been supplied with fresh water and provisions by American coastal vessels but on July 29 orders were issued by the Secretary of the Navy to prevent such intercourse and to seize offending vessels. On August 5 the War Department issued similar instructions to the army.

Beckwith made two further landings from Warren's fleet with his continuing troops. Both were abortive, but the whole coastline of Virginia and Maryland was kept in a state of alarm. However, no major change was made in American troop dispositions because of the activities of Warren's expedition, so that his operations failed as a diversion in favour of Prevost's hard-pressed forces in Canada. In early September Warren's fleet went to Halifax for a short visit before returning to the West Indies for the winter.[11]

Prevost had actually been able to create more of a diversion by the operations he had planned on Lake Champlain. These were intended to destroy the enemy's remaining war vessels and his unprotected depots at

Plattsburgh and Swanton, and to prevent further transfer of troops from the town of Burlington in Vermont to the Niagara frontier. In a letter of July 4, Prevost asked the senior naval officer at Quebec to furnish temporary crews for the American armed schooners captured off Isle aux Noix and renamed *Broke* and *Shannon*. Commander Thomas Everard, R.N., of H.M.S. *Wasp*, which reached Quebec on July 21, agreed to undertake an operation on Lake Champlain that could be completed within the two weeks his sloop was scheduled to remain at Quebec. On the following day he set out with 50 members of his own crew and 30 volunteers from the naval transports then in port. At Montreal he met the more junior Lieutenant Daniel Pring, R.N., who was on his way to take command of the naval establishment on Lake Champlain in his locally approved rank of captain. Command of the troops accompanying the expedition, which left Isle aux Noix on July 29, was entrusted to Lieutenant-Colonel John Murray. The 39 officers and 907 other ranks included detachments from the 13th, 100th and 103rd Regiments of Foot and the Canadian Fencibles, 24 Royal Artillerymen with two 3-pr. field guns, and 35 members of the 1st Battalion of Select Embodied Militia to help man three gunboats.

On July 30 the troops landed at Plattsburgh from the two schooners, three gunboats and 47 bateaux, and the work of destruction began. This was unopposed, since the few American militia had fled. Blockhouse, barracks, and military storehouses were burned at this thriving little village, which was the principal shipping centre on the New York shore of Lake Champlain. Detachments were then sent to the much smaller village of Swanton, Vermont, to destroy military property only. Reports later published by *Niles' Weekly Register* suggest that there was a needless destruction of private property, which "was not limited to such as they could eat, drink and carry away."[12] Commander Everard continued to Burlington with the two schooners and one gunboat. Then, as now, the most important town in Vermont, its garrison of better than 3,000 regulars and volunteers was too strong to be attacked, but Everard managed to capture four small lake vessels. He then returned to Isle aux Noix briefly before starting on his return journey to Quebec. Captain Pring accompanied him to look for sailors, and was able to borrow 60 from the naval transport service for the balance of the inland navigation season.

Meanwhile, what had been happening on Lake Ontario was far less exciting than might have been expected. Commodore Chauncey had no intention of leaving Sackets Harbor until his new corvette *General Pike*, launched on June 20, was ready. She was being armed with 26 long 24-prs. and thus would be superior at long range to any ship or combination of vessels flying the British flag, since their main armament was short-range carronades. Sir James Yeo knew this, from intelligence gleaned by parties sent from Kingston to Sackets Harbor under a flag of truce. He also knew that Chauncey was receiving drafts of trained seamen from the Atlantic ports, while he could man his own new brig *Melville* only by taking sailors and soldiers from other vessels of his own squadron. Inevitably there were thoughts of raiding Sackets Harbor and destroying *General Pike*. One such scheme was cancelled after two members of the Royal Newfoundland Fencibles involved in it were reported to have deserted to the Americans. According to the *Kingston Gazette* of July 7: "Our brave tars, with a detachment of the Royal Scots, and 100th Regiment, lay concealed in the woods, within ten miles of the Enemy's squadron the whole of Thursday [July 1], and the attack was to have taken place on that night."[13] Stratagems to lure Chauncey out onto the lake had no success either. Yeo wrote the Secretary of the Admiralty on July 16: "I have used every device in my power to induce the Enemy's Squadron to come out, before his new Ship was ready, but to no effect. I am sorry to say she is now manned and will be ready for sea in a few days."[14]

U.S.S. *General Pike* was indeed ready for service on July 20; on the following evening Commodore Chauncey left Sackets Harbor and sailed with his squadron for Fort Niagara. Here he took on board enough troops for an attack on Brigadier-General Vincent's supply depot at Burlington. Finding this position too strongly defended, Chauncey sailed to nearby York, which was now completely defenceless. On July 31 the capital of Upper Canada was occupied for a second time. Provisions were seized and storehouses burned-in retaliation for Commodore Yeo's earlier activities along the American shore of Lake Ontario. Chauncey's squadron – two ships, one brig, and 10 schooners – then returned to Niagara, where Yeo finally appeared on the morning of August 7 with two ships, two brigs, and two schooners.

"It is scarcely possible that a decisive naval action can be avoided," Prevost had already written about Lake Ontario to the Secretary of State for War and the Colonies,

and I therefore humbly hope that His Royal Highness, the Prince Regent, will approve of it being courted by us, as a necessary measure for the

preservation of the advanced positions of this army, which I have determined to maintain until the naval ascendency on Lake Ontario is decided, convinced that a retrograde movement would eventually endanger the safety of a large proportion of the troops in Upper Canada and
convert the heart of that province into the seat of war.[15]

Yet the decisive naval action which seemed inevitable on August 7 was
avoided by both naval commanders. During the first night of manoeuvring, two of Chauncey's schooners capsized in a heavy squall and were
lost. Yeo refused to close with Chauncey's heavier ships, however, and kept
hoping for a chance to cut off American schooners. This game continued
through August 8 and 9, and until the evening of August 10. Then, through
an error in seamanship, Chauncey's two leading schooners became separated from the rest of his squadron and were captured during the small
hours of August 11. The loss of four schooners was, however, no great matter as they were only makeshift war vessels anyway, and Chauncey still possessed a decided superiority over Yeo. Chauncey remained cautious, and
Yeo's caution exceeded his. "From what I have been able to discover of the
movements of the enemy," Chauncey explained in a letter of August 18 to
the Secretary of the Navy, "he has no intention of engaging us, except he
can get decidedly the advantage of wind and weather, and as his vessels in
squadron sail better than our squadron, he can always avoid an action. ...
He thinks to cut off our small dull sailing schooners in detail."[16]

Commodore Yeo was able to convince Sir George Prevost that his eva-
sive tactics had been the proper course of action until continued unfavourable winds had made it obvious that he would not be able to close with
Chauncey's ships and might as well return to Kingston. Prevost also agreed
that "until the Enemy's Naval force can be reduced, the ships cannot with
prudence or safety cooperate with the Land forces to any extent."[17] This
truism put an end to the hopes which Prevost had entertained when he
joined Major-Generals de Rottenburg and Vincent before Fort George in
mid-August. There they were "cooping up" 4,000 Americans, with only
half that number of troops on the whole extended line of the Niagara frontier.[18] The only unusual events since the fight at the Beaver Dam had been
two successful raids on American stores depots, at Fort Schlosser on July 5,
and at Black Rock on July 11. Lieutenant Fitzgibbon's company of the 49th
Foot had formed part of the latter and larger raiding force, whose popular
commander, Lieutenant-Colonel Cecil Bisshopp, had been mortally

wounded while protecting the withdrawal. This had been delayed unduly in order to bring away several hundred bags of salt, which was then very scarce in Upper Canada. There had thus been time for a number of Tuscarora Indians from a nearby reservation in New York State to reach the scene as allies of the Americans and to attack the British rear guard.[19] British inactivity after these raids had been bad for morale, with 40 men deserting from the 104th Regiment of Foot alone. As the summer drew on hope became widespread that Prevost would order an assault on Fort George.[20]

Sir George Prevost did order Major-General Vincent to make a "general demonstration" on the morning of Tuesday, August 24. According to Prevost's subsequent despatch, this served but to show that the fort could not be taken by the means at his disposal:

> the Picquets were driven in, a great part of them being taken, with a very trifling loss, and I found myself close to the Fort, and the new entrenched Camp which is formed on the right of that Work, both of them crowded with men, bristled with Cannon, and supported by the Fire from Fort Niagara on the opposite side of the River; but no provocation could induce the American Army to leave their places of shelter, and Venture into the Field, where alone I could hope to contend with it successfully having made a display of my force in vain, a deliberate retreat ensued without a casualty; – I am now satisfied that Fort George is not to be reduced, strengthened and supported as it is by Fort Niagara, without more troops, the Co-operation of the Fleet, and a battering Train – to accomplish this object a double operation becomes necessary, Fort Niagara must be invested and both places be attacked at the same moment, but my resources and means do not allow me to contemplate so glorious a termination to the Campaign in Upper Canada.[21]

The sensible course was to return to Kingston, and there to try and persuade Commodore Yeo to seek out the American fleet and destroy it. This Prevost did. The Commander of the Forces was responsible for his actions only to the British Government, and the uncomprehending inhabitants of the Niagara Peninsula and the rank and file of Vincent's Centre Division of the Army of Upper Canada were left to think what they liked.[22]

Prevost had, however, earlier ordered Lieutenant-Colonel Bruyeres, R.E., to proceed from Kingston to York and arrange for the construction of better fortifications on the site of the present "Old Fort York." Since no instructions awaited his arrival on the morning of August 26, Bruyeres had to do as he thought best. The half company of Royal Sappers and Miners made available from the Kingston garrison for the project also constructed a more advanced defensive position at Burlington to protect its supply depot on the landward side. There were plenty of skilled axemen among the local inhabitants to lend a hand and both fortifications were completed in a few weeks.

The continued need for supplies at the head of Lake Ontario forced Yeo's squadron to return there on convoy duty. On Tuesday, September 7, Chauncey nearly caught up with him off the mouth of the Niagara River. For the next five days Chauncey endeavoured to force a general action, which Yeo steadily refused while the little fleets sailed over most of the broad waters of Lake Ontario. Midshipman David Wingfield, now an acting lieutenant because of Yeo's shortage of officers, later recorded the chase and how it was affected by the changeable wind:

light and frequent calms kept us … constantly at our guns, alternately chasing and being chased, as the wind gave either the advantage, which is very changeable at this season of the year – a sudden breeze opening up would give us the advantage and, before we could close, either shifting or dying away– sometimes we were becalmed for hours together, within 5 or 6 miles of each other, so that our minds were worked up to the highest pitch of enthusiasm, and our seamen were in excellent spirits, and eager for the engagement.

Between 8 and 9 o'clock on the evening of the 10th September, the two fleets were becalmed in such a situation [off the mouth of the Genesee River], that whichever way a breeze sprung up, an engagement appeared inevitable, and we all adjourned to our berth to take a parting glass together. …

Next day a breeze sprang up in favour of the enemy which allowed them to take the desired distance; so that our short guns would not tell, while their shot flew about us in all directions; after having laid in this galling situation upwards of two hours, we got a breeze in our favour, and immediately tried to close, while the Americans made all sail from us.[23]

Commodore Yeo's letter to Admiral Warren of the following day, September 12, claimed that he had been in this "mortifying situation for five hours having only six guns in all the Squadron that would reach the Enemy (not a carronade being fired)."[24] His casualties were 1 midshipmen and 3 seamen killed, and 7 wounded. The contest ended with Yeo's squadron gaining the shelter of a deep bay five miles west of Kingston.[25]

Sir George Prevost wrote from Kingston to Lord Bathurst in bitter disappointment at "the unexpected return of our Squadron into this Harbour ... almost chased in by the Enemy, – And I deplore the protracted Contest on Lake Ontario for Naval ascendancy, Sir James Yeo having detained for this important object, nearly the whole of the Officers and Seamen which were sent from England with himself, leaving Captain Barclay on Lake Erie to depend almost entirely on the exertions of Soldiers belonging to the 41st Regiment and Royal Newfoundland Fencibles."[26]

The naval situation on Lake Erie might well concern Prevost. When the Americans had first captured York in April, a good part of the naval stores and guns intended for the naval vessels under construction at Amherstburg had been destroyed or captured. Barclay's journey to take over his command had been delayed by the enemy occupation of the Niagara Peninsula a month later. During July he did not have the resources to man properly the war vessels already in commission. He had only seven British seamen and 108 members of the Provincial Marine; he had only 54 men of the Royal Newfoundland Fencibles and 106 soldiers of the 41st Foot. Brigadier-General Henry Procter was only too ready to agree that "if we lose the Superiority of this Lake it will not be recovered without difficulty."[27]

The point was pressed upon Prevost. In a letter of July 13 Procter entreated that "even an Hundred Seamen pushed on here immediately would, in all probability, secure the Superiority on this Lake; at all Events enable us to appear on it, until further Efforts may be made. I am already weakened on Shore by my Efforts to enable Captain Barclay to appear on the Lake."[28] Letters already on the way from Sir George Prevost would soon inform him that the remainder of the 41st Regiment was being ordered to Amherstburg: but "the Ordnance & Naval Stores you require must be taken from the Enemy whose resources on Lake Erie must become yours."[29]

Provisions were in very short supply and Procter had been contemplating a raid on Major-General Harrison's principal supply depot on the Sandusky River. This was guarded by only a few hundred raw recruits and

**Captain Robert H. Barclay
(1785-1837)**
The commander of the British squadron
on Lake Erie, Barclay was unable to
match his American naval opponents on
that lake. He gambled it all on one
action – and lost. (Courtesy, Toronto
Reference Library, T-15259)

the raid was therefore quite feasible, but Procter's unruly Indian allies insisted instead that Fort Meigs at the Maumee Rapids should again be attacked. For fear that they might otherwise desert, Procter unwisely changed objectives.[30]

The force of nearly 300 British regulars and 3,000 Indians that Procter moved across Lake Erie from Amherstburg reached Fort Meigs on July 20.[31] An attempt was made to trick the American garrison into coming out to do battle in the open, by a sham battle started in the woods by two parties of Tecumseh's warriors on the afternoon of July 26, but the trick failed. Procter decided against attempting an assault of the fort and re-embarked his force on July 28. It sailed along the lake to the mouth of the Sandusky River. Indians could never be depended on to continue with any expedition, however, and all but 200 or 300 had already drifted away. The continuing braves were anxious to storm the weakly defended Fort Stephenson which blocked the route up river to Harrison's supply depot, and Procter again unwisely bowed to their wishes. Major-General Harrison, being no more venturesome a soldier than Procter, had ordered Fort Stephenson to be evacuated, but Major George Croghan had refused to withdraw his 160 U.S. regulars. Procter's guns proved too small to do any real damage to either the stockade or blockhouses, so that once again he had either to make an unsupported frontal attack or do nothing.

On the afternoon of August 2 the redcoats advanced in the open against two sides of the fort. According to Procter's despatch, the troops "displayed the greatest Bravery, the greater part of whom reached the Fort and made every Effort to enter: but the Indians who had proposed the Assault, and had it not been assented to, would have ever stigmatized the British Character, scarcely came into Fire, before they ran off out of its Reach."[32] The British suffered 96 casualties before Procter called off the assault. Major-General Harrison remained in safety a few miles distant, listening to the cannonade, until he received a message from Major Croghan that the British were re-embarking in their boats.

When Sir George Prevost wrote to Procter on August 22 about this engagement, it was to an officer whose promotion to the rank of major-general had been promulgated recently in London. Prevost, however, was caustic:

> I cannot refrain from expressing my regret at your having allowed the clamour of the Indian Warriors to induce you to commit a part of your valuable force in an unequal & hopeless conflict.
>
> You cannot be ignorant of the limited nature of the force at my disposal, for the defence of an extensive frontier & *ought therefore* not to count too largely upon my disposition to strengthen the right division.[33]

Yet Prevost had no better officer to send to this distant theatre and still had no real reason to doubt Procter's ability to command. He therefore was sending what reinforcements could be spared to Amherstburg. These were the 2nd Battalion of the 41st Regiment, admittedly understrength, and a detachment of Royal Artillerymen. Of more importance was the news in this letter that an officer and 50 or 60 British seamen were finally moving forward from Kingston. These were part of the crew of a naval transport detained at Quebec on Prevost's request; Commodore Yeo had insisted on retaining at Kingston for his own needs the 300 seamen ordered forward from Halifax by Admiral Warren.

Captain Barclay had an uneasy command of Lake Erie while the Americans were rushing two large brigs to completion at Presque Isle. He had thoughts of interfering with this work, but a sandbar in the harbour mouth had prevented him from sailing in and shooting up the dockyard. During August 2-4, while Barclay was elsewhere, the Americans managed to float the two brigs over the sandbar by removing their guns and raising their hulls on floats. There was no longer any need to retain in service the worthless Pennsylvania militia which had been garrisoning nearby Erie

after their own fashion. Neither was there any justification for the lauda-
tory farewell order issued by the militia's commanding general:

> Called out *en masse*, at the commencement of harvest, and after a long
> continuance of rainy weather, he was, with many others, surprised to see
> so great a proportion of the brigade assembled in arms. On the one side
> there was presented the probable loss of crops, just ripe, and the great
> privations of domestic pursuits, when the whole effective population *is*
> called away; on the other, the destruction of the shipping and means of
> defence for the north western army, the invasion of our territory, and
> the honor of the country invaded and degraded. In this alternative you
> embraced the cause of your country by suffering personal inconven-
> iences, and losses, far greater than has been suffered by any portion of
> this state, since the commencement of the war.[34]

This *fait accompli* at Presque Isle gave naval superiority to the squadron
commanded by Master-Commandant Oliver Hazard Perry, U.S.N., as a
captain, and forced Barclay to return to Amherstburg to hurry the completion of his own new brig *Detroit*.

Captain Perry was correspondingly almost as short of seamen as Barclay
because Commodore Chauncey, like Yeo, was looking after his own needs
first. Chauncey had agreed that 740 American seamen were required to
man the two new brigs and the eight schooners on Lake Erie, but Perry had
only 490 men, including nearly 100 soldiers and a number of landsmen engaged for four months' service. Yet Major-General Harrison needed his
support, so Perry now established a base at Put-in-Bay, in the Bass Islands
about 30 miles southeast of Amherstburg. His squadron appeared off Fort
Malden on both August 25 and September 1, but Barclay had no intention
of venturing forth until after the promised naval reinforcements had arrived from Kingston and his new *Detroit* was ready.[35]

Barclay was, however, being pressed by Major-General Procter to do
something to re-open communication with Long Point, where much
needed supplies of every description were waiting for vessels to transport
them along Lake Erie to Amherstburg and Detroit. Barclay's letter of September 1, addressed to Sir James Yeo, conceded that the "quantity of Beef,
and flour consumed here is tremendous, there are such hordes of Indians
with their *Wives*, and *children*."[36] A letter written by Procter on September
6 to Prevost's Military Secretary emphasized that the long expected

Supplies cannot any longer be delayed, without the most frightfull Consequences. The Indian and his Family, suffering from Cold, will no longer be amused with Promises. His Wants he will naturally attribute to our Neglect at least; and Defection is the least of Evils we may expect from him. There have not been among the Indians, with whom we are concerned, any Traders; consequently their Necessities can be supplied by us only, or the Enemy who are not inattentive to any circumstances respecting the Indians, that may be turned to their Advantage.[37]

Procter had become more insistent following the receipt of a letter from Prevost dated August 22, with its peculiar comment that "the experience obtained by Sir James Yeo's conduct towards a fleet infinitely Superior to the one under his Command [on August 11] will satisfy Captain Barclay that he has only to dare and the enemy is discomfitted."[38]

On September 6 two lieutenants, one master's mate, two gunners and 36 seamen reached Amherstburg, these apparently being all there was of a reinforcement mentioned in Prevost's letter of August 22. Barclay's proper naval rank was still only lieutenant; and Procter, a newly promoted major-general, was urging action of which the Commander of the Forces and Governor-in-Chief apparently approved. Commodore Yeo's original instructions to Barclay had directed him to exercise his own discretion at all times, and this neglected subordinate now wrote to him, on the same September 6, to set forth the unhappy dilemma he was placed in with supplies so short but his resources for acquiring them so meagre:

that some thing must be attempted by me to enable us to get Supplies, by the Lake – particularly as the Season is rapidly closing.

That such a thing is necessary, there can be no doubt and in consequence if I find that no further re-enforcements are likely to arrive immediately, and I know something of the few that have arrived – I shall sail and risk every thing to gain so great a point – as that of opening the communication by water.

That the Risk is very great I feel very much, but that in the present state of this place, without provisions, without stores – & without Indian Goods (which last is a matter of the highest importance,) it is necessary, I fully agree with the Genl.

Less can be expected, (if any thing at all) than if I had received re-enforcements, which I judge absolutely necy. more I have never asked from you.

I am certain of being well supported by the Officers, which gives me almost all the confidence I have in the approaching battle.

The Enemy has not appeared for some days, but I believe they are at the Islands.[39]

On the morning of Thursday, September 9, Barclay decided that weather conditions would be in his favour so he gamely left Amherstburg in the recently completed *Detroit*, accompanied by the smaller *Queen Charlotte* and *Lady Prevost* and by his three armed schooners. The armament intended for *Detroit* had been lost at York, and in desperation she had been armed with a variety of guns from the ramparts of Fort Malden. Since 17 of these were long guns, they gave her the advantage of being able to fight at a greater range than the American brigs, which had only carronades. Otherwise each of Perry's brigs possessed a greater armament and he had six schooners to Barclay's three. Perry's flagship, U.S.S. *Lawrence*, carried a fighting flag bearing the words "Don't give up the ship" attributed to the dying Captain Lawrence of U.S.S. *Chesapeake*.

Unfortunately for Barclay's gamble, the wind shifted completely to give the Americans the windward position, or weather gauge, and this enabled them to close with their opponents. Barclay opened fire first, around noon, with his long guns, on *Lawrence*, but Perry was able to close with the wind until his carronades could be effective against *Detroit*. By two o'clock in the afternoon both flagships were badly battered and a seriously wounded

Commodore Oliver Hazard Perry (1785-1819)
Representative of the small but superbly trained American naval officer corps, Perry was the victor on Lake Erie in 1813. (Lossing, *Field-Book*, 1869)

Barclay had been carried below. Perry now left the useless *Lawrence*, which promptly struck its colours, and took over the brig U.S.S. *Niagara*. Fire from her carronades was soon able to force both *Detroit* and *Queen Charlotte* to surrender. Captain Finnis of the last named, and Barclay's second-in-command since his arrival on Lake Erie, had been killed early in the battle. The remaining British vessels continued an unequal contest for as long as possible, but finally *Lady Prevost* and the three schooners also surrendered.[40]

The long guns of the American schooners had been engaged throughout, but Perry's decisive victory was a result of his larger vessels having closed boldly so that their heavy carronades could inflict the most damage. British and Canadian casualties were 41 killed and 94 wounded. American losses were 27 killed and 96 wounded, mostly on board U.S.S. *Lawrence*. The captured vessels were sailed to Put-in-Bay, with their surviving crew members as prisoners below decks. Perry now penned a dramatic message to the Secretary of the Navy in Washington: "It has pleased the Almighty to give to the arms of the United States a signal victory over their enemies on this Lake."[41] By return mail Perry was notified that the President had been pleased to promote him to the rank of captain in the United States Navy.

Commodore Sir James Yeo was almost as prompt to advise Admiral Sir John Warren that Barclay had "heroically devoted himself and the Squadron entrusted to his charge to the safety of the Army, the preservation of the Province, and what was equally dear to him the Honor of the British flag."[42] In consequence, and even though he was critically wounded and a prisoner, Barclay's name was included in the Admiralty list of officers promoted to the rank of Commander on November 15, 1813. Barclay's remaining but shattered arm was still in bandages when he was repatriated to England during the summer of 1814 and had to face an automatic court-martial because he had lost his squadron. The Court Martial, however, assembled at Portsmouth in September, "most fully and most honourably acquitted" him and his surviving officers and men. Sir James Yeo's own conclusion had been that Barclay "was not justified in seeking a contest the result of which he almost foresaw would prove disastrous" and that there had been "no necessity for General Procter to urge Captain Barclay to so hazardous, and unequal a contest."[43]

Sir George Prevost's letters to Major-General Procter after the Battle of Lake Erie also were in a critical vein. They recognized, however, that Procter could not continue at Forts Detroit or Malden and would have to retreat on the Centre Division of the Army commanded by Major-General Vincent.

Procter decided to withdraw along the line of the Thames River, which flowed into Lake St. Clair. About seventy miles up river was the Moravian Town. Here he could safely make a stand, since it was far enough inland to escape interference by the United States Navy. Actually, despite the considerable casualties from the futile attacks on Fort Meigs and Fort Stephenson, and the loss of soldiers on Barclay's war vessels, Procter still had nearly 900 troops, mostly of the 41st Regiment and including the recently arrived officers and other ranks of its second battalion. These did not have any illusions about Procter's ability as a battlefield commander, but his recent discomfitures had been partly the result of the Indians' failure to fight. Tecumseh and his immediate followers had a burning hatred for the Americans, but most of the other Indian braves were quite content merely to sit around and consume British rations. The Indians were, however, vehemently opposed to retreat, when the matter was finally broached in council on September 18. Tecumseh could see no reason for it, when there were no American soldiers in sight and Procter had never been defeated in a pitched battle. It was perhaps unfair to expect him to understand the importance attached by Procter to the fact that the Americans were now supreme on Lake Erie. Tecumseh was certain of only one thing, the British were planning to desert their Indian allies, as they had done both in 1783 and in 1794.[44]

Even after Tecumseh finally agreed to accompany Procter as far as the Moravian Town, nothing was hurried. Ordnance and other stores were started on their way, but the remaining bulk supplies at Detroit were burned only on September 24, when the garrison crossed over the Detroit River to Sandwich. Fort Malden's installations were similarly fired on September 26, after Captain Perry's naval squadron was reported to be entering the Detroit River. Not until the following morning, however, did Procter's retreat actually begin.

A few hours later Major-General Harrison's troops began landing at Amherstburg from Perry's vessels. Harrison, however, was as cautious as Procter was inept as a field commander. The letter that Harrison addressed to the Secretary of War on the evening of September 27, after occupying the deserted Fort Malden, stated that "I will pursue the enemy to-morrow, although there is no probability of my overtaking him, as he has upwards of 1,000 horses, and we have not one in the army."[45] His pursuing force numbered only slightly more than 3,000 regulars and volunteers, because sizable garrisons were left at Detroit, Sandwich and Fort Malden in case Indians might return to the attack. The Kentucky volunteers were led in person by 66-year-old Governor Isaac Shelby. On October 1 Lieutenant-Colonel Richard M. Johnson's regiment of 500 mounted riflemen finally caught up with Harrison and they provided a greater measure of mobility for the army. Harrison knew that many of the easily discouraged Indians had deserted Procter, and underestimated his adversary's force as having only 580 redcoated soldiers.

Harrison's reluctance to catch up with Procter seemed almost to be foiled by the British themselves. The failure of their rear guard to destroy bridges over small rivers and streams enabled the American advanced guard to keep close behind and reach the mouth of the Thames River late on October 2. Here it was joined by Captain Perry's gunboats which had travelled up the Detroit River and across Lake St. Clair. The next morning the whole American force started up the Thames River, which runs roughly parallel to Lake Erie. The gunboats accompanied the troops only part way, but Captain Perry himself continued as a "volunteer." Good time was made because their guide, Mathew Dolsen, was a former resident of the area. Most of the residents, needless to say, stayed out of sight and hoped that their homes would not be plundered. Near Chatham the American advanced guard came upon three abandoned British gunboats, recently set on fire to prevent capture. On the morning of October 5 two gunboats loaded with ammunition and several bateaux were captured.

Procter had been too busy reconnoitring possible defensive positions to the rear to keep a firm control over his slow-moving column. He also had his own family to worry about. On the morning of October 5 his rear guard was still two miles from the Moravian Town, but now that the Americans were so close he would have to make a temporary stand at once and hope to continue his retreat along the right or north bank of the river as soon as he had repulsed them. Procter therefore formed his regulars in two lines across the road and among the trees, with the river on his left and a large swamp on his right flank. There was no ammunition with the single 6-pr. field gun, however, and no thought seems to have been given to felling trees and forming abattis in front of this hastily assumed position. The Indians, who were in the swamp on his right flank, had a far stronger natural position.[46]

Major-General Harrison also did not follow the rules of frontier warfare. Frontier custom would have suggested that he use his mounted riflemen to ride down the Indians who had never developed a defence against horsemen. But in Harrison's case non-observance of the rules was fortunate and Procter's dispositions were to be his undoing. At the last moment Harrison moved his mounted troops to the centre of his line and "refused" his left flank; that is, he pulled back his left flank from possible contact with the Indians in the swamp. The Kentucky mounted riflemen, unlike European cavalrymen, were accustomed to ride their horses through wooded country and they did so boldly when the order was given by Harrison at Lieutenant-Colonel Johnson's suggestion. The tired and discouraged ranks of the 41st Foot, unprotected by abattis, barely able to see the American horsemen coming, gave them only a scattered fire, instead of the usually devastating volleys, before they had ridden through both lines.[47] While the disorganized redcoats were surrendering in small groups, Johnson turned his attention to the swamp. Here his men had to dismount, and here they found real opposition. It was only after a stiff fight, in which Tecumseh and his immediate followers were killed, that the rest of the Indians retreated. The 246 British officers and other ranks who managed to escape from the

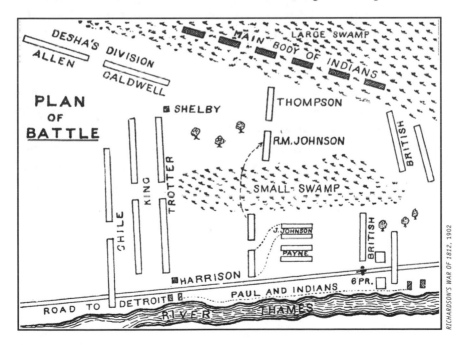

The Battle of Moravian Town, October 5, 1813

battle soon formed themselves into groups and made a proper retreat to the head of Lake Ontario; 28 officers and 606 men were killed or captured. Harrison reported that the Indians had managed to remove all but 33 of their own dead. American losses were 7 killed and 22 wounded.

There could be no doubt about the result. Since there was no other British force to try conclusions with, Harrison's whole army returned to the Detroit area with their captures, and the Kentucky volunteers were discharged and on their way home by October 13. On the following day Harrison signed an armistice with the Indians now gathered at Detroit, and accepted a number of squaws and children as hostages for their continued good behaviour. On October 17 Harrison issued a proclamation which permitted the civil officials of the Western District of Upper Canada to continue in office provided they took an oath to remain faithful to the United States during the period of occupation. Security of property and persons was pledged. Captain Perry agreed with Harrison, however, that it was too late in the season to attempt the recapture of Mackinac. Harrison therefore sailed with Perry for Buffalo with nearly 1,200 regulars, leaving only 400 U.S. regulars and 1,300 Ohio militia to garrison Detroit, Sandwich and Amherstburg.[48] Perry made a slow but triumphant progress to Baltimore, where he was to take command of a frigate then under construction. Harrison and his men loudly proclaimed their eagerness for further fighting.

The first, exaggerated reports of Procter's defeat reaching Kingston had persuaded Major-General de Rottenburg that everything to the westward would have to be abandoned.[49] Later news that the enemy had withdrawn to the Detroit frontier, however, soon persuaded him that York and Burlington should be held "so long as may be found practicable with reference to supplies of provisions &c."[50] A letter of November 1, nevertheless, advised Major-General Vincent that future operations must be governed by the outcome of the American campaign then being waged in the St. Lawrence region. For the moment, Procter continued at Burlington to command those officers and men who had retreated with him from the Battle of the Thames.[51]

CHAPTER TEN

The Autumn of 1813

BURLINGTON BAY / CHÂTEAUGUAY / CRYSLER'S FARM / NEWARK

Kingston and the upper St. Lawrence Valley had experienced a quiet summer. Knowledge that the American troops left at Sackets Harbor had fitted out a number of gunboats for service among the Thousand Islands had compelled Commodore Yeo to station three gunboats at each of Prescott, Gananoque, and Kingston to give added protection to convoys of bateaux moving up river from Montreal. American gunboats did capture one convoy of 15 bateaux and its escort on July 18, and defeat an expedition sent from Kingston to recover them in Goose Creek along the American shore, but these operations had little effect on the conduct of the war.

The hazards of the convoy system would have been lessened if shore travel had been easier. Efforts to have the road improved on both sides of Gananoque, and at other stretches along the St. Lawrence River, were made during the summer but failed because the sedentary militia to whom this work was assigned were busy with the harvest. Early in August, Colonel Joel Stone of the 2nd Leeds Militia optimistically promised to have detachments of 20 men each complete the Gananoque sections in short order; but a month later he had to confess that only seven men had reported to the detachment assigned to work west of that hamlet, and that three of these had soon deserted to their homes. Military pay and a rum ration were hardly sufficient to compete with civilian wages and opportunities.[1]

Below the Thousand Islands, all remained peaceful and private intercourse continued between Prescott and Ogdensburg. On August 9 Lieutenant-Colonel Thomas Pearson, once again commanding at Prescott, sent a local merchant across to Ogdensburg under a flag of truce to discover what news of the outside world Mr. David Parish might have brought from Washington. Pearson must have been slightly disconcerted, however, to be given a letter from Parish requesting that Sir George Prevost grant immunity for an ironworks being erected nearby "for country work only."[2]

Pearson's covering letter to the Commander of the Forces pointed out that a number of deserters from the Prescott garrison had gained employment at this ironworks, which had been started before the war but had been bedevilled by bad luck. Yet David Parish had influential friends, even in Montreal. A leading merchant named Isaac Todd having vouched for him, Prevost granted this request for immunity. Lieutenant-Colonel "Red George" Macdonell, now in command of the lst Light Infantry Battalion at Kingston, was directed to write privately to Ogdensburg that Sir George Prevost was "as much disposed as ever to respect every species of private property if not forced by western aggressions to retaliate, which I trust will never be the case."[3] Macdonell's letter, addressed to Parish's nephew and dated September 4, added that he made "frequent enquiries about my Ogdensburg acquaintances" and, should the war end shortly, he hoped to see some of them "even without a white handkerchief."[4]

Yet trouble was brewing. Realizing that he had been right all along, and wrong to let Commodore Chauncey and Major-General Dearborn ruin his spring plans, Secretary of War John Armstrong spelled out another plan to a new commanding general on August 8: "Operations westward of Kingston, if successful, leave the strength of the enemy unbroken. It is the great depot of his resources. So long as he retains this, and keeps open his communication with the sea, he will not want the means of multiplying his naval and other defences, and of reinforcing or renewing the war in the West."[5] Kingston should either be captured that autumn by direct action, or cut off from communication with Montreal by an army moving down the St. Lawrence River and securing both its banks in the vicinity of the present town of Morrisburg. The rest of the army could then continue against Montreal, being joined by the lesser army from Lake Champlain. Armstrong informed his senior general that, "in conducting the present campaign, you will make Kingston your primary *object*, and that you will *choose* (as circumstances may warrant), between a *direct* and *indirect* attack upon that post."[6]

President Madison had approved this plan in outline, but he had also approved the appointment of Major-General James Wilkinson to command Military District No. 9. Its 14,357 American regulars, including 2,528 non-effectives, were divided between Lake Champlain (4,053), Sackets Harbor (3,668) and the Niagara frontier (6,636). Wilkinson was now next in seniority to Dearborn, but practically every regular officer regarded him with antipathy or contempt. A veteran of the Revolutionary War, Wil-

Major-General James Wilkinson (1757-1826)
An officer with a very unsavoury background, Wilkinson became the senior American general on the northern frontier in the summer of 1813. (National Portrait Gallery, NPG 75.15)

kinson had been appointed to the regular army in 1791. Subsequently he had quarrelled with "Mad Anthony" Wayne, had been involved in Aaron Burr's conspiracy to separate Louisiana from the United States, and had been the centre of several lesser intrigues of which courts-martial had been unable to convict him.[7]

To make matters worse, a personal enemy of Wilkinson's, Major-General Wade Hampton, had previously agreed to assume command of the Lake Champlain region, on the distinct understanding that his was a separate command with direct communication to Washington; only in the event of a combined movement of armies would he have to accept direction from another field general. The Secretary of War pacified Hampton, when he learned of Wilkinson's appointment, by promising that all orders and reports should pass through the War Department, but Hampton declared that he would resign as soon as the coming campaign ended. Hampton, who had managed to become a man of means following his brief service in the Revolutionary War, had accepted appointment to the regular army only in 1808 and was generally considered to be a competent officer. *Niles' Weekly Register* announced with "great pleasure" on August 14 that

Hampton is busily employed in making *soldiers* of the *officers* of the army at *Burlington* [in Vermont]. They are frequently and severely drilled; and given to understand that they must and shall ascertain and perform their several duties. This is striking at the very root of our disasters. The best materials for an army that the world could furnish, have been sacrificed to the pompous ignorance or inconsiderable courage of those who should have applied them to victory.[8]

Hampton's main failing, and one that was not uncommon on the American frontier, was a "too free use of spiritous liquors."[9]

A council of war summoned by Major-General Wilkinson soon after his arrival at Sackets Harbor on Friday, August 20, unanimously agreed to the following version of Armstrong's plan:

> To rendezvous the whole of the troops on the lake in this vicinity, and in co-operation with our squadron to make a bold feint upon Kingston, slip down the St. Lawrence, lock up the enemy in our rear to starve or surrender, or oblige him to follow us without artillery, baggage, or provisions, or eventually to lay down arms; to sweep the St. Lawrence of armed craft, and in concert with the division under Major-General Hampton to take Montreal.[10]

Wilkinson then departed for Niagara, where he became incapacitated by fever. Only on October 2 did he finally return to Sackets Harbor, where during this month the Secretary of War had been personally supervising preparations for the forthcoming operations. Commodore Chauncey's fleet shortly followed, bringing with it the U.S. regulars then at Niagara.[11] This left only Brigadier-General George McClure's brigade of New York militia to garrison Fort George and the several posts on the American side of the Niagara river.

Chauncey's squadron had chased Yeo's ships into Burlington Bay on September 28. There Yeo lost 5 killed and 13 wounded. He wrote Admiral Warren that "the great advantage the Enemy has over us from their long 24 Pounders almost precludes the possibility of success, unless we can force them to close Action, which they have ever avoided with the most studied circumspection."[12] According to Chauncey's report to Washington, however, his own U.S.S. *Pike* had her main topgallant mast shot away early in the action and 27 killed or wounded among her crew. "At the time I gave up the chase," he wrote, "this ship was making so much water, it took all our pumps to keep her free, owing to us receiving several shot so much below the water edge that we could not plug the holes from the outside."[13]

Commodore Chauncey had better luck on October 5, when he captured six of seven schooners transporting the two flank companies of De Watteville's Regiment and a considerable number of sick and wounded from York to Kingston. Major-General de Rottenburg, having learned from American deserters of Wilkinson's concentration at Sackets Harbor, had decided to reinforce Kingston. He had already transferred to Kingston his military headquarters for Upper Canada. Travelling by bateaux from York along the north shore of Lake Ontario, the 49th and 104th Regiments of Foot and the Canadian Voltigeurs arrived there safely on the following Thursday and Friday.[14]

Sir George Prevost had removed to Montreal from Kingston on September 25, because of the news that Major-General Hampton had crossed the border of Lower Canada near Odelltown six days earlier. This was an effort to distract attention from American activity at Sackets Harbor. Prevost had then ordered Lieutenant-Colonel "Red George" Macdonell to follow him from Kingston with his lst Light Infantry Battalion. Major-General Sheaffe had already called out 3,000 sedentary militia in Lower Canada. Prevost now requisitioned 5,000 more. Dr. William Dunlop, who was travelling from Montreal by road to join the 89th Regiment of Foot in Upper Canada, encountered several of these French-speaking units of sedentary militia and later wrote:

> We came up with several regiments of militia on their line of march. They had all a serviceable effective appearance – had been pretty well drilled, and their arms being direct from the tower [of London], were in perfectly good order, nor had they the mobbish appearance that such a levy in any other country would have had. Their capots and trowsers of home-spun stuff, and their blue *tuques* (night caps) were all of the same cut and color, which gave them an air of uniformity that added much to their military look, for I have always remarked that a body of men's appearance in battalion, depends much less on the fashion of their individual dress and appointments, than on the whole being in strict uniformity.
>
> They marched merrily to the music of their voyageur songs, and as they perceived our [scarlet] uniform as we came up, they set up the Indian War-whoop, followed by a shout of *Vive le Roi* along the whole line. Such a body of men in such a temper, and with so perfect a use of their arms as all of them possessed, if posted on such ground as would preclude the possibility of regular troops out-manoeuvering them, and such positions are not hard to find in Canada, must have been rather a formidable body to have attacked.[15]

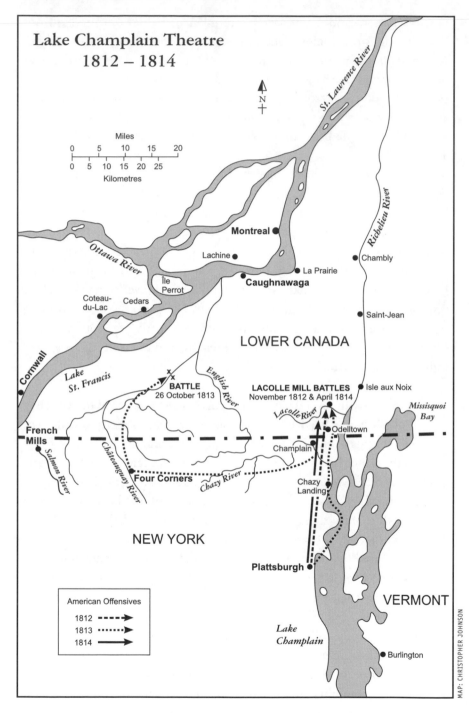

Lake Champlain Theatre
1812 – 1814

N

Miles
0   5   10   15   20
0   5 10 15 20 25
Kilometres

St. Lawrence River

Ottawa River

Montreal ●

Lachine ●

Île Perrot ●

Coteau-du-Lac ●   Cedars ●

Caughnawaga

La Prairie ●

Richelieu River

Chambly ●

Saint-Jean ●

LOWER CANADA

Cornwall ●

Lake St. Francis

English River

X X
BATTLE
26 October 1813

LACOLLE MILL BATTLES
November 1812 & April 1814

Isle aux Noix ●

Lacolle River

Odelltown ●

Missisquoi Bay

French Mills ●

Salmon River

Châteauguay River

Four Corners ●

Chazy River

Champlain ●

Chazy Landing ●

NEW YORK

Plattsburgh ●

VERMONT

American Offensives	
1812	---▶
1813	·····▶
1814	——▶

Lake Champlain

Burlington ●

MAP: CHRISTOPHER JOHNSON

The American advance into Lower Canada had, however, been discouraged both by the offensive-minded activities of nearby Canadian outposts and by a lack of drinking water for both men and horses. A summer of scanty rainfall had caused the wells and small streams in the area to become dry. A council of war agreed, however, that there should be enough water along the more circuitous route of the Châteauguay River. Major-General Hampton therefore led his army back into New York state and marched about 40 miles westward to the Châteauguay River. Here plenty of water was found. The Secretary of War approved both this change and Hampton's request for reinforcements. Colonel Robert Purdy, who had taken command of the 4th U.S. Infantry Regiment on September 18, later wrote of Hampton's force: "The army, consisting of about 4,000 men, was composed principally of recruits who had been but a short time in the service, and had not been exercised with that rigid discipline so essentially necessary to constitute the soldier. They had indeed been taught various evolutions, but a spirit of subordination was foreign to their views."[16]

Sir George Prevost could not be expected to divine this. On October 8 he wrote Lord Bathurst from Montreal about his concern at the threat to communications with Upper Canada:

> The position of Major-General Hampton at the Four Corners on the Châteauguay River, and which he continues to occupy, either with the whole or a part of his force, from the latest information I have been able to obtain from hence, is highly judicious, – as at the same time that he threatens Montreal and obliges me to concentrate a considerable body of troops in this vicinity to protect it, he has it in his power to molest the communication with the Upper Province, and impede the progress of the supplies required there for the Navy and Army.[17]

The same letter added that "His Majesty's [French-] Canadian Subjects have a second time answered the call to arms in defence of their Country with a zeal and alacrity beyond all praise." Yet the greater part of these 8,000 sedentary militia were not issued muskets, since they were intended to handle the supply and transport needs of the nearly 6,000 regulars, fencibles and select embodied militia stationed along the Montreal frontier or in reserve. Command of the line of frontier was now exercised by the Swiss-born Major-General de Watteville, who had accompanied his own foreign regiment to Canada in the past spring, while Major-General

Sheaffe commanded the reserve.[18] The two battalions of Royal Marines, with their artillery companies, which Admiral Warren had despatched from Halifax when he received news of the naval defeat on Lake Erie, were moving up river from Quebec.

On October 16 the American Secretary of War wrote Hampton respecting Wilkinson's approaching move down the St. Lawrence River. Hampton was ordered to "approach the mouth of the Châteauguay, or other point which shall better favour our junction, and hold the enemy in check."[19] Therefore on Thursday morning, October 21, Hampton for the second time crossed the border into Lower Canada with 4,000 infantry, 200 dragoons and 10 field guns. The two brigade columns were accompanied by a large number of loaded farm wagons and moved slowly, because the bridges over every small stream had been destroyed earlier. By late Friday evening, however, the advanced guard was within 15 miles of where the Châteauguay River empties into the St. Lawrence. The next two days were spent improving the roads and waiting for the remainder to catch up. As was by now becoming customary, practically the whole of Hampton's 1,400 New York militia had refused to cross into Canada.

Meanwhile Lieutenant-Colonel de Salaberry was preparing a defensive position nearby, where the Châteauguay River made a fairly sharp bend. Here the river was 40 yards wide and five or six feet deep, but there was a ford a short distance farther down stream. The road, which ran about 300 yards from the left bank of the river, was intersected at the bend by a ravine; a tract of cleared land here provided a limited field of fire for the de-

Lieutenant-Colonel Charles de Salaberry (1778-1829)

A regular officer in the British army, the French-Canadian de Salaberry was the victor at Châteauguay on October 26, 1813, which blunted the American drive on Montreal from the Lake Champlain area. (Sketch by Anson Dickinson, after engraving by A.B. Durand, National Archives of Canada, C-9226)

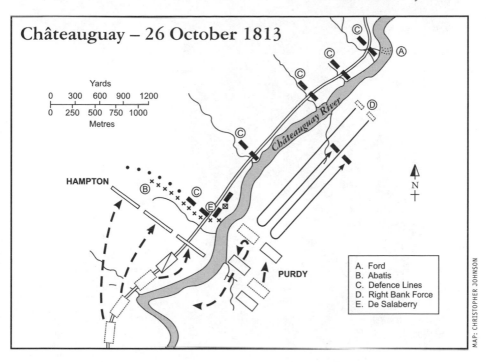

Châteauguay – 26 October 1813

Yards
0 300 600 900 1200
0 250 500 750 1000
Metres

HAMPTON

Châteauguay River

N

PURDY

A. Ford
B. Abatis
C. Defence Lines
D. Right Bank Force
E. De Salaberry

MAP: CHRISTOPHER JOHNSON

fenders of a line of breastworks and abattis which were erected at the edge of the continuing forest. They also built a blockhouse. Second and third lines were subsequently constructed from the river's edge to a marshy thicket on the far side of the road, to provide the necessary defence in depth (B on map).

De Salaberry posted 50 Canadian Fencibles, 150 of his own Canadian Voltigeurs, 100 sedentary militia and a few Indians behind this first line of defence. Two companies of select embodied militia and a company of sedentary militia, with a total strength of about 160 all ranks, were deployed on the right bank to cover the ford (A and D on map). About a mile and a half to the rear, on the left bank, was Lieutenant-Colonel George Macdonell with a supporting force of 300 Canadian Voltigeurs, 480 of the 2nd Battalion, Select Embodied Militia, 200 sedentary militia and about 150 Indians. These dispositions were visited and approved by Major-General de Watteville, and the men awaited the American advance with some confidence.[20]

On the Monday afternoon of October 25, American reconnaissance patrols reported to Hampton that the defences to their front were held by only 350 men, mostly militia, and that the position could be turned by a

185

Canadian Voltigeur and warrior ally
The Voltigeurs were a long-service provincial unit raised in Lower Canada that often fought alongside their native allies during the war. (Painting by G.A. Embleton, courtesy Parks Canada)

flanking force skirting the right bank of the river as far as the ford and wading across it. Hampton ordered Colonel Purdy to execute such a flanking movement during the night with 1,500 officers and men of the lst Infantry Brigade. Even the best troops in the world, however, would have found difficulty covering 15 miles on such a night, stumbling along a narrow, winding trail through dense woods. Only about six miles were covered. Thoroughly lost by daylight, the guides then led the Americans to the river bank almost opposite De Salaberry's forward defences. Here they came under fire.

Hampton's main body advanced in mid-morning for a frontal attack, but postponed any determined assault of the abattis in the hope that Purdy's brigade would still be able to execute the planned manoeuvre. Some time after noon, Purdy's advanced guard did finally get near the ford, only to come under fire from the three Canadian militia companies on the right bank. The Americans also now discovered the existence of Macdonell's supporting force to the rear. Surprised and alarmed by the racket deliberately created by Macdonell's men, Purdy's force of Americans soon began to retreat. This action proved to be contagious as soon as it was observed from the other bank by Hampton's main body. Both American columns retired in an orderly manner, however, and only a few Indians attempted to pursue them. The main body of Americans had hardly been involved and their casualties were about 50 officers and men; De Salaberry lost 5 killed, 16 wounded and reported 4 missing.[21]

Prevost and De Watteville arrived on the scene in time to justify their submission of despatches, and their action made it impossible for De Salaberry to submit an official report of his own on the victory he had won. The Legislative Assembly of Lower Canada, however, thanked him officially. The Prince Regent decided to provide colours for each of the five battalions of Select Embodied Militia in recognition of the part played by various companies and individuals during this skirmish at the ford which came to be called the Battle of Châteauguay. Yet too little attention has been paid to the fact that at least one company of partially trained sedentary militia was as heavily engaged as the Canadian Voltigeurs and Select Embodied Militia, both of whom were trained to the same standard as the British regulars serving elsewhere in Lower Canada. Undoubtedly the most important thing to note about the Battle of Châteauguay is that all the successful defenders were Canadians, whether they were English-speaking or French-speaking.[22]

Major-General Hampton retreated back across the border to the village of Châteauguay, New York. Convinced that there was no longer any sense in the Secretary of War's grandiose plan for cutting the Canadas in two, he put the question to a council of war and received the following answer:

> It is the unanimous opinion of this council, that it is necessary for the preservation of this army and the fulfilment of the ostensible views of the government, that we immediately return by orderly marches to such a position as will secure our communications with the United States, either to retire into winter quarters, or to be ready to strike below.[23]

Hampton was correct in assuming that the Secretary of War no longer expected Major-General Wilkinson to capture either Kingston or Montreal. Intelligence that Major-General de Rottenburg had managed to increase the garrison of Kingston had caused Armstrong to agree with Wilkinson that it was now too strong to be attacked. The Secretary of War also believed, although he did not bother to inform Wilkinson, that it was too late in the season to attack Montreal with any real hope of success. He had issued orders on October 16 that winter quarters should be constructed on Canadian soil above Montreal.[24]

Wilkinson did not know this when his army of between 7,000 and 8,000 officers and men left Sackets Harbor on the night of October 17, bound for an attack on Montreal. There were Major Forsyth's riflemen to spearhead the advance, 14 regiments of infantry, two regiments of dragoons and three regiments of artillery. There were 300 bateaux and other small boats for transportation, and 12 gunboats for protection. Yet gale-like winds and snowstorms kept the expedition among the Thousand Islands until November 5, when the weather was finally good enough to continue down river. Wilkinson was now bothered by a recurrence of fever and was not well enough to exert effective command.

News of the continued American movement reached Kingston the same evening; only then did De Rottenburg implement the instructions issued by Sir George Prevost as early as October 12. Prevost had then directed that, if the American force moved down river, the 49th and 89th Regiments should be sent in pursuit, under the command of Lieutenant-Colonel Joseph W. Morrison of the 89th. Morrison had been in action only as a lieutenant in the Netherlands campaign of 1799, when he had been badly wounded, but Prevost regarded him as an "active and intelligent officer."[25] His force amounted to 630 rank and file: the nine companies of the 89th totalled about 450 men, but the battalion companies of the 49th Foot had been reduced by casualties to a total of about 160 men and there were less

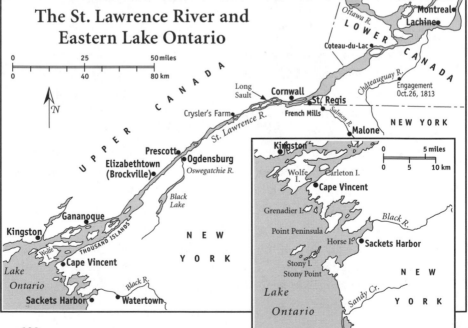

The St. Lawrence River and Eastern Lake Ontario

MAPS: ROBIN BRASS STUDIO

than a score of artillerymen with two 6-pr. field guns. This force embarked in the schooners *Lord Beresford* and *Sir Sydney Smith*, seven gunboats and a number of bateaux on Saturday night, November 6. Naval command was entrusted by Sir James Yeo to his favourite subordinate, Commander William Howe Mulcaster, R.N., who was serving as a captain on Lake Ontario.[26]

Wilkinson's expedition was now approaching Prescott. Since the guns of Fort Wellington commanded the St. Lawrence at Prescott, Wilkinson landed his army above Ogdensburg, floated the empty boats down river in the dark, and then re-embarked the troops. The Canadian farmers were turning out as militiamen to take pot shots at the expedition wherever the river narrowed, so Wilkinson ordered 1,200 troops to land on the Canadian shore at Iroquois, below Prescott, as an advanced guard and drive them off. This they succeeded in doing. On the following night, November 8, after the troops had camped on shore, he called a council of war to consider whether the expedition should proceed. Four of the brigadier-generals voted to attack Montreal; the other two declared that "we proceed from this place under great danger ... but we know of no other alternative."[27] Brigadier-General Jacob Brown was ordered to land his brigade of 2,500 men, with detachments of artillery and dragoons, on the Canadian shore and combine with the advanced guard to clear the way to Cornwall. Brigadier-General John Parker Boyd was detailed to form the troops not needed to navigate the boats through the Long Sault Rapids into a rear guard to oppose the pursuing British force, whose existence had finally been reported to Wilkinson.

Lieutenant-Colonel Morrison's pursuing force landed at Prescott on Tuesday morning, November 9. His "corps of observation" was augmented there by a detachment of 240 troops commanded by Lieutenant-Colonel Pearson. These consisted of the two flank companies of the 49th Foot, a detachment of Canadian Fencibles, three companies of Canadian Voltigeurs, a handful of militia artillerymen with a 6-pr. gun and half a dozen Provincial Dragoons to serve as couriers. Morrison now had a force of roughly 900 officers and men.[28] Captain Mulcaster had to leave his armed schooners at Prescott but his gunboats pressed on to harass the American boats farthest in the rear.

Rain and sleet fell almost continuously during the night November 10/11 and the troops of both armies huddled under any shelter they could find. The Americans were within sight of the Long Sault Rapids, with the British close enough to interfere with their further movements. Lieutenant-

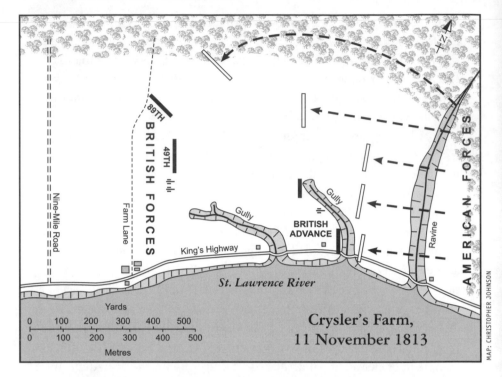

Crysler's Farm,
11 November 1813

MAP: CHRISTOPHER JOHNSON

Colonel Morrison, who had established his headquarters in John Crysler's spacious farmhouse, decided that he had a good defensive position should the Americans choose to turn on him. From the farmhouse a dirt road ran at right angles to the river as far as an impassable swamp about half a mile inland. The log fences lining this road provided cover for the battalion companies of the 49th Regiment and six companies of the 89th. To their front was a large field sprouting fall wheat; beyond that were a ploughed field, two gullies and a sizeable ravine. Between the two gullies and astride the road to Montreal was Pearson's detachment from Prescott. The right flank of his advanced position rested on the steep river bank; his left flank was protected by the 89th Regiment's remaining three companies which were arranged in echelon (or staggered) under the command of Captain George West Barnes. One of the force's three 6-pr. guns supported each of the unequally sized commands. The three companies of grey clad Canadian Voltigeurs were extended farther forward as skirmishers, in the vicinity of the large ravine. About 30 Indians from Tyendinaga were in the woods.

About eight o'clock on the Thursday morning of November 11, which was bleak and grey with an east wind but no more rain, the alarm was sounded. An Indian had fired on an American reconnaissance patrol, causing each side to believe that the other was about to attack. Wilkinson took the report seriously and ordered Brigadier-General Boyd to advance his 2,000 U.S. regulars in three columns, outflank the British and capture their field guns. Naturally such a force had no difficulty driving back the skirmish line of Canadian Voltigeurs during the early afternoon. At two o'clock, however, the advancing Americans were stopped by the volley firing of the companies of the 49th and 89th Regiments. The Americans then tried to turn Morrison's left flank, but he swung the 89th's companies around almost 90 degrees to counter this successfully. The Americans were also considerably disconcerted to discover that the men wearing grey greatcoats belonged to the famous 49th Foot, and not to a militia unit. By this time Captain Mulcaster's gunboats were shelling Wilkinson's headquarters area. According to Morrison's very concise report of the battle, it was won by a combination of spirited charges by the 49th and 89th Regiments and accurate fire by the artillery:

> The 49th was then directed to charge their [American] Guns posted opposite to ours, but it became necessary when within a short distance of them to check the forward movement, in consequence of a charge from their Cavalry on the right lest they should wheel about and fall upon their rear, but they were received in so gallant a manner by the Companies of the 89th under Captn. Barnes and the well directed fire of the Artillery that they quickly retreated and by an immediate charge from those Companies one Gun was gained. The Enemy immediately concentrated their Force to check our advance but such was the steady countenance and well directed fire of the Troops and Artillery that about 9 past four they gave way at all points from an exceeding strong position, endeavouring by their Light Infy. to cover their retreat, who were soon driven away by a judicious movement made by Lt. Col. Pearson.[29]

Morrison reported his own casualties for the Battle of Crysler's Farm as being 22 killed, 148 wounded and 9 missing. Boyd had foolishly committed his columns in a piecemeal fashion and in consequence had to report 102 killed and 237 wounded. Considerably more than 100 Americans became prisoners.[30]

Meanwhile the American advanced guard, capably led by Brigadier-General Brown, had cleared away the few Canadian defenders of the bridge over Hoople's Creek and opened the road to Cornwall. Yet how could

Wilkinson, even though his main force was still intact, hope to cope with the forces Sir George Prevost was gathering in front of Montreal?

This question was answered by the letter which reached him from Major-General Hampton on the following morning, November 12, after his troops had re-embarked and negotiated the Long Sault Rapids. Convinced that the Secretary of War did not count on Montreal being captured in 1813, Hampton refused to join Wilkinson near St. Regis. This made it easy for Wilkinson's inevitable council of war to blame Hampton for the abandonment of an attack on Montreal. Wilkinson then wrote Hampton that "such resolution defeats the grand objects of the campaign in this quarter, which, before the receipt of your letter, were thought to be completely within our power, no suspicion being entertained that you would decline the junction directed, it will oblige us to take post at French Mills, on Salmon river, or in their vicinity for the winter."[31] Knowing that the Secretary of War had issued orders as early as October 16 to have such winter quarters constructed on the shore of the St. Lawrence, Hampton had already tendered his resignation. He had no intention of being made the scapegoat. Wilkinson in the end did spend the winter with his army at French Mills, while most of the British troops returned to either Prescott or Kingston.[32]

Commodore Sir James Yeo was anxious to claim credit for Wilkinson's failure. "Had any part of this [British] Squadron been lost, taken, or rendered unserviceable, nothing could have saved Upper Canada," he explained in a private letter to the First Lord of the Admiralty on December 6.[33] "Your Lordship can have no idea what a wretched class of Vessels I found on this Lake – all with flat bottoms like our River Barges, and no one in good property belonging to them. Gun Brigs are very far superior to them. The Moira has at least twenty 24 pdr Shot thro' her Hull, and I verily believe not a shot of hers ever reached the Enemy. – I have always been obliged to tow her in, and out of action to prevent her being cut off by the numerous small Vessels of the Enemys Squadron." With the navigation season now at an end, Yeo's whole attention was being directed to the completion of two frigates, which he looked upon "as the foundation of a force that will for ever Command the Naval Superiority on Lake Ontario." Since both would be too large for anyone to command in the rank of commander, he had authorized Captain Mulcaster to act as a post captain and now requested approval for this appointment.[34]

The 300 seamen requested from Halifax in the spring had finally reached Kingston in September, and had been followed by 150 more in October, in consequence of Barclay's defeat on Lake Erie. Yet wastage had been considerable and Yeo would need an additional 250 seamen to meet his greater commitments for the coming year, when he hoped to destroy Commodore Chauncey's opposing squadron.[35]

Chauncey's last act of the season had been to transfer from Niagara to Sackets Harbor the brigade recently brought by Harrison from Detroit. These troops were needed to protect Chauncey's naval base, which had been virtually without defenders since Wilkinson's departure. In consequence there were no U.S. regular garrisons between the Detroit River and Sackets Harbor, and only a few hundred New York militia guarding the whole Niagara frontier. Since the New York militia refused to serve beyond their specified engagement, by December 10 Brigadier-General McClure had only about 100 men left at Fort George.

McClure wisely abandoned Fort George and re-crossed the river to Fort Niagara when he heard a rumour that the British "were advancing in force" to recover the Niagara frontier.[36] Unfortunately, however, he saw fit to burn the village of Newark, and much of nearby Queenston, after turning the inhabitants out into a cold winter night with only a few minutes' notice and leaving them to find shelter as best they could at the nearest farmhouses. "This step has not been taken *without counsel*," he wrote the Secretary of War, "*and is in conformity with the views of your Excellency expressed in a former communication*." Admittedly a letter of Armstrong's of October 4 had included the following sentence: "Understanding that the defense of the post committed to your charge, *may* render it proper to destroy the town of Newark, you are hereby directed to apprize its inhabitants of this circumstance, and to invite them to remove themselves and their effects to some place of greater safety."[37] Yet Armstrong obviously had meant McClure to burn Newark only in the event that he meant to defend the adjacent Fort George and needed to improve his field of fire, and he certainly had intended the inhabitants to be given more consideration. Possibly McClure was encouraged in his nefarious act by Lieutenant-Colonel Joseph Willcocks, a member of the Upper Canada Legislative Assembly who had defected earlier in the year and formed a renegade corps of Canadian Volunteers. Certainly Willcocks and his 70 fellow traitors played a major role in the actual burning of Newark.[38]

The United States Government promptly disavowed McClure's action, but the damage had been done and bitterness remained. "The enemy is much exasperated, and will make an attack on this frontier if possible," McClure reported to the Secretary of War from Fort Niagara on December 13;

> but I shall watch them close with my handful of men until a reinforcement of militia and volunteers arrives. ... I am not a little apprehensive that the enemy will take advantage of the exposed position of Buffalo and our shipping there. My whole effective force on this extensive frontier does not exceed two hundred and fifty men.[39]

McClure was right in assuming that the British had offensive operations in mind. On December 16 Lieutenant-General Gordon Drummond reached the Niagara Peninsula and relieved Major-General de Rottenburg as Administrator of Upper Canada. The 41-year-old Drummond had seen active service in The Netherlands, West Indies, and Egypt; he had been a major-general in the Canadas from 1808 to 1811 and subsequently a lieutenant-general commanding troops in southern Ireland.[40] He was accompanied by Major-General Phineas Riall, who replaced Major-General Vincent in command of all troops west of Kingston. This command now become the Right Division of the Army.[41] The 38-year-old Riall was an Irishman who had experienced battle only in the West Indies, but had been promoted to the rank of major-general in the preceding June. Vincent was in ailing health, but he temporarily took command of the Centre Division based on Kingston and the Upper St. Lawrence. De Rottenburg resumed command of the larger troop concentration in Lower Canada, now designated the Left Division of the Army. Major-General Sir Roger Sheaffe was conveniently returned to England, while Major-General Procter was relegated to the command of whatever troops might be at York until Sir George Prevost could further investigate his sorry conduct at the Battle of the Thames.[42,43]

No time was now wasted. During the early morning hours of December 19, Lieutenant-Colonel John Murray led 550 British regulars across the Niagara River. The Canadian militia navigated the bateaux across the rapidly flowing river, and the regulars then bayoneted the sentries and rushed the main gate of Fort Niagara. Not a shot was fired, but 67 Americans were killed and 11 wounded. British casualties were only 5 killed and 3 wounded. Fort Niagara was retained by the British for the balance of the war.

Major-General Riall followed with the battalion companies of the Royal

Scots and 41st Foot and a band of Indians to destroy the village of Lewiston. During the night of December 29, Riall again crossed the Niagara River, this time above the Falls and with about 1,500 British regulars and Indians. These burned the villages of Black Rock and Buffalo; they then destroyed four armed schooners and large quantities of American supplies before returning to the Canadian shore.

Sir George Prevost, in a proclamation of January 12, 1814, deprecated the need for such action, which had been taken in retaliation for the American burnings at Newark and Queenston. This proclamation also assured the inhabitants of Upper Canada that they would be "powerfully assisted at all points by the troops under His Excellency's command, and that prompt and signal vengeance will be taken for every fresh departure by the Enemy, from that system of warfare, which ought alone to subsist between enlightened and civilized nations."[44]

Prevost could not yet afford to relax his efforts but he would soon know that they were appreciated in London. Lord Bathurst's despatch of December 15, 1813, written before the good news of either Châteauguay or Crysler's Farm had reached London, magnanimously absolved him of blame for earlier misfortunes. Lord Bathurst did, however, take him to task for complaining about receiving no detailed instructions, since distant campaigns could not be directed from London on the basis of intelligence that would be several months old by the time orders could get to Canada. "It was therefore in every point of View considered expedient," this letter continued,

> to place at your disposal such means of defence as the Exigency of the Service required, & to leave their direction or distribution to your own discretion, more especially as the correct View which you expressed on the two points most essential to the Defence of the Canadas, the maintenance of a Naval Superiority on the Lakes, & the uninterrupted Communication with our Indian allies had at an early period received the Sanction of H. M. Government, & had been repeatedly recalled to your attention during the course of the preceding campaign.[45]

In view of what had happened to Barclay's squadron on Lake Erie, however, Lord Bathurst wrote that he could only approve of Commodore Sir James Yeo's discretion in avoiding battle under conditions which did not afford a fair prospect of success:

The preservation of the fleet under his Command is (next to the destruction of that of the Enemy) the object most essential for the Security of Canada. So long as it remains entire the Enemy are precluded from attempting with any hopes of Success the attack for which their means are preparing & their Troops collected – of the Numbers of the Enemy's force, tho' considerably increased, I confess that I feel but little apprehension, when I consider the Number & Composition of the force by which they will be opposed. It is as you observe not sufficient to conceive the idea of moving armies in Concert from different Quarters to act simultaneously on a given point, & I cannot but hope that previous to the Execution of this Project an opportunity may yet be afforded you of separately attacking one of these Armies before it can be supported and thus either repairing the failure of this Campaign or of opening the next with Vigour and Success.[46]

After learning that the American armies of Hampton and Wilkinson had been separately beaten at Châteauguay and Crysler's Farm, Lord Bathurst wrote that Prevost should continue to act on his own good judgment:

I am aware of the weight of your Responsibility, of the Clamour which will at times arise at any failure, or the advance of the Enemy on any part of the wide extended frontier of the Canadas.

But Justice will always be done you. The Result of Campaigns is that to which the Public will always look. Against occasional failures no man can guard. An extended line of frontier cannot be everywhere defended, against the Troops which the Enemy may be able, with their resources on the spot, to collect; with a force double what you have, if Great Britain could afford it, it might be imprudent to undertake it. The very advance of the Enemy to a given point may in many Cases be desirable, as furnishing the fairest opportunity of bringing on a decisive engagement in an open country, where your collected force might have the means of being employed to the greatest advantage.[47]

At the end of 1813 American troops held Amherstburg and controlled the whole Detroit frontier, and American sailors had undisputed command of Lake Erie, but the Union Jack still waved over every location on "the wide extended frontier" that was essential for a successful defence of the rest of Canada during the next year's campaigning season.

PART IV

1814: On the Offensive

Royal Marine recruiting poster, c. 1812-1814

H.M.S. *Prince Regent*, **1814**
Launched in April 1814, this powerful frigate, armed with 58 guns and carronades,
assured Yeo naval superiority on Lake Ontario in the early summer of 1814.
(Watercolour by H.T. Davies, courtesy of the National Archives of Canada, C-138986)

CHAPTER ELEVEN

Occasional Enterprises: December 1813 to May 1814

OSWEGO / SANDY CREEK

The conduct of this strange little war took an unexpected turn after the British ship *Bramble* arrived at Annapolis, Maryland, on December 30, 1813.

As early as the autumn of 1812, while Napoleon was advancing on Moscow, the Czar of Russia had proposed himself as mediator of the Anglo-American conflict. President Madison was moved to accept the offer when news came of Napoleon's retreat from Moscow, since this event opened up the possibility of there being a French defeat in Europe which would release large British armies for service in North America. Madison sent his Secretary of the Treasury, Albert Gallatin, and a leading Federalist politician, James A. Bayard, as a special mission to Russia on May 9, 1813. Lord Castlereagh was too astute a Foreign Secretary to risk offending Britain's most powerful ally in the European war, but there could be no thought of permitting the Czar to mediate this dispute over maritime rights. Britain and Russia had differences in the past over similar issues and might again in the future; Russia could not be disinterested. Lord Castlereagh evaded the issue as long as possible and then advised the Czar that Great Britain would prefer to negotiate a settlement directly with the United States. Hence *Bramble* brought a letter from Lord Castlereagh, dated November 4, 1813, suggesting that British and American commissioners should meet to negotiate a peace settlement.

The London newspapers brought to the United States by *Bramble* contained official reports of the three-day Battle of Leipzig, in which Napoleon had been so badly beaten by the Allies that he would probably have to abandon Germany completely. Except for France, the coastline of Europe was now open to British commerce. This knowledge would encourage American Federalists to become more vehement in their opposition to what had always seemed to them an ill-advised challenge to British interests in Europe. President Madison, further depressed by the latest news from the Niagara frontier, was able to persuade Congress to accept Lord Castlereagh's offer. The Senate approved his nomination of John Quincy Adams, Albert Gallatin, John A. Bayard, Jonathan Russell, and Henry Clay as peace commissioners. The first four Americans were already in Europe and Henry Clay sailed on January 9 to join them. Some months would, however, be taken up in travel and negotiation; meanwhile the war would go on.

Madison's Secretary of State, James Monroe, suggested to Sir George Prevost the desirability of concluding an armistice for the interval in North America. The approach was made through Brigadier-General William Winder, who had been captured at Stoney Creek but later permitted to return to the United States on parole, in an effort to secure better treatment for the 23 British soldiers held in close confinement as hostages for 23 American prisoners captured in 1812 and shipped to England for trial as being treasonable native-born British subjects. It will be remembered that three known deserters from the British Army had been found among the captured garrison of Fort Mackinac and others had been among the Ohio volunteers serving at Detroit. But no system of identification then known was perfect, and mistakes could just as easily be made about soldiers as they were about American seamen wrongly impressed into the Royal Navy. The American prisoners in England had not been brought to trial, for fear of American retaliation against the hostages held in the United States; however, Sir George Prevost had subsequently been ordered to place double that number of Americans in close confinement in Lower Canada. Both sides realized, of course, that there had to be an end to such petty reprisals.

Once again Colonel Edward Baynes negotiated on behalf of Sir George Prevost, and quickly agreed with Winder to a convention that would lead to an exchange of all prisoners held in Canada and the United States, except for the actual hostages. Sir George Prevost did not have authority to accept the armistice suggested by the American Government, but he stressed the desirability of such a step in letters to both Commodore Sir James Yeo and Admiral Sir John Warren, and in despatches to Lord Bathurst. At this late date, however, the British Government was determined to negotiate an advantageous peace with the United States and did not want its bargaining position undermined by any act of Sir George Prevost, who was curtly advised by return mail merely to continue the war as he was directed.

Prevost's judgment had been influenced by the purely military difficulties of the coming campaign. He was discouraged by the belief that only one of the four British regiments promised him was likely to reach Canada in the early spring. "Experience has taught me that reinforcement even by the most direct route to this Country cannot arrive in time to give a decided Character to the Campaign," he had written to Lord Bathurst on January 14, "as inevitably the principal events must have occurred before they can ascend the St. Lawrence to their destination."[1] The number of British regulars and fencibles (including as usual the Canadian Voltigeurs) already in the Canadas was nearly 900 officers and 15,000 other ranks, but many were sick or recuperating from wounds and all were exhausted by the rigours of the preceding campaign. Major-General Glasgow's minimum artillery requirement for 1814 had been estimated as three more companies of Royal Artillery and enough drivers for five or six field brigades. He had pointed out to Sir George Prevost that, although he had five companies of regular artillery totalling 585 gunners and 144 gunner-drivers, he had been unable to man the batteries on the extensive frontiers of the Canadas without employing regular infantry and the militia, leaving his brigades of field artillery with only half their regular complement. Only the two battalions of Royal Marines and their artillery companies, totalling about 1,600 all ranks, were really in good condition. Following the example of a year earlier, therefore, Prevost had ordered the 2nd Battalion of the 8th (or King's) Regiment of Foot to march overland from New Brunswick to Quebec City as an immediate reinforcement.

Wishing to improve his position in any way possible, Prevost was agreeable to a suggestion advanced by Lieutenant-General Gordon Drummond and Commodore Sir James Yeo that they lead a winter expedition to destroy the American naval vessels frozen into the ice at the far end of Lake Erie, but emphasized in his letter of January 29 to Drummond that troops already in Upper Canada would have to be employed. The balance of his letter was incapable of being misunderstood:

Whilst the Enemy continues to concentrate a large disposable Force near the frontier of Lower Canada situated between Lakes St. Francis and Champlain, thereby indicating his Intention, that the Pressure of the approaching Campaign should fall upon that Province, You must be sensible of my total inability of augmenting your present Force. I give you this information that you may regulate your measures accordingly.[2]

As early as February 3, however, Drummond had changed his mind. On February 19 he wrote Prevost that it was "totally impracticable, from the lateness of the Season, and the unusually mild weather during the entire of this winter, to make an attempt, with any reasonable hope of success, against the Enemy's Vessels, upon Lake Erie, and their Force at Detroit."[3]

While this correspondence was going on, comparably mild weather had made the overland journey from New Brunswick of the 2nd Battalion of the 8th Regiment far less rigorous than that of the 104th Regiment a year earlier. The same journey by sleighs and snowshoes was also made by Commander Edward Collier with 216 officers and men of the Royal Navy and Royal Marines. These comprised the crews of four war vessels, which had to be laid up, and volunteers from other vessels wintering at Halifax. According to the *Quebec Gazette* of March 10, the people of New Brunswick had shown fine public spirit in their efforts to assist those making the journey:

> The liberality of the people of New-Brunswick, in the assistance they have afforded to the 2nd battalion of the King's Regiment, and to the detachment of Seamen, recently arrived at Quebec overland from that Province, deserves public thanks. The inhabitants of the City of St. John, alone, gave three hundred pounds for the hire of sleighs to carry the Seamen and Soldiers from that place to Fredericton; and the House of Assembly of the Province voted an equal sum (£300) to convey them on their route from Fredericton as far as it was possible for sleighs to proceed.[4]

Commander Collier's detachments, minus three deserters and 23 sick men, who would follow later, continued on foot to Kingston and reached their final destination during the fourth week in March. They had been on the road for 53 days.

This naval reinforcement of 191 officers and men solved Commodore Yeo's immediate manpower needs, already assisted by the Admiralty's authorization of the dissolution in Canada of the 2nd Battalion of Royal Marines and the employment of its personnel on his ships. The almost completed frigates *Prince Regent* and *Princess Charlotte* would be more than a match for the two brigs nearing completion at Sackets Harbor, but Yeo was alarmed by reports that work had begun there on two larger ships. He persuaded Sir George Prevost to ask for 30 long 32-pr. guns and 30 32-

pr. carronades from the Halifax navy yard for a ship of the line which he proposed to lay down as soon as the frigates were launched.[5]

Meanwhile Sir George Prevost had been sorely tried by the squabbles in the Legislature of Lower Canada which he had opened on January 13. The Assembly was determined to impeach Chief Justices James Monk and Jonathan Sewell for the "wrong doings" of the *Château Clique* during "Craig's Reign of Terror." This English-speaking minority, which still had a majority of members in the Legislative Council, fought back: inspired by Bishop Mountain of the Church of England, it prepared to send both denunciations and delegates to London as soon as the navigation season opened. "The Catholic Clergy are my firmest supports & the Salary I obtained for the Bishop," Prevost would later write to a friend in England on July 29, "has strengthened my claim on their loyalty, zeal & influence over the people which has given great offence to the Head of our Church." Weary as he was of Canadian politics when he closed the Legislature's session on March 31, 1814, Prevost nevertheless had managed to preserve something of a philosophical calm. It was this personal tranquillity of mind that enabled him to see the impeachment proceedings in their proper colonial setting: differences between the legislative branches, and disputes over judicial appointees, were common and had recently occurred in other British colonies. He had agreed to forward the Assembly's request to London, but refused to suspend Monk and Sewell in the meantime. "Amidst all the Contests which have taken place between the two Branches of the Legislature," he would write Lord Bathurst on September 4,

> it is but justice to the House of Assembly to say that I have invariably found a disposition on their part to forward the Views of Government by promoting the measures I have submitted for their consideration, and when those measures have failed of being carried through, it has been more owing to differences between the House and Council upon points of privilege and of a personal nature, than from any desire on the part of the former to embarrass the Government, or to withhold that assistance I was entitled to expect from them.[6]

It was unfortunately true that the latest squabble had resulted in no revenue bill being passed, but Prevost could fall back on his military chest until after a new Assembly had been chosen in the elections scheduled for April, 1814.

The Legislative Council had also been intransigent in refusing to amend the Militia Act. This act permitted the service of substitutes and, as a result, certain more affluent citizens bought immunity after the ballot had been made to replenish the Select Embodied Militia and keep its strength at roughly 4,000 men. The 5th Battalion, nicknamed the "Devil's Own" because most of the original officers had been Montreal lawyers or *avocats*, had made a very poor showing during 1813, since these officers had resigned their commissions for business reasons when the battalion was moved away from Montreal and given an operational role.[7] New blood had now to be injected and the continuing six companies were reorganized as Canadian Chasseurs. This new unit was brigaded with the Canadian Voltigeurs and the Frontier Light Infantry, under the superintendence of Lieutenant-Colonel de Salaberry who now became Inspecting Field Officer of Militia Light Infantry.

The sedentary militia continued to be employed from time to time on *corvée*. According to the *Quebec Gazette* of March 10:

> The Militia of Col. Taché's division distinguished themselves in forwarding the Troops lately arrived from New-Brunswick. They conducted the 6th and 7th divisions in their carioles and sleighs, from the River du Loup to St. Roe. Several Gentlemen along the road presented refreshments to the Soldiers as they passed their houses, and had dinner for the whole of the Officers.[8]

In Upper Canada, Lieutenant-General Drummond was also preoccupied about manpower. He toyed with the idea of incorporating further battalions of militia, but was sceptical of finding the necessary men: the Volunteer Incorporated Militia Battalion raised the year before was now reduced to only 39 officers and 386 other ranks, and there were militia flank companies to be continued. His Legislature, which met from February 15 to March 14, gave him no trouble and approved the measures which he thought necessary for prosecuting the war. An act was even passed to suspend *habeas corpus*, which would make it easier to deal with treason cases. There were many of these: indictments were to be brought against more than 70 former residents of the Niagara, London and Western Districts. In the event only the 17 men actually held in custody would be tried that spring, between May 23 and June 21. One seriously ill prisoner pleaded guilty; 14 others were convicted by jury trial and sentenced to be hanged by what came to be known as the "Bloody Assize of Ancaster." Eight were hanged forthwith; the others being considered less culpable were recommended to mercy and reprieved by Drummond until the pleasure of the Prince Regent could become known.[9]

There was difficulty of another sort in the eastern part of Upper Canada where farmers were demanding exorbitant prices for provisions and forage. Drummond was forced to proclaim martial law and set prices. Lieutenant-Colonel Pearson at Prescott had put a temporary halt to trade with Ogdensburg during the winter, since he had become convinced that enemy agents were entering Upper Canada on the sleighs loaded with food and forage. Yet Drummond was to write Lord Bathurst on April 12 that he had authorized the purchase of an old printing press at Ogdensburg to replace the one earlier destroyed at York. Of course the British were active in intelligence themselves. That their agents were busy in the United States seems evident from the following order issued at Sackets Harbor on April 7, 1814:

The commanding officers of the navy and army, from recent information, know that the enemy have spies in and about the harbor. To detect and bring them to punishment is the duty of every good and honest citizen.

Any person or persons who will apprehend and cause them to be prosecuted to conviction through the commanding officer of the navy or army, shall receive five hundred dollars.

Every officer in the navy and army is ordered to apprehend all suspicious persons and every citizen is earnestly requested to report such Persons to the navy or army, that they may be immediately secured.

By April there had been considerable changes in the dispositions and intentions of the American military forces along the Canadian border. Until February 1, Major-General Wilkinson's army remained at French Mills, where it was well placed to interfere with communications between Lower and Upper Canada. Orders from the Secretary of War then sent Brigadier-General Brown to Sackets Harbor with 2,000 men and caused Wilkinson to withdraw on Plattsburgh with the remainder.

After the American forces had moved, a small force of Royal Marines and Select Embodied Militia crossed the St. Lawrence River from Cornwall on February 6 and raided the nearby village of Madrid. It brought back a considerable quantity of merchandise plundered from Canadian merchants during the previous autumn. Between February 19 and 24, larger raiding parties brought back booty by the sleigh load from Salmon River, Malone, and the Four Corners.

A month later Major-General Wilkinson made his last military effort. After some preliminary manoeuvring his three brigades, totalling 4,000 effectives, advanced from Champlain and occupied Odelltown on March 30. He then moved against the small garrison guarding the crossing of the nearby Lacolle River, about 10 miles from Isle aux Noix. His troops blundered about in the heavy snow, and his two 12-pr. guns were unable to make any impression against the thick stone mill which served as a blockhouse. At the same time the defenders' rocket artillery, manned by a detachment of Royal Marines, caused considerable casualties among the attackers. According to *Niles' Weekly Register*, "Gen. Wilkinson seems to have exposed his life with great prodigality. By a flag that came in, it appears the British officer enquired what person it was they had so repeatedly fired at, who it seems was the general."[10] The spring thaw soon forced the Americans to retire to Plattsburgh, wading through mud and water to their knees.

Wilkinson had had enough. In order to get relieved of duty without actually resigning, he requested a court of inquiry to rule on his conduct of the 1813 campaign. Orders from Washington dated March 24 granted his request. Once again he managed because of technicalities to secure a verdict of acquittal, but never again did he soldier.[11] On May 1 the newly promoted Major-General George Izard assumed command at Plattsburgh. Only 37 years old and considered by many to be the most promising officer in the United States Army, he had received his military training in Europe and had performed creditably under Major-General Hampton during 1813.[12]

Another new major-general was the erstwhile amateur, Jacob Brown. His defects in military education were to be supplied by two of the newly promoted brigadier-generals, Winfield Scott and Eleazer W. Ripley, who had been selected on their merits as regular officers. Major-General William Henry Harrison now disappeared from the United States Army. Believing him to be weak and pretentious, the Secretary of War had left him only a nominal command by transferring nearly all his troops from Military District No. 8. Harrison did the expected and tendered his resignation on May 11, 1814. It was promptly accepted and the vacancy quickly given to Major-General Andrew Jackson of the Tennessee Volunteers.

This self-taught lawyer had made quite a name for himself on the frontier prior to the outbreak of war. As Major-General of the Tennessee Militia he had organized a force of 2,000 volunteers to seize East Florida from Spain; but Spain was an ally of the Czar who wanted to act as a mediator between Britain and the United States, so the Secretary of War sent orders on February 5, 1813, for Jackson to disband his command. Only after a portion of the Creek Indians, prodded by emissaries from Tecumseh, decided in July of that year to fight the white men who were greedily trying to dispossess them of their hunting grounds did Andrew Jackson get his chance for action. The Creeks were not particularly warlike Indians and only part of the Confederacy went on the warpath. Jackson's campaign, which terminated in April 1814, had resulted in the virtual extermination of the Creeks, without the need for him to display any particular military ability or for his men to do more than shoot down and massacre Indians who were mostly without muskets. The greater part of Jackson's force had been state militia and volunteers, and they returned home as soon as their time had expired.[13]

Experience had proved that only American regulars were useful in the war against Canada. Yet in the past there had never been more than half the authorized establishment of 58,254 enlisted men fit for actual service. Congress now learned even worse news from the Adjutant General's Office: "although the numerical force in January, 1814, was 23,614, the actual strength of the army at that time was less than half that number, arising from the expiration of the term of service of the troops raised in 1809 and enlisted for five years, and of the twelve and eighteen-months men enlisted in 1812-1813." In consequence, Congress raised the enlistment bounty to $124.00, to add to the inducement of a grant of 320 acres of land on discharge. But a private soldier's pay remained unchanged at $10.00 per month. The Secretary of War could only hope that recruits would be forthcoming.

Secretary Armstrong, still convinced, and rightly so, that Kingston was a prime target, now pursued once more his endeavour to have it captured. As early as February 28 he had sent two sets of instructions to Major-General Brown at Sackets Harbor. The first suggested that Brown proceed to Niagara with the 2,000 troops he had brought from French Mills. Brigadier-General Scott had already been sent to organize a force for the recapture of Fort Niagara. Actually the Secretary of War hoped that the contents of this letter would become known to Sir George Prevost. His other, and secret, letter to Brown was intended as an operation order:

It is obviously Prevost's policy, and probably his intention, to re-establish himself on Lake Erie during the ensuing month. But to effect this other points of his line must be weakened, and these will be either Kingston or Montreal. If the detachment from the former be great, a moment may occur in which you may do, with the aid of Commodore Chauncey, what I last year intended ... and what we now all know was very practicable, viz to cross the river, or head of the Lake, on the ice, and carry Kingston by a *coup de main.*[14]

Chauncey and Brown, however, were not too ready to acquiesce. They agreed that the operation was not feasible with less than 4,000 troops and that Armstrong's other letter could be taken as an alternative plan of campaign. Therefore Brown departed from Sackets Harbor for Niagara in mid March, leaving behind less than 1,000 effective troops.

This news encouraged Lieutenant-General Drummond to contemplate an attack on Sackets Harbor, but he was unable to collect the minimum force considered necessary for such an enterprise. But by the time Drummond had journeyed to Kingston from York to look into possibilities further, the situation had again changed. On April 14 Commodore Yeo launched the frigates *Prince Regent* and *Princess Charlotte*, which would give his fleet a definite superiority over Commodore Chauncey's. H.M.S. *Prince Regent* would mount 30 long 24-pr. guns, eight 68-pr. carronades and 20 32-pr. carronades. H.M.S. *Princess Charlotte* would carry 24 long 24-pr. guns and 16 32-pr. carronades. Encouraged, on April 26 Drummond wrote Prevost suggesting an early attack on Sackets Harbor to destroy the ships and vessels there. This would be the best way of ensuring naval control of Lake Ontario and the shipment of adequate provisions to the more westerly points of Upper Canada, where the Indian allies were rapidly depleting what the Commissariat Department had in its stores. According to a further letter, written on the following day, Commodore Yeo was in complete agreement with Drummond. They might also destroy nearby Oswego. They would, however, need 800–1,000 regulars from Lower Canada in addition to the 4,000 rank and file which could be spared from the garrisons already at Kingston and to the westward.

Sir George Prevost's answer was a decided "no" to what he felt was only a gamble. He did not believe that Drummond could reduce the other garrisons in Upper Canada sufficiently to collect 4,000 regulars and fencibles at Kingston. Thus more than 1,000 troops would have to be sent from Lower Canada. According to Prevost's reply of April 30, the force in this Country is insufficient to enable me to concentrate at any one point in Upper Canada, the number of regulars you require for this important Service, without stripping Lower Canada of nearly the whole of those that are at present in it, and committing its defence to provincials and Militia. The views of His Majesty's Government respecting the mode of conducting the war with America, do not justify my exposing too much on one shake. It is by wary measures and occasional daring enterprizes with apparently disproportionate means, that the character of the war has been sustained, and from that policy I am not disposed to depart.[15]

Both H.M.S. *Prince Regent* and H.M.S. *Princess Charlotte* were finally ready for service on May 3, and Yeo and Drummond decided to make an immediate attack on Oswego "where the Enemy had, by river navigation, collected from the interior several heavy Guns, and Naval Stores for the Ships and large depots of Provisions for their Army."[16] Actually most of the long guns and naval stores had been detained at the falls about 12 miles up the Oswego River until there should be a favourable moment for small boats to carry them along the edge of Lake Ontario in safety to Sackets Harbor.

Not realizing this, but aware that Fort Oswego had been recently reoccupied by 290 American regulars, Drummond and Yeo decided that they possessed sufficient manpower resources to succeed against this illprepared fort. They had six companies of De Watteville's regiment under the command of Lieutenant-Colonel Victor Fischer, the light company of the Glengarry Light Infantry Fencibles, the not yet disbanded 2nd Battalion of Royal Marines and sizable detachments of Royal Artillery, Royal Sappers and Miners, and Royal Marine Artillery with Congreve rockets.

About noon on Thursday, May 5, Commodore Yeo's fleet arrived off Oswego. A heavy gale blew up from the northwest and delayed the assault landing until the following morning, but this time delay proved of no benefit to the American defenders. Supported by the guns of the fleet, Lieutenant-Colonel Fischer stormed ashore with 140 troops and 400 marines; Captain Mulcaster landed with 200 seamen who were armed with pikes. They had to climb a long and steep hill, under heavy fire from the small American garrison which was mostly composed of artillerymen; but once they reached the top the rest was easy. The American commander withdrew his men in good order into the countryside. He was to report 6 killed,

Attack on Oswego, 6 May 1814
Although successful, this hard-fought action did not result, as hoped, in the destruction of supplies for Chauncey's squadron at Sackets Harbor. (Lossing, *Field-Book*, 1869)

38 wounded and 25 missing. British casualties totalled 18 killed and 73 wounded; Captain Mulcaster was severely wounded while charging the enemy guns. Drummond and Yeo had accompanied the second wave of troops ashore and their staffs superintended the task of loading 2,400 barrels of flour, pork, salt and bread, seven long guns and a quantity of ordnance stores into captured schooners for removal to Kingston. The next day, May 7, the combined force returned to Kingston.[17]

Spies soon brought word to Kingston that the bulk of the 32-pr. long guns for Chauncey's recently launched ship, U.S.S. *Superior*, and a smaller brig under construction, were still at Oswego Falls. To prevent their transfer by water to Sackets Harbor, Commodore Yeo immediately established a close blockade there. On May 20 Commodore Chauncey had to report to Washington that "five sail were now anchored between Point Peninsula and Stoney Island, about ten miles from the harbor, and two brigs between Stoney Island and Stoney Point, completely blocking both passes. ... This is the first time that I have experienced the mortification of being blockaded on the lakes."[18]

Chauncey's able subordinate at Oswego, Master-Commandant Melancthon Woolsey, decided to make an attempt to reach Sackets Harbor on the night of May 28/29, with 19 bateaux carrying 21 long 32-pr. guns, 13 smaller guns and 10 heavy cables for use by the fleet. Major Daniel Appling and 130 regular riflemen went along as escort. By daybreak 18 bateaux had covered 20 miles and were met by 120 Oneida Indians who were to move along the shore as additional protection. A further 10 miles were covered that Sunday morning. With only eight miles left to travel, they pulled into Sandy Creek to await a further escort of marines and troops being despatched from Sackets Harbor, and news of Sir James Yeo's blockading vessels.

One of these had captured the other American bateau, some of whose crew had then betrayed the whole operation. Commander Stephen Popham, R.N., was sent in pursuit with two gunboats and smaller craft; *en route* he absorbed a small force under Commander Francis B. Spilsbury. This increased Popham's strength to three gunboats, four smaller craft and nearly 200 sailors and marines. Soon after daylight on Monday, May 30, he spied the masts of the American bateaux some way up Sandy Creek and decided to land and attack them. Popham had no idea that the American bateaux had a strong escort and thought that the prize to be gained was worth breaking Commodore Yeo's injunction never to enter a creek in an effort to capture enemy stores. After small parties were landed on each bank the British boats cautiously started up Sandy Creek. About half a mile below where the bateaux were now guarded by the marines and dragoons sent from Sackets Harbor, the advancing British were ambushed by the American riflemen and Indians. After losing 14 killed and 28 wounded, Popham quite sensibly surrendered: "The winding of the creek, which gave the enemy a great advantage in advancing to intercept our retreat, rendered further resistance unavailing."[19]

Tactically this was only a minor skirmish, but it had important results. Immediately Commodore Yeo was short the boats captured but, much more serious, 200 officers and men from his inadequate naval establishment. The American bateaux safely reached Sackets Harbor with the remaining guns for U.S.S. *Superior*. This 62-gun ship would give Chauncey command of Lake Ontario as soon as it was ready for action. Since Lieutenant-General Drummond agreed with Commodore Yeo's contention that there was no longer any purpose in blockading Sackets Harbor, the naval squadron returned to Kingston on June 6. "The Enemy are not in

Lieutenant-General Gordon Drummond (1772-1854)
The fourth British commander in Upper Canada, he proved the most capable after Brock. (Courtesy, McCord Museum, M400)

sufficient force to undertake any expedition in the face of our present Squadron," Yeo had written to Drummond three days earlier, "but any disaster on our Side, might give them a serious ascendancy."[20] By this time both Drummond and Yeo knew that, with Napoleon defeated in Europe, the British Government would be sending considerable reinforcements to Canada. A "fleet in being" would be most necessary to carry out whatever orders Sir George Prevost would be receiving from London, and Drummond therefore advised Yeo that

> there exists at present no motive or object connected with the security of this Province which can make it necessary for you to act otherwise than cautiously on the *defensive* (but at the same time closely watching all their movements) until the moment arrives, when by the addition of the large Ship now on the Stocks, you may bring the naval contest on this Lake fairly to issue, or by a powerful combined Expedition (if the Enemy, as is probable, should decline meeting you on the Lake) we may attack and destroy him in his stronghold.[21]

Once more there was the familiar recommendation for caution. The early months of 1814 had not been particularly favourable to the British defenders of Canada, but now at long last there was every expectation that offensive action would soon be possible.

CHAPTER TWELVE

Summer Stalemate in Upper Canada:
June to September 1814

CHIPPAWA / LUNDY'S LANE /
FORT ERIE / MACKINAC

The worst fears of President Madison were to be realized in this spring of 1814. On March 31 the armies of the European Allies had made a triumphal entry into Paris; the Duke of Wellington's Peninsular Army was still fighting its way northward from Bordeaux and had one more battle to win, at Toulouse on April 10. On the day following, at Fontainebleau, Napoleon abdicated unconditionally and was permitted to retire to the tiny island of Elba. On April 14 Lord Bathurst wrote Sir George Prevost that this favourable turn of events would make it possible to send a large reinforcement of artillery and infantry to North America.

Barely ten weeks before, on January 28, Lord Bathurst had sought the Duke of Wellington's opinion as to what might be attempted in North America once the fighting in Europe was concluded. The Duke had replied truthfully on February 22 that he knew little about American affairs or topography, but just the same the views he expressed were most cogent:

> I believe that the defence of Canada, and the co-operation of the Indians, depends upon the navigation of the lakes; and I see that both Sir G. Prevost and Commodore Barclay complain of the want of the crews of two sloops of war. Any offensive operations founded upon Canada must be preceded by the establishment of a naval superiority on the lakes.
>
> But even if we had that superiority, I should doubt our being able to do more than secure the points on those lakes at which the Americans could have access. In such countries as America, very extensive, thinly peopled, and producing but little food in proportion to their extent, military operations by large bodies are impracticable, unless the party carrying them on has the uninterrupted use of a navigable river, or very

extensive means of land transport, which such a country can rarely supply.

I conceive, therefore, that were your army larger than the proposed augmentation would make it, you could not quit the lakes; and, indeed, you would be tied to them the more necessarily in proportion as your army would be large.

Then, as to landings upon the coast, they are liable to the same objections, though to a greater degree, than an offensive operation founded upon Canada. You may go to a certain extent, as far as a navigable river or your means of transport will enable you to subsist, provided your force is sufficiently large compared with that which the enemy will oppose to you. But I do not know where you could carry on such an operation which would be so injurious to the Americans as to force them to sue for peace, which is what one would wish to see.[1]

The plan of campaign finally decided upon was not committed to paper in final form by Lord Bathurst until June 3, and Sir George Prevost did not receive it until the second week in July. This lengthy secret document is printed in the Appendix, but the gist of it must be given here. In doing so, however, it is important to emphasize that the British Government had two objects in mind. The first was to guarantee the safety of Canada during the balance of the war. The second was to secure the basis of a satisfactory boundary rectification by enabling British peace commissioners to argue *uti possidetis* (or, for retention of conquered territory).

The 4th Battalion of the lst (or Royal Scots) Regiment had already sailed from England for Quebec, where it would be joined by the Nova Scotia Fencibles from Newfoundland and the 90th Regiment from the West Indies. The 1/6th and 1/82nd Regiments had sailed from Bordeaux and would be followed by "twelve of the most effective Regiments of the Army under the Duke of Wellington together with three Companies of Artillery on the same service."[2] Thus Prevost would shortly receive an increase of 3,127 rank and file, and ultimately 10,000 further British troops. With these he might well carry out the designated operations in the Canadas:

When this force shall have been placed under your command, His Majesty's Government conceive that the Canadas will not only be protected for the time being against any attack which the enemy may have the means of making, but it will enable you to commence offensive operations on the Enemy's Frontier before the close of this Campaign. At the same time it is by no means the intention of His Majesty's Government to encourage such forward movements into the Interior of the American Territory as might commit the safety of the Force placed under your command. The object of your operations will be; first, to give immediate protection: secondly, to obtain if possible ultimate security to His Majesty's Possessions in America.

The entire destruction of Sackets Harbour and the Naval Establishments on Lake Erie and Lake Champlain come under the first description.

The Maintenance of Fort Niagara and so much of the adjacent Territory as may be deemed necessary: and the occupation of Detroit and the Michigan Country come under the second.

If our success shall enable us to terminate the war by the retention of the Fort of Niagara, and the restoration of Detroit and the whole of the Michigan Country to the Indians, the British Frontier will be materially improved. Should there be any advanced position on that part of our frontier which extends towards Lake Champlain, the occupation of which would materially tend to the security of the Province, you will if you deem it expedient expel the Enemy from it, and occupy it by detachments of the Troops under your command, always however taking care not to expose His Majesty's Forces to being cut off by too extended a line of advance.

If you should not consider it necessary to call to your assistance the two Regiments which are to proceed in the first instance to Halifax, Sir J. Sherbrooke will receive instructions to occupy so much of the District of Maine as will secure an uninterrupted intercourse between Halifax and Quebec.[3]

Four other regiments from Europe would be employed in a direct operation against the American coast. A "considerable force" would also be concentrated at Cork for employment in "a more serious attack on some part of the Coasts of the United States" later in the year. "These operations," this letter advised Prevost, "will not fail to affect a powerful diversion in your favour."

On July 5 the Military Secretary wrote to Prevost from the Horse Guards in London that all of the fourteen regiments from Wellington's army were now on their way across the Atlantic Ocean. The Duke of Wellington had selected Major-Generals Thomas Brisbane, James Kempt,

Manley Power and Frederick Philipse Robinson – all of whom had performed creditably under his command – to lead the brigades in which they were grouped. Rumours of the coming of men from the Peninsula flew about in the United States: one report, untrue, had it that Lieutenant-General Sir Thomas Picton of Peninsular fame had been selected as an overall field commander.

As early as April 30, the Secretary of War in Washington had advanced a plan which would make the most of the time available before British reinforcements could get to Canada, but President Madison could not get agreement for it from the members of his Cabinet until June 7. The decision was again, mistakenly, to direct the main effort against the Northwest and the Niagara Peninsula, instead of against Kingston or Montreal, because, it was held, the U.S. Navy had undisputed command of Lake Erie but was still inferior on Lake Ontario. Then Major-General Jacob Brown could easily land an army of 5,000 regulars and 3,000 volunteers on the Canadian shore close to where Lake Erie empties into the Niagara River. After capturing Fort Erie, he could move through the Niagara Peninsula against Burlington and York. The Secretary of War, however, had bitterly but unsuccessfully opposed another decision to send the garrison of Detroit against Fort Mackinac rather than use it to increase Brown's army. "Burlington and York carried," he had argued,

> a barrier is interposed which completely protects Detroit and Malden, makes doubtful and hazardous the enemy's intercourse with the western Indians, reduces Mackinac to a possession perfectly useless, renders probable the evacuation of Fort Niagara, and takes from the enemy half his motive for continuing the naval conflict on Lake Ontario. On the other hand, take Mackinac, and what is gained but Mackinac itself?[4]

The rest of the American Cabinet were also responsible for the suggestions that Major-General George Izard's army should make a feint from Plattsburgh against Montreal, and that several posts should be occupied along the St. Lawrence River from which 15 gunboats would be made available to attack convoys of supplies moving up river from Montreal. Commodore Chauncey's letter of June 15 to the Secretary of the Navy mentioned that 200 boats had passed Ogdensburg for Kingston during the previous week. Lieutenant-General Drummond's letter of June 28 to Sir George Prevost stated that Sir James Yeo "has taken measures for affording

Brigadier-General Winfield Scott (1786-1866)
One of the most aggressive American commanders of the war, Scott was representative of a new generation of American generals who had gained their experience on actual service. (*Portfolio Magazine*, 1816)

to every Brigade of Batteaux or Craft, a suitable convoy of Gun boats; which I trust will preserve it from injury, if not from insult."[5] Izard was not in the event ordered to take any action, however, and Commodore Yeo later reported this to the British Admiralty as an "extreme stupidity" which had cost the Americans the war.[6]

The American Cabinet was led to believe that Commodore Chauncey's fleet would be able to support Major-General Brown's army in its final advance along the shore of Lake Ontario. By then the long guns of U.S.S. *Superior* should have guaranteed him superiority over Yeo's frigates, while the new U.S.S. *Mohawk* of 42 guns would also be available. "I shall sail the first week in July to offer the enemy battle," Chauncey wrote on June 24; but this extremely cautious officer was to manufacture various reasons to avoid leaving Sackets Harbor until August 1.[7]

The strength estimated for Brown's army proved to be yet another miscalculation. He had barely 3,500 regulars and volunteers, instead of 8,000. Winfield Scott's brigade had only 65 officers and 1,319 enlisted men present for duty. These, mostly from New England, were being turned into first class troops by their young commander. The second brigade of regulars, commanded by Brigadier-General Eleazer Ripley, numbered 1,027 officers and men. There were 327 regular artillerymen, and about 600 Pennsylvania volunteer militia commanded by Brigadier-General Peter B. Porter. There were also 600 Indian warriors of the Six Nations living on reservations in New York State, but these were no more dependable than the braves eating British rations on the opposite shore of the Niagara River.[8]

The British troops scattered in garrisons along the Niagara Frontier were now less effective than in the winter when Lewiston, Black Rock and Buffalo had been raided successfully. The 8th (or King's) Regiment at Fort Niagara was plagued by illness and desertion, the latter actually being on the increase because the men were finally getting their arrears of pay. "The Men are Sick of the place," Major-General Phineas Riall had earlier reported to Drummond at Kingston, "tired & disgusted with the constant labor to which they see no end & have got sulky & dissatisfied."[9] The usual antidote, a "Ration of Spirits," was not having the desired effect. He wished to destroy all but one segment of Fort Niagara, which could be garrisoned by 85 regulars, and make the remaining troops available for mobile operations. Drummond's answer was that retention of Fort Niagara was extremely important, since it provided a secure harbour for Commodore Yeo's squadron at the western end of Lake Ontario. Furthermore, a British garrison of 500-600 men at Fort Niagara might induce the Americans to divert up to ten times that number for its capture.

This letter of March 23, actually written by the Deputy Adjutant General, Lieutenant-Colonel John Harvey, explained in considerable detail what Major-General Riall should do if the Americans invaded the Niagara Peninsula. If they came in sufficient numbers, Riall would have to leave the garrisons of the mutually supporting Forts Niagara and Fort George to look after themselves and concentrate the balance of his troops as a field force. The enemy would have to detach men to besiege these forts and this should reduce the main American army sufficiently for Riall to meet it on even terms in the open. The poor opinion held of American troops caused Harvey to instruct this newcomer to the war that his troops could be left strung out along the length of the Niagara River until the last moment, when they could still be concentrated more rapidly than the enemy would be able to move:

> In the disposition of so comparatively small a force, as you are likely to have for the defence of the Niagara Frontier, the arrangement would naturally strike a Military Man unacquainted with the character of the Enemy he has to contend with, or with the events of the last two Campaigns on that Frontier, would be to concentrate the Troops in some Central Position from whence they could be moved to either extremity, or to whatever Point was invaded.

Such an arrangement however would leave the extremities of the

Line open to Attack and would actually invite Invasion, and the Persons and Property of the Inhabitants would be left exposed to the outrages of the smallest Parties of the Enemy's marauders. – Experience moreover has proved that a small Force may be distributed along the Frontier without any great risque of being cut Off – It is therefore Lt. General Drummonds wish, that the Distribution of the Force should be made with reference to that of the last and preceding Campaigns (previous to the Attack of the Enemy on Fort George on the 27th of May last) and that all the Stations which were then occupied from Fort George to Fort Erie (but no further) should be now occupied.[10]

About 800 American marauders, as Harvey feared, did land, at Port Dover on the afternoon of May 14, and they burnt every building between there and Turkey Point within the next 24 hours. Once again the worst of the depredations, at the village of Long Point, were the work of the renegade Canadian Volunteers, this time led by Major Abraham Markle who also had been a member of the Upper Canada Legislative Assembly. These renegades were out to settle old scores with former neighbours and anxious to convince the American authorities of their zeal for the new cause. Five days later a small party of Americans raided nearby Port Talbot. Colonel Thomas Talbot was absent when they called at the backwoods manor house from which he administered his extensive Talbot Settlement, and fortunately for him he was absent on every occasion during the summer when American raiders from Amherstburg visited Port Talbot. These were led by former residents who bore personal grudges against this unpopular autocrat. Throughout the London and Western Districts of Upper Canada, the raiders pursued a policy of disorganizing local militia units by kidnapping their officers, before setting fire to the houses and barns of the most loyal residents.[11]

Lieutenant-General Drummond had planned to build some war vessels for service on Lake Erie, but by June 7 he had decided that it was too late in the season to attempt it. Once naval command of Lake Ontario had been guaranteed by the completion of Commodore Sir James Yeo's 102-gun ship of the line at Kingston, stores could be forwarded by water to the head of the lake for transfer by land during the winter of 1814-15 to Turkey Point, where a dockyard could then be established. Drummond, however, did become alarmed by the reported activities of Major-General Brown's American army. The 103rd Regiment had been forwarded from Kingston to Burlington, and the Glengarry Light Infantry Fencibles sent to York as a further reserve for Major-General Riall's Right Division of the Army, but in a letter of June 21 Drummond begged Sir George Prevost to provide more troops for the Niagara Peninsula. "I am of opinion," he wrote,

> that the Enemy's principal designs are intended against that [the Niagara] Frontier, a reoccupation of which would prove of such essential service to them, and of such incalculable injury to us; and that they will strain every nerve to effect so desirable an object – and I conceive their manoeuvres in the neighbourhood of Plattsburg to be merely for the purpose of preventing our sending sufficient reinforcements for the security of their intended point of attack.[12]

Prevost was, however, not impressed by this line of reasoning. Although it happened to be correct, it ran counter to the defensive strategy he had been practising for the past two years. "Very much obliged to Genl. D. for his opinion," Prevost scribbled on the letter; "unfortunately for him it is not founded on fact as not one soldier intended for U.C. has been prevented moving forward by the Enemy's Demonstrations in the vicinity of Odle Town [in Lower Canada]."[13]

On July 2 Drummond wrote again from Kingston that he was sending on the recently arrived 90th Regiment of Foot to Niagara. "At present the proportion of disposable force is very inconsiderable," this letter went on to explain, "when the number of those employed in the Forts and Batteries is deducted."[14] About 600 effectives of the 41st Regiment were now occupying Fort Niagara; 1,500 regulars of the lst Royal Scots and the 100th Regiment were garrisoning the several posts along the Canadian shore from Fort George to Fort Erie. Also on the Niagara frontier were a detachment of the 19th Light Dragoons, two troops of Provincial Dragoons, the flank companies of Lincoln Militia and a dwindling company of militia artillery. About 500 effectives of the 103rd Regiment were in reserve at Burlington, and nearly 1,000 rank and file of the 8th Regiment and Glengarry Light Infantry Fencibles at York.

Major-General Jacob Brown wisely decided to leave Fort Niagara alone and took his army across the river above Niagara Falls on the early morning of July 3. Scott's brigade landed below Fort Erie; Ripley's brigade landed above; the Indians gained the open rear of the weakly defended fort. The garrison of only two companies of redcoats surrendered late that day.

As soon as news of the invasion reached Fort George, Major-General Riall rode to Chippawa, followed by five companies of the Royal Scots to reinforce its garrison. The 8th Regiment, which was due to return that day from a period of rest at York, was to join him there. Meanwhile Lieutenant-Colonel Thomas Pearson had moved forward from Chippawa with the flank companies of the 100th Regiment, some militia, and a few Indians to establish contact with the enemy.

On the morning of July 4, Brigadier-General Winfield Scott's brigade led the American advance along the road towards Chippawa. Late in the afternoon, as Scott neared the Chippawa River, he discovered Riall's force positioned on its far bank. Since this river was 150 yards wide, and crossable only by the road bridge close to where it flows into the Niagara River, Scott withdrew two miles to Street's Creek for the night. The flat plain between the two water obstacles and the two forces was split longitudinally by a strip of thick woods extending to within less than a mile of the Niagara River.

Brown was anxious to attack on the following day, July 5, before the inferior British force could be reinforced. The Pennsylvania volunteers and Indians were sent to clear the intervening woods of Canadian militia and Indians but they were driven back in confusion. The 8th Regiment now having arrived on the scene, Riall decided to attack with his 1,500 regulars, 300 militia and Indians. His ignorance of the surrender of Fort Erie led him to assume incorrectly that a strong enemy force must be investing it and that he was not opposed by more than 2,000 Americans. Riall was also encouraged in his action by the instructions from Harvey previously quoted: these had indicated liberties might be taken with an enemy army of amateur soldiers.

He was facing a new enemy, however, and Brigadier-General Winfield Scott had no intention of shirking a fight. Instead of retiring behind Street's Creek, he deployed his three battalions on the plain beyond. Throwing his flanks obliquely forward, to prevent being outflanked and to enable them to take the British centre in enfilade, he also ordered an advance. According to his own report, Riall "immediately moved up the Kings Regiment to the right while the Royal Scots and 100th Regt. were directed to charge the Enemy in front, for which they advanced with the greatest Gallantry, under a most destructive fire. I am sorry to say, however, in this attempt they suffered so severely that I was obliged to withdraw them, finding that their further Efforts against the superior numbers of the

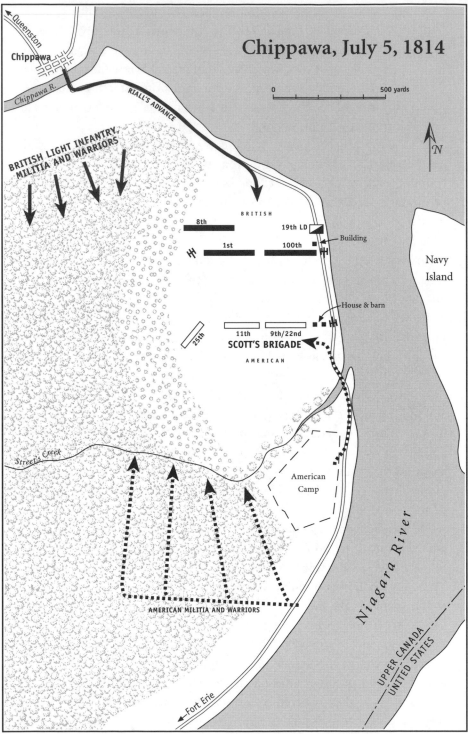

Chippawa, July 5, 1814

0   500 yards

N

Queenston

Chippawa

Chippawa R.

RIALL'S ADVANCE

BRITISH LIGHT INFANTRY, MILITIA AND WARRIORS

BRITISH

8th

19th LD

Building

1st   100th

Navy Island

House & barn

25th

11th   9th/22nd

SCOTT'S BRIGADE

AMERICAN

Street's Creek

American Camp

Niagara River

AMERICAN MILITIA AND WARRIORS

Fort Erie

UPPER CANADA
UNITED STATES

Enemy would be unavailing."[15] Actually Scott's brigade was slightly smaller than Riall's command, but the American musketry and artillery fire had proved far more accurate and destructive. Riall reported 148 killed, 321 wounded and 46 missing; Scott's brigade had only 48 killed and 227 wounded in this Battle of Chippawa.[16]

Major-General Riall managed to withdraw his troops across the Chippawa River to safety. Two days later, however, the Americans crossed at two places some distance higher up the river and he had to withdraw farther to Fort George in order to avoid being surrounded. Thereupon the Americans occupied Queenston and began to fortify the Heights, until such time as Commodore Chauncey's squadron should appear off Fort George and force the British to retreat to Burlington. The overly cautious Chauncey had not left Sackets Harbor, however, being afraid of what Sir James Yeo might attempt in his absence.

Lieutenant-General Drummond now ordered the Volunteer Incorporated Militia Battalion of Upper Canada to proceed from Kingston to Fort George and the 89th Regiment to York; the flank companies of the 104th Regiment were also to go to the provincial capital. Drummond wrote Sir

The Battle of Chippawa, 5 July 1814
American victory in this action made British commanders realize that, after two years of war, the United States army had become an opponent that had to be respected.
(Painting by C.H. McBarron, U.S. Army Center of Military History)

223

George Prevost on July 13 that, as soon as the five companies of the Canadian Fencibles reached Kingston from Lower Canada, he would go to Burlington himself. According to this letter, the need for reinforcements and the supplies to maintain them was urgent:

> The Royals, & 100th Regt. are in the greatest want for Officers. – The latter has but one Captain, & 3 Subalterns doing duty, and about 250 effective Men.
>
> Major-General Riall calls upon me strongly for, and indeed expects, reinforcements; But Your Excellency must be well aware, that I have not a man to send him; and that those expected from the Lower Province

Upper Canada Militia officer, 1814
On campaign, soldiers of the time dressed as comfortably as possible and this militia officer's broad-brimmed hat was a useful item. (Painting by G.A. Embleton, DND, Canada)

Soldier, Incorporated Militia of Upper Canada, 1814
This unit, enlisted for the duration of the war and led and trained by regular British officers, saw hard service in the Niagara in 1814. (Painting by G.A. Embleton, DND, Canada)

cannot be calculated at arriving higher than Cornwall, before the latter end of this week. – I have, however, ordered the Glengarry Light Infantry to proceed to Burlington, and the 89th on its arrival at York, leaving there its Boy Companies to follow the same Route. ...

And as Troops cannot be forwarded without Provisions, I have requested Sir James Yeo to send his two Brigs up, immediately, with as much Flour & Pork, as they can carry, to York and Burlington.[17]

The day before, Sir George had written Lord Bathurst that the 6th, 82nd and 90th Regiments newly arrived at Montreal were on their way to Upper Canada. As soon as they arrived, Drummond should be able to take the offensive.

Drummond reached York in company with the 89th Regiment on the evening of July 22, and almost immediately reported to Prevost on the desperate supply situation, and the measures he was taking to deal with it:

The two Brigs the Star and Charwell got up in safety to this place with their cargoes, which has in a great measure assisted us in our straightened circumstances as regards Provisions, tho' even this additional Supply is by no means adequate to the necessary consumption. Two Brigades of Batteaux are on their way up loaded with Provisions, which if they arrive in safety will further relieve us, tho' even then our Supply will be very far from sufficient. I have therefore been under the necessity of ordering all the Women and children, of the Troops, to be sent down from Niagara, Burlington, and York, and the families of the Indians to be placed on Half Allowance, with a view of decreasing as much as possible the issues. The sedentary Militia have been for some time called out for service at this Post, but I find it absolutely impracticable to keep them any longer, as the whole produce of the neighbouring country is in the greatest danger of being lost.[18]

Commodore Chauncey had made no attempt to interfere with this movement by water, or to send forward from Sackets Harbor the 24-pr. guns needed for an American siege of Fort George and the new but smaller fortification on Mississauga Point. Major-General Brown was becoming increasingly aware of his own growing weakness at Queenston. His field force was reduced by casualties and sickness to 2,644 effectives and there was no source from which reinforcements might be obtained. On July 24 he suddenly retreated to Chippawa and camped on the battlefield there. Brown planned to bring supplies across the river from Fort Schlosser, and transfer all his surplus baggage there, before continuing his offensive by an advance across country towards Burlington.[19]

As soon as Brown had left Queenston, Major-General Riall had immediately pushed forward an advanced guard of 1,000 regulars under Lieutenant-Colonel Pearson. Early on the Monday morning of July 25, it took up a defensive position on a hill where Lundy's Lane intersected the portage road, about a mile inland from Niagara Falls. There was open countryside for about a mile and a half on both sides of Lundy's Lane, which then entered a considerable wood as it continued inland. About the same time Lieutenant-General Drummond reached Fort George from York with the 89th Regiment and decided on another course of action: 500 regulars and Indians were ordered to advance from Fort Niagara along the American shore of the river and attack enemy installations at Lewiston, while Lieutenant-Colonel Joseph W. Morrison led his 89th Regiment to the support of Major-General Riall. The latter was now moving the balance of his 1,500 troops, with four guns, to join Pearson's advanced guard. Riall's force reached Lundy's Lane shortly after seven o'clock on Monday morning.

When Major-General Brown learned that a British force was advancing towards Lewiston, he naturally became alarmed about the safety of his supplies at Fort Schlosser and decided that the most effective counter was to advance himself towards Queenston. Therefore Brigadier-General Scott's brigade of 1,072 officers and men moved forward from Chippawa again about five o'clock on Monday afternoon.

Unknown to the Americans, the British expedition against Lewiston had been cancelled and the force of 500 redcoats and Indians by now had re-crossed the Niagara River at Queenston, where it found Morrison and also Drummond who had come on from Fort George. Most of the force was sent back to Fort George, but detachments of the Royals and King's Regiments and the light company of the 41st continued forward with the 89th Regiment. This increased Morrison's strength to nearly 800 rank and file. A few miles further back Colonel Hercules Scott of the 103rd Regiment was on the road with 1,200 regulars and militia and two 6-pr. guns, from Burlington.

It was early evening by the time Winfield Scott reached Lundy's Lane. A hasty reconnaissance suggested that he was opposed by an equal number of redcoats, but he deployed his brigade into line anyway and prepared to

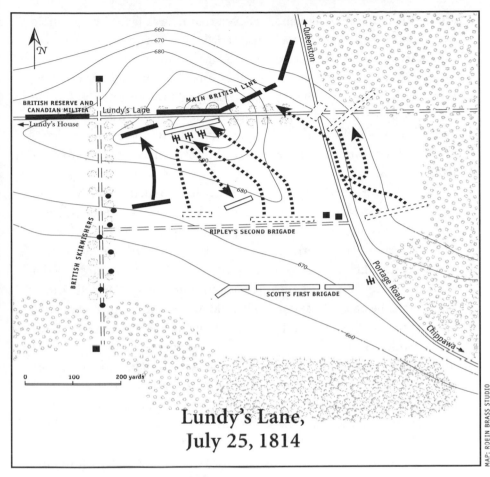

Lundy's Lane,
July 25, 1814

MAP: ROEIN BRASS STUDIO

This map shows the crucial event of the battle – the capture of the British artillery by Ripley's Second Brigade. After Scott's First Brigade had been decimated by the British guns, Ripley arrived and moved forward to the base of the hill and then attacked out of the dark. One of his regiments was repulsed but the other two accomplished their task. At this point, Drummond withdrew north of the hill and the latter stage of the battle saw him launch a series of unsuccessful counter-attacks to recapture his artillery.

attack. Riall, on the other hand, believed that he was faced by the whole American army and ordered a retreat. Fortunately Drummond, who had ridden on ahead from Queenston, arrived in time to countermand this last order. Within a few minutes Morrison's force also arrived. Drummond formed what were now slightly more than 1,600 troops into line on the northern slope of the hill where Lundy's Lane crosses it. Riall's two brass 24-pr. guns were advanced to the crest of the rise; two 6-prs. and an artillery detachment with Congreve rockets were also to be engaged in this defensive battle.

The initial American attack around 7 P.M. drove back the British left and reached the lane. Major-General Riall, badly wounded, was captured when his stretcher-bearers became confused by the twilight and headed in the wrong direction. The Americans failed to make any impression on the centre of the line, however, despite repeated attempts. "Of so determined a Character were their attacks directed against our Guns," reported Drummond after the battle, "that our Artillery Men were bayonetted by the Enemy in the Act of loading, and the muzzles of the Enemy's Guns were advanced within a few Yards of ours."[20] Yet each time the redcoated infantry drove them back. By nine o'clock, when the American brigades of Ripley and Porter arrived on the scene, Scott's brigade was reduced to about 600 effectives. One regiment of Ripley's brigade managed to capture the British guns on the crest, by advancing silently under cover of some shrubbery until within a few yards of the top, while British attention was concentrated on the frontal attack being launched by the battalion next in line. The balance of Ripley's tiny brigade succeeded in pushing back the weary defenders of the British left still further and defeat seemed possible, until Colonel Hercules Scott's 1,200 footsore redcoats and militia finally arrived to restore the situation.

It was now 10 o'clock at night and the battle became even more confused. Drummond reported that the guns were recaptured, together with an American 5.5-in howitzer and a 6-pr. gun; "and in limbering up our Guns at one period, one of the Enemy's Six Pounders was put, by mistake, upon a limber of ours, and one of our six limbered on one of his, by which means the pieces were exchanged, and thus, though we captured two of his Guns, yet, as he obtained one of ours, we have gained only one Gun."[21] Attack and counter-attack continued until midnight, with the opponents firing at musket flashes and mostly at ranges of only 10 to 15 yards.

By this time both Brown and Scott were suffering from severe wounds and the American command had devolved on Brigadier-General Ripley. "While retiring from the field," Brown would later report,

> I saw and felt that the victory was complete on our part, if proper measures were promptly adopted to secure it. The exhaustion of the men was, however, such as made some refreshment necessary. They particularly required water. I was myself extremely sensible of the want of this necessary article. I therefore believed it proper that General Ripley and the troops should return to camp, after bringing off the dead, the wounded, and the artillery; and in this I saw no difficulty, as the enemy has ceased to act.[22]

Such an evaluation of the British and Canadians appears absurd since in the first place they had been fighting a defensive battle, were now dead tired, and could hardly do anything further in the dead of the night.

Thus ended in disengagement what was to become known as the Battle of Lundy's Lane. American casualties were reported as being 171 killed, 572 wounded, and 110 missing. Drummond, who himself was severely wounded, admitted to having had 84 killed, 559 wounded, 193 missing, and 42 taken prisoner. The hardest hit unit was the 89th Foot, with 254 casualties. The Incorporated Militia Battalion of Upper Canada suffered 142 casualties, but the 500 Lincoln and York militiamen had only one killed and 19 wounded.

More British reinforcements were *en route* to Upper Niagara, but the American army on the Niagara frontier could not be replenished. This became painfully obvious to Brigadier-General Ripley in the cold light of the following morning. Therefore, as Drummond wrote, the enemy "abandoned his Camp, threw the greater part of his Baggage, Camp Equipage and Provisions into the rapids, and having set fire to Streets Mills, and destroyed the Bridge at Chippawa, continued his retreat in great disorder, towards Fort Erie."[23] Americans may argue with some reason that the hard fought Battle of Lundy's Lane was a draw, but Ripley's hasty retreat made it a tactical victory for Drummond. Had he followed closely on the heels of the retreating Americans and forced them to fight again, victory might have been complete.[24]

Ripley favoured a return to the American shore of the Niagara River, but the wounded Major-General Brown insisted that Fort Erie be retained as a bridgehead. If Drummond's recent experience and heavy losses had not made him overly cautious, the unfinished works of Fort Erie could have been overrun quickly and easily. There was still only an incomplete earthwork, about 150 yards distant from the shore, mounting three guns, but open in the rear. American engineers, however, now quickly built rear bastions. A wide ditch and seven-foot earthwork stretching to the shore completed the defences on the right. A similar earthwork was extended westwards in a long curving line to encompass what became a fortified camp with its open rear on Lake Erie. Brigadier-General Edmund P. Gaines had been called from Sackets Harbor to command the American army, now only 2,200 officers and men, until Major-General Brown should recover. The more junior Brigadier-General Ripley resumed command of his brigade.

All this was done before August 3, when Drummond at last approached Fort Erie. De Watteville's Regiment having finally arrived from Kingston, Drummond now had well over 3,000 regulars with him, and about 2,000 more elsewhere in the Right Division of the Army. Yet he felt obliged to write Prevost on the following day that "the inefficient State & composition of many of the Regiments are such as to detract greatly from the confidence which their numbers might otherwise inspire."[25] He would therefore not attempt an assault until heavy guns could be brought from Fort George to batter a breach in the defences.

On August 5 Commodore Chauncey's naval squadron finally appeared off Fort George. He was too late to co-operate with the American army which, he now hastened to point out to Major-General Brown, had never been able to approach Lake Ontario at any point nearer than Queenston; but Chauncey left small war vessels to blockade Forts George and Niagara when he sailed his new ships back to the eastern end of the lake to resume the blockade of Kingston and prevent further troops and supplies reaching Lieutenant-General Drummond by water. As Sir George Prevost explained in a despatch of August 14 to Lord Bathurst, "the Naval Ascendancy possessed by the Enemy on Lake Ontario enables him to perform in two days what our Troops going from Kingston to reinforce the Right Division required from Sixteen to Twenty of severe marching to accomplish; their Men arrived fresh whilst ours are fatigued, and with an exhausted equipment; the route from Kingston to the Niagara Frontier exceeds Two Hundred and Fifty Miles and passes in several places through a tract of Country impenetrable for the conveyance of Extensive supplies."[26] Actually there were no American reinforcements to send to Fort Erie, but Prevost

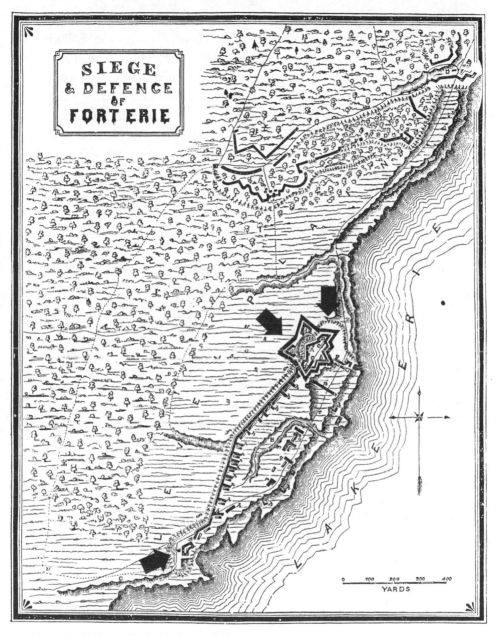

Assault on Fort Erie, August 15, 1814
The arrows show the areas where the three British columns attacked. (Based on
Lossing, *Field-Book*, 1869)

was right on all other points. "The most pressing and important Service to be performed by the Commodore [Yeo], as soon as his Squadron shall have acquired the ascendancy," Prevost reported [to Bathurst] on August 27, "Is the Conveyance of fresh Troops, with a large proportion of Provisions and supplies of every description to York and the Niagara Frontier, before the Navigation closes, and to bring from those places to Kingston, the exhausted Corps, the disabled and the sick who can endure Transport."[27]

This last was most important as a consequence of Drummond's loss of 57 killed, 309 wounded and 539 missing or prisoners in a futile assault of Fort Erie on August 15. Believing that a mere two days' bombardment had made "sufficient impression," he launched separate columns against each of the two lines of earthworks and against Fort Erie proper, some two hours before daylight. Another delusion was included in the operation order: "The Lt. General most strongly recommends a free use of the Bayonet – The Enemy Force does not Exceed 1500 fit for Duty – and those are represented as much dispirited."[28]

The largest column of 1,300 men attacked on the extreme right. One of its sub-units was stopped by the abattis and failed to reach the earthwork; another got misdirected in the darkness and suffered heavy casualties; members of the third waded along the shore line of Lake Erie and got into the American camp, and all were then captured. The other two columns missed their original objectives, but became joined together and managed to fight their way into the northeast bastion of Fort Erie. These 600 continuing redcoats tried repeatedly to advance against the rest of the fort, but each time were driven back by the defenders' musketry and artillery fire. Soon after daylight the sudden explosion of the ammunition stored in a ground floor magazine caused a large number of casualties and made the survivors flee back to their own lines. The total American casualties were only 84 officers and men, whereas for the British it was an extraordinarily bloody operation.[29]

In a private letter to Sir George Prevost of August 16, Drummond blamed the "failure on the present disgraceful, and unfortunate, conduct of the Troops."[30] For the most part, however, these had fought bravely, against an alert and determined enemy, and it seems more likely that the plan of attack was faulty. Drummond had very little command experience and had never directed siege operations. Obviously his prior bombardment of Fort Erie was inadequate; surprise was lacking because, as soon as the British gunfire had ceased, the Americans had stood to their defences.

Fortunately for Lieutenant-General Drummond, he was able to call up two fresh regiments, totalling about 1,200 all ranks, and thus continue the siege. On August 29 a British shell exploded in the quarters of Brigadier-General Gaines, wounding him severely and making it necessary for the still convalescent Major-General Jacob Brown to resume command. Drummond was, however, soon to find himself in new difficulties. On September 8 he believed it necessary to prepare Sir George Prevost for the "possibility of my being compelled by sickness or suffering of the troops, exposed as they will be to the effects of the wet and unhealthy Season which is fast approaching, to withdraw them from their present Position to one which may afford them the means of cover. Sickness has, I am sorry to say, already made its appearance in several of the Corps, particularly the 82nd."[31] On September 11 he wrote that his batteries had been almost silent for several days from the "reduced State of the ammunition."[32] The "sudden and most unlooked for return to the Head of Lake Ontario of the two [American] brigs by which the Niagara has been so long blockaded," he wrote on September 14, "and my communication with York cut off, has had the effect of preventing the junction of the 97th Regiment, which arrived at York on the 10th, and probably would have been here the following day, but for this unlucky circumstance."[33] The same letter added that the rain had been incessant: "as the whole of the Troops are without Tents, and the Huts in which they are placed are wholly incapable of affording Shelter against such severe weather, their situation is most distressing." "It was rather a bivouac than a camp," according to the recollections of Dr. William Dunlop, "the troops sheltering themselves under some branches of trees that only collected the scattered drops of rain, and sent them down in a stream on the heads of the inhabitants, and as it rained incessantly for two months, neither clothes nor bedding could be kept dry."[34]

Yet the besiegers persevered. On September 15 they managed to complete their third battery, on the edge of the woods and about half a mile inland from the first battery on the shore. The line of these batteries, about 600 yards from the old Fort Erie, was covered by abattis but defended only by a single brigade serving in rotation. For reasons of health, Drummond's main force was camped about a mile distant, behind two further intervening lines of abattis.

Major-General Brown feared that this third battery "would rake obliquely the whole American encampment." He wanted "to storm the batteries, destroy the cannon, and roughly handle the brigade upon duty, before those in reserve could be brought into action."[35] As early as September 9 a council of war had endeavoured to discourage any such sortie, but Brown had persisted in his idea and brought 1,000 New York militia volunteers across the river to participate.

Lieutenant-General Drummond had been warned by deserters that Brown was planning a sortie, but inexplicably he took no precautions. His engineers even left standing the dense woods within pistol shot of the flank and rear of the No. 3 Battery. All day long on September 16 American fatigue parties worked to open a path through the forest to this point. The following afternoon, at three o'clock and covered by a heavy rain, about 1,600 American militia and regulars suddenly erupted against the blockhouse covering this No. 3 Battery. Both were quickly captured from the defending De Watteville's Regiment; the guns were spiked and the magazine was blown up. The Americans then advanced on Battery No. 2, in conjunction with 400 more regulars of Winfield Scott's old brigade. This also was captured. The Royal Scots, 6th, 82nd and 89th Regiments now arrived on the scene, and the Americans were unable to capture the remaining Battery No. 1. A sharp fight ensued, and Brown's reserve had to be committed before he could extricate the whole and withdraw within Fort Erie. Most of the American senior officers were wounded. The Americans reported 79 killed and 432 wounded or missing. British casualties were considerably heavier – 115 killed, 176 wounded, and 315 missing. Moreover, three of Drummond's six siege guns were disabled and their ammunition destroyed.

Drummond had been caught napping. There could be no doubt on that score. It was equally clear that a continuation of the siege would now be pointless. "Within the last few days," he wrote to Prevost on September 21, ignoring his own error,

the sickness of the troops has increased to such an alarming degree, and their situation has really become one of such extreme wretchedness from the torrents of rain which have continued to fall for the last 13 days, and from the circumstance of the Division being entirely destitute of camp equipage, that I feel it my duty no longer to persevere in a vain attempt to maintain the blockade of so vastly superior and increasing a force of the enemy [which he persisted in estimating at more than 5,000] under such circumstances. I have therefore given orders for the troops to fall back toward the Chippewa, and shall commence my movement at eight o'clock this evening.[36]

The American army was in no condition to follow and bring on another battle. The Niagara campaign thus came to an end, after casualties heavier than in other seasons, but without any great effect on the battle lines. Most of the American troops soon re-crossed the Niagara River to Buffalo, while Drummond's units reverted to garrison duty at the forts along the Niagara frontier, at Burlington, and at York.

All that remains is to describe briefly the other part of the American plan for 1814: the re-capture of Fort Mackinac, along with which went smaller operations in the Northwest. Sir George Prevost had anticipated trouble, and Lieutenant-Colonel Robert McDouall of the Royal New-foundland Regiment had much earlier been ordered to Mackinac with re-inforcements, supplies and trade goods for the Indians. His party travelled overland during the winter from Lake Ontario, via Lake Simcoe to the Nottawasaga River. Near where it empties into Georgian Bay, his detach-ment of 30 carpenters and 20 seamen from the Kingston navy yard man-aged to build 30 bateaux, four of which were armed with carronades. It was found impracticable to build larger vessels, however, so the naval officer commanding the detachment from Kingston was without proper employ-ment. The whole party continued to Mackinac, where McDouall assumed command on May 18. Under his direction a blockhouse was built on the hitherto unoccupied highest point of the island.

On June 21 McDouall learned that a small American force of regulars and volunteers had occupied the Canadian fur trading post at Prairie du Chien, on the Mississippi River and in what is now the State of Wisconsin. Since a number of Winnebago Indians had been killed and his own west-ern Indian allies began clamouring for vengeance, McDouall had to act. A leading fur trader named William McKay was given the local rank of lieu-tenant-colonel and sent to recapture Prairie du Chien. His force consisted of one Royal Artilleryman with a 3-pr. gun, 12 local militiamen known as Michigan Fencibles, two companies of Canadian voyageurs and 300 Indi-ans. *En route* by canoe, McKay was joined by more voyageurs and Indians, and reached his destination on July 17 with a strength of 120 Canadians and 530 Indians. The American garrison numbered only 60 regulars and ammunition was running low; its commander agreed on July 20 to surren-der, on condition that he and his men be protected from the Indians and be sent home on parole.

Lieutenant-Colonel George Croghan had meanwhile sailed from Detroit with 700 U.S. regulars and Ohio militia on July 3 for Mackinac. His five small naval vessels, however, made poor time.[37] Only on July 20 did they reach St. Joseph's Island. Here he burned the now deserted fort and buildings. The Americans next captured a North West Company vessel and burned the fur trading post at the present Sault Ste. Marie. It was July 26 before Croghan's force anchored off Mackinac. The guns of the American vessels could not be elevated sufficiently to engage the fort, or the even higher new blockhouse, so Croghan was afraid to attempt an assault landing. On August 4, he finally decided to land at the other end of the island, as Captain Roberts had done in 1812, and entice Lieutenant-Colonel McDouall into leaving his fort and fighting in the open.

McDouall did just that, even though his disposable force numbered only 140 redcoats and possibly double that number of local militia and Indians. There was no point in being cooped up in a small fort unless a relief force could be expected shortly, and the nearest British troops were then busy besieging Fort Erie. His redcoats and militia were disposed behind a low breastwork, in an open space in the dense woods, and were supported by two small field guns. The Americans presented too good a target as they advanced in the open, and they retreated after having 13 killed and 51 wounded. The next day the Americans boarded their schooners and sailed away: Croghan had concluded his men could not be depended on to make another attack on McDouall's strong position. On their way back to Detroit, however, they shot up the tiny British post near the mouth of the Nottawasaga River and destroyed the schooner *Nancy*, the only British vessel in those waters. It had been maintaining communication with Mackinac.

The *Nancy's* commander, Lieutenant Miller Worsley, and his seamen managed to reach Mackinac by canoe. Here he persuaded Lieutenant-Colonel McDouall to let him make a night attack upon two American schooners still blockading that island. On the night of September 3, four boatloads of sailors and fencibles surprised *Tigress* and captured her by boarding, with the loss of only 2 killed and 8 wounded. Two nights later Lieutenant Worsley sailed *Tigress* close enough for her crew to board and capture *Scorpion*. These acquisitions provided the Royal Navy with a makeshift force on Lake Huron for the balance of the navigation season. No further American attempt against Mackinac was launched from Detroit and two American expeditions against Prairie du Chien were scattered *en route*.

In the Northwest at least, the British flag waved undisputed. On the Niagara frontier, after a great deal of effort, marching and fighting on both sides, the Americans managed to retain only Fort Erie.

CHAPTER THIRTEEN

On American Territory: April to September 1814

MAINE / WASHINGTON / BALTIMORE

Bᵣᵢₜᵢₛₕ **B**ritish plans for more vigorous offensive operations along the Atlantic seaboard during 1814 were made well before the end of the war against Napoleon in Europe. The first step was an adjustment in command. Late in January 1814, the Admiralty decided to separate the Royal Navy's combined North America and West Indies Command, as had been recommended unsuccessfully almost a year earlier by Admiral Sir John Borlase Warren who had then felt that he could not properly give his personal attention to both. Warren was now advised that the continuing North America Station would not warrant having a full admiral as commander-in-chief, so a more junior officer would be despatched to succeed him. Yet only on April Fool's Day did Warren actually hand over command to Vice-Admiral Sir Alexander Inglis Cochrane. The 55-year-old Cochrane had served in North American waters during the Revolutionary War; since 1793 he had seen considerable action elsewhere.[1] Promoted to the rank of Vice-Admiral in 1809, Cochrane's latest appointments had been Commander-in-Chief of the Leeward Islands Station and Governor of Guadeloupe.

Undoubtedly Cochrane was more offensive-minded than his predecessor, who had been originally instructed to try for an armistice with the Americans. "I have it much to heart," Cochrane would later write Lord Bathurst, "to give them a complete drubbing before peace is made, when I trust their northern limits will be circumscribed and the command of the Mississippi wrested from them."[2] The day after he assumed command he directed the following proclamation at negro slaves in the United States:

WHEREAS it has been represented to me, that many persons now resident in the United States, have expressed a desire to withdraw therefrom, with a view to entering into His Majesty's service, or of being received as free settlers into some of His Majesty's colonies,

This is therefore to give notice

That all those who may be disposed to emigrate from the United States, will with their families, be received on board His Majesty's ships or vessels of war, or at the military posts that may be established upon or near the coast of the United States, when they will have their choice of either entering into His Majesty's sea or land forces, or of being sent as FREE settlers, to the British possessions in North America or the West Indies, where they will meet with all due encouragement.[3]

The subsequent escape of many slaves to British ships did cause alarm among southern plantation owners, while the transfer of these negroes to Nova Scotia momentarily caused Lieutenant-General Sir John Sherbrooke to imagine that they might be enlisted in the New Brunswick Fencibles and thus finally bring that regiment to full strength.[4]

Sherbrooke was, however, soon busier with weightier matters. Vice-Admiral Cochrane issued a proclamation on April 25 which extended the "strict and rigorous blockade" to include New England. "I have stationed off the said Ports and Places," it read, "a Naval Force adequate to maintain the said Blockade in the most rigorous and effective manner."[5] On April 7, six British barges had already ascended the Connecticut River for eight miles and destroyed 20 vessels. "The eastern coast," reported *Niles' Weekly Register* in a subsequent issue, "is much vexed by the enemy. Having destroyed a great portion of the coasting craft, they seem determined to enter the little outports and villages, and burn everything that floats."[6] To top

Vice-Admiral Sir Alexander Cochrane (1758-1832)
Cochrane was the senior officer of the Royal Navy in American waters during the last months of the war. (Brenton's *Naval History of Great Britain*)

it off, Sir Alexander Cochrane cancelled the licences which had made possible a most lucrative coastal trade between New England and the provinces of New Brunswick and Nova Scotia. Repeated protests by the merchants of Halifax and Saint John were of no avail, but a solution to their difficulties gradually dawned on Sir John Sherbrooke.

The Legislature of New Brunswick had sent an Address to the Prince Regent during the course of its winter session of 1814, praying that "when a negotiation for Peace shall take place between Great Britain and the United States of America, His Royal Highness will be graciously pleased to direct such measures as he may think proper, to alter the boundary between those States and this Province, so that the important line of communication between this and the neighbouring Province of Lower Canada, by the River St. John may not be interrupted."[7] Events of 1812 and 1813 had already convinced the British Government that the salient of northern Maine was a danger to the normal portage route, and caused the Secretary of State for Foreign Affairs, Lord Castlereagh, to exclaim that the Treaty of 1783 had been "very hastily and improvidently framed in this respect."[8] Lord Bathurst therefore instructed Sir John Sherbrooke in a letter of June 6, 1814, to "occupy so much of the District of Maine, as shall ensure an uninterrupted communication between Halifax & Quebec."[9]

Sherbrooke decided that an occupation of northern Maine presented too many difficulties, because of its isolation from any considerable settlement. He believed, however, that the same object could be achieved by occupying the Penobscot coast "with a respectable force, and to take that river (which was the old frontier of the state of Massachusetts), as our boundary, running a line from its source in a more westerly direction than that which at present divides us from the Americans."[10] Such action would also make possible the resumption of the New England coastal trade with New Brunswick and Nova Scotia, because the place of origin of American lumber and provisions need not concern the British customs officials of any occupied port such as Castine, so long as they were legally cleared for shipment to a port in British North America.

While waiting for this project to be approved, Sir John Sherbrooke sent a small expedition to occupy disputed islands in Passamaquoddy Bay. Moose Island had always been claimed by Great Britain, but its American town of Eastport had long been the base for New England smuggling operations. No resistance was offered on July 11 when the 102nd Regiment, specially brought from Bermuda, began landing at Moose Island from the ships

Major-General Robert Ross (1768-1814)
A veteran of Wellington's Peninsular army, Ross commanded the land component of the British attack on Washington and Baltimore in the late summer of 1814. (Editor's collection)

commanded by Captain Thomas Hardy, in whose arms Lord Nelson had died at Trafalgar. The military commander, Lieutenant-Colonel Andrew Pilkington, gave the inhabitants seven days in which to take the oath of allegiance to King George III, which most of them did, or to quit the island.

By this time Major-General Robert Ross was on his way across the Atlantic Ocean with a brigade, consisting of the 1/4th, 44th and 85th Regiments, and a company of Royal Artillery from Wellington's army. He was to "effect a diversion on the coasts of the United States of America in favor of the army employed in the defence of Upper and Lower Canada."[11] The point of attack was to be decided by Vice-Admiral Cochrane. Ross had every intention of conducting more than a mere marauding expedition, but Cochrane had other views. Cochrane had been requested by Sir George Prevost to retaliate for the wanton destruction of private property in Upper Canada during the American raid on the village of Long Point on May 15 as a warning to deter the enemy from a repetition of similar outrages."[12]

Major-General Ross reached Bermuda on July 24. Here he added the 21st Regiment and the 3rd Battalion of Royal Marines to his force, whose strength was now nearly 4,000 rank and file. On August 3 this force sailed for Chesapeake Bay. Baltimore was the obvious objective, once a flotilla of gunboats commanded by Commodore Joshua Barney, U.S.N., had been destroyed first in the Patuxent River where it had taken refuge. Yet Rear-Admiral Sir George Cockburn suggested that they make a dash for Washington itself.

This move was not nearly as reckless as it sounded, in view of the defenceless state of the city. Only on July 2 had the American Government finally become alarmed by the extent to which the nation's capital was exposed to attack. A new Military District No. 10 was then created, but President Madison gave the command to the same Brigadier-General William H. Winder who had been captured at Stoney Creek – because he was related to the Governor of Maryland whose co-operation was now most necessary. Since there were less than 1,000 U.S. regulars and 120 marines directly available for this District, Winder was given an allocation on paper of 15,000 militia. The President and his Secretary of State, James Monroe, kept interfering in purely military matters, however, so Secretary of War Armstrong washed his hands of the defence of Washington and left Winder to do what he liked. This proved to be nothing.

On August 19 Major-General Ross landed his troops and began marching up the Patuxent River, supported by Rear-Admiral Cockburn with a naval division of light vessels. Three days later Commodore Barney destroyed his own gunboats, to prevent their capture, and withdrew his 400 seamen to defend the road leading from the village of Bladensburg to Washington.

Still Brigadier-General Winder did nothing. Others were responsible for collecting a scratch regular force of 300 infantry and 120 dragoons, 250 Maryland militia and about 1,200 militia living in the District of Columbia. This force joined Barney's seamen. Shortly before the British approached Bladensburg on the morning of August 24, nearly 5,000 further American militia began arriving on the battlefield that Winder had finally selected on the Washington side of the village.

Major-General Ross was unduly impressed by the American defensive position encountered at noon just past Bladensburg. "They were strongly posted on very commanding heights, formed in two lines," he wrote later, "the advance occupying a fortified house, which with artillery covered the

Rear-Admiral George Cockburn (1772-1853)
Cockburn, who commanded the inshore squadron of the Royal Navy off the middle Atlantic coast in 1813-1814, was hated by Americans for his enthusiastic raiding of coastal towns. (Naval Historical Center, Washington)

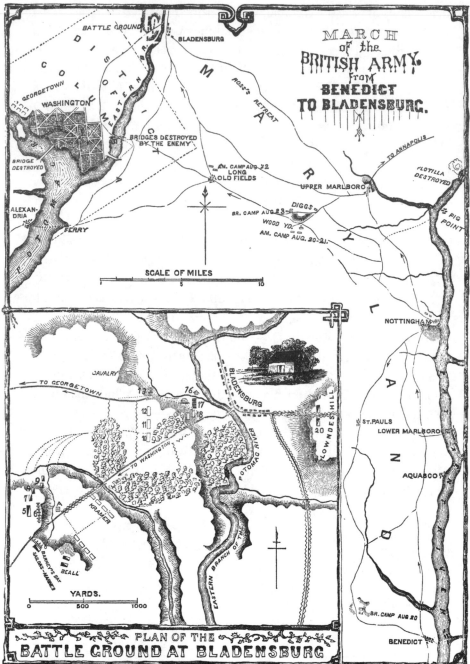

Bladensburg and Washington, August 1814

This map shows the course of Ross's army as it marched on Washington and the dispositions of the opposing sides at the battle of Bladensburgh, August 24, 1814.

bridge over the Eastern Branch, across which the British troops had to pass."[13] The American Secretary of War, however, was more of a realist and told President Madison who had also ridden out to view the battlefield that, "as it was between regulars and militia, the latter would be beaten."[14]

The greater number of American militia quickly took to their heels after a few rockets roared overhead and the red-coated infantry were seen to be crossing the bridge. Only Barney's seamen made a real fight of it, until ordered to retreat by their badly wounded commander to avoid capture. The charging British had 64 killed and 185 wounded at the "Bladensburg Races." American losses were 10 or 12 killed and about 40 wounded.[15]

After two hours' rest the British regiments re-formed into column of route and continued on to Washington. The American commander of the navy yard burned it as the British approached, but the Capitol and the President's official residence were set on fire by British troops acting under orders. The flames from these three conflagrations lit up the countryside for the fleeing President Madison and members of his cabinet. Other public buildings were subsequently destroyed.

When Ross's troops abandoned Washington and President Madison's government returned to begin the work of restoration, John Armstrong became its scapegoat. James Monroe was made acting Secretary of War to appease the angry citizens. The bungling Brigadier-General Winder did not return from Baltimore, his home town, whose defence he now decided to supervise in his capacity as commander of Military District No. 10. Subsequently the President's residence in Washington was rebuilt, and it now received the name "White House" since the walls were whitewashed to hide the marks of fire.

American newspapers, even those supported by the anti-war Federalist party, condemned the burning of Washington and the barbarism of war now being brought home to Americans. Their sentiments were expressed by the Editor of *Niles' Weekly Register* on September 10:

The hate with which *we* have always said *Great Britain* regarded us, is now exhibiting by a Goth-like war, which the late strange events in *Europe* enables her to carry on with extraordinary force and energy. The barriers with which civilized nations have circumscribed their military operations, are cast down by the foe; and the contest, begun for unalienable rights on the sea, is becoming a struggle for liberty and property on the land. The shores of the *Chesapeake* are lighted by the flames of farm houses and cottages, hitherto respected in war; and the fruits of the earth are wantonly consumed by the invader's torch. Whatever of private property pleases him, he lays hold of as a prize; and wickedly destroys what he cannot carry away.

Household furniture has been a favorite object of his vengeance, and *negroes* and *tobacco* are his darling spoils! His late capture of *Washington City* is an honor to the valor of his soldiery; but his conduct in burning the capitol, the president's house and the public offices, is a disgrace that he will not wipe away more easily than we shall. ... The capitals of the greatest empires and kingdoms of the old world were frequently captured by the contending parties, in the late wars. The *outlaw, Bonaparte*, entered *Lisbon, Madrid, Amsterdam, Berlin, Vienna,* (several times) *Moscow, Turin, Rome, Naples,* and the capitals of ten or fifteen of the minor states of Europe, but never, in the case of the *Kremlin* excepted, destroyed a public building undevoted to military purposes; and *that* was not demolished until it was evident that the people of *Moscow* would themselves destroy the city.[16]

Several London newspapers condemned the needless destruction of public buildings in Washington. "The Cossacks spared Paris," wrote the Editor of the *Statesman*, "but we spared not the Capitol of America. Is it certain, that the destruction of the public edifices for destruction sake alone, is a legitimate method of warfare."[17] Samuel Whitbread, a wealthy brewer, told his fellow members of the House of Commons on November 4, that it was "abhorrent to every principle of legitimate warfare."[18] Fortunately the British Government could conveniently explain it away as retaliation for American excesses at York in Upper Canada. "Although a small town," the Chancellor of the Exchequer explained in the House of Commons, "it [York] was a capital, and among other public and private buildings, the house of assembly and the house of the governor had been burnt to the ground."[19] American destruction of the *York Gazette's* office and printing press had deprived the provincial capital of its only newspaper for the rest of the war, so it is difficult to judge what must have been the reaction of its inhabitants to the news of similar destruction at Washington. Human nature being what it is, however, there probably was a general feeling of satisfaction for a job well done. The formidable Reverend John Strachan certainly did not mince words in the open letter he addressed to ex-President Jefferson of the United States on January 30, 1815. Strachan, as Treasurer of the Loyal and Patriotic Society of Upper Canada, brushed aside Jefferson's earlier charge that British "vandalism" had "triumphed at Washington." Strachan insisted that the destruction of its public buildings "was a small retaliation after redress had been refused for burnings and depredations, not only of public but private property, committed by them [Americans] in Canada."[20]

On the evening of August 25, Major-General Ross withdrew his British troops from Washington as quietly as they had come. On the following day they regained contact with the naval force in the Patuxent River. Another small naval force, which had entered the Potomac River, occupied Alexandria for three days and then brought away all the shipping and merchandise found there.

Cochrane's main fleet and the army slowly moved up Chesapeake Bay to make "a demonstration upon the City of Baltimore, which might be converted into a real attack should circumstances appear to justify it."[21] The army was landed 12 miles from the city on the morning of September 12. This time 3,200 American militia made a better fight of it before fleeing. They lost 24 killed, 139 wounded and 50 as prisoners. The British reported 46 killed and 273 wounded. Major-General Ross, however, was among those mortally wounded and was succeeded by Colonel Arthur Brooke of the 44th Regiment. The British advance continued on the following day, but the citizens of Baltimore had been labouring mightily to surround the city with entrenchments on the landward side and these looked very formidable to Colonel Brooke. Vessels sunk in the harbour and commanded by shore batteries prevented Cochrane's large ships from getting close enough for their long guns to do any real damage to the defences during a lengthy bombardment. This continued until after midnight and inspired Francis Scott Key, a young American lawyer attempting to arrange an exchange of prisoners, to write what would later become the National Anthem of the United States:

> O! say can you see by the dawn's early light.
> What so proudly we hailed at the twilight's last gleaming,
> Whose broad stripes and bright stars through the perilous fight,
> O'er the ramparts we watch'd were so gallantly streaming?
> And the Rocket's red glare, the Bombs bursting in air,
> Gave proof through the night that our Flag was still there;
> O! say does that star-spangled Banner yet wave,
> O'er the Land of the free, and the home of the brave.[22]

During this morning of September 14, while Francis Scott Key was scribbling down on paper the opening words of "The Star Spangled Banner," Vice-Admiral Cochrane and Colonel Brooke agreed that, a demonstration having been made, they would abandon their attempt to capture Baltimore. The British army was re-embarked on the following day. It headed for Jamaica, and Sir Alexander Cochrane sailed to Halifax.

Here he learned of the success achieved by Lieutenant-General Sir John Sherbrooke and Rear-Admiral Edward Griffith. On the morning of September 1, their fleet of warships and transports had arrived off the town of Castine, at the mouth of the Penobscot River, with a landing force consisting of the 29th, 62nd, and 98th Regiments of Foot, two companies of the 7th Battalion, 60th (or Royal American) Regiment and a detachment of Royal Artillery. While these 2,000 regulars were being landed the Americans abandoned their fort, after blowing up its magazine, and retreated up river.

Griffith and Sherbrooke then made plans to capture the frigate U.S.S. *Adams*, which had run 30 miles up the river to Hampden in the hope of there effecting much-needed repairs. Captain Robert Barrie's two sloops, one transport, and collection of armed boats transported up river the expedition's seven flank companies and 20 artillerymen, who had a 53-in. howitzer. The troops, under the command of Lieutenant-Colonel Henry John, landed three miles below Hampden on the morning of September 3 and quickly routed 1,400 local militia, with a loss of only one killed, eight wounded and one missing. Thereupon the captain of the U.S.S. *Adams* set her on fire to avoid capture and retreated with her crew. After securing the fleeing enemy's 20 cannon, the British expedition continued up river. "On approaching Bangor," Captain Barrie reported, "the Inhabitants who had opposed us at Hampden, threw off their Military character, and as Magistrates, select men, &c. made an unconditional surrender of the Town."[23] These, and other militiamen who subsequently surrendered, were released on parole. Fresh meat and bread were a welcome change from salt beef and biscuit, and both wine and spirituous liquors were found; but looting was prohibited and the local populace had little reason to complain. On September 9 the expedition returned down river to Castine.

That same day Lieutenant-Colonel Pilkington left Castine with the battalion companies of the 29th Foot and the remaining company of the 60th "to take possession of Machias, the only place occupied by the Enemy's Troops, between this and Passamaquoddy Bay."[24] The expedition arrived off Machias on the following evening. The troops were landed along the

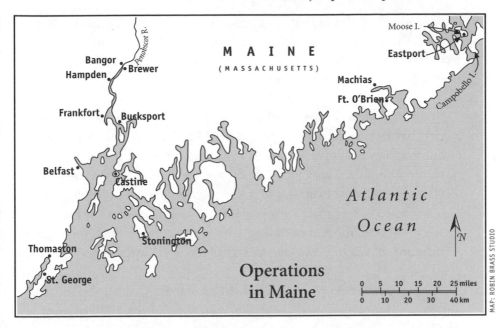

Operations
in Maine

MAP: ROBIN BRASS STUDIO

shore and spent the night thrashing through the woods so as to approach the fort from the rear. The advanced guard found at dawn, however, that the American garrison had fled. The town of Machias was also occupied without a fight. Lieutenant-Colonel Pilkington was preparing to advance inland on September 13, when he received a letter of capitulation from the senior American militia officers of the county:

> The Forces under your Command having captured the forts in the neighbourhood of Machias and taken possession of the Territory adjacent within the County of Washington, and the situation of the County being such between the Penobscot river and Passamaquoddy Bay as to preclude the hope that an adequate force can be furnished by the United States for its protection. We propose a capitulation and offer for ourselves and on behalf of the officers and Soldiers of the Brigade within the County of Washington to give our Parole of honor that we will not directly or indirectly bear Arms, or in any way serve against His Britannic Majesty King George … during the present war between Great Britain and the United States; upon condition we have your assurance that while we remain in this Situation and Consider ourselves under the British Government until further Orders, we shall have the safe and full enjoyment of our Private property, and be protected in the exercise of our usual occupations.[25]

247

Acceptance of this capitulation brought Sherbrooke's campaign to a close. Trade between New England and the ports of New Brunswick and Nova Scotia was officially resumed following a proclamation by Rear-Admiral Edward Griffith on September 15:

> The territory lying between the bay of Passamaquoddy and the Penobscot river having been taken possession of by H.M's forces: All vessels clearing out from any port of H.M's North American provinces, for any port or place within the territory, including the port of Castine, and the ports and places situated on the east side of the Penobscot river, are to pass free and unmolested, to bring back cargoes of lumber and provisions; also any vessels being from the port of Castine with a licence issued from the commanding officers of H.M's land and naval forces at Castine.[26]

Another proclamation, issued jointly by Lieutenant-General Sherbrooke and Rear-Admiral Griffith on September 21, appointed a military governor for this new British territory and a customs official for Castine. The inhabitants could take either the formal oath of allegiance or a lesser oath "to behave peaceably and quietly, and while inhabiting and residing within that country, not to carry arms, or in any respect act hostilely against His Majesty, or any of his subjects."[27] The inhabitants acquiesced in the new regime and no hostile acts were committed against the considerable British garrison left at Castine or the small one on Moose Island. The people of Maine were too busy resuming the interrupted trade with New Brunswick and Nova Scotia to care about a war they had not wanted in the first place.

British graffitti, Castine, 1814. Scratched into a window pane with a British officer's diamond ring, it was a reminder that, by September 1814, Britain occupied much American territory. (Lossing, *Field Book*, 904)

CHAPTER FOURTEEN

Defeat on Lake Champlain

PLATTSBURGH, SEPTEMBER 1814

On July 12, 1814 Sir George Prevost wrote Lord Bathurst from Montreal that, as soon as all the promised troops arrived, he would start to implement the secret instructions dated June 3 (see Chapter 12 and Appendix 1). Until complete naval command of Lakes Ontario and Champlain could be obtained, however, he would still have to confine himself to defensive operations.

On July 29 Prevost was able to report the arrival at Quebec of the 4/1st Royal Scots and the 97th Regiment from Ireland, and Major-General Manley Power's brigade of the 3rd, 5th, 1/27th and 58th Regiments, with a brigade of artillery, from Bordeaux. A week later Major-General James Kempt's brigade of the 9th, 37th, 57th and 81st Regiments, also accompanied by a brigade of artillery, reached Montreal. According to Prevost's despatch of August 5, time would still be needed to get this new force properly organized and the inland naval squadrons ready for action:

> The Transports with the two last Brigades of Troops from Bordeaux, are approaching Quebec, where arrangements have been made for their being pushed forward without a moments delay;– But notwithstanding every exertion it will be impossible to collect the whole force in the neighbourhood of this place, before the end of the present Month.
>
> This circumstance is the less to be regretted as our Fleets on the Lakes cannot attain a sufficient strength to co-operate with the Divisions of the Army assembling for the destruction of Sackets Harbour, and the occupation of Plattsburg, before the 15th of next Month, and without their Aid and protection, nothing could be undertaken affording a reasonable hope of substantial Advantage.[1]

Prevost, following his instructions dated June 3, considered Plattsburgh to be the "advanced position on that part of our frontier which extends towards Lake Champlain, the occupation of which would materially tend to the security of the Province." The Americans themselves were expected to be a help in certain areas: "The State of Vermont having Shown a decided opposition to the War, and very large supplies of Specie coming in daily from thence, as well as the whole of the Cattle required for the use of the Troops, I mean for the present to confine myself in any offensive Operations which may take place to the Western side of Lake Champlain."[2]

Smuggling into Lower Canada from Vermont had achieved the ultimate on June 28, when American naval personnel intercepted and destroyed on Lake Champlain two spars intended for the British frigate being built at Isle aux Noix; yet the "persons who were towing them made their escape on shore."[3] A watch was continued for the possible passage down Lake Champlain of a main mast, but only four further spars were intercepted, on the night of July 7. Although there was no shortage of timber for spars and masts in Lower Canada, dragging them up the rapids of the Richelieu River or over the rough intervening country would have been a slow and difficult process. As it was, the movement of guns and naval stores was taxing available resources.

Prevost's despatch of August 17 reported that all the troops from Bordeaux had arrived. His total increase in strength from all sources was better than 13,000 officers and men, and his next monthly strength return would show 29,437 effective other ranks in the Canadas, exclusive of militia.

Three infantry brigades were being organized into a division under the command of Major-General de Rottenburg for operations against Plattsburgh.[4] Major-General Robinson's lst Brigade, consisting of the 3/27th, 39th, 76th and 88th Regiments, totalled 2,495 all ranks. Major-General Brisbane's 2nd Brigade of troops on duty for some time in Lower Canada, the 2/8th, 13th and 49th Regiments of Foot, De Meuron's Regiment, the Canadian Voltigeurs and Canadian Chasseurs, numbered 3,785 regulars and militia. Major-General Power's 3rd Brigade of the 3rd, 5th, 1/27th and 58th Regiments amounted to 3,226 officers and men. Each brigade was supported by an artillery brigade of five 6-pr. guns and one 5.5-in. howitzer, for a grand total of 536 Royal Artillerymen. There were also 309 officers and other ranks of the 19th Light Dragoons to increase the division's combatant strength to 10,351 all ranks. Major-General Kempt's veteran brigade of the 9th, 37th, 57th and 81st Regiments from Bordeaux was destined for Kingston and a possible attack on Sackets Harbor.[5] It was to remain temporarily at Montreal as Army Reserve, however, because of the continued delay in the launching of Commodore Yeo's ship of the line at Kingston. Sir George Prevost wrote Lord Bathurst on August 27 that "in consequence all hopes of using our Squadron on Lake Ontario, before the first week in October have vanished."[6]

There had been no attempt all summer at a naval engagement on Lake Ontario. First Chauncey and then Yeo had remained in port, and let the other rule the lake with the ship then carrying the most and heaviest long guns. Sir James Yeo was bound to win this shipbuilder's campaign, however, because his new three-decked ship *St. Lawrence* would be considerably more powerful than even Lord Nelson's flagship at Trafalgar. Approval had only been given for a much smaller ship, but the opportunity to do what he liked at far-off Kingston was too much to resist for this young commander-in-chief who had never commanded anything bigger than a frigate. The ultimate result would be a monster carrying 112 guns and a crew of 837 officers and seamen.[7]

Where the crew would come from, however, was a vexing question. The North American Station was short 3,000 seamen. Rear-Admiral Edward Griffith at Halifax could not send forward any officers and men not authorized by the Admiralty in London; but 400 seamen were eventually ordered to Kingston by the port captain at Quebec City, from among the crews of 15 naval transports which had arrived there. Another 150 seamen from these naval transports at Quebec were ordered to Isle aux Noix at the insistence of Sir George Prevost. He had been disturbed all summer by the extent to which Commodore Yeo was funnelling naval personnel, stores and guns to Kingston for his own immediate use.

In consequence, work had progressed but slowly at Isle aux Noix on the frigate which was to be named *Confiance*, for the French ship which Commodore Yeo had captured much earlier in his career. This, it was hoped, would wrest supremacy on Lake Champlain from the American squadron of Captain Thomas Macdonough, who now had the actual naval rank of master-commandant.[8] His new frigate, U.S.S. *Saratoga*, carried 8 24-pr. long guns and 18 larger carronades. U.S.S. *Eagle*, was comparable to the British brig *Linnet*, which had 16 12-pr. long guns. It did not really matter that the remaining American schooner, two small sloops and 10 gunboats were somewhat inferior to the British three sloops and 12 gunboats. Completion of H.M.S. *Confiance* would, however, change the picture completely. Her 27 24-pr. long guns would be able to destroy U.S.S. *Saratoga* and the rest of Macdonough's squadron at a range which would leave her

Captain Thomas Macdonough, U.S.N. (1783-1825)
On 11 September 1814, Macdonough won an important American victory that halted the major British offensive of the war. (Lossing, *Field-Book*, 1869)

immune to any but lucky American cannon balls. In addition, Confiance was to be armed with four 32-pr. and six 24-pr. carronades.

By the time H.M.S. *Confiance* was launched on August 25, Sir James Yeo had decided to replace the very junior and bad-tempered post captain, Peter Fisher, in command on Lake Champlain. Captain Daniel Pring, advanced officially from lieutenant to the rank of commander in November 1813, would, however, remain in command of H.M.S. *Linnet*. Captain George Downie, R.N., arrived from Kingston on September 2 to take over the squadron. This young post captain of 20 months standing had brought 700 officers and seamen from England to join Commodore Yeo in the spring; he also brought a number of complimentary letters about his previous service which had been mostly in 18-gun sloops. Downie did not waste any time after his arrival at Isle aux Noix. On the day following, September 3, he ordered Captain Pring to take the gunboats and support the advance of the British army which was then underway.

Plattsburgh was a far simpler objective than Sackets Harbor, despite what Lord Bathurst and his Parliamentary Under-Secretary of State for War and the Colonies, Henry Goulburn, might imagine. Letters now being received by Prevost from Bathurst assumed that expeditions must already have been set in motion against both Plattsburgh and Sackets Harbor. Goulburn was suggesting to his political chief that Prevost should be able to secure naval supremacy on both Lakes Champlain and Ontario by attacking the respective American bases on the landward side while the enemy troops were still only raw material. Exactly how even British veterans would be able to cross the water obstacle between Kingston and Sackets Harbor, while Chauncey's fleet was blockading the former, does not seem to have been considered by Goulburn. On the other hand, Plattsburgh could be reached by an army marching on foot from the border of Lower Canada.

This last operation had been made even easier of accomplishment by American stupidity. Major-General George Izard, who it will be remembered had succeeded Wilkinson in early May, had erected strong fortifications at Plattsburgh during the summer; strong enough, it was hoped, to resist a combined military and naval attack for up to three weeks if Macdonough's squadron was in Plattsburgh Bay. On August 10, however, Izard received a letter from the Secretary of War suggesting that he move his army towards the St. Lawrence River to threaten communications between Montreal and Kingston. This would provide a diversion on behalf of Major-General Jacob Brown's army at Fort Erie. Izard had, however, learned enough about Sir George Prevost's concentration of troops to become convinced that it would be directed down Lake Champlain and therefore immediately replied from his advanced headquarters at Chazy that a movement away from Plattsburgh would seriously endanger the American position on Lake Champlain:

> I will make the movement you direct, if possible; but I shall do it with the apprehension of risking the force under my command, and with the certainty that everything in this vicinity but the lately erected works at Plattsburgh and Cumberland Head [across the bay] will in less than three days after my departure be in the possession of the enemy. He is in force superior to mine in my front; he daily threatens an attack on my position at Champlain; we are in hourly expectation of a serious conflict. That he has not attacked us before this time is attributable to caution on his part, from exaggerated reports of our numbers, and from his expectation of reinforcements.[9]

Yet Major-General Izard decided he must obey the Secretary of War's next letter dated August 12. This directed him "to carry the war as far to the westward as possible, particularly while we have an ascendency on the Lakes."[10] Izard perforce set out with 4,000 regulars on August 29 for Sackets Harbor, whence he might continue on to Niagara if the situation seemed to warrant it.

Left behind were 1,500 effectives and an equal number of recruits and convalescent soldiers. Their commander, Brigadier-General Alexander Macomb, was a promising young regular who had conducted himself well during the St. Lawrence campaign of the previous autumn, but four companies of infantry and three companies of artillery were the only formed units he now had.

Sir George Prevost also was faced with problems, despite the imposing sight presented by the 10,351 officers and men who began to cross the border at Champlain on September 1. The Peninsular veterans, who comprised two of the three brigades, had not been happy about being sent to fight in a mere colonial war, instead of being allowed to enjoy life in a European army of occupation or some leave at home. Officers had been further alienated by petty matters. The otherwise strict Duke of Wellington had never worried about what was worn on active service and had himself affected a blue frock-coat and pantaloons of civilian cut. According to Lieutenant William Grattan of the 88th Regiment, the Duke had

> never harassed us with reviews, or petty annoyances, which, so far from promoting discipline, or doing good in any way, have a contrary effect. A corporal's guard frequently did duty at Headquarters, and every officer who chose to purchase a horse might ride on a march. Provided we brought our men into the field well appointed, and with sixty rounds of good ammunition each, he never looked to see whether their trowsers were black, blue, or grey, and as to ourselves [i.e. officers], we might be rigged out in all colours of the rainbow if we fancied it.[11]

Sir George Prevost was a lesser man, however, and believed that discipline was discipline. Hence the following General Order about proper dress issued by his Adjutant General on August 23:

> The Commander of the Forces has observed in the dress of Several of the Officers of Corps & Departments, lately added to this Army from that of Field Marshal the Duke of Wellington, a fanciful vanity inconsistent with the rules of the Service, and in Some instances without Comfort or Convenience and to the prejudice of the Service, by removing essential distinctions of Rank and description of Service.
>
> His Excellency deems it expedient to direct that the General Officers in Charge of Divisions & Brigades do uphold His Majesty's Commands

in that respect, and only admit of such deviations from them as may be justified by particular causes of Service and Climate – and even then uniformity is to be retained.

Commanding Officers are held responsible that the Established Uniform of their Corps is strictly observed by the Officers under their Command.[12]

There were other factors that affected morale. All the newcomers were annoyed that the Adjutant General, Edward Baynes, although he had experienced very little fighting in his career, was now a major-general. The Quartermaster General, Major-General Sir Sidney Beckwith, had served in the early campaigns of the Peninsular War, but even he became suspect. The elderly Major-General De Rottenburg was well known and respected in the British Army, but he had never commanded more than a light infantry brigade within a large army, and that only for the few months of the unsuccessful Walcheren campaign of 1809. On the other hand, Major-Generals Brisbane, Power and Robinson were all fresh from the battles of Wellington's successful campaigns and older in years than Prevost himself, who had made his reputation in the West Indies and was not even of British origin.

"It appears to me," Major-General Robinson later wrote in his Journal, "that the army moved against Platsburg without any regularly digested plan by Sir George Prevost. There were neither Guides, Spies or Plans. ... A strange infatuation seems to have seized on the mind of Sir George Prevost as well as the Heads of Departments that it was impossible to gain any intelligence that could be depended upon, and therefore it was throwing money away to attempt it – for which reason Secret Service money was with-held from the Generals commanding at the out posts."[13] This, of course, was in striking contrast to the way things had been done in Spain, where officers had been employed as spies to verify and enlarge upon the information purchased from the inhabitants. Yet the Americans were impressed by the manner of the British advance, if Brigadier-General Macomb's official report to the Secretary of War in Washington can be believed. Macomb wrote that the hurriedly mobilized 700 New York militia, who blocked the roads with felled trees on September 6, "skirmished with his [Prevost's] advanced parties, [but] except a few brave men, fell back most precipitately in the greatest disorder, notwithstanding the British troops did not deign to fire on them, except by their flankers and advanced patrols…. So undaunted was the enemy, that he never deployed in his whole march, always pressing on in column."[14]

That evening, September 6, the British entered Plattsburgh. Macomb retreated across the Saranac River, which divided the village into unequal portions as it emptied into Lake Champlain. He ordered the planking removed from the two bridges and disposed his hodge-podge of regulars and militia in the fortifications erected earlier on the orders of Major-General Izard. These consisted of three open redoubts and two blockhouses. Captain Macdonough's frigate, brig, two sloops and 10 gunboats were then riding at anchor in the bay. From then on, Macomb's report of the battle continued,

> the enemy was employed in getting on his battering-train, and erecting his batteries and approaches and constantly skirmishing at the bridges and fords. By this time the militia of New York and the volunteers of Vermont were pouring in from all quarters. I advised general Mooers [of the New York militia] to keep his force along the Saranac to prevent the enemy's crossing the river, and to send a strong body in his rear to harass him day and night, and keep him in continual alarm. The militia behaved with great spirit after the first day, and the volunteers of Vermont were exceedingly serviceable. Our regular troops, notwithstanding the constant skirmishing … kept at their work day and night, strengthening the defences, and evinced a determination to hold out to the last extremity. It was reported that the enemy only waited the arrival of his flotilla to make a general attack.[15]

Sir George Prevost's first thought on reaching Plattsburgh was to order Major-General Robinson's brigade to attack immediately. This order he postponed until the morning of September 7, however, after admitting to Robinson that he did not know either the whereabouts of the fords across the Saranac River or the distance that the American fortifications were beyond its far bank. This information was subsequently obtained by the staff, but Prevost then told Robinson that he had decided to wait for co-operation from Captain Downie's naval squadron before venturing on an assault. H.M.S. *Linnet* and the gunboats which had accompanied the army's advance were capable of taking on the enemy shore batteries, but would be blown out of the water by the American naval squadron. "Your share in the operation in the first instance," Prevost wrote to Downie at Isle aux Noix, "will be to destroy or to Capture the Enemy's Squadron, if it should wait for a Contest, and afterwards Co-operate with this division of the Army, but if it should run away and get out of your reach, we must meet here to consult on Ulterior Movements."[16]

Captain Downie immediately replied to Prevost's letter that H.M.S. *Confiance* was far from ready for action, but that he would do his best. However, "until she is ready, it is my duty not to hazard the Squadron before an Enemy who will be superior in Force."[17] The 180 marines assigned to naval service on Lake Champlain now joined the seamen from Quebec on board *Confiance* and she was towed slowly up stream from Isle aux Noix, against both the current and a head wind. The following night of September 9, *Confiance* joined Captain Pring and the balance of the squadron off Chazy. Here her crew was completed with a company of soldiers from the 39th Foot. Gun crews now got their first chance to drill together, while artificers and carpenters still worked feverishly to complete the essentials for action.

Sir George Prevost had known for a month that *Confiance* could not be made ready before September 15 and he should have realized that every day's respite would result in added proficiency. Yet Prevost's succession of letters seemed to be designed to rush the much younger and junior Downie into a hasty decision. In consequence Downie wrote Prevost on the evening of September 9 that he intended to get underway about midnight, "in the Expectation of rounding into the Bay of Plattsburg about dawn of day, and commence an immediate attack upon the Enemy, if they should be found Anchored in a position that will offer chance of success. I rely on any assistance you can afford the Squadron."[18]

A strong head wind blowing down the lake made it impossible for Downie to approach Plattsburgh Bay, yet Prevost wrote on September 10: "In consequence the Troops have been held in readiness since 6 o'clock this morning to storm the Enemy's Works at nearly the same moment as the Naval Action should commence in the Bay. I ascribe the disappointment I have experienced to the unfortunate change of wind, & shall rejoice to learn that my reasonable expectations have been frustrated by no other cause."[19]

This was going too far, and Captain Downie said as much to the *aide-de-camp* who delivered the letter to him at Chazy. "I am surprised Sir George should think it necessary to urge me upon this subject: he must feel assured, that I am as desirous of proceeding to active operations as he can be; but I am responsible for the Squadron I command, and no man shall

257

make me lead it into action before I consider it in a fit condition."[20] The *aide-de-camp* could tell Sir George Prevost that the approach of the naval squadron would be signalled to the army by the scaling of the guns in H.M.S. *Confiance* (i.e., firing cartridges without shot). Captain Pring, who was present, later testified that Downie said to him that "this Letter does not deserve an Answer but I will convince him that the naval Force will not be backward in their share of the attack."[21] Downie also told Pring that "when the Batteries are stormed and taken possession of by the British Land Forces which the Commander of the Land Forces had promised to do at the moment the naval action commences the Enemy will then at all events be obliged to quit their position whereby we shall obtain decided Advantage over them during their Confusion. I would otherwise of course prefer fighting them on the Lake and would wait until our Force is in an efficient state but I fear they would if I waited take shelter up the Lake, and not meet me on equal Terms."

The wind being fair, and from the northeast, on the following morning, September 11 and a Sunday, Downie set sail from Chazy, which was about

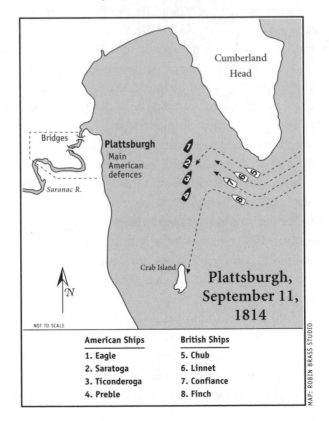

Cumberland Head

Bridges

Plattsburgh
Main American defences

Saranac R.

Crab Island

Plattsburgh, September 11, 1814

N

NOT TO SCALE

MAP: ROBIN BRASS STUDIO

American Ships	British Ships
1. Eagle	5. Chub
2. Saratoga	6. Linnet
3. Ticonderoga	7. Confiance
4. Preble	8. Finch

12 miles from Plattsburgh Bay. The agreed signal of scaling his guns was given at 5 A.M. The squadron subsequently hove-to off Cumberland Head and Captain Downie entered a small boat to reconnoitre the American position. Captain Macdonough had anchored his vessels in a line parallel to the Plattsburgh defences, but slightly closer to Cumberland Head. Their order from north to south was *Eagle* (20 guns), *Saratoga* (26 guns), *Ticonderoga* (seven guns) and *Preble* (seven guns). Macdonough's 10 gunboats, mounting a total of 16 guns, were disposed in groups closer to the Plattsburgh shore.

Captain Downie, on his return from viewing the enemy, decided that *Confiance* should sail far enough up the bay to pass along *Eagle* and give her a broadside before anchoring head and stem across the stern and bows of *Saratoga*. H.M.S. *Linnet*, supported by *Chub*, would then take on *Eagle*. Finch was to attack the American rear, supported by the 11 gunboats. The order to proceed was given at 8:30. As H.M.S. *Confiance* rounded Cumberland Head, all hands were ordered aft to listen to Captain Downie. "There are the Enemy's Ships," he told them; "our Army are to storm the Enemy's works at the moment we engage, and mind don't let us be behind."[22]

Sir George Prevost's subsequent excuse for insisting on a joint attack was to draw the American gunboats farther away from shore; otherwise they would fire on the British troops as they stormed across the Saranac River. Yet his attack plan does not substantiate this. Major-General Brisbane's brigade was intended primarily to create only a demonstration at the two plankless bridges over the Saranac, supported by artillery fire from the British siege batteries; Major-General Robinson was to lead a much larger force across a ford about three miles up river and assault the American defences from the flank and rear.

Robinson's assault force had been waiting since an hour before dawn. It consisted of his own 3/27th and 76th Regiments, Major-General Power's brigade of the 3rd, 5th, 1/27th and 58th Regiments, the light companies of the 39th and 88th Regiments, two squadrons of the 19th Light Dragoons, and an artillery detachment with two 6-pr. field guns and a supply of Congreve rockets. While riding to Sir George Prevost's headquarters to receive his final orders, Major-General Robinson could hear the scaling of Captain Downie's guns. Yet Prevost told Robinson not to march off his men until 10 o'clock. The advance was at that hour led by the eight light companies of the force, moving in column of route for Pike's Ford, under the guidance officers of the Quartermaster General's department. Then, according to Major-General Robinson's Journal, confusion arose as to the route to be followed:

> Having marched nearly a mile and a half, the road branched off into a number of cart roads into a thick wood, and the officers of the Quartermaster General's department were divided in opinion whether we were on the right road or not. Major Thorn, Assistant Quartermaster-General to my brigade, came to me and assured me we were wrong, and that he would undertake to conduct to Pike's Ford, without fear of any further mistake.
>
> We accordingly retraced our steps, and in about an hour we arrived on the banks of the Saranac.[23]

As Major-General Robinson neared the ford "we heard three cheers from the Plattsburg side. I then sent Major Cochrane to ascertain the cause."[24]

The cause was the naval battle, to which Captain Downie had become committed without military support. To make matters worse, the wind also failed as H.M.S. *Confiance* headed up Plattsburgh Bay. Downie's whole plan of alignment now went wrong. The best he could do was anchor *Confiance* some 500 yards from Macdonough's line of battle, about 9 A.M., and pour a broadside from 14 24-pr. long guns into U.S.S. *Saratoga*. It killed or wounded about one-fifth of *Saratoga*'s crew. Within 15 minutes, however, Captain Downie was killed and Lieutenant James Robertson had to take command of *Confiance*. By this time H.M.S. *Linnet* was hotly engaged with the brig *Eagle*, which she eventually forced to leave the American line of battle, with some help from the forward guns of *Confiance*. Neither British schooner contributed anything to the battle: *Chub*, which was to have supported *Linnet*, drifted helplessly off course through the American line and hauled down her colours; *Finch* also got off course and finally ran aground on Crab Island. The British officer commanding the gunboats proved to be a coward (he was subsequently sent off to Kingston to face a court-martial, and escaped on the way there) and many of the Select Embodied Militia making up nearly half the crew of each persisted in lying on the bottom of the boats instead of doing their duty. Only four of the 11 gunboats made a fight of it.

At 10:30 A.M. *Confiance* and *Linnet* were still hotly engaged with *Saratoga* and *Eagle*. The last-named then managed to get turned about, so that the guns on her undamaged side could bear on *Confiance*, while she herself was no longer a target for either British ship. Macdonough managed to get *Saratoga* hauled around also and to fire broadsides from her hitherto silent row of carronades into *Confiance*, which now had only four guns firing. Lieutenant Robertson tried to swing *Confiance* around likewise, so that his 13 other 24-pr. long guns could fire. This was a slow process, however, and the fresh carronades of *Saratoga* and *Eagle* were inflicting still more damage. The surviving crew members were loath to continue the fight, so Lieutenant Robertson decided to surrender before *Confiance* should sink under them. Captain Pring struck *Linnet's* colours a bare 15 minutes later. British casualties were reported as being 57 killed and 72 wounded; American losses were 52 killed and 58 wounded. Macdonough had done well; as soon as news of the Battle of Lake Champlain reached the Secretary of the Navy in Washington, action was taken to promote him to the rank of captain.

The naval battle had been closely watched from the shore by Sir George Prevost. After H.M.S. *Linnet* was seen to strike, he decided to call off his own attack "because the most complete success would have been unavailing, and the possession of the Enemy's Works offered no advantage to compensate for the loss we must have sustained in acquiring Possession of them."[25] Major-General Baynes sent the following message to Major-General Robinson:

The Battle of Plattsburgh, September 11, 1814
Although overshadowed by victories at Baltimore and New Orleans, Plattsburgh was the most important American success of the War of 1812. (National Archives of Canada, C-10928)

I am directed to inform you that the "Confiance" and the Brig having struck their colours in consequence of the Frigate having grounded, it will no longer be prudent to persevere in the Service committed to your charge, and it is therefore the Orders of the Commander of the Forces that you immediately return with the Troops under your command.[26]

This order took Robinson completely by surprise. Power was "equally astonished."[27] At Pike's Ford the Saranac River was about 70 yards wide, but only two or three feet deep, and the light troops had got quickly across and chased the American defenders to a distant wood. Most of the troops had now crossed and were about to continue in column of route for what the two major-generals considered to be a relatively simple attack – one not to be compared with the two occasions when the 50-year-old Robinson had been wounded at the head of his brigade while assaulting French positions. Orders were orders, however. Robinson ordered a retirement.

If the American military commander fully understood what had been the British plan, he certainly gave no evidence of it in the report sent to the Secretary of War in Washington. Instead he converted the British failure to make any serious attack into a military victory for his own men. "Three efforts were made by the enemy to pass the river at the commencement of the cannonade and bombardment, with a view of assaulting the works, and they had prepared for that purpose an immense number of scaling-ladders," wrote Brigadier-General Macomb.

One attempt to cross was made at the village bridge, another at the upper bridge, and a third at a ford about three miles from the works. At the first two he was repulsed by the regulars – at the ford by the brave volunteers and militia, where he suffered severely in killed, wounded, and prisoners: a considerable body crossed the stream, but were either killed, taken, or driven back. The woods at this place were very favorable to the operations of the militia. A whole company of the 76th regiment was here destroyed, the three lieutenants and 27 men prisoners, the captain and the rest killed.[28]

During the course of the same evening of September 11, Sir George Prevost issued orders for his troops to destroy their surplus stores and munitions, and to retire into Lower Canada. The retirement was conducted with little interference from the Americans, but during a drenching rain which caused tempers to become even shorter. Casualties for the whole campaign were only 35 killed, 47 wounded and 72 taken prisoner; but 234 men were officially acknowledged to have deserted to the enemy. These deserters had enough of soldiering and their motive was the one that had always plagued the British Army in Canada – the possibility of achieving a greater measure of material success in the prosperous economy of the United States of America.[29]

The officers who had served under the Duke of Wellington continued to feel injured and argued that, by capturing Plattsburgh, they could have maintained their reputations and with smaller casualties than had attended several of their victories in Spain. Naturally on their return to Lower Canada they associated with the English-speaking minority which had grown to hate Sir George Prevost and was actively campaigning for his recall and replacement by someone more like Sir James Craig. Correspondents at Quebec fed the London and Glasgow newspapers with tirades against the "timid, temporizing policy" of Sir George Prevost. These were much worse and sillier than even the following extract from a letter written by an English gentlewoman and officer's wife named Alicia Cockburn:

The governor who has hitherto made his own story good in England, & by a course of art, & deception, almost unexampled, contrived to blind the eyes of Ministers at borne, is now at his wits' end. – too surely convinced that his infamous behaviour can no longer be concealed, he is taking every step to soften down as much as possible, the tales which will be told, & using the meanest arts to get them conveyed (since told they must be) in as favourable a manner as he can – for this purpose, he is sending home creatures who are dependent on him, and whom neither truth nor common honesty, will induce to swerve from the path of interest, such as can only be obtained by the most servile flattery. ...

Had any man with common abilities been at the head of this Government, unbiased by the invidious counsels of fools and sycophants, we must long ago have taught the Yankees submission, & been at Peace. Such is the *decided opinion of every military man* in the Province, whether his rank be high or low, so glaring are the state of affairs at this moment. The Civil Government of the Province is in a state no less deplorable than the military. ...[30]

Sir George Prevost's explanation of his failure was sent to Lord Bathurst in a private letter of September 22. For the most part it was a plausible effort, pointing to the hazard created by the naval defeat for his army in enemy territory, but it revealed the defensive mentality that had been developed by his having hitherto had to conduct a war with very limited resources:

> Your Lordship must have been aware from my previous despatches that no Offensive Operations could be carried on within the Enemy's Territory for the destruction of his Naval Establishments without Naval Support. ...
>
> The disastrous and unlooked for result of the Naval Contest by depriving me of the only means by which I could avail myself of any advantage I might gain, rendered a perseverance in the attack of the Enemy's position highly imprudent, as well as hazardous.
>
> Under the circumstances I had to determine whether I should consider my own Fame by gratifying the Ardor of the Troops in persevering in the attack, or consult the more substantial interest of my Country by withdrawing the Army which was yet uncrippled for the security of these Provinces.
>
> The most ample success on shore after the loss of the Flotilla could not have justified the sacrifice I must have made to obtain it.
>
> Had I failed, & such an event was possible after the American Army had been cheered by the sight of a Naval Victory, the destruction of a great part of my Troops must have been the consequence. & with the remainder I should have had to make a precipitate and embarrassed retreat, one very different from that which I have made.[31]

What Prevost's letter had evaded was to be the subject of a protest by Commodore Yeo of September 29 to the Admiralty. By this time Yeo had been able to study the reports of surviving naval officers and talk to Captain Pring, who had been released on parole. Yeo now wrote that the naval misfortune was largely the result of Prevost's urging Downie to premature action and his failure to support him as promised:

> It appears very evident that Capt Downie was urged, and even goaded on to his fate, by His Excelly [Prevost] who appears to have assumed the direction of the Naval Force.

His Excellency assured Capt Downie that the Army should attack the Enemy's Batteries at the same moment that the Naval Action commenced; and under this persuasion alone, did Capt Downie go in to attack them. Had His Excellency adhered to his previous arrangement, the Enemy's Squadron must have quitted their Anchorage, particularly their Gun Boats that lay close under their Shore, and whose heavy Metal and cool fire did more execution to our Vessels than their Ship or Brig.

Had His Excellency taken the Batteries even after the Action it must have led to the recapture of our Vessels; if not those of the Enemy as it is Notorious, and a fact, that the Enemy's Vessels were so cut up and disabled as to be incapable of taking possession of our Ship and Brig for upwards of three hours after the Action; and as the wind was directly on Shore, our Ships could have run under the Works had they been in our possession.[32]

Yeo had earlier written to the Admiralty that "had our Troops taken their Batteries first, it would have obliged the Enemy's Squadron to quit the Bay and give ours a fair chance."[33] By this he meant that in the open lake the long guns of H.M.S. *Confiance* could have battered the whole of the American squadron into submission from a range too great for carronades to damage her.

Not being aware of this correspondence, Sir George Prevost decided to visit Commodore Yeo at Kingston. There, according to the *Kingston Gazette* of Friday, September 16: "On Saturday last was launched from His Majesty's Dock Yard at Point Frederick, the fine Ship St. Lawrence, of 104 Guns, on which occasion a Royal Salute was fired from the Batteries."[34] The situation along the upper St. Lawrence River, as Prevost journeyed to the strongly garrisoned Kingston in early October, was vastly different from that of 1812. Now there were substantial numbers of blue-coated artillerymen and redcoated infantry on duty: 12 officers and 224 other ranks at Coteau-du-Lac, 25 officers and 507 other ranks at Cornwall, and another 19 officers and 421 other ranks divided between Prescott and Gananoque.

On October 11 Sir George Prevost wrote Lord Bathurst that H.M.S. *St. Lawrence* would not be ready to sail until October 15, but that Commodore Chauncey had already abandoned his blockade of Kingston. Eight more guns had been crowded on H.M.S. *St. Lawrence*, so that she now mounted 112 guns. So much of the stores tediously brought up river from Montreal had gone into the equipment of this monster ship, however, that there were insufficient quantities to outfit otherwise an expedition against Sackets Harbor. Moreover the navigation season was drawing to a close. Therefore *St. Lawrence* would be employed as escort for a convoy of stores badly needed by Lieutenant-General Drummond on the Niagara frontier.

Here Major-General George Izard's American army had arrived on October 5, having continued from Sackets Harbor in response to an urgent appeal from Major-General Jacob Brown. Izard's 5,500 regulars and 800 militia should be able to capture or destroy the continuing British army on the Niagara frontier, which now numbered only about 2,500 effectives – or so both Izard and the now subordinate Brown thought. Yet Izard found that the British defences in front of Chippawa were too strong for a frontal attack, when he advanced against them on October 15. The following day he learned that "Commodore Chauncey with the whole of his fleet has re-tired into port [Sackets Harbor], and is throwing up batteries for its pro-tection."[35] Izard's next bad news was of Sir James Yeo's arrival in the mouth of the Niagara River. "I confess I am greatly embarrassed," Izard now wrote the Secretary of War. "At the head of the most efficient army the United States have possessed during this war, much must be expected from me; and yet I can discern no object which can be achieved at this point worthy of the risk which will attend its attempt." On October 21 Izard retreated and prepared to break up his army. Major-General Brown marched his division to Sackets Harbor, close to his own home and where the next fighting might be expected. The remainder of the American army re-crossed the Niagara River to take up winter quarters at Buffalo on November 5, after blowing up Fort Erie.[36]

The Royal Navy shortly began the building of two schooner-gunboats, *Tecumseth* and *Newash*, at Chippawa for service on the upper lakes in 1815. This was in addition to a frigate and other naval construction planned for the incipient base at Penetanguishene. At Kingston work was beginning on two more ships of the line to carry 120 guns each, since the Americans had commenced a similar pair at Sackets Harbor. A 55-gun frigate, whose frame had been shipped across the Atlantic Ocean in pieces and then transported up the St. Lawrence river during the previous summer, was launched on Christmas Day as H.M.S. *Psyche*. Plans for 1815 also included the construction of three frigates and two heavy brigs at Isle aux Noix to regain naval supremacy on Lake Champlain.

Had Sir George Prevost had his way, the Admiralty would have been asked to send a rear-admiral to command on the inland waters, leaving

Commodore Sir James Yeo responsible only for the squadron on Lake Ontario, where his attention had been unduly concentrated. In London, however, Sir George Prevost was now held in ill favour. As early as October 30, the Duke of Wellington had replied to Lord Bathurst's request for an opinion: "It is very obvious to me that you must remove Sir George Prevost. I see he has gone to war about trifles with the general officers I sent him, which are certainly the best of their rank in the army; and his subsequent failure and distresses will be aggravated by that circumstance; and will probably with the usual fairness of the public be attributed to it."[37] Yet on December 22, the Duke of Wellington wrote in support of Prevost's course of action to his former Quartermaster General, Major-General Sir George Murray, who was being sent to North America as a local lieutenant-general for the specific purpose of telling Lieutenant-General Sir George Prevost to return to London and to explain his conduct of the Plattsburgh campaign.

I believe your opinions and mine are not far different as to the war in America. I approve highly, indeed I go further, I admire, all that has been done by the military in America, as far as I understand it generally. Whether Sir George Prevost was right or wrong in his decision at Lake Champlain is more than I can tell; but of this I am very certain, he must equally have retired to Kingston [a slip of the pen for Montreal] after our fleet was beaten, and I am inclined to believe he was right.

I have told the Ministers repeatedly that a naval superiority on the lakes is a *sine qua non* of success in war on the frontier of Canada, even if our object should be solely defensive.[38]

Unfortunately for the sake of Canadian history, the Duke of Wellington refrained from commenting on what to him must have seemed obvious. The Plattsburgh fiasco was the result of leaving a defensively minded general in charge of operations once the tide had turned and there no longer was any need to hesitate about doing battle merely because several hundred casualties might be suffered in a single action. Had one of Wellington's senior subordinates been sent to command Prevost's reinforced troops in the field, the story of Plattsburgh could have had a different ending.

CHAPTER FIFTEEN

The Treaty of Status Quo:
July 1814 to January 1815

NEGOTIATING THE TREATY OF GHENT /
NEW ORLEANS

Lord Castlereagh's offer in November 1813 to negotiate a peace settlement and President Madison's prompt acceptance of negotiation in January 1814 had not been followed by an early conference. Napoleon had abdicated by the time Henry Clay and Jonathan Russell had joined the American delegation of John Quincy Adams, James A. Bayard, and Albert Gallatin in Europe. London newspapers were then demanding vengeance against the United States. The British Government was preparing to send victorious troops to North America and would soon direct Sir George Prevost to prosecute the war with "all possible vigour" until the moment peace should finally be concluded.[1]

The instructions finally issued to British peace commissioners on July 28, 1814, emphasized that *uti possidetis*, or "retention of conquered territory," must be the starting point for negotiations.[2] In view of the offensive operations planned, this could mean a boundary rectification involving British retention of northern Maine, Plattsburgh, Sackets Harbor, Fort Niagara, Detroit and Mackinac. The future security of Canada was to be further ensured by the creation of an Indian buffer state in the Old Northwest: a step which would also undo the harm done in 1783 when Indian allies had been forgotten by the British negotiators.

The American delegation had been directed to demand that the Royal Navy put an end to its practice of impressing sailors; it was to negotiate about blockades, contraband and the maritime rights of neutrals; and it was to try and secure the cession of the two Canadas to the United States. The five American commissioners, being extremely able men, soon realized how silly these instructions were. Contrary to President Madison's belief, even the Baltic states had no intention of challenging Britain on the question of maritime rights. The President's particular friend, Albert Gallatin, therefore wrote on June 13 "that under the existing unpropitious circumstances of the world, America cannot by a continuance of the war compel Great Britain to yield any of the maritime points in dispute, and particularly to agree to any satisfactory arrangement on the subject of impressment; and that the most favourable terms of peace that can be expected are the status *ante bellum*."[3]

Whether even this might be secured would depend upon the outcome of the 1814 campaign and the ability of the American commissioners to outwit the British delegates who had no experience in diplomacy. Admiral Lord Gambier was to be almost a nonentity during the protracted negotiations at Ghent and allow Henry Goulburn, the Parliamentary Under-Secretary of State for War and the Colonies, to act as spokesman. The third member of the delegation, William Adams, was a Doctor of Civil Law. Their shortcomings were fully known to Lord Castlereagh, who was personally occupied by the Congress at Vienna, but he seems to have considered that no harm could be done because all their actions would have to be referred to the Prime Minister in London for approval.

Since neither delegation was empowered to admit the initial claims of the other, nothing was accomplished during the opening session on August 8. The second session on August 19, called to consider the British delegation's new instructions from London, was just as unsatisfactory. Yet the British Government did not wish the world to believe that it desired continuation of the war for purposes of conquest, so ameliorating instructions were soon sent to Ghent.

Another factor influencing the British Government's policy was the swarm of American privateers now operating in home waters, where merchant ships had been sailing without adequate naval protection. Indignation meetings were held by the shipowners and manufacturers of several large British ports. The following resolutions were passed at Glasgow on September 10, declaring the injury to British commerce and British naval pride:

> That the number of American privateers with which our channels have
> been infested, the audacity with which they have approached our coasts,
> and the success with which their enterprise has been attended, have

proved injurious to our commerce, humbling to our pride, and discreditable to the directors of the naval power of the British nation, whose flag of late waved over every sea and triumphed over every rival.

There is reason to believe, in the short space of twenty-four months, above eight hundred vessels have been captured by the Power whose maritime strength we have hitherto impolitically held in contempt.[4]

The Secretary of the Admiralty might reasonably point out that the number of merchant ships had deserted from naval convoys when close to port and thus had only themselves to blame. Yet members of the general public would agree with the prevailing sentiment that, with a navy of nearly a thousand vessels of various types, it was not safe for a British merchantman to sail in home waters.

The news of the capture of Washington, which was published in London newspapers on September 27, correspondingly discouraged the American commissioners at Ghent, as did the subsequent news that the British had occupied part of Maine. Should the offensive launched from Canada also prove successful, they would have no counter to the British claim of *uti possidetis*. Fortunately for them, the next news from North America was that of the American naval victory on Lake Champlain.

By this time the British Government was beginning to worry about the possibility of a European war being revived and the continuing safety of its Ambassador in Paris, the Duke of Wellington. Bonapartists had threatened his life and obviously were planning the overthrow of King Louis XVIII. The British Government decided to get Wellington away by offering him the military command in North America.

The Duke of Wellington's reply to the Prime Minister, dated November 9, discouraged the whole idea, but gave the British Government the answer it really needed about the claims it should press. The most interesting portions of this letter give Wellington's firm view of the importance of sea power on the inland lakes, his commendation of a defensive role for the army (even if led by himself), and his recommendation that no claims for territory were warranted:

I have already told you and Lord Bathurst that I feel no objection to going to America, though I don't promise to myself much success there. I believe there are troops enough there for the defence of Canada forever, and even for the accomplishment of any reasonable offensive plan that could be formed from the Canadian frontier. I am quite sure that all the American armies of which I have ever read would not beat out of a field of battle the troops that went from Bordeaux last summer, if common precautions and care were taken of them. That which appears to be wanting in America is not a General, or General Officers and troops, but a naval superiority on the Lakes. Till that superiority is acquired, it is impossible, according to my notion, to maintain an army in such a situation as to keep the enemy out of the whole frontier, much less to make any conquest from the enemy, which with those superior means, might, with reasonable hopes of success, be undertaken. I may be wrong in this opinion, but I think the whole history of the war proves its truth.... The question is, whether we can acquire this naval superiority on the Lakes. If we can't, I shall do you but little good in America; and I shall go there only to prove the truth of Prevost's defence, and to sign a peace which might as well be signed now....

Considering every thing, it is my opinion that the war has been a most successful one, and highly honourable to the British arms; but from particular circumstances, such as the want of naval superiority on the Lakes, you have not been able to carry it into the enemy's territory, notwithstanding your military success, and now undoubted military superiority, and have not even cleared your own territory of the enemy on the point of attack [Fort Erie and Fort Malden]. You cannot, then, on any principle of equality in negotiation, claim a cession of territory [Northern Maine, Fort Niagara and Fort Mackinac] excepting in exchange for other advantages which you have in your power.[5]

The British Government took the Duke's advice. On November 18 the Prime Minister wrote to Lord Castlereagh that "I think we have determined, if all other points can be satisfactorily settled, not to continue the war for the purpose of obtaining, or securing any acquisition of territory. We have been led to this determination by the consideration of the unsatisfactory state of the negotiations at Vienna, and by that of the alarming situation of the interior of France."[6]

By this time the American commissioners at Ghent had received instructions which permitted them to modify their own stand. Internally the United States was in a bad way. Trade was at a standstill; banks were failing and paper money was being heavily discounted; only a fraction of the federal government's latest war loan was subscribed; the regular army was declining in strength because there were not enough recruits to make good its wastage; worst of all, there was a growing movement in New England for secession from the United States and creation of its own confederation. In consequence the American commissioners were able to submit for consideration by the British delegation a draft treaty based on the *status quo ante bellum.*

Nine of the 15 articles in this draft were finally acceptable, in a more or less amended form, to both parties. The Treaty of Ghent, written as 11 articles in all, was signed on Christmas Eve, 1814. All conquests were to be returned; hostilities against the Indians were to be terminated by both sides; the British abandoned the idea that the Old Northwest might be an Indian buffer state and the boundary stretching from the Bay of Fundy to the Lake of the Woods was to be defined by subsequent international commissions. Nowhere in the Treaty was there any reference to the causes that had led to war.[7]

There was no quick way of halting the last of the scheduled British offensives. This had begun on December 10 with the landing of troops from Vice-Admiral Cochrane's fleet on the left or east bank of the Mississippi River some distance from its mouth. The intention was to capture New Orleans, with its storehouses full of sugar and cotton, and to close the mouth of the Mississippi River to American traffic. Had the British advanced guard of 1,600 troops pushed resolutely forward along its left bank on December 23, for the last seven miles, New Orleans could have been secured, because Major-General Andrew Jackson had not yet taken any steps for its defence. By Christmas Day, however, when Major-General Sir Edward Pakenham finally caught up with the British army he had been sent from England to command, it was too late for boldness. American troops and local negro slaves had time to construct a breastwork of sugar barrels and earth behind a wide but empty ditch, which stretched for three-fifths of a mile between the river bank and an impassable swamp. Behind this, Major-General Jackson massed the bulk of his regulars and militia, with four guns. A naval battery on the right, or west, bank provided supporting fire.

Sir Edward Pakenham was a competent soldier.[8] He had served as Adjutant General to the Duke of Wellington's Peninsular Army (he was also the Duke's brother-in-law), but he was now placed in a difficult situation. The heavy guns brought with great difficulty from Vice-Admiral Cochrane's ships proved unable to breach the American breastworks. Rather than give

Major-General Sir Edward Pakenham (1778-1815)
Wellington's brother-in-law, the veteran Pakenham only reluctantly assumed command in Louisiana and was killed at the battle of New Orleans. (Editor's collection)

up and go away, since he now had about 6,000 British regulars and 1,000 negro soldiers of two of the West India Regiments, Pakenham decided to make a strong feint against this impregnable earthwork on January 8, 1815, while Colonel William Thornton crossed the river with 1,500 regulars and advanced up its west bank to outflank the American position.

Thornton's party succeeded both in driving off the 800 Kentucky militia stationed there and in seizing the American naval guns; it then managed to advance far enough up river to be behind Jackson's position. This operation was badly behind schedule, however, and a holding attack by the rest of the army had already come to grief, since the dense columns were thinned by the American artillery as the men tried to negotiate the muddy ditch made greasy by recent rain. Sir Edward Pakenham was killed by a piece of grapeshot while watching the attack go forward; Major-General Samuel Gibbs was mortally wounded and Major-General John Keane was seriously wounded. There were more than 2,000 other British casualties, while the American defenders of the earthworks had only 71 killed and wounded. The surviving British major-general, John Lambert, recalled Colonel Thornton's party and subsequently retreated down river with what was still actually a powerful army. On February 8 it invested Fort Bowyer at the entrance to Mobile Bay. Three days later the American garrison surrendered.[9]

LIEU: GEN: SIR GEORGE PROVOST
GOVERNOR OF CANADA.

Caricature of Sir George Prevost, 1815
Although he had carried out his difficult task of defending British North America during the war, Prevost's reverse at Plattsburgh led to him becoming the butt of ridicule and, eventually, to his recall to Britain. (Toronto Reference Library, T-15460)

That was the day news of peace reached New York. Everywhere it was greeted with enthusiasm, even before the terms were made public. These indicated that nothing had been achieved by the war, yet the United States Senate confirmed the Treaty unanimously on February 16. Victory tidings had already arrived from New Orleans, so there was something at the end to be proud of. By the time news of this British defeat reached England, Napoleon had left Elba and was beginning his triumphal return to Paris; there would be another war in Europe and there was no time to waste in looking back at North America.

On March 1, Sir George Prevost learned at Quebec that the Treaty of Ghent had been ratified by representatives of the British and American Governments in Washington. The following day, however, Lieutenant-General Sir George Murray reached Quebec, via the overland route across New Brunswick, with the personal message from Lord Bathurst that Prevost's commission as Governor-in-Chief was revoked and that he was to return to London to explain his conduct of the Plattsburgh campaign. That this was a bitter and unexpected blow is evident from the letter Prevost addressed to Lord Bathurst on March 3:

This is the first & only notice I have received from your Lordship respecting my conduct at Platsburg, and I cannot but express the surprise excited by the nature, as well as the mode of this communication. Conscious of no fault I dread not the strictest investigation, but it appears adding unnecessary poignancy to the unexpected blow, that the mortification you have judged proper to inflict should be conveyed through a third person & this an officer so much my junior in the Service.

Your Lordship states that the revocation of my commission as Governor General is not meant to mark His Royal Highness the Prince Regent's displeasure: unfortunately the distinction will be very difficult for the world to discover, and I must confess that to my own feelings the circumstance is acutely painful. The consequence may probably be that I may remain some time from severity of climate, or other circumstances (as your Lordship observes) seeing myself deprived of every authority and every emolument after four years of the most arduous duties I have performed in the course of the five & thirty I have devoted to His Majesty's Service, unless to avoid such an interval I should prefer passing through the United States like a fugitive.[10]

Sir George Prevost issued orders at once to put an end to hostilities and to disband the militia. On March 25 he prorogued the Legislature of Lower Canada. On April 3 he left Quebec, travelling to Saint John on foot by the winter route across New Brunswick. He was succeeded in the government

The Duke of Wellington (1769-1852)
The greatest soldier of his time, Wellington consistently approved Sir George Prevost's conduct of the war although he also approved Prevost's recall to Britain. (Charles Oman, *Wellington's Army*, 1913)

by Lieutenant-General Gordon Drummond who arrived from Upper Canada a few hours after his departure. Prevost reached England on May 11. His explanation was accepted by the British Government, which undoubtedly was greatly impressed by the Duke of Wellington's opinion and by Prevost's successful conduct of the war prior to the advance on Plattsburgh.

Five days later Commodore Sir James Yeo also reached England, having been replaced in Canada on March 22 by Commodore E.W.C.R. Owen, R.N. During mid-August Sir James Yeo was a leading participant in the naval court-martial of the surviving officers of the Battle of Lake Champlain. The court "honourably acquitted" the survivors, and decided that the defeat "was principally caused by the British Squadron having been urged into Battle previous to it being in a proper state to meet its Enemy by a promised Cooperation of the Land Forces, which was not carried into Effect and by the very pressing Letters and communications of their Commander in Chief."[11]

Sir George Prevost protested the publication of this finding in a letter to the Commander-in-Chief, H.R.H. Frederick, Duke of York, and requested a court-martial so that he might have a public opportunity of justifying his conduct. A General Court-Martial was summoned for January 12, 1816, which would allow time for witnesses to travel from Canada. Sir George Prevost was in ill health, however, as a consequence of his recent strenuous duties and worries, and died a week before the court-martial was due to assemble. Nothing could now be done legally to clear Sir George Prevost's reputation, but the Prince Regent did, at the behest of his widow, confer upon her and succeeding baronets a lasting memorial in the form of supporters for the Prevost coat of arms, holding banners inscribed "West Indies" and "Canada" respectively, and a motto *servatum cineri*.[12]

Yet the harm already done could not be obliterated. Only four days after Prevost had left Quebec, *The Letters of Veritas* began appearing in the *Montreal Herald*. These 10 letters, republished as a pamphlet in July 1815, purported to be "a succinct narrative of the military administration of Sir George Prevost, during his command in the Canadas; whereby it will appear manifest, that the merit of preserving them from Conquest belongs not to him."[13] *Veritas* proved to be a Montreal merchant named John Richardson, who twisted fact and rumour to suit the ends of the English-speaking faction that had grown to hate Prevost. This perversion of truth formed a basis for the contention in the *Quarterly Review* (London, July 1822) that the British Army should have shown to greater advantage.

Prevost's former Civil Secretary replied with *Some Account of the Public Life of the late Lieutenant-General Sir George Prevost, Bart. particularly of his services in the Canada's; including a reply to the strictures on his military character, contained in an article in The Quarterly Review for October 1822* (London, 1823). This was buttressed by extensive quotations from Prevost's personal papers, but the book was badly written and citing the wrong issue of the *Quarterly Review* was merely one factual error which did not help its case.[14]

Canadians have preferred the version by *Veritas*, probably because his first letter contributed to the myth that American invasion attempts were thwarted by the bravery of the local militia, with some help from the British Army. What was best remembered in the Canadas, as the years passed and personal recollections became blurred, were the occasions, relatively few in number, on which militia had come face to face with the enemy without the support of regulars. These encounters were magnified in number and naturally tended, in almost every instance, to become victories. After American raiders had been deterred from landing at Turkey Point on May 16, 1814, Colonel Thomas Talbot did report that he had "every Confidence in the determined Spirit of the Militia to oppose the Enemy," but he added that "Their ardour is greatly increased by the Support of the [British] 19th Light Dragoons."[15] No one in an official position ever thought it necessary to explain that the sedentary militia satisfactorily performed the principal roles expected of it. These were transporting supplies, building roads and fortifications, guarding prisoners and providing mounted couriers – necessary tasks that could be performed by men who had little or no formal military training and which are nowadays performed by what is known as the administrative "tail" of a field force. On the other hand, the small units of volunteer militia in both provinces and the battalions of Select Embodied Militia of Lower Canada became well enough trained to fight alongside the British regulars and acquit themselves well.[16]

The desire of most New Englanders to stay out of the war, and the unquestioned supremacy of the Royal Navy in the North Atlantic, made it unnecessary for the militias of New Brunswick, Nova Scotia and Prince Edward Island to take an active part in the war. All that the people of New Brunswick and Nova Scotia could later boast about were the exploits of the 37 privateers and 12 armed traders, which had received letters of marque and brought into port 207 American prizes for disposal by Vice-Admiralty

Courts. Yet the illicit trade encouraged with New England helped greatly to feed and maintain Sir George Prevost's military forces in the Canadas: supplies and troops surplus to local requirements were either moved overland across New Brunswick and into Lower Canada, or transferred by sea from Halifax to Quebec.

British soldiers and sailors must have been appalled by the vastness of the wilderness to be traversed, mostly on foot or in bateaux, before they could reach the scene of actual fighting. Yet they quickly managed to adapt themselves to local conditions and cope with the insects and fever of the hot summers and frostbite during the long, cold winters, as well as poor food most of the time. By the time British servicemen got back to Great Britain, however, the general public had heard so much about the victories of the Peninsular War and Waterloo that they did not want to hear about a little war in North America. Although decisive and hard fought victories had been won there, they were mostly mere engagements or skirmishes by European standards. Half-pay officers like Lieutenant-Colonel "Red George" Macdonell might later rail against the indifference shown their efforts and the favouritism extended to the "P and W" boys, but only officers who had actually served under the great Duke of Wellington got the best appointments during his long tenure as Commander-in-Chief of the British Army.[17]

The Duke of Wellington became firmly convinced, from his study of Canadian despatches and maps, that the failure of the Americans to conquer Canada had been caused by their own inadequacy. On April 15, 1828 he said as much to a Select Committee of the House of Commons dealing with colonial defence expenditure:

> I have never been in that country [Canada], but I must add that I have been astonished that the officers of the army and navy employed in that country were able to defend those provinces last war; and I can attribute their having been able to defend them as they did only to the inexperience of the officers of the United States in the operations of war, and possibly likewise to the difficulty which they must have found in stationing their forces as they ought to have done, upon the right bank of the St. Lawrence.[18]

Secretary of War Armstrong in Washington had recognized the importance of cutting the line of the St. Lawrence as the most certain way to conquer Upper Canada, but he could not get action from his generals. His successor, James Monroe, found Major-General Jacob Brown more co-operative and prepared to act if the war had continued into the summer of 1815. It seems unlikely that the 29,000 British regulars in the country could have been defeated in the field by what forces Brown might gather; even if they were, the Royal Navy could have subsequently brought to Quebec sufficient reinforcements from the army with which Wellington defeated Napoleon at Waterloo to restore the British position in Canada.

The Duke of Wellington can hardly have realized, however, how badly the United States Army lacked competent young regimental officers, without which it is impossible to have good soldiers and units. British regimental officers may have been lacking in imagination in most cases, but they were well grounded in elementary tactics and their men had been well drilled by experienced drill sergeants.[19] Of the British general officers only Procter managed to blunder consistently; Sheaffe, Riall, and Drummond all had good as well as bad days.[20]

The importance of sea power on the large inland lakes was recognized in both London and Washington, and neither Yeo nor Chauncey was censured for avoiding battle on Lake Ontario when the odds were unfavourable. The American commanders on Lake Champlain and Lake Erie were not abler than their British counterparts; rather they were lucky not to be hounded into battle by army officers who were older and much more senior in rank.

What is surprising is the absence of anything resembling a national war effort on either side. Life went on as usual, unless there was imminent danger from an immediate enemy. Both Americans and Canadians were willing to leave the real fighting to professionals and to the patriotic or adventurous minority who volunteered their services. Many Americans were vehemently opposed to a war in which the United States was plainly the aggressor and insisted that their duty as militia men was legally limited to the defence of their own state. Because the Americans were the aggressors, both English-speaking and French-speaking Canadians were mostly prepared to defend the country against them, once it was realized that the British were determined to put up a real fight. There was far less active disloyalty than the authorities feared.

As a result of the war, hostility towards the United States was very real in British North America for many years. It was most pronounced in Upper Canada. Conservative elements persisted in labelling all reformers as pro-

American and desirous of introducing the worst excesses of Jacksonian democracy. The manifestation of the growing importance of the common man in American politics had been brought to Washington by the victor of New Orleans, Andrew Jackson, who served as President of the United States from 1829 to 1837. Americans paused little in their efforts to expand their nation westward and achieve greater material prosperity, but when they did look back on the War of 1812, they thought first of the interference with their maritime rights which had caused them to fight and then of the successful exploits of their own privateersmen. Since the Treaty of Ghent conveniently coincided with the end of European interference in American affairs, they were able to imagine it as a second successful conclusion of the War for Independence. Herbert Agar suggests in *The Price of Union* (1950), that perhaps this illusion was useful:

> Perhaps it is well that no one told America that her new freedom depended not on the Treaty of Ghent, but on the Treaty of Paris which had been signed on May 30, 1814, after Napoleon's abdication at Fontainebleau. It was not the little war against England which won for America the blessing of being left alone; it was the enormous war against Europe's conqueror. With Napoleon beaten, and England supreme at sea, the world was to know relative peace for a hundred years; and within that peace the United States was safe, and grew strong.[21]

Nowadays the conflict on the inadvertent battleground of Canada is no longer a national issue, although interest in its men and events and its setting continues. Increasingly since 1871, when the Treaty of Washington issued in an era of continuing good relations, Canadians and Americans have become proud of the undefended boundary that separates them and now try their best to forget, or excuse, the incredible little War of 1812.

Despatches Respecting Defensive and Offensive Policy

The two despatches printed below provide the basis for a reasoned explanation of Sir George Prevost's conduct of the War of 1812, but one which seems to have escaped Canadian historians. The first was addressed by Prevost on May 18, 1812 to the Earl of Liverpool, who shortly became Prime Minister, however, and was succeeded as Secretary of State for War and the Colonies by Earl Bathurst. It is preserved at the Public Record Office, London, England in C.O. 42/146. The second, sent by Bathurst to Prevost on June 3, 1814, was copied into C.O. 43/23 in 1910 from the original despatch loaned to the Public Record Office for the purpose by Sir Charles Prevost. There are microfilm copies of C.O. 42/146 and C.O. 43/23 in the National Archives of Canada.

I. PREVOST TO LIVERPOOL

Quebec 18th May 1812.

My Lord,

In obedience to the Commands signified to me in your Lordship's dispatch No. 7 of the 13th February, I now have the honor to report upon the Military position of His Majesty's North American Provinces, and the means of defending them.

UPPER CANADA

Commencing with Upper Canada, as the most contiguous to the Territory of the United States and frontier to it along its whole extent, which renders it, in the event of War, more liable to immediate attack.

Fort St Joseph. Fort St Joseph, distant about 1500 miles from Quebec, consists of Lines of Strong Pickets enclosing a Block House. – It stands on the Island St Joseph within the detour communicating the head of Lake Huron with Lake Superior:– It can only be considered as a Post of Assemblage for friendly Indians, and in some degree a protection for the North West Fur Trade:– The Garrison at St Joseph's consists of a small Detachment from the Royal Artillery, and one Company of Veterans.

Fort Amherstburg. Fort Amherstburg, situated on the River Detroit at the head of Lake Erie, is of importance from it's being the Dock Yard and Marine Arsenal for the Upper Lakes:– It is also a place of reunion for the Indians inhabiting that part of the Country, who assemble there in considerable numbers to receive Presents:– The Fort has been represented to me as a temporary Field Work in a ruinous State; it is now undergoing a repair to render it tenable:– The Garrison at Amherstburg consists of Subaltern's Detachment of Artillery, and about 120 men of the 41st Regiment-the whole Commanded by Lieutenant Colonel St. George an Inspecting Field Officer:– The Militia in its Vicinity amounts to about 500 men.

Fort George. Fort George is a temporary Work at the head of Lake Ontario, now repairing to render it tenable, but in its most improved State, it cannot make much resistance against an Enemy in considerable force:– The Garrison at Fort George consists of a Captain's Command of Artillery, and about 400 men of the 41st Regiment, the whole Commanded by Colonel Procter:– The Militia Force in the, Neighborhood of Fort George, does not exceed 2,000 Nominal men.

Fort Erie, Chippawa and Fort George form the chain of Communication between Lake Erie and Lake Ontario.

Fort Erie. At Fort Erie, there is a Captains Command from the 41st Regiment, and at Chippawa a Subaltern's. – The American Posts directly opposed to this Line are Fort Niagara, Fort Schlosser, Black Rock, and Buffalo Creek:– In the event of Hostilities, it would be highly advantageous to gain possession of Fort Niagara to secure the Navigation of the River Niagara.

York. York is situated on the North Shore of Lake Ontario, has a good Harbour, and is the position in Upper Canada best adapted for a deposit of Military Stores, whenever it is converted into a Post of defence, and also for a Dock Yard and Marine Arsenal for this Lake. Its retired situation from the American frontier, makes it a position particularly desirable for those purposes:– The project of fortifying and strengthening this Post has been submitted for consideration:– York is the Head Quarters of Upper Canada, – its Garrison consists of three Companies of the 41st Regiment:– The Militia in its vicinity is computed at 1500 men.

Kingston. Kingston is situated at the head of the Boat Navigation of the St Lawrence, contiguous to a very flourishing Settlement on the American frontier, and is exposed to sudden attack, which, if successful, would cut off the communication between the Upper and Lower Province, and deprive us of our Naval resources:– The Garrison of Kingston consists of Four Companies of the 10th

Royal Veteran Battalion, under the Command of Major Macpherson:– The Militia in the Neighborhood about 1500 men.

The Americans have Posts in the vicinity of Kingston, not only opposite, but both above & below with good Harbours, which are open to the resources of a very populous Country:– In the event of Hostilities it will be indispensably necessary for the preservation of a Communication between the Lower and the Upper Province, to establish some strong Post for the Regulars and Militia, to secure the Navigation of the St. Lawrence above the Rapids to Lake Ontario:– The total number of Militia in Upper Canada is calculated at 11,000 men, of which it might not be prudent to Arm more than 4,000.

LOWER CANADA

Montreal. Montreal is the principal commercial city in the Canadas, and in the event of War, would become the first object of Attack:– It is situated on an extension Island, and does not possess any means of defence:– Its security depends upon our being able to maintain an impenetrable line on the South Shore, extending from La Prairie to Chambly, with a sufficient Flotilla to command the Rivers St: Lawrence and the Richelieu.

The Garrison of Montreal at present, consists of a Brigade of Light Artillery, and the 49th Regiment:– The Militia in its neighborhood, and easily collected, would exceed 12,000 men, ill armed and without discipline, and 600 embodied, now assembled for training at La Prairie.

St John's. St John's is considered a frontier Post:– there ends the Navigation from Lake Champlain:– It is occupied by a Company of Royal Veterans and one of the 49th Regiment:– The Field Works formerly erected for the defence of this Post, are now in ruins, and could not be resumed to much advantage, as they are commanded by ground contiguous, and the Post can be turned by following the New Roads leading from the United States to Montreal

Chambly. Chambly is unimportant, but as a Post of Support to St Johns, and a place of assemblage for the Militia and a Depot for their Arms and Ammunition:– It is occupied by about 300 Voltigeurs, and a Detachment of Artillery having two Field Guns.

William Henry [Sorel]. William Henry is 13 leagues from Chambly, and is situated at the junction of the Richelieu & St Lawrence:– It is the most important position on the South Shore for Depots, and for a rendezvous for the Armed Vessels and Boats required for the defence of the St. Lawrence:– It is unquestionably a position which deserves being made tenable against a sudden or irregular attack:– From thence down the St. Lawrence are many excellent positions for arresting the progress of an Enemy marching on either Shore upon Quebec, particularly if he is not in possession of the Navigation of the River:– The Garrison

THE INCREDIBLE WAR OF 1812

at William Henry consists of one Field Officer and four Companies of the 100th Regiment.

Quebec. Quebec is the only permanent Fortress in the Canadas:– It is the Key to the whole and must be maintained:– To the final defence of this position, every other Military operation ought to become subservient, and the retreat of the Troops upon Quebec must be the primary consideration: -The means of resistance afforded by the Fortifications in their present imperfect State, are not such as could justify a hope of its being able to withstand a vigorous and well conducted siege. – It requires Bomb proof Casmates for the Troops, as the Town is completely commanded from the South Shore at Point Levi, a position which it has frequently been recommended to occupy in force:– The Casmates ought to be erected on Cape Diamond, a position that points itself out for a Citadel:– It is advisable that the whole circumference of the summit of this Hill should be occupied, being the only elevation within the Walls not commanded by the height of Land on the plains of Abraham:– Such a Work would essentially defend the extension Line of Fortification, sloping from Cape Diamond to the Artillery Barrack which is old and imperfect, is commanded from the high land opposite, and is besides seen in reverse and open to an enfilade fire from positions on the bank of the St. Charles River.

The Garrison of Quebec at present consists of about 2500 Rank and File:– The Militia of Lower Canada amounts to 60,000 men, a mere posse, ill arm'd, and without discipline, where of 2,000 are embodied for training.

In framing a general out line of Cooperation for defence with the Forces in Upper Canada, commensurate with our deficiency in strength, I have considered the preservation of Quebec as the first object, and to which all others must be subordinate:– Defective as Quebec is, it is the only Post that can be considered as tenable for a moment, the preservation of it being of the utmost consequence to the Canadas, as the door of entry for that Force The King's Government might find it expedient to send for the recovery of both, or either of these Provinces, altho' the pressure of the moment in the present extended range of Warfare, might not allow the sending of that force which would defend both, therefore considering Quebec in this view, its importance can at once be appreciated.

If the Americans are determined to attack Canada, it would be in vain the General should flatter himself with the hopes of making an effectual defence of the open Country, unless powerfully assisted from Home:– All predatory or ill concerted attacks undertaken presumptuously and without sufficient means, can be resisted and repulsed: Still this must be done with caution, that the resources, for a future exertion, the defence of Quebec, may be unexhausted.

NEW BRUNSWICK & NOVA SCOTIA

The Province of New Brunswick and the peninsula of Nova Scotia present so many vulnerable points to an invading Army, that it is difficult to establish any precise Plan for the defence of either, and consequently much must depend upon Contingencies in the event of Invasion:— Their security very materially depends upon the Navy, and the vigilance of our Cruizers in the Bay of Fundy.

In the event of Hostilities with America, it would be an advisable measure to take possession of Moose Island, in the Bay of Passamaquoddy, improperly occupied by a small American Garrison, where we should derive great advantage from the cooperation of our Navy, and should remove the scene of Warfare to the American frontier.

Fredericton. The defence of Fredericton is out of the question, and the course of the River St John must be defended at the discretion of the Officer Commanding that Garrison, according to the description and number of the assailing Army:— The Garrison at Fredericton at present consists of a small Detachment of Artillery, and Six Companies of the 104th Regiment.

St John. The Town of St John is totally indefensible on the land side, it would therefore be requisite to make provision for the removal of the Ordnance and Stores from thence:— Two or three small Vessels of War stationed in the River St John (part of whose Crews might Man Gun Boats) would very much conduce to its security, and in case of a hasty retreat might bring away the Ordnance and Stores:

St John is at present Garrisoned by two Companies of the 104th Regiment, and a proportion of the Artillery:— The Militia of New Brunswick amount to about 4,000 men, much scattered, and but few of them have been trained to the use of Arms.

Halifax. In the event of an Enemy approaching Halifax by Land, Nature has done much for its protection:— At the Isthmus near Cumberland, the Militia supported by a proportion of regular Troops, may make a very protracted defence, were its Flanks secured by the Navy: No point can be fixed upon for the defence of the Basin of Minas, as the entrance of that Bay is too wide to admit of being fortified:— If the Enemy escapes the squadron stationed in the Bay of Fundy, he may have his choice of Ground for debarkation, but must look to the destruction of his Flotilla, and no further support by water. Margaret's Bay on the Eastern Coast of Nova Scotia, offers a spacious and safe Harbour, and should any Enemy meditate the capture of Halifax, that point would probably attract his attention:— The attempt however would be very hazardous, and he must not calculate either on a Retreat, or Succour, which it is presumed would be prevented by the Squadron from Halifax:— The approach from this Bay is through a Country easily defended, and unfavorable for the Transport of Ordnance or

Stores of any Kind:– The Sea defences of the Harbour of Halifax offer much to rely on, but the Land defences are so imperfect as to be undeserving of notice:– The Garrison of Halifax at present consists of about 1500 men, including three Companies of Artillery:– The Militia of Nova Scotia amounts to upwards of 11,000 men; about 6000 of whom have been furnished with Arms and accoutrements, and from the assistance and instruction afforded them by the Inspecting Field Officers in that District, they have made as much progress in training and discipline, as could be expected from a Class of People, who are so much scattered.

CAPE BRETON AND PRINCE EDWARD ISLAND

The Islands of Cape Breton & Prince Edward Island, dependencies of the British North American Provinces, are Garrisoned by small Detachments of Troops stationed at the principal Town in each, but their Works of defence are so insignificant, as to be unworthy of Observation; – Nor does their Militia amount to any considerable number deserving to be noticed:

NEWFOUNDLAND

The Island of Newfoundland, also a dependency of this Command, is principally defended by the Navy upon that Station during the Summer:– The Chief Town and Military depot, St. Johns, is Garrisoned by the Nova Scotia Fencible Regiment, and a Company of Artillery.

BERMUDAS

Of the Bermudas, their strength and resources against an attack, I cannot as yet presume to report upon, to your Lordship, as they have but recently been made a part of this Command.

I have the honor to be My Lord,

Your Lordship's Most Obedient and most humble Servant

GEORGE PREVOST

Quebec lst June 1812

P.S. The following alterations have taken place since the foregoing Report was prepared – Five Companies of the Royal Newfoundland Fencibles have proceeded from Quebec, and are now on their Route to York in Upper Canada, for the Marine Service.

Four hundred Recruits belonging to the Glengary Levy are assembled at Three Rivers in Lower Canada, to be formed into a Regiment, trained and disciplined.

The Detachment of the Royal Newfoundland Fencibles from Quebec, has been replaced by an equal number of the 100th Regiment from Three Rivers.

II. BATHURST TO PREVOST

Secret

Downing Street,
3rd June, 1814.

Sir,

I have already communicated to you in my despatch of the 14th of April the intention of His Majesty's Government to avail themselves of the favourable state of Affairs in Europe, in order to reinforce the Army under your command. I have now to acquaint you with the arrangements which have been made in consequence, and to point out to you the views with which His Majesty's Government have made so considerable an augmentation of the Army in Canada.

[R. & F. 768] The 4th Battalion of the Royal Scots of the strength stated in the margin sailed from Spithead on the 9th ulto. direct for Quebec, and was joined at Cork by the 97th Regiment destined to relieve the Nova Scotia Fencibles at Newfoundland; which latter will immediately proceed to Quebec.

[R. & F. 6th 980, 82. 837] The 6th and 82nd Regiments of the strength as per margin sailed from Bordeaux on the 15th ulto. direct for Quebec. Orders have also been given for embarking at the same port, twelve of the most effective Regiments of the Army under the Duke of Wellington together with three Companies of Artillery on the same service.

This force, which (when joined by the detachments about to proceed from this Country) will not fall far short of ten thousand infantry, will proceed in three divisions to Quebec. The first of these divisions will be embarked immediately, the second a week after the first and the third as soon as the means of Transport are collected. The last division however will arrive at Quebec long before the close of the year.

Six other Regiments have also been detached from the Gironde and the Mediterranean, four of which are destined to be employed in a direct operation against the Enemy's Coast, and the other two are intended as a reinforcement to Nova Scotia and New Brunswick; available (if circumstances appear to you to render it necessary) for the defence of Canada, or for the offensive operations on the Frontier, to which your attention will be particularly directed. It is also in contemplation at a later period of the year to make a more serious attack on some part of the Coasts of the United States; and with this view a considerable force will be collected at Cork without delay. These operations will not fail to effect a powerful diversion in your favor.

[R. & F. 3127] The result of this arrangement, as far as you are immediately concerned, will be to place at your disposal the Royals, The Nova Scotia Fencibles, the 6th & the 82nd Regiments amounting to three thousand one hundred

and twenty seven men: and to afford you in the course of the year a further reinforcement of ten thousand British Troops. [10,000]

When this force shall have been placed under your command, His Majesty's
Government conceive that the Canadas will not only be protected for the time
against any attack which the enemy may have the means of making, but it will
enable you to commence offensive operations on the Enemy's Frontier before
the close of this Campaign. At the same time it is by no means the intention of
His Majesty's Government to encourage such forward movements into the Interior of the American Territory as might commit the safety of the Force placed
under your command. The object of your operations will be; first, to give immediate protection: secondly, to obtain if possible ultimate security to His Majesty's Possessions in America.

The entire destruction of Sackets harbour and the Naval Establishments on
Lake Erie and Lake Champlain come under the first description.

The maintenance of Fort Niagara and so much of the adjacent Territory as
may be deemed necessary: and the occupation of Detroit and the Michigan
Country come under the second.

If our success shall enable us to terminate the war by the retention of the Fort of
Niagara, and the restoration of Detroit and the whole of the Michigan Country to
the Indians, the British Frontier will be materially improved. Should there be any
advanced position on that part of our frontier which extends towards Lake Champlain, the occupation of which would materially tend to the security of the Province,
you will if you deem it expedient expel the Enemy from it, and occupy it by detachments of the Troops under your command, always however taking care not to expose His Majesty's Forces to being cut off by too extended a line of advance.

If you should not consider it necessary to call to your assistance the two Regiments which are to proceed in the first instance to Halifax, Sir J. Sherbroke will
receive instructions to occupy so much of the District of Maine as will secure an
uninterrupted intercourse between Halifax and Quebec.

In contemplation of the increased force which by this arrangement you will
be under the necessity of maintaining in the Province directions have been given
for shipping immediately for Quebec, provisions for ten thousand men for six
months.

The Frigate which conveys this letter has also on board one hundred thousand pounds in Specie for the use of the Army under your command. An equal
sum will also be embarked on board the Ship of War which may be appointed to
convoy to Quebec the fleet which is expected to sail from this Country on the
10th or at the latest on the 15th instant.

I have the honor etc.,

BATHURST

Order of Battle and Service

BRITISH REGULAR UNITS AND CORPS
IN NORTH AMERICA, 1812-1815

Key to Theatre

CH: Chesapeake area including the middle Atlantic coast

LA: Louisiana

LC: Lower Canada

ME: Castine expedition, 1814

MP: Maritime Provinces (including Newfoundland)

NW: Old Northwest (Ohio, Michigan, Illinois Territories)

UC: Upper Canada

Unit	Title in 1814 Army List	Service
Cavalry		
14th Light Dragoons[1]	Duchess of York's Own Regiment	LA: 1814-1815
19th Light Dragoons	-	UC, LC: 1813-1815
Infantry of the Line		
1st Foot, 1st Bn	The Royal Scots	UC, LC: 1814-1815
1st Foot, 4th Bn	The Royal Scots	LC: 1814-1815
3rd Foot, 1st Bn	East Kent Regiment, or the Buffs	LC: 1814-1815
4th Foot, 1st Bn	King's Own Regiment	CH, LA: 1814-1815
5th Foot, 1st Bn	Northumberland Regiment	LC, UC: 1814-1815
6th Foot, 1st Bn	1st Warwickshire Regiment	LC, UC: 1814-1815
7th Foot, 1st Bn	Royal Fuzileers	LA: 1814-1815
8th Foot, 1st Bn	King's Regiment	LC, UC: 1812-1815
8th Foot, 2nd Bn	King's Regiment	MP, LC: 1812-1815
9th Foot, 1st Bn	East Norfolk Regiment	LC, UC: 1814-1815
13th Foot	1st Somersetshire	LC: 1813-1815
16th Foot	Bedfordshire Regiment	LC: 1814-1815
21st Foot	Royal North British Fuzileers	CH, LA: 1814-1815
27th Foot, 1st Bn	Iniskilling Regiment	LC, 1814-1815
27th Foot, 3rd Bn	Iniskilling Regiment	MP, LC: 1814-1815
29th Foot	Worcestershire Regiment	MP, ME: 1814-1815
37th Foot, 1st Bn	North Hampshire Regiment	LC, UC: 1814-1815
39th Foot, 1st Bn	Dorsetshire Regiment	LC: 1814-1815
40th Foot, 1st Bn	2nd Somersetshire Regiment	LA: 1814-1815
41st Foot, 1st Bn	-	LC, UC, NW: 1813-1815
41st Foot, 2nd Bn	-	LC, UC: 1813-1815
43rd Foot, 1st Bn	Monmouthshire Regiment (Light Infantry)	LA: 1815
44th Foot, 1st Bn	East Essex Regiment	CH, LA: 1814-1815

49th Foot	Hertfordshire Regiment	LC, UC, 1812-1815
57th Foot	West Middlesex Regiment	LC, UC: 1814-1815
58th Foot, 1st Bn	Rutlandshire Regiment	LC: 1814-1815
60th Foot, 7th Bn	Royal American Regiment	MP, ME: 1814-1815
62nd Foot, 1st Bn	Wiltshire Regiment	MP, ME: 1814-1815
64th Foot, 1st Bn	2nd Staffordshire Regiment	MP: 1813-1815
70th Foot	Glasgow Lowland Regiment	LC, UC: 1813-1815
76th Foot	Hindoostan Regiment[2]	LC: 1814-1815
81st Foot, 1st Bn	Loyal Lincoln Volunteers	LC, UC: 1814-1815
82nd Foot, 1st Bn	Prince of Wales's Volunteers	LC, UC: 1814-1815
85th Foot	Bucks Volunteers (Light Infantry)	CH, LA: 1814-1815
88th Foot, 1st Bn	Connaught Rangers	LC: 1814-1815
89th Foot, 2nd Bn	-	MP, LC, UC: 1812-1815
90th Foot, 1st Bn	Perthshire Volunteers	LC, UC, 1814-1815
93rd Foot, 1st Bn	-	LA: 1814-1815
93rd Foot, 2nd Bn	-	MP: 1814-1815
95th Foot, 3rd Bn	Riflemen	LA: 1814-1815
97th Foot	Queen's Own Regiment	LC, UC: 1814-1815
98th Foot	-	MP, ME: 1812-1815
99th Foot	Prince of Wales's Tipperary Regiment	MP: 1812-1815
100th Foot	Prince Regent's City of Dublin Regiment	LC, UC: 1812-1815
102nd Foot	-	CH, MP: 1813-1815
103rd Foot	-	LC, UC: 1812-1815
104th Foot	-	MP, LC, UC: 1812-1815

Other Infantry Units

1st West India Regiment of Foot	LA: 1814-1815
2nd West India Regiment of Foot	CH: 1814-1815
5th West India Regiment of Foot	LA: 1814-1815
4th Garrison Battalion	Bermuda: 1813-1815
10th Royal Veteran Battalion	LC, UC, NW: 1812-1815
Royal Newfoundland Fencible Infantry	LC, UC, NW: 1812-1815
Nova Scotia Fencible Infantry	LC, UC, NW: 1812-1815
Canadian Fencible Infantry	LC, UC: 1812-1815
Glengarry Light Infantry Fencibles	UC: 1812-1815
New Brunswick Fencible Infantry	MP: 1812-1815
De Meuron's Regiment of Foot	LC: 1813-1815
De Watteville's Regiment of Foot	LC, UC: 1813-1815
1st Independent Company of Foreigners[3]	CH, MP: 1813
2nd Independent Company of Foreigners	CH, MP: 1813

Royal Marines

1st Battalion[4]	CH, MP, LC, UC: 1813-1815
2nd Battalion[5]	CH, MP, LC, UC: 1813-1815
3rd Battalion (became 2nd Battalion in 1814)[6]	CH: 1814-1815
3rd Battalion (Colonial Marines)[7]	CH: 1814-1815
Shipboard Marine Detachments[8]	CH, LA: 1813-1815

Artillery
Royal Horse Artillery

Capt. H.B. Lane's Troop (2nd Troop), Rocket Brigade	LA: 1814-1815

Royal Artillery
  2nd Battalion

Capt W. Payne's Coy	MP: 1812-1814
Capt D. Story's Coy	MP, UC: 1812-1815

  4th Battalion

Capt P.M. Wallace's Coy	LC: 1812-1815
Capt J.S. Sinclair's Coy	LC: 1812-1815
Capt J.T. Caddy's Coy	LC: 1812-1815
Capt W. Holcroft's Coy	UC: 1812-1815
Capt S. Maxwell's Coy	LC: 1814-1815

  5th Battalion

Capt H. Phillot's Coy[9]	MP: 1812-1815
Capt G. Crawford's Coy	MP: 1812-1815
Capt H. Trelawney's Coy	LC: 1814-1815

  7th Battalion

Capt J.P. St. Clair's Coy	MP, LC, UC: 1812-1815

  8th Battalion

Capt R. Pym's Coy	CH, LA: 1814-1815
Capt L. Carmichael's Coy	CH, LA: 1814-1815

  9th Battalion

Capt J. Michell's Coy	CH, LA: 1814-1815
Capt G. Turner's Coy	UC, LC: 1814-1815

  10th Battalion

Capt J. Maclachlan's Coy	UC: 1814-1815
Capt J. Addams's Coy	UC, LC: 1814-1815

Royal Marine Artillery

1st Company	MP, CH, LC, UC: 1813-1815
2nd Company	MP, CH, LC, UC: 1813-1815
3rd Company[10]	CH, LA: 1814-1815
Rocket Company[11]	MP, CH, LC, UC, 1813-1815

Engineer Units
Royal Engineers[12]   UC, LC, MP, CH, LA: 1812-1815
Royal Sappers and Miners[13]

Company in Newfoundland	MP: 1812-1815
Company at Halifax	MP, ME: 1812-1815
7th Coy of 1st Bn	LA: 1814-1815
3rd Coy of 3rd Bn	LC, UC: 1813-1815
2nd Coy, 4th Bn	CH, LA: 1814-1815
4th Coy, 4th Bn	LC, UC: 1814-1815
8th Coy, 2nd Bn	LA: 1815[14]

Royal Staff Corps[15]   LA: 1814-1815

Sources

The major source for this appendix is found in the records of the army in Public Record Office, War Office 17, Muster Rolls, 1812-1815, for North America, Record Group 8 I of the National Archives of Canada, and the *Army Lists*, 1812-1815. Useful secondary sources consulted were Henry M. Chichester and George Burges-Short, *The Records and Badges of Every Regiment and*

Corps in the British Army (London, 1900) John Fortescue, History of the British Army, Vol 9 (London, 1920); M.E.S. Laws, Battery Records of the Royal Artillery (Woolwich, 1952); Charles Stewart, ed. The Service of British Regiments in North America (Ottawa, 1964); Stuart Sutherland, His Majesty's Gentlemen (publication forthcoming); and Arthur Swinson, ed., A Register of the Regiments and Corps of the British Army (London, 1972). Also consulted were a great number of published regimental, unit and corps histories – for references, see the bibliography that follows.

Notes

1. Detachment served in Louisiana in a dismounted capacity, 1814-1815.
2. The name "Hindoostan" granted for the 76th Foot's exceptional service in India was not their official title but was permitted to be worn on their colours and appointments.
3. Raised in 1812 from French prisoners of war for garrison duty in the West Indies, the two companies of foreigners participated in the Chesapeake expedition of 1813 and behaved so badly that they were returned to Halifax and disbanded in the spring of 1814.
4. Organized in 1813, this battalion participated in the Chesapeake expedition in the spring of 1813 before being sent to Canada in the autumn. In the summer of 1814 it was broken up for service on the warships of the squadrons on the lakes but was reconstituted in November of that year and detachments participated in amphibious operations in the Chesapeake over the winter of 1814-1815.
5. Organized in early 1813, the 2nd Battalion of Royal Marines participated in the operations in the Chesapeake before being sent to the Canadas where it was broken up in June 1814 for service on the warships of the lakes' squadrons.
6. Organized in early 1814 in Holland, the 3rd Battalion was renumbered the 2nd when the original unit of that number was broken up in June 1814. Detachments from this battalion served in the Creek territory over the winter of 1814-1815.
7. Formed in the summer of 1813 from three companies of the 3rd (later 2nd) Battalion and three companies of liberated black slaves from Virginia (who proved very enthusiastic soldiers) and a varying number of companies of shipboard marines.
8. The complements of British warships included detachments of Royal Marines, varying in number from 25 privates on a sloop to 100 on a first rate line of battle ship. This provided RN commanders operating in American coastal waters with a ready-made amphibious landing force and detachments of shipboard marines participated in many operations on the Atlantic coast and in the Gulf of Mexico.
9. Became Capt. H. Gardner's coy in 1813.
10. Raised in early 1814 with the 3rd Battalion in Holland. Detachments from this company fought in the Creek territory and in Louisiana in 1814-1815.
11. Raised with the two companies of RMA in early 1813 for field service in North America, participated in operations in the Chesapeake in 1813 before being transferred to the Canadas.
12. During this time the Royal Engineers consisted of officers only.
13. At the outbreak of the war in June 1812, this organization was known as the Royal Military Artificers or Sappers and Miners." This title was changed to that shown above in March 1813.
14. This company arrived in the theatre too late to see action.
15. The Royal Staff Corps was created in 1799 to provide the British army with its own engineers as, at this time, the Royal Engineers were under the control of the Board of Ordnance. Their function was to construct field works and to undertake other duties for the quarter master's department. The corps was later incorporated into the Royal Engineers.

The Troop Strength of the British Army in North America, 1812-1814

OVERVIEW OF BRITISH COMBAT UNITS IN NORTH AMERICA, 1812-1815

Area	Infantry Bns (or Part)	Artillery Coys (or Part)	Cavalry Regts (or Part)
Canadas and the North West	40	15	1
Maritime Provinces	13	8	-
American Territory (Maine, Chesapeake and Louisiana)	25	8	1

Note: Units that served in more than one area have been included in the totals for all areas in which they served. These figures do not include embodied or provincial Upper and Lower Canadian units or shipboard detachments of the Royal Marines.

STRENGTH AND DISPOSITION, BRITISH ARMY IN NORTH AMERICA, 1812-1815

	1812 25 June	1812 25 Dec.	1813 25 Dec.	1814 25 Dec.
Upper and Lower Canada and the North West[1]	6,034	8,136	14,623	30,728
Maritime Provinces (including Newfoundland[2] and Bermuda)	3,743	4,519	4,854	6,588
American Territory[3]				
Maine	-	-	-	2,144
Chesapeake[4]	-	-	(2,280)[5]	4,200
Louisiana	-	-	-	4,503
Total British Strength	9,777	12,655	19,477	48,163

The British army was mustered and paid on the 25th of every month and the table above is extracted from these monthly musters. Officers were mustered separately from enlisted personnel but their totals have been combined in the figures above.

This table clearly shows that, for Britain, the main theatre of war was Upper and Lower Canada.

Sources

The major source for this appendix is found in the records of the army in Public Record Office, War Office 17, Muster Rolls, 1812-1815, for North America, Record Group 8 I of the National Archives of Canada, and the *Army Lists*, 1812-1815. Useful secondary sources consulted were Henry M. Chichester and George Burges-Short, *The Records and Badges of Every Regiment and Corps in the British Army* (London, 1900)John Fortescue, *History of the British Army*, Vol 9 (London, 1920); M.E.S. Laws, *Battery Records of the Royal Artillery* (Woolwich, 1952); and Charles Stewart, ed. *The Service of British Regiments in North America* (Ottawa, 1964).

Notes

1. Note that the Upper and Lower Canada figures do not include the various Upper and Lower Canada embodied or provincial units with the exception of the *Voltigeurs Canadiens* who were mustered as regulars throughout the war. The strength of these units would add about 4,000 to the annual figures for 1813 and 1814 in Upper and Lower Canada.
2. The figures for the Newfoundland garrison have been included in the total for the maritime provinces although Newfoundland, as a military garrison and naval station, was a separate establishment and units and warships in that colony were not used in the active defence of mainland British North America.
3. Not included in the figures for the Maine, Chesapeake and Louisiana are detachments of Royal Marines serving on board warships. The three battalions of marines formed for land service in Britain and the three companies of Colonial Marines recruited from escaped black slaves in Virginia are included.
4. The strength figures for the Chesapeake on 25 December 1813 and 25 December 1814, as noted, are actually for earlier periods during those years. They have been included to provide a more accurate basis for the wartime distribution of British military units.
5. This was the force that attacked Craney Island and Hampton in the Chesapeake area in June 1813 and consisted of the 102nd Foot, the 1st and 2nd Battalions of Royal Marines, the 1st and 2nd Companies of Royal Marine Artillery and the 1st and 2nd Companies of Independent Foreigners, see John Fortescue, *History of the British Army*, Vol 9 (London, 1920), 321. When this expedition had ended, the 102nd Foot was sent to Nova Scotia and the Royal Marine units to Upper and Lower Canada and their strengths appear in the figures for those areas on 25 Dec 1813. The Independent Companies of Foreigners were broken up.
6. This figure excludes the 2,995 troops who transferred from the Chesapeake to Louisiana in the autumn, their numbers are included in the total for the Chesapeake. The total number of regular troops who participated in the Louisiana campaign was 7,195.

Canadian Military Units, Upper and Lower Canada, 1812-1815

Note: Units that actually saw combat are indicated with an asterisk (*).

LOWER CANADA

The military organization of Lower Canada was a three-tiered structure. At the top were the various provincial units raised for the duration of the war from volunteers, officered by professional British officers, and uniformed, trained and equipped as regular units. In this category were the Voltigeurs Canadiens (arguably the most effective Canadian unit of the war), the Canadian Light Dragoons and the Corps of Artillery Drivers.

The second tier were the volunteer units and the select embodied units (raised either by draft or ballot from males of young military age for varying periods of service). These were trained, armed and equipped as regular troops but were not quite as effective as the provincial units. Some volunteer units served for such a long time that they can be regarded as embodied units.

The third tier was the sedentary militia which basically consisted of every male of military age (16 to 60) and called out as needed. Occasionally some sedentary units volunteered for brief periods of service and, still more rarely, some were embodied for longer periods.

Provincial and Embodied Units

Cavalry
Canadian Light Dragoons[*1]
Dorchester Provincial Light Dragoons[2]
Quebec Volunteer Cavalry[3]

Infantry
Provincial Corps of Light Infantry
(Voltigeurs Canadiens)[*4]
Frontier Light Infantry[*5]
Chasseurs Canadiens (Canadian
Chasseurs)[*6]
1st Battalion, Select Embodied Militia[*7]
2nd Battalion, Select Embodied Militia[*8]
3rd Battalion, Select Embodied Militia[*9]
4th Battalion, Select Embodied Militia[10]
5th Battalion, Select Embodied Militia[11]
6th Battalion, Select Embodied Militia[12]
7th Battalion, Select Embodied Militia[13]
8th Battalion, Select Embodied Militia[14]
1st Militia Light Infantry Battalion[*15]
2nd Militia Light Infantry Battalion[16]
Quebec Volunteers (infantry)[17]

Other
Corps of Provincial Royal Artillery Drivers[18]
Corps of Canadian Voyageurs[*19]
Provincial Commissariat Voyageurs[*20]

Volunteer Militia Units

Cavalry
Royal Montreal Troop of Cavalry[21]
Compagnie des Guides[22]

Infantry
Montreal Militia Battalion[23]
Montreal Incorporated Volunteers (infantry)[24]

Artillery
Quebec Volunteers (artillery)
Royal Militia Artillery[25]
Montreal Incorporated Volunteers (artillery)[26]

Sedentary Militia Units
Note that the "divisions" are really districts

Montreal District
1st Battalion, City of Montreal, Montreal
British [English-speaking] Militia

2nd Battalion, City of Montreal
  2nd Battalion, Pointe-Claire company
3rd Battalion, City of Montreal
  3rd Battalion, Longue-Pointe Company
Argenteuil Division
Vaudreuil Division
Vaudreuil Battalion
Rivière-Duchesne Battalion
L'Isle Jésus Division
L'Isle Jésus Battalion
Terrebonne Battalion
Blainville Battalion
L'Assomption Division
Lavaltrie Division
Berthier Division
Saint-Ours Division
Chambly Division
1st Boucherville Division
2nd Boucherville Division
Beauharnois Division*[27]

Eastern Townships District
1st Battalion
2nd Battalion
3rd Battalion
4th Battalion
5th Battalion
6th Battalion

Trois-Rivières District
Northern Division
  Trois-Rivières Battalion
  Rivière-du-Loup (Louiseville)
  Battalion
  Sainte-Anne Battalion
Southern Division
  Yamaska Battalion
  Nicolet Battalion
  Bécancour Battalion

Quebec District
1st Battalion, City of Quebec
  1st Battalion, Parish of L'Île d'Orléans
2nd Battalion, City of Quebec
  2nd Battalion, Parish of Lotbinière
3rd Battalion, City of Quebec, Quebec
  British [English-speaking] Militia
Quebec Division
Beauport Division
Baie-Saint-Paul Division
Saint-Thomas Division
Rivière-Ouelle Division

Gaspé District
Gaspé District Division
Îles de la Madeleine Company

UPPER CANADA

The military organization of Upper Canada also consisted of several components. The most effective units were the incorporated or provincial units raised from volunteers for the duration of the war. The distinction between the two was largely artificial and somewhat confusing even during the period as provincial units are often called incorporated units in period documents or *vice versa*.

The sedentary militia consisted of the bulk of the male population aged 16 to 60 organized by counties and political ridings — thus the 5th Lincoln Regiment was the fifth political riding of Lincoln County. These units were called out as needed. In 1812 flank companies, consisting of younger men, were organized in most regiments of sedentary militia and these were given increased training. Some sedentary units, which possessed the resources, also organized rifle or artillery companies and cavalry troops which saw service.

Provincial and Incorporated Units

Cavalry
Niagara Light Dragoons (Niagara
  Guides)*[28]
Niagara Provincial Light Dragoons*[29]
Provincial Light Dragoons*[30]

Infantry
Battalion of Incorporated Militia*[31]

Artillery
The Provincial Artillery Company*[32]
The Incorporated Artillery Company[33]

Canadian Military Units, Upper and Lower Canada, 1812-1815

Other

Royal Provincial Artillery Drivers (The Car Brigade)*[34]

Corps of Artificers (The Coloured Corps)*[35]

Sedentary Militia Units

Eastern District

1st Glengarry Regiment*
  Flank Coy*
2nd Glengarry Regiment*
  Flank Coy*
1st Prescott Regiment*
1st Stormont Regiment*
  Flank Coy*
1st Dundas Regiment*
  Flank Coy*

Johnstown District

1st Grenville Regiment*
  Flank Coy*, Rifle Coy
2nd Grenville Regiment*
  Flank Coy*, Cavalry Trp*
1st Leeds Regiment*
  Flank Coy*, Cavalry Trp, Rifle Coy*
2nd Leeds Regiment*
  Flank Coy, Rifle Coy

Midland District

1st Frontenac Regiment
  Flank Coy, Artillery Coy
1st Lennox Regiment
  Flank Coy, Cavalry Trp
1st Addington Regiment
  Flank Coy, Cavalry Trp
1st Hastings Regiment
  Flank Coy
1st Prince Edward Regiment
  Flank Coy, Cavalry Trp

Newcastle District

1st Northumberland Regiment
  Flank Coy
1st Durham Regiment
  Flank Coy

Home District

1st York Regiment*
  Flank Coy*, Cavalry Trp*, Rifle Coy*
2nd York Regiment*
  Flank Coy*
3rd York Regiment*
  Flank Coy*

Niagara District

1st Lincoln Regiment*
  Flank Coy*, Cavalry Troop*, Artillery Coy*
2nd Lincoln Regiment*
  Flank Coy*, Cavalry Trp*, Artillery Coy*
3rd Lincoln Regiment
  Flank Coy*
4th Lincoln Regiment*
  Flank Coy*
5th Lincoln Regiment*
  Flank Coy*

London District

The Loyal London Volunteers
1st Norfolk Regiment*
  Flank Coy*
2nd Norfolk Regiment*
1st Oxford Regiment*
  Flank Coy*, Rifle Coy*
1st Middlesex Regiment*
  Flank Coy*

Western District

The Western Rangers (Caldwell's Rangers)*
1st Essex Regiment*
  Flank Coy,*
2nd Essex Regiment*
  Flank Coy*, Cavalry Trp*
1st Kent Regiment"
  Flank Coy*, Cavalry Trp*

The Indian Country (British Lake Superior Area and the old North West)

Infantry

Michigan Fencibles*[36]
Mississipi Volunteers*[37]
Dease's Mississippi Volunteers* (Prairie-du-Chien Militia)[38]
Canadian Volunteers* (Canadian Voyageurs)[39]
Green Bay Militia*[40]

Artillery

Mississippi Volunteer Artillery*[41]

Sources

William Gray, *Soldiers of the King: The Upper Canada Militia 1812-1815* (Toronto, 1997); Lukin H. Irving, *Officers of the British Forces in Canada During the War of 1812-1815* (Welland, 1908); Luc Lépine, *Les Officiers de milice du Bas-Canada 1812-1815* (Montreal, 1996)

Notes

1. Authorized in January 1813 this troop of cavalry was raised by Captain Thomas Colman in the Montreal area and saw extensive service in the Niagara and western Upper Canada in 1813. This troop was disbanded in May 1815.
2. Embodied in March 1813 and disbanded in March 1815, this was actually a volunteer unit but it served for such a long time that it became a provincial unit.
3. Raised at Quebec City in April 1812 and disbanded in August 1813, but it served for such a long time that it can be regarded as an embodied or provincial unit.
4. Authorized in March 1812 this eight-company regiment of light infantry saw extensive combat in Upper and Lower Canada during the war, playing a prominent role in the 1813 battles of Crysler's Farm and Châteauguay. It was regarded by the British army as a regular unit and appeared on the monthly returns of the regular forces in the Canadas. The Voltigeurs were disbanded in March 1815.
5. The Frontier Light Infantry consisted of two companies drawn from the six battalions of sedentary militia in the Eastern Townships. In August 1813 they were attached to the Canadian Voltigeurs, becoming Nos. 9 and 10 Coys of that unit.
6. Formed in March 1814 with a strength of six companies provided by drafts from the 1st through 4th Select Embodied Battalions, this unit was brigaded with the Voltigeurs Canadiens and the Frontier Light Infantry under the command of Lieutenant Colonel Charles de Salaberry.
7. Embodied in May 1812 and disbanded in March 1815.
8. Battalion embodied in May 1812 and broken up in March 1815.
9. Battalion embodied in May 1812 and disbanded in March 1815.
10. Battalion embodied in May 1812 and disbanded in March 1815.
11. Battalion authorized in the Montreal area in September 1812 and reorganized as the Chasseurs Canadiens in March 1814. This unit was known as "The Devil's Own" either because of the large number of lawyers among its officers or because of its propensity for thieving.
12. Embodied in February 1813 from three battalions of Quebec City sedentary militia, this unit did garrison duty until disbanded in September 1814.
13. Embodied in November 1813 from sedentary militia units in the Richelieu area, disbanded that same month.
14. Embodied from sedentary militia units in the Trois Rivières area in November 1813 and disbanded that same month.
15. Formed at Kingston, Upper Canada, from the flank companies of the 2nd and 5th Select Embodied Battalions and the first flank company of the 3rd Battalion. Elements of this battalion, which was broken up in November 1813, saw action at the battle of Châteauguay on 26 October 1813.
16. Formed in April 1813 from the flank companies of the 1st and 4th Battalions, Select Embodied Militia, and the second flank company of the 3rd Battalion. Broken up in November 1813.
17. Raised from the 1st through 3rd Battalions, Quebec City Militia, and did garrison duty in rotation from the summer of 1812 through to the spring of 1813. Although it was a volunteer unit, it served for such a long time that it can be regarded as a provincial unit.
18. Formed in January 1813 and attached to the Royal Artillery in the Montreal area, this corps was disbanded in March 1815.
19. Formed from the skilled boat and canoemen of the North West Fur Company to man the boat convoys transporting troops and supplies along the St. Lawrence River. Raised in the autumn of 1812, the Canadian Voyageurs were disbanded in March 1813, their task taken over by the Commissariat Voyageurs.

20. Formed in April 1813 to carry on the work of the Canadian Voyageurs.

21. Raised in November 1813 and disbanded that same month.

22. Authorized in August 1812 and disbanded in March 1815.

23. Formed from the flank companies of the Montreal City sedentary militia battalions and served throughout the war as a garrison unit.

24. Three companies of infantry and one of artillery embodied in September 1812 and relieved the following month; embodied again in November 1813 and stood down that same month.

25. Very little is known about this unit which appears to have been composed of volunteers of the various Montreal sedentary militia units.

26. Embodied in the autumn of 1812 for one month and again in November 1813 for one month's service.

27. Elements of the 2nd Battalion of this division saw action at the battle of Châteauguay, 26 October 1813.

28. Authorized in June 1812, this cavalry troop saw action in the Niagara in the following summer and autumn. It was disbanded in February 1813.

29. Authorized in April 1813, this cavalry troop was the successor to the Niagara Light Dragoons and saw considerable action in the Niagara campaigns of 1813 and 1814. It was disbanded in March 1815.

30. Two troops under Captains Richard D. Fraser and Andrew Adams were raised in the Eastern and Johnstown Districts in March 1813 and were combined into one troop the following September. This troop did useful work as despatch riders along the St. Lawrence and elements were present at the battle of Crysler's Farm, 11 November 1813. Disbanded in March 1815.

31. Raised in March 1813, this infantry battalion saw heavy fighting in the Niagara in the summer of 1814, being present at the battle of Lundy's Lane on 25 July and during the siege of Fort Erie in August and September.

32. Authorized in March 1813 under the command of Captain Alexander Cameron of the Lincoln militia, this company saw action at Ft. George in May 1813 and was disbanded in March 1815. To make matters confusing, Cameron's company was also known as the "Incorporated Artillery Company."

33. Authorized in March 1813 under the command of Lieutenant William Jarvis, this company served at York until February 1814 when it was disbanded and its personnel transferred to the Incorporated Militia Battalion.

34. Authorized in March 1813 this corps was intended to provide drivers for the Royal Artillery field brigades (batteries) serving in Upper Canada. It saw action in the Niagara in the summer of 1814 and was disbanded in March 1815.

35. Also known as "Captain Runchey's Company of Coloured Men," this unit of free blacks was raised from the Lincoln sedentary militia in the autumn of 1812 as a labour unit but saw action at Queenston Heights in October 1812. In March 1813 it appears to have been made a provincial unit and its members were to function as skilled craftsmen. It saw action at the attack on Fort George in May 1813 and was disbanded in March 1815.

36. Raised in 1813 at Mackinac Island and embodied for the duration of the war, this unit was somewhere between a fencible unit (a regular unit raised for local service) and a provincial unit.

37. Raised in 1814 from fur trappers and voyageurs.

38. Raised in 1814 from fur trappers and voyageurs.

39. Raised in 1812 from voyageurs of the North West Fur Trading Company, this unit fought at Mackinac in both that year and 1814.

40. Participated in the attack on Prairie-du-Chien in 1814.

41. Raised in 1814 for the attack on Prairie-du-Chien, this consisted of one 6-pdr. gun commanded by Sergeant James Keating, RA, (who was given the local rank of lieutenant and a gun detachment).

Native Military Forces in the Great Lakes Theatre, 1812-1815

COMPILED BY CARL BENN

Determining native military strength is difficult, partly because of poor quality and conflicting statistical data, especially for the nations of the Old Northwest. Therefore, the figures below ought to be considered as mere estimates. Furthermore, only a fraction of the warrior population ever took to the field at any one time, and the native nations allowed their members to exercise considerable freedom in a conflict, with the result that some people might ally with opposing sides while others might choose to be neutral. Enthusiasm for hostilities varied from year to year as changing circumstances determined how a group might act to protect its interests, and it typically was at the village level rather than the tribal level that native groups would make their most important foreign policy decisions. Some individuals from far-off nations, such as the Dakotas, also travelled to the Great Lakes theatre to fight, but it is very difficult to estimate the extent of their participation. Beyond the Great Lakes, other native nations participated in the war, a prime example being the Creek confederacy far to the south, with 2,000 warriors, which fought its own disastrous war against the United States.

Some explanation of terminology is needed. The terms "Algonkian," "Iroquoian" and "Siouan" below refer to language/cultural groups. The "Iroquois," on the other hand, were a confederacy of Six Iroquoian nations. (Most of the Iroquoians that existed in the Great Lakes at the time of the first white exploration, such as the Neutrals and Eries, were destroyed as independent societies in the mid-1600s.)

With all this in view, the following is a list of the native nations allied with either Britain or United States in the Great Lakes area during the War of 1812.

A. NATIONS GENERALLY ALLIED WITH GREAT BRITAIN

Lower Canada (est. 1,100 warriors)
Algonkian
    Abenakis of St. Francis
    Algonkins from the Ottawa River area and Lac-des-deux-Montagnes (Kanesetake)
    Nipissings of Trois-Rivières and Lac-des-deux-Montagnes (Kanesetake)
Iroquoian
    Iroquois – largely Mohawks – of St. Regis (Akwesasne), Caughnawaga (Kahnawake),
        and Lac-des-deux-Montagnes (Kanesetake)

Upper Canada (est. 700-800 warriors)
Algonkian
    Ottawas from the upper lakes
    Ojibways (Chippewas) from the upper lakes, Lake Simcoe, and neighbouring
        regions

Mississaugas from various parts of the province
Delawares, Nanticokes, Tutelos, and others, from the Grand River tract
Mixed Algonkian Delawares (including Munsees and Moravians)
Iroquoian
    Wyandots (Hurons), and other nations from the Thames River valley and south-
        western Upper Canada
    Iroquois Mohawks from Tyendinaga
    Iroquois Cayugas, Mohawks, Oneidas, Onondagas, Tuscaroras, and Senecas, from
        the Grand River tract

Old North West: Ohio, Michigan and Illinois Territories, and surrounding areas (est.
9.000 warriors)
Algonkian
    Delawares, Kickapoos, Menominees, Mesquakies (Foxes), Miamis (including
        Kaskaskias), Mississaugas, Ojibways (Chippewas), Ottawas, Piankshaws,
        Potawatomis, Sauks (Sacs), Shawnees and Weas
Iroquoian
    Iroquois Mingoes (a Six Nations tribe that had formed in the mid-eighteenth
        century from immigrants from New York and Canada
Siouan
    Winnebagos

B. NATIVE NATIONS GENERALLY ALLIED WITH THE UNITED STATES

New York and Pennsylvania (est. 1,050 warriors)
Algonkian
    Brothertowns, Delawares, and Stockbridges, largely from an area near Rome, New
        York, or living among the Irouqois
Iroquoian
    Iroquois Cayugas, Mohawks, Oneidas, Onondagas, Tuscaroras, and Senecas from
        fourteen reservations in New York and the Cornplanter tract in Pennsylvania

Ohio (est. 700 warriors)
Algonkian
    Delawares and Shawnees
Iroquoian
    Wyandots (Hurons)
    Sandusky Senecas (a tribe of various Six Nations people which formed in the Ohio
        country in the late eighteenth century)

Sources
The figures for the military strength of the First Nations of the Canadas and the Old Northwest
are extracted from: NAC, RG 10, vol 10, 16106; AO, MS 35, Strachan Papers, State of the Indian
Tribes, October 1812, a "List of Indian Warriors as they Stood in 1812 at the time war was de-
clared; Carl Benn, *The Iroquois in the War of 1812* (Toronto, 1998), 51, 195-200; Helen Hornbeck
Tanner, ed., *Atlas of Great Lakes Indian History* (Norman, 1987), 96-121; Bruce G. Trigger, ed.,
Handbook of North American Indians, vol 15, "The Northeast", (Washington, 1978). A good map
showing tribal locations by village sites is published in Tanner, 98-99.

British and Canadian Military Heritage
of the War of 1812

BRITISH ARMY

War of 1812 Unit or Corps	Postwar Fate or 1999 Successor
Cavalry	
14th Light Dragoons	The King's Royal Hussars
19th Light Dragoons	The Light Dragoons
Infantry of the Line	
1st Foot	The Royal Scots (The Royal Regiment)
3rd Foot	The Princess of Wales's Royal Regiment (Queen's and Royal Hampshires)
4th Foot	The King's Own Royal Border Regiment
5th Foot	The Royal Regiment of Fusiliers
6th Foot	The Royal Regiment of Fusiliers
7th Foot	The Royal Regiment of Fusiliers
8th Foot	The King's Regiment
9th Foot	The Royal Anglian Regiment
13th Foot	The Light Infantry
16th Foot	The Royal Anglian Regiment
21st Foot	The Royal Highland Fusiliers
27th Foot	The Royal Irish Regiment
29th Foot	The Worcestershire and Sherwood Foresters Regiment (29th/45th Foot)
37th Foot	The Princess of Wales's Royal Regiment (Queen's and Royal Hampshires)
39th Foot	The Devonshire and Dorset Regiment
40th Foot	The Queen's Lancashire Regiment
41st Foot	The Royal Regiment of Wales
43rd Foot	The Royal Green Jackets
44th Foot	The Royal Anglian Regiment
49th Foot	The Royal Gloucestershire, Berkshire and Wiltshire Regiment
57th Foot	The Princess of Wales's Royal Regiment (Queen's and Royal Hampshires)
58th Foot	The Royal Anglian Regiment
60th Foot	The Royal Green Jackets
62nd Foot	The Royal Gloucestershire, Berkshire and Wiltshire Regiment
64th Foot	The Staffordshire Regiment (The Prince of Wales's)

70th Foot	The Princess of Wales's Royal Regiment (Queen's and Royal Hampshires)
76th Foot	The Duke of Wellington's Regiment (West Riding)
81st Foot	The Queen's Lancashire Regiment
82nd Foot	The Queen's Lancashire Regiment
85th Foot	The Light Infantry
88th Foot	*Disbanded in 1922 as The Connaught Rangers*
89th Foot	The Royal Irish Regiment
90th Foot	*Disbanded in 1968 as The Cameronians (Scottish Rifles)*
93rd Foot	The Argyll and Sutherland Highlanders (Princess Louise's)
95th Foot	The Royal Green Jackets
97th Foot	*Disbanded in 1818 as the 96th Foot*
98th Foot	The Staffordshire Regiment (The Prince of Wales's)
99th Foot	*Disbanded in 1818 as the 98th Foot*
100th Foot	*Disbanded in 1922 as The Prince of Wales's Leinster Regiment (Royal Canadians)*
102nd Foot	*Disbanded in 1818 as the 100th Foot*
103rd Foot	*Disbanded in 1817*
104th Foot	*Disbanded in 1816* (see below)

Infantry – Other Units

1st West India Regiment	*Disbanded 1927*
2nd West India Regiment	*Disbanded 1927*
5th West India Regiment	*Disbanded 1817*
4th Garrison Battalion	*Disbanded 1816*
10th Royal Veteran Battalion	*Renumbered 4th in 1815. Disbanded 1821*
Royal Newfoundland Fencible Infantry	*Disbanded 1816* (see below)
Nova Scotia Fencible Infantry	*Disbanded 1816* (see below)
Canadian Fencible Infantry	*Disbanded 1816* (see below)
Glengarry Light Infantry Fencibles	*Disbanded 1816* (see below)
New Brunswick Fencible Infantry	*Disbanded 1816* (see below)
De Meuron's Regiment of Foot	*Disbanded 1816*
De Watteville's Regiment of Foot	*Disbanded 1816*
1st Independent Company of Foreigners	*Disbanded 1814*
2nd Independent Company of Foreigners	*Disbanded 1814*
Royal Marines	The Royal Marines

Artillery

Royal Horse Artillery	The Royal Horse Artillery
Royal Regiment of Artillery	The Royal Regiment of Artillery
Royal Marine Artillery	The Royal Marines

Other Units and Corps

Corps of Royal Engineers	Corps of Royal Engineers
Royal Sappers and Miners	Corps of Royal Engineers
Royal Staff Corps	*Disbanded 1838*

Canadian Forces

No unit of the modern Canadian Forces (with the possible exception of the Royal New-foundland Regiment) can officially trace its lineage back to a predecessor unit of the War of 1812. This is because of a decision made in the 1960s by the Department of National Defence that the cut-off point for lineage and battle honours would be 1855, the date of union of the provinces of Ontario and Quebec into the nucleus of what would evolve into the modern nation of Canada. This *fiat* has effectively deleted the War of 1812 from the heritage of the modern Canadian Forces and defence department bureaucrats have expended more energy in defending it than they have in reconsidering its merits. The exception is the Royal Newfoundland Regiment, which has had a continuous existence from 1795 to 1870, thus bridging both periods of this arbitrary cut-off date.

Nonetheless, many Canadian militia units can quite easily trace an unofficial lineage to a War of 1812 predecessor by means of close geographical links. For example, any militia unit on the current order of battle can claim a link with a War of 1812 sedentary militia unit that existed in its geographical area in 1812-1815. Some units have more specific claims:

Modern (1999) Unit or Corps	War of 1812 Unit or Corps
Royal Regiment of Canadian Artillery	Wartime militia artillery units in all provinces
Maritime Provinces	
The Princess Louise Fusiliers	Nova Scotia Fencible Infantry
The Royal New Brunswick Regiment	104th Regiment of Foot New Brunswick Fencible Infantry
The West Nova Scotia Regiment	Nova Scotia Fencible Infantry
The Royal Newfoundland Regiment	Royal Newfoundland Fencible Infantry
Quebec (Lower Canada)	
Any militia armoured unit that had a predecessor in existence in 1812-1815	Canadian Light Dragoons
4ᵉ Bataillon, Royal 22ᵉ Régiment (Châteauguay)	Chasseurs de Châteauguay
All militia infantry units that had predecessors in existence in 1812-1815	Voltigeurs Canadiens Select Embodied Militia Battalions Canadian Fencible Infantry
Ontario (Upper Canada)	
All militia armoured units that had predecessors in existence in 1812-1815	Niagara Light Dragoons (Niagara Guides) Niagara Provincial Light Dragoons Provincial Light Dragoons
All militia infantry units that had predecessors in existence in 1812-1815	Incorporated Militia Battalion
The Stormont, Dundas & Glengarry Highlanders	The Glengarry Light Infantry Fencibles

Sources

Information on affiliations of modern British army units was kindly supplied by Lieutenant-Colonel R.C.B. Nutting of the Defence Liaison Staff, British High Commission, Ottawa and Major Andrew Hart of The Royal Irish Regiment, serving at Gagetown, New Brunswick. Other sources were: H.M. Chichester and G. Burges-Short, *The Records and Badges of Every Regiment and Corps in the British Army* (London, 1900); J.M. Hitsman and Alice Sorby, "Independent Companies of Foreigners or Canadian Chasseurs," *Military Affairs* 25 (1961); Charles Stewart, *The Service of British Regiments in Canada and North America* (Ottawa, 1964); Arthur Swinson, ed., *A Register of the Regiments and Corps of the British Army* (London, 1972; G. Tylden, "The West India Regiments, 1795 to 1927, and from 1958," *JSAHR* 40 (1962); A.S. White, "Garrison, Reserve and Veteran Battalions and Companies," *JSAHR* 38 (1960); R.L. Yaples, "The Auxiliaries: Foreign and Miscellaneous Regiments in the British Army, 1802-1817, *JSAHR* 50 (1972).

Information on modern Canadian units from M. Mitchell, *Ducimus. The Regiments of the Canadian Infantry* (Ottawa, 1992).

Statements on the affiliations of modern units of the Canadian Forces with predecessor units of the War of 1812 are the sole opinion of the editor and do not reflect in any way the lineage policies of the Department of National Defence of Canada, which continues to refuse to acknowledge the participation of Canadian soldiers in the War of 1812.

British and American Naval Forces in North American Waters, 1812-1814

COMPILED BY ROBERT MALCOMSON

The following is a general listing of the number and type of British warships in North American waters. It excludes vessels assigned to the Newfoundland Station, minor vessels such as cutters and tenders, and non-fighting vessels such as troop ships, receiving ships and prison ships.

For comparison, a summary has also been provided for the United States Navy.

BRITISH NAVAL FORCES

The Royal Navy Rating System for Warships

During the Napoleonic period, all major British warships were classified or rated by the number of guns they carried. A rated vessel was a suitable command for a full, or "post," captain. Warships of the 5th and 6th rates were usually of the frigate type.[1] The system was as follows:

Rate	Qualities
1st	100+ guns
2nd	90-98 guns
3rd	64-80 guns on two gundecks
4th	50-60 guns
5th	30-44 guns
6th	20-30 guns

Smaller warships were not rated. These vessels were:

Type	Qualities
Sloop	Two or three masts, 16-24 guns, suitable for an officer of the rank of commander
Brig of war	Two masts, 10-24 guns, commanded by a lieutenant
Schooner	Two masts, fore and aft rig, usually commanded by a lieutenant
Bomb	Two masts, fitted with 1-2 large mortars, built with reinforced construction to absorb the recoil. Royal Marine Artillery detachments often served on board.

The Royal Navy in the Atlantic and Gulf of Mexico

Flag Officers, North American and West Indies Station

1812-1813	Vice Admiral Herbert Sawyer
1813-1814	Admiral Sir John Borlase Warren
1814-1815	Vice Admiral Sir Alexander Cochrane

Number and Type of Rated and Unrated Warships

	1812	1813	1814
3rd	1	11	10
4th	-	-	4
5th	5	16	17
6th	1	2	2
Sloops	9	25	23
Brigs	1	-	-
Schooners	1	-	-
Bomb	-	-	5
Rocket Ship[2]	-	-	1

British Naval Force on the Great Lakes

At the outbreak of war, the British naval force on Lakes Ontario and Erie was the Provincial Marine, actually part of the army quartermaster's department, not the Royal Navy. In the spring of 1813, the RN assumed control of all naval forces on the inland seas. It should be noted that the list below includes only the major vessels and not the numerous small gunboats constructed by both nations during the war.

Lake Ontario

1812: Provincial Marine, Master and Commander Hugh Earl, Senior Officer

Rate	Number of Vessels
Sloop	2
Schooner	2

1813-1814: Royal Navy, Commodore Sir James Lucas Yeo

Number and Type of Rated Warships[3]

	1813	1814
1st	-	1
4th	-	1
5th	-	1
6th	-	2
Sloop	2	2
Brig	2	2
Schooner	2	2

Lake Erie and Upper Lakes

1812: Provincial Marine, Master and Commander George Hall, Senior Officer

Type	Number
Sloop	1
Brig	3
Schooner	1

1813: Royal Navy, Commander Robert Barclay
1814: Royal Navy, Lieutenant Miller Worsely

Number and Type of Rated and Unrated Warships

Rate or Type	1813	1814
Sloop	2	-
Brig	1	-
Schooner	1	2
Sloop-rig (single-mast)[4]	1	-

Lake Champlain
1813: Royal Navy, Commander Daniel Pring, Senior Officer
1814: Royal Navy, Commander Daniel Pring, Captain Peter Fisher (July-August),
Captain George Downie (August-11 September)

Number and Type of Vessels

Rate or Type	1813	1814
5th	-	1
Sloop	-	1
Sloop Rig (Single mast)	2	2

AMERICAN NAVAL FORCES

Atlantic Seaboard

United States Navy warships on the Atlantic Seaboard operated independently or in small squadrons rather than operating as a fleet under a flag officer. The USN system for rating vessels differed from that used by the Royal Navy.

Type	1812	1813	1814
Frigate, 44 guns	3	3	3
Frigate, 36 guns	3	4	3
Frigate, 32 guns	2	1	1
Corvette[5], 24 guns	1	2	2
Sloop, 18 guns	2	3	7
Sloop, 16 guns	-	-	3
Brig, 16 guns	2	1	1
Brig, 14 guns	4	2	2
Brig, bomb vessel	-	-	1
Schooner, 14 guns	-	1	2

The Great Lakes

Lake Ontario
1812-1814: Commodore Isaac Chauncey, Senior Officer

Type	1812	1813	1814
Frigate, 58 guns	-	-	1
Frigate, 42 guns	-	-	1
Corvette, 24-26 guns	-	2	2
Brig	1	2	4
Schooner	6	12	1

Lake Erie and Upper Lakes
1812: Lieutenant Samuel Angus, Senior Officer
1813: Master Commandant[6] Oliver H. Perry
1814: Commodore Arthur Sinclair

Type	1812	1813	1814
Brig	1	3	3
Schooner	-	5	2
Sloop-Rig (Single Mast)	-	1	-

Lake Champlain
1812-1814: Master Commandant Thomas Macdonough, Senior Officer

Type	1812	1813	1814
Sloop, 20+ guns	-	-	2
Schooner	-	-	1
Sloop rig (single mast)	3	1	3

Sources

The major sources for British naval forces in North American waters are the *Naval Chronicle*, 1812-1815; William L Clowes, *The Royal Navy: A History from the Earliest Times to 1900*, vols. 4 and 5 (London, 1899, 1900); William Dudley, ed., *The Naval War of 1812: A Documentary History* (2 vols, Washington, 1985, 1992); Donald E. Graves, *Sir William Congreve and the Rocket's Red Glare* (Bloomfield, 1989); Robert and Thomas Malcomson, *HMS Detroit: The Battle for Lake Erie* (Annapolis, 1991), Robert Malcomson, *Lords of the Lake: The Naval War on Lake Ontario, 1812-1814* (Toronto, 1998); Theodore Roosevelt, *The Naval War of 1812* (New York, 1882).

The sources for the United States Navy were *American State Papers: Naval Affairs*, Vol 1 (Washington, 1834); Howard Chapelle, *The History of the American Sailing Navy: Their Ships and Their Development* (New York, 1949); William Dudley, ed., *The Naval War of 1812: A Documentary History*, 2 vols. (Washington, 1985, 1992); Robert and Thomas Malcomson, *HMS Detroit: The Battle for Lake Erie* (Annapolis, 1991); Robert Malcomson, *Lords of the Lake: The Naval War on Lake Ontario, 1812 1814* (Toronto, 1990), Theodore Roosevelt, *The Naval War of 1812* (New York, 1882).

Notes

1. A frigate was a three-masted vessel with a single gun deck having more than 24 guns.
2. H.M.S. *Erebus* was one of two sloops fitted to fire Congreve rockets from scuttles (apertures) in her sides. It was the Royal Marine Artillery detachment on *Erebus* under the command of Lieutenant Theophilus Beauchant, RMA, who provided the "rocket's red glare" during the bombardment of Fort McHenry in September 1814.
3. Note that this list contains only operational vessels and excludes prizes not employed as warships and vessels that were laid up.
4. A single-masted, fore and aft rigged vessel. In this instance "sloop" refers to the vessel's rig rather than its rate.
5. A flush-decked vessel with a single gun deck, carrying fewer guns than a frigate.
6. During the War of 1812 the rank of master commandant in the USN was equivalent to the rank of commander in the RN.

British and Canadian Battle Honours, Medals and Awards of the War of 1812

BATTLE HONOURS

Only five engagements of the war were regarded by the Horse Guards as important enough to warrant the grant of a battle honour to be borne on the colours of the units involved.

Honour	Units Receiving Honour	Modern (1999) Equivalent
Detroit, 16 Aug. 1812	41st Foot	The Royal Regiment of Wales
Queenstown[1], 13 Oct. 1812	41st Foot	The Royal Regiment of Wales
	49th Foot	The Royal Gloucestershire, Berkshire and Wiltshire Regiment
Miami[2], 23 Apr. 1813	41st Foot	The Royal Regiment of Wales
Niagara[3], 25 Jul. 1814	19th Light Dragoons	The Light Dragoons
	Royal Artillery	Royal Artillery
	8th Foot	The King's Regiment
	41st Foot	The Royal Regiment of Wales
	89th Foot	The Royal Irish Regiment
	100th Foot	*Disbanded in 1819*
	103rd Foot	*Disbanded in 1817*
	104th Foot	The Royal New Brunswick Regiment
	Glengarry Light Infantry Fencibles	The Stormont, Dundas and Glengarry Highlanders
Bladensburg, 24 Aug. 1814	Royal Artillery	Royal Artillery
	Royal Engineers	Royal Engineers
	4th Foot	The King's Own Royal Border Regiment
	21st Foot	The Royal Highland Fusiliers
	44th Foot	The Royal Anglian Regiment
	85th Foot	The Light Infantry
	Royal Marines	Royal Marines

Note: Although the Glengarry Light Infantry and 104th Foot, Canadian units, received a battle honour for Niagara, their modern successors are unable to officially receive these honours because of the lineage policy of the Canadian Forces (see Appendix 6).

In 1819 the 89th Regiment of Foot applied to the War Office for an honour for the battle of Crysler's Farm, 11 November 1813. This request was denied as, while the unit's record at Crysler's Farm were regarded as "meritorious," the engagement did not fall under that "description of actions, for which it has been usual to grant honorary distinctions."[4]

Royal Artillery "Niagara" Honour

In appreciation for their conduct during the fighting in the Niagara Peninsula between 1812 and 1814, Captain William Holcroft's company, Royal Artillery, was "permitted to bear the word 'Niagara' on its appointments." That company is still in existence as 52 ("Niagara") Battery, 4th Regiment, Royal Artillery.

MEDALS

Large Army (General Officer's) Gold Medal

General officers who played a distinguished role in "brilliant and distinguished events in which the success of His Majesty's arms has received royal approbation" might be awarded a gold medal which was worn suspended around their neck by a red ribbon with a blue edge. Only one such medal was awarded for the War of 1812 and it went to Major General Sir Isaac Brock for his victory at Detroit in August 1812.

Small Army (Field Officer's) Gold Medal

Field grade officers (major to colonel) who participated in "brilliant and distinguished events" (i.e. notable victories) might be eligible for the Small Army Gold Medal which was a reduced version of the general officer's medal but was worn hanging from a buttonhole on a red ribbon with blue edging. Officers of lower rank were also eligible for this medal providing they commanded their units or corps or served on the staff during the engagement for which it was awarded.

In January 1814, Sir George Prevost was asked to nominate those officers under his command "who had been most distinguished" in actions against "superior numbers" of the enemy who would be eligible for this medal. He nominated the following:

Action	Officer
Detroit, Aug. 1812	Lieutenant Colonel Matthew Elliott, Indian Department
	Lieutenant Colonel John Macdonell, Upper Canada Militia
	Lieutenant Colonel Robert Nichol, Upper Canada Militia
	Lieutenant Colonel Thomas St. George, Inspecting Field Officer
	Major Peter Chambers, Staff
	Major Adam Muir, 41st Foot
	Major Joseph Tallon, 41st Foot
	Captain John B. Glegg, Staff
	Captain M.C. Dixon, Royal Engineers
	Lieutenant Felix Troughton, Royal Artillery
Châteauguay, Oct. 1813	Lieutenant Colonel George MacDonell, Glengarry Light Infantry
	Lieutenant Colonel Charles de Salaberry, Voltigeurs Canadiens
Crysler's Farm, Nov. 1813	Lieutenant Colonel John Harvey, Deputy Adjutant General
	Lieutenant Colonel Joseph W. Morrison, 89th Foot
	Lieutenant Colonel Thomas Pearson, 23rd Foot

Lieutenant Colonel Charles Plenderleath, 49th Foot
Major Miller Clifford, 89th Foot
Major Frederick G. Heriot, Voltigeurs Canadiens
Captain Henry G. Jackson, Royal Artillery

Military General Service Medal, 1793-1814: War of 1812 Clasps

In 1847 it was decided to issue a medal to all surviving officers and soldiers who had fought in the battles of the revolutionary and Napoleonic wars. It was also decided to issue clasps for each engagement that had been recognized by the earlier award of a large or small Gold Medal. Three War of 1812 actions – Detroit, Châteauguay and Crysler's Farm – were so distinguished. The Military General Service Medal is enscribed "To the British Army/1793-1814" and the recipient's name (if he bothered to apply for the medal) was stamped on its edge. In all, 911 of these medals and clasps were issued for service at these three actions during the war.

Naval General Service Medal, 1793-1840: War of 1812 Clasps

To mark the valour of the officers and men of the Royal Navy and Royal Marines, a parallel Naval General Service Medal was instituted in 1848 and issued the following year to those who applied for it. A number of clasps for War of 1812 naval actions were issued with this medal:

Clasp	Description of Action
Boat Service, April and May 1813	Operations in the Chesapeake, April and May 1813
Shannon vs. *Chesapeake*	Capture of USS *Chesapeake* by HMS *Chesapeake*, 1 June 1813
Pelican, 14 August 1813	Capture of USS *Argus* by HMS *Pelican*, 14 August 1813
Phoebe, 28 March 1814 *Cherub*, 28 March 1814	Two clasps for the same action, the capture of USS *Essex* by HMSS *Phoebe* and *Cherub*, 28 March 1814
Boat Service, 8 April 1813	Destruction or capture of 27 American privateers or merchantmen in the Chesapeake area
Boat Service, 6 May 1814	Attack on Oswego, New York, 6 May 1814
The Potomac, 17 August 1814	Operations of a squadron under Captain James Parker on the Potomac River*
Boat Service, 3 and 6 September 1814	Capture of USS *Tigress* and *Scorpion* on Lake Huron, 2 and 6 September 1813
Boat Service, 14 December 1814	Naval action on Lake Borgne, Louisiana, resulting in destruction of American squadron
Endymion vs. *President*	Capture of USS *President* by HMS *Endymion*, 15 January 1815

The "Upper Canada Preserved" Medal

Following the war, the Loyal and Patriotic Society of Upper Canada, an organization formed by some of the leading citizens of the province, decided to cast and distribute a medal to commemorate the war and reward those Upper Canadian militiamen who had displayed conspicuous gallantry during it. The Society had a number of medals struck which had the legend "For Merit. Presented by a Grateful Country" on the obverse side and "Upper Canada Preserved" on the reverse side and a scene representing a "Streight [sic] between two lakes, on the north side a Beaver (emblem of peaceful industry), the ancient armorial bearing of Canada" with "an English lion slumbering" in the back-

Field Officer's Small Gold Medal for the surrender of Detroit, 1812
Awarded to Lieutenant-Colonel John Macdonell for his services in the Detroit campaign. (Richardson, *War of 1812*, 1902)

Military General Service Medal, 1793-1814, with Crysler's Farm clasp
This medal was instituted in 1847 for all surviving veterans who had participated in the Napoleonic Wars. Some engagements, including Crysler's Farm, were commemorated by a clasp worn on the ribbon of the medal.

The ill-fated "Upper Canada Preserved" Medal
Created to reward deserving militiamen from the province, this medal was never distributed because of controversy on the part of the awards committee. (Editor's collection)

ground. On the south side of the "streight" was "an American eagle planeing [sic] in the air, as if checked from seizing the Beaver by the presence of the Lion."

The Society had a number of such medals cast and asked the commanding officers of wartime militia units to recommend the names of deserving militia officers and men to receive them. They shortly discovered they had more names than medals and therefore had another batch struck but internal squabbles in the Society (including a wish to award each other medals), politics and other problems led to the result that the medals were never properly distributed and most were destroyed in 1840.

Sources

C.B. Norman, *Battle Honours of the British Army ...* (London, 1911); Donald E. Graves, *Field of Glory: The Battle of Crysler's Farm, 1813* (Toronto, 1999); Theodore Roosevelt, *The Naval War of 1812* (New York, 1882); George Sheppard, *Plunder, Profit and Paroles: A Social History of the War of 1812 In Upper Canada* (Toronto, 1995); George Stanley, *The War of 1812: Land Operations* (Ottawa, 1983).

Notes

1. The battle of Queenston Heights.
2. Action at the Maumee Rapids near Fort Meigs.
3. The battle of Lundy's Lane.
4. See Donald E. Graves, *Field of Glory: The Battle of Crysler's Farm, 1813* (Toronto, 1999), 375-376.

Endnotes

Abbreviations Used in the Notes and Bibliography

Adm — Admiralty
AHR — *American Historical Review*
AIQ — *American Indian Quarterly*
Amer Nept — *American Neptune*
AO — Archives of Ontario, Toronto
AR — *Alabama Review*
ASPMA — *American State Papers, Class V: Military Affairs* (vol 1, Washington, 1832)
BHM — *Bulletin of the History of Medicine*
BHSP — *Buffalo Historical Society Proceedings*
CDQ — *Canadian Defence Quarterly*
CGJ — *Canadian Geographical Journal*
CHA — Canadian Historical Association
CHAR — *Canadian Historical Association Report*
CHR — *Canadian Historical Review*
CMH — *Canadian Military History*
CO — Colonial Office
DAB — *Dictionary of American Biography*, (22 vols, New York, 1958-1964)
DCB — *Dictionary of Canadian Biography*, (vols 5-9, Toronto, 1976-1988)
DH — Ernest A. Cruikshank, ed., *The Documentary History of the Campaign on the Niagara Frontier ... 1812[-1814]* (9 vols, Welland, 1902-1908)
DNB — *Dictionary of National Biography* (63 vols, London, 1885)
FHQ — Florida Historical Quarterly
FO — Foreign Office
HA — Parks Canada, History and Archaeology Series
HK — *Historic Kingston*
IMH — *Indiana Magazine of History*
IS — *Inland Seas*
JCHA — *Journal of the Canadian Historical Association*
JES — *Journal of Erie Studies*
JRAMC — *Journal of the Royal Army Medical Corps*
JSAHR — *Journal of the Society for Army Historical Research*
LQ — *Louisiana Quarterly*
MA — *Military Affairs*
MCH — *Military Collector and Historian*
MFRS — Parks Canada, Microfiche Report Series

MG — Manuscript Group
MHM — *Maryland History Magazine*
Micro — Microfilm
MIHR — *Michigan Historical Review*
MM — *Mariner's Mirror*
MRS — Parks Canada, Manuscript Report Series
MVHR — *Mississippi Valley Historical Review*
NAC — National Archives of Canada, Ottawa
Naval War — William Dudley, ed., *The Naval War of 1812: A Documentary History* (Washington, 1992)
NSHSP — *Proceedings of the Nova Scotia Historical Society*
NHSP — *Niagara Historical Society Publications*
NHST — *Niagara Historical Society Transactions*
NWR — *Niles' Weekly Register*
NYHS — New York Historical Society
OH — *Ontario History*
OHPA — Parks Canada, *Occasional Papers in History and Archaeology*
OHSPR — *Ontario Historical Society, Papers and Records*
PRO — Public Record Office, Kew, Surrey
RB — Parks Canada, Research Bulletin
RG — Record Group
RSC — *Royal Society of Canada, Transactions*
SBD — William H. Wood, ed., *Select British Documents of the Canadian War of 1812* (3 vols in 4, Toronto, 1920-1928)
SPCMI — *Selected Papers, Canadian Military Institute*
Tupper — Ferdinand B. Tupper, *The Life and Correspondence of Major-General Sir Isaac Brock, K.B ...* (London, 1847)
USNA — United States National Archives, Washington
USNIP — *United States Naval Institute Proceedings*
vol — volume
WCHO — *Women's Canadian Historical Society of Ottawa*
WCHT — *Women's Canadian Historical Society of Toronto*
WHC — *Wisconsin Historical Collections*
WMQ — *William and Mary Quarterly*
WO — War Office

CB = Carl Benn. RM = Robert Malcomson. SS = Stuart Sutherland

Introduction and Editorial Note

1. Information on Hitsman's family provided by George Henderson of Queen's University Archives in Kingston, other information by Canon Tony Hitsman of Harrington Harbour, Quebec. Unless otherwise noted, all personal information about Mac Hitsman is from this latter source.
2. In fact, the remaining five volumes would never see publication as the project was scrapped in 1946. In 1964, a one volume official history by G.W.L. Nicholson was released with the title *Canadian Expeditionary Force, 1914-1919*.
3. The list of Canadian military historians who have served in the Army Historical Section or its successor, the Directorate of History, is lengthy and impressive. Among those who have published on the War of 1812 alone, it includes W.A.B. Douglas, D.B. Goodspeed, B. Greenhous, A.M.J. Hyatt, J.M. Hitsman, G.W.L. Nicholson, A.O. Sorby, C.P. Stacey, G.F.G. Stanley, S.F. Wise – and the editor.
4. Editor's conversation, 15 July 1999, with Professor S.F. Wise, Director of History during the latter years of Mac Hitsman's life, and biographical information provided by Canon Tony Hitsman.
5. An Exhortation pronounced after the Sermon …, York, 22 Dec. 1812 in *Report of the Loyal and Patriotic Society of Upper Canada* (Montreal, 1817) appendix.
6. William James, *Full and Correct Account of the Chief Naval Occurrences of the Late War Between Great Britain and the United States …* (2 vols, London, 1817) and *A Full and Correct Account of the Military Occurrences of the Late War between Great Britain and the United States* (2 vols, London, 1818).
7. Egerton Ryerson, *The Loyalists of America and Their Times, from 1620 to 1816* (2 vols, Toronto, 1880), 2, 316, quoted in S.F. Wise, "The War of 1812 in Popular History," in Arthur Bowler, ed., *War Along the Niagara: Essays on the War of 1812 and Its Legacy* (Youngstown, 1991), 117.
8. Henry Adams, *History of the United States of America [during the Administrations of Thomas Jefferson and James Madison]* (9 vols, New York, 1889-1891 and many subsequent editions) and Alfred Thayer Mahan, *Sea Power in Its Relations to the War of 1812* (2 vols, New York, 1905). A very useful single-volume condensation of Adams's *History*, containing those sections dealing solely with military and naval matters and edited by Henry De Weerd, appeared in 1944.
9. James Hannay, *History of the War of 1812* (Toronto, 1905) vii, quoted in S.F. Wise, "The War of 1812 in Popular History," 107, in Bowler, *War Along the Niagara*.
10. Such is Cruikshank's publication record that the editor has never seen a complete bibliography of the man's work. Indeed, such a task would be very difficult as Cruikshank often published the same article with a different title in different periodicals appearing in different countries. His main 1812 publications were a series of pamphlets on the various military actions in the Niagara area; a series of articles on Canadian military units of the war; several articles covering political disaffection in Canada and operations in Lower Canada; and three document collections concerned with the war in Upper Canada generally, the campaign on the Detroit River and the 1814 campaign on the Niagara. Details for some of these publications will be found in the bibliography that follows.
11. Cruikshank's three documentary collections were: *The Documentary History of the Campaign on the Niagara Frontier in 1812 [-1814]* (9 vols, Welland, 1902-1908; *Documents Relating to the Invasion of Canada and the Surrender of Detroit* (Ottawa, 1912); and *Documents Relating to the Invasion of the Niagara Peninsula by the United States Army, commanded by General Jacob Brown, in July and August* (Niagara-on-the-Lake, 1920). The nine-volume series (known to *cognoscenti* of the War of 1812 as the "Doc Hist") actually covers operations from Cornwall to Detroit.
12. William H. Wood, ed., *Select British Documents of the Canadian War of 1812* (3 vols in 4, Toronto, 1920-1928).
13. It might not be out of place to add a few further facts about the energetic Ernest Cruikshank's life and work. Despite his good record in the militia, where he rose from lieutenant to brigadier-general largely on the strength of his ability to maintain high standards of discipline (he was actually a martinet), Cruikshank was considerably less successful on the one occasion when he was placed in charge of regular troops. Appointed to command Military District 13 in Alberta in 1914, he came close to inciting a mutiny and was quickly transferred.

   He was then given the task of supervising the writing of the official history of the Canadian Expeditionary Force in the First World War. In the early 1920s, the chief of the general staff, not having heard of any progress on the project for some time, asked Cruikshank for a situation report. Cruikshank's response was that the first volume, which brought the story up to 1784, would soon be in print. He left the army shortly thereafter but that book, a collection of documents relating to military matters in Canada from the end of the Seven Years' War to the close of the Revolutionary War, saw print as *A History of the Military and Naval Forces of Canada from 1763 to 1784.*

In his later years Cruikshank was chairman of the Historic Sites and Monuments Board of Canada. In May 1939, at the age of eighty-six, he made a rigorous tour of eastern Ontario to select sites for historic plaques but caught a chill that led to his death a month later.

14. C.P. Stacey, "The War of 1812 in Canadian History," *OH* 50 (1958), 154.

15. These articles were: "David Thompson and Defence Research," *CHR* 40 (1959), 315-318; "Alarum on Lake Ontario, Winter 1812-1813," *Military Affairs* 23 (Fall, 1959), 129-138; "Spying at Sackets Harbor, 1813," *Inland Seas* 15 (1959), 120-122; "Independent Foreigners or Canadian Chasseurs," *Military Affairs* 25 (1961), 11-19; "The War of 1812 in Canada," *History Today* 12 (Sep. 1962), 632-639; "Sir George Prevost's Conduct of the Canadian War of 1812, *Report* of the Canadian Historical Association (1962), 34-43; "David Parish and the War of 1812," *Military Affairs* 26 (Winter 1962), 171-177. An eighth article on a War of 1812 topic, "Kingston and the War of 1812," appeared in *Historic Kingston* 15 (1967), 50-60.

Notable among the 1812 publications contributed by historians associated with the Army Historical Section were Charles Stacey's article, "The War of 1812 in Canadian History," discussed in the text and his "Naval Power on the Lakes," in Philip P. Mason, ed., *After Tippecanoe: Some Aspects of the War of 1812* (Toronto, 1963), 49-59. George Stanley published two interesting articles on the native peoples in the war: "The Indians in the War of 1812," *CHR* 31 (1950), 145-165; and "The significance of the Six Nations participation in the War of 1812," *Ontario History* 55 (1963), 215-231; and also "The Contribution of the Canadian Militia During the War," in Mason, *After Tippecanoe,* 28-48.

16. J.M. Hitsman, *Safeguarding Canada, 1763-1871* (Toronto, 1968).

17. Author's preface to the original edition of *The Incredible War of 1812.*

18. J.M. Hitsman, "Sir George Prevost's Conduct of the Canadian War of 1812," *Annual Report* of the Canadian Historical Association 1962, 34-43.

19. Unfortunately this is no longer the case as funding cutbacks have forced the National Archives to curtail its hours, and its reading room is no longer open twenty-four hours a day, every day of the year. In the early 1980s, when the former cheerful situation held true, the editor once visited the reading room on Christmas Day just to see if anyone would actually be there – he found three determined researchers happy at their labours.

20. Editor's conversations with Dr. Francess G. Halpenny, 5 Aug. 1999; and Ted Hitsman, 28 June 1999; and information supplied by Canon Tony Hitsman.

21. Obituary of J.M. Hitsman by C.P. Stacey, *CHR* 51 (June 1970).

22. NAC, CO 42, vol 23, Prince Regent's Instructions to Prevost, 22 Oct. 1811.

23. It should not be overlooked that, almost from the day the war started, military operations took place against a background of diplomatic efforts by both combatant nations to end it peacefully. Even before the United States declared war, Britain repealed many of the infamous orders-in-council concerning maritime restrictions that formed one of America's outstanding grievances, although news of this step did not reach Washington until after the declaration of war on 18 June 1812. When Prevost learned of this event, he arranged a temporary armistice along the northern frontier in August and September 1812 in the expectation that the war would be brought to a negotiated conclusion. Madison's refusal to take such a step doomed this hope but in early 1813 the president accepted an offer by the Czar of Russia to mediate a solution and sent diplomats to St. Petersburg. Throughout most of 1813 there was anticipation in Washington that Britain would accept the Czar's proposal, but Britain turned it down in December. The next month, however, Britain made an offer of direct negotiations to end the war which was quickly accepted by the United States. Peace commissioners from both nations met in the Dutch city of Ghent (Belgium did not exist at that time) in early July and, after much discussion, a definitive treaty of peace was signed on 24 December 1814.

24. Prevost entry in *DNB,* vol 5.

25. As Hitsman notes in his preface to the 1965 edition, Mahan, in his *Sea Power in its Relations to the War of 1812,* also felt that Prevost had done the best he could under the circumstances, see Vol 2, 381-382, 430-431.

26. Hitsman, *Safeguarding Canada*, 108.
27. The updated bibliography appended to this new edition contains a listing of recent scholarship on the native peoples and the war, and the war and Canadian civilian society.
28. Editor's conversation with Francess Halpenny, 5 Aug. 1999 and Halpenny to editor, 6 Sep. 1999.
29. All quotations from reviews of *The Incredible War of 1812* are from those reproduced on the dust jacket of *Safeguarding Canada*.
30. An American edition of *Incredible War* was published in 1966. The last Canadian printing was 1972.
31. Obituary of John Mackay Hitsman by C.P. Stacey, *CHR* 51 (June 1970). Mac Hitsman was a member of the Canadian Historical Society, the Royal Historical Society, the Commonwealth Society, the American Military Institute, the Company of Military Historians, the Professional Institute of Canada, and the Royal Canadian Legion. He was also the recipient of Canada Council and Centennial Commission awards.

  Besides *The Incredible War* and *Safeguarding Canada*, Hitsman produced three other books. His M.A. thesis was published as *Canadian Naval Policy* by Queen's University in Kingston in 1940; *A History of Medical Inspection Services in Canada* (Ottawa, 1962); and, with J.L. Granatstein, *Broken Promises; a History of Conscription in Canada* (Toronto, 1977).
32. G.F.G. Stanley, *The War of 1812. Land Operations* (Ottawa, 1983), xvii. The planned companion volume to this book covering naval operations has not yet appeared. In its continued absence the interested reader is directed to William Dudley's excellent multi-volume series, *The Naval War of 1812: A Documentary History*.
33. Kate Caffrey, *The Twilight's Last Gleaming; The British Against America, 1812-1815* (London, 1977); Alan Lloyd, *The Scorching of Washington: The War of 1812* (London, n.d., c. 1975); Wesley B. Turner, *The War of 1812: The War Both Sides Won* (Toronto, 1990); and Pierre Berton, *The Invasion of Canada, 1812* (Toronto, 1980) and *Flames Across the Border, 1813-1814* (Toronto, 1981). Berton's books, written in a highly dramatic fashion in (curiously enough) the present tense, were the best-selling of these popular histories. They contain a good bibliography, which their author might have used to better advantage.
34. Among the major works published by British or Canadian scholars since 1966, the editor has contributed book length studies of the St. Lawrence campaign of 1813 and the Niagara campaign of 1814 while Sandor Antal has examined the western campaigns of 1812-1813 in *A Wampum Denied: Procter's War of 1812* (Ottawa, 1997) The 1812 battle of Queenston Heights has been studied by Carol Whitfield in *The Battle of Queenston Heights* (Ottawa, 1974) and Victor Suthren has discussed the 1813 action at Châteauguay in *The Battle of Châteauguay* (Ottawa, 1974). Michelle Guitard's *The Militia of the Battle of Châteauguay: A Social History* (Ottawa, 1983) is at one and the same time an excellent example of good social and military history combined with incisive historiographical analysis. Robin Reilly's *The British at the Gates: The New Orleans Campaign in the War of 1812* (New York, 1974) written by a Briton resident in the United States, is a very good campaign study that incorporates strategical, operational and tactical elements in its analysis.

  The role played by the native peoples of North America in the war has deservedly received more attention in recent years from British and Canadian historians. The Briton John Sugden has brought out two fine studies of Tecumseh and his confederation: *Tecumseh's Last Stand* (Norman, 1985) and *Tecumseh: A Life* (New York, 1997), while Carl Benn has studied the involvement of one group of native peoples and the war in *The Iroquois and the War of 1812* (Toronto, 1998).

  The effects of the war on Canadian society have been examined by Jane Errington in *The Lion, the Eagle, and Upper Canada: a Developing Colonial Ideology* (Montreal, 1987) and George Sheppard in *Plunder, Profit and Paroles: a Social History of the War of 1812 in Upper Canada* (Montreal, 1995)). Wesley Turner has contributed a useful study of British military command problems and personalities, *British Generals in the War of 1812. High Command in the Canadas* (Montreal, 1999), which is counterbalanced by Robert Malcomson's study of naval command problems and operations on Lake Ontario in *Lords of the Lake* (Toronto, 1998). William Gray has studied the militia of Upper Canada in *Soldiers of the King: the Upper Canadian Militia, 1812-1815* (Erin, 1995) while Luc Lépine has chosen the militia of Lower Canada in *Les Officiers de Milice du Bas-Canada, 1812-1815* (Montreal, 1996).

  These are only the major titles; see the bibliography for a more complete listing of British and Canadian scholarship on the War of 1812 since 1965.

35. William Gray, *Soldiers of the King: the Upper Canadian Militia, 1812-1815* (Erin, 1995), 7.
36. Take the case of the editor's personal copy as an example. Acquired secondhand while he was an undergraduate, it has seen such hard service over a quarter of a century that it has been reduced to a handful of loose pages, profusely covered with annotations and marginal comments, and held together by a fat elastic band. Long past honourable retirement, it has only been kept in the traces because of the difficulty and expense of acquiring a replacement. Other historians have stated that their copies of *The Incredible War* are in a similar state of disintegration.

Author's Preface
1. Although the illustrations and maps in this edition of *The Incredible War* have been changed and are no longer the work of the persons the author thanks, his acknowledgements have been left in place as a matter of record.

Chapter 1: Years of Tension: The Road to War, 1783-1811
1. For a biography of Haldimand, see *DCB*, vols 4 and 5.
2. Journals of the Continental Congress, vol 27, 524, quoted in James R. Jacobs, *The Beginning of the U.S. Army, 1783-1812* (Princeton, 1947), 14.
3. For a biography of Dorchester, see *DCB*, vol 5.
4. For a biography of Simcoe, see *DCB*, vol 5.
5. *Habitants* was one of the names commonly given to the French-speaking subjects of the Crown in the Canada. The other, more common term, was *Canadiens*.
6. At this time, British officers whose units were disbanded could be placed on half pay (actually about 40 per cent of their annual salary). Since a lieutenant made about as much in a year as a small shopkeeper or a minor clergyman, his half pay would keep him just above the poverty line in Britain but would allow him to live much better in the Canadas, where there was always a shortage of hard cash.
7. The form of the oath of loyalty given in Upper Canada is contained in NAC, RG 9I, B1, vol 2, 1812, Miscellaneous.
8. The most recent study of the Upper Canada militia during the war is William Gray, *Soldiers of the King: The Upper Canadian Militia, 1812-1815* (Erin, 1995). For a survey of the non-combat duties of the militia, see Glenn Steppler, "A Duty Troublesome Beyond Measure: Logistical Considerations in the Canadian War of 1812," MA Thesis, McGill University, 1074.
9. The author's description of the vessels and ranks of the Royal Navy in 1812 needs some elaboration. First rate warships carried 100 guns or more. Sloops were vessels under commission to a commander and could be corvettes (ship-rigged, three-masted vessels) or brigs (two-masted vessels) or schooners (two masts but fore-and-aft rigged). A "sloop rigged" vessel had one mast and fore-and-aft sails. A post captain earned that rank when his name was posted on the seniority list of commanding officers in the Royal Navy and this occurred when he was given the command of a sixth-rate or larger warship. See Brian Lavery, *Nelson's Navy: The Ships, Men and Organization* (London, 1898). RM
10. Pioneers were infantry soldiers who undertook elementary field and garrison engineering and construction tasks.
11. NAC, CO 42, vol 318, Simcoe to Dundas, 23 Feb. 1794.
12. This is a reference to the ill-fated American invasion of Quebec in the summer of 1775 which foundered against the walls of Quebec City in the following winter and ended when navigation resumed on the St. Lawrence and the Royal Navy exerted its presence. See George F.G. Stanley, *Canada Invaded, 1775-1776* (Ottawa, 1973).
13. NAC, CO 42, vol. 318, Simcoe to Dundas, 23 Feb. 1794.
14. NAC, CO 42, vol 101, Dorchester to Dundas, 24 May 1794.
15. While it is true that Brant tried to create a pan-tribal confederacy after the American Revolution, the tribes of the Northwest, particularly in the Ohio country, were leery of their Six Nations Iroquois neighbours and the confederacy they formed to fight the Americans never really included official Mohawk or other Iroquoian participation. In effect, the western alliance was formed without reference to Brant and the Iroquois. **CB.**
16. "Shattering defeats" is no exaggeration. In Oct. 1790 the native peoples of the North West defeated a military force under General Josiah Harmar. A year later, a second and larger American army under General Arthur St. Clair was nearly destroyed at the battle of Fallen Timbers of 4

Nov. 1791, suffering 908 casualties. This was the worst defeat the native peoples inflicted on the armed forces of the United States.

17. The term "fencible" is often a source of confusion and needs to be better defined than it is in the text. Fencible regiments were regular units of the British army raised for local, as opposed to "universal" or overseas service, otherwise they were indistinguishable. The fencible regiments raised in the North American colonies were only liable for service in British North America (which also included Bermuda).

18. Brock to York, n.d. (c. Jan. 1806) in Ferdinand B. Tupper, The *Life and Correspondence of Major-General Sir Isaac Brock, K.B.* (London, 1847), 33.

19. PRO, FO 5, vol 52, no. 21, Erskine to Canning, 17 July 1807.

20. For a biography of Brock, see *DCB*, vol 5.

21. A *mandement* is a decree issued by a bishop of the Roman Catholic Church to his diocese.

22. *Quebec Mercury*, 31 Aug. 1808.

23. Brock to Gordon Brock, 6 Sep. 1807, in Tupper, 64.

24. The Board of Ordnance, under the nominal control of the Master-General of Ordnance, was in charge of the procurement, storage and distribution of weapons for the British army in this period. It also controlled the so-called "ordnance troops": the Royal Artillery and Royal Engineers, who were trained, commissioned and promoted separate from the officers of the "horse and foot" (cavalry and infantry), who came under the control of the commander-in-chief at the Horse Guards, Frederick, Duke of York, second son of George III.

25. For a biography of Gore, see *DCB*, vol 8.

26. A "stand of arms" was a musket and bayonet (with scabbard and belt), cartridge box and belt.

27. NAC, CO 42, vol 347, Gore to Castlereagh, 7 Oct. 1807.

28. For a biography of Craig, see *DCB*, vol 5.

29. Militia General Order, 24 Nov. 1807, quoted in J.M. Hitsman, *Safeguarding Canada 1763-1871* (Toronto, 1968) 72.

30. H.W. Wilkinson to John Macaulay, 3 Jan. 1808, in R.A. Preston, ed., *Kingston before the War of 1812* (Toronto, 1959), 256.

31. NAC, CO 42, vol 136, Craig to Gore, 6 Dec. 1807.

32. Militia Act, Upper Canada, 16 Mar. 1808, contained in *DH*, vol 3, 3.

33. NAC, CO 42, vol 136, Gore to Craig, 5 Jan. 1808.

34. NAC, CO 42, vol 136, Craig to Gore, 6 Dec. 1807.

35. The Horse Guards was the popular name for the office of the Duke of York, the commander-in-chief of the army, located near the Horse Guards parade ground in London – hence, the origin of the expression "from the horse's mouth" to mean information from the best possible source. The Duke of York may have commanded the army but he certainly did not control it as he shared responsibility with the Master-General of Ordnance (ordnance and fortifications), the Secretary of State for War and the Colonies (higher strategical and colonial direction), the Secretary at War (financial control) and a bewildering array of lesser departments and individuals with semi-independent and often overlapping jurisdictions such as the Paymaster General, Barrackmaster General, Transport Board, Commissariat, Storekeeper General, Quartermaster General, Military Secretariat, Commissary General for Musters, the Medical Board, Commissioners for Chelsea Hospital. For a discussion of the complicated military machinery of Great Britain during this period, see Richard Glover, *Peninsular Preparation: The Reform of the British Army, 1795-1809* (Cambridge, 1963), 14-45, and Michael Glover, *Wellington as Military Commander* (London, 1973), 13-19.

36. NAC, CO 42, vol 136, Gore to Craig, 5 Jan. 1808.

37. Michael Smith, *A Geographical View of the Province of Upper Canada and Promiscuous Remarks on the Government* .... (Boston, 1813). This book went through many editions, each of which varies slightly.

Chapter 2: "A General Outline for Defence": Preparations for War, 1811-1812

1. See his biography in *DCB*, vol. 5, and Edward Brenton, *Some Account of the Public Life of the Late Lieutenant-General Sir George Prevost, Bart.* ... (London, 1823), 5-12.

2. Such has been Sir George Prevost's reputation among Canadian historians that it is often overlooked that he had a distinguished combat record in the West Indies, where he served almost continuously from 1791 to 1805 and again in 1808-1809, see Brenton, *Account of the Public Life*,

6-11. As a battalion commander in 1796, he was badly wounded during the defence of St. Vincent; as a brigadier general in 1805 he was responsible for the successful defence of Dominica; and as a major general in 1809 he commanded a division during the conquest of Martinique – and commanded it well. Prevost was far from being a desk soldier.

3. For a biography of Sherbrooke, see *DCB*, vol. 6.

4. For a biography of de Rottenburg, see *DCB*, vol 6.

5. *Regulations for the Exercise of Riflemen and Light Infantry, and Instructions for their Conduct in the Field, 1st August, 1798, with Plates and Music* (London, 1798, 2nd edn in 1803). Rottenburg apparently published this manual in German in 1797 and it was translated into English by Sir William Fawcett, the adjutant general of the British army, see Glover, *Peninsular Preparation*, 128. It was one of a number of semiofficial manuals used to train British light infantry and rifle units during this period, another popular work being Francis Jarry, *Instruction concerning the Duties of Light Infantry in the Field* (London, 1803).

6. Brock to his brothers, 19 Nov. 1808, in Tupper, 72.

7. Brock to Prevost, 12 Feb. 1812, in Tupper, 151.

8. Madison to Congress, 4 Nov. 1811, in *Annals of Congress: Debates and Proceedings in the Congress of the United States, 1789-1834* (42 vols, Washington, 1834-1836), 12th Congress, Session 11.

9. The most recent biography is John Sugden, *Tecumseh. A Life* (New York, 1997).

10. On Harrison, see Richard C. Knopf, *William Henry Harrison and the War of 1812* (Columbus, 1957).

11. The *Queen Charlotte* was about the same size as the *Royal George* and was also ship-rigged. The other British vessels on Lake Ontario were the ship-rigged *Earl of Moira* (14 guns), the aging schooner *Duke of Gloucester* (6 guns), the replacement for which, the schooner *Prince Regent* (8), was launched in July 1812. See Robert Malcomson. *Lords of the Lake. The Naval War on Lake Ontario* (Toronto, 1998). **RM**

12. Formed in 1807 from discharged or time-expired soldiers who wished to emigrate to North America, the 10th Royal Veteran Battalion was sent to Canada in 1808 to do service in outlying posts. It was felt that veterans, many of whom had families, would be less likely to be lured into deserting across the border. This unit saw action in the opening months of the war but was thereafter shifted to garrison duties in Lower Canada. It was renumbered the 4th Battalion and disbanded in 1816. See René Chartrand, Brian Dunnigan and Dirk Gringhuis, "10th Royal Veteran Battalion, Fort Mackinac, 1812," *Military Historian* 23 (1972), 47-48, 82; and A.S. White, "Garrison, Reserve and Veteran Battalions," *JSAHR* 38 (1959), 156-157.

13. British military terminology can be confusing for readers who are not familiar with it. Unlike most armies, where a regiment is a unit made up of two or more battalions, in the British army (and in modern Commonwealth armies), the word "regiment" is part of a unit's title and has nothing to do with its administrative and tactical organization. The basic tactical and administrative British infantry unit in 1812 (and today) was a battalion commanded by a lieutenant-colonel. The British equivalent to a regiment in the French or American armies of 1812 was a brigade. During the Napoleonic period, the British army consisted of 104 "regiments of the line," each having at least one battalion and some as many as six. To make things more confusing, the terms "regiment" and "battalion" were often used interchangeably.

14. Artificers were skilled craftsmen who worked under the direction of officers of the Royal Engineers to erect military buildings and fortifications. The name of this corps would shortly be changed to the Royal Sappers and Miners.

15. In fact, the duties of a modern chief of staff were split between Baynes and Captain Noah Freer, Prevost's military secretary throughout the war.

16. Hitsman's comment that Edward Macdonnell, quartermaster general, at the beginning of the war, was a "nonentity" who "would not long continue in his new duties" is somewhat unfair. Macdonnell was an experienced staff officer and did not continue long in his appointment because he died in Oct. 1812. **SS**

17. The expressed desire of all ranks of the New Brunswick Fencibles to extend their service beyond North America had led to this unit being placed on the regular British establishment as the 104th Regiment of Foot in 1810.

18. During this period, the wives of soldiers and their children often accompanied them on campaign. In the British army, six wives were allowed for each company on foreign service and they and their children were given rations at a reduced rate. This meant that a battalion in Canada would have, on average, 60 wives and approximately 100 children accompanying it. These were

the official dependants with a recognized status who were fed and transported by the Crown; there were often other unofficial dependants who had to get by as best they could.

19. "Brown Bess" was the generic term for the British military longarm of the musket period (c. 1700-1850), possibly because of the custom of staining or "browning" the barrels of these weapons. The two most common weapons in service during the War of 1812 were the Short Land Pattern (42-inch barrel) and the India Pattern (39-inch barrel), both with a .75 calibre bore.

Hitsman's statement that British muskets were superior to those of other nations is contested by some historians who point out that the .69 calibre French musket, although it fired a smaller round, had a similar range and expended less powder with each discharge. See Brent Nosworthy, *Battle Tactics of Napoleon and his Enemies* (London, 1996), 196-197.

20. Despite the inadequacies of the individual weapon, the musket could be devastating if used in numbers at short range. At the battle of Talavera in 1809, it has been calculated that twenty effective volleys by British infantry inflicted some 1,250 to 1,300 French casualties. See Donald E. Graves, *Where Right and Glory Lead; The Battle of Lundy's Lane, 1814* (Toronto, 1997), 31.

21. Hitsman's comments on the British officer corps in this paragraph reflect the state of scholarship on the subject at the time he was writing and are not correct. By 1812, more than 60 per cent of the officers were being created from middle-class candidates who joined without purchasing a commission. Only about 20 per cent of new officers purchased their first commission; the remaining 20 per cent were appointed from deserving noncommissioned officers, and in the case of paymasters, directly from civilian life. Promotion up through the ranks by purchase was also becoming extremely uncommon, since by regulations only a commission that had been bought and which was up for sale, could be sold, and then only in strict seniority in the regiment or battalion. The rise of an officer therefore did not depend "upon his having the purchase price available whenever a vacancy occurred in his own regiment, or in any one whose colonel would accept him," while purchase into another regiment was extremely uncommon, indeed almost nonexistent at this time. Given the strict regulation of promotion, exchanges and purchase instituted by the Duke of York beginning in the late 1790s, it is doubtful that officers wishing to transfer out of regiments ordered on colonial service could do so for a financial consideration. This was illegal by regulation in 1812, and although some transactions of this sort may have taken place, they were quite uncommon and would have earned the transgressors dismissal from the army had they been caught. Officers served in distant colonies because they had to, not because they were "run-of the-mill" or "keen."

On promotion and purchase in the British army, see Michael Glover, "The Purchase of Commissions: A Reappraisal," *JSAHR* 58 (1980), 223-235; and "Purchase, Patronage and Promotion in the Army at the Time of the Peninsular War," *Army Quarterly* 103 (1972-1973), 211-215, 355-362; and Stuart Sutherland, *His Majesty's Gentlemen: A Directory of the Regular British Army Officers* (publication forthcoming). SS.

22. This paragraph also needs considerable correction. The colonel of a regiment was always a general officer in this period. The issuance of brevet rank was not because the holder was a staff officer away from regimental duty; it was for distinguished service or because the officer had had the same rank for a number of years, commonly ten. This rank was only called "brevet rank," not "army rank," which latter applied when an officer transferred to another regiment (i.e. he took his rank with him). The date of his first commission in that rank was called army rank, but the date of his commission in the new regiment determined his seniority in that unit, and he was commonly the most junior of his rank on his transferral. As to Procter, he was a lieutenant-colonel commanding the 1st Battalion of the 41st Foot in 1812 and only a brevet colonel by virtue of seniority; the latter rank had nothing to do with his staff appointment. For sources on British officer ranks, promotion and appointment see the titles listed in note 21. SS.

23. Again, Hitsman did not have access to recent scholarship and his comments need correction. Vacancies created by death were always filled without purchase, no matter how the commission had been awarded. Battlefield commissions did not exist; the time between a recommendation for a deserving and intelligent sergeant or sergeant-major and an award of a commission was frequently several months. At this period, the appointment of paymaster was either given to a serving officer (usually a lieutenant), or much more frequently to a candidate straight from civilian life, but most adjutants and quartermasters were drawn from noncommissioned officers. For sources on promotion in the officer corps of the British army in the Napoleonic period, see note 21. SS.

24. Although on paper engineer and artillery officers were primarily responsible to the Board of Ordnance, by 1812 they were *de facto* subservient to the commander-in-chiefs in all theatres. It would have been politic for senior officers to respect the separate reporting system of the Royal Engineers and Artillery but no officer of these corps flouted his main commander with impunity. It did happen occasionally – in 1814 the RA officers attached to the Right Division in the Niagara complained about their commander, Major-General Phineas Riall, directly to the Commander, Royal Artillery in British North America, Major-General George Glasgow. The result was an exchange of correspondence that ended up on Prevost's desk. SS.

25. NAC, CO 42, vol 146, Prevost to Liverpool, 18 May 1812.

26. Hitsman's claim that inspecting field officers of militia did not take their job seriously is not supported by a more intensive examination of the activities of these officers. For example, Colonel Thomas Pearson in the Canadas and Colonel Joseph Gubbins, both experienced combat veterans, laboured long and hard to correct the deficiencies of the militia, see Howard Temperley, ed., *Lieutenant Colonel Joseph Gubbins. New Brunswick Journals of 1811 & 1813* (Fredericton, 1980). SS.

27. NAC, CO 42, vol 146, Prevost to Liverpool, 18 May 1812.

28. For a biography of Macdonell, see *DCB*, vol. 9.

29. NAC, RG8 I, vol. 1218, Prevost to Bathurst, 26 May 1812.,

30. *Quebec Gazette*, 28 May 1812.

31. For a biography of de Salaberry, see *DCB*, vol 6, and Patrick Wohler, *Charles de Salaberry, Soldier of the Empire, Defender of Quebec* (Toronto, 1984).

32. He was related to many of his officers, see Michelle Guitard, *The Militia of the Battle of the Châteauguay: A Social History* (Ottawa, 1983), 16-23.

33. *Quebec Gazette*, 23 Apr. 1812.

34. NAC, RG 8 I, vol 676, 92, Brock to Prevost, 25 Feb. 1812.

35. 1812 Upper Canada Militia Act in *DH*, vol 4, 5.

36. NAC, RG 8 I, vol 12031/2a, Brock to Butler, 8 Apr. 1812.

37. Militia General Order, 29 Apr. 1812 in *York Gazette*, 8 May 1812.

38. NAC, RG 8 I, vol 1218, 139, Brock to Freer, 23 Jan. 1812.

39. NAC, RG 8 I, vol 673, 171, Brock to Prevost, 11 Dec. 1811.

40. NAC, CO 42, vol. 23, Prince Regent's Instructions to Prevost, 22 Oct. 1811.

41. Prevost to Brock, 14 Dec. 1811, in Tupper, 133.

42. NAC, CO 42, vol 146, 188, Prevost to Liverpool, 18 May 1812. All subsequent quotations are from this document, which is reproduced in full in Appendix I.

43. At this time, artillery pieces were denominated by the weight of the roundshot they fired, if they were guns or carronades, or their bore diameter, if they were mortars or howitzers. Thus a 6-pdr. gun fired a 6 pound iron shot while a 5.5-in. howitzer fired a shell of that diameter.

44. On Dearborn, see Richard Erney, *The Public Life of Henry Dearborn* (New York, 1979).

45. Madison to Congress, 1 June 1812, in *Annals of Congress: Debates and Proceedings in the Congress of the United States, 1789-1834* (42 vols, Washington, 1834-1836), 12th Congress, Session 11.

46. PRO, Foreign Office 5, vol 86, Foster to Castlereagh, 20 June 1812.

Chapter 3: Opening Moves: June and July 1812

1. Brigade was the period British term for a field or mobile battery of artillery. The Royal Artillery was organized in companies and each company usually provided the personnel for one brigade of field artillery. The infantry used the term "brigade" differently: an infantry brigade was a formation consisting of two or more battalions of infantry.

2. For a biography of Glasgow, see *DCB*, vol 5.

3. *Corvée* was forced labour, either by the crown or seigneur, and usually involved road construction or transportation tasks.

4. Army Bills were paper currency.

5. USNA, RG 107, Micro 6, vol 5, Secretary of War Eustis to Dearborn, 16 June 1812.

6. NAC, MG 11, A21, NB, Hunter to Liverpool, 27 June 1812. Although they lived in amity with their neighbours in Maine throughout the next two years, the people of New Brunswick made a substantial contribution to the British war effort. Of a male population of military age numbering no more than 5,000, at least 1,300 New Brunswickers enlisted in either the 104th Foot or the New Brunswick Fencibles, regular units of the British army, see David Facey-Crowther, *The New*

Brunswick Militia, 1787-1867 (Fredericton, 1990), ch. 2. Several privateers, including the *Brunswicker, General Smythe, Herald, Hare, Snap Dragon, Dart* and *Star*, operated out of Saint John during the war and depredated the American coasting trade in the Bay of Fundy area.

7. NAC, MG 11, A21, NB, Smyth to Liverpool, 4 July 1812. For a biography of Smyth, see *DCB*, vol 6.

8. NAC, CO 42, vol 90, Proclamation, 3 July 1812, contained in Sherbrooke to Bathurst, 2 Aug. 1812.

9. NAC, CO 188, vol 18, Smyth to Liverpool, 4 July 1812.

10. Licence dated 4 Aug. 1812 contained in Alfred T. Mahan, *Sea Power in Its Relations to the War of 1812* (2 vols, New York, 1905) vol 1, 410.

11. *Naval Chronicle*, vol 29.

12. Rodgers to Hamilton, 1 Sep. 1812, in *Naval War*, 1985 and 1990), vol 2, 262.

The term "super-frigate" is rarely used now to describe the four largest American warships in 1812 but it is perhaps an apt one. Constructed in the 1790s, the frigates *Constitution, President, United States* and *Philadelphia* were rated at 44 guns (a large proportion of which were heavy 24-pdr. weapons), which made them among the most heavily-armed frigates of the period. This, combined with their large dimensions and heavy construction, created very formidable vessels.

Though rated at 44 guns, the *Constitution* actually carried 55 long guns and carronades throwing a broadside of 692 pounds of shot while the *Guerrière*, rated a "heavy 38," mounted 49 long guns and carronades throwing a broadside of 581 pounds, which gave it about 20 per cent disadvantage in weight of shot. Other circumstances, such as the poor physical state of the British frigate, affected the outcome of the engagement. See Tyrone G. Martin, *A Most Fortunate Ship: A Narrative History of Old Ironsides* (Chester, 1980). **RM.**

13. On Warren, see *DNB*.

14. On Tompkins, see *DAB*.

15. On Stephen Van Rensselaer, see *DAB*.

16. On Solomon van Rensselaer, see Benson Lossing, *Pictorial Field Book of the War of 1812* (New York, 1869), 408.

17. On Brown, see John Morris, *Sword of the Border; Major-General Jacob Jennings Brown, 1775-1828* (publication forthcoming).

18. In Upper Canada, the sedentary militia was organized into regiments by political ridings and thus the 1st Frontenac Regiment was the regiment of the first riding of that county. For a full listing of the Upper Canada militia, see Appendix 4.

19. NAC, MG 24, L8, Jacques Viger, "Ma Saberdache."

20. NAC, RG 8 I, vol 676, 122, Cartwright to Prevost, 5 July 1812.

21. NAC, RG 8 I, vol 688a, Baynes to Lethbridge, 10 July 1812.

22. The Corps of Voyageurs was formed in the autumn of 1812 to provide crews for the boats that carried supplies up the St. Lawrence. The personnel were taken from the skilled canoemen of the Northwest Fur Trading Company or former river boatmen. Under the command of regular British officers, the voyageurs carried out this vitally important but largely unsung service throughout the war.

23. NAC, RG 8 I, vol 688a, Baynes to Lethbridge, 10 July 1812.

24. The manual and platoon exercises were the basic fundamental training for infantry and encompassed the various movements for the movement and fire of an infantry company.

25. NAC, RG 8I, vol 676, 115, Brock to Prevost, 3 July 1812.

26. Brock to Prevost, 12 July 1812, in Tupper, 202.

27. Baynes to Brock, 10 July 1812, in Tupper, 199.

28. NAC, CO 42, vol 23, Bathurst to Prevost, 10 Aug. 1812.

29. NAC, CO 42, vol 23, Bathurst to Prevost, 10 Aug. 1812.

Chapter 4: Victories in the Old Northwest: August 1812

1. NAC, CO 42, vol. 146, 135, Proclamation, 12 July 1812.

2. USNA, RG 107, Micro 221, reel 46, Hull to Eustis, 21 July 1812.

3. NAC, RG 8 I, vol 676, 177, St. George to Brock, 21 July 1812.

4. It should be noted that the four hundred warriors at Detroit included members of the native peoples of Upper Canada who were not formally part of Tecumseh's confederacy. **CB.**

5. NAC, RG 8 I, vol 676, 203, Brock to Prevost, 20 July 1812.

6. NAC, RG 8 I, vol 676, 408, Brock to Prevost, 26 July 1812.

7. *New York Statesman*, 25 Aug. 1812.

8. The difficult position of the Six Nations people of the Grand River at the outbreak of war is succinctly delineated by Carl Benn in *The Iroquois in the War of 1812* (Toronto, 1998), 29-66.

9. NAC, CO 42, vol 315, 152, Brock's Proclamation, 22 July 1812.

10. NAC, RG 8 I, vol 676, 203, Brock to Prevost, 20 July 1812.

11. NAC, RG 8 I, vol 676, 408, Brock to Prevost, 26 July 1814.

12. For a biography of Procter, see *DCB*, vol 6. Procter wrote his own, somewhat confusing, memoir of the war which was published posthumously as *Lucubrations of Humphrey Ravelin* (London, 1823). A recent re-examination of the career of this officer and his operations in the North West in 1812-1813 is Sandor Antal, *A Wampum Denied: Procter's War of 1812* (Ottawa, 1997).

13. NAC, RG 8 I, vol 676, 408, Brock to Prevost, 26 July 1812.

14. Mahan, *Sea Power*, vol 1, 349.

15. USNA, RG 107, Micro 6, vol 6, Eustis to Hull, 24 June 1812.

16. USNA, RG 107, Micro 221, reel 46, Hull to Eustis, 9 July 1812.

17. Hull to Eustis, 22 July 1812, quoted in Henry Adams, *History of the United States during the First Administration of James Madison, 1813-1817* (3 vols, New York, 1931) vol 2, 34.

18. Brock to Roberts, 28 June 1812, in *SBD*, vol 1, 428.

19. Baynes to Roberts, 25 June 1812, in *SBD*, vol 1, 428.

20. Baynes to Roberts, 25 June 1812, in *SBD*, vol 1, 428.

21. Roberts's native force also included warriors from the Mohawk nations of Lower Canada so that the attack on Mackinac was the first action of the war for the Iroquoian peoples. CB.

22. NAC, RG 8 I, vol 676, 232, Roberts to Brock, 17 July 1812.

23. NAC, RG 8 I, vol 676, 232, Roberts to Brock, 17 July 1812.

24. NAC, RG 8 I, vol 676, 232, Roberts to Brock, 17 July 1812.

25. NAC, RG 8 I, vol 676, 217, Brock to Prevost, 28 July 1812.

26. NAC, RG 8 I, vol 676, 217, Brock to Prevost, 28 July 1812.

27. For a biography of Sheaffe, see *DCB*, vol 8.

28. A gentleman volunteer was an officer aspirant for whom there was no commissioned position available in a unit. He therefore served in the ranks of enlisted men but lived with the officers until an opening occurred, whereupon he became an officer.

29. John Richardson, for a biography, see John Richardson, *The War of 1812, with notes and a life of the author by A.C. Casselman*, (Toronto, 1902).

30. The quote on Tecumseh's opinion of Brock on first meeting comes from Tupper, 261, but the author does not provide a source for this information.

31. Brock to Bathurst, 29 Aug. 1812, in Ernest A. Cruikshank, *Documents Relating to the Invasion of Canada and the Surrender of Detroit* (Ottawa, 1912), 192.

32. The Wyandots actually crossed over to the British after the capture of Mackinac, abandoning their former policy of neutrality. CB.

33. District General Order, 14 Aug. 1812, in *DH*, vol 3, 179.

34. Brock to Hull, 15 Aug. 1812, in Richardson, *War of 1812*, 50.

35. Among those killed by this shell was the unfortunate Lieutenant Porter Hanks, who was undergoing a court of inquiry for his surrender at Mackinac.

36. Proclamation by Brock, 16 Aug. 1812 in Richardson, *War of 1812*, 69.

Chapter 5: Brock and the Niagara: September and October 1812

1. USNA, RG 107, Micro 221, reel 46, Dearborn to Eustis, 9 Aug. 1812.

2. NAC, CO 42, vol. 147, 133, Prevost to Bathurst, 17 Aug. 1812.

3. NAC, CO 42, vol 147, Prevost to Bathurst, 24 Aug. 1812.

4. NAC, CO 42, vol 352, Brock to Bathurst, 29 Aug. 1812

5. Brock to his brothers, 3 Sep. 1812, in Tupper, 284.

6. Van Rensselaer to Sheaffe, 20 Aug. 1812, in *DH*, vol 3, 87.

7. NAC, RG 8 I, vol 1218, 376, Prevost to Brock, 30 Aug. 1812.

8. Michael Smith, *A Geographical View of the Province of Upper Canada and Promiscuous Remarks on its Government …* (Trenton, 1813).

9. James Carmichael-Smyth, *Precis of the Wars in Canada, from 1755 to the Treaty of Ghent in 1814, with Military and Political Reflections* (London, 1862), 141.

10. USNA, RG 107, Micro 6, vol 6, Eustis to Dearborn, 13 Aug. 1812.

11. Adams, *History*, vol 2, 389.

12. NAC, RG 8 I, vol 677, 64, Brock to Prevost, 7 Sep. 1812.
13. NAC, RG 8 I, vol 677, 90, Brock to Prevost, 13 Sep. 1812.
14. Robinson to van Rennselaer, 12 Dec. 1812, *DH*, 4, 265.
15. On Winchester, see biography in *DAB*.
16. NAC, RG 8 I, vol 1218, Prevost to Brock, 27 July 1812.
17. For a biography of Vincent, see *DCB*, vol 7.
18. NAC, CO 42, vol 147, 133, Prevost to Bathurst, 17 Aug. 1812.
19. Prevost to Brock, 14 Sep. 1812, in Tupper, 308.
20. Prevost to Brock, 25 Sep. 1812, in Tupper, 317.
21. Brock to Savery Brock, 18 Sep. 1812, in Tupper, 315.
22. On Smyth, see *DAB*.
23. Letter to unknown recipient signed Thomas Evans, 15 Oct. 1812, in *SBD*, vol 1, 617.
24. Letter signed Thomas Evans, 15 Oct. 1812, in *SBD*, vol 1, 620.
25. "Push on the York Volunteers" was attributed to Brock just before he was killed, in a letter by Lieutenant Archibald Maclean, Brown's Point, 15 Oct. 1812, published in the *Quebec Mercury*, 27 Oct. 1812, see *DH*, vol 4, 114. "Push on, brave York Volunteers," according to the biography of Brock in the *DCB*, vol 5, first appeared in an article in the *York Gazette* on 17 Oct. 1812 as "the last words of the dying hero."

George Jarvis, a fifteen-year-old volunteer with the light company of the 49th Foot at Queenston was near the general when he was hit and saw "our gallant General fell on his left side, within a few feet of where I stood. Running up to him I enquired, 'Are you much hurt, Sir?' He placed his hand on his breast and made no reply and slowly sunk down." See *DH*, vol 4, 116.

Although at least three men have been named as the soldier who killed Brock, the testimony of Private Robert Walcot, First United States Artillery, most closely matches Jarvis's version of Brock's death, see Robert Walcot, "General Brock's Death," *Philadelphia Times*, 22 Nov. 1880, in Ludwig Kosche, "Relics of Brock: An Investigation," *Archivaria*, 9 (1979-80). **RM.**
26. Destined to become the dominant figure in the United States Army of the 19th century, Scott is the subject of a new and critical biography – Timothy Johnston, *Winfield Scott: The Quest for Military Glory* (Lawrence, 1998).
27. Captain Robert Runchey's company of "Coloured Men" was a militia unit raised from free blacks and indentured servants in the Niagara area to function as skilled artificers in the construction of fortifications. In the spring of 1813, it was made a provincial unit.
28. Recent research reveals that Hitsman's account of the battle of Queenston Heights is inaccurate is some aspects. Exact information is lacking about Brock's activities prior to his final attack. There is little evidence to support Hitsman's statement that he was present in the redan battery when Wool charged it. The small force Brock led to regain the battery numbered only about fifty. The flank companies of York militia marched to Queenston independent of Macdonell, who closely followed Brock to that place. Also omitted from the author's version of events is the role played by fewer than 100 Grand River warriors including John Brant, the son of Joseph Brant, led by John Norton, or the Snipe, war chief of the Mohawk peoples, and a detachment of RA gunners under Major William Holcroft who kept the Americans occupied and in check on the heights after they had gained control of Queenston. These two detachments had been sent into action by Sheaffe, who was, contrary to Hitsman, on the ground well before noon. On the Mohawks at Queenston, see Carl Benn, *Iroquois in the War of 1812*, 86-96. An account of the battle of Queenston Heights incorporating much new evidence is, at the date of this writing, in preparation – see Robert Malcomson, "The Battle of Queenston Heights, 13 Oct. 1812," in Donald E. Graves, ed., *Fighting For Canada: Seven Battles, 1758-1945* (in progress). **RM.**

Only a portion of the 300 native warriors at Fort George went into action at Queenston Heights. It should also be noted that while John Brant was one of the native leaders, the most important native commander was an older and more experienced man, Mohawk war chief John Norton, or the Snipe. Since *The Incredible War* was published before Norton's notable journal emerged on the scholarly horizon in 1970, Hitsman could not have known much about the man. On Norton, see C.F. Klinck and J.J. Talman, eds., *The Journal of Major John Norton* (Toronto, 1970). **CB.**
29. Sheaffe to Prevost, 23 Nov. 1812, in *DH*, vol 4, 229.
30. Livingston to Smyth, 4 Nov. 1812, in *DH*, vol 4, 180.
31. Smyth to Tannehill, 21 Nov. 1813, in *DH*, vol 4, 225.
32. Tannehill to Smyth, 22 Nov. 12, in *DH*, vol 4, 225.

33. General Order by Smyth, 10 Nov. 1812, in *DH*, vol 4, 193.
34. For a biography of Bisshopp, see *DCB*, vol 5.
35. Winfield Scott, *Memoirs of Lieut.-General Scott, LLD. Written by Himself* (2 vols, New York, 1864), vol 1, 31.
36. Smyth's statement, 3 Dec. 1812, in *DH*, vol 4, 270.
37. Proclamation by Sheaffe, 9 Nov. 1812, in *DH*, vol 4, 188.
38. "York, 22 Nov., 1812, An Exhortation pronounced after the Sermon, or rather in continuation of it, to induce the Inhabitants to contribute to the comfort of the Militia fighting upon the lines," attributed to John Strachan and contained in *Report of the Loyal and Patriot Society of Upper Canada* (Montreal, 1817). As noted in the introductory essay, this sermon has been identified as the beginning of the militia myth in Canadian historiography of the war.

Chapter 6: Supply Routes: August to December 1812

1. Hamilton to Chauncey, 23 Sep. 1812, in *Naval War*, vol 1, 297.
2. On Chauncey, see *DAB*.
3. On Forsyth, see Richard Patterson, "Lieutenant Colonel John Forsyth," *North Country Notes*, Nov. 1974.
4. *Kingston Gazette*, 11 Aug. 1812.
5. The abbreviation "U.S.S." means "United States Ship" although the largest American vessel on Lake Ontario at this time , being two-masted, was known officially as the U.S. Brig *Oneida*, except when commanded by Commodore Chauncey when its rate changed to that of a sloop, according to the same convention followed in the Royal Navy. RM.
6. *Kingston Gazette*, 29 Sep. 1812.
7. On David Parish, see J.M. Hitsman, "David Parish and the War of 1812," *Military Affairs*, 26 (No. 2, Winter 1962-1963), 171-177.
8. Brown to Tompkins, 7 Oct. 1812, in Franklin Hough, *A History of Jefferson County, New York* (Albany, 1854) 424.
9. *Montreal Herald*, 10 Oct. 1812.
10. Lieutenant-Colonel Thomas Pearson (1780-1847) was one of the most experienced officers serving in the British army in North America. He had fought in Holland in 1799, Egypt in 1801, at Copenhagen in 1807, in Martinique in 1809 and Spain in 1810-11. He suffered his third wound in Spain and was invalided out of the Peninsula to become inspecting field officer of militia in Canada. Before the war had ended, Pearson would fight at Crysler's Farm in 1813, and Oswego, Chippawa, Lundy's Lane and Fort Erie in 1814, receiving two more wounds and a gold medal. He ended his career as lieutenant general having spent, in all, 51 years on active service.
11. In fact, the native people of St. Regis or Akwesasne were much more evenly divided in their loyalties than Hitsman believes and, for the remainder of the war, the settlement became more or less neutral. In 1814, a survey of native military power compiled for the British Indian Department noted that at Akwesasne there were about 250 warriors who "were divided in Politiks [sic] and owing chiefly to our mismanagement one half of them at least were with the Enemy," see AO, MS 35 Strachan Papers, List of Indian Warriors as they Stood in 1812 at the time war was declared. For a discussion of the problems at Akwesasne, see Benn, *The Iroquois in the War of 1812* (Toronto, 1998), 30-31, 62-63. CB.
12. On this subject, see Walter R. Copp, "Nova Scotian Trade during the War of 1812," *CHR* 37 (1937), 143-146.
13. The term "carronade" originates with Caron company of Scotland, which was the first manufacturer of this type of ordnance in 1780s.
14. Chauncey to Hamilton, 10 Nov. 1812 in *Naval War*, vol 1, 344.
15. Gray to Prevost, 3 Dec. 1812, in *DH*, vol 4, 272.
16. NAC, CO 42, vol 147, 215, Prevost to Bathurst, 17 Oct. 1812.
17. There were actually only 230 warriors, see Benn, *Iroquois in the War of 1812*, 102.
18. NAC, CO 42, vol 23, Prevost to Bathurst, 28 Nov. 1812
19. NAC, RG 8 I, vol 728, 115, Gray to Prevost, 3 Dec. 1812.
20. Tompkins to Parish, 9 Oct. 1812, in *Public Papers of Daniel D. Tompkins, Governor of New York, 1807-1817, Military* (3 vols, Albany, 1902), vol 3, 163.
21. NAC, CO 42, vol 147, 201, Bathurst to Prevost, 16 Nov. 1812.

Chapter 7: Across the Ice: January and February 1813

1. On 12 June 1812, six days before the United States declared war on Great Britain, Napoleon had invaded Russia with an army of 600,000 men – by Jan. 1813 his troops were in full retreat.

2. De Watteville's and De Meuron's regiments were Swiss units that had formerly been in the service of Holland but had been brought into the British army.

3. On Yeo, see his biography in *DCB*, vol 5.

4. Yeo's detachment actually included four commanders (Richard O'Conor had volunteered to join the group) and 465 officers and men. They came from a wide variety of ships and stations rather than, as Hitsman states, from the Baltic gunboat squadrons. See Robert Malcomson, *Lords of the Lake*, 119-123. RM.

5. Admiralty to Yeo, 19 Mar. 1813, in *Naval War*, vol 2, 435.

6. NAC, RG 8 I, vol 688E, 22, Warren to Prevost, 5 Mar. 1813.

7. Barclay, Finnis and Pring were promoted to the rank of commander by Warren, a rank attributed to them in all the documents of the period, and were no longer considered to be lieutenants, the confirmation of their promotion by the Admiralty considered to be a formality. Barclay had lost his left arm in a small boat action against the French in 1809. See Robert and Thomas Malcomson, *H.M.S. Detroit: The Battle for Lake Erie* (Annapolis, 1991), 20-24. RM.

8. *NWR*, vol 3, 383.

9. Wellington to Bathurst, 10 Feb. 1813, in Henry Gurwood, *The Dispatches of Field Marsh the Duke of Wellington during his various Campaigns …* (12 vols, London, 1837-1838) vol 10, 103.

10. John Le Couteur, *New York Albion*, 26 Nov. 1812. An annotated version of this narrative is available, see Donald E. Graves, ed., *Merry Hearts Make Light Days: The War of 1812 Journal of Lieutenant John Le Couteur, 104th Foot* (Ottawa, 1993).

11. John Le Couteur's account, *New York Albion*, 26 Nov. 1831.

12. NAC, CO 42, vol 157, Prevost to Bathurst, 27 Aug. 1814.

13. NAC, CO 42, vol 150, Prevost to Bathurst, 8 Feb. 1813.

14. NAC, CO 42, vol 151, Prevost to Bathurst, 21 Apr. 1813.

15. At this time, the horses and vehicles of the Royal Artillery were under the control of a separate corps, the Royal Artillery Drivers. Shortly after the war ended, the artillery drivers were made part of the Royal Artillery.

16. NAC, CO 42, vol 150, Salaberry to Baynes, 11 Mar. 1813.

17. William H. Merritt, *Journal of Events, Principally on the Detroit and Niagara Frontiers During the War of 1812* (St. Catharines, 1867).

18. *Kingston Gazette*, 11 Dec. 1812. The full text of Roxburgh's advertisement makes for interesting reading:

Sharp-Shooters – Volunteers

Wanted for the *Glengarry Light Infantry Fencibles* – Brave and loyal young men of good character, who wish to defend their lives and property, their mothers and sisters from insult, their country from invasion and dishonour, can in no way discharge this sacred duty with so much advantage to themselves and benefit to their country, as by joining this highly favoured corps, in which young men of activity, and respectable character are sure to meet with encouragement and promotion. –

Those spirited young men who choose to join this fine young regiment during the American war only, will receive *Four Guineas Bounty*, and a complete set of regimental clothing consisting of

A Regimental Green Jacket
A Cloth Shell Jacket
A Pair of Cloth Pantaloons
A Pair of Shoes
A Regimental Cap
A Military Great Coat

As every man is liable to be called upon to carry arms during this *unjust* and *unprovoked* war, the advantages held out by this liberal offer, are too evident to require any comment. To those who engage to serve for three years, or til a general Peace, *Seven Guineas bounty*, one hundred acres of Crown Lands, and clothing as above, will be given. And his Excellency the commander of the Forces, sensible of the high valor and estimation in which a brave and loyal population merits being held by Government, and which is at this time evinced in the most honourable manner, by the patriotic and gallant exertions of the heroic Militia of the Province, assures the soldiers engaging in the Glengarry Light Infantry, that in selecting eligible situations for their future establishment in either Province, every consideration and indulgence will be paid to their comforts and ultimate advantage.

> Apply at Walker's Hotel,
> Alex. Roxburgh
> Capt. Glengarry Light Infantry

19. His Majesty's Sloop *Tartarus*, 20 guns, commanded by Captain John Pasco or Pascoe sailed for North America on 20 Apr. 1812. It carried Captain Foster Lech Coore, with the American colours captured at Detroit, from Quebec to Halifax and arrived there on 14 Sep. 1812. **RM.**

20. "Scuds like a Mudian and lays like a gannet" – the *Tartarus*, according to its captain, was a vessel with fine sailing qualities. When a vessel is sailing before a strong wind of almost gale force, the captain has the choice of scudding or lying. The former required the use of one or two large sails, the latter, no sails at all. A Mudian (sometimes Bermudian or Mugian) was a type of single-masted, heavily raked, fore and aft rigged vessel common in Bermuda and which was said to be among the fastest in the world. A gannet is a large sea bird common to the British Isles. Pasco is saying that the *Tartarus* would sail under a strong wind as fast as Mudian but with the ease of a seabird on water. It was probably all lies. **RM.**

21. *Acadian Recorder*, Feb. 1813.

22. Robert Christie, *Memoirs of the Administration of the Colonial Government of Lower-Canada, by Sir James Henry Craig and Sir George Prevost, from the year 1807 until the year 1815* (Quebec, 1818), 68-70.

23. Sandor Antal, in his recent study, *A Wampum Denied*, 168-182, disagrees with Hitsman's assessment of Procter's conduct during the Frenchtown campaign. Antal states that the element of surprise was lost at Frenchtown when American sentries spotted the approaching British troops and their native allies but feels that Procter's victory at Frenchtown "was one of the most complete of any in the war." A careful reading of his description of the action reveals, however, that Procter formed his infantry line within musket range of an enemy who were behind the cover of split rail fences and kept them there for more than two hours. The result was 185 casualties, or 40 per cent of Procter's force, most being regular troops of the 41st Foot which he could ill afford to lose. For a contrasting view of Procter's tactical handling of the battle, see Robert S. Quimby, *The U.S. Army in the War of 1812: An Operational and Command Study* (2 vols, East Lansing, 1998), vol 1 135-136, 198. John Richardson, who fought with the 41st in this engagement, later remarked that Procter's conduct at Frenchtown "has ever been a matter of astonishment to me, and on no one principle that I am aware of, can it be satisfactorily accounted for." See Richardson, *War of 1812*, 134. **Editor.**

On the subject of Procter's culpability for the massacre of the American prisoners after the action, Hitsman may not be fair by charging that Procter was nonchalant or negligent in not preventing the incident. This likely represents Hitsman's unexamined acceptance of partisan American criticism of the British commander. He or a subordinate did post a guard over the prisoners, but obviously this was inadequate, perhaps reflecting a tragic error in judgement rather than something more sinister. There are other parallels in North American history over how this sort of event could occur because of differing white and native concepts of war, such as is described in fascinating detail in Ian K. Steele's examination of the aftermath of the surrender of Fort William Henry in 1757, see that author's *Betrayals* (New York, 1990). **CB.**

24. John Armstrong, *Notices of the War of 1812* (2 vols, New York, 1840), I, 249.

25. General Staff Act of 3 Mar. 1813 in *Register, Rules and Regulations for the Army in 1813* (Washington, 1813).

26. On Armstrong, see Edward Skeen, *John Armstrong Jr., 1758-1843: A Biography* (Syracuse, 1981). For a discussion of American strategical planning in early 1813, see Donald E. Graves, *Field of Glory: The Battle of Crysler's Farm, 1813* (Toronto, 1999), 20-21, 30-33.

27. USNA, RG 45, Micro 125, reel 10, 231, Jones to Chauncey, 27 Jan. 1813.

28. On Perry, see John K. Mahon, "Oliver Hazard Perry: Savior of the Northwest," 126-46 in James C. Bradford, *Command Under Sail: Makers of the American Naval Tradition, 1775-1850* (Annapolis, 1985); Charles J. Dutton, *Oliver Hazard Perry* (New York, 1935) and Edwin P. Hoyt, *The Tragic Commodore: The Story of Oliver Hazard Perry* (London, 1966). **RM.**

29. Perry received his orders in Jan. 1813 but did not arrive on Lake Erie until the end of Mar. The

Lake Erie shipyard was established late in 1812 by Sailing Master Daniel Dobbins, USN, at Erie, Pennsylvania, a tiny village on the shore of Presque Isle Bay. It produced four gunboat-schooners and two 20-gun brigs, and was located in the village rather than on the sandy peninsula known as Presque Isle. See Malcomson, *HMS Detroit*, 42-45. RM.

30. Chauncey to Jones, 21 Jan. 1813, in *DH*, vol 7, 232.

31. USNA, RG 45, Micro 125, vol 25, 200, Chauncey to Hamilton, 1 Dec. 1812.

32. USNA, RG 45, Micro 125, vol 25, 200, Chauncey to Hamilton, 1 Dec. 1812.

33. *New York Evening Post*, 22 Jan. 1813.

34. Norman Lord, ed., "The War on the Canadian Frontier, 1812-1814: Letters Written by Sergeant James Commins, 8th Foot." *JSAHR* 18 (Winter, 1839), 203.

35. Comins is exaggerating here, the Americans retreated long before the British and Canadians had a chance to close with the bayonet.

36. Prevost to Macdonell, 22 Feb. 1813, in "Philalethes" [George Macdonell], "The Last War in Canada," *Journal of the United Service Institute*, 1848, 271-283.

37. Roseel to Parish, 26 Feb. 1812, Parish Papers, St. Lawrence University, Canton, New York.

38. Except for a brief period in the first weeks of Nov. 1813, when Wilkinson's large army moved down it by boat, the vitally important St. Lawrence communications route was under firm British control throughout the war. British commanders at Cornwall, Prescott and Kingston received a steady stream of intelligence from the American side of the river brought to them by men like Captain Reuben Sherwood of the Upper Canada militia. Sherwood, a prewar land surveyor, had worked both sides of the river and established a network of Americans who provided him with intelligence. He moved through New York state with ease for the entire war, on solitary missions and leading raiding parties and his activities deserve to be better known.

39. NAC, RG 8 I, vol 678, 95, Macdonell to Harvey, 22 Feb. 1813.

40. NAC, CO 42, vol 150, 76, Prevost to Bathurst, 27 Feb. 1813.

41. Chauncey to Jones, 8 Mar. 1813, in *DH*, vol 7, 233.

42. USNA, RG 45, Micro 125, reel 27, 33, Chauncey to Jones, 12 Mar. 1813.

43. USNA, RG 45, Micro 125, reel 27, 33, Chauncey to Jones, 12 Mar. 1813.

44. NAC, CO 42, vol 150, Prevost to Bathurst, 5 Mar. 1813.

Chapter 8: See-Saw in the Canadas: April to June 1813

1. Mahan, *Sea Power*, vol 2, 30.

2. Dearborn to Armstrong, 20 Mar. 1813, in Armstrong, *Notices*, vol 1, 129, note 2.

3. USNA, RG 107, Micro 6, reel 6, Armstrong to Dearborn, 29 Mar. 1813.

4. Bruyeres to Prevost, 19 Jan. 1813, in *Naval War*, vol 2, 414.

5. Bruyeres to Prevost, 13 Feb. 1813, in *SBD*, vol. 2, 71.

6. NAC, RG 8 I, vol 678, Sheaffe to Prevost, 5 Apr. 1813.

7. NAC, RG 8 I, vol 695a, 195, Sheaffe to Prevost, 5 May 1813.

8. Letter by Lieutenant Fraser in the *Philadelphia Aurora*, May 1813, in *DH*, vol 5, 192.

9. Patrick Finan, a young boy who was at York during the American attack, later recorded his recollection of the explosion at the magazine and its result:

A gun was aimed at one of the vessels, and the officers, desirous of seeing if the ball would take effect, ascended the bastion: in the mean time the artillery man, waiting for the word of command to fire, held the match behind him, as is usual under such circumstances; and the travelling magazine, a large wooden chest, containing cartridges for the great guns, being open just at his back, he unfortunately put the match into it, and the consequence, as may be supposed, was dreadful indeed! Every man in the battery was blown into the air, and the *dissection* of the greater part of their bodies was inconceivably shocking! The officers were thrown from the bastion by the shock, but escaped with a few bruises: the cannons were dismounted, and consequently the battery was rendered completely useless.

I was standing at the gate of the garrison when the poor soldiers, who escaped the explosion with a little life remaining, were brought in to the hospital, and a more afflicting sight could scarcely be witnessed. Their faces were completely black, resembling those of the blackest Africans; their hair frizzled like theirs, and their clothes scorched and emitting an effluvia so strong as to be perceived long before they reached one. One man in particular presented an awful spectacle: he was brought in a wheel-barrow, and from his appearance I should be inclined to suppose that almost every bone in his body was broken; he was lying in a powerless heap, shaking about with every motion of the barrow, from which his legs hung dangling down, as if only connected with his body by the skin, while his cries and groans were of the most heart-rending description.

See Patrick Finan, *Journal of a Voyage to Quebec in the Year 1825, with Recollections of Canada during the late American War in the Years 1812-1813* (London, 1828) quoted in *DH*, vol 5, 206.

10. Letter to Prevost dated 8 May 1813 signed by W. Chewett, W. Allan, D. Cameron, S. Smith, J. Strachan, A. Woods, W.W. Baldwin, in Cruikshank, *DH*, vol 5, 192.

11. Patrick Finan remembered "a tremulous motion in the earth resembling the shock of an earthquake, and looking toward the spot, I saw an immense cloud ascend into the air" containing "a great confused mass of smoke, timber, men, earth &c." See Finan, *Journal of a Voyage to Quebec*, quoted in *DH*, vol 5, 207.

The debris from the explosion of the main magazine did not just come down on the Americans but also on the defenders. Captain Eli Playter, whose militia company had taken shelter near the magazine because the American "Balls came so hott," remembered stones "falling as thick as Hail & large ones sinking into the very earth. [I] see Captn Loring a little distance from me fall with his Horse, & Mr Sanders also with one leg mashed by a stone; Captn Loring escaped but his Horse was Killed." See diary of Eli Playter, 27 Apr. 1813 in Edith Firth, *The Town of York, 1793-1815* (Toronto, 1962), 280.

12. The most recent study of the attack on York in Apr. 1813 is contained in Carl Benn, *Historic Fort York* (Toronto, 1993).

13. Beikie to Macdonell, 5 May 1813, in Edith Firth, ed., *The Town of York, 1793-1815* (Toronto, 1963), 300.

14. Dearborn to Armstrong, 13 May 1813, in *DH*, vol 5, 229.

15. The massacre of prisoners by native warriors at Fort Meigs was deplored by other aboriginal people. One man, Mohawk war chief John Norton, thought it "An Act of Cruelty" that was "perpetrated so suddenly as to prevent the interference of the humane." According to Norton, "A Worthless Chippawa of Detroit having with him a number of wretches like himself, who had not the courage to kill their Enemies while in arms, – but yet desirous of obtaining the repute of having killed them," attacked "the unfortunate prisoners and killed a Sentry of the 41st [Foot] – that stood forth in their defence." The murderers "made great havock [sic] before their ungenerous fury could be restrained" by Tecumseh. See Carl F. Klinck and J.J. Talman, eds., *The Journal of Major John Norton, 1816* (Toronto, 1970), 321-322. CB.

16. Procter to Prevost, 11 July 1813, in *SBD*, vol 2, 253.

17. NAC, MG 24, F18, David Wingfield, "Four Years on the Lakes …"

18. The merchant schooner, *Governor Simcoe*, was converted into the *Sir Sidney Smith*, 12 and a brig, *Lord Melville*, 14, was laid down at Point Frederick in May 1813 and launched in July. RM.

19. Yeo to Admiralty, 29 May 1813, in *Naval War*, vol 2, 469.

20. Yeo to Croker, 26 May 1813, in *Naval War*, vol 2, 246.

21. NAC, CO 42, vol 150, 181, Prevost to Bathurst, 26 May 1813.

22. NAC, RG 8 I, vol 1170, 244, General Order, 12 Apr. 1813.

23. A car brigade of artillery was a period term for mobile brigade or battery.

24. Actually, Fort George was out of range of Chauncey's warships and his squadron did not engage the British until the morning of the attack, 27 May 1813, when they covered the army's landing. RM.

25. NAC, RG 8 I, vol 678, 317, Vincent to Prevost, 28 May 1813.

26. NAC, RG 8 I, vol 678, 317, Vincent to Prevost, 28 May 1813.

27. Prevost to Bathurst, 1 June 1813, in *DH*, vol 5, 292.

28. Recent research has revealed that Lieutenant-Colonel Electus Backus of the United States regular army was in command of the defence of Sackets Harbor on 29 May 1813 not Jacob Brown. See Patrick Wilder, *The Battle of Sackett's Harbour, 1813* (Baltimore, 1994).

29. Prevost to Bathurst, 1 June 1813, in *DH*, vol 5, 292.

30. Norman Lord, ed., "The War on the Canadian Frontier, 1812-1814: Letters Written by Sergeant James Commins, 8th Foot." *JSAHR* 18 (Winter, 1839), 204. Lieutenant John Le Couteur of the 104th Foot, who participated in this attack, thought it was "a scandalously managed affair" and that the "murmurs against Sir George were deep, not loud." See Graves, *Merry Hearts*, 117. Although his editor got it wrong in the title, James Commins actually spelled his name with only one "m."

31. Brown to Armstrong, 1 June 1813, in *Naval War*, vol 2, 473. Brown claimed credit for a victory

that was actually the work of Backus who was mortally wounded during the fighting, see Wilder, *Sackett's Harbour*, 111-125.

32. The American naval officer in question was Lieutenant John Drury, who was subordinate to Lieutenant Wolcott Chauncey, the younger brother of the commodore, who was also present during the attack. Two courts of inquiry into the affair resulted in Drury's acquittal on charges of disobedience and resulted in whispers that the commodore had tried to cover up his brother's culpability as senior naval officer on the station. Drury ordered fires set in the shipyard and not directly on the new vessel. See Malcomson, *Lords of the Lake*, 135-136, 142-143.

33. USNA, RG 107, RG 45, Micro 125, reel 29, 14, Chauncey to Jones, 4 June 1813.

34. NAC, RG 8 I, vol 679, 83, Harvey to Baynes, 6 June 1813. For a biography of John Harvey, one of the most competent British officers to campaign in North America, see *DCB*, vol. 8.

35. Burn to Dearborn, 7 June 1813, in *DH*, vol 6, 23.

36. NAC, RG 8 I, vol 679, 76, Harvey to Baynes, 11 June 1813.

37. USNA, RG 107, Micro 221, reel 52, Dearborn to Armstrong, 8 June 1813. Among the Canadians who came into the American lines at this time was Joseph Willcocks, member of the legislative assembly of Upper Canada. He offered to raise a unit of Canadians to fight for the United States and Dearborn accepted this offer. Thus was born the Canadian Volunteers, a small corps of mounted scouts who rendered good service for the United States in the Niagara in 1813 and 1814 and created much misery for their former fellow citizens. On Willcocks and his followers, see Donald E. Graves, "Joseph Willcocks and the Canadian Volunteers: A Study of Political Disaffection during the War of 1812" (MA Thesis, Carleton University, 1982).

At York and Fort George, Dearborn granted paroles to 1,193 Canadian militiamen who promised not to take up arms against the United States until some formally exchanged (on paper) with Americans in British captivity (see Graves, "Joseph Willcocks," 38). As this amounted to just over 10 per cent of the Upper Canada militia, one historian has concluded that this "great parole rush" was evidence of widespread disinclination on the part of the militia to fight for the Crown, see George Sheppard, *Plunder, Profit, and Paroles: A Social History of the War of 1812 in Upper Canada* (Montreal, 1994), 75-90. Sheppard suggests that "at least a quarter and perhaps as many as a half of all the members of the provincial militia considered themselves exempt from service" on the basis of being parolees. If this statement is true, it cannot be based on the list of 1,193 parolees compiled by Dearborn in the early summer of 1813 as an intensive analysis of the names on the list by William Gray has revealed that a significant proportion did not appear on any of the wartime militia rolls, leading to the conclusion that the Americans were signing up boys younger than 16 and men older than 60. See Gray, *Soldiers of the King*, 39-41.

38. Chauncey to Jones, 11 June 1813, in *Naval War*, vol 2, 493.

39. *Quebec Gazette*, 10 June 1813.

40. NAC, RG 8 I, vol 1220, Prevost to York, 23 June 1813. Within five months, de Rottenburg would in turn be replaced in Upper Canada by Lieutenant-General Gordon Drummond. It has always been a matter of some puzzlement to the editor why, shortly after the war started, the British government did not send out younger generals with more recent experience of active service to assist Prevost. As it was, the two senior officers, Lieutenant-General Gordon Drummond and Major-General Phineas Riall, who were specially picked for service in North America, took their time getting there – Prevost was informed in June 1813 they were coming but they did not actually arrive in Lower Canada until the following Oct.

It was not that there was a shortage of generals in the British army, the *Army List* of 1812 contains the names of 83 full generals, 179 lieutenant-generals and 304 major-generals, a total of 566. Not all these officers were employed, however, as the happy situation prevailed in the British army at this time that a general officer was only paid as such when he had an appointment as such. Those who did not have appointments in their rank, or other positions such as a colonial governorship, might have to support themselves on the half pay of their substantive ranks, which in some cases were as low as major. Although he had been bothered by a shortage of generals during the early years of his campaign in the Peninsula (particularly competent men), by 1812-1813 Wellington was being deluged with senior officers sent out from Britain, many of whom proved of little use.

It was a problem that Prevost would have liked to have had but it would appear that service in North America with its rough living conditions, inclement weather, backward society and dismal career prospects, was not popular among the senior ranks of the army. Only in 1814 did experienced Peninsular veterans such as Robinson, Murray, Brisbane, Kempt, Power, Ross, Lambert and Pakenham arrive on the other side of the Atlantic.

41. NAC, CO 42, vol 151, 24, Prevost to Bathurst, 24 June 1813.
42. Letter to Prevost dated 8 May 1813 signed by W. Chewett, W. Allan, D. Cameron, S. Smith, J. Strachan, A. Woods, W.W. Baldwin, in *DH*, vol 5, 192.
43. The best account of Laura Secord and the controversy which arose over whether she made her perilous walk is contained in her biography in *DCB*, vol 9, as Laura Ingersoll.
44. The native force at Beaver Dams was: 180 Seven Nations warriors from Lower Canada; 203 Grand River warriors, 12 Thames River warriors, 70 Ojibway and Mississauga warriors. In his account of the battle Hitsman exaggerates somewhat the leadership role of the officers of the Indian Department over that of the native chiefs. CB
45. Fitzgibbon to Kerr, 30 Mar. 1818, in *DH*, vol 6, 120. For a biography of James Fitzgibbon, see *DCB*, vol 9.
46. Comment by Captain W. Hamilton Merritt, in *DH*, vol 6, 123.
47. Armstrong to Dearborn, 6 July 1813, in *ASPMA*, vol 1, 451.

Chapter 9: Defeats in the West: June to October 1813

1. Croker to Warren, 9 Jan. 1813, in *Naval War*, vol 2, 14.
2. On Cockburn, see James Pack, *The Man Who Burned the White House: Admiral Sir George Cockburn* (Annapolis, 1987).
3. *NWR*, vol 4, 159.
4. Mahan, *Sea Power*, vol 2, 126-127.
5. Mahan, *Sea Power*, vol 2, 127.
6. On Broke and the battle, see Peter Padfield, *Broke and the Shannon* (London, 1968) and H.F. Pullen, *The Shannon and the Chesapeake* (Toronto, 1970).

   One of the most interesting results of this action was the effect it had on the career of Lieutenant Provo Wallis from Halifax. The son of an RN dockyard official, Wallis had been born in 1791 and joined the service on paper a few days short of his fourth birthday but, in reality, as a 13-year-old midshipman in 1804. In 1811, he became the third lieutenant of the *Shannon* and, following the action with the *Chesapeake*, as Broke was badly wounded and the senior surviving lieutenant had taken over command of the American frigate, Wallis briefly commanded *Shannon* during the return voyage to Halifax. By the 1820s, he was a post captain but spent long periods on shore waiting on half pay between commands. He eventually made admiral's rank in 1851 at the age of 60 and finished his sea duty in 1858, having completed 54 years service afloat and ashore.

   At this point, Wallis would have gone on the retired list except that he qualified under an interesting exception in the rules. During the 1840s, the Admiralty, in a rare sentimental gesture but actually with the intention of clearing out the clogged upper reaches of the captains' seniority list, decided that officers who had commanded a ship during the Napoleonic wars, 1792-1815, would be kept on the active list at full pay during their lifetimes. This permitted such officers to take an honourable retirement under good financial conditions, and permitted the promotion of younger postwar captains. At the same time, as most of the surviving officers who qualified under this provision were by this time well into their sixties or even seventies, the Admiralty could rightfully expect that the grim reaper would eventually save the Crown money.

   Provo Wallis, having commanded *Shannon* for five days in 1813, qualified and went into "retirement" on full pay while retaining his position on the admirals' list. This led eventually to his becoming full admiral by seniority in 1863 and, fourteen years later, he became admiral of the fleet, the senior officer of the navy, at the age of 85. It was now 64 years after the battle between the *Shannon* and the *Chesapeake*, and Provo was an interesting and well respected relic of the golden age of fighting sail, and everyone expected him to go to his due reward in fairly short order.

   The problem was that Provo Wallis kept on going and, as long as he was alive, he would retain his rank as admiral of the fleet, holding up the promotion of everyone below him on the admirals list. As Wallis reached his 90s, the Admiralty became somewhat concerned and wrote him a polite letter pointing out the problem and asking him to retire voluntarily. Provo replied he was content with the current arrangement. The Admiralty then sent him another, perhaps less polite, letter pointing out that, as he was technically on full pay, he was liable for sea duty. Wallis responded by expressing his great pleasure at going to sea once more but noted that, as senior admiral, he would immediately command any ship or fleet in which he sailed and unfortunately all his experience was with sailing ships and he knew nothing about iron ships propelled by steam. This put a lid on the matter and Provo Wallis continued as admiral of the fleet until his death in 1892 at the age of 100. Officially, having been entered on the rolls in 1795, and being retained on them at full pay, Provo Wallis had completed 96 years of active service in the Royal Navy. It is unlikely that this record will ever be broken.

On Provo Wallis, see William Heine, *96 Years in the Royal Navy* (Halifax, 1987) and J.G. Brighton, *Admiral of the Fleet Sir Provo Wallis, G.C.B.* (London, 1892).

7. Thomas B. Akins, "History of Halifax City," *Nova Scotia Historical Society Collections*, 8 (1892-1894), 158. In Canada today the War of 1812 is best remembered in Ontario, where memorials mark the scenes of the many military actions that took place in the province between 1812 and 1814. In the Maritime provinces, memories of the war are more distant and somewhat different as the War of 1812 enhanced an economic boom that had been going on since the renewal of war with France in 1803. Between 1812 and 1814, 37 privateers operated out of the Maritimes (most from Liverpool, Nova Scotia) and they brought in 207 American prizes. Akins records that the numerous vessels being brought as prizes into Halifax by the Royal Navy and Nova Scotia privateers resulted in an Active Court of Vice-Admiralty and "the newspapers of the day appear filled with advertizements of sales of prizes and prize goods." On 19 Mar. 1813, "twelve full-rigged ships, eight brigs, seven schooners and ten or twelve small vessels, with their cargoes" were for sale in Halifax. "With all this bustle of business money became plenty, and the foundations of small fortunes began to be laid by the Crown lawyers and the prize agents." This resulted in a busy social life and Akins records the town being illuminated on the occasion of British victories and frequent dinner parties and assemblies.

The presence of a large military and naval garrison had a marked effect on life in Halifax. Beamish Murdoch, a wartime resident, recorded that rents doubled, then tripled, while a "constant bustle existed in our chief streets, cannon were forever noisy; it was a salute of a man-of-war entering or leaving, practising with guns or celebrating something or somebody." As Hitsman quotes in his text, the area around the citadel was a "resort" for 8,000 sailors and soldiers who lived in the little town along with 10,000 civilians and it "was well known through His Majesty's dominions for its evil reputation as the worst haunts of Plymouth or Portsmouth in England." On several occasions during the war, the Royal Navy secured a press warrant in Halifax, usually for a period of 48 hours, and press gangs roamed the streets looking for what Akins called "the idle and worthless vagabonds of the town" for service on His Majesty's warships where "they could be brought under wholesome restraint."

Another aspect of the wartime Halifax was the large number of French and American prisoners. Akins records that

A prison had been erected at Melville Island, at the head of the North West Arm, for their accommodation, and soon became crowded. Many of the French sailors were ingenious workers in wood and bone, and made articles of use as well as ornament, which they sold to the numerous visitors who were freely permitted access to Melville Island. It was the favourite resort of the young people on Sundays and holidays, where a pleasant hour could be passed in conversing with the French prisoners and examining their toys.

For accounts of prisoner of war experiences in Halifax, see the bibliography and J.A. Deveau, *Diary of a Frenchman. François Lambert Bourneuf's Adventures from France to Acadia, 1787-1871* (Halifax, 1990).

A brief summary of New Brunswick's participation in the War of 1812 is contained in the notes to Chapter 3 but, as it is often overlooked in Canadian history, some mention should be made here of Newfoundland's activities during the war. In 1812, the island was still somewhat backward in its political development as it had not yet received the right of a legislative assembly, but its 20,000 people generally benefited from the conflict along with their Maritime neighbours. There were ready markets for the fishermen and employment in support of the British garrison and naval squadron stationed in St. John's. Nearly 600 men served in the island's own unit, the Royal Newfoundland Fencibles, which saw considerable action in the Canadas during the war, and Newfoundlanders sailing in vessels like *Fly* and *Star* brought more than thirty American ships to the island as prizes.

8. William Napier, *The Life and Opinions of General Sir Charles James Napier, G.C.B.* (4 vols, Lon-

don, 1857), vol 1, 223. The Independent Companies of Foreigners were raised in 1812 from French prisoners of war in England. Intended as garrison troops in the West Indies, they were pressed into service for the Chesapeake expedition of 1812 and quickly proved to be a liability as they were singularly unruly soldiers who established a reputation for looting, mutiny and desertion. Embarrassed by their crimes at Hampton, the British army disbanded the Independent Foreigners in 1814. On the Independent Companies of Foreigners, see J.M. Hitsman and Alice Sorby, "Independent Companies of Foreigners or Canadian Chasseurs," *Military Affairs* 25 (Spring 1961), 11-17.

9. NAC CO 42, vol 151, 71, Beckwith to Warren, 5 July 1813.

10. Warren to Taylor, 29 June 1813, *NWR*, vol 5, 107. The American press capitalized on the excesses of the Independent Companies of Foreigners at Hampton – *NWR* (vol 5, 107-109, 291-293, 309-311, 333-337, 340) reported the incidents of looting and rape in detail that bordered on the salacious. "Remember Hampton!" became a rallying cry for the Virginia militia and convinced those Americans living on the Atlantic coast that the enemy was now at their gates, see Joseph Whitehorne, *The Battle of Baltimore, 1814* (Baltimore, 1997, 69-71.

11. Hitsman does not go into detail on British operations in the Chesapeake area in 1813 other than the Hampton expedition. Between Feb. and Sep. 1813, the Royal Navy made numerous incursions in the bay area, cutting out American merchant shipping and raiding coastal villages in an attempt to provide a diversion that would draw off American forces from the northern frontier. In this they failed and these operations caused resentment and a stiffening of public resolve. On the other hand, the British became increasingly aware of the vulnerability of Washington, which at this time was virtually undefended. On the Chesapeake in 1813, see Whitehorne, *Battle of Baltimore*, chs. 4-6.

12. *NWR*, vol 4, 388. This report may be close to the truth. Private George Ferguson of the 100th Foot, who participated in the raid on Plattsburgh, remembered that

> When we came to Plattsburgh, a flag of truce came from the town, surrendering the place. Their army had removed to Sackets Harbor, having vacated the town. This was a grand wealthy village. The few that remained in it were filled with fear and consternation. Most of the inhabitants had fled, and carried with them as much of their property as they could. No females in the town and everything wore a gloomy aspect. Our men began to plunder all they could get; but I was determined to take nothing. Every eye was upon me, and I resolved that no plunder should be found with me, as so much depended upon our circumspection and watchful piety.

It should be noted that Private Ferguson was a lay Methodist preacher who later proudly remarked that he had fired his musket only once during the entire war and was sure that he did not hurt anyone – thankfully, he was a rarity in the British army in North America. His memoir of his military service is in the United Church Archives, University of Toronto.

13. *Kingston Gazette*, 7 July 1813. This major operation, an attempt by Yeo to reverse the outcome of the May attack on Sackets Harbor, has been almost ignored by historians. The most complete account is in Malcomson, *Lords of the Lake*, 149-153.

14. Yeo to Croker, 16 July 1813, in *Naval War*, vol 2, 502.

15. NAC, CO 42, vol 151, Prevost to Bathurst, 1 Aug. 1813.

16. USNA, RG 45, Micro 125, reel 30, 99, Chauncey to Jones, 13 Aug. 1813.

17. Yeo to Prevost, 22 Aug. 1813, in *DH*, vol 7, 50.

18. Prevost to Bathurst, 25 Aug. 1813, in *DH*, vol 7, 62.

19. While there was (and is) a Tuscarora settlement near the site of Bisshopp's raid, the counter-attacking native force was a Seneca one from the Buffalo Creek settlement. The Tuscaroras largely remained neutral until Dec. 1813 when the British attacked the American side of the Niagara River. Their village was destroyed and they allied themselves with the Americans.

The participation of the Iroquoian peoples from New York state, in the Niagara campaigns of 1813 and 1814 saw them pitted against the Iroquoian peoples from the Grand River. Casualties were heavy and this civil war demoralized both groups, see Benn, *Iroquois in the War of 1812*, chs 5 and 6. CB.

20. The soldiers of neither army liked the Niagara during the summer of 1813 because of its hot humid weather, the high rate of sickness and the lack of action. For John Le Couteur of the 104th Foot, it was a place where "only misery, wretchedness, Broken heads and no honour or credit can be met with." See Le Couteur to Bouton, 24 Oct. 1813 in Graves, *Merry Hearts*, 146.

21. Prevost to Bathurst, 25 Aug. 1813, in *DH*, vol 7, 62.
22. Wesley Turner in his *British Generals in the War of 1812: High Command in the Canadas* (Montreal, 1999), 39-41, feels that the operations around Fort George raise questions about Prevost's "tactical discernment." It is Turner's belief that the British general should have either conducted a full-scale assault on the fort or, in the alternate, obtained information about its defences through "a reconnaissance or small-scale probes." Turner relies heavily on a statement by a junior officer, Lieutenant John Le Couteur, that his battalion commander wanted to convert the operations from a reconnaissance in force to a major attack (see Graves, *Merry Hearts*, 131-133) for evidence that such an operation could have been mounted.

Prevost's decision makes sense if the tactical situation that prevailed around the fort is examined in detail. The American picquets, or outposts, had to be pushed back on the main defences for Prevost to get a detailed look at those defences and this required a major effort. When Prevost got that look, he wisely decided not to mount a full-scale assault. His strength, as Turner points out, was about 3,000 men (of whom half were on the sick list); the strength of the American defenders was between 4,300 and 4,500, of whom half were also on the sick list – but the Americans had the advantage of position. The odds were certainly not in favour of a British success and, as always, Prevost had to be careful about incurring heavy casualties that could not be replaced.

Turner also criticizes Prevost for making "no attempt to coordinate the movement with Yeo" whose squadron was off the mouth of the Niagara. It is unclear to the editor how Yeo could have assisted in an attack on Fort George, which lies about a mile inland from Lake Ontario, well beyond range of his guns. If Yeo had tried to proceed up the Niagara River to get within range, his ships would have had to bypass the American-held Fort Niagara and also move against a very strong current. During the war, the Lake Ontario squadrons of neither nation attempted this movement when Fort Niagara was not held by friendly forces.

With all this in view, it would seem that the reconnaissance in force at Fort George in Aug. 1813 is an incident for which Prevost has been unfairly criticized. As Hitsman points out, Prevost was responsible to his superiors in London and not to the naturally dissatisfied troops and civilians in the Niagara area.
23. NAC, MG 24, F18, David Wingfield, "Four Years on the Lakes ..."
24. Yeo to Warren, 12 Sep. 1813, in *Naval War*, vol 2, 579.
25. The squadrons did not come in close enough contact to make an engagement possible as the two commodores manoeuvred around each other in the western approaches of the lake between 7 and 10 Sep. 1813. Chauncey finally caught Yeo inshore and becalmed on 11 Sep. See Malcomson, *Lords of the Lake*, chs 10 and 11. **RM.**
26. Prevost to Bathurst, 15 Sep. 1813, in *DH*, vol 7, 130.
27. NAC, RG 8 I, vol 679, 220, Procter to Prevost, 11 July 1813.
28. NAC, RG 8 I, vol 679, 224, Procter to Prevost, 13 July 1813.
29. NAC, RG 8 I, vol 679, 216, Prevost to Procter, 11 July 1813.
30. Strategically, Procter's "unruly Indian allies" wanted to destroy Fort Meigs because they believed it represented a larger threat to their hopes of establishing an independent homeland in the Old Northwest, and hence their desire to attack it was not without reason as Hitsman seems to imply. **CB.**
31. More recent research reveals that Tecumseh brought between two and three thousand warriors to the second siege of Fort Meigs, see John Sugden, *Tecumseh: A Life* (New York, 1997), 346.
32. NAC, RG 8 I, vol 679, 371, Procter to Prevost, 12 Aug. 1813. Although Procter was inclined to blame his native allies for his repulse, the disastrous frontal assault on Fort Stephenson on 2 Aug. 1814 furnishes another example of his tactical ineptitude. Following a two-hour bombardment which had little effect, Procter launched 500 regular infantry against the fort; they were completely repulsed with a loss of one-fifth their number. Procter exercised little control over the battle although one eyewitness recorded him crying over his heavy casualties. In *Wampum Denied*, 259-260, Antal, whose treatment of Procter is sometimes perilously close to the adulatory, attributes the heavy losses at Fort Stephenson not to Procter but to the "internal politics" of his officers. It is not clear to the editor from Antal's text how he arrived at this singular conclusion.

The native warriors with Procter's Right Division were just as unimpressed by British military leadership. Black Hawk, a chief of the Sac nation, recorded his impression of white generals and their tactics:

On my arrival at the village, I was met by the chiefs and braves, and conducted to a lodge that had been prepared to receive me. After eating, I gave an account of what I had seen and done. I explained to them the manner the British and Americans fought. Instead of stealing upon each other, and taking every advantage to *kill the enemy and save their own people*, as we do, (which, with us, is considered good policy in a war chief) they march out, in open daylight, and *fight*, regardless of the number of warriors they may lose! After the battle is over, they retire to feast, and drink wine, as if nothing had happened; after which, they make a *statement in writing*, of what they have done – *each party claiming the victory*! and neither give an account of half the number that have been killed on their own side. They all fought like braves, but would not do to *lead a war party with us*. Our maxim is, "*to kill the enemy and save our own men*." Those chiefs would do to *paddle* a canoe, but not to *steer* it. The Americans shoot better than the British, but their *soldiers* are not so well clothed, or provided for.

See Donald Jackson, ed., *Black Hawk, an Autobiography* (Urbana, 1964), 68.

33. NAC, RG 8 I, vol 679, 476, Prevost to Procter, 22 Aug. 1813.

34. Order [c. Aug. 1813] issued by Brigadier-General Adamson Tannehill, Orderly Book, General Tannehill's Brigade, Pennsylvania Militia, Clements Library, University of Michigan.

35. The *Detroit* was a 20-gun ship similar in design to the *Royal George*.

36. NAC, RG 8 I, vol 730, 126, Barclay to Yeo, 1 Sep. 13.

37. NAC, RG 8 I, vol 680, 26, Procter to Freer, 6 Sep. 1813.

38. NAC, RG 8 I, vol 679, 476, Prevost to Procter, 22 Aug. 1813.

39. Barclay to Yeo, 6 Sep. 1813, in *SBD*, vol 2, 292.

40. Perry's squadron consisted of the brigs *Lawrence* and *Niagara*, 20 guns (each rated as a sloop and equipped with a pair of 12-pdr. long guns) and *Caledonia*, 3 guns, (including two 24-pdr. long guns) and six schooners. Master Commandant Jesse Elliott commanded the *Niagara* and became the centre of a protracted controversy because he failed to get into the action until Perry was rowed aboard the brig to take command. See Malcomson, *HMS Detroit*, 71, 125. RM.

41. Perry to Jones, 10 Sep. 1813, in *Naval War*, vol 2, 287.

42. Yeo to Warren, 10 Oct. 1813, in *SBD*, vol. 2, 294.

43. Court martial of Barclay, Yeo's evidence, in *SBD*, vol 2, 289.

44. For two contrasting views on Procter's decision to retreat and the way in which he communicated that decision to his native allies, see Antal, *Wampum Denied*, ch. 13, and John Sugden, *Tecumseh's Last Stand* (Norman, 1985), ch. 3.

Hitsman's comments on the native peoples with Procter's Right Division are perhaps a little too harsh and reflect the time in which he was writing. Tecumseh and his followers were desperate for Procter's regulars to remain on the Detroit River as they rightly suspected that, if that general withdrew to the east, their lands would never be free from American occupation. Within their own terms the native confederacy of the North West had fought, and fought hard, since the outbreak of war. Tecumseh's anger at Procter's decision to retreat is clearly evident in the words he addressed to the British general:

> Our fleet has gone out, we know they have fought; we have heard the great guns; but know nothing of what has happened to our Father with one Arm [Captain Robert Barclay, RN]. Our ships have gone one way, and we are much astonished to see our Father tying up every thing and preparing to run the other, without letting his red children know what his intentions are. You always told us to remain here and take care of our lands; it made our hearts glad to hear that was your wish. Our Great Father, the King, is the head and you represent him. You always told us that you would never draw your foot off British ground; but now, Father, we see you are drawing back, and we are sorry to see our Father doing so, without seeing the enemy. We must compare our Father's conduct to a fat animal that carries its tail upon its back; but when affrighted, it drops it between its legs and runs off.

"We are determined to preserve our lands," the Shawnee warrior concluded and if it was the will of the Great Spirit, "we wish to leave our bones upon them." On Tecumseh's famous "yellow dog" speech, see Richardson, *War of 1812*, 205.

45. Harrison to Armstrong, 27 Sep. 1813, in Logan Esarey, ed., *Messages and Letters of William Henry Harrison* (2 vols, Indianapolis, 1922), vol 2, 251. Harrison's caution about British cavalry is difficult to understand because it is doubtful that Procter had one hundred horses in his small force.

46. Antal appears to blame Procter's poor tactical dispositions at Moraviantown on interference from Tecumseh, see *Wampum Denied*, 335. He states that the British infantry of Procter's first line were stationed with a 3-foot interval between each man and the result was that they were

quickly ridden down by Harrison's mounted troops. John Sugden, in *Tecumseh's Last Stand*, ch. 5, analyses Procter's dispositions using much of the same evidence but makes more use of the testimony presented at that officer's subsequent court martial. Sugden not only rejects the claim that Tecumseh interfered but notes that the British dispositions were "far from satisfactory." At his court martial, Procter was found guilty of "not on the said 5th day of October [1813], either prior to or subsequent to, the attack by the Enemy ... make the Military dispositions best adapted to meet or to resist the said attack." The weight of evidence would suggest that Procter bears the major responsibility for the defeat at Moraviantown.

47. Private Shadrach Byfield of the 41st Foot remembered that the battle of Moraviantown ended quickly:

> We were thus formed, in a wood, when the enemy came within 20 or 30 yards of us, and sounded the bugle to advance and attack.
>
> The attack commenced on the right, with the Indians, and very soon became general through the line. After exchanging a few shots, our men gave way. I was in the act of retreating, when one of our sergeants exclaimed, "For God's sake, men, stand and fight." I stood by him and fired one shot, but the line was broken, and the men were retreating. I then made my escape farther into the wood, where I met with some of the Indians, who said that they had beaten the enemy on the right, but that their prophet [Tecumseh] was killed, and they then retreated.

See Shadrach Byfield in John Gelner, ed., *Recollections of the War of 1812: Three Eyewitness Accounts* (Toronto, 1964), 26.

48. Harrison was unable to capitalize on his victory. Following the battle of the Thames, the militia component of his army dispersed to their homes in the United States, leaving him only 1,500 regular troops to continue his pursuit of Procter. He proceeded to Fort George, which he found held only by a New York militia brigade as the main army was at this time moving down the St. Lawrence against Montreal. He planned an attack on the British position at Burlington Heights but was ordered by Armstrong to transfer his troops to Sackets Harbor, which had been left weakly guarded. Harrison accordingly transferred his regulars to that place on board Chauncey's squadron but most of these troops, who had enlisted only for one-year, left the service in Feb. 1813. Harrison himself resigned from the army a few months later.

49. This is a reference to the actions of staff adjutant John Reiffenstein, a militia officer who served with Procter's Right Division but escaped the debacle at Moraviantown. One of the first survivors to reach British troops in the Niagara, he spread tales of disaster that de Rottenburg and Vincent, having no other information, were inclined to believe. As other survivors of the action appeared, the truth of the matter was gradually sorted out. On Reiffenstein, see his biography in *DCB*, vol 7, and Antal, *Wampum Denied*, 358-360.

50. NAC, RG 8 I, vol 681, 5, De Rottenburg to Vincent, 1 Nov. 1813.

51. Hitsman does not talk about the fate of the native peoples of the American Northwest, whose hopes of preserving their territory in the face of American encroachment were doomed by the British withdrawal from the Detroit and the defeats on Lake Erie and at Moraviantown. Thousands of native men, women and children followed the retreating British regulars to Burlington Heights on Lake Ontario and became wards for the Crown's not very generous assistance. Others camped near the British-held post at Mackinac for protection. Unable to hunt or plant crops to feed their families, their condition was pitiful. In June 1814 Chetanwakanmani or Little Crow, a chief of the Mdewkanton Sioux, appealed at Mackinac for reinforcements of British "big Guns and brave warriors" and supplies of foodstuffs as, "Although you give Assistance to all Your Children, Yet you have too many to care of, before it can reach us" and "We have of late not had much assistance through you, My Father, for one half of our Nation have died of hunger with shreds of skin in their mouths for want of other Nourishment." At the end of the war, in contravention of the terms of the Treaty of Ghent, the United States at first refused to re-admit into American territory those members of the Northwest nations who wished to return to their homes, but later relented after an exchange of diplomatic correspondence. Many of these peoples, fearing American vengeance, chose to remain on British soil.

Chapter 10: The Autumn of 1813

1. This is no exaggeration. A militia private in Upper Canada received about sixpence per day of duty – in contrast a farmer whose team was contracted to transport supplies received about forty

shillings (a shilling was twelve pence) per day and civilian labourers between five and ten shillings a day for manual labour. Given this disparity in income, it is small wonder that militia service was unpopular. See Gray, *Soldiers of the King*, 42.

2. NAC, RG 8 I, vol 14, Parish to Prevost, 10 Aug. 1813.

3. Macdonell to Parish, 4 Sep. 1813, Parish Papers, St. Lawrence University, Canton, New York.

4. Macdonell to Parish, 4 Sep. 1813, Parish Papers, St. Lawrence University, Canton, New York.

5. Armstrong to Wilkinson, 8 Aug. 1813, in *ASPMA*, vol 1, 464. American strategical planning for the campaigns of 1813 was a protracted and tortuous business, for a recent account see Graves, *Field of Glory*, Chs. 1-4.

6. Armstrong to Wilkinson, 8 Aug. 1813, in *ASPMA*, vol 1, 464.

7. For Wilkinson, see James R. Jacobs, *Tarnished Warrior. Major General James Wilkinson* (New York, 1938).

8. *NWR*, 14 Aug. 1813.

9. Purdy to Wilkinson, n.d., in *ASPMA*, vol 1, 461. There was some truth to Purdy's comments as Brigadier-General George Izard recorded in his diary an incident during the autumn 1813 campaign when Hampton unexpectedly arrived at his headquarters to dine and consumed so much alcohol that he fell off his chair and was unable to rise, see Graves, *Field of Glory*, 147.

10. Minutes of a Council of War, Sackets Harbor, 26 Aug. 1813, in James Wilkinson, *Memoirs of My Own Times* (3 vols, Philadelphia, 1816), vol 3, Appendix 1.

11. In fact, very few of the American troops at Fort George were transported to Sackets Harbor on Chauncey's squadron. Most embarked in a flotilla of small boats and made a hazardous and delayed journey in stormy weather to the rendezvous point, some units taking nearly two weeks to accomplish a voyage that normally took as little as thirty hours to complete. See Graves, *Field of Glory*, 61-62.

12. Yeo to Warren, 29 Sep. 1813, in *Naval War*, vol 2, 585.

13. Chauncey to Jones, 1 Oct. 1813, in *Naval War*, vol 2, 586. The action of 28 Sep. 1813, which began ten miles south of York and very nearly saw the two squadrons engage in a climactic battle, became known as the "Burlington Races" because Chauncey chased Yeo westward until storm conditions and tactical limitations forced the Americans to haul off. It has often been alleged that Yeo ran his squadron into safety on the Little Lake (modern Hamilton harbour) by riding the storm surge through the narrow, twisting and shallow channel in the wide isthmus that nearly encloses the harbour. No period documents support this legendary feat. Yeo actually anchored in Burlington Bay near the modern town of Oakville, Ontario, and hurriedly repaired the damage his vessels had suffered in action. RM.

For an account of this action, see Malcomson, *Lords of the Lake*, 200-211.

14. Lieutenant John Le Couteur was among the troops pulled out of the Niagara and sent in a convoy of small boats along the north shore of Lake Ontario to Kingston. He and his comrades made better progress than their American counterparts; Le Couteur left the Niagara on 3 Oct. and arrived in Kingston in the early morning hours of 8 Oct., see Graves, *Merry Hearts*, 136-137.

15. William Dunlop, *Tiger Dunlop's Upper Canada* (Ottawa, 1967), 10.

16. Purdy to Wilkinson, n.d., in *ASPMA*, vol 1, 461.

17. NAC, CO 42, vol 122, 199, Prevost to Bathurst, 8 Oct. 1813.

18. For a biography of de Watteville, see *DCB*, vol. 6.

19. Armstrong to Hampton, 16 Oct. 1813, in *ASPMA*, vol 1, 460.

20. The most thorough analysis of the number of Canadians who fought at Châteauguay was undertaken by Michelle Guitard in *The Militia of the Battle of Châteauguay: A Social History*. Guitard's conclusion is that of the 1,777 troops available to De Watteville, only 339 were in action on 26 Oct. 1813. Approximately 3,500 of Hampton's division saw action, see Graves, *Field of Glory*, 351.

21. The most complete account of this action from the British side is Victor Suthren, *The Battle of Châteauguay* (Ottawa, 1974). A recent examination of the action, which includes both sides, is Graves, *Field of Glory*, ch. 5.

The number of American casualties at Châteauguay is difficult to ascertain as the various sources disagree. Perhaps the most accurate statement is the comment by one Canadian officer that his men "buried upwards of forty" Americans after the action. See Graves, *Field of Glory*, 109.

22. There was much pride in Lower Canada about the fact that most of the British troops at Châteauguay were French-speaking *Canadiens*, the *Quebec Gazette* of 4 Nov. 1813 exulted that

the action was "the first in which any considerable number of the natives of this Province have been engaged with the Americans since the war" and "a few experiments of this kind, will probably convince the Americans that their project of conquering this Province is premature."

In later years, after both Macdonell and de Salaberry were dead, a dispute arose between English- and French-speaking Canadian historians over which officer was primarily responsible for the victory. It was a somewhat contrived controversy as Macdonell had never claimed to be the victor and de Salaberry had always acknowledged the support he had received from his English-speaking comrade in arms. See Guitard, *The Militia of the Battle of the Châteauguay*, 87-89, for a summary of this dispute and also for comments on Prevost's reporting of the action.

23. Hampton to Armstrong, 1 Nov. 1813, in *ASPMA*, vol 1, 461.

24. Following Wilkinson's defeat at Crysler's Farm on 11 Nov. 1813 and the end of the grandiose American autumn campaign of 1813, Wilkinson issued an arrest order for Hampton, who he was determined should bear the responsibility for the disaster. The officer carrying it arrived at Hampton's headquarters at Plattsburgh shortly after Hampton, who had been forewarned, had turned over command on Lake Champlain to Izard and decamped for Washington. There, he requested that Armstrong provide his official correspondence concerning the campaign, which, with Hampton's own evidence, he wanted laid before Madison. If the president thought that Hampton should undergo a court martial, Hampton was willing to do so but, if not, he requested from Armstrong a statement in writing expressing the government's confidence in his actions. In preference to a public court martial, which might bring forth evidence embarrassing to himself, Armstrong opted to ignore the arrest order and Hampton was allowed to retire from the army without penalty in the spring of 1814. See Graves, *Field of Glory*, ch. 14, for the recrimination among senior American officers and officials following the end of the 1813 St. Lawrence campaign.

25. NAC, RG 8 I, vol 1221, 179, Prevost to Rottenburg, 12 Oct. 1813. On Joseph Morrison, see William Patterson, "A Forgotten Hero in a Forgotten War," *JSAHR*, 78 (1990), 7-21.

26. On Mulcaster, see Henry J. Morgan, *Sketches of Celebrated Canadians, and Persons Connected with Canada* (Quebec, 1862), 226-227.

27. Council of War at the White House, 8 Nov. 1813, in Wilkinson, *Memoirs*, vol. 3, appendix 24.

28. More recent research has revealed that Morrison's strength at the battle of Crysler's Farm was just under 1,200 men, see Graves, *Field of Glory*, 362-364. Just over 3,000 American troops came into action on 11 Nov. 1813.

29. NAC, RG 8 I, vol 681, 82, Morrison to Rottenburg, 12 Nov. 1813. The charge of a squadron of the Second Regiment of Light Dragoons at Crysler's Farm on 11 Nov. 1813 was one of the few regular cavalry charges made during the war. A young Canadian officer, Lieutenant John Sewell of the 49th Foot, remembered that charge:

> About this time my Captain was killed. I assumed command of the company and now I could see the enemy and more of the field than in the supernumerary rank and to my no small anxiety I saw a squadron of Cavalry, galloping up the high road, towards our right front. Ellis who commanded the right company wheeled it four paces and poured in [a] volley and so did our flank companies that were posted on the other side of the road. I think also Jackson's guns had one round at them. Be that as it may, many saddles were emptied ere they went right about. Their leader was a gallant one; he leapt over the fence and was riding toward our right, but alone; some of the men rushed out to attack him with their bayonets fixed, but observing that he was unassisted he took the fence again in good hunting style and followed his men who were in good retreat.

See Recollections of the Battle of Crysler's Farm by Colonel John Sewell in AO, MU 1032, Kingsford Papers.

30. Recent research has revealed that the total British and Canadian casualties at Crysler's Farm were just over 200 or about a sixth of the force involved while American casualties were over 400 men or about 13 per cent of the force involved. See Graves, *Field of Glory*, 268-270.

31. Wilkinson to Hampton, 12 Nov. 1813, in John Brannan, ed., *Official Letters of the Military and Naval Officers of the United States during the War with Great Britain in the years 1812, 13, 14 & 15* (Washington, 1823), 263.

32. Wilkinson's army spent the next three months in a camp that they built at French Mills (modern Fort Covington, New York) not far from Cornwall. His troops were riddled with sickness and dispirited. The camp was an attractive objective for a major British attack and many British sen-

ior officers expected that Prevost would mount such an operation. In this they were disappointed as Prevost, always cautious about incurring heavy casualties that he could not replace, was content with having repulsed the invasion. When the Americans left French Mills in Feb. 1813, one division going to Plattsburgh, the other to Sackets Harbor, British and Canadian raiding parties scoured the south side of the St. Lawrence and from this time until the end of the war, the St. Lawrence valley was a British possession.

Another outcome of the campaign was an increase in the bad feelings between Prevost and his naval commander, Yeo. Yeo performed very badly in the autumn of 1813; despite his orders, he did not actively harass the American flotilla as it made its way down the river and, on the one occasion when he had a chance to bring the American naval squadron to battle, on 5 Nov. 1813 at French Creek, he refused to do so but returned to Kingston. The honour of the Royal Navy was upheld by his subordinate, Captain William Howe Mulcaster, who commanded the little squadron of gunboats attached to Morrison's force. Mulcaster not only made life miserable for the Americans as they moved down the river, but he sent raiding parties into their camp at French Mills to blow up their powder magazine.

On Prevost's decisions after the campaign and his dissatisfaction with Yeo, see Graves, *Field of Glory*, 286-292.

33. NAC, MG 24, F14, Yeo to Admiralty, 6 Dec. 1813. Yeo's claim had little validity; he passed up a chance to attack Chauncey's squadron in the St. Lawrence on 5 Nov. and was chastised by Prevost for his lack of aggression. It was his subordinate, Mulcaster, who had provided competent and timely support to Morrison's little force.

34. The *Princess Charlotte* was barely more than a keel and frames when Yeo placed Mulcaster in command of it. Because this 40-gun vessel was 6th rate according to Royal Navy conventions, it could only be commanded by a post captain. When Yeo gave Mulcaster command of *Princess Charlotte*, he automatically placed him at the bottom of the post captains' seniority list. RM.

35. Manpower continued to be a problem for Yeo during the autumn of 1813 as the reinforcements he received barely met his needs. About 75 seamen from merchant vessels at Quebec had been loaned to him during the summer, but their term ended in Oct. and they all left. About 40 men joined from the naval transport *Dover* in Sep. and, in Oct., 110 came from HMS *Marlborough*, sent from Halifax. During the summer, Commander Stephen Popham was ordered to Canada from Britain with 350 officers and men but they did not reach Quebec until late in Oct. and then were delayed at Montreal during the time that Wilkinson's army was descending the St. Lawrence. Nearly half of Popham's detachment were subsequently sent to the post at Isle aux Noix while the rest went to Kingston. For a detailed discussion of Yeo's manning problems, see Malcomson, *Lords of the Lake*. RM.

36. USNA, RG 107, Micro 221, reel 55, McClure to Armstrong, 12 Dec. 1813.

37. USNA, RG 107, Micro 6, reel 6, Armstrong to "Commanding Officer at Fort George," 4 Oct. 1813.

38. The actual conflagration was carried out by Joseph Willcocks and his renegade Canadian Volunteers. An American eyewitness described Willcocks (who had lived in Newark previous to the war) leading "a banditti through the town on that fatal night, ... applying the epithet of Tory to all who disapproved of this flagrant act of barbarity." See Col. Chapin to the Public, *Buffalo Gazette*, 14 June 1814.

39. USNA, RG 107, Micro 221, reel 55, McClure to Armstrong, 12 Dec. 1813.

40. For a biography of Drummond, see *DCB*, vol 8.

41. For a biography of Riall, see *DCB*, vol 7.

42. In Jan., 1815, a general court-martial held at Montreal found Major-General Procter guilty of carelessness in conducting his retreat and of making faulty dispositions on the field of battle, but acquitted him of the charges of incompetence and cowardice. It sentenced him merely to be publicly reprimanded and suspended from pay and rank for a period of six months. The Prince Regent was not pleased and directed that his own "high disapprobation" of Procter's conduct should be conveyed to him and included in the general order to be read at the head of every regiment in His Majesty' service.

43. Procter's court martial took place from Dec. 1814 to Jan. 1815 and it has been stated (Antal, *Wampum Denied*, 371-374) that it was unduly delayed by Prevost and that the board consisted of officers recently arrived from Europe who knew little of North American conditions.

In fact, the court martial was not deliberately delayed by Prevost but by the exigencies of war and the slowness of communications. Most of the witnesses had been taken prisoner at

Moraviantown and were not exchanged and available for testimony until the summer of 1814. Procter was informed in May of that year that charges would be preferred against him but a court martial board of an officer of his rank and record required officers of similar qualities and these were not available until the end of the campaign season in Nov. (For similar reasons, Major-General James Wilkinson of the United States Army, who was charged in June 1814, had to wait until Jan. 1815 before his legal proceedings could take place). Procter wanted the board to sit in Upper Canada, but as the greater part of the required officers were serving in Lower Canada in 1814, it made more sense to hold it in that province and it took place in Montreal. Procter's hearing was therefore not delayed because of manipulations on Prevost's part but because waging war was a higher priority than the personal situation, no matter how difficult, of one individual.

The board commenced sitting at Montreal in Dec. 1814 with Major-General Francis de Rottenburg as president. This officer was not appointed to this position by Prevost, because he was "an accessory to events" surrounding Procter's failures in the Northwest, as stated by Antal, but as the senior major-general in the Canadas, regulations required that he had to be present. It should also be noted that, by this time, Rottenburg was not on the best of terms with Prevost because he resented his own 1813 relief as commander in Upper Canada.

The board also included Major-Generals George Glasgow, Henry Conran, Thomas Brisbane and Louis de Watteville; Colonels John Murray, John Tucker, Henry Darling, Henry Tolley, John O'Neill and Edward Copson; and Lieutenant-Colonels Edward Pritchard, RA, Joseph Morrison, Jonathan Yates, George Robertson, Philip Hughes, RE, and Charles de Salaberry. Of these officers only four, – Brisbane, Tolley, Copson and Pritchard – had arrived in Lower Canada in the summer of 1814 while de Watteville, Tucker, Darling, O'Neill, Yates and Morrison had been in North America since 1813 and the remaining five had served in the Canadas throughout the war.

In terms of experience, the board was impressive. It contained officers who were not only fairly senior in their rank in North America but who had proven combat records. Morrison (victor of Crysler's Farm, 1813 and veteran of Lundy's Lane, 1814), de Salaberry (victor of Châteauguay, 1813 and many minor border actions), Murray (Plattsburgh and Fort Niagara, 1813) and Tucker (Fort Erie, 1814) had campaigned hard in the Canadas while Brisbane, Tolley and Copson were distinguished veterans of the Peninsula, and the foreign officers, Rottenburg and Watteville, possessed a wide variety of service. None of them, with the possible exception of Glasgow, were particularly close to Prevost – indeed Salaberry had come to detest him by late 1814. The board was also interesting because of the broad range of backgrounds displayed of its members. It consisted of the senior Royal Artillery officer in Canada (Glasgow) as well as a gunner officer of field grade (Pritchard) and a Royal Engineer officer (Hughes). Also present was the only cavalry regimental commander in the Canadas (O'Neill) and six very experienced infantry battalion commanders (Murray, Tolley, Copson, Morrison, Yates and Salaberry). The conclusion is inescapable that, far from being railroaded, Procter received a fair hearing from an intelligent and experienced group of officers very much his peers.

"Upon the whole," the board concluded, Procter had "in many instances during the retreat, and in the disposition of the Force under his Command, been erroneous in judgement, and in some, deficient in those energetic and active exertions, which the extraordinary difficulties of his situation so particularly required." They found Procter guilty of not taking proper measures for conducting the retreat from Amherstburg, not affording security to his ammunition, stores and supplies during that retreat, not fortifying the heights above Moraviantown, not forming his division properly to receive an attack on 5 Oct. 1813, and not taking the best dispositions to resist that attack.

As Hitsman notes, Procter was sentenced to be suspended from rank and pay for six months and be publicly reprimanded. The Prince Regent remitted the suspension from rank and pay but upheld the public reprimand, read out before every regiment in the army, which expressed his "high disapprobation" of Procter's conduct and his "regret, that any officer of the length of service, and of the exalted rank which he has attained, should be so extremely wanting in professional knowledge, and so deficient in those active and energetic qualities, which must be required of every officer, but especially of one in the responsible situation in which the *Major-General* was placed."

The evidence suggests that Procter was not ill used, as Antal claims, by being the only senior British officer of the War of 1812 subjected to such "public degradation on such selective pretexts." To the contrary, it indicates that Major-General Henry Procter got a fair hearing from his peers and they rendered a fair verdict. For further information, see NAC, MG 13, which contains the transcript of the court martial from PRO, WO 71. SS

44. Proclamation, 12 Jan. 1814, in *DH*, vol 9, 112.
45. NAC, CO 42, vol 23, Bathurst to Prevost, 15 Dec. 1813
46. NAC, CO 42, vol 23, Bathurst to Prevost, 15 Dec. 1813.
47. NAC, CO 42, vol 23, Bathurst to Prevost, 15 Dec. 1813.

Chapter 11: Occasional Enterprises: December 1813 to May 1814
1. NAC, CO 42, vol 158, Prevost to Bathurst, 14 Jan. 1814.
2. NAC, RG 8 I, vol 1222, 32, Prevost to Drummond, 29 Jan. 1814.
3. NAC, RG 8 I, vol 621, 1, Drummond to Prevost, 19 Feb. 1814.
4. *Quebec Gazette*, 10 Mar. 1813.
5. Hitsman does not mention here that the Admiralty decided to re-organize the Royal Navy on the lakes early in 1814 to conform with standard procedures. Part of this revision involved changing the names of the vessels on Lake Ontario as they duplicated the names of vessels in commission on the high seas. The *Prince Regent* and *Princess Charlotte* were added to the Admiralty list as were the former vessels identified with new names: *Montreal* (former *Wolfe*), *Niagara* (*Royal George*), *Star* (*Melville*), *Charwell* (*Moira*), *Netley* (*Beresford*, ex-*Prince Regent*, the 1812 schooner) and *Magnet* (*Sir Sydney Smith*). This change in names was not undertaken, as some thought at the time and since, to confuse the Americans about the true strength of Yeo's squadron. RM.
6. NAC, CO 42, vol 151, Prevost to Bathurst, 4 Sep. 1813.
7. It would seem that the legal profession was held in no greater respect in 1814 than it is today.
8. *Quebec Gazette*, 10 Mar. 1813.
9. For an account of this execution, see "Eight Men Were Sentenced To Be 'Hanged-Drawn-Quartered'," *Cuesta*, (Spring 1981), 31.
10. *NWR*, 23 Apr. 1814.
11. Actually, this is not correct. Wilkinson was acquitted of all charges and did not escape penalty because of technicalities. His court martial sat in Jan. and Feb. 1815 and he was charged with neglect of duty and unofficerlike conduct, drunkenness on duty, conduct unbecoming an officer and gentleman, and encouraging and countenancing disobedience of order. Although the evidence made it clear that he was a very reluctant warrior, it was also clear that former Secretary of War John Armstrong bore a large part of the responsibility for the failure of the autumn 1813 campaign. In the end, Wilkinson was acquitted on all charges but dropped from the rolls of the army a few months later. He was no great loss to the United States Army. On this court martial, see James Wilkinson, *Memories of My Own Times* (3 vols, Philadelphia, 1816), vol 3, which included a surprisingly full coverage of all the evidence brought forward during this proceeding.
12. On Izard, see *DAB*
13. The association of native peoples of the same culture, called the Creek Confederation, was one of the largest and most important First Nations within the United States, numbering about 18,000 person and located in Tennessee, Georgia and Mississippi. The Confederacy suffered from divisions and, when a group of anti-American warriors attacked a force of Mississippi militiamen in July 1813, it initiated the conflict that became known as the Creek War. Andrew Jackson made his military reputation as a military commander in a series of campaigns that ended in Mar. 1814 with the confederacy shattered and thousands of Creeks dead. Their military power broken, the Creeks signed a treaty ceding 20 million acres of land and accepting exile west of the Mississippi River.
14. Armstrong to Brown, 28 Feb. 1814 in Armstrong, *Notices*, vol 2, 213.
15. NAC, RG 8 I, vol 1222, 112, Prevost to Drummond, 30 Apr. 1813.
16. Yeo to Croker, 9 May 1813, in *SBD*, vol 3, part 1, 61.
17. On Oswego, see Robert Malcomson, "War on Lake Ontario: A Costly Victory at Oswego, May 1814," *The Beaver* 75 (1995), 4-13.
    Lieutenant Joseph Mermet of De Watteville's Regiment wrote a delightful letter to an officer in the *Voltigeurs Canadiens* that has some entertaining remarks on this action. Mermet was on the *Prince Regent* when it neared Oswego and remembered dining at 6 P.M. of 5 May 1814 "amidst a confusion of shouts, whistles [and] a thousand *God-damn[s]*. 'All hands, all *Royal Marines* upon deck, God-damn! All foreigners *below*, *God-damn*! Out and run; be quick, be quick!'" As his company landed from their boats, the enemy showed them "with his murderous shells and smaller shot – we answer with the triple cry of victory. 'Gentlemen, let us set the example!' We land. We arrive on the beach, helping one another; we form. Our [ammunition] pouches

are full of water – what does that matter? We have bayonets!" When it was all over, Mermet was at the victory party held on *Prince Regent*: "forty-two officers in a cabin, seated at their ease, ... babbling a Franco-Anglo-Italian patois (for all these naval officers have been around the world), and how they [talked] and how they listened, and how they sang – and how they drank! '*Gentlemen, a toast: Colonel Fischer and De Watteville's Regt.! – Colonel Malcolm and 2d B[attalio]n. R[oya]l. Marines! Our success! Gen[era]l. Drummond! Sir James Yeo!'* etc., etc., etc." See NAC, MG 24, L8, Jacques Viger, "Ma Saberdache," vol 4, Mermet to Viger, 23 May 1814.

One of the worst results of this action was the loss of Captain William Howe Mulcaster, captain of the *Prince Regent*, who was badly wounded. The 29-year-old Mulcaster was Yeo's most aggressive and professional subordinate. He was the only commanding officer to bring his vessel within range of the American position during the attack on Sacket's Harbor on 29 May 1813 and he did this by having it towed by its boats while the remainder of the squadron was becalmed. He had saved his superior during the naval battle of 28 Sep. by interposing his vessel between Yeo's crippled flagship and Chauncey's *Pike*. He mounted an attack on the American base at French Creek on 1 Nov. 1813 which was beaten off after hard fighting and commanded the little squadron of gunboats that trailed the Americans down the St. Lawrence that month, harassing them at every opportunity. During the winter he was stationed at Coteau du Lac with his gunboats and regularly harassed the American camp at French Mills with naval raiding parties. Mulcaster was an intelligent officer whose professional qualities went a long way to make up for the shortcomings of his superior.

18. USNA, RG 107, RG 45, Micro 125, reel 36, 82, Chauncey to Jones, 20 May 1814.
19. NAC, C0 42, vol 156, 327, Popham to Yeo, 20 May 1814.
20. NAC, RG 8 I, vol 683, 239, Yeo to Drummond, 3 June 1814.
21. NAC, RG 8 I, vol 683, 242, Drummond to Yeo, 6 June 1814

Chapter 12: Summer Stalemate in Upper Canada: June to September 1814

1. Wellington to Bathurst, 22 Feb. 1814, in John Gurwood, ed., *Dispatches of Field Marshal the Duke of Wellington During His Various Campaigns* ... (12 vols, London, 1838), vol 11, 525.
2. NAC, CO 42, vol 23, Bathurst to Prevost, 3 June 1814. All subsequent references to this letter are from this document, which is reproduced in full in Appendix 1.
3. Hitsman perhaps did not interpret these important instructions as fully as he might, for they carry a very mixed message. On the one hand, for the first time during the war Prevost was ordered to commence offensive operations; on the other, he is cautioned not to jeopardize the "safety of the Force placed under your command," particularly not "to expose His Majesty's Forces to being cut off by too extended a line of advance." The wording is not as such to inspire an offensive spirit in a defensive-minded general who had just spent nearly two years defending the Canadas with limited forces and who had always tried to avoid heavy casualties because he could not replace them.
4. Armstrong to Madison, 30 Apr. 1814, in *DH*, vol. 9, 320.
5. NAC, RG 8 I, vol 1222, 71, Drummond to Prevost, 28 June 1814.
6. NAC, MG 12, Adm 1, vol 2738, 83, Yeo to Croker, 30 May 1815.
7. USNA, RG 145, Micro 125, reel 37, 98, Chauncey to Jones, 24 June 1814
8. Brown's Left Division, which eventually consisted of two regular and one militia brigades, assembled slowly and reinforcements straggled in throughout July 1814. On 23 July 1814 Brown had 5,009 officers and men, with 4,232 fit for duty. From this total he had to provide garrisons for Buffalo, Fort Erie, Lewiston and Schlosser. See Donald E. Graves, *Where Right and Glory Lead: The Battle of Lundy's Lane, 1814* (Toronto, 1997), 258. **Editor.**

As well as including contingents from the Oneida, Tuscarora and Senecas, members of the Six Nation Iroquois living in the United States, the native contingent with Brown also included Algonkian Stockbridges who lived with the Oneida. Hitsman's comment that the American-allied warriors were "no more dependable than the braves eating British rations" is unfair (to say nothing of the critical importance of aboriginal forces in defending the Canadas successfully during the war). **CB.**
9. NAC, RG 8 I, vol 388, 44, Riall to Drummond, 15 Mar. 1814.
10. NAC, RG 8 I, vol 682, 269, Harvey to Riall, 23 Mar. 1814. When Harvey used the term "exposed to outrages," he meant that Drummond did not want to leave the Canadian side of the Niagara vulnerable to the depredations of Willcocks and his renegades as had happened in the autumn of 1813.
11. A local girl, Amelia Ryerse, remembered the American raid:

On the following morning, the 15th of May, as my Mother and myself were at Breakfast, the Dogs made an unusual barking. I went to the door to discover the cause. When I looked up I saw the hillside and the fields as far as the eye could reach covered with American soldiers. They had landed at Patterson's Creek, Burnt the Mills and village of Port Dover and then marched to Ryerse.

Two men stepped from the ranks, selected some large chips, came into the room where we were standing and took coals from the hearth, without speaking. My mother knew instinctively what they were going to do. She went out and asked to see the commanding officer, a gentleman rode up to her and said he was the person she asked for. She entreated Him to spare her property and said that she was a widow with a young family. He answered her civilly & respectfully and regretted that his orders were to Burn, but that He would spare the house, which He did, & said in justification that the Buildings were used as Barracks and the mill furnished flour for British Troops.

Very soon we saw [a] column of dark smoke arise from every Building and what at early morn had been a prosperous homestead, at noon there remained only smouldering ruins. The following day Col. Talbot and the Militia under his command marched to Fort Norfolk. The Americans were then safe on board their own ships & well on their way to their own shores.

See memoir of Amelia Harris, in James Talman, ed., *Loyalist Narratives from Upper Canada* (Toronto, 1946), 148.

The raids on the Long Point area had disastrous consequences for the United States. Prevost decided to retaliate but rather than do so along the northern frontier, which might begin a campaign of cross-border ravaging, he requested Vice-Admiral Alexander Cochrane to retaliate on the Atlantic coast. Cochrane then planned the campaign that resulted in the burning of Washington in Aug. 1814. See Graves, *Right and Glory*, 224-225.

12. NAC, RG 8 I, vol 683, 295, Drummond to Prevost, 21 June 1814.

13. Prevost's marginal comments scribbled on the margins of Drummond's letter of 21 June 1814.

14. NAC, RG 8 I, vol 684, 12, Drummond to Prevost, 2 July 1814.

15. NAC, RG 8 I, vol 684, 51, Riall to Drummond, 6 July 1814.

16. Because of his career longevity, his self-propaganda and his prominent status in the 19th-century army, Winfield Scott was able to obscure the fact that it was actually Brown, not he, who won the victory at Chippawa on 5 July 1814. Scott's brigade was successful in the climactic infantry action but there was other fighting at Chippawa that Hitsman does not cover in his text. For the most recent study, see Donald E. Graves, *Red Coats and Grey Jackets: The Battle of Chippawa, 5 July 1814* (Toronto, 1994).

17. NAC, RG 8 I, vol 684, 59, Drummond to Prevost, 13 July 1814.

18. NAC, RG 8 I, vol 684, 201, Drummond to Prevost, 22 July 1814.

19. Although Hitsman does not discuss this in the text, it is important to note that Riall withdrew from Chippawa to Fort George on 8 July after Brown outflanked his position. Brown then advanced to Queenston, where he waited in vain for Chauncey's squadron to appear. During the night of 13 July, Riall withdrew most of his troops from Fort George west to the Twenty-Mile Creek although he left a strong garrison in place. Brown, despairing of Chauncey's arrival, moved forward and demonstrated against the fort on 20-22 July, hoping to lure the defenders out into open battle. When this failed, he withdrew to Queenston on 23 July and the following day to his supply base at Chippawa, where he planned to re-supply and then march north to Burlington Bay, in the hopes it would bring on a general engagement. See Graves, *Right and Glory*, 93-104.

20. NAC, RG 8 I, vol 684, 235, Drummond to Prevost, 27 July 1814.

21. NAC, RG 8 I, vol 684, 235, Drummond to Prevost, 27 July 1814. Given the different construction of American and British artillery carriages, the veracity of this statement is doubtful. An American field gun could be connected to a British limber but those making that connection would quickly become aware of the difference in equipment. See *Right and Glory*, 302, note 39.

22. Brown to Armstrong, 7 Aug. 1814, Parker Papers, Historical Society of Pennsylvania.

23. NAC, RG 8 I, vol 684, 235, Drummond to Prevost, 27 July 1814.

24. The editor and Hitsman disagree over which side gained a tactical victory at Lundy's Lane. This battle has always been a controversial action, which is not surprising considering it was an unplanned meeting engagement, fought mostly in the dark, and with continuous reinforcement on both sides. It is the editor's conclusion, as expressed in *Where Right and Glory Lead*, that the battle was a tactical American victory because Brown's troops seized the central terrain feature of the

field, the hill, and Drummond's artillery, and held them against repeated British counter-attacks. In the confusion of the American withdrawal, the captured artillery, the proofs of this victory, were left on the ground, where they were repossessed, not recaptured, by the British the next morning (except for one brass 6-pdr. gun currently on display at Fort McNair in Washington). In operational terms (what effect it had on the outcome of the 1814 Niagara campaign) Lundy's Lane can only be seen as a British victory because it resulted in Brown's division advancing no further but withdrawing to Fort Erie, its initial crossing point. Drummond, however, threw away this operational success by his desultory advance to Fort Erie – by the time he approached, the Americans had converted it into a strong defensive position that he was unable to overcome. In strategical terms (what effect it had on the outcome of the war) Lundy's Lane had none whatsoever.

25. NAC, RG 8 I, vol 685, 38, Drummond to Prevost, 4 Aug. 1814. Following Lundy's Lane, Drummond withdrew his army seven miles north to Queenston, where he stayed for nearly a week before advancing to Fort Erie. This backward movement permitted the Americans time to construct a strong position at that place and doomed his troops to six frustrating weeks, see Graves, *Right and Glory*, 211-212.

For a contrasting view, see Turner, *British Generals*, 126-127, who feels that Drummond's actions after the battle were "methodical and prudent." Turner also suggests (227, note 75) that Drummond took up a position that was closer to Fort Erie than Queenston. He bases this statement on Norton's *Journal*, 358, in which Norton states that he was sent in pursuit of the Americans on 26 July, and on Le Couteur's journal (see Graves, *Merry Hearts*, 176) in which Le Couteur states that the light troops were sent in pursuit of the enemy on that same day. Unfortunately for this thesis, Norton also records (359-360) that the entire army retired to Queenston on 26 July and although his warriors, accompanied by a small party of regular cavalry, moved south again on 27 July, they came no closer to Fort Erie than the ferry at Black Rock, where they were on 2 Aug. Le Couteur, while noting that the warriors and light troops were sent in pursuit of the Americans on 26 July (this was Norton's party which was withdrawn to Queenston that same day) also records (176) that the army withdrew to Queenston on the 26 July. The subsequent movements of the main body of Drummond's force are recorded in a letter written by Le Couteur on 6 Sep. 1814. Le Couteur, whose light infantry company was part of the army's advance guard, notes that it was only "on the 2d [of Aug. 1814] that we followed them up, and took up a position about a mile from the Fort [Erie] on a large clear space opposite Black Rock", see D.E. Graves, ed., "The Assault on Fort Erie, 15 August 1814: A New Le Couteur Letter from the War of 1812," *Camp Stew*, July 1996, 1-4.

It was only on 3 Aug., eight days after the battle of Lundy's Lane, that Drummond's troops drove in the American pickets at Fort Erie so that he could have a close look at the defences. The week's grace he had granted his enemy had been put to good use. Ripley made the decision to entrench at Fort Erie on 28 July and, by 3 Aug., a strong defensive position was in place. By his *extremely desultory pursuit*, Drummond gave up any claim he might have had to an operational success at Lundy's Lane.

It is important to understand that Drummond did not possess the strength to fully invest the extended American position at Fort Erie. The best he could do was to establish a position on the northern flank of the American defences and the remainder of the perimeter was only covered by pickets, while the defenders enjoyed unrestricted water communication to Buffalo, which permitted them to receive supplies and reinforcements. In effect, the operations at Fort Erie in Aug. and Sep. 1814 were not a siege but an attack on a fortified bridgehead. The most recent examination of the "siege" of Fort Erie in Aug. and Sep. 1814 is Joseph Whitehorne, *While Washington Burned: The Battle of Fort Erie, 1814* (Baltimore, 1992).

26. NAC, CO 42, vol 157, 42, Prevost to Bathurst, 14 Aug. 1814.

27. NAC, CO 42, vol 157, Prevost to Bathurst, 27 Aug. 1814.

28. NAC, RG 8 I, vol 685, 83, Arrangement for the attack on Fort Erie, 14 Aug. 1814.

29. The most recent examination of this ill-fated assault is Donald E. Graves, "William Drummond and the battle of Fort Erie," *Canadian Military History* 1 (Autumn 1991), 31-39.

30. NAC, RG 8 I, vol 685, 101, Drummond to Prevost, 16 Aug. 1814.

31. NAC, RG 8 I, vol 685, 179, Drummond to Prevost, 8 Sep. 1814.

32. NAC, RG 8 I, vol 685, 192, Drummond to Prevost, 11 Sep. 1814.

33. NAC, RG 8 I, vol 685, 197, Drummond to Prevost, 14 Sep. 1814.

34. Dunlop, *Tiger Dunlop's Upper Canada*, 37.

35. Brown to Monroe, 29 Sep. 1814, in *DH*, vol 2, 211.
36. NAC, RG 8 I, vol 685, 261, Drummond to Prevost, 21 Sep. 1814. In fairness to Drummond, Brown could not sustain a claim that the sortie of 17 Sep. 1814 resulted in the British decision to withdraw from Fort Erie. That decision had been made several days before and the British were engaged in removing the heavy artillery from the siege batteries when the Americans attacked from the fort. See Graves, *Right and Glory*, 223.
37. Croghan's force was transported to their objective by part of the Lake Erie squadron then under Commander Arthur Sinclair. The vessels included the brigs *Lawrence, Niagara,* and *Caledonia* and the schooners *Tigress* and *Scorpion*. RM.

Chapter 13: On American Territory: April to September 1814

1. For a biography of Cochrane, see *DNB*.
2. PRO, WO 1, vol 141, Cochrane to Bathurst, 14 July 1814.
3. PRO, Adm 1, vol 508, 577, Proclamation by Cochrane, 2 May 1814.
4. Cochrane organized a small battalion of "Colonial Royal Marines" numbering 600 men from these ex-slaves, which performed well in Chesapeake operations. These marines and their families were later settled in freedom in the West Indies. A large number of the black refugees were transported to Nova Scotia, where they were given their freedom and land near Halifax. Ironically, they were clothed in American uniforms which had been captured by the Sep. 1814 expedition to Castine, Maine, see Akins, "History of Halifax City," 163. On the colonial marines, see John M. Weiss, "The Corps of Colonial Marines, 1814-1815: A Summary," *Immigrants & Minorities* 15 (1996), 80-90.

   Slavery had never been a popular institution in British North America after 1783 and it was progressively dismantled until 1834 when it was abolished completely throughout the British empire. It is ironic that Cochrane anticipated Abraham Lincoln's Emancipation Proclamation by some forty-eight years.
5. Proclamation by Cochrane, 25 Apr. 1814, in *Naval Chronicle* 31 (1814), 475.
6. *NWR*, vol 6, 317.
7. NAC, MG 11, A23, New Brunswick Joint Address, 3 Mar. 1814.
8. Castlereagh to British commissioners, 28 July 1814, in Charles W. Vane, ed., *Correspondence, Despatches, and other Papers of Viscount Castlereagh* (4 vols, London, 1848-1853), series 3, vol 2, 69.
9. NAC, MG 11, A23, Bathurst to Sherbrooke, 6 June 1814
10. NAC, MG 11, A151, Sherbrooke to Bathurst, 18 Sep. 1814.
11. PRO, WO 6, vol 2, 1, Bathurst to Ross, n.d. [c. May 1814]. For a biography of Major General Robert Ross, see W.A. Maguire, *Major General Ross and the Burning of Washington* (Ulster, n.d.).
12. NAC, RG 8 I, vol 684, 221, Prevost to Cochrane, 11 May 1814.
13. Ross to Bathurst, 30 Aug. 1814, in William James, *A Full and Correct Account of the Military Occurrences of the Late War between Great Britain and the United States of America* (2 vols, London, 1818), vol 2, 496.
14. Attorney-General Richard Rush's statement, *ASPMA*, vol 1, 542.
15. Bladensburg was a British victory but the casualty figures suggest that it was no walkover by Ross's army. British officers who were veterans of the Peninsula were disgusted by what they thought were unnecessary high casualties. Captain Harry Smith felt that the losses at the battle were six times higher than they would have been if Wellington had been in command, see G.C.M. Smith, ed., *The Autobiography of Lieutenant General Sir Henry Smith* (London, 1901), 198. A later British historian remarked there was "little merit in the generalship, for the British troops were sent into action in dangerous driblets, and the frontal attack" was "pure bludgeon work." See John Buchan, *The History of the Royal Scots Fusiliers (1678-1918)* (London, 1926), 171. The most recent scholarly examination of the action is Whitehorne, *The Battle of Baltimore*, 127-144.
16. *NWR*, 10 Sep. 1814.
17. *NWR*, 31 Dec. 1814.
18. Great Britain, *Parliamentary Debates* (1st series, London, 1815), vol 29, 47.
19. Great Britain, *Parliamentary Debates* (1st series, London, 1815), vol 29, 59.
20. Strachan to Jefferson, 30 Jan. 1815, in William Coffin, *The War and Its Moral* (Montreal, 1864), 284.
21. PRO, Adm 1, vol 507, 171, Cochrane to Croker, 17 Sep. 1814.
22. Words to "The Defence of Baltimore" (later "The Star-Spangled Banner") by Francis Scott Key.

Key set the words to a popular drinking song of the time, "To Anacreon in Heaven," sung by American soldiers campaigning on the northern frontier, see Graves, *Field of Glory*, 36.

23. Barrie to Griffith, 3 Sep. 14, *SBD*, vol 3, part 1, 323.

24. NAC, MG 11, A 151, Pilkington to Sherbrooke, 14 Sep. 1814.

25. NAC, MG 11, A 151, Capitulation at Machias, 13 Sep. 1814.

26. NAC, MG 11, A 151, Proclamation by Griffith, 15 Sep. 1814.

27. NAC, MG 11, A 151, Proclamation by Griffith and Sherbrooke, 21 Sep. 1814. The British forces continued to collect the customs and excise taxes in those areas of Maine they controlled and, after the war, the proceeds were used to build an officer's library for the garrison at Halifax and to found Dalhousie University in that city.

Chapter 14: Defeat on Lake Champlain

1. Prevost to Bathurst, 5 Aug. 1814, in *SBD*, vol 3, part 1, 345.

2. Prevost to Bathurst, 5 Aug. 1814, in *SBD*, vol 3, part 1, 345.

3. For an account of this and other smuggling incidents on Lake Champlain, see Alan Everest, *The War of 1812 in the Champlain Valley* (Syracuse, 1981), 152.

4. Although de Rottenburg had not performed all that well in Upper Canada from June to Dec. 1813, Prevost had no choice but to offer him the command of this division largely composed of veterans. De Rottenburg was the senior major-general in North America and could not be by-passed in favour of a younger and more aggressive, but more junior, officer. SS.

5. The veteran Peninsula regiments that arrived in North America from Bordeaux in the early summer of 1814 were not very happy soldiers. After almost six years of continuous campaigning in Portugal, Spain and France, they expected to be returned to the British Isles, and their gloom was not lightened by the sight of their Spanish and Portuguese wives, and their children, wading out into the surf in vain attempts to stop the boats taking them out to the transports for passage to America. See William Grattan, *Adventures with the Connaught Rangers, 1809-1814* (London, 1902, 1989), 330-334.

6. NAC, CO 42, vol 157, Prevost to Bathurst, 27 Aug. 1814. Montreal during the summer of 1814 was a scene of concentrated martial activity as Alicia Cockburn wrote to a correspondent in England:

> We are expecting an attack hereabouts. It is something like the French invasion; the war is at an end without its ever having come to pass, & such will be the case here. All is bustle however in the neighbouring Camp – Guns – Drums – Bugles – Horse – Foot – Brigadiers – Grenadiers – & Fuzileers – Right – Left – here – there – march – halt – wheel – double-quick – tumble down – tumble up – fire away – thus they "keep moving" and a most moving scene it is

See Alicia Cockburn to Charles Sandys, 28 June 1814, *SBD*, vol 3, pt 1, 385.

7. The *St. Lawrence* only mounted 104 guns during its brief active career in Oct. and Nov. 1814. It had a broadside of 1,564 pounds compared to the *Victory*'s broadside of 1,052 pounds at Trafalgar. Nelson's flagship was 20 feet shorter than Yeo's, but less than one foot narrower. Though it had a much deeper hull and higher stern than the *St. Lawrence*, the *Victory* was nearly 200 tons less in burthen. Malcomson, "H.M.S. *St. Lawrence*: The Freshwater First-Rate," *Mariner's Mirror* 83 (1997), 419-433. RM.

8. On Macdonough, see *DAB*.

9. USNA, RG 107, Micro 221, reel 62, Izard to Armstrong, 12 Aug. 1814.

10. Armstrong to Izard, 12 Aug. 1814, in George Izard, *Official Correspondence with the Department of War* (Philadelphia, 1816), 69.

11. Grattan, *Adventures with the Connaught Rangers*, 50.

12. Order quoted in William Kingsford, *History of Canada* (10 vols, Toronto, 1887), vol 8, 532n. This unfortunate order (which caused a sensation when it was issued) was directed squarely at the officers of the units from Wellington's army who had just arrived in Canada. If Prevost was not impressed with their appearance, the civilian population certainly was – the *Quebec Gazette* noted on 30 June 1814 that "the city witnessed the extraordinary sight of a number of transports with British troops on board, arriving from Bordeaux ... who came on shore wearing the white cockade, which we understand, was universally worn by our people in France." A week later the same paper praised the newly landed men of the 82nd Foot "Notwithstanding their ... worn uniforms which covered them in so much glory in France." The white cockade was the symbol of

the Bourbon crown of Spain and also the symbol of the Stuarts of England. British troops at this time normally wore the black cockade of the Hanoverians.

13. C.W. Robinson, ed., "The Battle of Plattsburgh, Upper Lake Champlain, Canada, 1814," *Journal of the Royal United Service Institution* 61 (Aug. 1916), 10 Sep. 1814. See also Richard Preston, ed., "The Journals of Sir F.P. Robinson, G.C.B.," *CHR* 37 (Dec. 1956).

14. Macomb to Armstrong, 15 Sep. 1814, in Brannan, *Official Letters*, 418. On Macomb, see *DAB*

15. Macomb to Armstrong, 15 Sep. 1814, in Brannan, *Official Letters*, 418.

16. NAC, CO 42, vol 158, Prevost to Downie, 7 Sep. 1814.

17. NAC, CO 42, vol 158, Downie to Prevost, 8 Sep. 1814.

18. NAC, CO 42, vol 158, Downie to Prevost, 9 Sep. 1814.

19. NAC, CO 42, vol 158, Prevost to Downie, 10 Sep. 1814.

20. NAC, CO 42, vol 158, Downie to ADC, 10 Sep. 14.

21. NAC, CO 42, vol 158, Statement of Captain Daniel Pring.

22. NAC, CO 42, vol 158, Statement of Lieutenant Robertson.

23. Robinson, "The Battle of Plattsburgh," 10 Sep. 1814.

24. Robinson, "The Battle of Plattsburgh," 10 Sep. 1814.

25. NAC, CO 42, vol 158, Prevost to Bathurst, 11 Sep. 1814.

26. Robinson, "The Battle of Plattsburgh," 10 Sep. 1814.

27. Robinson, "The Battle of Plattsburgh," 10 Sep. 1814.

28. Macomb to Armstrong, 15 Sep. 1814, in Brannan, *Official Letters*, 418.

29. It is notable that most of the desertion occurred during the withdrawal from Plattsburgh, not during the advance, which may be an indication of low morale in the army. Desertion was the plague of the British army in North America – during the war, 1,570 British regulars deserted while stationed in the Canadas as opposed to 2,733 lost due to combat or disease, see WO 17, Muster Rolls, June 1812 to Dec. 1814.

30. Alicia Cockburn to Charles Sandys, 20 Oct. 1814, *SBD*, vol 3, part 1, 386. Alicia Cockburn was the wife of Lieutenant-Colonel Francis Cockburn, the commanding officer of the Canadian Fencibles, and she was prominent in the anti-Prevost camp that emerged in the higher circles of the British military in Canada in 1814, collecting information and documentation about Sir George that was sent back to London. Her poor opinion of Prevost predated the Plattsburgh campaign – on 28 June 1814, she was complaining that, if she commanded the army, she would "move it a *little nearer the enemy*" but that "there are some worthy people who have the happy knack of discovering *danger* long before its approach, and *wisely* determine to take every measure save that of running into it, – they bear in mind the *old Poem*

He who fights & runs away,
May live to fight another day,
But he who is in Battle slain,
Will never rise to fight again.

See Alicia Cockburn to Charles Sandys, 28 June 1814, *SBD*, vol 3, pt 1, 385

31. Prevost to Bathurst, 22 Sep. 1814, in *SBD*, vol 3, part 1, 364.

32. Yeo to Croker, 24 Sep. 1814, in Wood, *SBD*, vol 3, part 1, 377.

33. NAC, MG 12, Adm 1, vol 2737, 173, Yeo to Croker, 16 Sep. 1814.

34. *Kingston Gazette*, 16 Sep. 1814.

35. Izard to Monroe, 16 Oct. 1812, *DH*, vol. 2, 251.

36. It was unfortunate for the United States that Izard, being senior to the more aggressive Brown, assumed command on the Niagara frontier in the autumn of 1814, as he proved to be a singularly cautious officer despite the fact that he commanded 8,000 trained regular troops, the largest army of regulars fielded by the U.S. during the war.

Izard, however, was not backward in coming forward in print. He tendered his resignation in late 1814 and, by early 1816, had published his own version of events as *Official Correspondence with the Department of War* (Philadelphia, 1816).

37. Wellington to Bathurst, 30 Oct. 1814, in Francis Bickley, ed., *Historical Manuscripts Commission: Report on the Manuscripts of Earl Bathurst present at Cirencester Park* (London, 1923), 302.

38. Wellington to Murray, 22 Dec. 1814, in Gurwood, ed., *Despatches of Field Marshal the Duke of Wellington*, vol 12, 224.

Chapter 15: The Treaty of Status Quo: July 1814 to January 1815

1. NAC, CO 42, vol 23, Bathurst to Prevost, 3 June 1814.
2. Castlereagh to British commissioners, 28 July 1814, in Charles W. Vane, *Correspondence, Despatches, and other Papers of Viscount Castlereagh* (4 vols, London, 1848-1853), Series 3, vol 2, 69.
3. Gallatin to Madison in Henry Adams, ed., *The Writings of Albert Gallatin*, (3 vols, Philadelphia, 1879), vol 1, 627.
4. NAC, CO 42, vol 160, Petition of merchants, etc, of Glasgow and Newark, 10 Sep. 1814.
5. Wellington to Goulbourn, 9 Nov. 1814, in the Duke of Wellington, *Supplementary Dispatches, Correspondence and Memoranda of the Duke of Wellington* (14 vols, London, 1858-1872), vol 10, 425.
6. Goulbourn to Castlereagh, 18 Nov. 1814, quoted in Mahan, *Sea Power*, vol 2, 431.
7. A copy of the "as signed" version of the Treaty of Ghent is contained in *SBD*, vol 3, part 1, 515-524.
8. On Pakenham, see John Fortescue, "Sir Edward Pakenham," *Blackwood's Magazine* 235 (1934), 33-54 and Valerie Scott, *Major General Sir Edward Pakenham* (New Orleans, 1965).
9. The best account of the New Orleans campaign because it removes many of the mythological weeds that have sprouted up around this operation and connects it, as it should be connected, to events on the Canadian frontier, is Robin Reilly, *The British at the Gates. The New Orleans Campaign in the War of 1812* (New York, 1974).
10. NAC, CO 42, vol 159, 71, Prevost to Bathurst, 3 Mar. 1815.
11. Verdict of Court Martial in *SBD*, vol 3, part 1, 401.
12. In fact, it occurred somewhat differently than Hitsman has suggested. After "an enquiry to clear Sir George's name was refused, restitution of a tangible nature was made to the General's family, for the Prince Regent, acting for the King, offered his widow a Peerage for his son as a sign of royal approval. This was not accepted, as his estate was not such as to uphold the dignity and 'Supporters' to the crest were substituted." See W.A.J. Prevost, *The Records of the Prevost Family* (private, 1949), 36.

 Catherine Anne Prevost wanted nothing from the Crown but an inquiry to clear her husband's name. When the Crown turned down her request but offered a peerage in lieu, she refused it because she did not feel her family was wealthy enough to maintain that situation but did accept an award of supporters to the Prevost armorials. The granting of supporters for the coat of arms is a very rare distinction and the Prevost award is the oldest such honour in England given to a Baronet (an untitled gentleman received a similar award in 1815), see A.C. Fox-Davies, *A Complete Guide to Heraldry* (London, 1909, revised 1985), 318.

 The translation of the Prevost family motto is "Faith Kept with the Dead" which, under the circumstances, is an apt one.

 Sir George Prevost was survived by his wife, his son of the same name and his two daughters, Anne Elinor and Harriet. His brother William was a major-general in the army and his brother James was a captain in the Royal Navy.

 Catharine Prevost erected a memorial to her husband in Winchester Cathedral which testified to Sir George Prevost's services as governor-general and commander-in-chief of British North America and, in part, reads: "In which command, by his wise and energetic measures, And with a very inferior force, He preserved the Canadas to the British Crown, From the repeated invasions of a powerful Enemy." Sir George Prevost is buried in the graveyard of St. Mary the Virgin church at East Barnet in Hertfordshire.

 I am indebted to Sir Christopher Prevost of London for this information.
13. The full title of this work (which tells it all) is *The Letters of Veritas. Re-Published from the Montreal Herald, Containing a Succinct Account of the Military Administration of Sir George Prevost, during his Command in the Canadas, Whereby it Will Appear Manifest, that the Merit of Preserving Them from Conquest, Belongs Not to Him* (Montreal, 1815).
14. The authorship of the article entitled "Campaigns in the Canadas" which appeared on pages 405-449 of the *Quarterly Review* for July 1822 has been attributed to Henry Procter, see Antal, *Wampum Denied*, 393. According to Antal, after leaving the army in 1816, Procter "lived for several years in quiet semiretirement until he learned that the Prince Regent had honoured Prevost's services in Canada," whereupon he set pen to paper. This is apparently a reference to the Prince Regent's award of supporters for the Prevost coat of arms, and, if so, then Procter waited six years after that award was made in 1816. The *Review* article, couched in inflammatory language, was a dedicated exercise in character assassination that was highly critical of Prevost's conduct of the war but singled out for particular censure his supposed lack of preparations for the defence of

Canada, his mismanagement of naval affairs on the lakes, the abortive attack on Sackets Harbor, and the Plattsburgh expedition. It is very probable that Procter was the author as almost a third of the article (and the most vehement part) was devoted to Prevost's alleged lack of support for the Right Division on the Detroit and Barclay's squadron on Lake Erie. Concerning these latter matters the author states that, "in the whole course of that vacillation and error, which unhappily distinguished the administration of Sir George Prevost, his imbecility of judgement and action was most flagrant and palpable, in the circumstances which led to the destruction of our marine on Lake Erie."

Prevost's wife, Catharine Anne, had died before the *Quarterly Review* attack was published but his children and brothers responded with a small monograph written by his wartime civil secretary, Edward B. Brenton, entitled *Some Account of the Public Life of Sir George Prevost*, and published in 1823. As Hitsman notes, it was a badly written book and poorly organized but Brenton succeeded in rather clumsily refuting point by point almost every criticism made by the author of the *Review* article, with the possible exception of his failure at Plattsburgh. To counter the charge that Prevost was responsible for the destruction of the squadron on Lake Erie, the family called upon Captain Robert Barclay, the commander of that squadron, for his opinion. Barclay, who regretted "that an article so ungenerous and severe, should have been written," had no hesitation in declaring that, "as far as relates to Lake Erie, nothing can be more false." There was no reply to Brenton's counter-attack from the author of the *Review* article and this silence would tend to support the thesis that Procter was its author as Procter died in Oct. 1822 some four months after it was published. Henry Procter was a bitter man. His career was destroyed when he was found guilty of ineptitude during the retreat from Amherstburg after a fair trial by his peers and, as one of his former officers (NAC, MG 40, G4, Cochran narrative) remarked: "This wretched man was of course never again employed" but "slunk away into obscurity and we never heard of him more." Procter, however, avenged himself on Prevost, whom he held primarily responsible for his troubles.

The most recent scholarly examination of Sir George Prevost's conduct of the defence of British North America (Turner, *British Generals*, 97) gives credit to Prevost for "his quiet persistence, strategic ability, and administrative achievements."

15. NAC, RG 8 I, vol 683, 171, Talbot to Riall, 16 May 1814.
16. As noted in the introduction, an elaborate myth evolved in Upper and Lower Canada in the decades after the war which held that the successful defence of the two colonies was primarily the work of the Canadian militia, occasionally assisted by a few British regulars. This "militia myth" was in full flower by the end of the 19th century when most of the major 1812-1814 battlefields in Canada were marked as historic sites, and their inscriptions bear witness to that fact. This myth has been progressively debunked by historians in the last half century but it should not be forgotten, as Hitsman notes, that the militia did play an important role in providing administrative and logistical support for the regulars. Another aspect of the war that should not be overlooked is the service of the long-service Canadian units, including the 104th Foot and the five fencible regiments of the British army, and the provincial corps such as the Voltigeurs Canadiens, the Select Embodied battalions of Lower Canada and the Incorporated Militia Battalion of Upper Canada. For a complete listing of these units, see Appendix 4.
17. "P and W" or "Peninsula and Waterloo." The British army that fought in North America in 1812-1814 was in a similar situation to the British Fourteenth Army that campaigned in Burma and Malaysia in 1943-1945 – its achievements were overshadowed by events in Europe that received more publicity. British veterans of the War of 1812 tended to take a humorous view of the business – as Surgeon William Dunlop of the 89th Foot remarked about Wellington and Waterloo: "thank God he managed to do without us." See Dunlop, *Tiger Dunlop's Upper Canada*, 62.
18. Wellington to the House of Commons, 15 Apr. 1828, *British Parliamentary Papers* (3rd series, London, 1828), no. 493.
19. Hitsman may be a little harsh in his assessment of British regimental officers when he terms them "lacking in imagination." As the events of the war demonstrated, the British army quickly adapted itself to North American conditions and performed creditably in a number of unconventional roles in the most difficult of circumstances. For an insight into what life was like for the British officer in North America during the war, see the lively journal of John Le Couteur of the 104th Foot published as Donald E. Graves, ed., *Merry Hearts Make Light Days: The War of 1812 Journal of Lieutenant John Le Couteur, 104th Foot* (Ottawa, 1993). Another excellent first-

hand account by a junior officer is that left by Ensign George Gleig of the 85th Foot, who fought at Washington and New Orleans in 1814, see *Campaigns of the British Army at Washington and New Orleans*, (London, 1972).

20. Hitsman's criticism of Procter is not shared by the most recent author to study his wartime record, see Antal, *A Wampum Denied: Procter's War of 1812* (Ottawa, 1997). The editor inclines toward Hitsman's opinion of Procter.

The most recent examination of British military leadership during the war which, unfortunately, does not include such principal commanders on the northern frontier as Procter and Vincent, nor those in other theatres such as Ross and Pakenham, is Wesley B. Turner, *British Generals in the War of 1812. High Command in the Canadas* (Montreal, 1999).

21. Agar, *The Price of Union*, (Boston, 1950), 182.

A Bibliography of the British, Canadian and Native War of 1812

COMPILED BY DONALD E. GRAVES

The following bibliography takes Mac Hitsman's note on sources in the original edition of *The Incredible War of 1812*, widens it to include topics such as the First Nations and civilian society and the war not covered in the first edition, and extends it to embrace major titles that have appeared since 1966. Unpublished secondary sources have been included with published sources in their respective subject areas.

In compiling entries, emphasis was put on British, Canadian and First Nation involvement in the War of 1812. Readers interested in the American side of the war are directed to John C. Fredriksen, *Free Trade and Sailors' Rights: A Bibliography of the War of 1812* (Westport, 1985), *Shield of the Republic/Sword of Empire. A Bibliography of United States Military Affairs, 1783-1846* (Westport, 1990) and *War of 1812 Eyewitness Accounts. An Annotated Bibliography* (Westport, 1997). Also useful in this respect is Dwight Smith, *The War of 1812; An Annotated Bibliography* (1985).

Those interested in the British, Canadian and native war have not been so well served. Beyond a basic listing compiled by Wesley Turner for Morris Zaslow's *The Defended Border* (Toronto, 1964) and the War of 1812 section in Claude Thibeault's now very dated *Bibliographica Canadiana* (Don Mills, 1973), there is no available bibliography to the literature. There are published guides which cover related topics. For example, useful references may be found in Donald E. Graves and Anne E. MacLeod, *Nova Scotia Military History: a Resource Guide* (Halifax, 1982); Jacques Rouillard, *Guide d'histoire du Québec; du Régime français à nos jours; bibliographie commentée* (Montreal, 1991); Brooke Taylor, *Canadian History: a Reader's Guide. Volume 1: Beginnings to Confederation* (Toronto, 1994) and Owen A. Cooke, *The Canadian Military Experience 1867-1995: A Bibliography* (Ottawa, 1997). In addition historians working for Parks Canada have produced a substantial amount of work on the archaeological, architectural and material history aspects of the war and many of their efforts are included below,while a complete listing may be found in *Parks Canada Research Publications: Catalogue* (Ottawa, 1998). Finally, British military history of the Napoleonic period is covered in Robin Higham, *A Guide to the Sources of British Military History.* (Hamden, 1975) and Gerald Jordan, *British Military History: A Supplement to Robin Highams's Guide to the Sources* (New York, 1988).

Some comments about contents and arrangement are in order. The list of archival sources is very preliminary and by no means exclusive – it only gives a brief overview of what is available. Because of space restrictions, the citations below are minimal and considerable use of abbreviations has been made. Full titles for these abbreviations can be found in the list that precedes the endnotes section of this book.

D.E.G.

I. PRIMARY SOURCES

1. ARCHIVAL SOURCES: RECORDS AND MANUSCRIPTS

1.1 American Repositories
Buffalo and Erie County Historical Society, Buffalo
   Manuscripts Collection, War of 1812, letterbook of Major General Phineas Riall
Burton Historical Library, Detroit
   Charles Askins papers
   John Askins papers
   Diary of Ensign Andrew Warffe, Incorporated Militia
Chicago Historical Society, Chicago
   Captain Billy Caldwell papers
Clements Library, University of Michigan, Ann Arbor
   Captain Robert Barrie, RN, papers, 1814
   General Sir Thomas Brisbane papers, Plattsburgh 1814
   Henry Goulbourn papers (Treaty of Ghent negotiations)
   Rear Admiral George Cockburn papers
   John Wilson Croker papers, Admiralty, 1812-1815
   Admiral Pulteny Malcom papers, 1814-1815
Fort McHenry National Monument and Historic Shrine, Baltimore
   Logs of HM Ships *Tonnant, Erebus, Seahorse, Volcano, Surprize*, 1814
Gelman Library, George Washington University, Washington
   Major General Robert Ross papers
Indiana University, Bloomington
   Memoir "Campaigns of a British Officer in Europe and America"
   Journal of Capt R. Saumarez, RN, Penobscot 1814
Minnesota Historical Society, St. Paul, Minnesota
   Robert Dickson papers
National Archives of the United States, Washington
   Record Group 45
     Log of HMS *Wolfe*, 1813-1814
   General Henry Procter papers
Naval Historical Foundation, Washington
   Rear Admiral George Cockburn papers, 1813-1815
New York Historical Society, New York
   Papers of Thomas Barclay, British Prisoner Agent in the US
   Journal of Lt. Peter Brooke, RN, 1814
   Diary of Admiral Alexander Cochrane
New York State Library, Albany
   Order Book, 6th Foot, Ft. Erie, 1814
Perkins Library, Duke University, Durham, North Carolina
   Diary of Capt. Robert Barrie, RN
   Diary of Lt. John Lang, 19th Light Dragoons, 1812-1815
St. Lawrence University, Canton, New York
   David Parish papers
United States Library of Congress, Washington
   Admiral Alexander Cochrane papers, 1813-1815
   Rear Admiral George Cockburn papers, 1813-1815
   John Henry papers
   Memoir by Captain Charles Napier, RN, 1814
United States Naval Academy, Library, Annapolis
   British officer's journal of the Chesapeake campaign, 1813
University of Chicago, Chicago
   Papers of Sir Thomas Duckworth, Governor of Newfoundland

1.2 British Repositories
East Riding County Records Office, Beverly, Yorkshire
   Admiral Henry Hotham papers
Hertfordshire County Archives, Kingston-upon-Thames
   Letters of Midshipman John Johnson, 1813
Ipswich and East Suffolk Record Office
   Captain Philip Broke papers
Lord Coutanche Library, Société Jersiaise, St. Helier, Jersey
   Journal of Sir John Le Couteur, 1811-1816
   Diary of Sir John Le Couteur, 1815
National Library of Scotland, Edinburgh
   Admiral Alexander Cochrane papers
   Admiral Edward Codrington papers
   Memoir by Sir George De Lacy Evans on Chesapeake Operations, 1814
   General Sir George Murray papers
National Maritime Museum, Greenwich
   Admiral John Warren papers
Public Record Office, Belfast, Northern Ireland
   Diary of Col. Arthur Brooke, 1814-1815
Public Record Office, Kew, Surrey (* indicates copies in National Archives of Canada)
   Admiralty 1, In-Letters, Reports of Court Martials, 1812-1815*
   Admiralty 2, Secretariat, Secret Letters*
   Admiralty 37, Musters, Establishments,
   Admiralty 51, Captains' Logs*
   Admiralty 52, Masters' Logs*
   Admiralty 103, Prisoner of War Records
   Admiralty 106, Navy Board In-Letters from Yards, Canada*
   Colonial Office 5, Indies Trade
   Colonial Office 23, West Indies
   Colonial Office 42, Secretary of State Correspondence, In-Letters, Canada*
   Colonial Office 43, Secretary of State Correspondence, Out-Letters, Canada*
   Colonial Office 45, Sessional and Council Papers
   War Office 1, Secretary at War, In Letters
   War Office 17, Monthly Returns of the British Army in North America*
   War Office 25, Officer's Registers, Various
   War Office 27, Inspection Returns
   War Office 31, Correspondence of the Adjutant-General
   War Office 42, Pension Records*
   War Office 44, Ordnance Office, In-Letters*
   War Office 55, Ordnance Office, Out-Letters*
      Journal of Lt. Phillpotts, RE, Ft. Erie, September 1814*
   War Office 57, Commissariat, In-Letters, Canada*
   War Office 71, Court Martial Records
   War Office 97, Chelsea Hospital Pension Records*
Royal Artillery Institution, Woolwich
   Col. Alexander Dickson papers
   Journal of Major C.R. Forrest, 1814-1815
   Diary of Major John Michell, 1814-1815
Royal Regiment of Wales Museum, Cardiff
   Lt. James Cochran, "The War in Canada, 1812-1815"
   Cochran's annotations to Richardson's *War of 1812*

1.3. Canadian Repositories
Archives of Ontario, Toronto
   Robert Baldwin papers
   Brock Monument papers
   MS 35, Bishop John Strachan papers

MS 109, Major General Henry Procter papers
MS 199, Isaac Wilson diary
MS 496, F.B. Tupper papers
MS 520, Solomon Jones papers
MS 842, Journal of a Staff Officer (Lt. Colonel John Harvey)
MU 572, Daniel Clark papers
MU 1057, Colley L. Foster papers
MU 2036, Military Records
MU 2825, Sir David Smith papers
MU 3027, F.B. Tupper papers.
MU 7253, Givins Family papers
MU 8191, General Gordon Drummond Letterbook
MU 1032, William Kingsford papers
MU 1054, Ford papers
MU 2057, John Harvey papers
MV 2118, Abraham Nelles papers
Niagara Historical Society papers
John Norton papers
Eli Playter diary, 1813
Anne Powell correspondence
Sir George Prevost, correspondence and letter books
John B. Robinson papers
Captain David Thorburn, memoir
Commodore Sir James Yeo correspondence
McCord Museum, Montreal
Captain R.H. Barclay papers
Cuthbert Family papers
War of 1812 papers
National Archives of Canada, Ottawa
Manuscript Group 9
Kent County Historical Society Records
Norfolk County Historical Society Records
Manuscript Group 11 (Colonial Office 42), Original Correspondence, Canada, 1811-1815
Manuscript Group 13, War Office 71, Transcript of Court Martial of Major General Henry Procter
Manuscript Group 19
A39, Duncan Clark papers
Account of the Battle of Lundy's Lane
Order Book, 1813-1814
F1, William Claus papers
Manuscript Group 23
D2, Edward Winslow papers
G3, Murray papers
G11, Sewell papers
H1, John Graves Simcoe papers
Manuscript Group 24
A1, Brock papers
A9, Prevost Family papers
A41, Drummond letterbook
B3, Ryland letterbook
C2, Joseph Willcocks papers
E1-4, Merritt papers
F14, Lord Melville papers
F15, Correspondence of Colonel Hercules Scott, 103rd Foot, 1814
F17, Livre de voyage, Surgeon Francis Hall, 1816
F18, "Four Years on the Lakes" by Lt. David Wingfield, RN
F21, William H. Robinson, letter on Plattsburgh
F23, Gustavus Nicolls papers

vol. 1, Memoir by de Gaugreben
F24, Jonas Simonds papers
F25, Great Britain, Lakes papers
F78, General Francis de Rottenburg papers
F95, Ms. biography of Capt. W.H. Mulcaster, RN
F96, De Watteville papers
    Diary, 1812-1815
F112, Charles K. Gardner papers
F113, Henry Shrapnel papers
G5, Vassal de Monviel papers
G6, John Moorehead papers
G7, Servos papers
G9, Jean-Baptiste Juchereau-Duchesnay papers
G13, Montreal militia papers
G17, Memory Book of Lieutenant Joseph Baker, Canadian Volunteers, 1814
G18, J.A. Cartier papers
G21, Muster Roll of Captain Hall's Company, Canadian Fencibles
G45, De Salaberry Correspondence
G46, Mahlon Burwell Journal
G59, John Macdonell papers, 1813
J48, John William Whittaker papers
L8, Captain Jacques Viger, Voltigeurs Canadiens, "Ma Saberdache", vols 2-5
Manuscript Group 30
    E1, Audet papers
    E66, Ernest Cruikshank papers
Manuscript Group 40
    E1, House of Lords papers
    R110, Holmes, Pedestrian Tour to the Falls of Niagara
National Map Collection (contains wartime maps)
Record Group 1, Records of the Executive Council, Upper Canada, 1812-1815
Record Group 5, Records of the Civil Secretary's Office, Upper Canada, 1812 1815
Record Group 7, Governor-General's Office, 1812-1815
Record Group 8 I, British Military Records, 1811-1815
Record Group 9, Pre-Confederation Militia Records, 1811-1815
Record Group 10, Indian Department
Record Group 19, E5, War of 1812 Loss Claim Records
National Archives of Quebec, Montreal
    Correspondence of Lt. Maurice Nowlan, 100th Foot, 1812-1813
Niagara Historical Society, Niagara-on-the-Lake,
    Standing Orders for the 2nd West York Regiment.
Queen's University Archives, Kingston
    Papers and Diaries of Richard Cartwright
    Diary of Private Richard Ringer, 100th Foot, 1813-1814
Royal Canadian Military Institute, Toronto
    Manuscript Notebook of Captain Paul, RA
Toronto Reference Library
    William Allan papers
    Robert Baldwin papers
    Journal of Lieutenant Christopher Hagerman, ADC to Major General Drummond
    S.P. Jarvis papers, B 65, Militia.
    Sir George Prevost letterbook
United Church Archives, Toronto
    Memoir of Reverend George Ferguson (private, 100th Foot, 1812-1815)
University of Montreal Archives
    Baby family papers
University of Western Ontario, London
    Aeneas Shaw papers

2. PUBLISHED DOCUMENT COLLECTIONS

[Brock, Isaac] "District General Orders of Maj.-Gen. Sir Isaac Brock from June 27th, 1812 -Oct. 16th, 1812." *WCHT* 19 (1920), 5-48.

Cockburn, George. "Admiral Cockburn's plan." *Maryland Historical Society,* 6 (1911), 16-19.

"Court Martial of Commodore Barclay." *Journal of American History* 8 (1914), 129-148

Cruikshank, Ernest A., ed. *Documentary History of the Campaigns upon the Niagara Frontier in 1812-1814* [titles vary slightly]. 9 vols, Welland, 1896-1908.

————, ed. *Documents Relating to the Invasion of Canada and the Surrender of Detroit, 1812.* Ottawa, 1913.

————, ed. *Documents Relating to the Invasion of the Niagara Peninsula by the United States Army, commanded by General Jacob Brown in July and August, 1814.* Niagara-on-the-Lake, 1920.

————, ed., *Records of Niagara. A Collection of Contemporary Documents and Letters. 1812.* Niagara-on-the-Lake, 1934.

Dudley, William S., ed. *The Naval War of 1812: A Documentary History. Vol 1: 1812; Vol 2: 1813.* Washington, 1985 and 1992.

Firth, Edith, ed. *The Town of York, 1793-1815. A Collection of Documents of Early Toronto.* Toronto, 1962.

Gurwood, John, ed. *The Dispatches of Field Marshal the Duke of Wellington During His Various Campaigns* .... 12 vols, London, 1838.

Johnston, Charles M. ed. *The Valley of the Six Nations: A Collection of Documents on the Indian Lands of the Grand River.* Toronto, 1964.

[Lethbridge, Robert]. "Dispatch from Col. [Robert] Lethbridge to Major General Brock." *OHSPR* 18 (1913), 57-59.

Murdock, Richard K., ed. "A British Report on West Florida and Louisiana, November, 1812." *FHQ* 43 (July 1964), 36-51

Official Letters with Comments and Observations Relative to the Capture of the President, American Frigate. Bermuda, 1815.

Preston, Richard, ed. *Kingston Before the War of 1812.* Toronto, 1959.

[Procter, Henry]. "War of 1812. Reports and Correspondence From the Canadian Archives at Ottawa." *NOQ* 2 (1930), 1-14.

Proceedings of the Court Martial Held on the Officers and Crew of His Majesty's Late Ship the Java. N.p., 1813.

Upper Canada, Legislative Assembly. "Journals and Proceedings of the House of Assembly of the Province of Upper Canada, 1812-1818." *Ninth Report of the Bureau of Archives of the Province of Ontario,* Toronto, 1912.

Upper Canada, Legislative Council. "Journals of the Legislative Council of the Province of Upper Canada." [1792-1819] *Seventh Report of the Bureau of Archives of the Province of Ontario.* Toronto, 1910.

Wellington, Duke of. *Supplementary Despatches, Correspondence and Memoranda of the Duke of Wellington.* 14 vols, London, 1858-1871.

Wood, William, ed. *Select British Documents of the Canadian War of 1812.* 4 vols. Toronto, 1920-1928.

3. NEWSPAPERS AND PERIODICALS

Acadian Recorder
Annual Register, or a View of the History, Politics, and Literature for the year 1812 ... 1813 ... 1814 ... 1815. London, 1822-1825.
Canadian Courant and Montreal Advertizer
Edinburgh Annual Register
Halifax Gazette
Kingston Gazette
Montreal Gazette
Montreal Herald
Niagara Herald
Quebec Gazette
Quebec Mercury
Quarterly Review
York Gazette

**4. PUBLISHED PERSONAL ACCOUNTS, DIARIES, CORRESPONDENCE, MEMOIRS
AND JOURNALS**

4.1 British Military (Upper and Lower Canada and the Northwest)

Allen, Robert S., ed. "The Bisshopp Papers during the War of 1812." *JSAHR* 61 (1983), 22-29.

Anonymous. "The Assault on Fort Erie; or, Two ways of Telling a Story." *United Service Journal*, (1841), 84-90.

Brymner, Douglas, ed. "Capture of Fort McKay, Prairie du Chien, in 1814." *WHC* 11 (1888), 254-271

Bulger, Andrew H. *An Autobiographical Sketch of the Services of the late Captain Andrew Bulger of the Royal Newfoundland Fencible Regiment.* Bangalore, 1865. [Captain, Royal Newfoundland Fencibles]

Carnochan, Janet, ed. "Letters of 1812." *NHSP* 31 (1919), 6-10. [lieutenant, 49th Foot].

Cruikshank, Ernest A., ed. "Campaigns of 1812-1814." *NHSP* 9 (1902), 1-46. [Captain Matthew Elliott]

Dunlop, William. *Tiger Dunlop's Upper Canada.* Toronto, 1967. [surgeon, 89th Foot]

Gellner, John, ed. *Recollections of the War of 1812: Three Eyewitness Accounts.* Toronto, 1964. [Private Shadrach Byefield, 41st Foot and Patrick Finan, civilian]

Graham, Gerald S., ed. "Views of General Murray on the Defense of Upper Canada, 1815." *CHR* 34 (1953), 158-165.

Grattan, William. *Adventures with the Connaught Rangers, 1809-1814.* London, 1902, reprinted 1989. [lieutenant, 88th Foot]

Graves, Donald E. ed., *Merry Hearts Make Light Days: The War of 1812 Journal of Lieutenant John Le Couteur, 104th Foot.* Ottawa, 1993.

———., ed. "The Assault on Fort Erie, 15 August 1814: A New Le Couteur Letter from the War of 1812." *Camp Stew* 8 (1996), 1-4. [Lieutenant John Le Couteur, 104th Foot]

Hay, George. "Recollections of the War of 1812 by George Hay, Eighth Marquis of Tweeddale, Contributed by Lewis Einstein." *AHR* 32 (1926), 69-78. [lieutenant-colonel, 100th Foot]

Holmden, H.R., ed. "Baron de Gaugreben's Memoir on the Defence of Upper Canada." *CHR* 11 (1921), 58-68. [captain, RE]

Howison, John. *Sketches of Upper Canada.* Edinburgh, 1821.

Jackson, Henry G. in *The Bath Archives. A Further Selection from the Diaries and Letters of Sir George Jackson, K.C.H., from 1809 to 1816.* 2 vols, London, 1873. [captain, RA]

Lighton, William B. *Narrative of the Life and Sufferings of a Young British Captive.* Concord, 1836. [private soldier]

Lord, Norman, ed. "The War on the Canadian Frontier, 1812-1814: Letters Written by Sergeant James Commins, 8th Foot." *JSAHR* 18 (1939).

Lowry, Dr. "Fort Niagara, 1814." *NHSP* 30 (1917), 38-39. [Surgeon, 8th Foot].

"Philalethes," [George R. Macdonell]. "The Last War in Canada." *Journal of the United Service Institute*, 1848, 271-283, 425-441. [staff]

McKay, William. "Capture of Fort McKay, Prairie du Chien, in 1814." *PAC Annual Report, 1887*, 104-109.

Mills, George H., ed. "Documents relating to the battle of Stoney Creek." *Wentworth Historical Society Papers and Records*, 2 (1899), 94-102.

Morgan, J.C. *The Emigrant's Notebook and Guide, with Recollections of Upper and Lower Canada During the Late War.* London, 1824, 332-346. [lieutenant, Royal Marines]

Preston, Richard A., ed. "The Journals of Sir F.P. Robinson, G.C.B." *CHR* 37 (1956), 352-355.

[Procter, Henry and George] "Campaigns in the Canadas." *Quarterly Review* 27 (1822), 405-449.

[———]. *Defence of Major General Procter Tried at Montreal by a General Court-martial Upon Charges Reflecting His Character as Soldier.* Montreal, 1842.

[———]. *The Lucubrations of Humphry Ravelin, esq., Late Major in the xx Regiment of Infantry.* London, 1823. [staff]

"Battle of Stoney Creek." *Grimsby Historical Society Proceedings* No. 1 (1950), 57-59. [Officer of the 49th Foot]

[Sheaffe, Sir Roger] "Documents Relating to the War of 1812: The Letter Book of Sir Roger Hale Sheaffe [1812-1813]." *BHSP* 17 (1913), 271-381.

Temperly, Howard, ed. *Lieutenant Colonel Joseph Gubbins. New Brunswick Journals of 1811 & 1813.* Fredericton, 1980. [inspecting field officer of militia, New Brunswick]

"Truth". "Sir Roger Sheaffe and the Defence of York." *Anglo-American Magazine* 3 (1853), 565-566.

Tupper, Ferdinand B., ed. *The Life and Correspondence of Major General Sir Isaac Brock, K.B.* London, 1847.

Upham, C.W., ed. "The Capture of General Riall." *Historical Magazine* 1 (1872), 252-253. [Captain Richard Leonard, 104th Foot].

[Wood, James] "Plattsburgh, 1814." *WCHT* 5 (1905), 10-16. [captain, RA]

4.2 British Military (Other Theatres)

[Brown, David]. *Diary of A Soldier, 1805-1827; by David Brown, Sergeant, 21st Royal North British Fusiliers.* Ardrossan, n.d.

Chartrand, René, ed. "An Account of the Capture of Washington, 1814." *MCH* 37 (1985), 182. [Lieutenant David Dennear, Royal Artillery Drivers].

[Chesterton, George]. *Peace, War and Adventure: An Autobiography of George Laval Chesterton.* 2 vols, London, 1853. [captain, RA]

Cooke, John H. *A Narrative of Events in the South of France and the Attack on New Orleans in 1814 and 1815.* London, 1835. [captain, 43rd Foot]

Cooper, John S. *Rough Notes of Seven Campaigns in Portugal, Spain, France and America During the Years, 1809-10-11-12-13-14-15.* London, 1869, reprinted 1914. [sergeant, 7th Foot]

Dickson, Alexander. "Artillery Services in North America in 1814 and 1815." *JSAHR* 8 (1929), 79-113; 178-197; 213-227. [colonel, RA]

[Evans, George D]. *Facts Relating to the Capture of Washington.* London, 1829. [colonel, quartermaster general]

Ewart, James. *James Ewart's Journal, Covering His Stay at the Cape of Good Hope (1811-1814) and His Part in the Expedition to Florida and New Orleans I.*

Forrest, C.R. *The Battle of New Orleans – A British View: The Journal of Major C.R. Forrest, Asst. QM General, 34th Foot.* New York, 1961.

———. "Journal of Operations against New Orleans in 1814 and 1815." *LHQ* 44 (1961).

George, Christopher T. "The Family Papers of Major General Robert Ross, The Diary of Col. Arthur Brooke, and the British Attacks on Washington and Baltimore of 1814." *MHM* 88 (1993), 300-316.

Gleig, George R. *A Narrative of the Campaigns of the British Army* …. London, 1821. [lieutenant, 85th Foot]

———. "Letter of Mr. George R. Gleig." *Magazine of American History* 15 (1886), 508-509.

———. *The Campaigns of the British Army at Washington and New Orleans.* London, 1847, reprinted New York, 1972.

[Hill, Benson Earle] *Recollections of An Artillery Officer, Including Scenes and Adventures in Ireland, America, Flanders and France.* 2 vols, London, 1836. [captain, RA]

Holmes, J.D.L. "Robert Ross's Plan for the Invasion of Louisiana." *Louisiana History*, 5 (1964).

[Michell, John]. "Diary of Major J. Michell." *LHQ* 44 (1961), 127-130. [major, RA]

Moore-Smith, G.C. ed. *The Autobiography of Lieut. General Sir Harry Smith.* 2 vols, London, 1902.

[Mullins [sic], Thomas] *General Court Martial for Trial of Brevet Lieutenant-Colonel Thomas Mullens.* Dublin, 1815. [lieutenant-colonel, 44th Foot]

[Mullins [sic], Thomas]. "Court-Martial Held at the Royal Barracks, Dublin, For the Trial of Brevet Lieutenant Colonel Thomas Mullins." *LHQ* 9 (1926), 33-110.

Napier, William. *The Life and Opinions of General Sir Charles Napier, G.C.B.* London, 1857. [lieutenant-colonel, 102nd Foot]

Pakenham, Thomas, ed., *Pakenham Letters 1800-1815.* London, 1914.

Pakenham, Valerie. "Sir Edward Pakenham and the Battle of New Orleans." *Irish Sword* 9 (1975), 32-37.

[Pringle, Norman]. *Letters by Major Norman Pringle, Late of the 21st Royal Scots Fusiliers, Vindicating the Character of the British Army Employed in North America in the Years 1814-1815, From Aspersions Cast Upon it in Stuart's 'Three Years in North America'.* Edinburgh, 1834.

[Simpson, Robert] "The Battle of New Orleans." *Blackwood's Magazine* 24 (1828), 354-357. [captain, 43rd Foot]

Smith, G.C. Moore, ed. *The Autobiography of Lieutenant-General Sir Harry Smith, Baronet of Aliwal on the Sutlej G.C.B.* 2 vols, London, 1902.

Surtees, William. *Twenty-Five Years in the Rifle Brigade.* 1833, reprinted London, 1973. [quarter-master, 95th Foot]

Thornton, William. Diary in C.R.B. Barrett, ed., *The 85th King's Light Infantry.* London, 1913. [lieu-tenant-colonel, 85th Foot]

Verner, Willoughby, ed. "Diary of a Private Soldier in the Campaign of New Orleans." *Macmillan's Magazine* 77 (1908), 321-333. [Private John Timewell]

Wrottesley, George. *Life and Correspondence of Field Marshal Sir John Burgoyne.* 2 vols, London, 1873. [colonel, RE]

[Wylly, Edward E.]. *Pakenham Letters, 1800 to 1815.* London, 1914.

4.3 Canadian Military

Anderson, Thomas G. "Anderson's Journal at Fort McKay, 1814." *WHC* 9 (1882), 207-261. [captain, militia]

[———] "Personal Narrative." *WHC* 7 (1882), 137-260.

Anonymous. "An Account of the Expedition Against Fort Shelby on the Mississippi Undertaken in 1814, under the Command of Lieutenant Col. McKay, then Major of the Michigan Fencibles." *Canadian Magazine and Literary Repository* 4 (1825), 323-326, 400-405.

Anonymous. *The Battle of Frenchtown.* Detroit, 1937.

Carman, Francis A. "Chateauguay and De Salaberry: An Account of the Famous Campaign Taken from De Salaberry's Own Letters." *Canadian Magazine* 42 (1913), 22-28.

Carnochan, Janet, ed. "Col. Daniel MacDougal and Valuable Documents." *NHSP* 23 (1912), 26-41. [colonel, militia]

Casselman, A.C., ed. *Richardson's War of 1812.* Toronto, 1902. [Lieutenant John Richardson, 41st Foot]

Crooks, A.D. "Recollections of the War of 1812. From a manuscript of the late Hon. James Crooks." *WCHT,* 13 (1913-1914), 11-24.

Cruikshank, Ernest A., ed. "Reminiscences of Colonel Claus." *Canadiana* 1 (1889), 177-182; 2 (1890), 7-11, 24-28, 127-130, 203-206.

———, ed. "Campaigns of 1812-14: Contemporary Narratives by Captain W.H. Merritt, Colonel William Claus, Lieut.-Colonel Matthew Elliott and Captain John Norton." *NHST* 9 (1902).

———, ed. "Letters of 1812." *NHSP* 23 (1912), 42-47.

———, ed. "A Memoir of Colonel The Honourable James Kerby, His Life in letters." *Welland County Historical Society, Papers and Records* 4 (1931), 17-37.

———, ed. *Campaigns of 1812-1814: Contemporary Narratives by Captain W.H. Merritt, Colonel William Clause, Lieut.-Colonel Matthew Elliott and Captain John Norton.* Niagara, 1902.

[DeCew, John]. "Reminiscences of the Late Captain John DeCew." *Annual Transactions of the Empire Loyalists Association* 4 (1901), 93-99.

Edgar, Matilda. *Ten Years of Upper Canada in Peace and War, 1805-1815; Being the Ridout Letters with Annotations.* Toronto, 1890.

[Grignon, August]. "Seventy-Two Years' Recollections of Wisconsin." *WHC* 3 (1857), 107-295.

[Jarvis, Steven] in J.J. Talman, ed. *Loyalist Narrative From Upper Canada* Toronto, 1946, 251-259. [Adjutant General, Upper Canada Militia]

[Jarvis, William M.]. "Extracts from the Jarvis Papers." *WCHT* 5 (1905), 3-9. [private, Upper Canada militia]

[Kilborn, John]. "Biographical Sketch," in Thaddeus Leavitt, *History of Leeds and Grenville, Ontario, From 1749 to 1879,* Brockville, 68-71. [lieutenant, Incorporated Militia]

Lampman, John. "Memoirs of Captain John Lampman (1790) and his Wife Mary Secord (1797)." *Welland County Historical Society, Papers and Records,* 3 (1927), 126-134. [Incorporated Militia officer]

Land, John, ed. "Tales of the War: Queenston Heights." *Wentworth County Historical Society Journal and Transactions* 6 (1915), 59-63. [Privates George Hughson and Joseph Birney of the Upper Canada Militia]

"Lawe and Grignon Papers." *WHC* 10 (1888), 90-141.

McCollom, W.A. "McCollom Memories." *OHSPR* 6 (1909), 90. [militia private]

Merritt, William H. *Journal of Events Principally on the Detroit and Niagara Frontiers during the War of 1812.* St. Catharines, 1863. [captain, light dragoons]

Mills, George H., comp. "Documents Relating to the Battle of Stoney Creek." *Wentworth County Historical Society Papers*, vol. 2, 1899.

Neilson, J.L. Hubert, trans. *Reminiscences of the War of 1812-1814; Being Portions of the Diary of a Captain of the "Voltigeurs Canadiens" while in Garrison at Kingston, etc.* Kingston, 1895. [Captain Jacques Viger, Canadian Voltigeurs]

O'Sullivan, Michael, "An Eye Witness's Account." *Montreal Gazette*, 9 November 1813. [Canadian Voltigeur officer, Châteauguay, 1813]

Playter, Ely, diary in Edith Firth, ed. *The Town of York, 1793-1815*, Toronto, 1961. [captain, militia]

Quaife, Milo, ed. "Charles Askins' Journal of the Detroit Campaign, July 24 to September 12, 1812." in *The John Askins Papers*, Detroit, 1928 & 1931, vol. 2, 711-742. [militia officer]

Quaife, Milo M., ed. *War on the Detroit; The Chronicles of Thomas Verchères de Boucherville and The Capitulation by an Ohio Volunteer.* Chicago, 1940.

Ruttan, Henry, "Memoir" in James J. Talman, ed., *Loyalist Narratives from Upper Canada.* Toronto, 1946, 302-311. [Incorporated Militia Battalion]

[Slater, D.] "An Old Diary: Entries of D. Slater's Diary, Stoney Creek." *Wentworth Historical Society Transactions* 5 (1908), 31-33. [Upper Canada Militia]

Stacey, C.P. "Upper Canada at War: Captain Armstrong Reports." *OH* 48 (1956), 37-42. [captain, Nova Scotia Fencibles]

Sulté, Benjamin, ed. "Deux lettres écrites dans les tentes de Châteauguay." *Les Soirées canadiennes*, 4 (1864), 91-96. [Lieutenant Charles-Casimir Pinguet, Canadian Fencibles]

Thompson, Mabel W., ed., "Billy Green, the Scout." *OH* 44 (1942), 173-181.

Thwaites, Reuben G. "Dickson and Grigon Papers, 1812-1815." *WHC* 11 (1888), 271-315.

4.4 British and Canadian Naval: Great Lakes

Ellison, David, ed. "David Wingfield and Sacketts Harbour." *Dalhousie Review* 52 (1972), 407-13. [midshipman, RN]

Malcomson, Robert. "The Barclay Correspondence: More from the Man Who Lost the Battle of Lake Erie." *JES* 20 (Spring 1991), 18-35. [captain, RN]

———, ed., *Sailors of 1812: Memoirs and Letters of Naval Officers on Lake Ontario.* Youngstown, 1997. [James Richardson of the Provincial Marine]

Richardson, James. "Reminiscences of Lieut. James Richardson, Naval Officer during the War of 1812." *WCHT* 15 (1915-1916), 13-38.

Ritchie, M.K. and C., eds. "A Laker's Log." *Amer Nept* 17 (July 1957), 203-211. [Midshipman Frederick J. Johnston, 1813]

Snider, Charles H., ed. *Leaves From the War Log of the Nancy, Eighteen Hundred and Thirteen.* Toronto, 1936. [Alexander Mackintosh].

[Stockell, William]. *The Eventful Narrative of Captain William Stockell, Comprising An Authentic and Faithful Detail of His Travels in Different Countries.* Cincinnati, 1840. [lieutenant, RN, on Lake Ontario].

4.5 British and Canadian Naval: Other Waters

Anonymous ("Old Sub"). "Recollections of the Expedition to the Chesapeake and Against New Orleans in the Years 1814-1815." *Colburn's United Services Magazine* (April 1840), 443-456; (May, 1840), 25-36; (June 1840), 192-195; (July 1840), 337-352.

Anonymous. "We Must Fight Her." *United States Naval Institute Proceedings* 99 (March 1973), 90-93. [*United States* vs. *Macedonian*].

Anonymous. "Narrative of Naval Operations in the Potomac." *Colburn's United Services Magazine*, 53 (1833), 469-481.

Anonymous. "The War of 1812 Battle of the Patuxent (Two sides of the same war)." *Calvert Historian* 9 (1994), 7-20.

Barrett, Robert J. "Naval Recollections of the Late American War." *Colburn's United Services Magazine* (April 1841), 455-467; (May 1841), 13-23.

———. "A White Squall off the Chesapeake." *United Service Magazine*, Part 1 (January 1831), 57-59.

Bourchier, Lady. *Memoir of the Life of Admiral Sir Edward Codrington.* London, 1873.

Brindley, H.H., ed. "Loss of the Lapwing, Post Office Packet." *MM* 16 (January 1930), 18-47. [Ensign Henry Senior, 60th Foot]

A Curtailed Memoir of Incidents in the Life of John Surman Carden, Vice Admiral of the British Navy. Oxford, 1912. [Captain of HMS *Macedonian*]

Chaumier, Frederic. *The Life of a Sailor.* London, 1839. [Chesapeake, 1814]

Hayman, Henry, ed. "The Shannon and the Chesapeake." *United Service Magazine* 2 (October 1890), 9-16. [Midshipman G. Raymond, RN]

Hayman, Henry, ed. "Some Notes from New Orleans in 1814-15: From the Private Memoranda of an Eyewitness." [Notes of Midshipman G. Raymond, RN]

Holman, Louis A., ed. "The Log of a Canadian Privateer." *Canadian Magazine* 31 (September 1908), 435-440.

Hume, Edgar E., ed. "Letters Written During the War of 1812 By the British Naval Commander in American Waters." *WMQ* 10 (October 1930), 281-301. [correspondence of Vice-Admiral David Milne, 1811-1815]

Hussey, John A., ed. *The Voyage of the Raccoon: A "Secret" Journal of a Visit to Oregon.* San Francisco, 1958. [Pacific coast, 1813-1814].

Lingel, Robert, ed. "The Manuscript Autobiography of Gordon Gallie MacDonald." *New York Public Library Bulletin* 34 (March 1930), 139-147. [lieutenant, RN]

[Loftus, Charles]. *My Youth By Land and Sea from 1809 to 1816.* 2 vols, London, 1876.

[Lovell, William Stanhope]. *Personal Narrative of Events from 1799-1815, With Anecdotes.* London, 1879. [lieutenant, HMS *Melpomme*]

[Milne, David] "Letters Written During the War of 1812 by a British Naval Commander in American Waters." *WMQ* 10 (1930).

Murdock, Richard K., ed. "British Documents on the Stonington Raid." *Connecticut Historical Society Bulletin* 37 (July 1972), 65-75. [Captain Thomas Hardy, RN]

Napier, Edward H.D.E. *The Life and Correspondence of Admiral Sir Charles Napier.* 2 vols, London, 1862.

Napier, Henry E. *New England Blockade in 1814; The Journal of Henry Edward Napier ....* Salem, 1939.

[Nepture, W.J.] *The Life and Adventures of W.J. Neptune, Commonly Called General Jarvis, Written By Himself.* Hull, 1832.

Pouchin-Mold, Daphne D., ed. "What It Was Like to Be Shot Up By 'Old Ironsides.'" *American Heritage* 34 (April/May 1983), 65-67. [Alfred Strangeways in HMS *Cyane*]

[Roche, Douglas]. "Dockyard Reminiscences: An Account of the Action Between the Chesapeake and the Shannon." *NSHSC* 18 (1919), 59-67.

Rowbotham, W.B., ed. "Robert Fulton's Turtle Boat." *USNIP* 62 (December 1936), 1746-1749. [Captain, HMS *Maidstone*].

Rowley, Peter, ed. "Robert Rowley Helps to Burn Washington, D.C." *MHM* 82 (1987), 24-250; 83 (1988), 247-253. [Captain Robert Rowley, RN]

Scott, James. *Recollections of a Naval Life.* 3 vols, London, 1834.

Williams, Noel H. *The Life and Letters of Admiral Sir Charles Napier.* London, 1917.

4.6 Civilian

"The Surrender of Amelia." *FHQ* 4 (October, 1925), 90-95. [George F. Clarke]

Bickley, Francis, ed. *Historical Manuscripts Commission: Report on the Manuscripts of Earl Bathurst present at Cirencester Park.* London, 1923.

Broughton, Lord. *Recollections of a Long Life.* London, 1911.

Coffin, William F. *1812. The War and Its Moral: A Canadian Chronicle.* Montreal, 1864.

"Correspondence Between Hon. William Dickson, Prisoner of War, and General Henry Dearborn, 1813." *NHST* 28 (1916), 1-5.

Coues, Henry, ed. *New Light on the Early History of the Greater Northwest: The Manuscript Journals of Alexander Henry and David Thompson.* 3 vols, New York, 1897.

Coyne, James H., ed. "The Talbot Papers." *RSC,* (1907), 15-210.

Davis, Richard B. ed. *Jeffersonian American: Notes of the United States Collected in the Years, 1805-6-7 and 11-12 by Sir Augustus John Foster, Bart.* San Marino, 1954. [Diplomat].

———. ed. *Jeffersonian American: Notes of the United States Collected in the Years, 1805-6-7 and 11-12 by Sir Augustus John Foster, Bart.* San Marino, 1954. [diplomat]

Dickson, Robert. Thwaites, Reuben G. "Dickson and Grignon Papers, 1812-1815." *WHC* 11 (1888), 271-315.

"The Panton-Leslie Papers: Letters of Edmund Doyle, Trader." *FHQ* 16 (April 1938), 251-264.

[Franchere, Gabriel]. *A Voyage to the Northwest Coast of America.* New York, 1854.

Gellner, John, ed. *Recollections of the War of 1812: Three Eyewitness Accounts* . Toronto, 1964. [Patrick Finan]

Goulburn, Henry. Jones, Wilbur D., ed. "A British View of the War of 1812 and the Peace Negotiations." *MVHR* 45 (December 1958), 481-488.

Hall, Francis. *Travels in Canada and the United States, in 1816 and 1817.* London, 1818.

Harris, Amelia, "Memoir," in James J. Talman, ed. Loyalist *Narratives from Upper Canada. Toronto,* 1946, 144-148.

Howison, John. *Sketches of Upper Canada.* Edinburgh, 1821.

[Kemp, Andrew]. "Recollections of a Boy of 1812." *NHSP* 11 (1904), 1-6.

Klinck, Carl F. "Some Anonymous Literature of the War of 1812." *OH* 49 (1957), 49-60.

Moir, J.S. "An Early Record of Laura Secord's Walk." *OH* 51 (1959), 105-108.

Morrison, Robert, "What an Eye-Witness said of the Engagement and What Followed It." *Montreal Gazette,* 11 May 1895. [Châteauguay, 1813]

Murray, John M., ed. "A Recovered Letter: W.W. Baldwin to C.B. Wyatt, 6th April, 1813." *OHSPR* 35 (1943), 49-55. york

Parish, John C. ed. *The Robert Lucas Journal of the War of 1812 during the Campaign under General William Hull.* Iowa City, 1906.

Parker, D.W. "Secret Reports of John Howe 1808." *AHR* 17 (1911).

Quaife, Milo M. *The John Askins Papers.* 2 vols, Detroit, 1928-1931.

Raymond, W.O., ed. *Winslow Papers A.D. 1776-1826.* St. John, 1901.

[Reynolds, Squire] in William Coffin, *1812: The War and Its Moral: A Canadian Chronicle.* Montreal, 1864, 196-214 [commissariat, Ft. Malden]

Rives, George L., ed. *Selections From the Correspondence of Thomas Barclay. Formerly British Consul-General at New York.* New York, 1894.

Spragge, G.W. *The John Strachan Letter Book, 1812-1834.* Toronto, 1946.

Vane, Charles W., ed. *Correspondence, Despatches, and other Papers of Viscount Castlereagh.* 4 vols, London, 1848-1853.

[Vernon, J.B.]. *Early Recollections of Jamaica with Particulars of An Eventful Passage Home via New York and Halifax at the Commencement of the American War of 1812.* London, 1848.

5. PERIOD MILITARY REGULATIONS, MANUALS AND TREATISES

5.1 General Regulations and Orders

Great Britain, Adjutant-General. *General Regulations and Orders, 1st November 1804.* London, 1805.

———. *General Regulations and Orders for the Army.* London, 1811, reprinted 1970.

Great Britain. Admiralty. *Regulations and Instruction Relating to His Majesty's Service at Sea.* London, 1808.

Nova Scotia, Adjutant-General. *Rules and Articles for the better government of the Militia Forces of this Province, while embodied on actual service.* Halifax, 1812.

———. *Militia Law of the province of Nova Scotia, in force in the year of our Lord, 1813.* Halifax, 1813.

Prince Edward Island, Adjutant-General. *Militia General Order ... orders, rules and regulations ... to be strictly observed by the militia throughout Prince Edward Island ...* Charlottetown, 1814.

5.2 Authorized Tactical Manuals

Great Britain, Adjutant-General. *Rules and Regulations for the Formation, Field-Exercise, and Movements of His Majesty's Forces. London,* 1808.

———. *The Manual and Platoon Exercises.* Halifax, 1812.

———. *Rules and Regulations for the Cavalry.* London, 1795.

———. *Light Infantry Exercise: As ordered in His Majesty's Regulations for the Movements of the Troops.* London, 1797.

———. *General Orders and Observations on the Movements and Field Exercise of the Infantry, 1st September 1804 ....* London, 1805.

———. *Regulations for the Exercise of Riflemen and Light Infantry, and Instructions for their Conduct in the Field....* London, 1798.

Great Britain, Admiralty. *Regulations and Instructions Relating to His Majesty's Service at Sea, Established by His Majesty in Council.* London, 1808.

Jarry, Francois. *Instruction concerning the Duties of Light Infantry in the Field*. London, 1803.

Lower Canada, Adjutant General. *Rules and Regulations for the Militia Forces of Lower Canada*. Quebec, 1812.

Rottenburg, Francis de. *Regulations for the Exercise of Riflement and Light Infantry, and Instructions for their Conduct in the Field, 1st August 1798, with Plates and Music*. London, 1798.

5.3 Officers' Lists

Great Britain, Admiralty. *The Navy List*. London, 1812, 1813, 1814, 1815.

Great Britain, War Office. *A List of all the Officers of the Army and Royal Marines on Full and half-pay*. London,, 1812, 1813, 1814, 1815.

5.4 Technical Treatises and Literature

Adye, Ralph W. *The Bombardier and Pocket Gunner*. London, 1813.

Congreve, William. *The Details of the Rocket System*. London, 1814, reprinted Ottawa, 1970.

Cooper, T.H. *A Practical Guide for the Light Infantry Officer*. London, 1806, reprinted 1970.

James, Charles. *A New and Enlarged Military Dictionary, in French and English*. 2 vols, London, 1810.

———. *The Regimental Companion, Containing the Pay, Allowances and Relative Duties of Every Officer in the British Service*. 2 vols, London, 1811.

Naval Pocket Gunner; or; Compendium of Information Relating to Sea Service Gunnery, Including Proportions of Guns and Stores for Every Class of Ships and Vessels in the British Navy. London, 1814.

Smith, George. *An Universal Military Dictionary, Or A Copious Explanation of the Technical Terms &c. Used in the Equipment, Machinery, Movements, and Military Operations of an Army*. London, 1789.

II SECONDARY SOURCES

1 GENERAL WORKS

1.1 American Histories

Adams, Henry. *History of the United States during the Administration of James Madison*. 4 vols, New York, 1930.

Beirne, Francis F. *The War of 1812*. Hamden, 1965.

Elting, John. *Amateurs, to Arms! A Military History of the War of 1812*. Chapel Hill, 1991.

Heidler, David S. and Heidler, Jeanne T., eds. *Encyclopedia of the War of 1812*. Santa Barbara, 1997.

Hickey, Donald. *The War of 1812: A Forgotten Conflict*. Chicago, 1989.

Horsman, Reginald. *The War of 1812*. London, 1969.

Mahan, Alfred T. *Sea Power in Its Relations to the War of 1812*. 2 vols, London, 1905.

Mahon, John K. *The War of 1812*. Gainesville, 1972.

Quimby, Robert S. *The U.S. Army in the War of 1812. An Operational and Command Study*. 2 vols, East Lansing, Michigan, 1997.

Stagg, John. *Mr. Madison's War: Politics, Diplomacy, and Warfare in the Early American Republic*. Princeton, 1983.

Tucker, Glenn. *Poltroons and Patriots: A Popular Account of the War of 1812*. 2 vols, New York, 1954.

1.2 British and Canadian Histories

Auchinleck, Gilbert. *A History of the War between Great Britain and the United States in the years 1812-1814*. Toronto, 1855.

Berton, Pierre. *The Invasion of Canada, 1812-1813*. Toronto, 1980.

———. *Flames Across the Border, 1813-1814*. Toronto, 1981.

Caffrey, Kate. *The Twilight's Last Gleaming; The British Against America, 1812-1815*. London, 1977.

Christie, Robert. *The Military and Naval Operations in the Canadas, during the Late War with the United States ....* Quebec, 1818.

———. *History of the Late Province of Lower Canada, Parliamentary and Political ....* 5 vols, Quebec, 1848-1855.

Fortescue, John. *A History of the British Army*. Vols 7-10, London, 1911-1920.

Hannay, James. *History of the War of 1812 between Great Britain and the United States of America.* Toronto, 1905.

James, William. *A Full and Correct Account of the Military Occurrences of the Late War Between Great Britain and the United States of America.* 2 vols, London, 1818.

Lloyd, Alan. *The Scorching of Washington: The War of 1812.* London, 1975.

Lucas, Charles P. *The Canadian War of 1812.* Oxford, 1906.

Thompson, David. *History of the Late War between Great Britain and the United States of America.* Niagara, 1832.

Turner, Wesley B. *The War that Both Sides Won.* Toronto, 1990.

1.3. Essay Collections

Bowler, R. Arthur, ed. *War Along the Niagara: Essays on the War of 1812 and its Legacy.* Youngstown, 1991.

Mason, Philip. ed., *After Tippecanoe: Some Aspects of the War of 1812.* Toronto, 1963

Skaggs, David C. and W.J. Welsh, eds., *War on the Great lakes: Essays Commemorating the 175th Anniversary of the Battle of Lake Erie.* Kent, 1991.

Turner, Wesley B., ed. *The Military in the Niagara Peninsula.* St. Catharines, 1986.

Zazlow, Morris. *The Defended Border. Upper Canada and the War of 1812.* Toronto, 1964.

2. BIOGRAPHICAL ENCYCLOPEDIAS, REGISTERS, DIRECTORIES AND GUIDES

Askwith, W.H. *List of Officers of the Royal Regiment of Artillery from the Year 1716 to the Year 1899.* London, 1899.

Baillie, Laureen, ed. *American Biographical Index.* London, 1993.

Callahan, Edward,. ed. *List of Officers of the Navy of the United States and of the Marine Corps from 1775 to 1900.* Washington, 1901, reprinted New York, 1969.

Dictionary of Canadian Biography. Volumes V-IX, Toronto, 1976-1988

Dictionary of National Biography. 65 vols, London, 1885.

Gray, William. *Soldiers of the King. The Upper Canadian Militia 1812-1815. A Reference Guide.* Toronto, 1995.

Irving, L. Homfray. *Officers of the British Forces in Canada during the War of 1812-15.* Welland, 1908.

Lépine, Luc. *Les Officiers de milice du Bas-Canada, 1812-1815/Lower Canada's Militia Officers, 1812-1815.* Montreal, 1996.

Marshall, John, ed. *Royal Navy Biography.* 4 vols and 4 supplements, London, 1823-1835.

Morgan, Henry J. *Sketches of Celebrated Canadians, and Persons Connected with Canada.* Quebec, 1862.

O'Byrne, William R. *A Naval Biographical Dictionary.* London, 1849.

Philippart, John, ed. *The Royal Military Calendar, or Army Service and Commission Book, containing the Services and Progress of Promotions of the Generals, Lieutenant-Generals, Major-Generals, Colonels, Lieutenant-Colonels and Majors of the Army.* 5 vols, London, 1820.

Ralfe, J. *The Naval Biography of Great Britain.* 4 vols, London, 1828.

Robertson, H.H. "Some Historical and Biographical Notes on the Militia within the limits now constituting the County of Wentworth in the years 1804, 1821, 1830, 1838 and 1839 with the Lists of the Officers." *Journal and Transactions of the Wentworth County Historical Society* 4 (1905), 25-65.

Smith, D.B., ed. *The Commissioned Sea Officers of the Royal Navy, 1660-1815.* 3 vols, London, 1954.

Sutherland, Stuart. *His Majesty's Gentlemen. A Directory of British Regular Army Officers of the War of 1812.* Toronto, forthcoming.

3. THE ORIGINS AND DIPLOMACY OF THE WAR

Bartlett, C. J., "Gentlemen versus Democrats: Cultural Prejudice and Military Strategy in Britain in the War of 1812." *War in History* 1 (1994), 140-159.

Burt, Alfred L. *The United States, Great Britain and British North America from the Revolution to the Establishment of Peace after the War of 1812.* New York, 1961.

Carr, Albert H.Z. *The Coming of War: An Account of the Remarkable Events Leading to the War of 1812.* New York, 1960.

Clifford, Egan. "The Origins of the War of 1812." *MA* 38 (1974).

Cruikshank, E.A. *The Political Adventures of John Henry: the Record of an International Imbroglio.* Toronto, 1936.

Engelman, Fred L. *The Peace of Christmas Eve.* New York, 1962.

Gates, Charles M. "The West in American Diplomacy, 1812-1815." *MVHR* 26 (1940), 499-510.

Horsman, Reginald. "Western War Aims, 1811-1812." *IMH* 53 (1957), 1-18.

———. *The Causes of the War of 1812.* Philadelphia, 1962.

———. *The Diplomacy of the New Republic, 1776-1815.* Arlington Heights, 1985.

———. "On to Canada: Manifest Destiny and the United States in the War of 1812." *MIHR* 13 (1987), 1-24.

Jones, Wilbur D. "A British View of the War of 1812 and the Peace Negotiations." *MVHR* 45 (1958-1959), 481-487.

Manning, William R., ed. *Diplomatic Correspondence of the United States: Canadian Relations, 1784-1860.* 4 vols, Washington, 1912.

Perkins, Bradford, ed. *The Causes of the War of 1812: National Honour or National Interest?* New York, 1963.

Pratt, Julius. *Expansionists of 1812.* 1925, reprinted Gloucester, 1957.

Reuter, Spencer C. and Frank T. *Injured Honor: The Chesapeake-Leopard Affair, June 22, 1807.* Annapolis, 1996.

Selement, George. "Impressment and the American Merchant Marine, 1782-1812: An American View." *MM* 59 (1973), 409-418.

Stagg, John. "James Madison and the 'Malcontents': The Political Origins of the War of 1812." *WMQ*, October 1976.

———. "The Politics of Ending the War of 1812," in R.A. Bowler, ed., *War Along the Niagara. Essays on the War of 1812 and Its Legacy,* Youngstown, 1991, 93-104.

Strum, Harvey. *War Scare of 1807 and the Embargo.* Lockport, 1986.

Webster, C.K. *British Diplomacy, 1813-1815, Select Documents.* London, 1921.

———. *The Foreign Policy of Castlereagh, 1812-1815.* London, 1934.

4 THE WAR ON LAND

4.1 Higher Strategical Direction

Hitsman, John M. "Sir George Prevost's Conduct of the Canadian War of 1812." *CHAR* 1962, 34-43.

Kimball, Jeffrey. "Strategy on the Northern Frontier." PhD Thesis, University of Louisiana, Baton Rouge, 1969.

Mahon, John K. "British Command Decisions in the Northern Campaigns of the War of 1812." *CHR* 66 (1965), 219-237.

———. "British Command Decisions Relative to the Battle of New Orleans." *Louisiana History* 6 (1965).

Owsley, Frank L. "The Role of the South in British Grand Strategy of the War of 1812." *Tennessee Historical Quarterly* (1972), 22-35.

Roberts, Stephen G. "Imperial Policy, Provincial Administration as a Defence in Upper Canada, 1796-1812." DPhil. dissertation, Oxford University, 1975.

Stacey, C.P. "Halifax as an International Strategic Factor, 1749-1949." *CHAR*, 1949.

Turner, Wesley B. *British Generals in the War of 1812: High Command in the Canadas.* Montreal, 1999.

4.2 Logistics

Greenhous, Brereton, "A Note on Western Logistics in the War of 1812." *MA* 34 (1970), 41-44.

Kimball, Jeffrey, "The Fog and Friction of Frontier War: The Role of Logistics in American Offensive Failures during the War of 1812." *Old Northwest,* 5 (1979-1980), 323-343.

McKee, Marguerite M. "Service of Supply in the War of 1812: Organization for Supplying the Army in the War of 1812." *Quartermaster Review* 6, (1927), 53-76.

Risch, Erna. *Quartermaster Support of the Army: A History of the Corps, 1775-1939.* Washington, 1962.

Steppler, Glenn A. "A Duty Troublesome Beyond Measure: Logistical Considerations in the Canadian War of 1812." MA thesis, McGill University, Montreal, 1974.

Stickney, Kenneth. "Logistics and Communication in the 1814 Niagara Campaign." MA thesis, University of Toronto, 1976.

4.3 Campaigns

4.3.1 LOWER CANADA AND LAKE CHAMPLAIN THEATRE

Bilow, John. *Chateaugay, N.Y., and the War of 1812.* N.p., 1984.

Cruikshank, Ernest A. "From Isle aux Noix to Chateauguay. A Study of Military Operations on the Frontier of Lower Canada in 1812 and 1813." *RSC* 1 (1913), 129-173; 2 (1914), 25-102.

David, Laurent O. *Les Héros de Châteauguay.* Montreal, 1883.

Everest, Alan S. *The War of 1812 in the Champlain Valley.* Syracuse, 1981.

Guitard, Michelle. *The Militia of the Battle of the Châteauguay: A Social History.* Ottawa, 1983.

McKell, Wayne. "The Battle of Chateaugay." *Chateaugay Valley Historical Association Annual Report* 6 (1973), 81-86.

Sellar, Gordon. *The U.S. Campaign of 1813 to Capture Montreal.* Huntington, 1913.

Sulté, Benjamin. *La Bataille de Châteauguay.* Quebec, 1899.

Suthren, Victor. *The Battle of Châteauguay.* OPHA 11, Ottawa, 1974.

Wood, J.H. "Plattsburgh, 1814." *WCHT* 5 (1905), 10-16.

4.3.2 UPPER CANADA AND ADJACENT UNITED STATES TERRITORY

"The American Invasion, 1812-1813." *Canadian Antiquarian and Numismatic Journal* 7 (1879), 128-136.

Babcock, Louis. "The Siege of Fort Erie." *New York Historical Association Proceedings* 8 (1909), 38-59.

———. *The War of 1812 on the Niagara Frontier.* Buffalo, 1927.

Benn, Carl. *The Battle of York.* Belleville, 1984.

———. *Historic Fort York.* Toronto, 1993. [York, 1813]

Boeth, David J. "Battle of Sacket's Harbor." *Soldiers* 40 (1985), 44-45.

Boyd, John P. *Documents and Facts Relative to Military Events During the War.* Boston, 1816.

Boylen, J.C. "Strategy of Brock Saved Upper Canada: Candid Comments of a U.S. Officer Who Crossed at Queenston." *OH* 58 (1966), 59-60.

Buell, W.S. "Military Movements in Eastern Ontario during the War of 1812." *OH* 10 (1913), 60-71.

Coleman, Margaret. *The American Capture of Fort George.* HA 13, Ottawa, 1977.

Couture, Paul M. *A Study of the Non-Regular Forces on the Niagara Frontier, 1812-1814.* MFRS 193, Ottawa, 1985.

Cresswell, D.K.R. "A Near-Run Thing on the Niagara: The Battle of Lundy's Lane," in Corlene Taylor, ed., *Sharing Past and Future: Proceedings of the Ontario Genealogical Society,* Toronto, 1988, 33-56.

Croil, James. *Dundas, or, A Sketch of Canadian History.* Montreal, 1861. [Crysler's Farm, 1813]

Cruikshank, Ernest A. *The Fight in the Beechwoods.* Niagara, 1889. [Beaver Dams]

———. *The Battle of Queenston Heights.* Niagara Falls, 1891.

———. *The Battle of Lundy's Lane, 25th July, 1814.* Welland, 1893.

———. *Drummond's Winter Campaign 1813.* Niagara Falls, 1900. [Fort Niagara]

———. *The Siege of Fort Erie, August 1st – September 23d, 1814.* Welland, 1905.

———. "The County of Norfolk in the War of 1812." *Proceedings of the Ontario Historical Society,* 20 (1923), 9-40.

Elliott, James. *Billy Green and the Battle of Stoney Creek.* Hamilton, 1994.

Evans, Jack. "A Forgotten Battle of the War of 1812 [Sandy Creek]." *Magazine of American History* 29 (1893).

Fairlie Wood, Herbert. "The Many Battles of Stoney Creek." *CGJ* 64 (1962).

Frazer, John. "The Battle of Queenston Heights." *Magazine of American History* 24 (1890), 203-211.

Graves, Donald E. "William Drummond and the Battle of Fort Erie." *CMH* 1 (1992), 25-44.

———. *Redcoats and Grey Jackets. The Battle of Chippawa, 1814.* Toronto, 1994.

———. *Where Right and Glory Lead. The Battle of Lundy's Lane, 1814.* Toronto, 1997.

———. *Field of Glory: The Battle of Crysler's Farm, 1813.* Toronto, 1999.

Hitsman, John M. "Spying at Sackets Harbor, 1813." *IS* 15 (1959), 120-122.

Hough, Franklin B. *A History of St. Lawrence and Franklin Counties, New York.* Albany, 1853, reprinted Baltimore, 1970.

————. *A History of Jefferson County.* Albany, 1854.

Humphries, Charles W. "The Capture of York." *OH* 51 (1959), 1-21.

Hyatt, A.M.J. "The Defence of Upper Canada in 1812." MA thesis, Carleton University, 1961.

Kerr, W.B. "The Occupation of York (Toronto), 1813." *CHR* 5 (1924), 9-21.

Kimball, Jeffrey. "The Battle of Chippewa: Infantry Tactics in the War of 1812." *MA* 31 (1967-1968), 168-186.

Kirby, William. *Annals of Niagara.* Niagara Falls, 1896, reprinted 1972.

Kosche, Ludwig, "Relics of Brock: An Investigation." *Archivaria*, 9 (1979-1980).

Land, J.H. "The Battle of Stoney Creek." *Wentworth Historical Society* 1 (1892), 21-27.

Leslie, J.H. "Chrysler's [sic] farm, 11 November, 1813." *Journal of the Royal Artillery*, 63 (1936), 188-199.

Malcomson, Robert. "Upper Canada Preserved: Isaac Brock's Farewell to Arms, Queenston Heights 1812." *Beaver* 73 (1993), 4-15.

————. *The Battle of Queenston Heights.* Niagara-on-the-Lake, 1994.

————. "War on Lake Ontario: A Costly Victory at Oswego, 1814." *Beaver* 75 (1995), 4-13.

Mather, J.D. "The Capture of Fort Niagara, 19 December 1813." *CDQ* 3 (1925), 271-275.

McConnell, David. *The Location of the Site of the Battle of Beaver Dams.* RB 47, Ottawa, 1977.

Near, Irwin W. "The Causes and Results of the Failure of the American Campaigns on the Niagara Frontier in the Second War with England." *New York Historical Association Proceedings* 8 (1909), 91-102.

Oman, Charles. "How General Brock Saved Canada." *Blackwood's Magazine*, December 1912.

"Papers relating to the burning of Buffalo, and to the Niagara Frontier prior to and during the War of 1812." *BHSP* 9 (1906), 309-406.

Pringle, J.F. *Lunenburgh, or the Old Eastern District.* Cornwall, 1890.

Quaife, Milo M. *The Yankees Capture York.* Detroit, 1955.

Salisbury, George Cook. *The Battle of Chrysler's [sic] Farm, War of 1812-1814.* n.p., n.d. [c. 1955].

Scott, Winfield. *Memoirs of Lieut -General Scott, LL.D. Written by Himself.* 2 vols, New York, 1864.

Stacey, Charles P. "The Defence of Upper Canada, 1812" in C.P. Stacey, ed., *Introduction of the Study of Military History for Canadian Students*, Ottawa, 1960.

Walcot, Robert. "General Brock's Death." *Philadelphia Times*, 22 November 1880.

Way, Ronald. "The Day of Crysler's Farm." *CGJ* 62 (1961), 184-217.

Whitehorne, Joseph. *While Washington Burned: The Battle for Fort Erie, 1814.* Baltimore, 1992.

Whitfield, Carol. *The Battle of Queenston Heights.* OPHA 11, Ottawa, 1974.

Wilder, Patrick. *The Battle of Sackett's Harbour.* Baltimore, 1994.

Wright, Ross P. *The Burning of Dover.* Erie, 1948.

4.3.3 DETROIT FRONTIER, OLD NORTH WEST, MISSISSIPPI AND THE PACIFIC

Adventures of the First Settlers on the Oregon or Columbia River. London, 1849.

Allen, Robert S. "Canadians on the Upper Mississippi." *MCH* 31, (1979), 120. [Prairie du Chien]

Antal, Sandor. *A Wampum Denied: Procter's War of 1812.* Ottawa, 1997.

Bird, Harrison. *War for the West, 1790-1813.* New York, 1971.

Bourne, Alexander. "The Siege of Fort Meigs, Year 1813." *NOQ* 17 (1945), 139-154; 18 (1946), 39-48.

Bowlus, Bruce, "A 'Signal Victory:' The Battle for Fort Stephenson, August 1-2, 1813." *NOQ* 63 (1991), 43-57.

Carter-Edwards, Dennis. "The War of 1812 along the Detroit Frontier." *MIHR* 13 (1987), 25-30.

Couture, Paul M. *War and Society on the Detroit Frontier, 1791 to 1815.* MFRS 289, Ottawa, 1986.

Cruikshank, Ernest A. "Harrison and Procter: the River Raisin." *RSC* 4 (1910).

————. "The County of Norfolk in the War of 1812." *Proceedings of the Ontario Historical Society*, 20 (1923), 9-40.

Dudley, Thomas P. "Battle and Massacre at Frenchtown, Michigan, January 1813, by Rev. Thomas P. Dudley, One of the Survivors." *Western Reserve and Northern Ohio Historical Society Publications* 1, 1870.

Ermatinger, Charles. "The Retreat of Procter and Tecumseh." *OHSPR* 17 (1919), 11-21.

Evelyn, George J. "A Feather in the Cap? The Affair at River Canard, 16th July, 1812." *MCH* 39 (1987), 169-171.

Gilpin, Alec R. *The War of 1812 in the Old Northwest.* Toronto, 1958.

Hamil, Fred C. *Michigan in the War of 1812.* Lansing, 1969.

Kellogg, Louise P. "The Capture of Mackinac in 1812." *Proceedings of the State Historical Society of Wisconsin* (1912), 124-145.
Landon, Fred. *Western Ontario and the American Frontier.* Toronto, 1967.
Lauriston, Victor. "The Case for General Procter." *Kent Historical Society Papers and Records* 7 (1951).
Nelson, Larry L. *Men of Patriotism, Courage and Enterprize! Fort Meigs in the War of 1812.* Canton, 1985.
Pearkes, George R. "Detroit and Miami." *CDQ* 11 (1933), 456-466.
Poole, J.L. "The Fight at Battle Hill." *Transactions of the London and Middlesex Historical Society,* 1911-1912.
Russel, Nelson V. *The British Regime in Michigan and the Old Northwest, 1760-1796.* Northfield, 1939.
Spencer, Rex L. "The Gibraltar of the Maumee: Fort Meigs in the War of 1812." PhD. dissertation, Ball State University, 1988.
Wright, Ross P. *The Burning of Dover.* Erie, 1948.
Young, Bennett. *The Battle of the Thames.* Louisville, 1903.

4.3.4 NOVA SCOTIA AND MAINE
Copp, Walter R. "Nova Scotia and the War of 1812." MA thesis, Dalhousie University, 1935.
———. "Military Activities in Nova Scotia During the War of 1812." *NSHSC,* 24 (1938), 57-74.
Haliburton, Thomas C. *An Historical and Statistical Account of Nova Scotia.* 2 vols, Halifax, 1829.
Harvey, D.C. "The Halifax-Castine Expedition." *Dalhousie Review,* 18 (1938), 207-213.
MacNutt, W.S. *The Atlantic Provinces: The Emergence of Colonial Society.* Toronto, 1965.
Stanley, George F. "The Defence of the Maritime Provinces during the War of the French Revolution." *CDQ* 14 (1937), 437-447.
Trenholm, Donald T. "The Military defence of Nova Scotia during the French and American Wars (1789-1815)." MA thesis, Mt. Allison University, 1939.
Weeks, W.A., "Military History of Prince Edward Island," in D.A. MacKinnon and A.B. Warburton, eds., *Past and Present of Prince Edward Island,* Charlottetown, 1906, 327-343.

4.3.5 THE ATLANTIC SEABOARD
Anderson, Russell. *The British Raid on Essex, April 8, 1814.* Essex,
Brooks, Charles B. *The Siege of New Orleans.* Seattle, 1961.
Byron, Gilbert. *The War of 1812 in Chesapeake Bay.* Baltimore, 1964.
Carter, Samuel. *Blaze of Glory: The Fight for New Orleans, 1814-1815.* New York, 1971.
Coker, William S. "The Last Battle of the War of 1812: New Orleans, No. Fort Bowyer!" *Alabama Historical Quarterly* 43 (1981), 42-63.
Hadel, Albert Kemperly. "The Battle of Bladensburg." *MHM* 1 (1906), 155-167.
Huntsberry, Thomas V. *North Point, War of 1812.* Baltimore, 1985.
Lord, Walter. *The Dawn's Early Light.* New York, 1972.
Lynch, Frank C. "The Battle of Stonington in Retrospective: Its Strategy, Politics, and Personalities." *Stonington Historical Society Historical Footnotes* 1 (1964), 5-14.
Maguire, W.A. "Major General Ross and the Burning of Washington." *The Irish Sword* 14 (No. 55), 1-12.
Marine, William M. *The British Invasion of Maryland, 1812-1815.* Hatboro, 1965.
Mogilka, Gerard H. "The British Campaign in the Chesapeake during the latter part of August, 1814." MA thesis, De Paul University, 1975.
Muller, Charles G. *The Darkest Day: 1814, the Washington-Baltimore Campaign.* Philadelphia, 1963.
Murdock, Richard K. "The Battle of Stonington: A New Look." *Stonington Historical Society Historical Footnotes* 10 (1973), 1-3, 6-9.
Pitch, Anthony S., *The Burning of Washington: The British Invasion of 1814* (Annapolis, 1998).
Sheads, Scott. "Defending Baltimore in the War of 1812: Two Sidelights." *MHM* 84 (1989), 252-258.
Simmons, Edwin S. *The Rocket's Red Glare: The Maritime Defenses of Baltimore in 1814.* Centreville, 1986.
Stahl, John M. *The Invasion of the City of Washington, A Disagreeable Study in and of Military Unpreparedness,* Argos, 1918.
Whitehorne, Joseph. *The Battle for Baltimore, 1814.* Baltimore, 1997.

Williams, J.S. *History of the Invasion and Capture of Washington and of the Events Which Preceded and Followed.* New York, 1857.

4.3.6 FLORIDA AND LOUISIANA

Adams, Reed. "New Orleans and the War of 1812." *LHQ* 16 (1933), 221-234, 479-503, 681-703; 17 (1934), 169-182, 349-363, 502-523.

Brown, Wilburt S. *The Amphibious Campaign for West Florida and Louisiana, 1814-1815: A Critical Review of Strategy and Tactics at New Orleans.* Alabama, 1969.

Chidsey, Donald Barr. *The Battle of New Orleans.* New York, 1961.

Cox, Isaac J. *The West Florida Controversy, 1798-1813: A Study in American Diplomacy.* Baltimore, 1918.

Lord, Walter. *The Dawn's Early Light.* New York, 1972.

Owsley, Frank L. "Jackson's Capture of Pensacola." *AR* 19 (1966), 175-185.

———. *Struggle for the Gulf Borderlands.* Gainesville, 1981.

Patrick, Rembert W. *Florida Fiasco: Rampant Rebels on the Georgia-Florida Border, 1810-1815.* Athens, 1954.

Pickles, Tim. *New Orleans 1815. Andrew Jackson Crushes the British.* London, 1993

Rankin, Hugh F. "The British at New Orleans: Strategy or Blunder." *Louisiana Studies* 4 (1965), 179-186.

Reilly, Robin. *The British at the Gates. The New Orleans Campaign in the War of 1812.* New York, 1974.

Ricketts, Robert, "The Men and the Ships of the British Attack on Fort Bowyer – February 1815." *Gulf Coast Historical Review* 5 (1990), 7-17.

5 THE ARMIES AT WAR

5.1 General

Bruce, Anthony G. *The Purchase System in the British Army, 1660-1871.* London, 1980.

Blanco, Richard L. *Wellington's Surgeon-General: Sir James McGrigor.* Durham, 1974. [Medical practice and organization in the army]

Clode, Charles M. *The Military Forces of the Crown: Their Administration and Government.* 2 vols, London, 1869.

Glover, Michael. "Purchase, Patronage and Promotion in the Army at the Time of the Peninsular War." *Army Quarterly* 103 (1972-1973), 211-215, 355-362.

———. *Wellington as Military Commander.* London, 1973.

———. "The Purchase of Commissions: A Reappraisal." *JSAHR* 58 (1980), 223-235.

Glover, Richard. *Peninsular Preparation: The Reform of the British Army, 1795-1809.* Cambridge, 1963.

Gray, William. *Soldiers of the King. The Upper Canadian Militia 1812-1815: A Reference Guide.* Erin, 1995.

Oman, Charles. *Wellington's Army, 1809-1814.* London, 1912, reprinted 1986.

Pimlott, J.L. "The Administration of the British Army, 1783-1794." Unpublished PhD. dissertation, University of Leicester, 1975.

Sutherland, Stuart. *His Majesty's Gentlemen: A Directory of British Regular Army Officers of the War of 1812.* Publication forthcoming. [Staff organization and promotion patterns]

Ward, S.G.P. *Wellington's Headquarters: A Study of the Administrative Problems in the Peninsula, 1809-1814.* Oxford, 1957. [Staff organization]

Weigley, Russell F. *History of the United States Army.* New York, 1967.

5.2 Unit and Corps Histories

5.2.1 BRITISH UNITS AND CORPS

Barrett, C.R.B., ed. *The 85th King's Light Infantry.* London, 1913.

Biddulph, John. *The Nineteenth and their Times; being an Account of the Four Cavalry Regiments in the British Army that have borne the number Nineteen and of the Campaigns in which they Served.* London, 1899.

Brenton, J.M. *A History of the Royal Regiment of Wales (24th/41st Foot) and its Predecessors, 1689-1989.* Cardiff, 1989.

Brinckman, Rowland. *Historical Record of the Eighty-Ninth Princess Victoria's Regiment.* Chatham, 1888.

Buchan, John. *The History of the Royal Scots Fusiliers, 1678-1918.* London, 1925. [21st Foot]

Buckley, R.N. *Slaves in Red Coats: The British West India Regiments, 1793-1815.* New Haven, 1979.

Butler, L.W.G., and S.W. Hare. *The Annals of the King's Royal Rifle Corps.* 5 vols, London, 1913-1921, vol 3. [60th Foot]

Carter-Edwards, Dennis. *The Royal Artillery at Fort George, 1796-1812.* MFRS 246, Ottawa, 1986.

———. *The 41st (the Welch) Regiment 1700-1815.* MFRS 250, Ottawa, 1986.

Caulfield, J.E. *One Hundred Years' History of the 2nd Batt. West India Regiment from date of raising, 1795 to 1898.* London, 1899.

Cavendish, A.E. *An Reismeid Caitach, The 93rd Sutherland Highlanders, now 2nd Bn. The Argyll and Sutherland Highlanders (Princess Louise's) 1799-1927.* n.p., 1928.

Chartrand, René. "African-Americans Who Fought for the British." *Camp Stew* 9 (1996), 1-2.

Clark, James, comp. *Historical Record and Regimental Memoir of The Royal British Fusiliers ....* Edinburgh, 1885. [21st Foot]

Connolly, T.W.J. *The History of the Corps of Royal Sappers and Miners.* 2 vols, London, 1855.

Cope, William H. *The History of the Rifle Brigade.* London, 1877. [95th Foot]

Cotton, James. "His Majesty's Regiment de Meuron." *Calcutta Review,* vol 117 (1903), 192-234.

Cowper, L.I. *The King's Own, The Story of a Royal Regiment.* 2 vols, Oxford, 1939. [4th Foot]

Cunliffe, Marcus. *The Royal Irish Fusiliers, 1793-1950.* London, 1950. [89th Foot]

Duncan, Francis. *History of the Royal Regiment of Artillery.* 2 vols, London, 1873.

Ellis, A.B. *The History of the First West India Regiment.* London, 1885.

Elting, John R. "Those Independent Companies of Foreigners." *MCH* 40 (1988), 124-125.

Everard, H. *History of Thos. Farrington's Regiment, Subsequently Designated the 29th ....* Worcester, 1891. [29th Foot]

Everett, Henry. *The History of the Somerset Light Infantry (Prince Albert's), 1685-1914.* London, 1934. [13th Foot]

Field, Cyril. *Britain's Sea Soldiers: A History of the Royal Marines.* 2 vols, Liverpool, 1924.

Fraser, Edward and L.G. Carr-Laughton. *The Royal Marine Artillery 1804-1923.* London, 1930.

Haarman, Albert W. "The Independent Companies of Foreigners at Hampton, Virginia, June 1813." *MCH* 38 (1986), 178-179.

Hamilton, Henry B. *Historical Record of the 14th (King's) Hussars from A.D. 1715 to A.D. 1900.* London, 1901.

Hill, Maurice. "A Short History of the New South Wales Corps, 1789-1818." *JSAHR,* 13, (1935), 135-140. [102nd Foot]

Hitsman, John M. and Alice Sorby. "Independent Foreigners or Canadian Chasseurs." *MA* 25 (1961), 11-17.

Kendrick, N.C.E. *The Story of The Wiltshire Regiment (Duke of Edinburgh's); the 62nd and 99th Foot, 1756-1959.* Aldershot, 1960.

Kingsford, Charles L. *The Story of the Royal Warwickshire Regiment (formerly the 6th Foot).* London, 1921.

Koke, Richard J. "The Britons Who Fought on the Canadian Frontier." *NYHS Quarterly,* 45 (1961), 141-194.

Laws, M.E.S. *Battery Records of the Royal Artillery, 1716-1859.* Woolwich, 1952.

Leask, J.C., and H.M. McCance. *The Regimental Records of The Royal Scots (The First or The Royal Regiment of Foot).* Dublin, 1915.

Levinge, Richard G.A. *Historical Records of The Forty-Third Regiment, Monmouthshire Light Infantry ....* London, 1868.

Lomax, D.A.N. *A History of the Services of the 41st (the Welch) Regiment (now 1st Battalion The Welch Regiment) ... 1719 to 1895.* Devonport, 1899.

Martin, J.D.P. "The Regiment de Watteville: Its Settlement and Service in Upper Canada." *OH* 52 (1960), 17-30.

Muir, Augustus. *The First of Foot; the History of The Royal Scots (The Royal Regiment).* Edinburgh, 1961.

Newbolt, Henry. *The Story of the Oxfordshire and Buckinghamshire Light Infantry (The old 43rd and 52nd Regiments).* London, 1915.

Nicola, Paul H. *Historical Record of the Royal Marine Forces.* 2 vols, London, 1845.

Petre, Francis L. *The Royal Berkshire Regiment (Princess Charlotte of Wales). Vol. 1, 1743-1914.* Reading, 1925. [49th Foot]

Rioux, Christian. *The Royal Regiment of Artillery in Quebec City, 1759-1871.* HA 57, Ottawa, 1982.

Robertson, A.C. *Historical Record of The King's Liverpool Regiment of Foot ....* London, 1883. [8th Foot]

Sharpe, Tony. *Garrisons Stationed at Chambly, 1760-1869.* MRS 167, Ottawa, 1970.

Stewart, Charles, ed. *The Service of British Regiments in Canada and North America; A Resume.* Ottawa, 1964.

Threfall, T.R. *The Story of The King's (Liverpool Regiment) formerly the Eighth Foot.* London, 1917

Tylden, G. "The West India Regiments, 1795 to 1927, and from 1958." *JSAHR* 40 (1962), 42-49.

Weiss, John McNish. "The Corps of Colonial Marines, 1814-1815: A Summary." *Immigrants & Minorities* 15 (1996), 80-90.

Whitton, Frederick E. *The History of The Prince of Wales Leinster Regiment (Royal Canadians).* 2 vols, Aldershot, 1924. [100th Foot]

White, A.S. "Garrison, Reserve and Veteran Battalions." *JSAHR* 38 (1960), 156-167.

Wickes, H.L. *Regiments of Foot.* London, 1974.

Wylly, H.C. *History of the Manchester Regiment.* London, 1923 [97th Foot]

———. *The Loyal North Lancashire Regiment.* London, 1933. [10th Foot]

Yaples R.L. "The Auxiliaries: Foreign and Miscellaneous Regiments in the British army, 1802-1817." *JSAHR* 50 (1970), 10-28.

5.2.2. CANADIAN UNITS AND CORPS

Baldry, W.Y. and A.S. White. "The New Brunswick Fencibles – afterwards the 104th Foot." *JSAHR* 1 (1922), 90-92.

Baxter, John B. *Historical Records of the New Brunswick Regiment Canadian Artillery.* Saint John, 1896.

Boss, W. *The Stormont, Dundas and Glengarry Highlanders, 1783-1951.* Ottawa, 1952.

Chartrand, René. "Canadian Voyageurs During the War of 1812." *JSAHR* 72 (1994) 184-186.

——— and Eric Manders. "Upper Canadian Militia and Provincials, 1812 1815." *MCH* 28 (1976), 14 16.

——— and Eric Manders. "Lower Canada Select Embodied Militia Battalions, 1812-1815." *MCH* 31 (Fall 1979), 127.

Crowther, David R.F. "The New Brunswick Militia, 1784-1871." MA thesis, University of New Brunswick, 1965.

Cruikshank, Ernest A. *The Origin and Official History of the Thirteenth Battalion of Infantry and a Description of the Early Militia of the Niagara Peninsula in the War of 1812 and Rebellion of 1837.* Hamilton, 1899.

———. "Record of the Services of Canadian Regiments in the War of 1812" appearing in *SPCMI,* 1893 to 1916.

———. "I. The Royal Newfoundland Regiment." *SPCMI* 5 (1893-1894), 5-15.

———. "II. The Glengarry Light Infantry." *SPCMI* 9 (1897-1899), 70-80.

———. "III. The 104th Regiment." *SPCMI* 7 (1895-1896), 9-20.

———. "IV. The Provincial Cavalry." *SPCMI* 8 (1896-1897), 9-26.

———. "V. The Incorporated Militia." *SPCMI* 6 (1894-1895), 9-23.

———. "VI. The Canadian Voltigeurs." *SPCMI* 10 (1899-1900), 9-21.

———. "VII. The Canadian Fencibles." *SPCMI* 11 (1901), 9-22.

———. "VIII. The Frontier Light Infantry." *SPCMI* 12 (1902), 9-19.

———. "IX. The Lincoln Militia." *SPCMI* 13 (1904), 9-41.

———. "X. The Militia of Essex and Kent." *SPCMI* 14 (1906), 43-60.

———. "XI. The Militia of Norfolk, Oxford and Middlesex." *SPCMI* 15 (1907), 47-71.

———. "XII. The York Militia." *SPCMI* 16 (1908), 31-54.

———. "XIII. The Militia of the Eastern District." *SPCMI* 21 (1916), 69-98.

Edwards, Joseph P. *The Militia of Nova Scotia.* Halifax, 1913.

Facey-Crowther, David. *The New Brunswick Militia, 1787-1867.* Fredericton, 1990.

Fortier, Paul. "Fraser's Troop, Incorporated Provincial Light Dragoons in Upper Canada During the War of 1812." *Campaigns* 47 (1984), 42-48.

Henderson, Robert, "His Majesty's Canadian Regiment of Fencible Infantry, 1803-1816." *Military Illustrated* 37 (June 1991), 18-25; 38 (July 1991), 27-33.

Hitsman, John M. "Military Defenders of Prince Edward Island, 1775-1864." *CHAR* 1966, 25-37.

Howe, Jonas. "The King's New Brunswick Regiment, 1793-1802." *Collections of the New Brunswick Historical Society* 1 (1894), 13-62.

Legault, Roch. "Les aléas d'une carrière militaire pour les membres de la petite noblesse seigneuriale de la révolution américaine à la guerre de 1812-1815." MA thesis, University of Montreal, 1986.

———. "Les officiers de milice francophones (1760-1862), À l'oeuvre et à l'epreuve." *Cap-aux-Diamants* 43 (1995).

Lépine, Luc. "Non-francophone members of the Canadian Voltigeurs." *Connections*, September 1991.

———. "Officers of the Canadian Voltigeurs during the War of 1812." *Connections*, June 1992.

Maunsell, G.J. "The New Brunswick Militia." *New Brunswick Magazine*, 2 (1899).

Muir, J. Lloyd. "The New Brunswick Militia, 1787-1867." *Dalhousie Review*, 44, no. 3 (1964-1965), 333-338.

Nicholson, G.W.L. *The Fighting Newfoundlanders; a History of the Royal Newfoundland Regiment.* St. John's, 1964.

Ouellet, Fernand. "Officiers de milice et structure sociale au Québec, 1660-1815." *Histoire Sociale* 12 (1979).

Russell, Bill. *The 104th New Brunswick Regiment.* MRS 165, Ottawa, 1975.

Squires, W. Austin. *The 104th Regiment of Foot (The New Brunswick Regiment), 1803-1817.* Fredericton, 1962.

———. "The Trail of the 104th." *Atlantic Advocate*, 53 (1962).

Stanley, George F. "The Royal Nova Scotia Regiment, 1793-1802." *JSAHR* 21 (1942), 157-170.

———. "The Canadian Militia during the colonial period." *JSAHR* 24 (1946), 30-41.

———. "The Contribution of the Canadian Militia During the War." in Philip Mason, ed., *After Tippecanoe: Some Aspects of the War of 1812*, Toronto, 1963, 28-48.

Sulté, Benjamin. *Histoire de la milice canadienne-française, 1760-1897.* Montreal, 1897.

———. *A Thousand Young Men. The Colonial Volunteer Militia of Prince Edward Island. 1775-1874.* Charlottetown, 1990.

5.3 Tactics, Weapons, Uniforms and Equipment

"'Artillero Viejo', or, How to Fight Brother Jonathan." *Museum of Foreign Literature, Science and Art* 42 (1841), 210-214.

Bailey, De Witt. *British Military Longarms 1715-1865.* London, 1986.

Blackmore, Howard. *British Military Firearms, 1650-1850.* London, 1961.

Calver, William L. and Reginald Bolton. *History Written with Pick and Shovel.* New York, 1950.

Chartrand, René. *Canadian Military Heritage. Vol. II.* Ottawa, 1995.

——— and Jack L. Summers. *Military Uniforms in Canada 1665-1970.* Ottawa, 1981.

Darling, Anthony. *Red Coat and Brown Bess.* Ottawa, 1970.

Dunnigan, Brian L. *The British Army at Mackinac, 1812-1815.* Mackinac, 1980.

———. "To Make a Military Appearance. Uniforms of Michigan's Militia and Fencibles." *MIHR* 15 (1989), 29-43.

Gates, David. *The British Light Infantry Arm, c. 1790-1815: Its Creation, Training and Operational Role.* London, 1987.

Gooding, S. James. *An Introduction to British Artillery in North America.* Ottawa, 1965.

Graves, Donald E. *Sir William Congreve and the Rocket's Red Glare.* Bloomfield, 1989.

———. "Field Artillery of the War of 1812: Equipment, Organization, Tactics and Effectiveness." *AC* 30 (1992), 39-48.

Grazebrook, R.M. "The Wearing of Equipment, 1801." *JSAHR* 24 (1946), 38.

Griffith, Paddy. *Forward into Battle: Fighting Techniques from Waterloo to Vietnam.* Strettington, 1981.

Greener, William. *The Gun; or, A Treatise on the Various Descriptions of Small Fire-Arms.* London, 1835.

Haythornewaite, Philip. *Weapons and Equipment of the Napoleonic Wars.* Poole, 1979.

Hofschromb, Peter. "Flintlocks in Battle." *Military Illustrated* 1 (1986), 29-36.

Hughes, B.P. *British Smooth-Bore Artillery. The Muzzle-Loading Artillery of the 18th and 19th Centuries.* London, 1969.

———. *Firepower: Weapons Effectiveness on the Battlefield, 1630-1850.* London, 1974.

———. *Open Fire: Artillery Tactics from Marlborough to Wellington.* Strettington, 1983.

McConnell, David. *British Smooth-Bore Artillery: A Technological Study to Support Identification, Acquisition, Restoration, Reproduction, and Interpretation of Artillery at National Historic Sites in Canada.* Ottawa, 1988.

Milne, Samuel. *The Standards and Colours of the Army from the Restoration, 1661 to the Introduction of the Territorial System.* Leeds, 1893.

Muir, Rory. *Tactics and the Experience of Battle in the Age of Napoleon.* New Haven, 1998.

Nosworthy, Brent. *Battle Tactics of Napoleon and His Enemies.* London, 1995.

Priest, Graham. *The Brown Bess Bayonet.* Norwich, 1986.

Reid, Stuart and Graham Turner. *British Redcoat (2), 1793-1815.* London, 1998.

Robson, Brian. *Swords of the British Army: The Regulation Patterns.* London, 1975.

Winter, Frank H. *The First Golden Age of Rocketry.* Washington, 1990.

5.4 Life of the Soldier

Brett-James, Anthony. *Life in Wellington's Army.* London, 1972.

Burroughs, Peter. "Tackling Army Desertion in British North America." *CHR,* 61 (1980), 28-68.

Carter-Edwards, Dennis. *Men at Work: Military and Civilian Artificers at Niagara.* MFRS 290, Ottawa, 1985.

———. *At Work and Play: The British Junior Officer in Upper Canada, 1796-1812.* MFRS 291, Ottawa, 1985.

De Watteville, H. *The British Soldier: His Daily Life from Tudor to Modern Times.* London, 1954.

Glover, Michael. *Wellington's Army in the Peninsula, 1808-1814.* Newton Abbot, 1977. [Military daily life]

Graves, Donald E. *Fort George Historical Study.* MRS 353, Ottawa, 1979.

Guitard, Michelle. *The Militia of the Battle of Châteauguay. A Social History.* Ottawa, 1981.

Hare, John S. "Military Punishments in the War of 1812." *Journal of the American Military Institute* 4 (1940), 225-239.

Lacelle, Claudette. *The British Garrison in Quebec City as Described in Newspapers from 1760-1840.* HA 23, Ottawa, 1979.

Lépine, Luc. "Les cours martiales durant la guerre de 1812." *Cap-aux-Diamants* 43 (1995).

Massicotte, Etienne-Zodiac. "Chansons militaires de 1812." *Bulletin des récherches historiques* 25 (1911), 188-191.

Oman, Charles. *Wellington's Army, 1809-1814.* London, 1913, reprinted 1986.

Price, Karen. *Glimpses of Soldiering at Coteau-du-Lac, 1780-1856.* HA 15, Ottawa, 1977.

Rioux, Christian. *The British Garrison at Quebec 1759-1871.* Ottawa, 1996.

Whitfield, Carol. *Tommy Atkins: The British Soldier in Canada, 1759-1870.* Ottawa, 1981.

Winstock, Lewis. *Songs and Music of the Redcoats, 1642-1902.* London, 1972.

5.5. Military Fortifications, Architecture and Archaeology

Allen, Robert S. *A History of Fort George, Upper Canada.* OPHA 11, Ottawa, 1974.

Ashworth, Michael J. *Fort St. Joseph.* MRS 35, Ottawa, 1971.

Baker, Raymond F. *Early Citadels at Halifax, 1749-1815.* MRS 107, Ottawa, 1970.

Bayliss, Joseph and Estelle. *Historic St. Joseph Island.* Cedar Rapids, 1938.

Benn, Carl. *Historic Fort York, 1793-1993.* Toronto, 1993.

Burns, Robert J. *Fort Wellington: A Narrative and Structural History, 1812-1838.* MRS 296, Ottawa, 1979.

Cadieux, Pierre-B. *Les Constructions militaires du Haut-Richelieu.* St. Jean-sur-Richelieu, 1977.

———. *Le Fort Lennox.* St. Jean-sur-Richelieu, 1986.

Charbonneau, André. *The Fortifications of Ile aux Noix: A Portrait of the Defensive Strategy on the Upper Richelieu Border in the 18th and 19th Centuries.* Ottawa, 1994.

Dendy, J.O. "The Fortifications of Kingston, 1790-1850: Plans and Commentaries." Honours BA thesis, Royal Military College of Canada, 1964.

Desloges, Yvon. *Structural History of Fort George.* MRS 189, Ottawa, 1977.

Eames, F. "Gananoque Block House, 1813-1859." *OHSPR* 32 (1937), 85-91.

Flemming, David. *Fort Mississauga, Ontario (1814-1972).* HA 37, Ottawa, 1982.

Guitard, Michelle. *La Camp militaire de Chambly (1812-1869).* MRS 416, Ottawa, 1980.

Hooper, Thomas. *The Royal Navy Station at Isle-aux-Noix (1812-1839).* MRS 167, Ottawa, 1970.

Ingram, George. *A Narrative History of the Fort at Coteau-du-Lac.* MRS 186, Ottawa, 1977.

———. *The Fort at Coteau-du-Lac: Structures and Other Features.* MRS 186, Ottawa, 1977.

Lee, David E. *Ile-aux-Noix: 1759-1870.* MRS 40, Ottawa, 1965.

———. *The Fort on St. Joseph's Island.* MRS 131, Ottawa, 1969.

———. *Preliminary Report on Fort Malden, Amherstburg, Ontario.* MRS 157, Ottawa, 1974.

———. *Fort Wellington: A Structural History.* HA 8, Ottawa, 1976.

Lindo, Patrick Richard. "The History of the Fredericton Military Compound." MA thesis, University of New Brunswick, 1965.

McConnell, David. *A Study of the British Military Buildings at Niagara-on-the-Lake, 1814-1837.* MRS 191, Ottawa, 1977.

Mecredy, Stephen D. "Crisis Confronting Construction: The History of Point Henry During the War of 1812." *HK* 33 (1984), 3-14.

Owen, David. *Fort Erie (1764-1823). An Historical Guide.* Fort Erie, 1986.

Piers, Harry. *The Evolution of the Halifax Fortress, 1749-1928.* Halifax, 1947.

Ray, Frederic. *Old Fort Niagara, An Illustrated History.* Youngstown, 1988.

Saunders, Ivan. *A History of Martello Towers in the Defence of British North America, 1796-1871.* OPHA 15, Ottawa, 1976.

Stanley, George F. "Historic Kingston and its Defences." *OH* 46 (1954), 21-35.

Steppler, Glenn A. *Quebec, The Gibraltar of North America?* MRS 224, Ottawa, 1976.

Vincent, Elizabeth. *Fort St. Joseph: A History.* MRS 335, Ottawa, 1978.

Way, Ronald L. "Defence of the Niagara Frontier, 1764-1870." MA thesis, Queen's University, Kingston, 1938.

Young, Richard J. *Blockhouses in Canada, 1749-1841: A Comparative Report and Catalogue.* OPAH 23, Ottawa, 1980.

5.6 Medals, Awards and Battle Honours

Blatherwick, F.J. *Canadian Orders, Decorations and Medals.* Toronto, 1994.

Irwin, R.W. *War Medals and Decorations of Canada.* Toronto, 1969.

Jocelyn, Arthur. *Awards of Honour.* London, 1956.

Long, W.H. *Medals of the British Navy and How They were Won.* London, 1895.

McCall, Clayton W. "A British Medal of Michigan Interest." *Michigan History* 29 (1945), 51-58.

Mullen, A.L.T. *The Military General Service Roll, 1793-1814.* London, 1990.

Norman, C.B. *Battle Honours of the British Army from Tangier 1662, to the Commencement of the Reign of Edward VII.* London, 1911.

Payne, A.A. *British and Foreign Orders, War Medals and Decorations.* Sheffield, 1911

Tancred, G. *Historical Record of Medals and Honorary Distinctions.* London, 1891.

Wilson, Barbara. *Military General Service Medal 1793-1814 (Canadian Regiments), Egypt Medal 1882-1889 (Canadian Recipients), North West Canada 1885.* London, 1975.

6 THE NAVAL WAR OF 1812

6.1 General Naval Histories

Brenton, Edward P. *The Naval History of Great Britain from the Year 1783 to 1836.* London, 1837.

Clowes, William, ed. *A Naval History of Great Britain from the Earliest Times to the Present.* 7 vols, London, 1901, volume 6.

Gardiner, Robert, ed. *The Naval War of 1812.* London, 1998.

James, William. *The Naval History of Great Britain from the Declaration of War by France in 1793 to the Accession of George IV.* London, 1902.

Lewis, Michael. *The History of the British Navy.* London, 1957.

Little, C.H. "Naval Activities on the Lakes: Past and Present." *CGJ* 67 (1963), 202-215.

Mahan, Alfred T. *Sea Power in its Relations to the War of 1812.* 2 vols, London, 1902.

Maloney, Linda. "The War of 1812: What Role for Sea Power?" in Kenneth J. Hagan, ed., *In War and Peace: Interpretations of American Naval History, 1775-1978,* Westport, 1978.

Naval Chronicle for 1812 … 1813 … 1814 … 1815. London, 1812-1815.

Roosevelt, Theodore. *The Naval War of 1812.* Annapolis, 1987.

Stacey, Charles P. "Naval Power on the Lakes," in Philip P. Mason, ed., *After Tippecanoe: Some Aspects of the War of 1812* (Toronto, 1963), 49-59.

6.2 Naval Command and Control

Douglas, W.A.B. "The Anatomy of Naval Incompetence: The Provincial Marine in Defence of Upper Canada before 1813." *OH* 71 (March, 1979), 3-25.

Drake, Frederick. "Commodore Sir James Lucas Yeo and Governor General George Prevost: A Study in Command Relations, 1813-14," in William B. Cogar, ed., *New Interpretations in Naval History: Selected Papers from the Eighth Naval History Symposium,* Annapolis, 1989, 156-171.

Lohnes, Barry. "British Naval Problems at Halifax during the War of 1812." *MM,* 59 (1973), 317-333.

6.3 Naval Operations and Engagements

6.3.1 LAKE CHAMPLAIN

Bellico, Russell P. *Sails and Steam in the Mountains: A Maritime and Military History of Lake George and Lake Champlain.* New York, 1992.

Bredenberg, Oscar. *The Battle of Plattsburgh Bay, The British Navy's View.* Plattsburgh, 1978.

Heinrichs, W.H. "The Battle of Plattsburgh – the Losers." *Amer Nept* 21 (January 1961), 42-56.

Milgram, James W., "Battle of Lake Champlain Mementos." *Manuscripts* 43 (1991), 106-116.

6.3.2 LAKE ONTARIO AND THE ST. LAWRENCE

Cruikshank, Ernest A. "The Contest for the Command of Lake Ontario in 1812 and 1813." *Transactions of the Royal Canadian Institute* 6 (1899), 75-126; 10 (1916), 161-223.

———. "The Contest for the Command of Lake Ontario in 1814." *OHSPR* 21 (1924), 99-159.

Hitsman, J. Mackay. "Alarum on Lake Ontario, Winter 1812-1813. *MA* 23 (1959), 129-138.

Malcomson, Robert. "War on Lake Ontario: A Costly Victory on Lake Ontario." *Beaver* 75 (1995), 4-13.

———. *Lords of the Lake; The Naval War on Lake Ontario, 1812-1814.* Toronto, 1998.

Malcomson, Thomas. "September, 1813: The Decidedly Indecisive Engagements between Chauncey and Yeo." *IS* 47 (1991), 299-313.

———. "Muster Table for the Royal Navy's Establishment on Lake Ontario during the War of 1812." *Northern Mariner* 9 (1999), 41-68.

Nelson, Dan. "Sinking of the Hamilton and Scourge: How Many Men were Lost?" *Freshwater* 2 (1987), 4-7.

Palmer, Richard F. "The Captures of the Schooner *Julia/Confiance.*" *Amer Nept* 51 (1991),83-90.

Stacey, Charles P. "Commodore Chauncey's Attack on Kingston, November 10, 1812." *CHR* 32 (1961), 126-138.

6.2.2 LAKE ERIE AND THE UPPER LAKES

Altoff, Gerard T. and David Skaggs. *A Signal Victory: The Lake Erie Campaign, 1812-1813.* Annapolis, 1997.

Burt, A. Blanche. "Captain Robert Heriot Barclay, R.N." *OH* 14 (1916), 169-178.

Buckie, Robert. "His Majesty's Flag Has Not Been Tarnished: The Role of the Robert Heriot Barclay." *JES* 17 (1988), 85-102.

Cruikshank, Ernest A. "The Context for the Command of Lake Erie in 1812-1813." *Transactions of the Royal Canadian Institute* 6 (1899).

———. "An Episode of the War of 1812: the Story of the Schooner *Nancy.*" *OHSPR* 9 (1908).

Dillon, Richard. *We Have Met the Enemy.* Toronto, 1978.

Drake, Frederick C. "A Loss of Mastery: The British Squadron on Lake Erie, May-September, 1813." *JES* 17 (1988), 47-75.

Jury, Elsie M. "USS Tigress – HMS Confiance, 1813-1831." *IS* 28 (1972), 3-16.

Malcomson, Robert, "Controversial Relationships among the British before and after the Battle of Lake Erie." *IS* 46 (1990), 187-197.

———. "The Crews of the British Squadrons at Put-in-Bay: A Composite Muster Roll and its Insights." *JES* 20 (1991), 18-35.

————. "The Barclay Correspondence: More from the Man Who Lost the Battle of Lake Erie." *JES* 20 (1991), 18-35.

————. "George Inglis: Insights About the Man Who Hauled Down the British Flag at Put-In-Bay." *JES* 24 (1995), 71-80.

Malcomson, Robert and Thomas. *HMS Detroit: The Battle for Lake Erie.* Annapolis, 1991.

Saunders, Robert. *Newfoundland's Role in the Historic Battle of Lake Erie.* Poole, 1954.

Stacey, Charles P. "Another Look at the Battle of Lake Erie." *CHR* 39 (1958).

Stevens, John R. *The Story of HM Armed Schooner Tecumseh.* Halifax, 1961.

Welsh, Jeffrey William and David Curtis Skaggs. eds. *War on the Great Lakes: Essays Commemorating the 175th Anniversary of the Battle of Lake Erie.* Kent, 1991.

6.2.3 THE HIGH SEAS

Barnes, J. *Naval Actions of the War of 1812.* New York, 1896.

Carr, H.J. "Naval History of Bermuda." *Bermuda Historical Quarterly,* 8 (1951).

Collins, F. "The Chesapeake and the Shannon, June 1, 1813." *United Service Journal,* October 1879.

Crosse, John, comp., "The arrival of the *Chesapeake* in Halifax in 1813 as described by Thomas Haliburton ('Sam Slick')." *Amer Nept* 57 (1997), 161-165.

De Kay, James T. *The Battle of Stonington: Torpedoes, Submarines and Rockets in the War of 1812.* Annapolis, 1990.

————. *Chronicles of the Frigate Macedonian: 1809-1922.* New York, 1995

Dennis, D.L. "The Action between the Shannon and the Chesapeake." *MM* 45 (1959).

Dye, Ira. *The Fatal Cruise of the Argus: Two Captains in the War of 1812.* Annapolis, 1994.

Garbett, H. "The Shannon and the Chesapeake." *Royal United Service Institute Journal,* 1913.

James, William. *An Inquiry into the Merits of the Principal Naval Actions between Great Britain and the United States.* Halifax, 1816.

Martin, Tyrone G. *A Most Fortunate Ship: A Narrative History of "Old Ironsides".* Chester, 1980.

Macmechan. A.M. "The Glory of the Shannon." *Canadian Magazine,* 32 (1913).

McCleary, J. R., "Lost by Two Navies: HMS *Epervier,* a most un-fortunate ship." *Nautical Research Journal* 41 (1996), 81-87, 131-141.

Poolman, K. *Guns off Cape Ann.* London, 1961. [Shannon vs. Chesapeake]

Pullen, Hugh F. *The Shannon and the Chesapeake.* Toronto, 1970.

Ralph, James J., ed. *Naval Chronology of Great Britain ... 1803-1815.* 3 vols, London, 1820.

Snider, C.J.H. *The Glorious 'Shannon's' Old Blue Duster and other Faded Flags of Fadeless Fame.* Toronto, 1923.

Squires, W. Austin. "War in the Bay of Fundy, 1812." *Atlantic Advocate,* 53 (1963).

6.2.4 PRIVATEERS

Cruikshank, Ernest A. "Colonial Privateers in the War of 1812." *Canadiana* 1 (1889), 129-137.

————. "Cruises of a Nova Scotia Privateer." *Canadiana* 1 (1889), 81-86.

Kert, Faye M. *Prize and Prejudice: Privateering and Naval Prize in Atlantic Canada in the War of 1812.* St. John's, 1997.

Snider, C.J.H. *Under the Red Jack.* Toronto, 1928.

Stewart, J. *Reports of cases, argued and determined in the Court of Vice-Admiralty at Halifax, in Nova Scotia ... in the time of Alexander Croke.* London, 1814.

Vice-Admiralty Court, Halifax. American Vessels Captured by the British during the Revolution and the War of 1812. Salem, 1911.

6.3 Naval Construction and Armament

Amer, Christopher F. *The Brown's Bay Vessel: Its Design and Construction.* RB 307, Ottawa, 1994.

Beattie, Judith. *Gunboats on the St. Lawrence River (1763-1839).* MRS 15, Ottawa, 1967.

Breithaupt, William H. "Some facts about the schooner 'Nancy' in the War of 1812." *OHSPR* 23 (1926), 5-7.

Brunelle, David. "H.M.S. Nancy and the War of 1812." *Camp Stew* 9 (1996), 3-8.

Cain, Emily. "Building the Lord Nelson." *IS* 41 (1985), 121-129.

Colledge, James J. *The Ships of the Royal Navy, An Historical Index.* 2 vols, Annapolis, 1987-1988.

Congreve, William. *An Elementary Treatise on the Mounting of Naval Ordnance.* London, 1811, reprinted Ottawa, 1970

Crisman, Kevin. *The Eagle: An American Brig on Lake Champlain during the War of 1812.* Annapolis, 1987.

———. *The Jefferson: The History and Archaeology of an American Brig from the War of 1812.* Ann Arbor, 1989.

Donaldson, Gordon. "When Kingston Built the World's Mightiest Ships." *CGJ* 103 (1984), 55-61.

Hogg, Ian and John Batchelor. *Naval Gun.* Poole, 1978.

Lavery, Brian. *The Arming and Fitting of English Ships of War, 1600-1815.* Annapolis, 1987.

———. *Nelson's Navy: The Ships, Men and Organization, 1793-1815.* London, 1989.

Lord, Barry. "Two Armed Schooners from the War of 1812." in David L. Materson, ed., *Naval History: The Sixth Symposium of the United States Naval Academy,* Wilmington, 1987, 354-358.

Malcomson, Robert. "Gunboats on Lake Ontario in the 1812 War." *Seaways: Ship in Scale* 7 (1996), 1:31-38; 2:27-31; 3:40-44.

———. "Xebecs for the Great Lakes War." *Model Ship Builder* 101 (1996), 51-4

———. "HMS *St. Lawrence*: The Freshwater First-Rate." *MM* 83 (1997), 419-33.

Malcomson, Thomas. "HMS *Psyche*: A Frigate in Frame." *Seaways' Ships in Scale* 4 (1993), 16-21.

Nelson, Daniel. "Ghost Ships of the War of 1812." *National Geographic* 163 (1983), 288-313.

Padfield, Peter. *Guns at Sea.* New York, 1974.

Robertson, F.L. *The Evolution of Naval Armament.* London, 1968.

Snider, Charles H. "Recovery of H.M.S. Tecumseth." *OH* 46 (1954), 97-105.

Stacey, Charles P. "The Ships of the British Squadron on Lake Ontario, 1812-1814." *CHR* 34 (December 1953), 311-323.

Stevens, John R. "HM Provincial Marine Schooner 'General Hunter'." *Nautical Research Journal* 3 (1952), 125-127.

Tucker, Spencer C. "The Carronade." *USNIP* 99 (1973), 65-70.

———. "Mr. Jefferson's Gunboat Navy." *Amer Nept* 43 (1983), 135-141.

———. "U.S. Navy Gun Carriages from the Revolution Through the Civil War." *Amer Nept* 47 (1987), 108-118.

———. *Arming the Fleet: U.S. Navy Ordnance in the Muzzle-Loading Era.* Annapolis, 1989.

———. *The Jeffersonian Gunboat Navy.* Columbia, 1993.

Winton-Clare, C. "A Shipbuilder's War." *MM* 29 (1943).

Wishart, Bruce. "Sir James Yeo and the St. Lawrence: 'A Remarkably Fine Ship,' Sea-Dogs at War, 1812-1814." *Beaver* 72 (1992), 12-22.

6.4 The Life of Sailors

Byrn, John D. *Crime and Punishment in the Royal Navy: Discipline on the Leeward Islands Station, 1784-1812.* Aldershot, 1989.

Claver, Scott. *Under the Lash: A History of Corporal Punishment in the British Armed Forces.* London, 1954.

Lavery, Brian. *Nelson's Navy: The Ships, Men, and Organization, 1793-1815.* Annapolis, 1994.

Lewis, Michael. *A Social History of the Royal Navy, 1793-1815.* London, 1960.

Pope, Dudley. *The Black Ship.* London, 1963.

7 THE FIRST NATIONS AND THE WAR OF 1812

7.1 General

———. *His Majesty's Indian Allies: British Indian Policy in the Defence of Canada, 1774-1815.* Toronto, 1992.

Calloway, Colin G. *Crown and Calumet: British-Indian Relations, 1763-1815.* Norman, 1987.

Chalou, George C. "The Red Pawns Go To War." PhD. dissertation, Indiana University, 1971.

Cruikshank, Ernest A. "The Employment of Indians in the War of 1812." *Annual Report of the American Historical Association for the year 1895* (1895).

Debo, Angie. *The Road to Disappearance.* Norman, 1941.

Dowd, Gregory Evans. *A Spirited Resistance. The North American Indian Struggle for Unity, 1745-1815.* Baltimore, 1992.

Gilman, Carolyn. *When Two Worlds Meet: The Great Lakes Fur Trade.* St. Paul, 1982.

Hatheway, G.G. "The Neutral Indian Barrier States." PhD. dissertation, University of Minnesota, 1957.

Heath, Herschell. "The Indians as a Factor in the War of 1812." PhD. dissertation, Clark University, 1926.

Horsman, Reginald. *Expansionism and American Indian Policy, 1783-1812*. Norman, 1967.

———. *The Frontier in the Formative Years, 1783-1815*. New York, 1971.

Stanley, George F. "The Indians in the War of 1812." *CHR* 31 (1950), 145-165.

Tanner, Helen. *Atlas of Great Lakes Indian History*. Norman, 1987.

Trigger, Bruce, ed. *Handbook of North American Indians 15 (Northeast)*. Washington, 1978.

White, Richard. *The Middle Ground: Indians, Empires, and Republics in the Great Lakes Region, 1650-1815*. New York, 1991.

Wilcomb E., ed. *Handbook of North American Indians 4 (History of Indian-White Relations)*. Washington, 1988.

7.2 Tecumseh and the Northwest

[Anonymous]. "Death of Tecumseh." *WHC* 4 (1857-1858), 375-376.

Antal, Sandor. "The Salina, a Stubborn Patriot." *JES* 20 (1991), 12-17.

———. *A Wampum Denied: Procter's War of 1812*. Ottawa, 1997.

Armstrong, Perry. *The Sauks and the Blackhawk War*. Springfield, 1887.

Black Hawk. *Life of Black Hawk*. 1834, revised by Milo M. Quaife, 1916, reprinted New York, 1994.

Clarke, Peter D. *Origin and Traditional History of the Wyandotts*. Toronto, 1870.

Clifton, James A. "Merchant, Soldier, Broker, Chief. A Corrected Obituary of Captain Billy Caldwell." *Journal of the Illinois State Historical Society* 71 (1978), 185-210.

Council Fires on the Upper Ohio: A Narrative of Indian Affairs in the Upper Ohio Valley until 1795. Pittsburgh, 1940

Doane, Robinson, ed. "A Sioux Indian View of the Last War with England." *South Dakota Historical Collections* 5 (1910), 397-401. [John Sioux].

Drake, Benjamin. *Life of Tecumseh and of His Brother, the Prophet*. Cincinnati, 1841.

Duffy, Dennis. "The Fate of Tecumseh." *The Beaver* 73 (1993), 20-23.

Eckart, Allan W. *A Sorrow in Our Heart: The Life of Tecumseh*. Toronto, 1992.

Edmunds, R. David. *The Potawatomis*. Norman, 1978.

———. *The Shawnee Prophet*. Lincoln, 1983.

———. *Tecumseh and the Quest for Indian Leadership*. Boston, 1984.

———. "Main Poc, Potawatomi Wabeno." *AIQ* 9 (1985), 259-272.

———. "The Thin Red Line, Tecumseh, the Prophet and the Shawnee Resistance." *Timeline* 4 (1988), 2-19.

Eid, Leroy V. "American Indian Military Leadership: St. Clair's 1791 Defeat." *Journal of Military History* 57 (1993).

Galloway, William A. *Old Chillicothe: Shawnee and Pioneer History*. Xenia, 1934.

Gifford, Jack L. "The Northwest Indian War, 1784-1795." PhD dissertation, University of Southern California, 1964.

Goltz, Herbert. "Tecumseh, The Prophet, and the Rise of the Northwestern Indian Confederacy." PhD. dissertation, University of Western Ontario, 1973.

Hagan, William. *The Sac and Fox Indians*. Norman, 1958.

Hauser, Raymond E. "An Ethno-History of the Illinois Indian Tribe, 1672-1832." PhD. dissertation, Northern Illinois University, 1973.

Hickerson, H. *The Chippewas and Their Neighbours*. New York, 1970.

Hickling, William. "Caldwell and Shabonee." *Addresses Delivered at the Annual Meeting of the Chicago Historical Society, 1868*. Chicago, 1877.

Horsman, Reginald. "British Indian Policy in the Northwest, 1807-1812." *MVHR* 45, 1958.

———. *Matthew Elliott, British Indian Agent*. Detroit, 1964.

Howard, Dresden W., ed. "The Battle of Fallen Timbers as Told by Chief Kin-jo-i-no." *NOQ* 20 (1948), 37-49.

Indian Johnson. "Narrative of the Battle of the Thames." in O.K. Watson, "Moraviantown." *OHSPR* 28 (1932), 125-131.

Kinzie, J.H. *Wau-Bun, The 'Early Day' in the North-West*. ed. Milo M. Quaife, Chicago, 1932.

Kirkland, Joseph. *The Chicago Massacre of 1812*. Chicago, 1893.

Lanfried, Helen M. "The Indian Campaigns in the Ohio Country, 1787-1795." MA thesis, University of Cincinnati, 1944.

Lauriston, Victor. "Tecumseh." *Kent Historical Society Papers and Addresses* 3 (1917), 24-37.

Libby, Dorothy R. *An Anthropological Report on the Piananshaw Indians.* New York, 1974.

Lynd, William F. "Fallen Timbers: the Effect of a Single Battle on the Course of American History." MA thesis, University of California, 1951.

Marson, Nehemiah. *Memories of Shaubena.* Chicago, 1878.

McCullough, Almeda, ed. *The Battle of Tippecanoe.* Lafayette, 1973.

Melhorn, Donald F. "'A Splendid Man'": Richardson, Ft. Meigs and the Story of Metoss." *NOQ* 69 (1997), 133-160.

Metoss. "Speech of Metawth." *WCHT* 4 (1903), 11-12.

Mouton, Gary E., ed. *The Papers of Chief John Ross.* 2 vols, Norman, 1985. [Cherokee chief]

Nelson, Paul D. "Anthony Wayne's Indian War in the old Northwest, 1792-1795." *NOQ* 56 (1984), 115-140.

Norris, Caleb H. "Tarhee, the Crane, Chief of the Wyandots." *NOQ* 7 (1935), 1-13.

Pokagon, Simon. "The Massacre of Fort Dearborn at Chicago." *Harper's New Monthly Magazine* 98 (March 1899), 649-656. [Pottawatomi chief]

"William Powell's Recollections." *Wisconsin Historical Society Proceedings* (1912), 146-179. [Menomonee nation]

Quaife, Milo M. *Chicago and the Old North-west, 1637-1835.* Chicago, 1913.

Robinson, Doane. *A History of the Dakota or Sioux Indians.* 1904, reprinted Minneapolis, 1967.

Shipman, Fred W. "The Indian Council of 1793: A Clash of Policies." MA thesis, Clark University, 1933.

Smelser, Marshall. "Tecumseh, Harrison and the War of 1812." *IMH* 45 (March 1969), 25-44.

Smith, Dwight L. "Wayne's Peace Treaty with the Indians of the Old Northwest," *Ohio Archaeological and Historical Society Quarterly* 55 (1946), 1-11.

———. "Indian Land Cessions in the Old Northwest, 1795-1809." PhD. dissertation, Indiana University, 1949.

———. "Wayne and the Treaty of Greenville." *Ohio Archaeological and Historical Society Quarterly* 63 (1954), 1-7.

Stout, David B. *The Piankashaw and Kaskaskia and the Treaty of Greenville.* New York, 1974.

Sugden, John. *Tecumseh's Last Stand.* Norman, 1985.

———. "Early Pan-Indianism: Tecumseh's Tour of the Indian Country, 1811-1812." *AIQ* 10 (1986), 273-304.

———. *The Shawnees in Tecumseh's Time.* Nortorf, 1990.

Tebbel, John W. *The Battle of Fallen Timbers, August 20, 1794.* New York, 1972.

Tucker, Glenn, *Tecumseh. Vision of Glory.* Indianapolis, 1956.

Walsh, G. Mark. "We Have Heard the Great Guns: British Indian Policy and the Battle of Lake Erie." *JES* 17, no. 2 (1988), 27-38.

Walsh, William P. "The Defeat of Major General Arthur St. Clair, November 4, 1791: A Study in the Nation's Response, 1791-1793." PhD. dissertation, Loyola University, 1977.

Warner, Michael S. "General Josiah Harmar's Campaign Reconsidered: How the Americans lost the battle of Kekionga." *IMH* 83 (1987), 43-64.

Whicker, J. Wesley, ed. "Shabonee's Account of Tippecanoe." *IMH* 17 (1921), 353-363.

Sword, Wiley. *President Washington's Indian War; The Struggle for the Old Northwest, 1790-1795.* Norman, 1985.

7.3 The Lake Ontario and St. Lawrence Theatres

Benn, Carl. *The Iroquois in the War of 1812.* Toronto, 1998.

———, ed. *Memoirs of a Mohawk War Chief: John Norton/Teyoninhokarawen, 1812-1814.* Publication forthcoming.

Claus, William. "An Account of the Operations of the Indian Contingent with Our Forces on the Niagara Frontier, 1812-1813." *NHSP* 9 (1902), 23-46.

Cooper, Virginia. "A Political History of the Grand River Iroquois, 1784-1880." MA thesis, Carleton University, Ottawa, 1975.

Devine, E.J. *Historic Caugnawaga.* Montreal, 1922.

Houghton, Frederick. *The History of the Buffalo Creek Reservation.* Buffalo, 1920.

Johnson, Elias. *Legends, Traditions and Laws of the Iroquois, or Six Nations, and History of the Tuscarora Indians.* Lockport, 1881.

Johnson, Evelyn H. "Chief John Smoke Johnson. Sakayegwaraton – 'Disappearing of the Indian Summer Mist.'" *OHSPR* 12 (1914), 102-113.

Johnston, Charles M. "William Claus and John Norton: A Struggle for Power in Old Ontario." *OH* 57 (1965).

Kelsay, Isabel Thompson. *Joseph Brant, 1743-1807: Man of Two Worlds.* Syracuse, 1984.

Klinck, Carl F. "New Light on John Norton." *RSC* 4 (1966).

――― and J.J. Talman, eds. *The Journal of Major John Norton, 1816.* Toronto, 1970.

Marcous, Joseph. "Mémoire pour la défense de la neutralité des Sauvages de S. Regis pendant la dernière guerre avec les Américans." *Le Bulletin des recheches historiques* 67 (1961).

Parker, Arthur C. "The Senecas in the War of 1812." *New York History* 15 (1916).

Richter, Daniel. *Ordeal of the Longhouse: The Peoples of the Iroquois League in the Era of European Colonization.* Chapell Hill, 1992.

Smith, Donald B. "The Dispossession of the Mississauga Indians: A Missing Chapter in the Early History of Upper Canada." *OH* 72 (1980), 67-87.

Snow, Dean R. *The Iroquois.* Cambridge, 1994.

Snyder, Charles M., ed. *Red and White on the New York Frontier: A Struggle for Survival; Insights from the Papers of Erastus Granger, Indian Agent.* Harrison, 1978.

Stanley, George F. "The Significance of the Six Nations Participation in the War of 1812." *OH* 55 (1963), 215-231.

Stone, William L. *Life of Joseph Brant – Thayendanegea.* 1838, reprinted Secaucas, 1972.

―――. *The Life and Times of Sa-go-ye-wat-ha, or Redjacket.* Albany, 1866.

Wallace, A.F.C. *The Death and Rebirth of the Seneca.* New York, 1973.

7.4 The Creek War

Akers, Frank H. "The Unexpected Challenge: The Creek War of 1813-1814." PhD. dissertation, Duke University, 1975.

Barber, Douglas. "Council Government and the Genesis of the Creek War." *AR* 38 (1985), 163-174.

Caughey, John Walton. *McGillivray of the Creeks.* Norman, 1938.

Cotterill, Robert S. "Federal Indian Management in the South, 1789-1825." *MVHR* 20 (1933-1934), 333-352.

―――. *The Southern Indians: The Story of the Civilized Tribes Before Removal.* Norman, 1954.

Halbert, Henry S. and Timothy H. Ball. *The Creek War of 1813 and 1814.* 1895, reprinted Alabama, 1969.

Hall, Arthur H. "The Red Stick War: Creek Indian Affairs during the War of 1812." *Chronicle of Oklahoma* 12 (September 1934), 264-293.

Hassig, Ross. "Internal Conflict in the Creek War of 1812-1814." *Ethnohistory* 21 (1974), 251-271.

Holland, James W. "Andrew Jackson and the Creek War: Victory at the Horshoe." *AR* 21 (1968), 243-275.

Mahon, John K. "British Strategy and the Southern Indians' War of 1812." *FHQ* 44, no. 4 (April 1966), 285-302.

Owsley, Frank L. "British and Indian Activities in Spanish West Florida during the War of 1812." *FHQ* 46 (1967), 111-123.

―――. "The Fort Mims Massacre." *AR* 24 (1971), 192-204.

―――. "Prophet of War: Josiah Francis and the Creek War." *AIQ* 11 (1985), 273-293.

Sugden, John. "The Southern Indians in the War of 1812: The Closing Phase." *FHQ* 61 (1982), 273-312.

Thomson, Hugh M. "Governor Peter Early and the Creek Frontier, 1813-1815." *Georgia Historical Quarterly* 45 (1961), 223-227.

West, Elizabeth H. "A Prelude to the Creek War of 1813-1814." *FHQ* 18 (1940), 247-266.

Wright, J. Leitch. *Creeks and Seminoles: The Destruction and Regeneration of the Muskogulge People.* Lincoln, 1986.

7.5 Native Culture, Costume, Weapons and Warfare

Bailey, De Witt. "Those Board of Ordnance Indian Guns – Again!" *Museum of the Fur Trade Quarterly* 21 (1985).

———. "Those Board of Ordnance Indian Guns – Again! – Supplement." *Museum of the Fur Trade Quarterly* 21 (1985).

Benn, Carl. "Iroquois Warfare, 1812-1814." in Arthur Bowler, ed., *War along the Niagara: Essays on the War of 1812 and its Legacy*, Youngstown, 1991.

Boyce, Douglas W, ed. "A Glimpse of Iroquois Cultural History through the Eyes of Joseph Brant and John Norton." *Proceedings of the American Philosophical Society* 117 (1973).

Burke, Lee. "Wilson Cypher Guns – Chiefs' Guns of the Revolution." *American Society of Arms Collectors Bulletin* (1996).

Eccles, Ross. "Canadian Indian Treaty Guns." *AC* 14 (1976).

Eid, Leroy V. "'National' War among Indians of Northeastern North America." *Canadian Review of American Studies* 16 (1985).

Guthman, William H. "Frontiersmen's Tomahawks of the Colonial and Federal Periods." *Antiques* 119 (1981).

Hadlock, Wendell S. "War among the Northeastern Woodland Indians." *American Anthropologist* 44 (1947).

Hamilton, T.M. *Colonial Frontier Guns.* Chadron, 1980.

Johnson, Michael G. and Richard Hook. *American Woodland Indians.* London, 1990.

Mahon, John K. "Anglo-American Methods of Indian Warfare, 1676-1794." *MVHR* 45 (1958-9).

Malone, Patrick M. *The Skulking Way of War: Technology and Tactics among the New England Indians.* Lanham, 1991.

Nadeau, Gabirel. "Techniques of Indian Scalping." *BHM* 10 (1941).

Otterbein, Keith F. "Why the Iroquois Won: An Analysis of Iroquois Military Tactics." *Ethnohistory* 11 (1964).

Richter, Daniel. "War and Culture: The Iroquois Experience." *WMQ* 40 (1983).

8 BIOGRAPHICAL STUDIES

Anderson, William J. *The Life of F.M., H.R.H. Edward, Duke of Kent, Illustrated by His Correspondence with the De Salaberry Family … from 1791 to 1841.* Ottawa, 1870.

Antal, Sandor. "Myths and Facts Concerning General Procter." *OH* 79 (Sep 1987), 251-262

Booth, Alan D. "Research Note: Confusion in the Chronological Record of General Brock's Life." *OH* 83 (1991), 224-229.

Brenton, Edward. B. *Some account of the Public Life of the late Lieutenant-General Sir George Prevost, but particularly of his services in the Canadas including a reply to the strictures on his military character.* London, 1823.

Brighton, J.G. *Admiral Sir P.B.V. Broke, Bart, K.C.B., etc.,; a Memoir.* London, 1866.

———. *Admiral of the Fleet Sir Provo W.P. Wallis, G.C.B., etc.,; a Memoir.* London, 1892.

Brode, Patrick. *Sir John Beverly Robinson, Bone and Sinew of the Compact.* Toronto, 1984.

Burt, A. Blanche. "Captain Robert Heriot Barclay, R.N." *OH* 14 (1916), 169-178.

Butler, William F. *Sir Charles Napier.* London, 1890.

Cruikshank, Ernest A. "A Sketch of the Public Life and Services of Robert Nichol." *OH* 19 (1922), 6-79.

———. "Sir Gordon Drummond, K.C.B." *OHSPR* 29 (1933).

Curzon, Sarah. *Laura Secord, the Heroine of 1812: A Drama and other Poems.* Toronto, 1887.

———. "The Story of Laura Secord, 1813." *OH* 51 (1959).

Eayrs, Hugh. *Sir Isaac Brock.* Toronto, 1924.

Ermatinger, E. *Life of Colonel Talbot & the Talbot Settlement.* Belleville, 1972.

Fitzgibbon, Mary Agnes. *A Veteran of 1812 … The Life of James Fitzgibbon.* Toronto, 1894.

Flint, David. *John Strachan, Pastor and Politician.* Toronto, 1971.

George, Christopher T. "The Family Papers of Maj. Gen. Robert Ross, the Diary of Col. Arthur Brooke, and the British Attacks on Washington and Baltimore of 1814." *MHM* 88 (1993), 300-316.

Graves, Donald E. "William Drummond and the Battle of Fort Erie." *Canadian Military History* 1 (1992), 1-18.

Henderson, John L. *John Strachan, 1778-1867.* Toronto, 1969.

Heriot, J.C.A. "Major General, The Hon. Frederick George Heriot, C.B." *Canadian Antiquarian and Numismatic Journal*, 8 (April 1911), 49-72.

Horsman, Reginald. *Matthew Elliott, British Indian Agent.* Detroit, 1964.

Howe, Jonas, "Colonel Henry Ormond: The Career of a New Brunswick Soldier." *Acadiensis*, 2 (1902), 19-23.

Ingram, George. "The Story of Laura Secord Revisited." *OH* 57 (June 1965), 85-97.

Jarvis, Julia. *Three Centuries of Robinsons: The Story of a Family*. Toronto, 1967.

Kerr, James E. "Sketch of the Life of the Honourable William Dickson." *Waterloo Historical Society Papers* 4 (1916), 26-32.

Lehmann, Joseph H. *Remember You are an Englishman: A Biography of Sir Harry Smith, 1787-1860*. London, 1977.

McKenna, Katherine M. *A Life of Propriety: Anne Murray Powell and Her Family, 1755-1849*. Montreal, 1994.

McKenzie, Ruth. *Laura Secord: The Legend and the Lady*. Toronto, 1972.

Merritt, J.P., ed. *Biography of the Hon. W.H. Merritt ... Compiled Principally from His Original Diary and Correspondence*. St. Catharines, 1875.

Moir, J.S. "An Early Record of Laura Secord's Walk." *OH* 51 (1959), 105-108.

———. "Laura Secord Again." *OH* 54 (1962), 190.

Morgan, Cecilia, "Of Slender Frame and Delicate Appearance: the Placing of Laura Secord in the Narratives of Canadian Loyalist History." *JCHA* 5 (1994), 195-212.

Neale, Graham, "Colonel John Crysler of Crysler's Farm." *Journal of the Orders and Medals Research Society*, 21 (Autumn 1982), 50-54.

Pack, James. *The Man Who Burned the White House: Admiral Sir George Cockburn, 1772-1853*. Annapolis, 1987.

Patterson, William. "A Forgotten Hero in a Forgotten War." *JSAHR* 68 (1990), 7-20.

Raudzens, George. "'Red George Macdonell', Military Saviour of Upper Canada." *OH* 62 (1970), 199-212.

Read, David B. *Life and Times of Major-General Sir Isaac Brock, K.B.* Toronto, 1894.

Riddell, William R. *The Life of William Dummer Powell, First Judge at Detroit and Fifth Chief Justice of Upper Canada*. Lansing, 1924.

Robertson, H.H. "Major Titus Geer Simons at Lundy's Lane." *Transactions of the Wentworth County Historical Society* 11 (1899), 49-54.

Robinson, C.W. *The Life of Sir John Beverly Robinson*. Toronto, 1904.

Simons, John R. "The Fortunes of a United Empire Loyalist Family." *OHSPR* 23 (1926), 470-482.

Spurr, John W. "Sir James Lucas Yeo: A Hero on the Lakes." *HK* 30 (1982), 30-45.

Stevens, Joan. *Victorian Voices: An Introduction to the Papers of Sir John Le Couteur, Q.U.A.D.C, F.R.S.* St. Helier, 1969.

Thomas, Earle. *Sir John Johnson, Loyalist Baronet*. Toronto, 1986.

Tucker, Lillian H. "Sir Peter Parker, Commander of HMS *Menelaus*." *Bermuda Historical Quarterly*, 1 (1944), 189-195.

Turner, Wesley B. "The Career of Isaac Brock in Canada, 1802-1812." MA thesis, University of Toronto, 1961.

Ward, S.G.P. "General Sir George Murray." *JSAHR* 58 (1980), 191-208.

Williams, Jack. *Merritt: A Canadian Before His Time*. St. Catharines, 1985.

Wohler, Patrick. *Charles de Salaberry. Soldier of the Empire, Defender of Quebec*. Toronto: Dundurn, 1984.

Wrong, George. *A Canadian Manor and Its Seigneurs*. Toronto, 1926.

9 PRISONERS OF WAR

Beal, Vernon L. "John McDonnell and the ransoming of American captives after the River Raisin massacre." *Michigan History*, 35 (1951), 331-351.

Deveau, J.A., ed. *Diary of a Frenchman. Francois Lambert Bourneuf's Adventures from France to Acadia, 1787-1871*. Halifax, 1990.

Dye, Ira. "American Maritime Prisoners of War, 1812-1815." in Timothy J. Runyan, *Ships, Seafaring and Society. Essays in Maritime History*. Detroit, 1987, 293-320.

Fairchild, George, ed. *Journal of an American Prisoner at Fort Malden and Quebec in the War of 1812*. Quebec, 1909.

Gilje, Paul A., ed., "A Sailor Prisoner of War during the War of 1812." *MHM* 85 (1990), 58-72.

Rives, George L., ed. *Selections From the Correspondence of Thomas Barclay. Formerly British Consul-General at New York.* New York, 1894.

Robinson, Ralph. "Retaliation for the Treatment of Prisoners in the War of 1812." *AHR* 49 (1943), 65-70.

10. MEDICINE

Anderson, Fanny J. "Medical Practices During the War of 1812." *BHM* 16 (1944), 261-275.

Ashburn, P.M., "American Army Hospitals of the Revolution and the War of 1812." *Bulletin of the Johns Hopkins Hospital*, 46 (1920), 47-60.

Billroth, Theodore. *Historical Studies on the Nature and Treatment of Gun-shot Wounds from the 15th Century to the Present Time.* New Have, 1933

Cantlie, Neil. *A History of the Army Medical Department.* 2 vols, Edinburgh, 1974.

Chaplin, Arnold. *Medicine in the Age of George III.* London, 1920.

Douglas, John. *Medical Topography of Upper Canada.* Canton, 1985.

Dunlop, William. *Tiger Dunlop's Upper Canada.* Toronto, 1967.

Eaton, Leonard. "Military Surgery in the Battle of Tippecanoe." *BHM* 25 (1951), 460-463.

Estes, J. Worth and Ira Dye. "Death on the *Argus*: American Medical Malpractice *versus* British Chauvinism in the War of 1812." *Journal of the History of Medicine and Allied Sciences* 44 (1989), 179-185.

Ewell, James. *The Medical Companion; Treatment, According to the Most Successful Practices ....* Philadelphia, 1817.

Guthrie, George. *A Treatise on Gun-Shot Wounds.* London, 1827.

———. *Commentaries on the Surgery of War.* London, 1855.

Hennen, John. *Principles of Military Surgery.* London, 1820.

Horner, William [Surgeon], "Surgical Sketches: A Military Hospital at Buffalo, New York, in the Year 1814." *Medical Examiner and Record of Medical Service*, 16 (1852), 753-774, 17 (1853), 1-25.

Howell, H.A.L. "The Story of the British Army Surgeon and the Care of the Sick and Wounded." *JRAMC* 22 (1914), 320-334, 445-471, 643-658.

Hunter, John. *Treatise on the Blood, Inflammation and Gunshot Wounds.* London, 1794.

———. *Observations on the Diseases of the Army in Jamaica and on the Best Means of Preserving the Health of Europeans in the Climate ....* London, 1808.

Huntt, Henry. "An Abstract Account of the Diseases Which Prevailed Among the Soldiers, Received into the General Hospital, at Burlington, Vermont, During the Summer and Autumn of 1814." *Medical Recorder* 1 (1818), 176-179.

Jackson, Robert. *A System of Arrangement and Discipline for the Medical Department of Armies.* London, 1805.

Keevil, J.J. and Christopher Lloyd and Jack Coulter. *Medicine and the Navy, 1200 1900.* 4 vols, London, 1957-1963.

Kempthorne, G.A. "The American War, 1812-1814." *JRAMC* 62 (1934), 139-140.

———. "The Army Medical Services at Home and Abroad, 1803-1808." *JRAMC* 61 (1933), 144-146, 223-232.

———. "The Medical Department of Wellington's Army." *JRAMC* 54 (1930), 65-72, 131-146, 213-220.

Litt, Paul, and Ronald Williamson and Joseph Whitehorne, eds., *Death at Snake Hill. Secrets from a War of 1812 Cemetery.* Toronto, 1993.

Lloyd, Christopher, ed. *The Health of Seamen; Selections from the Works of Dr. James Lind, Sir Gilbert Blane, and Dr. Thomas Trotter.* London, 1965.

Mann, James. *Medical Sketches of the Campaigns of 1812, 1813, and 1814.* Dedham, Mass., 1816.

Monro, John. *Observations on the Means of Preserving the Health of Soldiers and of Constituting Military Hospitals and On the Diseases Incident to Soldiers.* 2 vols, London, 1816.

Pfeiffer, Susan and Ronald Williamson, eds. *Snake Hill. An Investigation of a Military Cemetery from the War of 1812.* Toronto, 1991.

Phalen, James. "Landmarks in Surgery. Surgeon James Mann, U.S. Army; Observations on Battlefield Amputations." *Surgery* 66 (1938), 1072-1073.

———. "Surgeon James Mann's Observations on Battlefield Amputations." *Military Surgeon* 87 (1940), 463-466.

[Raney, John]. *The Nature and Treatment, of Gun-Shot Wounds. By John Raney, Esquire; Surgeon-General to the British Army.* Philadelphia, 1776

Roland, Charles G. "War Amputations in Upper Canada." *Archivaria* 10 (1980), 73-84.

Tilton, James. *Economical Observations on Military Hospitals and the Prevention and Cure of Diseases Incident to an Army* .... Wilmington, 1813.

Wangensteen, Owen H. and Sarah, and Jacqueline Smith. "Some Highlights in the History of Amputation Reflecting Lessons in Wound Healing." *BHM* 41 (1967), 97-123.

———. and Sarah D. "Successful Pre-Listerian Antiseptic Management of Compound Fracture, Crowther (1802), Larrey (1824), and Bennion (ca. 1840)." *Surgery* 69 (1971), 819.

11 THE WAR AND CIVILIAN SOCIETY

Akins, Thomas Beamish. "History of Halifax City." *NSHSC* 8 (1892-1894), 3-272.

Biggar, C.L. *A Tale of Early Days on Lundy's Lane.* Niagara Falls, n.d. [c. 1960]

Bouchette, Joseph. *A Topographical Description of the Province of Lower Canada and Remarks upon Upper Canada.* London, 1815.

Bowler, R.A. "Propaganda in Upper Canada: A Study of the Propaganda Directed at the People of Upper Canada during the War of 1812." MA thesis, Queen's University, Kingston, 1964.

Couture, Paul M. *War and Society on the Detroit Frontier, 1791 to 1815.* MFRS 289, Ottawa, 1986.

Croil, James. *Dundas, or, A Sketch of Canadian History.* Montreal, 1861.

Errington, Jane. "Friends and Foes – the Kingston Elite and the War of 1812: A Case Study in Ambivalence." *Journal of Canadian Studies* 20 (Spring 1985), 58-79.

———. *The Lion, the Eagle, and Upper Canada: A Developing Colonial Ideology.* Montreal, 1987.

Fabel, Robin F.A. "The Laws of War in the 1812 Conflict." *Journal of American Studies* 14 (August 1980), 199-218.

Firth, Edith, ed., *The Town of York, 1793-1815.* Toronto, 1963.

Fraser, Robert L. "Like Eden in Her Summer Dress: Gentry Economy and Society, Upper Canada, 1812-1840." PhD. dissertation, University of Toronto, 1979.

Garland, M.A. and J.J. Talman. "Pioneer Drinking Habits and the Rise of Temperance Agitation in Upper Canada Prior to 1840." *OHSPR* 27 (1931), 341-364.

Glazebrook, G.P. de T. *Life in Ontario: A Social History.* Toronto, 1968

Green, Ernest. "Township No. 2: Mount Dorchester, Stamford." *OHSPR* 25 (1929), 248-338.

Hein, Edward B. "The Niagara Frontier and the War of 1812." PhD. dissertation, University of Ottawa, 1949.

Hitsman, John M. "David Thompson and Defence Research." *CHR* 40 (1959), 315-318;

Lanctot, Gustave, ed. *Les Canadiens français et leurs voisins du sud* .... Montreal, 1941.

Lépine, Luc. "La participation des canadiens-français à la guerre de 1812-1815." MA thesis, University of Montreal, 1986.

Martell, James S. "Halifax During and After the War of 1812." *NSHSC* 23 (1943), 289-304.

Mecredy, Stephen. "Some Military Aspects of Kingston's Development during the War of 1812." MA thesis, Queen's University, Kingston, 1982.

Ouellet, Fernand, *Lower Canada 1791-1840: Social Change and Nationalism.* Toronto, 1980.

———. *Economic and Social History of Quebec, 1760-1850.* Toronto, 1983.

[Richardson, John]. *The Letters of Veritas, Re-Published from the Montreal Herald, Containing a Succinct Account of the Military Administration of Sir George Prevost* .... Montreal, 1815.

Riddell, William R. "The First Canadian War-Time Prohibition Measure." *CHR*, 1 (1920), 187-190.

Ryerson, Egerton. *The Loyalists of America and Their Times, from 1620 to 1816.* 2 vols, Toronto, 1880.

Seibel, George. *The Portage Road; 200 Years, 1790-1990.* Niagara Falls, 1990.

Sermon Preached at York, Upper Canada on the Third of June, Being the Day Appointed for a General Thanksgiving. Montreal, 1814.

Sheppard, George. *Plunder, Profit, and Paroles. A Social History of the War of 1812 in Upper Canada.* Kingston, 1994.

———. "'Wants and Privations:' Women and the War of 1812 in Upper Canada." *Social History* 28 (1995), 159-179.

Smith, Alison. "John Strachan and Early Upper Canada, 1799-1814." *OH* 52 (1950), 159-173.

Smith, Michael. *A Geographical View of the Province of Upper Canada.* Philadelphia, 1813 [various editions]

Smyth Carter, J. *The Story of Dundas, Being a History of the County of Dundas from 1784 to 1903.* Iroquois, 1905.

Sulté, Benjamin. *Histoire des canadiens-français, (1608-1880).* Montreal, 1882.

Sutherland, Maxwell. "The Civil Administration of Sir George Prevost 1811-1815: A Study in Conciliation." MA thesis, Queen's University, Kingston, 1959.

11.1 Wartime Economy

Alcock, Donald G., "The Best Defence is … Smuggling? Vermonters during the War of 1812, *Canadian Review of American Studies* 25 (1995), 73-91.

Copp, Walter R., "Nova Scotian Trade during the War of 1812, *CHR* 37 (1937), 143-146.

Cruikshank, Ernest A. "A County Merchant in Upper Canada 1800-1812." *OHSPR* 25 (1920), 145-190.

Easterbrook, W.T. and W.H. Watkins. *Approaches to Canadian Economic History.* Toronto, 1967.

Hitsman, J. Mackay. "David Parrish and the War of 1812." *MA* 26, 1962-1963.

McCalla, Douglas. "The 'Loyalist' Economy of Upper Canada, 1784-1806." *Histoire sociale/Social History,* 16 (1983), 279-304.

———. *Planting the Province: The Economic History of Upper Canada, 1784-1870.* Toronto, 1993.

Muller, H.N. "A Traiterous and Diabolical Traffic: The Commerce of the Champlain-Richelieu Corridor during the War of 1812." *Vermont History* 44 (Spring 1976), 78-96.

Ouellet, Fernand. *Economic and Social History of Quebec, 1760-1850.* Toronto, 1983.

Resources of the Canadas or Sketches of the Physical and Moral Means which Great Britain and her Colonial Authorities Will Successfully Employ … against the Government of the United States. Quebec, 1813.

Sheppard, George. *Plunder, Profit, and Paroles. A Social History of the War of 1812 in Upper Canada.* Kingston, 1994.

Shortt, Adam. "The Economic Effect of the War of 1812 on Upper Canada." *OHSPR* 10 (1913).

Stevenson, James. "The Circulation of Army Bills with Some Remarks upon the War of 1812." *Literary and Historical Society of Quebec Transactions* 21 (1891-1892), 1-79.

Walter, Philip G. and Raymond Walters. "The American Career of David Parish." *Journal of Economic History* 4 (1944), 149-166.

Wilson, Bruce G. *The Enterprises of Robert Hamilton.* Ottawa, 1984.

11.2 Political Disaffection, Treason and Repression

Colquhoun, A.H.U. "The Careers of Joseph Willcocks." *CHR* 7 (1926), 287-293.

Cruikshank, E.A.C. "A Study of Disaffection in Upper Canada." *RSC* 6 (1912), 55-65.

———. "John Beverly Robinson and the Trials for Treason in 1814." *OH* 25 (1929), 191-219.

"Eight Men Were Sentenced To Be 'Hanged-Drawn-Quartered'." *Cuesta* (Spring 1981).

Graves, Donald E., "Joseph Willcocks and his Canadian Volunteers. A Study of Political Disaffection in Upper Canada During the War of 1812." M.A. thesis, Carleton University, Ottawa, 1982.

Muir, Robert C. *The Early Political and Military History of Burford.* Quebec, 1913.

———. "Burford's First Settler, Politician and Military Man – Benajah Mallory." *OHSPR* 26 (1930), 492-497.

Riddell, William R. "The Ancaster 'Bloody Assize' of 1814." *OHSPR* 20 (1923), 108-125.

———. "An Echo of the War of 1812." *OHSPR* 24 (1927), 476-499.

———. "Joseph Willcocks: Sheriff, Member of Parliament, and Traitor." *OH* 24 (1928), 475-499.

Stray, Albert. "Canadian Volunteers Burn Old Niagara." *Canadian Genealogist* 6 (December 1984), 220-242.

Weekes, William M. "The War of 1812: Civil Authority and Martial Law in Upper Canada." *OH* 48 (1956), 147-161.

12 THE AFTERMATH OF THE WAR

Address by Canon Houston, 25th July, 1893. Niagara Falls, 1893.

Ahearn, M.H. "Battlegrounds of the Niagara Peninsula." *WCHO* 5 (1912), 19-36.

Bethune, John. *A Sermon Preached at Brockville … June, 1816 Being a Day of General Thanksgiving.* Montreal, 1816.

Brief Account of a Third Military Re-Enactment at Lundy's Lane, Oct. 13th, 1899, with Notes, etc. Niagara Falls, 1899.

Burpee, Lawrence. "Influence of the War of 1812 upon the Settlement of the Canadian West." *OHSPR* 12 (1914), 114-120.

Calloway, Colin G. "The End of an Era: British-Indian Relations in the Great Lakes Region after the War of 1812." *MVHR* 12 (Fall 1986), 1-20.

Centenary Celebration of the Battle of Lundy's Lane. July Twenty-Fifth, Nineteen Hundred and Fourteen. Niagara Falls, 1919.

Craig, H. "The Loyal and Patriotic Society of Upper and Canada and Its Still-Born Child – the 'Upper Canada Preserved' Medal". *OH* 52 (March 1960), 31-52.

Centenary Celebration of the Battle of Lundy's Lane. July Twenty-Fifth, Nineteen Hundred and Fourteen. Niagara Falls: Lundy's Lane Historical Society, 1919.

Cruikshank, Ernest A. "The Negotiation of the Agreement for Disarmament on the Lakes." *RSC* 30 (1936), 151-184.

Earl, D.W.L. "British Views of Colonial Upper Canada, 1791-1841." *OH* 53 (1961), 117-136.

Fraser, Alexander. *Brock Centenary, 1812-1912: Account of the Celebration of Queenston Heights, Ontario, on the 12th of October, 1912.* Toronto, 1913.

Furber, Holden, ed. "How William James came to be a Naval Historian." *AHR* 38 (1932), 74-85.

Hitsman, John M. *Safeguarding Canada, 1763-1871.* Toronto, 1965.

Jarvis, Eric. "Military Land Granting in Upper Canada following the War of 1812." *OH* 67 (1975), 121-134.

Magill, M.L. "William Allan and the War of 1812." *OH* 64 (1972), 132-141.

Manning, Helen T. *The Revolt of French Canada, 1800-1835.* New York, 1962.

Martell, James. "Nova Scotia's Contribution to the Canadian Relief Fund in the War of 1812." *CHR* 23 (1942), 297-302.

———. "Military Settlements in Nova Scotia after the War of 1812." *CHR,* 23 (1942), 297-302.

McConnell, Jennie. "The Effect of the War of 1812 on Canada." *WCHO* 1 (1901), 177-188.

Military Re-Interment of Eleven Soldiers (of the 89th and 103rd Regiments) killed in battle at Lundy's Lane, July 25th, 1814. Niagara Falls, 1891.

Militia and Defence Department, Canada. *Statement showing the name, age, and residence of militiamen of 1812-1815 who have applied to participate in the gratuity voted by Parliament in 1875, with the name of the corps or division and rank in which they served.* Ottawa, 1876.

Morden, James C. *Historical Monuments and Observatories of Lundy's Lane and Queenston Heights.* Niagara Falls, 1929.

Pfeiffer, Susan and Ronald Williamson, eds. *Snake Hill: An Investigation of a Military Cemetery from the War of 1812.* Toronto, 1991.

Report [of the] Commissioners appointed to investigate the Claims of Certain Inhabitants of this Province for losses sustained … during the Late War …. York, 1825.

Report of the Loyal and Patriotic Society of Upper Canada, with an appendix, and a list of subscribers and benefactors. Montreal, 1817.

Sheppard, George. "'Deeds Speak': Militiamen, Medals and the Invented Traditions of 1812." *OH* (Sept 1990), 207-392.

Stacey, Charles P. "The War of 1812 in Canadian History." *OH* 50 (1958), 153-159.

Strachan, James. *A Visit to the Province of Upper Canada in 1819.* Dundee, 1820, reprinted Toronto, 1968.

Symons, John, ed. *The Battle of Queenston Heights … with Notices of the Life of Major-General … Brock … and description of the Monument erected to His Memory.* Toronto, 1859.

Upper Canada, Legislative Assembly. *Report of the Select Committee on … Certain Medals.* Toronto, 1840.

Walden, K. "Isaac Brock, Man and Myth: A Study of the Militia Myth of the War of 1812 in Upper Canada, 1812-1912." MA thesis, Queen's University, 1971.

Warner, Mabel. "Memorials at Lundy's Lane." *OH* 51 (1959), 43-48.

Index

About the author

A native of Kingston, J. Mackay Hitsman (1917-1970) served as a captain in the Second World War and was afterward chief archivist of the Army Historical Section in Ottawa. Besides *The Incredible War of 1812: A Military History*, he also produced *Safeguarding Canada, 1763-1871* and, with J.L. Granatstein, *Broken Promises: A History of Conscription in Canada*.

About the editor

Donald E. Graves is an internationally recognized expert on the War of 1812 and has written or edited five previous books on that conflict, including *Field of Glory: The Battle of Crysler's Farm, 1813*, of which *Quill & Quire* said, "This is history at its best: exciting, entertaining, and readable." Graves's study of the bloody 1814 battle of Lundy's Lane, *Where Right and Glory Lead!*, has been called "an excellent example of the 'sharp end' of military history." Don Graves's other War of 1812 titles are: *Redcoats and Grey Jackets: The Battle of Chippawa, 1814; Merry Hearts Make Light Days: The War of 1812 Journal of Lieutenant John Le Couteur, 104th Foot*; and *Soldiers of 1814: American Enlisted Men's Memoirs of the Niagara Campaign*. He served as an historical consultant for the War of 1812 segment of the Canadian Broadcasting Corporation's "People's History of Canada." His most recent book as author is *Century of Service: The History of the South Alberta Light Horse*, the centennial history of Alberta's senior militia regiment. Donald Graves is the director of Ensign Heritage, a company specializing in heritage consulting and travel, and lives with his author wife, Dianne, near Ottawa.

About the cover artist

Peter Rindlisbacher, who painted the cover art, is a full-time marine artist specializing in sailing navy subjects. Museums and historic sites in the U.S. and Canada have purchased many of his oil paintings, while prints of his work are sold as fundraisers for various historical groups. His images have appeared on book and magazine covers and in a number of public television programs. Recent books with cover illustrations by Peter Rindlisbacher include *Guns Across the River: The Battle of the Windmill, 1838* and *Field of Glory: The Battle of Crysler's Farm, 1813*, both by Donald E. Graves, and *Lords of the Lake: The Naval War on Lake Ontario, 1812-1814* by Robert Malcomson. The artist lives in Amherstburg, Ontario, with his wife and two children.

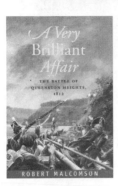

A Very Brilliant Affair: The Battle of Queenston Heights, 1812

by Robert Malcomson

The story of the famous engagement, when American forces invaded across the Niagara River. The British defeated the intruders but their revered General Isaac Brock was killed. This is the first full-length study of this well known battle.

352 pages • 6 x 9 inches • about 60 pictures and maps • hardcover • (Published in U.S.A. by Naval Institute Press)

The British at the Gates: The New Orleans Campaign in the War of 1812

by Robin Reilly

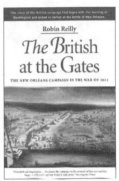

The highly acclaimed account of the final campaign of the war. As well as covering the events in detail from the burning of Washington to the climactic battle at New Orleans that made Andrew Jackson famous, he describes the origins and early events of the war, and the protracted peace negotiations that took place in Europe.

"Detailed and impressive … he places the campaign in the context of the war and the larger world scene against which it took place." *Los Angeles Times*

420 pages • 6 x 9 inches • about 45 pictures and maps • paperback

Lords of the Lake: The Naval War on Lake Ontario, 1812-1814

by Robert Malcomson

Of all the struggles that took place along the border between the United States and the British provinces of Canada in the War of 1812, the longest was the battle for control of Lake Ontario.

Winner of the 1998 John Lyman Prize for Best Work in Canadian Naval and Maritime History.

"All in all, this is an outstanding book, beautifully produced, and it should be read by anyone interested in the War of 1812." *The Mariner's Mirror.*

432 pages • 6 x 9 inches • about 100 pictures, maps • paperback • (Published in U.S.A. by Naval Institute Press)

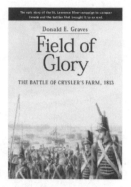

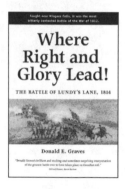